T0211777

More information about this series at http://www.springer.com/series/7407

Lecture Notes in Computer Science 11955

Tom Gedeon · Kok Wai Wong ·
Minho Lee (Eds.)

Neural
Information Processing

26th International Conference, ICONIP 2019
Sydney, NSW, Australia, December 12–15, 2019
Proceedings, Part III

Editors
Tom Gedeon ⓘ
Australian National University
Canberra, ACT, Australia

Kok Wai Wong ⓘ
Murdoch University
Murdoch, WA, Australia

Minho Lee ⓘ
Kyungpook National University
Daegu, Korea (Republic of)

ISSN 0302-9743   ISSN 1611-3349   (electronic)
Lecture Notes in Computer Science
ISBN 978-3-030-36717-6   ISBN 978-3-030-36718-3   (eBook)
https://doi.org/10.1007/978-3-030-36718-3

LNCS Sublibrary: SL1 – Theoretical Computer Science and General Issues

This Springer imprint is published by the registered company Springer Nature Switzerland AG
The registered company address is: Gewerbestrasse 11, 6330 Cham, Switzerland

Preface

Welcome to the proceedings of the 26th International Conference on Neural Information Processing of the Asia-Pacific Neural Network Society (APNNS 2019), held in Sydney during December 12–15, 2019.

The mission of the Asia-Pacific Neural Network Society is to promote active interactions among researchers, scientists, and industry professionals who are working in Neural Networks and related fields in the Asia-Pacific region. APNNS had Governing Board Members from 13 countries/regions – Australia, China, Hong Kong, India, Japan, Malaysia, New Zealand, Singapore, South Korea, Qatar, Taiwan, Thailand, and Turkey. The society's flagship annual conference is the International Conference of Neural Information Processing (ICONIP).

The three-volume set of LNCS 11953–11955 includes 177 papers from 645 submission, and represents an acceptance rate of 27.4%, reflecting the increasingly high quality of research in Neural Networks and related areas in the Asia-Pacific.

The conference had three main themes, "Theory and Algorithms," "Computational and Cognitive Neurosciences," and "Human Centred Computing and Applications." The three volumes are organized in topical sections which were also the names of the 20-minute presentation sessions at the conference. The topics were Adversarial Networks and Learning; Convolutional Neural Networks; Deep Neural Networks; Feature Learning and Representation; Human Centred Computing; Hybrid Models; Artificial Intelligence and Cybersecurity; Image Processing by Neural Techniques; Learning from Incomplete Data; Model Compression and Optimisation; Neural Learning Models; Neural Network Applications; Social Network Computing; Semantic and Graph Based Approaches; Spiking Neuron and Related Models; Text Computing Using Neural Techniques; Time-Series and Related Models; and Unsupervised Neural Models.

Thanks very much in particular to the reviewers who devoted their time to our rigorous peer-review process. Their insightful reviews and timely feedback ensured the high quality of the papers accepted for publication. Finally, thank you to all the authors of papers, presenters, and participants at the conference. Your support and engagement made it all worthwhile.

October 2019

Tom Gedeon
Kok Wai Wong
Minho Lee

Organization

Program Chairs

Tom Gedeon   The Australian National University, Australia
Kok Wai Wong   Murdoch University, Australia
Minho Lee   Kyungpook National University, South Korea

Program Committee

Hussein Abbass	UNSW Canberra, Australia
Hosni Adil Imad Eddine	Beijing Institute of Technology, China
Shotaro Akaho	AIST, Japan
Alaa Al-Kaysi	University of Technology, Iraq
Bradley Alexander	The University of Adelaide, Australia
Georgios Alexandridis	National Technical University of Athens, Greece
Usman Ali	Shanghai Jiao Tong University, China
Ahmad Ali	Shanghai Jiao Tong University, China
Abdulrahman Altahhan	Leeds Beckett University, UK
Muhamad Erza Aminanto	NICT, Japan
Ali Anaissi	The University of Sydney, Australia
Khairul Anam	University of Jember, Indonesia
Emel Arslan	Istanbul University, Turkey
Sunil Aryal	Deakin University, Australia
Arnulfo Azcarraga	De La Salle University, Philippines
Donglin Bai	Shanghai Jiao Tong University, China
Hongliang Bai	Beijing Faceall Technology Co., Ltd., China
Mehala Balamurali	The University of Sydney, Australia
Mohamad Hardyman Barawi	Universiti Malaysia Sarawak, Malaysia
Younès Bennani	Université Paris 13 and Université Sorbonne-Paris-Cité, France
Christoph Bergmeir	Monash University, Australia
Gui-Bin Bian	Chinese Academy of Sciences, China
Larbi Boubchir	University of Paris 8, France
Amel Bouzeghoub	Télécom SudParis, France
Congbo Cai	Xiamen University, China
Jian Cao	Shanghai Jiaotong University, China
Xiaocong Chen	University of New South Wales, Australia
Junsha Chen	UCAS, China
Junjie Chen	Inner Mongolia University, China
Qingcai Chen	Harbin Institute of Technology, Shenzhen, China

Gang Chen	Victoria University of Wellington, New Zealand
Junya Chen	Fudan University, USA
Dong Chen	Wuhan University, China
Weiyang Chen	Qilu University of Technology, China
Jianhui Chen	Institute of Neuroscience, Chinese Academy of Science, China
Girija Chetty	University of Canberra, Australia
Sung-Bae Cho	Yonsei University, South Korea
Chaikesh Chouragade	Indian Institute of Science, India
Tan Chuanqi	Tsinghua University, China
Yuk Chung	The University of Sydney, Australia
Younjin Chung	The Australian National University, Australia
Tao Dai	Tsinghua University, China
Yong Dai	Hunan University, China
Popescu Dan	UPB, Romania
V. Susheela Devi	Indian Institute of Science, India
Bettebghor Dimitri	Expleo Group, France
Hai Dong	RMIT University, Australia
Anan Du	University of Technology Sydney, Australia
Piotr Duda	Czestochowa University of Technology, Poland
Pratik Dutta	IIT Patna, India
Asif Ekbal	IIT Patna, India
Mounim El Yacoubi	Télécom SudParis, France
Haytham Elghazel	LIRIS Lab, France
Zhijie Fang	Chinese Academy of Sciences, China
Yuchun Fang	Shanghai University, China
Yong Feng	Chongqing University, China
Raul Fernandez Rojas	UNSW Canberra, Australia
Junjie Fu	Southeast University, China
Bogdan Gabrys	University of Technology Sydney, Australia
Junbin Gao	The University of Sydney, Australia
Guangwei Gao	Nanjing University of Posts and Telecommunications, China
Tom Gedeon	The Australian National University, Australia
Ashish Ghosh	Indian Statistical Institute, India
Heitor Murilo Gomes	The University of Waikato, New Zealand
Iqbal Gondal	Federation University, Australia
Yuri Gordienko	National Technical University of Ukraine, Ukraine
Raju Gottumukkala	University of Louisiana at Lafayette, USA
Jianping Gou	Jiangsu University, China
Xiaodong Gu	Fudan University, China
Joachim Gudmundsson	The University of Sydney, Australia
Xian Guo	Nankai University, China
Jun Guo	East China Normal University, China
Katsuyuki Hagiwara	Mie University, Japan
Sangchul Hahn	Handong Global University, South Korea

Tae Joon Jun	Asan Medical Center, South Korea
H. M. Dipu Kabir	Deakin University, Australia
Kyunghun Kang	Kyungpook National University Hospital, South Korea
Asim Karim	Lahore University of Management Sciences, Pakistan
Kathryn Kasmarik	UNSW Canberra, Australia
Yuichi Katori	Future University Hakodate, Japan
Imdadullah Khan	Lahore University of Management Science, Pakistan
Zubair Khan	Shanghai Jiaotong University, China
Numan Khurshid	Lahore University of Management Sciences, Pakistan
Matloob Khushi	The University of Sydney, Australia
Shuji Kijima	Kyushu University, Japan
Rhee Man Kil	Sungkyunkwan University, South Korea
SangBum Kim	Seoul National University, South Korea
Mutsumi Kimura	Ryukoku University, Japan
Eisuke Kita	Nagoya University, Japan
Simon Kocbek	University of Technology Sydney, Australia
Hisashi Koga	University of Electro-Communications, Japan
Tao Kong	Tsinghua University, China
Nihel Kooli	Solocal, France
Irena Koprinska	The University of Sydney, Australia
Marcin Korytkowski	Czestochwa University of Technology, Poland
Polychronis Koutsakis	Murdoch University, Australia
Aneesh Krishna	Curtin University, Australia
Lov Kumar	BITS Pilani Hyderabad Campus, India
Takio Kurita	Hiroshima University, Japan
Shuichi Kurogi	Kyushu Institute of Technology, Japan
Hamid Laga	Murdoch University, Australia
Keenan Leatham	University of District of Columbia, USA
Xiaoqiang Li	Shanghai University, China
Yantao Li	Chongqing University, China
Ran Li	Shanghai Jiaotong University, China
Jiawei Li	Tsinghua University, China
Tao Li	Peking University, China
Li Li	Southwest University, China
Xiaohong Li	Tianjin University, China
Yang Li	Tsinghua University, China
Nan Li	Tianjin University, China
Mingxia Li	University of Electronic Science and Technology of China, China
Zhixin Li	Guangxi Normal University, China
Zhipeng Li	Tsinghua University, China
Bohan Li	Nanjing University of Aeronautics and Astronautics, China
Mengmeng Li	Zhengzhou University, China
Yaoyi Li	Shanghai Jiao Tong University, China
Yanjun Li	Beijing Institute of Technology, China
Ming Li	La Trobe University, Australia

Mingyong Li	Donghua University, China
Chengcheng Li	Tianjin University, China
Xia Liang	University of Science and Technology, China
Alan Wee-Chung Liew	Griffith University, Australia
Chin-Teng Lin	UTS, Australia
Zheng Lin	Chinese Academy of Sciences, China
Yang Lin	The University of Sydney, Australia
Wei Liu	University of Technology Sydney, Australia
Jiayang Liu	Tsinghua University, China
Yunlong Liu	Xiamen University, China
Yi Liu	Zhejiang University of Technology, China
Ye Liu	Nanjing University of Posts and Telecommunications, China
Zhilei Liu	Tianjin University, China
Zheng Liu	Nanjing University of Posts and Telecommunications, China
Cheng Liu	City University of Hong Kong, Hong Kong, China
Linfeng Liu	Nanjing University of Posts and Telecommunications, China
Baoping Liu	IIE, China
Guiping Liu	Hetao College, China
Huan Liu	Xi'an Jiaotong University, China
Gongshen Liu	Shanghai Jiao Tong University, China
Zhi-Yong Liu	Institute of Automation, Chinese Academy of Science, China
Fan Liu	Beijing Ant Financial Services Information Service Co., Ltd., China
Zhi-Wei Liu	Huazhong University of Science and Technology, China
Chu Kiong Loo	University of Malaya, Malaysia
Xuequan Lu	Deakin University, Australia
Huimin Lu	Kyushu Institute of Technology, Japan
Biao Lu	Nankai University, China
Qun Lu	Yancheng Institute of Technology, China
Bao-Liang Lu	Shanghai Jiao Tong University, China
Shen Lu	The University of Sydney, Australia
Junyu Lu	University of Electronic Science and Technology of China, China
Zhengding Luo	Peking University, China
Yun Luo	Shanghai Jiao Tong University, China
Xiaoqing Lyu	Peking University, China
Kavitha MS	Hiroshima University, Japan
Wanli Ma	University of Canberra, Australia
Jinwen Ma	Peking University, China
Supriyo Mandal	Indian Institute of Technology Patna, India
Sukanya Manna	Santa Clara University, USA
Basarab Matei	University of Paris 13, France

Xiaolian Wang	University of Chinese Academy of Sciences, China
Zeyuan Wang	The University of Sydney, Australia
Dong Wang	Hunan University, China
Qiufeng Wang	Xi'an Jiaotong-Liverpool University, China
Chen Wang	Institute of Automation, Chinese Academy of Sciences, China
Jue Wang	BIT, China
Xiaokang Wang	Beihang University, China
Zhenhua Wang	Zhejiang University of Technology, China
Zexian Wang	Shanghai Jiao Tong University, China
Lijie Wang	University of Macau, Macau, China
Ding Wang	Chinese Academy of Sciences, China
Peijun Wang	Anhui Normal University, China
Yaqing Wang	HKUST, China
Zheng Wang	Southwest University, China
Shuo Wang	Monash University and CSIRO, Australia
Shi-Lin Wang	Shanghai Jiaotong University, China
Yu-Kai Wang	University of Technology Sydney, Australia
Weiqun Wang	Institute of Automation, Chinese Academy of Sciences, China
Yoshikazu Washizawa	University of Electro-Communications, Japan
Chihiro Watanabe	NTT Communication Science Laboratories, Japan
Michael Watts	Auckland Institute of Studies, New Zealand
Yanling Wei	University of Leuven, Belgium
Hongxi Wei	Inner Mongolia University, China
Kok-Wai Wong	Murdoch University, Australia
Marcin Woüniak	Silesian University of Technology, Poland
Dongrui Wu	Huazhong University of Science and Technology, China
Huijun Wu	University of New South Wales, Australia
Fei Wu	Nanjing University of Posts and Telecommunications, China
Wei Wu	Inner Mongolia University, China
Weibin Wu	Chinese University of Hong Kong, Hong Kong, China
Guoqiang Xiao	Shanghai Jiao Tong University, China
Shi Xiaohua	Shanghai Jiao Tong University, China
Zhenchang Xing	The Australian National University, Australia
Jianhua Xu	Nanjing Normal University, China
Huali Xu	Inner Mongolia University, China
Peng Xu	Jiangnan University, China
Guoxia Xu	Hohai University, China
Jiaming Xu	Institute of Automation, Chinese Academy of Sciences, China
Qing Xu	Tianjin University, China
Li Xuewei	Tianjin University, China
Toshiyuki Yamane	IBM, Japan
Haiqin Yang	Hang Seng University of Hong Kong, Hong Kong, China

Bo Yang   University of Electronic Science and Technology of China,
                              China
Wei Yang   University of Science and Technology of China, China
Xi Yang   Xi'an Jiaotong-Liverpool University, China
Chun Yang   University of Science and Technology Beijing, China
Deyin Yao   Guangdong University of Technology, China
Yinghua Yao   Southern University of Science and Technology, China
Yuan Yao   Tsinghua University, China
Lina Yao   University of New South Wales, Australia
Wenbin Yao   Beijing Key Laboratory of Intelligent Telecommunications
                              Software and Multimedia, China
Xu-Cheng Yin   University of Science and Technology Beijing, China
Xiaohan Yu   Griffith University, Australia
Yong Yuan   Chinese Academy of Science, China
Ye Yuan   Southwest University, China
Yun-Hao Yuan   Yangzhou University, China
Xiaodong Yue   Shanghai University, China
Seid Miad Zandavi   The University of Sydney, Australia
Daren Zha   Chinese Academy of Sciences, China
Yan Zhang   Tianjin University, China
Xiao Zhang   Huazhong University of Science and Technology, China
Yifan Zhang   CSIRO, Australia
Wei Zhang   The University of Adelaide, Australia
Lin Zhang   Beijing Institute of Technology, China
Yifei Zhang   University of Chinese Academy of Sciences, China
Huisheng Zhang   Dalian Maritime University, China
Gaoyan Zhang   Tianjin University, China
Liming Zhang   University of Macau, Macau, China
Xiang Zhang   University of New South Wales, Australia
Yuren Zhang   ByteDance Ltd., China
Jianhua Zhang   Zhejiang University of Technology, China
Dalin Zhang   University of New South Wales, Australia
Bo Zhao   Beijing Normal University, China
Jing Zhao   East China Normal University, China
Baojiang Zhong   Soochow University, China
Guoqiang Zhong   Ocean University, China
Caiming Zhong   Ningbo University, China
Jinghui Zhong   South China University of Technology, China
Mingyang Zhong   Central Queensland University, Australia
Xinyu Zhou   Jiangxi Normal University, China
Jie Zhou   Shenzhen University, China
Yuanping Zhu   Tianjin Normal University, China
Lei Zhu   Lingnan Normal University, China
Chao Zhu   University of Science and Technology Beijing, China

Xiaobin Zhu   University of Science and Technology Beijing, China
Dengya Zhu   Curtin University, Australia
Yuan Zong   Southeast University, China
Futai Zou   Shanghai Jiao Tong University, China

Contents – Part III

Semantic and Graph Based Approaches

Spiking Neuron and Related Models

Text Computing Using Neural Techniques

Time-Series and Related Models

Unsupervised Neural Models

Semantic and Graph Based Approaches

GL2vec: Graph Embedding Enriched by Line Graphs with Edge Features

Hong Chen$^{(\boxtimes)}$ and Hisashi Koga

Graduate School of Informatics and Engineering,
The University of Electro-Communications, Tokyo 1828585, Japan
{chen,koga}@sd.is.uec.ac.jp

Abstract. Recently, several techniques to learn the embedding for a given graph dataset have been proposed. Among them, Graph2vec is significant in that it unsupervisedly learns the embedding of entire graphs which is useful for graph classification. This paper develops an algorithm which improves Graph2vec. First, we point out two limitations of Graph2vec: (1) Edge labels cannot be handled and (2) Graph2vec does not always preserve structural information enough to evaluate the structural similarity, because it bundles the node label information and the structural information in extracting subgraphs. Our algorithm overcomes these limitations by exploiting the line graphs (edge-to-vertex dual graphs) of given graphs. Specifically, it complements either the edge label information or the structural information which Graph2vec misses with the embeddings of the line graphs. Our method is named as GL2vec (Graph and Line graph to vector) because it concatenates the embedding of an original graph to that of the corresponding line graph. Experimentally, GL2vec achieves significant improvements in graph classification task over Graph2vec for many benchmark datasets.

Keywords: Line graph · Graph embedding · Graph-based pattern recognition

1 Introduction

Graph is a powerful tool for representing complex objects and is widely used in many fields such as social network analysis and chemo-informatics.

Recently, to apply graph data to the existing machine learning algorithms, the problem to represent a graph as a numeric feature vector called a graph embedding has received extensive attention. Inspired by the success of embedding techniques such as Word2vec [1] and Doc2vec [2] in natural language processing, many graph embedding algorithms based on the language model have been proposed. For example, Node2vec [3] learns the embedding of nodes which is useful for node classification, node clustering, link prediction and so on.

Whereas many previous works focused on the embedding of graph substructures like nodes, Graph2vec [4] is unique and remarkable, because it learns the embedding of entire graphs which can be applied to graph classification and graph clustering. Specifically, given a set of graphs with node labels, Graph2vec outputs the embeddings of all the graphs in an unsupervised manner. Graph2vec is founded on Doc2vec [2].

© Springer Nature Switzerland AG 2019
T. Gedeon et al. (Eds.): ICONIP 2019, LNCS 11955, pp. 3–14, 2019.
https://doi.org/10.1007/978-3-030-36718-3_1

While Doc2vec regards a document as a set of words, Graph2vec views a graph as a set of rooted subgraphs. Then, the embeddings of the graphs are obtained by the skip-gram language model [1].

This paper purposes to improve Graph2vec. We first point out that Graph2vec has two limitations to be improved: (1) Edge labels cannot be handled. (2) When Graph2vec quantizes the subgraphs of a graph G, it bundles the node label information and the structural information. Thus, the resultant subgraph IDs for a graph G do not always maintain enough structural information to evaluate the structural similarity between G and other graphs.

To overcome these limitations, we exploit the line graph (edge-to-vertex dual graph) of G. Conceptually, the line graph $L(G)$ of a graph G is created by mapping every edge in G to a node in $L(G)$. Thus, the nodes in $L(G)$ can hold the edge features in G as the node labels. Moreover, because $L(G)$ discards the node labels in G, $L(G)$ is suitable to treat the structural information about G independently of the node labels in G.

Our method constructs the embedding of the line graph $L(G)$ and uses it to complement either the edge label information or the structural information of G which Graph2vec misses. Specifically, if the graph dataset has edge labels, we specify the edge labels in G as the node labels in $L(G)$ so that the embedding of $L(G)$ may hold the edge label information of G. On the other hand, for graph datasets without edge labels, so that the embedding of $L(G)$ may express the structural information about G, we specify the degrees of edges in G as the node labels in $L(G)$. Here, the degree of an edge e is an edge feature and defined as the number of incident edges to e. Since the embedding of $L(G)$ alone cannot consider the node labels in G, we append the embedding of G capturing the node label information to it. Due to this property, our method is named as GL2vec (Graph and Line graph to vector). Experimentally, GL2vec achieves significant improvements in graph classification task over Graph2vec for many benchmark datasets.

This paper is organized as follows. Section 2 explains the conventional Graph2vec. In Sect. 3, we clarify the two shortcomings of Graph2vec. Section 4 describes our GL2vec to overcome these shortcomings. Section 5 reports the experimental results. Section 6 briefs the related works and Sect. 7 is the conclusion.

2   Graph2vec

This section explains Graph2vec in [4]. Given a set of graphs $\{G_1, G_2, \ldots G_N\}$ and a positive integer δ which determines the dimensionality of embedding, Graph2vec learns a mapping which maps the graphs to a set of δ-dimensional vectors $\{f(G_1), f(G_2), \ldots, f(G_N)\}$. $f(G_i)$ is called the embedding of G_i. In particular, Graph2vec tries to learn a mapping which satisfies the condition that, as two graphs G_i and G_j are semantically more similar, $f(G_i)$ and $f(G_j)$ become closer in the δ-dimensional vector space.

Graph2vec assumes that graphs have node labels. A graph G with node labels is represented as $G = \{V, E, \lambda\}$. Here, V is a set of nodes and $E \subseteq (V \times V)$ be a set of edges. $\lambda : V \to \mathcal{L}$ is a function which assigns a unique label from the alphabet $\mathcal{L}$ to every node $v \in V$.

Graph2vec is inspired by Doc2vec [2]. As Doc2vec represents a single document as a set of words, Graph2vec represents a single graph as a set of rooted subgraphs. After expressing every graph as a group of rooted subgraphs, Graph2vec learns the embedding of each graph by the skip-gram language model [1]. In the subsequence, Sect. 2.1 explains the extraction of rooted subgraphs in a single graph. Then, Sect. 2.2 describes how Graph2vec learns the embedding of all the graphs.

2.1   Extraction of Rooted Subgraphs

Let H be a non-negative integer parameter which defines the maximum height (maximum hop) of rooted subgraphs. Usually, the users must specify H. For every node v in a graph G, Graph2vec generates $(H+1)$ rooted subgraphs whose roots are v. For $0 \le t \le H$, the t-th subgraph rooted at v describes the surroundings around v within t hops, and its height equals t. After all, if G consists of n nodes, Graph2vec enumerates the set of $n(H+1)$ rooted subgraphs denoted by $c(G) = \{ sg_1^{(o)}, sg_2^{(0)}, \ldots, sg_n^{(0)},$ $sg_1^{(1)}, sg_2^{(1)}, \ldots sg_n^{(1)}, \ldots, sg_1^{(H)}, sg_2^{(H)}, \ldots, sg_n^{(H)} \}$

These subgraphs are quantized into subgraph IDs according to the WL (Weisfeiler-Lehman) relabeling strategy [5].

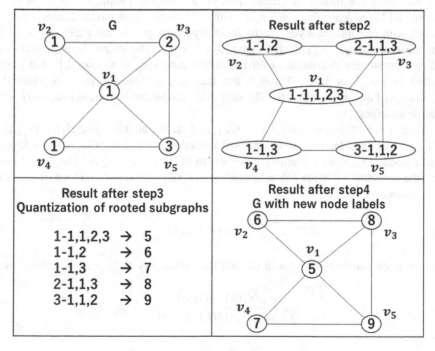

Fig. 1. WL relabeling for graph G

Below, we depict the procedure of the WL relabeling at the t-th iteration in which the t-th rooted subgraphs are created for all the nodes and quantized into subgraph IDs. In this algorithm, $\lambda^t(v)$ symbolizes the node label of v which expresses the ID of the t-th subgraph rooted at v, i.e., $sg_v^{(t)}$.

1. For every node v in G, collect the labels of the nodes adjacent to v and create the multiset of node labels $M^t(v) = \{\lambda^{t-1}(u)|u \in \text{Neighbors}(v)\}$
2. Sort the elements in $M^t(v)$ in ascending order and concatenate them into a string $S^t(v)$. Then, insert $\lambda^{t-1}(v)$ into $S^t(v)$ as the prefix.
3. $S^t(v)$ is mapped to a new ID using some hash function such that $\text{Hash}(S^t(v)) = \text{Hash}(S^t(w))$ iff $S^t(v) = S^t(w)$.
4. Replace the label of v with $\lambda^t(v) = \text{Hash}(S^t(v))$.

Here, the second step constructs $sg_v^{(t)}$ by combining the $(t-1)$-th subgraphs rooted at the neighbors of v with the $(t-1)$-th subgraph rooted at v itself. Then, the third step quantizes $sg_v^{(t)}$ to the subgraph ID "$\lambda^t(v)$". Figure 1 shows an example of the execution of the WL relabeling strategy. For instance, the rooted subgraph for v_5 is first described as "3-1,1,2", where "3" is the label of the root and "1,1,2" expresses the labels of nodes adjacent to v_5. Then, this subgraph is quantized to a new subgraph ID "9".

2.2   Learning Embeddings of Entire Graphs

After extracting the rooted subgraphs from all the graphs, Graph2vec uses the skip-gram model [1] to learn the graph embedding. The skip-gram model adopts a neural network with one hidden layer. At the input layer, the graphs for which we want to learn the embeddings are encoded as one-hot vectors. The output layer outputs the predicted probability distribution over the rooted subgraphs conditioned by the graph inputted at the input layer. Through the learning, the hidden layer acquires the embeddings of the inputted graphs. The skip-gram model can be trained efficiently with negative sampling [1].

Given a set of graphs $\{G_1, G_2, \ldots G_N\}$ and their subgraphs $\{c(G_1), c(G_2), \ldots, c(G_N)\}$, Graph2vec learns a δ-dimensional embedding $f(G_i)$ for G_i, and a δ-dimensional embedding for each member subgraph in $c(G_i)$ for $1 \leq i \leq N$. The model considers the probability that the j-th subgraph sg_j in $c(G_i)$ occurs in G_i and maximizes the log-likelihood in Eq. (1).

$$\sum_{j=1}^{n_i(H+1)} \log P_r\left(sg_j|G_i\right), \tag{1}$$

where n_i is the number of nodes in G_i, and the probability $P_r\left(sg_j|G_i\right)$ is defined as

$$\frac{\exp\left(f(G_i) \cdot f\left(sg_j\right)\right)}{\sum_{sg \in Voc} \exp(f(G_i) \cdot f(sg))}. \tag{2}$$

In Eq. (2), *Voc* denotes the vocabulary of subgraphs across all the graphs. After the training converges, graphs which share many common rooted subgraphs are mapped to similar positions in the vector space.

3 Limitations of Graph2vec

Although Graph2vec is helpful for graph classification and graph clustering, we claim that it has two limitations which motivate us to initiate this research.

The first limitation is simple. Graph2vec cannot handle edge labels, even if they are available on the graph dataset. This limitation is trivial, as the WL relabeling strategy in Graph2vec ignores them.

The second limitation is related to the quantization of subgraphs in Graph2vec. When Graph2vec quantizes the rooted subgraphs of a graph G, it bundles the node label information and the structural information. As a result, the resultant subgraph IDs for G do not always maintain enough structural information to evaluate the structural similarity between G and other graphs. Because this problem is rather complicated, let us explain it with a motivating example in Fig. 2. This figure shows two graphs G and G^* which have exactly the same graph shape. Only one difference between them is the label of the central node. Generally speaking, the similarity between two node-labeled graphs should be judged from both the node label similarity and the structural similarity (i.e. the shape similarity). In this sense, the fact that G and G^* have the same shape is valuable.

However, the WL relabeling strategy in Graph2vec makes it impossible to recognize this fact by bundling the node labels and the structural information. Suppose that H, the maximum height of rooted subgraphs is set to 1. After extracting rooted subgraphs, Graph2vec represents G and G^* as the lists $c(G)$ and $c(G^*)$ of subgraph IDs.

- $c(G) = \{1, 1, 1, 2, 3, 5(1-1, 1, 2, 3), 6(1-1, 2), 7(1-1, 3), 8(2-1, 1, 3), 9(3-1, 1, 2)\}$
- $c(G^*) = \{1, 1, 2, 3, 4, 10(1-2, 4), 11(1-3, 4), 12(2-1, 3, 4), 13(3-1, 2, 4), 14(4-1, 1, 2, 3)\}$

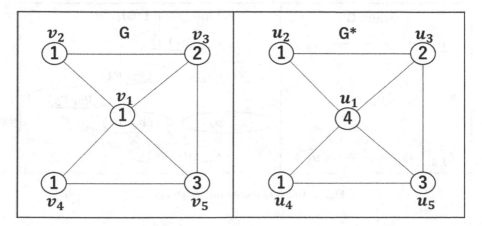

Fig. 2. Two graphs which are identical in structure but differ only in the label of central node

Here, for instance, the subgraph rooted at v_5 in G whose height is 1 is "3-1,1,2" and the WL relabeling quantizes it to a subgraph ID "9". Similarly, the subgraph rooted at u_5 in G^* whose height is 1 is "3-1,2,4" and the WL relabeling quantizes it to a different subgraph ID "13".

From $c(G)$ and $c(G^*)$, we can only tell that G and G^* share four nodes with the same node labels whose IDs are "1", "1", "2" and "3" respectively. We cannot recognize that the shapes of G and G^* are exactly the same by examining $c(G)$ and $c(G^*)$. We cannot even understand that the degrees of v_5 and u_5 are the same, after the two rooted subgraphs "3-1,1,2" and "3-1,2,4" are quantized into different subgraph IDs.

The above inconvenience is caused because two subgraphs with the same shape are quantized into different IDs, even if only one node label is different. Thus, the approach in Graph2vec to treat the node labels and the structural shapes at once hinders the pure evaluation of structural similarity.

4 Proposed Method

This section presents our proposed method named GL2vec which overcomes the limitations of Graph2vec in Sect. 3 helped by the line graphs. Before describing GL2vec in Sect. 4.2, Sect. 4.1 explains the notion of line graph [6].

4.1 Line Graph (Edge-to-Vertex Dual Graph)

Given a graph $G = (V, E)$, its line graph $L(G) = (LV, LE)$ represents the adjacency relationship between edges in G. To construct $L(G)$, the edges in G are converted to the nodes in $L(G)$. Namely, $LV = \{v(e) | e \in E\}$. In $L(G)$, two vertices $v(e_i)$ and $v(e_j)$ are connected by an edge, if e_i and e_j share a common endpoint in G. See Fig. 3. In this example, because edge (v_1, v_2) and edge (v_1, v_4) share the same endpoint v_1 in G, an edge connects the node (v_1, v_2) and the node (v_1, v_4) in $L(G)$.

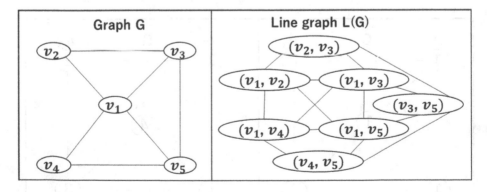

Fig. 3. Graph G and its line graph $L(G)$

In graph theory, the number of edges incident to a node v is called the degree of v and denoted by $deg(v)$. Similarly, the number of edges incident to an edge e is referred to as the degree of e and symbolized as $deg(e)$. When an edge e has two endpoints v_a and v_b, it holds that $deg(e) = deg(v_a) + deg(v_b) - 2$.

In $L(G)$, the degree of a node $v(e)$ is known to be identical with the degree of e in G. That is, $deg(v(e)) = deg(e)$.

4.2 GL2vec

As stated in Sect. 3, Graph2vec fails to deal with the edge labels. It also fails to preserve enough structural information to evaluate the structural similarity by bundling the node label information and the structural information in quantizing subgraphs.

Our GL2vec aims to complement such edge label information and structural information which Graph2vec misses by making use of the line graphs. The line graph has an attractive property that the edge features of a graph G can become the node labels in $L(G)$. Furthermore, because $L(G)$ discards the node labels in G, $L(G)$ is suitable to treat the structural information about G independently of the node labels in G. In the same way as Graph2vec, GL2vec assumes that graphs are accompanied by node labels. GL2vec is able to process both graph datasets with edge labels and those without edge labels.

If the graph dataset has edge labels, GL2vec specifies the edge label of an edge e in G as the node label of $v(e)$ in $L(G)$. Thus, the embedding of $L(G)$ takes the edge label information in G into account.

On the other hand, for a graph dataset without edge labels, GL2vec makes the embedding of $L(G)$ represent the structural information about G without influenced by the node labels in G. This mechanism is realized by specifying another edge feature, the degrees of edges in G as the node labels in $L(G)$. Note that the degree of an edge is dominated by the shape of G and, therefore, an edge feature which describes the structure of G.

Here, one may think that the structural information about G can also be extracted from the original graph G without $L(G)$, if we modify the label of a node v in G to deg (v), the degree of v. Although this is correct, $L(G)$ is capable of describing the structure of G more finely: Since there usually exist more edges than nodes in G, $L(G)$ can characterize the structure of G with more arithmetic values (i.e., degrees of edges) than G which counts on the degrees of nodes. Thus, the line graph evaluates the structural similarity at a finer level than the original graph.

Since $L(G)$ alone cannot consider the node labels in G, GL2vec appends the embedding of $L(G)$ to that of G into which the node labels in G are reflected. The operation of GL2vec is written as follows.

1. Given a set of graphs $\{G_1, G_2, \ldots G_N\}$, we construct their line graphs $\{L(G_1), L(G_2), \ldots, L(G_N)\}$. We change the node labels in $L(G_i)$, depending on if the graph dataset has edge labels or not.

   - If G_i has edge labels, a node $v(e)$ in $L(G_i)$ is assigned the edge label of e in G_i as the node label.

- If G_i does not have edge labels, a node $v(e)$ in $L(G_i)$ is assigned deg(e) in G_i as the node label.

2. By applying Graph2vec to $\{G_1, G_2, \ldots G_N\}$, the embedding $f(G_i)$ of each G_i is derived.
3. By applying Graph2vec to $\{L(G_1), L(G_2), \ldots L(G_N)\}$, we create the embedding $g(L(G_i))$ of each $L(G_i)$.
4. By appending $f(G_i)$ to $g(L(G_i))$ the final embedding of G_i is made.

In the last of this section, let us discuss the handling of a graph dataset without node labels. For such a graph dataset, Graph2vec [4] recommends to label a node v with its degree $deg(v)$. In this case, the embedding of G presents the structural information about G like that of $L(G)$. However, as discussed in the above, $L(G)$ captures the structure of G more finely than G. Hence, GL2vec assesses the structural similarity between graphs at two different resolutions by combining the embedding of G with that of $L(G)$.

5 Experimental Evaluations

We evaluate our GL2vec in the task of graph classification on several benchmark datasets. We compare GL2vec with Graph2vec in terms of classification accuracy.

5.1 Graph Datasets

We prepare 10 graph datasets which are categorized into 2 types. The first type consists of 6 datasets in which graphs do not have edge labels. The second type consists of 4 datasets in which graphs have edge labels. Table 1 summarizes the number of samples, the average graph size, the number of distinct node labels, and the number of distinct edge labels for all the datasets. From now on, we describe these 2 types of datasets in details.

(Type 1) Datasets without edge labels:
The six datasets classified into (Type 1) are MUTAG, PTC, PROTEINS, NCI1, NCI109 and IMDB-B. The first five of them have already been used to evaluate Graph2vec in [4].

MUTAG, PTC, NCI1, and NCI109 originate from chemo-informatics field. The chemical data are converted to graphs, where nodes represent atoms and edges represent chemical bonds. Nodes are labeled by atoms types. In MUTAG, chemical compounds are divided into two classes according to their mutagenic effect on a bacterium. In PTC, the classes indicate the carcinogenicity on rats. NCI1 and NCI109 are composed of chemical compounds screened for activity against non-small cell lung cancer and ovarian cancer cell lines, respectively.

PROTEINS expresses proteins as graphs, where nodes represent secondary structure elements (SSEs) and edges indicate neighborhood in amino-acid sequence or in 3D spaces.

IMDB-B [8] is a special graph dataset in which graphs have neither node labels nor edge labels. This dataset stores graphs converted from movie collaboration database. More specifically, two movie collaboration networks are built for two genres "Action" and "Romance", where nodes represent actors/actresses and there is an edge between them if they appear in the same movie. Then, ego-networks for actors/actresses are extracted from these networks. We must judge which of the two genres an ego-network graph belongs to.

(Type 2) Datasets without edge labels:
The members of (Type 2) are MUTAG*, NCI33, NCI83 and DBLP.

MUTAG* [8] is an extension of MUTAG by labeling the edges. NCI33 [7] and NCI83 [7] are composed of chemical compounds screened for activity against melanoma cancer and breast cancer cell lines, respectively. For these datasets, edges are labeled with chemical bond types.

DBLP dataset [7] creates graphs from bibliography data in computer science, where an individual paper is represented as a graph. A graph for a paper P consists of the primary paper node which represents P itself, other paper nodes which correspond to the papers having the citation relationship with P and the keyword nodes. There exist three kinds of edge labels, that is, (paper-paper), (keyword-paper) and (keyword-keyword). We have to predict whether the field of the paper is DBDM (database and data mining) field or CVPR (computer vision and pattern recognition).

Table 1. Dataset statistics

Dataset	#samples	#nodes (avg.)	#distinct node labels	#distinct edge labels
MUTAG	188	17.9	7	–
PTC	344	25.5	19	–
PROTEINS	1113	39.1	3	–
NCI1	4110	29.8	37	–
NCI109	4127	29.6	38	–
IMDB-B	1000	19.8	–	–
MUTAG*	188	17.9	7	4
NCI33	2843	30.2	29	4
NCI83	3867	29.5	28	4
DBLP	19456	10.5	41324	3

5.2 Experimental Setup

Our implementation of GL2vec calls the existing Graph2vec software package as a subroutine. As for the parameters in Graph2vec, the maximum height H of rooted subgraph is set to 3, and the dimensionality of embedding $\delta = 1024$. As GL2vec concatenates the embeddings of G and $L(G)$, the dimensionality of embedding grows 2048 for GL2vec.

The graphs are classified with the Linear SVM classifier to which their embeddings are inputted. For each dataset, we randomly choose 90% of the samples as the training data. The remaining 10% of the samples serve as the testing data. The hyper-parameters of SVM are tuned by 5-fold cross validation. We repeat the experiments 20 times and report the average classification accuracy.

5.3   Results and Discussions

Table 2 presents the classification accuracy for Graph2vec and GL2vec for the (Type 1) six datasets without edge labels. While five of these datasets have been already used in [4] to evaluate Graph2vec, Graph2vec in our experiments classifies graphs with almost the same accuracy as [4] for such datasets. Table 2 shows that GL2vec outperformed Graph2vec for 4 datasets (MUTAG, NCI1, NCI109 and IMDB-B) and worked comparably to Graph2vec for the PTC dataset. On the other hand, GL2vec is defeated by Graph2vec for the PROTEINS dataset. From these results, we claim that the approach in GL2vec to complement the structural information with the embedding of line graphs without being affected by the node labels is promising, which is not conclusive yet though.

Regarding the IMDB-B dataset, since it originally does not have node labels, Graph2vec uses the degree of nodes as the node labels in the original graphs. According to the discussion in the last of Sect. 4.2, the result is interpreted as follows: GL2vec examining the structural similarity at two different resolutions for the original graphs and for the line graphs works more effectively than Graph2vec based on the single-level structural similarity.

Table 2. Classification accuracy (mean ± std dev.)% for datasets without edge labels

Datasets	MUTAG	PTC	PROTEINS	NCI1	NCI109	IMDB-B
Graph2vec	83.68 ± 7.02	61.00 ± 5.58	72.50 ± 6.16	75.82 ± 2.72	75.87 ± 2.27	72.80 ± 3.42
GL2vec	**86.58 ± 5.78**	60.57 ± 4.41	70.09 ± 5.52	**77.77 ± 2.34**	**79.69 ± 2.04**	**74.10 ± 4.44**

Table 3. Classification accuracy (mean ± std dev.)% for datasets with edge labels

Datasets	MUTAG*	NCI33	NCI83	DBLP
Graph2vec	83.68 ± 7.02	78.95 ± 1.82	75.90 ± 1.66	90.63 ± 0.59
GL2vec	**87.63 ± 7.50**	**81.30 ± 2.17**	**77.29 ± 1.31**	**92.27 ± 0.62**

The results for the (Type 2) datasets with edge labels are shown in Table 3: GL2vec outperforms Graph2vec for all the 4 datasets. These results prove that GL2vec adequately settles down a limitation of Graph2vec that it cannot handle the edge labels by complementing the edge labels with the embeddings of line graphs. They also reveal that the edge labels are useful for the graph classification tasks.

Overall, GL2vec outperforms Graph2vec for 8 out of the 10 datasets. Therefore, we consider that the line graphs succeed in complementing the embeddings of the original graphs, which improves the classification accuracy.

6   Related Works

This section introduces two recent related works in the literature which leverage the concept of line graphs for graph-based pattern recognition.

Bai *et al.* [9] developed an edge-based matching graph kernel EMBK which measures the similarity between two graphs from the number of matched edge pairs. To judge if two edges match, they represent an edge *e* as a feature vector derived from the line graph: The *i*-th coordinate value in the feature vector is determined from the *i*-hop surroundings around $v(e)$ in the line graph. They show that the edge-based matching kernel outperforms the node-based matching kernel which operates on the original graph. The main differences between our method with EMBK are: (1) EMBK is a graph kernel and does not generate feature vectors directly, while GL2vec outputs feature vectors which can be applied to any vector-based machine learning algorithms. (2) EMBK uses the line graph solely with ignoring the original graph, while our method combines the features of the original graph and the line graph.

DPGCNN [10] is a Dual-Primal graph convolutional networks. DPGCNN is an extension of GAT (Graph Attention Networks) [11]. Whereas GAT computes attention scores from the node features, DPGCNN computes them from the edge features. DPGCNN treats the edge features in the original graph as the node features in the line graph, which is similar to our method. The main difference between our GL2vec and DPGCNN is that DPGCNN is an end-to-end model which learns the property of graph substructures such as nodes and edges in a supervised or in a semi-supervised manner, while GL2vec learns the features of entire graphs in an unsupervised manner.

7 Conclusion

This paper proposed GL2vec which extends Graph2vec. First, we make clear the two shortcomings of Graph2vec that edge labels cannot be handled and that structural information is not kept enough to evaluate the structural similarity, as Graph2vec mixes the node label information with the structural information in extracting subgraphs. By contrast, our GL2vec can complement such information missed by Graph2vec with the embeddings of the line graphs. This property is realized by converting the edge features in the original graph such as edge labels and degree of edges to the node features in the corresponding line graph. To cover the node label similarity in addition, GL2vec concatenates the embedding of the original graph to that of the line graph. Experimentally, GL2vec achieves higher graph classification accuracy than Graph2vec for many benchmark datasets. One future direction of this research is to examine the characteristics of graph datasets for which GL2vec works best. Another interesting research issue is about the handling of dense graphs. If the original graph is dense, the number of vertices increases up to the square of the original graph in its line graph. Thus, the line graphs may not be obtained due to lack of computing resources. How to extend GL2vec for such cases is worth studying.

Acknowledgments. This work was supported by JSPS KAKENHI Grant Number JP18K11311, 2019.

References

1. Mikolov, T., Sutskever, I., Chen, K., Corrado, G., Dean, J.: Distributed representations of words and phrases and their compositionality. Adv. Neural. Inf. Process. Syst. **26**, 3111–3119 (2013)
2. Le, Q., Mikolov, T.: Distributed representations of sentences and documents. In: Proceedings of the 31st International Conference on Machine Learning, PMLR, vol. 32, no. 2, pp. 1188–1196 (2014)
3. Grover, A., Leskovec, J.: node2vec: scalable feature learning for networks. In: KDD 2016 Proceedings of the 22nd ACM SIGKDD International Conference on Knowledge Discovery and Data Mining, pp. 855–864 (2016)
4. Narayanan, A., Chandramohan, M., Venkatesan, R., Chen, L., Liu, Y., Jaiswal, S.: graph2vec: Learning Distributed Representations of Graphs. arXiv preprint arXiv:1707. 05005. (2017)
5. Shervashidze, N., Schweitzer, P., van Leeuwen, E.J., Mehlhorn, K., Borgwardt, K.M.: Weisfeiler-Lehman graph kernels. J. Mach. Learn. Res. **12**, 2539–2561 (2011)
6. Harary, F.: Graph Theory, pp. 71–83. Addison-Wesley, Boston (1972)
7. Zhu, X., Zhang, C., Pan, S., Yu, P.: Graph stream classification using labeled and unlabeled graphs. In: Proceedings of the 2013 IEEE 29th International Conference on Data Engineering, pp. 398–409 (2013)
8. Benchmark Data Sets for Graph Kernels. http://graphkernels.cs.tu-dortmund.de. Accessed 20 June 2019
9. Bai, L., Zhang, Z., Wang, C., Hancock, E.R.: An edge-based matching kernel for graphs through the directed line graphs. In: Proceedings of the International Conference on Computer Analysis of Images and Patterns, pp. 85–95 (2015)
10. Monti, F., Shchur, O., Bojchevski, A., Litany, O., Günnemann, S., Bronstein, M.M.: Dual-primal graph convolutional networks. arXiv preprint arXiv:1806.00770. (2018)
11. Veličković, P., Cucurull, G., Casanova, A., Romero, A., Lio, P., Bengio, Y.: Graph attention networks. arXiv preprint arXiv:1710.10903. (2017)

Joint Semantic Hashing Using Deep Supervised and Unsupervised Methods

Kuan Xu[1], Yu Qiao[1(✉)], Yueyang Gu[1], Xiaoguang Niu[1], Suwei Ma[3],
Xiaobin Xiao[2], and Xingqi Fang[1]

[1] Intelligence Learning Laboratory, Department of Automation,
Shanghai Jiao Tong University, Shanghai, China
{whxk225,qiaoyu,guyueyang,2012657,xqfang}@sjtu.edu.cn
[2] Shanghai Science and Technology Network Communications Co., Ltd.,
Shanghai, China
Xiaoxb@stnc.cn
[3] Shanghai Stock Exchange, Shanghai, China
swma@sse.com.cn

Abstract. Deep hashing methods have achieved impressive results due
to the powerful nonlinear mapping ability brought by deep neural network. However, existing deep hashing algorithms treat label information
as the only measurement for image similarity, which degenerated the task
from retrieval to classification. In this paper, to address this problem,
we propose a joint learning framework that learns semantic hash codes
from both supervised and unsupervised information. We divide the K-
bits hash codes into semantic branch and content branch. The codes from
semantic branch are generated with general deep supervised training procedure, while the content branch constructs hash codes by autoencoder
incorporated within the hashing model. Experimental results show that
the semantic retrieval performance of our framework is compatible to the
state of the art. In addition, more semantic information can be embedded into the generated hash codes, which demonstrates the effectiveness
of our joint framework for CBIR tasks.

Keywords: Content-based image retrieval (CBIR) · Hashing method ·
Joint learning · Semantic codes · Content codes

1 Introduction

Hashing methods, as one of the most popular strategies for content-based image
retrieval (CBIR), try to represent images with binary hash codes. The compact
binary representation can boost the searching procedure and relieve the storage consumption as well. The key point for qualified hashing methods is the
construction of similarity-preserving hash functions.

This research is partly supported by NSFC, China (No:61375048).

T. Gedeon et al. (Eds.): ICONIP 2019, LNCS 11955, pp. 15–23, 2019.
https://doi.org/10.1007/978-3-030-36718-3_2

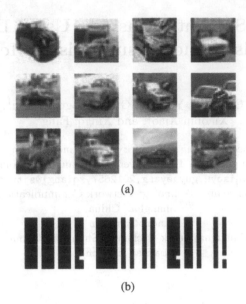

(a)

(b)

Fig. 1. Illustration for the overfitting problem existed in supervised hashing methods: (a) 12 samples randomly picked from CIFAR-10 dataset with the same label (i.e., the car category); (b) respective hash codes generated by deep supervised hashing algorithm SSDH [21].

Early hashing methods are performed independently from data distribution dataset [2,5], which limited the performance. To utilize data information, various unsupervised hashing [3,7,14,19,20] and supervised hashing methods [4,13,15, 16] are proposed to construct hash function based on data information. Among these methods, deep hashing performed best due to additional representation ability brought by deep neural network. Current deep hashing methods utilize supervised information mainly by constructing similarity pairwise matrix [18] or triplets [10,12] with labels. There is also a tendency to evaluate the performance of binary codes by their abilities for classification [11,21].

One problem of current supervised hashing methods is that the label information is the only guidance used during the optimization procedure. The content-based features within the same class will be wiped out from the generated hash codes, as shown in Fig. 1. The CBIR task will therefore downgrade to traditional classification task.

To address this issue, in this paper, we incorporate supervised and unsupervised hashing into one framework to obtain information from both image content and label. We divide hash codes bits into two branches. For the supervised coding branch, we using deep convolutional neural network (CNN) [9]. For the unsupervised branch we utilize feature maps obtained from the last fully connected layer of the network to train an autoencoder , which aimed at preserving image feature ignored by supervised learning procedure. The entire framework is presented in Fig. 2. Experimental results show that our joint learning framework can

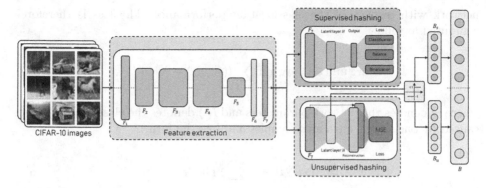

Fig. 2. The architecture of the proposed joint learning hashing framework. Features from F_7 layer is shared by both branches.

produce more perceptual retrieval results comparing to models using only label information or only raw pixel input. It demonstrates the practical value of this method. What's more, by combination of information from different levels, the latent semantic label could be discovered, even though it's not included within the supervise information.

2 Methodology

Given dataset $\mathcal{D} = \{x_n\}_{n=1}^N$ where $x_n \in \mathbb{R}^D$ and class labels set $\mathcal{Y} = \{y_n\}_{n=1}^N$. Our goal is to seek a set of hash functions $\mathbf{h}(x) = [h_1(x), h_2(x), ..., h_K(x)], h(x) :$ $\mathbb{R}^D \mapsto \{-1, +1\}$ that project images points from D-dimension space down to K-bits ($K \ll D$) codes and preserve the similarity relationship in original space in the same time. To achieve this, we divide the hash codes of K-bits B into two sub-codes B_s and B_u with length K_s and K_u respectively, where

$$B = [\underbrace{b_1, b_2, ..., b_{K_s}}_{K_s}, \underbrace{b_{K_s+1}, ..., b_K}_{K_u}]. \tag{1}$$

Based on the guided information used for construing hash function, out framework can be divided into two branches, i.e., supervised hashing branch and unsupervised hashing branch.

2.1 Deep Supervised Hashing

Shown in Fig. 2, we adopt the same CNN architecture in [21] for supervised hashing branch. The structure is similar to the one proposed by Krizhevsky et al. [9], except that a latent layer H is appended after the second fully connected layer F_7. The latent fully connect (FC) layer has K hidden units and uses $\tanh(\cdot)$ as the activation function. The hash codes can be obtained by binarizing the activation of this latent layer. The ideal codes can be learned by training the network with respect to the classification performance. The loss is therefore computed as follow.

$$\arg\min_{\Theta} \mathcal{L} = \arg\min_{\Theta} \sum_{i=1}^{N} l(\mathbf{y}_i, \hat{\mathbf{y}}_i) + \lambda \|\Theta\|^2, \tag{2}$$

where Θ denotes the network parameters and $l(\cdot)$ denotes the classification error caused by one singular training samples and has the form

$$l(\mathbf{y}_i, \hat{\mathbf{y}}_i) = -\sum_{i=1}^{N} \mathbf{y}_i \ln \hat{\mathbf{y}}_i, \tag{3}$$

where y_i and $\hat{y}_i$ are the ground-truth and prediction label vector for the i-th sample.

Additional constraint terms are added to the objective function to ensure the quality of the hash codes including

$$\mathcal{Q}_1 = -\frac{1}{2K} \sum_{i=1}^{N} \left\| \mathbf{a}_i^{Hs} \right\|_2^2, \tag{4}$$

$$\mathcal{Q}_2 = \frac{1}{2K} \sum_{i=1}^{N} \left\| \mathbf{a}_i^{Hs} \mathbf{1}_{K \times 1} \right\|_2^2, \tag{5}$$

where $\mathbf{a}^{Hs} \in \mathbb{R}^K$ denotes the activations from the latent layer H. Equation 4 try to maximize the absolute value of $\mathbf{a}^{Hs}$, which is equivalent to push the value of $\mathbf{a}^{Hs}$ to $\{+1, -1\}$, so that the information loss caused by the binarization operation can be reduced. Equation 5 expects that the distribution of $\mathbf{a}^{Hs}$ is zero-centered to fulfill the balance property [17]. The entire objective function that learns semantic codes is given as

$$\arg\min_{\Theta} \mathcal{O}_s = \mathcal{L} + \alpha_1 \mathcal{Q}_1 + \alpha_2 \mathcal{Q}_2. \tag{6}$$

2.2   Unsupervised Hashing

For the unsupervised branch, we want to find a stable binary embedding using only content information. Many unsupervised hashing methods are capable for this purpose. Most of those methods utilize hand-made features extracted from images contents. However, this feature extraction procedure can be well performed by deep network. In this paper, we construct the unsupervised hash function using an autoencoder, which project the data from original space into a representation space, followed by a dimension-expanding stage reconstructing the input feature using the compact codes. Intuitively, the basic structure of an autoencoder is similar to the latent layer module used in supervised branch. Both of them try to represent the input with low-dimensional features and try to recover information from them. In the supervised branch reconstructed features

(a) HOG

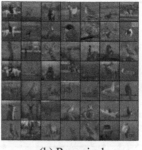

(b) Raw pixel

Fig. 3. Ground truth sets illustration computed with HOG feature and raw pixel Euclidean distance. Left corner denotes the query while remains are top 48 ground truths.

can be used to directly perform classification task. In the unsupervised branch, the input can be recovered from the embedding. In this way, the embedded codes will learn a compressed representation of the input feature, and preserve more perceptual information of the input.

Paralleling to the latent embedding layer 2, we append a hidden encoding layer H_u to the F_7 layer for embedding, followed by a decoder to reconstruct the input feature from the embedded vector. We choose $\tanh(\cdot)$ activation so that the output of the hidden layer ranges the same as the supervised latent layer. With the K_u units hidden layer, the objective function of the autoencoder can be formulated by

$$\arg\min_{\Theta_u} \mathcal{O}_u = \frac{1}{2} \sum_{i=1}^{N} \|\mathbf{a}_i^{H_U} - \hat{\mathbf{a}}_i^{H_U}\|_2^2 + \lambda_u \|\Theta_u\|^2, \qquad (7)$$

where Θ_u denotes the encoder and decoder weights, λ_u is the coefficient balance the regularization term and the mean squared error. $\mathbf{a}_i^{H_U}$ and $\hat{\mathbf{a}}_i^{H_U}$ denote the feature output from F_7 and the feature reconstructed by the autoencoder respectively.

3   Experiments

In this section we compare our proposed framework with original SSDH to test the effectiveness of our method. We first present the setup of our the experiment.

3.1   Setup

We choose CIFAR-10 benchmark [8] as the experiment dataset. It contains 60,000 color images with a fixed size of 32×32 categorized into 10 mutually exclusive classes. Following the setting adopted by [21], we randomly select 100 images from each class to compose a query set containing 1,000 samples in total, while

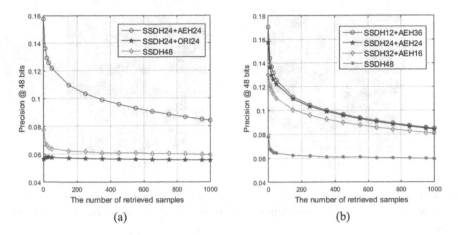

(a)   (b)

Fig. 4. (a) Precision comparison for SSDH and our proposed framework using the Euclidean distance in HOG space as the ground truth; (b) precision comparison with different sub-codes ratio of the proposed joint learning framework.

the remaining 59,000 samples as the database. The parameter setting is same as [21], i.e., $\alpha_1 = \alpha_2 = 1$. The model is trained on an Ubuntu desktop using NVIDA TITAN-X GPU, with Caffe deep learning framework [6].

3.2 Content-Based Retrieval Comparison

We generate a $64 \times 8 \times 8$ dimension HOG feature [1] and compute the Euclidean distance between images from queries and database. As shown in Fig. 3, the ground truth sets constructed with HOG features are better for retrieval performance evaluation because they preserves more perceptual information comparing to those with raw pixel features. For queries we traverse the database and retrieve top 5% nearest samples in HOG space as ground truth set. The top k nearest neighbors in Hamming space are selected as predict set. The overlap number of samples between the two sets denote the points that are retrieved correctly. The curve of retrieval precision versus number of returned images can be obtained by varying k. For comparison methods, we choose SSDH and our method integrated with different kinds of unsupervised features, which are denoted as "SSDH48", "SSDH24+AEH24" and "SSDH24+ORI24" receptively. The "ORI" abbreviation denotes the unsupervised codes generated by a LSH-like random projection using raw pixel input. "AEH" denotes the unsupervised codes from the hidden layer of the autoencoder. The number after the method abbreviation represents the code length used for that method. As can be seen from Fig. 4(a), our proposed method outperforms the original method significantly considering the content similarity preserving performance. To demonstrate the influence of unsupervised codes to the performance of content similarity preserving, we evaluate our method with different code length ratio between supervised and unsupervised branch. As shown in Fig. 4(b), the retrieval precision increases

Table 1. mAP evaluation for different method on CIFAR-10 dataset

Method	Mean average precision
SSDH48	89.46%
SSDH24+ORI24	89.35%
SSDH12+AEH36	89.45%
SSDH24+AEH24	89.35%
SSDH32+AEH16	89.49%

with the expansion in the length of content codes, while the length increasement of the semantic codes downgrades the precision.

3.3 Semantic Retrieval Performance Comparison

Given label information, we can evaluated the performance of the algorithm by the mean average precision (mAP) computed using the retrieval results. The results are given in Table 1. We can see that though the semantic codes are reduced by half in our method, the mAP is still comparable to the original method that uses full semantic codes, while our method can get additional gain from the content codes to obtain retrieval results with more perceptual consistency. As the semantic bits increasing, a slight improvement in the the label retrieval performance can be observed from Table 1. Combined with the tendency observed in Fig. 4(b), we can see that this ratio acts as a balance between the retrieval performance of semantic information and content information.

3.4 Subjective Comparison

To give a subjective visual evaluation of our method, we input a query image and return from CIFAR-10 dataset the top nearest 48 images using SSDH24+AEH24 and SSDH48, respectively. The results are shown in Fig. 5. Queries are displayed at the upper left, with rest 48 patches the retrieval results in ascending order based on the distance to the query in Hamming space. Obviously, the results retrieved from our proposed method are more semantically consistent with query image compared with those of the original SSDH. For example, in Fig. 5(a), given a query of a man riding a horse, most of the results (i.e., 38 out of the 48) returned by our method retain the same perceptual content (man riding horse). Moreover, 21 of them give exactly the same semantic information, i.e., a man in black riding a white horse. In contrast, only 11 out of the 48 retrieval images of SSDH involve content of both horse and a riding man. Only one of them preserve all of the semantic label of the query. Same results can be observed from Fig. 5(c)(d) and Fig. 5(e)(f), in which the retrieval images are of the same category of the query. The posture and appearance of the returned images are also consistent with the query, which is desired for content-based images retrieval task.

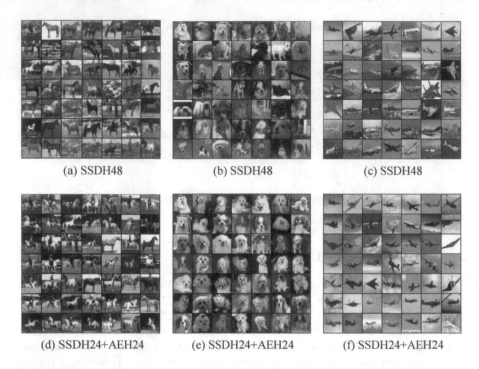

(a) SSDH48   (b) SSDH48   (c) SSDH48

(d) SSDH24+AEH24   (e) SSDH24+AEH24   (f) SSDH24+AEH24

Fig. 5. Subjective comparison between proposed joint learning framework and deep hashing using only supervised branch

4 Conclusion

In this paper, we propose a deep hashing framework that jointly learns a semantic-preserving and content information embedding hash codes. Experimental results show that our framework not only achieves comparable performance with the original model, but also improves content consistency comparing to the original method. Those results demonstrate the effectiveness of our method for CBIR task.

References

1. Dalal, N., Triggs, B.: Histograms of oriented gradients for human detection. In: 2005 IEEE Computer Society Conference on Computer Vision and Pattern Recognition (CVPR 2005), San Diego, USA, vol. 1, pp. 886–893. IEEE (2005). 24705
2. Gionis, A., Indyk, P., Motwani, R.: Similarity search in high dimensions via hashing. Vldb **99**(6), 12 (1999)
3. Gong, Y., Lazebnik, S.: Iterative quantization: a procrustean approach to learning binary codes. In: Computer Vision and Pattern Recognition (CVPR), pp. 817–824, June 2011

4. Hu, Z., Chen, J., Lu, H., Zhang, T.: Bayesian supervised hashing. In: Proceedings of the IEEE Conference on Computer Vision and Pattern Recognition, pp. 6348–6355 (2017)

5. Indyk, P., Motwani, R.: Approximate nearest neighbors: towards removing the curse of dimensionality. In: Proceedings of the Thirtieth Annual ACM Symposium on Theory of Computing, STOC 1998, pp. 604–613. ACM, New York (1998)

6. Jia, Y., et al.: Caffe: convolutional architecture for fast feature embedding. In Proceedings of the 22nd ACM international conference on Multimedia, pp. 675–678. ACM (2014). 09357

7. Jiang, Q.-Y., Li, W.-J.: Scalable graph hashing with feature transformation. In: IJCAI, pp. 2248–2254 (2015)

8. Krizhevsky, A., Hinton, G.: Learning multiple layers of features from tiny images, p. 03040. Citeseer, Technical report (2009)

9. Krizhevsky, A., Sutskever, I., Hinton, G.E.: Imagenet classification with deep convolutional neural networks. In: Advances in Neural Information Processing Systems, pp. 1097–1105 (2012)

10. Lai, H., Pan, Y., Liu, Y., Yan, S.: Simultaneous feature learning and hash coding with deep neural networks. In: Proceedings of the IEEE Conference on Computer Vision and Pattern Recognition, pp. 3270–3278. IEEE, June 2015

11. Li, Q., Sun, Z., He, R., Tan, T.: Deep supervised discrete hashing. pp. 2482–2491, June 2017

12. Li, W.-J., Wang, S., Kang, W.-C.: Feature Learning based Deep Supervised Hashing with Pairwise Labels. arXiv:1511.03855 [cs], November 2015

13. Li, X., Ma, C., Yang, J., Qiao, Y.: Teach to hash: a deep supervised hashing framework with data selection. In: Cheng, L., Leung, A.C.S., Ozawa, S. (eds.) ICONIP 2018. LNCS, vol. 11301, pp. 120–129. Springer, Cham (2018). https://doi.org/10.1007/978-3-030-04167-0_11

14. Liu, W., Mu, C., Kumar, S., Chang, S.-F.: Discrete graph hashing. In: Advances in Neural Information Processing Systems, pp. 3419–3427 (2014)

15. Liu, W., Wang, J.R., Ji, R., Jiang, Y.G., Chang, S.F.: Supervised hashing with kernels. In: 2012 IEEE Conference on Computer Vision and Pattern Recognition, pp. 2074–2081 (2012)

16. Shen, F., Shen, C., Liu, W.,Tao Shen, H. : Supervised discrete hashing. In: Proceedings of the IEEE Conference on Computer Vision and Pattern Recognition, pp. 37–45 (2015)

17. Weiss, Y., Torralba, A., Fergus, R.: Spectral hashing. In: Advances in Neural Information Processing Systems, pp. 1753–1760 (2009)

18. Xia, R., Pan, Y., Lai, H., Liu, C., Yan, S.: Supervised hashing for image retrieval via image representation learning. In: Proceedings of the 28th AAAI Conference on Artificial Intelligence, pp. 2156–2162. AAAI Press (2014)

19. Xu, K., Qiao, Y.: Randomized sampling-based fly local sensitive hashing. In: 2018 25th IEEE International Conference on Image Processing (ICIP), pp. 1293–1297. IEEE (2018). 00000

20. Xu, K., Qiao, Y., Niu, X., Fang, X., Han, Y., Yang, J.: Bone scintigraphy retrieval using sift-based fly local sensitive hashing. In: 2018 IEEE 27th International Symposium on Industrial Electronics (ISIE), pp. 735–740. IEEE (2018). 00000

21. Yang, H.F., Lin, K., Chen, C.S.: Supervised learning of semantics-preserving hash via deep convolutional neural networks. IEEE Trans. Pattern Anal. Mach. Intell. **99**, 1 (2017)

Label-Based Deep Semantic Hashing for Cross-Modal Retrieval

Weiwei Weng[1,2], Jiagao Wu[1,2(✉)], Lu Yang[1,2], Linfeng Liu[1,2], and Bin Hu[3]

[1] School of Computer, Nanjing University of Posts and Telecommunications,
Nanjing 210023, Jiangsu, China
[2] Jiangsu Key Laboratory of Big Data Security and Intelligent Processing,
Nanjing 210023, Jiangsu, China
weiweiweng325@163.com, jgwu@njupt.edu.cn, yanglu19951028@163.com,
liulf@njupt.edu.cn
[3] Key Laboratory of Virtual Geographic Environment, Ministry of Education,
Nanjing Normal University, Nanjing 210046, Jiangsu, China
hb_hubin@126.com

Abstract. With the arrival of the era of big data, multimodal data increases explosively and the cross-modal retrieval has drawn increasing research interests. Due to benefits of low storage cost and fast query speed, hashing-based methods have made great advancements in cross-modal retrieval. Most of the previous hashing methods design a similarity-preserving matrix based on labels to simply describe binary similarity relationship between multimodal data, i.e., similar or dissimilar. This method is applicable to single-label data, but it fails to make use of labels to explore rich semantic information for multi-label data. In this paper, we propose a new cross-modal retrieval method, called Label-Based Deep Semantic Hashing (LDSH). In this method, a new similarity-preserving matrix is given according to multi-label to describe the degree of similarity between multimodal data. Moreover, the last fully connected layer of the deep neural network is designed as a Block Structure (B-Structure) to reduce the redundancy between generated bits. In order to accelerate the convergence speed of neural network, the Batch Normalization Layer (BN-Layer) is adopted after the B-Structure. Extensive experiments on two real datasets with image-text modalities demonstrate the superiority of the proposed method in cross-modal retrieval tasks.

Keywords: Cross-modal retrieval · Multi-label · Deep semantic
hashing · Similarity · B-Structure

1 Introduction

With the rise of social network platforms such as micro-blog and Facebook, the amount of media data on the network has increased dramatically and the

Supported by National Natural Science Foundation of China under Grants Nos. 41571389 and 61872191, TIADMP of Chongqing under Grant No. cstc2018jszx-cyztzxX0015.

T. Gedeon et al. (Eds.): ICONIP 2019, LNCS 11955, pp. 24–36, 2019.
https://doi.org/10.1007/978-3-030-36718-3_3

forms of media presentation have also shown multimodality, such as images, texts and videos, etc. In order to make better use of these data, cross-modal information retrieval, such as searching images by text queries, or searching texts by image queries, has become one of the hot issues in recent years [1–3]. However, with the rapid growth of media data and the diversification of modality, traditional retrieval methods designed for single-modal data can no longer meet the needs of cross-modal retrieval. Therefore, cross-modal hashing methods have been proposed [4–6]. Hashing is an effective method to solve big data problems with its benefits of low storage cost and fast query speed, which projects original high-dimensional data into a common hash code space in such a way that makes close points more possibly collided than those far apart.

Most existing cross-modal hashing methods can be classified into unsupervised [5,7,8] and supervised hashing [6,9,10]. Supervised cross-modal hashing methods exploit semantic labels to retrieve different modal data, which achieves better performance than unsupervised hashing methods. However, almost all these existing methods use shallow architectures based on hand-crafted features, which may be not conducive to learning discriminant hash codes from samples and reduce the accuracy of retrieval.

In recent years, deep neural networks has achieved remarkable success in many vision and multimedia tasks, such as image classification [11], face recognition [12] and object detection [13], etc. The deep neural networks can automatically learn highly discriminative features and accurately capture the semantic structure of input data. Deep cross-modal hashing (DCMH) [14] uses two deep neural networks as hash functions and integrates feature learning and hash-code learning into the same framework, which extends traditional models for cross-modal retrieval. However, DCMH only preserves intra-modality similarity while lacking the inter-modality similarity preservation, which may result in inadequate retrieval results. Pairwise relationship guided deep hashing (PRDH) [15] makes an improvement, which exploits different pairwise constraints to discover the heterogeneous correlations across different modalities from intra-modality and inter-modality preserving. However, the similarity-preserving matrix they give is a binary similarity matrix, in which 0 and 1 are adopted to denote dissimilar and similar relationship between cross-modal data. This method is applicable to single-label data, but it fails to make use of labels to explore the rich semantic information for multi-label data. For example, there are three multi-label instances: image A labeled dog, sleep and white, text B labeled dog, sleep and yellow and text C labeled dog, run and black. We know that image A is similar to text B and C, but in fact image A and text B are more similar than A and C. Therefore, the previously proposed binary similarity matrix can no longer represent this similarity relationship.

In this paper, we propose a cross-modal hashing method, called Label-Based Deep Semantic Hashing (LDSH), for cross-modal retrieval. Specifically, LDSH adopts deep neural networks to simultaneously integrate feature learning and hash-code learning for each modality into the same framework. It makes full use of labels to construct a new similarity-preserving matrix to maximize the preservation of semantic information between modalities. Moreover, a classification loss is given to ensure that the generated hash code can preserve label information. At the same time, Block Structure (B-Structure) and Batch Normalization Layer (BN-Layer) [16] are also added to the model to solve the redundancy problem between hash bits and accelerate the convergence speed of the neural network respectively. The main contributions of this work can be summarized as follows:

1. We propose a new similarity-preserving matrix according to multi-label to capture the rich semantic information to the greatest extent possible between cross-modal data. It can characterize the degree of similarity between modalities, which can make two samples with more common labels more similar than those with less common labels.
2. We design the last fully connected layer of two deep neural networks with a B-Structure, which makes the generated hash bits independent and reduces the redundancy between them.
3. The BN-Layer is adopted after the B-Structure to accelerate the convergence speed of two deep neural networks, which will greatly reduce the time consumed in training neural networks.

The rest of this paper is organized as follows. Related works are briefly introduced in Sect. 2. Section 3 introduces problem definition of this paper and describes in detail our LDSH method. Section 4 gives the experimental results. Lastly, we conclude our work in Sect. 5.

2   Related Work

Cross-modal hashing methods can be roughly categorized into two groups: unsupervised methods [7,8] and supervised methods [6,10]. Unsupervised methods learn hashing functions without semantic labels. As one of representative methods, latent semantic sparse hashing (LSSH) [5] uses sparse coding and matrix factorization for each modality. It then maps these learned features to a joint abstraction space to generate the unified hash codes. Supervised methods can exploit available supervised information (such as semantic labels or semantic relevance) to enhance the data correlation from different modalities and reduce the semantic gap. Semantic correlation maximization (SCM) [6] utilizes label information to obtain the similarity matrix which describes semantic correlations and reconstructs it through the binary codes. Semantics-preserving hashing (SePH) [9] generates a unified binary code by transforming semantic affinities of training data into a probability distribution while at the same time minimizing the Kullback-Leibler divergence.

However, most of the previous hashing methods are based on hand-crafted features extracted by shallow architectures, which are unable to describe the complicated nonlinear correlations across different modalities. Recently, deep models for cross-modal embedding show that they can effectively exploit the heterogeneous relationships among modalities. The representative works adopting deep architectures to achieve cross-modal retrieval include deep cross-modal hashing (DCMH) [14], self-supervised adversarial hashing networks (SSAH) [17], pairwise relationship guided deep hashing (PRDH) [15], etc. In comparison to these methods with a similarity-preserving matrix to describe binary similarity relationship, we give a new similarity-preserving matrix to more accurately characterize the degree of similarity among modalities. Moreover, inspired by [18], we utilize two B-Structures, one for each modality, to reduce the redundancy between generated hash codes.

3   Label-Based Deep Semantic Hashing

In this section, we give problem definition and specify our LDSH method. The framework of the proposed LDSH is shown in Fig. 1, which consists of deep network architecture and hash code learning. The details are illustrated in Sects. 3.2 and 3.3.

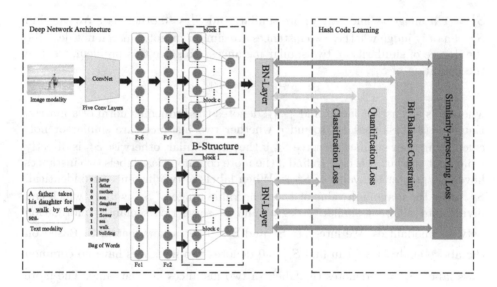

Fig. 1. Framework of LDSH.

3.1   Problem Definition

Although the proposed method is also applicable to more than two modalities, we only focus on cross-modal retrieval for two modalities in this paper. Assume that we have n training data points, each of which has two modalities of features. In this paper, we choose image and text modality for illustration. Image set is represented by $\mathbf{X} = \{\mathbf{x}_i\}_{i=1}^n$, text set is represented by $\mathbf{Y} = \{\mathbf{y}_i\}_{i=1}^n$, where $\mathbf{x}_i$ denotes the visual feature of image i, and $\mathbf{y}_i$ denotes the corresponding text feature. For the case of multi-label data points, let $\mathbf{L}^x = \{\mathbf{l}_i^x\}_{i=1}^n \in \{0,1\}^{k \times n}$ denote labels of n images and $\mathbf{L}^y = \{\mathbf{l}_i^y\}_{i=1}^n \in \{0,1\}^{k \times n}$ denote labels of n texts, where k is the total number of classes. $\mathbf{l}_i^x = \{l_{mi}^x\} \in \{0,1\}^k$ is the label vector for the ith image, where $l_{mi}^x = 1$ if the ith image belongs to the mth class and 0 otherwise, $m = 1, \cdots, k$. $\mathbf{l}_i^y$ is defined similarly to $\mathbf{l}_i^x$. We use $\widetilde{\mathbf{S}} \in [0,1]^{n \times n}$ to denote similarity-preserving matrix we proposed. Specifically,

$$\widetilde{\mathbf{S}} = (1 - \alpha)\mathbf{S}^1 + \alpha\mathbf{S}^2 \tag{1}$$

where $\mathbf{S}^1 \in \{0,1\}^{n \times n}$ and $\mathbf{S}^2 \in [0,1]^{n \times n}$ are used to preserve the binary similarity and the degree of similarity between cross-modal data respectively, α is a trade-off parameter. The specific forms of $\mathbf{S}^1$ and $\mathbf{S}^2$ are as follows:

$$S_{ij}^1 = \begin{cases} 1, & \text{if image } \mathbf{x}_i \text{ and text } \mathbf{y}_j \text{ share at least one class label} \\ 0, & \text{otherwise} \end{cases} \tag{2}$$

$S_{ij}^1 = 1$ if image $\mathbf{x}_i$ and text $\mathbf{y}_j$ are similar, and $S_{ij}^1 = 0$ otherwise. We can find S_{ij}^1 can only judge whether two instances are similar or not, but can not describe the degree of similarity of two similar instances. To solve this problem, we give the definition of S_{ij}^2.

$$S_{ij}^2 = S_{ij}^1 \cdot e^{-\|\mathbf{l}_i^x - \mathbf{l}_j^y\|_F^2 / \rho} \tag{3}$$

where ρ is a constant factor and $\|\cdot\|_F$ denotes the Frobenius norm of a matrix. Equation (3) first uses S_{ij}^1 to judge whether two instances are similar or not, calculating their similarity degree S_{ij}^2 if they are similar, otherwise S_{ij}^2 is directly 0, i.e., not similar. It is easy to find if the more common class labels two instances have, the greater the value of S_{ij}^2 is. When labels of two instances are identical, S_{ij}^2 takes the maximum value of 1. So the value range of S_{ij}^2 is $[0,1]$, which can divide into different similarity degree and preserve rich semantic information between modalities. We integrate $\mathbf{S}^1$ and $\mathbf{S}^2$ to get a new matrix $\widetilde{\mathbf{S}}$. Based on the above analysis, we can find $\widetilde{S}_{ij} = 0$ denotes two instances have no common class label. $\widetilde{S}_{ij} = 1$ denotes the labels of two instances are the same. The more common class labels two instances have, the more similar they are. Therefore, the new similarity-preserving matrix can describe the degree of similarity and capture the rich semantic information to the greatest extent possible between cross-modal data.

3.2   Deep Network Architecture

In this part, two deep neural networks are adopted to extract features for image and text modalities, respectively.

In extracting image features part, we use a refined CNN-F. CNN-F model [19] contains 5 convolutional layers and three fully-connected layers. The refined

CNN-F model of first seven layers are the same as CNN-F [19]. After the seventh layer Fc7, we conduct B-Structure. It takes 4096 output nodes from the seventh layer as input nodes and then divides the 4096 nodes into c blocks, where c is the length of hash code. Each block generates a node through its own full connected layer. Then these nodes are spliced together and the length is obviously c. Finally, a c-bit hash code is generated from the B-Structure. The B-Structure part of refined CNN model is illustrated as Fig. 1.

As for the part of text modality, we first represent text modality with bag-of-words (BOW) representation. Let it pass through two full connected layers and output 4096 nodes. Then, similar to the image modality part, the 4096 nodes are taken as input nodes and enter the B-Structure, resulting in a c-bit hash code.

Similar to the last three full-connection layers used by CNN-F [19], each hash bit generated will be related to all its input features, which may cause redundant information between these hash bits. However, the method of making each hash bit generated from a separate block can reduce bit and bit redundancy and maximize the information provided by each bit. Moreover, to accelerate the convergence speed of two deep neural networks, the BN-Layer [16] is adopted after the B-Structure, which will greatly reduce the time consumed in training neural networks.

3.3   Hash Code Learning

We adopt $\mathbf{P}_{*i} = p(\mathbf{x}_i; \omega_x) \in R^c$ to denote the learned image feature for a data point i, which corresponds to the output of the CNN for image modality; $\mathbf{T}_{*j} = t(\mathbf{y}_j; \omega_y) \in R^c$ denotes the learned text feature for a data point j, which corresponds to the output of the deep neural network for text modality. ω_x, ω_y represent the parameters of the CNN for image and the deep neural network for text, respectively. We also effectively use label information, learning a linear classifier $\mathbf{Z}$ to make hash codes $\mathbf{B}$ classified into different classes correctly [20], where $\mathbf{Z} \in R^{c \times k}$ and $\mathbf{B}$ is the unified hash codes from both modalities. In datasets, data appears as text-image pairs, so $\mathbf{L}^x$ and $\mathbf{L}^y$ are the same. We use $\mathbf{L}$ to represent them in our loss function.

The overall objective function of LDSH can be defined as follows:

$$\min_{\omega_x, \omega_y, \mathbf{B}, \mathbf{Z}} J = J_1 + \mu J_2 + \tau J_3 + \beta J_4 + \gamma J_5$$
$$s.t. \quad \mathbf{B} \in \{-1, 1\}^{c \times n} \tag{4}$$

where $J_1 = \|\mathbf{L} - \mathbf{Z}^T \mathbf{B}\|_F^2$, $J_2 = -\sum_{i,j=1}^{n} (\tilde{S}_{ij}\theta_{ij} - \log(1 + e^{\theta_{ij}}))$, $J_3 = \|\mathbf{B} - \mathbf{P}\|_F^2 + \|\mathbf{B} - \mathbf{T}\|_F^2$, $J_4 = \|\mathbf{P} \cdot \mathbf{1}\|_F^2 + \|\mathbf{T} \cdot \mathbf{1}\|_F^2$, $J_5 = \|\mathbf{Z}\|_F^2$ and μ, τ, β, γ are hyper-parameters.

The first term $J_1 = \|\mathbf{L} - \mathbf{Z}^T \mathbf{B}\|_F^2$ is a classification loss. Optimizing it enables $\mathbf{B}$ to preserve the label information and classified into different classes correctly.

The second term $J_2 = -\sum_{i,j=1}^{n}(\tilde{S}_{ij}\theta_{ij} - \log(1 + e^{\theta_{ij}}))$. This equation is derived from the following deduction.

$$J_2 = -\sum_{i,j=1}^{n} \log p(\tilde{S}_{ij}|\mathbf{P}_{*i}, \mathbf{T}_{*j})$$

$$= -\sum_{i,j=1}^{n} (\tilde{S}_{ij}\log(\sigma(\theta_{ij})) + (1 - \tilde{S}_{ij})(1 - \log(\sigma(\theta_{ij})))) \qquad (5)$$

$$= -\sum_{i,j=1}^{n} (\tilde{S}_{ij}\theta_{ij} - \log(1 + e^{\theta_{ij}}))$$

where $\theta_{ij} = \frac{1}{2}\mathbf{P}_{*i}^{T}\mathbf{T}_{*j}$, $\mathbf{P} \in R^{c \times n}$ and $\mathbf{T} \in R^{c \times n}$, $\mathbf{P}_{*i}$ denotes the ith column of matrix $\mathbf{P}$, $\mathbf{T}_{*j}$ denotes the jth column of matrix $\mathbf{T}$, $\mathbf{P}_{*i}^{T}$ is the transpose of $\mathbf{P}_{*i}$, $\sigma(\theta_{ij}) = \frac{1}{1+e^{-\theta_{ij}}}$. It is a similarity-preserving loss to preserve the degree of similarity between cross-modal data in $\tilde{\mathbf{S}}$. Optimizing this loss can reduce the Hamming distance of two more similar modalities and increase the Hamming distance of dissimilar modalities, which enables rich semantic information between modalities to be preserved.

The third term $J_3 = \|\mathbf{B} - \mathbf{P}\|_F^2 + \|\mathbf{B} - \mathbf{T}\|_F^2$ can make quantization loss reduce as much as possible. The fourth term $J_4 = \|\mathbf{P} \cdot \mathbf{1}\|_F^2 + \|\mathbf{T} \cdot \mathbf{1}\|_F^2$ balances the number of +1 and that of -1 for each bit of the hash code on all the training samples, where $\mathbf{1}$ to represent a vector with all elements being 1. The fifth term $J_5 = \|\mathbf{Z}\|_F^2$ denotes the regularization to avoid overfitting.

3.4 Optimization

It is intractable to optimize Eq. (4) directly since it is non-convex with variables $\omega_x, \omega_y, \mathbf{B}, \mathbf{Z}$. However, it is convex when taking one variable with the other three variables fixed. Therefore, we use an alternating learning strategy that fixing three parameters and updating the left one at a time until convergence. The whole alternating learning procedure is shown in Algorithm 1 and the detailed derivation will be introduced as follows:

1. Optimize $\mathbf{Z}$ with ω_x, ω_y and $\mathbf{B}$ fixed, then the problem shown in Eq. (4) becomes:

$$\min_{\mathbf{Z}} J = \|\mathbf{L} - \mathbf{Z}^T\mathbf{B}\|_F^2 + \gamma\|\mathbf{Z}\|_F^2 \qquad (6)$$

Let $\frac{\partial J}{\partial \mathbf{Z}} = 0$, then the closed-form solution of $\mathbf{Z}$ can be derived as:

$$\mathbf{Z} = (\mathbf{B}\mathbf{B}^T + \gamma\mathbf{I})^{-1}\mathbf{B}\mathbf{L}^T \qquad (7)$$

2. Optimize ω_x with ω_y, $\mathbf{B}$ and $\mathbf{Z}$ fixed. We use stochastic gradient descent (SGD) with a BP algorithm to optimize the CNN parameter ω_x of the image modality. For each sampled point $\mathbf{x}_i$, we can compute the gradient as follows:

$$\frac{\partial J}{\partial \mathbf{P}_{*i}} = \frac{1}{2}\mu(\sum_{j=1}^{n}(\sigma(\theta_{ij})\mathbf{T}_{*j} - \tilde{S}_{ij}\mathbf{T}_{*j}))$$
$$+ 2\tau(\mathbf{P}_{*i} - \mathbf{B}_{*i}) + 2\beta \mathbf{P} \cdot \mathbf{1} \tag{8}$$

Then $\frac{\partial J}{\partial \omega_x}$ can be computed with $\frac{\partial J}{\partial \mathbf{P}_{*i}}$ by using the chain rule, based on which BP can be used to update the parameter ω_x.

Algorithm 1. The learning algorithm for LDSH

Input: Image dataset $\mathbf{X}$, text dataset $\mathbf{Y}$, label set $\mathbf{L}$, and
   similarity-preserving matrix $\tilde{\mathbf{S}}$, bit length c, parameters μ, τ, β, γ.
Output: Parameters ω_x and ω_y of the deep neural networks for image and
   text modalities, hash codes $\mathbf{B}$.
Initialize network parameters ω_x and ω_y, mini-batch size $N_x = N_y = 128$, and
   iteration number $t_x = \lceil n/N_x \rceil, t_y = \lceil n/N_y \rceil$.
repeat
   Update $\mathbf{Z}$ according to Eq.(7).
   for $iter = 1, 2, \cdots, n_x$ **do**
      Randomly select N_x images from $\mathbf{X}$ to construct a mini-batch.
      For each sampled point $\mathbf{x}_i$ in the mini-batch, calculate $\mathbf{P}_{*i} = p(\mathbf{x}_i; \omega_x)$
         by forward propagation.
      Calculate the derivative according to Eq.(8).
      Update the parameter ω_x by back propagation.
   end
   for $iter = 1, 2, \cdots, n_y$ **do**
      Randomly select N_y texts from $\mathbf{Y}$ to construct a mini-batch.
      For each sampled point $\mathbf{y}_i$ in the mini-batch, calculate $\mathbf{T}_{*i} = p(\mathbf{y}_i; \omega_y)$
         by forward propagation.
      Calculate the derivative according to Eq.(9).
      Update the parameter ω_y by back propagation.
   end
   Update $\mathbf{B}$ bit by bit according to Eq.(12).
until *a fixed number of iterations;*

---

3. Optimize ω_y with ω_x, $\mathbf{B}$ and $\mathbf{Z}$ fixed. Then we also use SGD with a BP algorithm to optimize the neural network parameter ω_y of the text modality. For each sampled point $\mathbf{y}_i$, we compute the gradient as:

$$\frac{\partial J}{\partial \mathbf{T}_{*j}} = \frac{1}{2}\mu(\sum_{i=1}^{n}(\sigma(\theta_{ij})\mathbf{P}_{*j} - \tilde{S}_{ij}\mathbf{P}_{*j}))$$
$$+ 2\tau(\mathbf{T}_{*i} - \mathbf{B}_{*i}) + 2\beta \mathbf{T} \cdot \mathbf{1} \tag{9}$$

Then $\frac{\partial J}{\partial \omega_y}$ can be computed with $\frac{\partial J}{\partial \mathbf{T}_{*i}}$ by using the chain rule, based on which BP can be used to update the parameter ω_y.

4. Optimize $\mathbf{B}$ with ω_x, ω_y and $\mathbf{Z}$ fixed. The objective function shown in Eq. (4) can be reformulated as:

$$\min_{\mathbf{B}} J = \|\mathbf{L} - \mathbf{Z}^T\mathbf{B}\|_F^2 + \tau(\|\mathbf{B} - \mathbf{P}\|_F^2 + \|\mathbf{B} - \mathbf{T}\|_F^2)$$
$$s.t. \quad \mathbf{B} \in \{-1, 1\}^{c \times n} \tag{10}$$

which is rewritten as:

$$\min_{\mathbf{B}} J = \|\mathbf{Z}^T\mathbf{B}\|_F^2 - Tr(\mathbf{B}^T\mathbf{W})$$
$$s.t. \quad \mathbf{B} \in \{-1, 1\}^{c \times n} \tag{11}$$

where $\mathbf{W} = \mathbf{ZL} + \tau(\mathbf{P} + \mathbf{T})$ and $Tr(\cdot)$ denotes the trace of a matrix. Although it is challenging to address the optimization in Eq. (11) due to $\mathbf{B} \in \{-1, 1\}^{c \times n}$ is discrete, we can adopt a closed-form solution to optimize a single row of $\mathbf{B}$ by the other rows fixed. So we can directly use the discrete cyclic coordinate descent (DCC) approach [10] to learn $\mathbf{B}$ bit-by-bit iteratively. Specifically, let $\mathbf{h}^T$ be the qth row of the $\mathbf{B}$, $q = 1, \cdots, c$ and $\mathbf{B}'$ the matrix of $\mathbf{B}$ excluding $\mathbf{h}$. Analogously, let $\mathbf{v}^T$ be the qth row of the $\mathbf{Z}$ and $\mathbf{Z}'$ the matrix of $\mathbf{Z}$ excluding $\mathbf{v}$. Besides, let $\mathbf{w}^T$ be the qth row of the $\mathbf{W}$ and $\mathbf{W}'$ the matrix of $\mathbf{W}$ excluding $\mathbf{w}$. Then the problem can achieve optimal solution:

$$\mathbf{h} = sign(\mathbf{w} - \mathbf{B}'^T\mathbf{Z}'\mathbf{v}) \tag{12}$$

where the $sign(\cdot)$ is an element-wise sign function defined as $sign(u) = 1$ if $u \geq 0$, and $= -1$ otherwise.

4   Experiments

To verify the effectiveness of the proposed LDSH, we conduct sufficient experiments on two popular datasets. Two types of cross-modal retrieval tasks are designed to evaluate the performance of cross-modal retrieval: (1) Img2Text: querying related texts with images, and (2) Text2Img: querying related images with texts.

4.1   Datasets

The **MIRFLICKR-25K** dataset [21] contains 25,000 instances collected from the social photography site Flickr. Each instance includes an image and associated textual tags and is manually annotated with at least one of the 24 class labels. In our experiment, we select 20,015 instances which have at least 20 textual tags. The text for each instance is represented as a 1,386-dimensional bag-of-words vector. For the hand-crafted feature based methods, the image modality is represented as a 512-dimensional SIFT feature vector. For the deep hashing method, the raw pixels are directly used as the image modality inputs.

The **NUS-WIDE** dataset [22] is a public web image dataset composed of 269,648 instances which have an image with its associated textual tags. Each instance is manually annotated with one or multiple labels from 81 provided labels. We select 186,577 image-text pairs that belong to the top 10 most frequent concepts in our experiment. The text for each instance is represented as a 1,000-dimensional bag-of-words vector. For the hand-crafted feature based methods, a 500-dimensional bag-of-words vector is adopted for its image modality representation. For the deep hashing method, the raw pixels are directly used as the image modality inputs.

4.2 Baselines

To evaluate the effectiveness of our proposed method, we compare it with five state-of-the-art cross-modal hashing methods, including CVH [7], LSSH [5], STMH [4], SCM [6] and DCMH [14]. Among these methods, CVH, LSSH, STMH and SCM are based on shallow structure while DCMH and our method are based on deep structure. Source codes of these baselines are kindly provided by corresponding authors. In our experiments, all the parameters in these baselines are set based on the suggestion of the original papers.

Table 1. Comparison with baselines on MIRFLICKR-25K and NUS-WIDE in terms of mAP. The best accuracy is shown in boldface.

Task	Method	MIRFLICKR-25K			NUS-WIDE		
		16bits	32bits	64bits	16bits	32bits	64bits
Img2Text	CVH	0.5852	0.5861	0.5835	0.3797	0.3871	0.3893
	LSSH	0.5850	0.5887	0.5910	0.3831	0.3879	0.3916
	STMH	0.5943	0.5981	0.5983	0.4293	0.4350	0.4401
	SCM	0.6243	0.6305	0.6352	0.4786	0.4793	0.4854
	DCMH	0.7274	0.7298	0.7381	0.6231	0.6277	0.6401
	LDSH	**0.7366**	**0.7383**	**0.7522**	**0.6330**	**0.6380**	**0.6496**
Text2Img	CVH	0.5849	0.5851	0.5903	0.3682	0.3869	0.3776
	LSSH	0.5942	0.5961	0.5992	0.4099	0.4124	0.4118
	STMH	0.5865	0.5902	0.5961	0.3769	0.3893	0.4005
	SCM	0.6150	0.6216	0.6283	0.4453	0.4502	0.4599
	DCMH	0.7601	0.7642	0.7752	0.6571	0.6597	0.6740
	LDSH	**0.7680**	**0.7715**	**0.7858**	**0.6700**	**0.6713**	**0.6851**

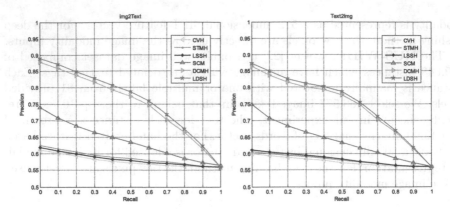

Fig. 2. Precision-recall curves with code length 64 on MIRFlickr-25K.

4.3 Settings and Performance Comparisons

For MIRFLICKR-25K dataset, we randomly sample 10,000 instances as the training set. For testing, we take 2,000 instances of this dataset as the test set and the rest as retrieval set. For NUS-WIDE dataset, we randomly sample 10,500 instances to train, 2,100 instances to test and the rest to retrieval. After multiple adjustments of parameters, we find that good performance can be achieved with $\rho = 10$, $\alpha = 0.5$, $\mu = \tau = \beta = 1$ and $\gamma = 0.01$ in our experiments. Moreover, the batch size is fixed to be 128 and the algorithm runs 300 times.

Mean average precision (mAP) and precision-recall curves are adopted to directly evaluate the performance of all compared methods in our experiment. As shown in Table 1, we can observe the mAP values of all the methods on MIRFlickr-25K and NUS-WIDE with 16, 32 and 64 bits, respectively. In addition, Fig. 2 shows the precision-recall curves of all the methods with code length 64 on MIRFlickr-25K. According to the experimental results, we find that the performance of LDSH and DCMH is far superior to other methods, because the features extracted by deep model are better than those extracted by hand-crafted methods. We can also find that LDSH performs better than DCMH, which indicates the similarity-preserving matrix we use can capture more rich semantic information in cross-modal data.

5 Conclusion

In this paper, we propose a label-based deep semantic hashing method for cross-modal retrieval. The proposed method gives a new similarity-preserving matrix according to multi-label to describe the degree of similarity, which can capture the rich semantic information to the greatest extent possible between cross-modal data. In addition, the last fully connected layer of the deep neural network is designed as a B-Structure to reduce the redundancy between generated bits and the BN-Layer is adopted after the B-Structure to accelerate the convergence speed of neural network. Extensive experiments on two datasets with image-text modalities show the superiority of our method in cross-modal retrieval tasks. In future, we intend to apply the generative adversarial networks to our model and optimize hash codes through adversarial learning.

References

1. Feng, F., Wang, X., Li, R.: Cross-modal retrieval with correspondence autoencoder. In: Proceedings of the 22nd ACM International Conference on Multimedia, pp. 7–16. ACM (2014)
2. Wang, K., He, R., Wang, L., Wang, W., Tan, T.: Joint feature selection and subspace learning for cross-modal retrieval. IEEE Trans. Pattern Anal. Mach. Intell. **38**(10), 2010–2023 (2015)
3. Wu, Y., Wang, S., Huang, Q.: Online asymmetric similarity learning for cross-modal retrieval. In: Proceedings of the IEEE Conference on Computer Vision and Pattern Recognition, pp. 4269–4278 (2017)
4. Wang, D., Gao, X., Wang, X., He, L.: Semantic topic multimodal hashing for cross-media retrieval. In: Twenty-Fourth International Joint Conference on Artificial Intelligence (2015)
5. Zhou, J., Ding, G., Guo, Y.: Latent semantic sparse hashing for cross-modal similarity search. In: Proceedings of the 37th International ACM SIGIR Conference on Research & Development in Information Retrieval, pp. 415–424. ACM (2014)
6. Zhang, D., Li, W.J.: Large-scale supervised multimodal hashing with semantic correlation maximization. In: Twenty-Eighth AAAI Conference on Artificial Intelligence (2014)
7. Kumar, S., Udupa, R.: Learning hash functions for cross-view similarity search. In: Twenty-Second International Joint Conference on Artificial Intelligence (2011)
8. Liu, W., Mu, C., Kumar, S., Chang, S.F.: Discrete graph hashing. In: Advances in Neural Information Processing Systems, pp. 3419–3427 (2014)
9. Lin, Z., Ding, G., Hu, M., Wang, J.: Semantics-preserving hashing for cross-view retrieval. In: Proceedings of the IEEE Conference on Computer Vision and Pattern Recognition, pp. 3864–3872 (2015)
10. Shen, F., Shen, C., Liu, W., Tao Shen, H.: Supervised discrete hashing. In: Proceedings of the IEEE Conference on Computer Vision and Pattern Recognition, pp. 37–45 (2015)
11. Wang, F., et al.: Residual attention network for image classification. In: Proceedings of the IEEE Conference on Computer Vision and Pattern Recognition, pp. 3156–3164 (2017)
12. Parkhi, O.M., Vedaldi, A., Zisserman, A., et al.: Deep face recognition. In: bmvc. vol. 1, no. 6 (2015)
13. Ren, S., He, K., Girshick, R., Sun, J.: Faster r-cnn: towards real-time object detection with region proposal networks. In: Advances in Neural Information Processing Systems, pp. 91–99 (2015)
14. Jiang, Q.Y., Li, W.J.: Deep cross-modal hashing. In: Proceedings of the IEEE Conference on Computer Vision and Pattern Recognition, pp. 3232–3240 (2017)
15. Yang, E., Deng, C., Liu, W., Liu, X., Tao, D., Gao, X.: Pairwise relationship guided deep hashing for cross-modal retrieval. In: Thirty-First AAAI Conference on Artificial Intelligence (2017)

16. Ioffe, S., Szegedy, C.: Batch normalization: accelerating deep network training by reducing internal covariate shift. arXiv preprint arXiv:1502.03167 (2015)
17. Li, C., Deng, C., Li, N., Liu, W., Gao, X., Tao, D.: Self-supervised adversarial hashing networks for cross-modal retrieval. In: Proceedings of the IEEE Conference on Computer Vision and Pattern Recognition, pp. 4242–4251 (2018)
18. Lai, H., Pan, Y., Liu, Y., Yan, S.: Simultaneous feature learning and hash coding with deep neural networks. In: Proceedings of the IEEE Conference on Computer Vision and Pattern Recognition, pp. 3270–3278 (2015)
19. Chatfield, K., Simonyan, K., Vedaldi, A., Zisserman, A.: Return of the devil in the details: Delving deep into convolutional nets. arXiv preprint arXiv:1405.3531 (2014)
20. Zhong, F., Chen, Z., Min, G.: Deep discrete cross-modal hashing for cross-media retrieval. Pattern Recogn. **83**, 64–77 (2018)
21. Huiskes, M.J., Lew, M.S.: The mir flickr retrieval evaluation. In: Proceedings of the 1st ACM International Conference on Multimedia Information Retrieval, pp. 39–43. ACM (2008)
22. Chua, T.S., Tang, J., Hong, R., Li, H., Luo, Z., Zheng, Y.: Nus-wide: a real-world web image database from national university of singapore. In: Proceedings of the ACM International Conference on Image and Video Retrieval, p. 48. ACM (2009)

HRec: Heterogeneous Graph Embedding-Based Personalized Point-of-Interest Recommendation

Yijun Su[1,3], Xiang Li[1,2,3], Daren Zha[3(✉)], Wei Tang[1,2,3], Yiwen Jiang[1,2,3], Ji Xiang[3], and Neng Gao[2,3]

[1] School of Cyber Security, University of Chinese Academy of Sciences, Beijing, China
{suyijun,lixiang9015,tangwei,jiangyiwen}@iie.ac.cn
[2] State Key Laboratory of Information Security, Chinese Academy of Sciences, Beijing, China
gaoneng@iie.ac.cn
[3] Institute of Information Engineering, Chinese Academy of Sciences, Beijing, China
{zhadaren,xiangji}@iie.ac.cn

Abstract. POI (point-of-interest) recommendation as an important location-based service has been widely utilized in helping people discover attractive locations. A variety of available check-in data provide a good opportunity for developing personalized POI recommender systems. However, the extreme sparsity of check-in data and inefficiency of exploiting unobserved feedback pose severe challenges for POI recommendation. To cope with these challenges, we develop a heterogeneous graph embedding-based personalized POI recommendation framework called HRec. It consists of two modules: the learning module and the ranking module. Specifically, we first propose the learning module to produce a series of intermediate feedback from unobserved feedback by learning the embeddings of users and POIs in the heterogeneous graph. Then we devise the ranking module to recommend each user the ultimate ranked list of relevant POIs by utilizing two pairwise feedback comparisons. Experimental results on two real-world datasets demonstrate the effectiveness and superiority of the proposed method.

Keywords: POI recommendation · Graph embedding · Personalized ranking

1 Introduction

Location-based social networks (LBSNs) have become popular recently because of the increasing proliferation of smart mobile devices with location-acquisition that make people easy to post their real location and location-related contents. These LBSNs like Foursquare, Facebook Places, and Yelp allow users to make friends and share their check-in experiences on Points-of-Interests (POIs), e.g.,

© Springer Nature Switzerland AG 2019
T. Gedeon et al. (Eds.): ICONIP 2019, LNCS 11955, pp. 37–49, 2019.
https://doi.org/10.1007/978-3-030-36718-3_4

restaurants, stores, and museums. Driven by a vast amount of check-in data collected, POI recommendation arises to improve the user experience. It has become an important location-based service to help people explore interesting and attractive places [3].

The task of POI recommendation is to model users' preferences and suggest novel POIs to users. It is a very challenging problem due to two major reasons. First, the check-in data are **extremely sparse**, which significantly increases the difficulty of POI recommender systems. In fact, a single user usually chooses only a small portion from millions of POIs to check in. This will make the user-POI matrix very sparse. In the literature, some researchers have sought to utilize **social information** and **geographical information** to supplement the highly sparse user-POI matrix. Most existing approaches have been proposed to incorporate social relations between users into collaborative filtering (CF) techniques, e.g., friend-based CF [16], matrix factorization with social regularization [1], and friend-based matrix factorization [2]. However, these methods provide considerably limited improvements on POI recommendation because social links of users are also sparse. On the other hand, most related works [1,5,10,12] attempt to establish independent geographical models to recommend POIs. Nonetheless, such modeling approaches only mean that the check-in activity is limited to the distance constraint and do not effectively represent users' preferences. Second, unobserved feedback is **implicit** and its number is **very large**, which will lead to the inefficiency of computation and the inaccuracy of prediction. Some researchers [2,6,8,13] have proposed to ranking-based models to alleviate this situation. Bayesian Personalised Ranking (BPR) [8] is a famous ranking-based model, which learns the ranking based on pairwise preference comparison over observed and unobserved feedback. However, due to the imbalance between users' visited POIs and non-visited POIs, the BPR model cannot successfully enhance prediction accuracy.

More recently, graph embedding methods which embed information networks into low-dimensional vector spaces have been widely adopted for a variety of tasks such as link prediction, text mining, and sentiment analysis [9]. Such low-dimensional representation is denser than the user-POI check-in matrix, so graph embedding is a potential and powerful solution to alleviate the problem of data sparsity. In this paper, we extend these efforts and propose a **H**eterogeneous graph embedding-based personalized POI **Rec**ommendation framework (HRec) to effectively address the aforementioned challenges. The overall architecture of HRec is shown in Fig. 1. Our recommendation framework consists of two modules, one of which is the **learning module** and the other is the **ranking module**. (1) The learning module is to generate a series of intermediate feedback from unobserved feedback by exploiting social and geographical information networks, which is treated as weak preference relative to positive feedback while as strong preference in comparison to other unobserved feedback. The module learns vector representations for the nodes (i.e., users and POIs embeddings) in the heterogeneous graphs and then uses the learned representations for generating intermediate feedback. (2) The ranking module is to recommend each

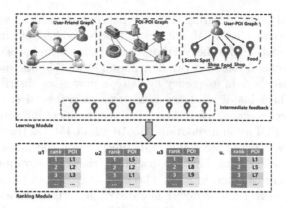

Fig. 1. The architecture framework of HRec.

user a ranked list of relevant POIs that the user might be interested in but has not visited before. In this module, we augment the ranking function of BPR by introducing the intermediate feedback generated by the learning module. Furthermore, we design a mini-batch gradient descent (MBGD) with the bootstrap sampling algorithm to optimize its objective function. Finally, we evaluate the proposed framework on two large-scale real-world datasets and prove its superiority to several state-of-the-art baselines.

To summarize, our work makes the following contributions:

1 We develop a Heterogeneous graph embedding-based personalized POI Recommendation framework (HRec) to overcome the data sparsity issue and inefficiency of exploiting unobserved feedback. The HRec consists of two modules: the learning module and the ranking module.
2 The learning module in HRec is devised for generating a series of intermediate feedback from unobserved feedback by learning the embeddings of users and POIs in the heterogeneous graph.
3 The ranking module in HRec is designed for recommending each user the ultimate ranked list of relevant POIs by utilizing two pairwise feedback comparisons.
4 We conduct extensive experiments on real-world datasets. Experimental results prove the effectiveness and efficiency of the proposed HRec framework.

2   Related Work

In this section, we discuss some existing works related to our research, particularly those employing social and geographical information for POI recommendation. As the main learning and ranking modules fall within the realm of graph embedding and personalized ranking, we also review these related techniques.

Based on the fact that friends are more likely to share common interests, social information is widely used in POI recommender systems [2]. In particular, friend-based collaborative filtering [12] and matrix factorization with social regularization [1] are two effective algorithms in LBSNs, which both integrate social relationship information into the collaborative filtering techniques to improve the quality of POI recommendation. Besides, Zhang et al. [15] designed a model to estimate the social check-in frequency by using a power-law distribution learned from historical check-ins of all users. Since the geographical characteristics of locations can affect users' check-in behavior, geographical information plays an important role in POI recommendation [1,5,10,12,13,15]. On the one hand, geographical distance between users and POIs limits users' check-in choice. On the other hand, as Tobler's First Law of Geography shown, geographical clustering phenomenon is very common in users' check-in activities. In particular, several representative models, such as power law distribution (PD) model [12], Multi-center Gaussian distribution model (MGM) [1], and Kernel Density Estimation (KDE) [14], are proposed to capture the geographical influence in POI recommendation.

Graph embedding techniques that embed information networks into low-dimensional vector spaces have attracted considerable attention and made great progress in recent years. For example, Xie et al. [11] proposed a graph embedding model for POI recommendations to systematically model the POI, user, and time relations and learned the representations. Zhao et al. [17] proposed a temporal POI embedding based on Skip-Gram model to capture users' temporal preference. However, few works based on graph embedding attempt to exploit social relations between users and geographical neighborhood characteristics between POIs for POI recommendations. From the perspective of ranking tasks, these collaborative filtering-based methods mentioned above can be viewed as point-wise methods. Indeed, empirical studies [6,13] have demonstrated that point-wise methods are generally less effective than pairwise ranking methods. Yuan et al. [13] proposed a GeoBPR model that injects users' geo-spatial preference. Manotumruksa et al. [6] developed a novel personalized ranking framework with multiple sampling criteria to enhance the performance of POI recommendation.

In this paper, our work distinguishes itself from previous researches in several aspects. First, to the best of our knowledge, it is the first effort that exploits social relations between users and geographical neighborhood characteristics between POIs to address the challenges of data sparsity and inefficiency of unobserved feedback in a unified way. Second, we generate a series of intermediate feedback from unobserved feedback in the learning module to augment the ranking function of Bayesian Personalised Ranking (BPR) [8]. Moreover, we integrate the embeddings of users and POIs and BPR in a systematic way for POI recommendations.

3   Problem Statement

Let users and POIs denoted by $\mathcal{U} = \{u_1, u_2, ...\}$ and $\mathcal{L} = \{l_1, l_2, ...\}$. Each user u checked in some POIs $\mathcal{L}_u$. Each POI has a location $l_j = \{lon_j, lat_j\}$ in terms of longitude and latitude. We use $\mathcal{F}_u = \{f_1, f_2, ...\}$ to represent the set of the user's friends. In this paper, we consider three different types of feedback, namely positive, intermediate, negative feedback. The positive feedback is defined as a set of POIs previously checked in by user u: $P_u = \mathcal{L}_u$. The intermediate feedback $I_u = \{l_1, ..., l_c\}$ is learned from unvisited POIs in the learning module. The remaining unvisited POIs are viewed as the negative feedback $N_u = \{l_1, ..., l_h\}$. Here *negative* only means no explicit feedback can be observed from the user and does not denote users' dislike of the POIs.

Definition 1. User-POI Graph, *denoted as $G_{ul} = (\mathcal{U} \cup \mathcal{L}, \mathcal{E}_{ul})$, is a bipartite graph where $\mathcal{E}_{ul}$ is the set of edges between users and POIs. The weight w_{ul} between user u and POI l is simply defined as the frequency of user u checked in POI l.*

Definition 2. User-Friend Graph, *denoted as $G_{uf} = (\mathcal{U} \cup \mathcal{F}, \mathcal{E}_{uf})$, is a social relation graph where $\mathcal{F}$ is a set of users' friends and $\mathcal{E}_{uf}$ is the set of edges between users and friends. The weight w_{uf} between user u and friend f is defined as common check-in ratio between user u and his friend f, which is measured by $\frac{|\mathcal{L}_u \cap \mathcal{L}_f|}{|\mathcal{L}_u \cup \mathcal{L}_f|}$.*

Definition 3. POI-POI Graph, *denoted as $G_{ll} = (\mathcal{L} \cup \mathcal{L}, \mathcal{E}_{ll})$, captures the geographical neighborhood characteristics between POIs. In general, if POI l_i is a geographical neighbor of POI l_j, there will be an edge between l_i and l_j. The weight w_{ij} of the edge between l_i and l_j is set to 1 when POI l_i is the neighbors in geographical space to POI l_j.*

Problem 1 **(POI Recommendation).** Given a user check-in record $\mathcal{L}_u$, the geographical coordinates of POIs and the user's social friends $\mathcal{F}_u$, the task of POI recommendation is to generate a ranked list of POIs that the user might be interested in but has not visited before in LBSNs.

4 POI Recommendation Framework

4.1 Learning Module

In this module, the aim is to generate a series of intermediate feedback from unobserved feedback by learning the user and POI embeddings of heterogeneous information networks. We adopt the bipartite graph embedding approach from Tang et al. [9], which is a representation learning method for heterogeneous text networks.

Bipartite Graph Embedding. Given a bipartite graph $G_{AB} = (\mathcal{V}_A \cup \mathcal{V}_B, \mathcal{E})$, where $\mathcal{V}_A$ and $\mathcal{V}_B$ are two disjoint sets of vertices of different types, and $\mathcal{E}$ is the set of edges between them. The conditional probability of vertex v_i in set $\mathcal{V}_A$ generated by vertex v_j in set $\mathcal{V}_B$ can be defined as:

$$p(v_i|v_j) = \frac{exp(z_i^T \cdot z_j)}{\sum_{v_k \in \mathcal{V}_A} exp(z_k^T \cdot z_j)} \tag{1}$$

where z_i denotes the embedding vector for vertex v_i, and z_j is the embedding vector of vertex v_j. For each vertex v_j in $\mathcal{V}_B$, Eq. (1) defines a conditional distribution $p(\cdot|v_j)$ over all the vertices in the set $\mathcal{V}_A$. For each edge e_{ij}, its empirical distribution is given by $\hat{p}(v_i|v_j) = \frac{w_{ij}}{deg_j}$, where w_{ij} is the edge weight between v_i and v_j and $deg_j = \sum_{i \in \mathcal{V}_A} w_{ij}$.

To learn embeddings, we make the conditional distribution $p(\cdot|v_j)$ closely approximates the empirical distribution $\hat{p}(\cdot|v_j)$. Hence, we minimize the following objective function over the graph G_{AB}:

$$O_{AB} = \sum_{j \in \mathcal{V}_B} \lambda_j d(\hat{p}(\cdot|v_j), p(\cdot|v_j)) \tag{2}$$

where $d(\cdot, \cdot)$ is the KL-divergence between two distributions, and λ_j is the importance of vertex v_j in the graph, which can be set as the degree deg_j. Omiting some constants, the objective function can be writen as:

$$O_{AB} = - \sum_{(i,j) \in \mathcal{E}} w_{ij} \log p(v_i|v_j) \tag{3}$$

Optimizing the objective function Eq. (3) is computationally expensive, which requires the summation over the entire set of vertices when calculating the conditional probability $p(\cdot|v_j)$. To overcome this problem, we use the techniques of edge sampling [9] and negative sampling [7]. For each edge e_{ij}, its final objective function is:

$$O_{AB} = - \sum_{(i,j) \in \mathcal{E}} \left[\log \sigma(z_i^T \cdot z_j) + \sum_{n=1}^{K} \mathcal{E}_{v_n \sim P_n(v)} \log \sigma(-z_n^T \cdot z_j) \right] \tag{4}$$

where $\sigma(x) = 1/(1 + \exp(-x))$ is the sigmoid function, K is the number of negative edges. In our implementation, we set $K = 5$, $P_n(v) \propto d_v^{3/4}$ from the empirical setting of [7], where d_v is the out-degree of node v.

Joint Training Learning. The heterogeneous information network is composed of three bipartite graphs: User-POI, User-Friend and POI-POI. To collectively embed the three bipartite graphs, minimizing the sum of all objective functions as following:

$$O = O_{ul} + O_{uf} + O_{ll} \tag{5}$$

where

$$O_{ul} = - \sum_{(i,j) \in \mathcal{E}_{ul}} w_{ij} \log p(u_i|l_j) \tag{6}$$

$$O_{uf} = - \sum_{(i,j) \in \mathcal{E}_{uf}} w_{ij} \log p(u_i|f_j) \tag{7}$$

$$O_{ll} = - \sum_{(i,j) \in \mathcal{E}_{ll}} w_{ij} \log p(l_i|l_j) \tag{8}$$

We learn user and POI embeddings by joint training the three bipartite graphs. In each step, we adopt the asynchronous stochastic gradient algorithm (ASGD) to update the model parameters. See Algorithm 1 for more details. Finally, we sort all unobserved POIs in accordance with their scores $s = z_u^T z_l$

to acquire the Top-t as intermediate feedback for each user, where z_u, z_l are embeddings for user u, POI l and t is the number of intermediate feedback we defined.

Algorithm 1. Joint training

Input: Bipartite graphs (User-POI graph G_{ul}, User-Friend graph G_{uf}, POI-POI graph G_{ll}), number of samples T, number of negative samples K, vector dimension d.
Output: users embeddings: $Z_u \in \mathbb{R}^{|U| \times d}$ and POI embeddings $Z_l \in \mathbb{R}^{|\mathcal{L}| \times d}$
1: **while** $iter \leq T$ **do**
2:     sample an edge from $\mathcal{E}_{ul}$ and draw K negative edges, and update the user and POI embeddings;
3:     sample an edge from $\mathcal{E}_{uf}$ and draw K negative edges, and update the user embeddings;
4:     sample an edge from $\mathcal{E}_{ll}$ and draw K negative edges, and update the POI embeddings;
5: **end while**

4.2 Ranking Module

In this module, we augment the ranking function of BPR by introducing the intermediate feedback. Specifically, we treat the intermediate feedback as weak preference relative to positive feedback while as strong preference in comparison to other unobserved feedback. Compared with the basic assumption of BPR, our assumption can mine more contribution information from unobserved POIs. Thus, for user u, the ranking order of her preference over positive feedback $i \in P_u$, intermediate feedback $c \in I_u$, and negative feedback $j \in N_u$ is given as the following:

$$
\begin{cases} \hat{r}_{ui} > \hat{r}_{uc} \\ \hat{r}_{uc} > \hat{r}_{uj} \end{cases} \Rightarrow \begin{cases} W_u H_i^T + b_i > W_u H_c^T + b_c \\ W_u H_c^T + b_c > W_u H_j^T + b_j \end{cases} \tag{9}
$$

where $\hat{r}_{ui}$ is the predicted users' preference score, which is modelled by matrix factorization, i.e., $\hat{r}_{ui} = W_u H_i^T + b_i$. The W_u and H_i^T denotes latent feature vectors of user u and POI i, respectively. The b_i is the bias term of POI i. Thus, model parameters $\Theta = \{W \in \mathbb{R}^{|U| \times k}, H \in \mathbb{R}^{|\mathcal{L}| \times k}, b \in \mathbb{R}^{|\mathcal{L}|}\}$.

Due to the BPR method gives equal weight to each POI pair, it does not distinguish between their different contributions in learning the objective function. To address this limitation, we assign a higher weight to highlight its contribution. To this end, we propose the augmented bayesian personalized ranking function based on matrix factorization to compute the ranking loss function, given by:

$$
J(\Theta) = \min_{W,H} - \sum_{u \in \mathcal{U}} \left[\sum_{i \in \mathcal{P}_u} \sum_{c \in \mathcal{I}_u} \ln \sigma \left(c_{uic}(\hat{r}_{ui} - \hat{r}_{uc}) \right) \right.
$$

$$
\left. + \sum_{c \in \mathcal{I}_u} \sum_{j \in \mathcal{N}_u} \ln \sigma (\hat{r}_{uc} - \hat{r}_{uj}) \right] \tag{10}
$$

$$
+ \lambda_\Theta ||\Theta||^2
$$

where c_{uic} denotes the weight of the difference between positive and intermediate feedback, and its value is determined by the difference of two visit frequencies $c_{uic} = 1 + \alpha f_{ui}$, where α is a tuning parameter and f_{ui} represents the check-in frequency of user u on POI i. λ_Θ are model specific regularization parameters and $\sigma(x)$ is the sigmoid function.

Algorithm 2. Ranking Algorithm

Input: feedback data: user $u \in \mathcal{U}$, positive feedback $\mathcal{P}_u$, intermediate feedback $\mathcal{I}_u$, and negative feedback $\mathcal{N}_u$

hyperparameters: sampling times st, batch size bs, learning rate η, and regularization parameters $\lambda_u, \lambda_i, \lambda_c, \lambda_j, \beta_i, \beta_c, \beta_j$

Output: model parameters $\Theta = \{W, H, b\}$

1: Initialization Θ with Normal distribution $\mathcal{N}(0,0.1)$
2: **for** $t = 1$ to st **do**
3:     Uniformly sample a user u from $\mathcal{U}$
4:     Uniformly sample a positive feedback i from $\mathcal{P}_u$
5:     Uniformly sample a intermediate feedback c from $\mathcal{I}_u$
6:     Uniformly sample a negative feedback j from $\mathcal{N}_u$
7: **end for**
8: $s = 0$
9: **while** $(s + 1) * bs \leq st$ **do**
10:     **for** $j = 1$ to bs **do**
11:         $\hat{r}_{uic} = (1 - \sigma(c_{uic}(\hat{r}_{ui} - \hat{r}_{uc}))) \cdot c_{uic}, \hat{r}_{ucj} = 1 - \sigma((\hat{r}_{uc} - \hat{r}_{uj}))$
12:         $W_u \leftarrow W_u + \eta\left([\hat{r}_{uic}(H_i - H_c) + \hat{r}_{ucj}(H_c - Hj)] - \lambda_u W_u\right)$
13:         $H_i \leftarrow H_i + \eta\left(\hat{r}_{uic}W_u - \lambda_i H_i\right)$
14:         $H_c \leftarrow H_c + \eta\left(-\hat{r}_{uic}W_u + \hat{r}_{ucj}W_u - \lambda_c H_c\right)$
15:         $H_j \leftarrow H_i + \eta\left(-\hat{r}_{ucj}W_u - \lambda_i H_i\right)$
16:         $b_i \leftarrow b_i + \eta\left(\hat{r}_{uic} - \beta_i b_i\right)$
17:         $b_c \leftarrow b_c + \eta\left(-\hat{r}_{uic} + \hat{r}_{ucj} - \beta_c b_c\right)$
18:         $b_j \leftarrow b_j + \eta\left(-\hat{r}_{ucj} - \beta_j b_j\right)$
19:     **end for**
20:     $s = s + 1$
21: **end while**
22: **return** Θ

We propose a Mini-batch Gradient Descent (MBGD) with the bootstrap sampling to optimize the objective function. See Algorithm 2 for more details.

5   Experimental Evaluation

5.1   Datasets

We make use of two publicly available real-world datasets, Gowalla [4] and Foursquare [2], to evaluate the performance of the proposed framework. Each check-in record contains a user ID, a location ID, a timestamp and geo-coordinates of the location. Also, data sets have social links information. The data statistics are shown in Table 1. In our experiments, we divide each dataset into training set, tuning set and test set in terms of the user's check-in time instead of choosing a random partition method. For each user, the earliest 70% check-ins are selected for training, the most recent 20% check-ins as testing, and the next 10% as tuning.

Table 1. Statistical information of the two datasets

Statistical item	Gowalla	Foursquare
Number of users	5,628	2,551
Number of POIs	31,803	13,474
Number of check-ins	620,683	124,933
Number of social links	46,001	32,512
User-POI matrix density	0.22%	0.291%

5.2   Evaluation Metrics

We use two widely-used metrics [4] to evaluate the performance of the model we proposed: precision (Pre@N) and recall (Rec@N), where N is the number of recommended POIs. Pre@N refers to the ratio of recovered POIs to the top-N recommended POIs and Rec@N measures the ratio of recovered POIs to the set of visited POIs in the testing data.

5.3   Baseline Methods

To illustrate the effectiveness of our recommendation framework, we compare it with the following state-of-the-art methods.

- **Random**: Random method is to recommend users with random POIs.
- **BPR-KNN**: This is a ranking-based adaptive model, which employs item-based k-nearest-neighbor to recommend POIs [8].
- **BPR-MF**: This is a classical pairwise ranking model based on matrix factorization [8].
- **GeoBPR**: This is a state-of-the-art method for POI recommendation, which incorporates the geographic feedback into the BPR model [13].

5.4   Parameter Settings

For all the compared baselines, we adopt the optimal parameter configuration reported in their works. In our experiments, all critical parameters are tuned through cross-validation. Empirically, for the learning module, the vector dimension d is set to 100, the tuning parameter α is set to 0.5 and the number of intermediate feedback $t = 2000$. In Foursquare dataset, the learning rate η is set to 0.001, the latent factor dimension $k = 40$, and regularization parameters $\lambda_u = 0.005$, $\lambda_i = \lambda_c = \lambda_j = 0.005$, $\beta_i = \beta_c = \beta_j = 0.006$. In Gowalla dataset, the learning rate η is set to 0.005, the latent factor dimension $k = 30$, and regularization parameters $\lambda_u = 0.005$, $\lambda_i = \lambda_c = \lambda_j = 0.005$, $\beta_i = \beta_c = \beta_j = 0.003$. The effect of the latent factor dimension k will be detailed later.

5.5   Experimental Results

Performance Comparisons. Results of all POI recommendation models in terms of Pre@N and Rec@N on Foursquare and Gowalla are presented in Figs. 2 and 3, respectively. One can observe that HRec framework always outperforms all the compared POI recommendation methods on the two datasets. On the one hand, compared with non-ranking algorithm Random, our recommendation framework presents an absolute advantage. In fact, Random model outputs the lowest performance. For example, in terms of Pre@5 and Rec@5, HRec attains 0.044, 0.0251 and 0.0298, 0.0134 on Foursquare and Gowalla datasets, respectively. On the other hand, our framework significantly outperforms other three ranking algorithms BPR-KNN, BPR-MF and GeoBPR. For instance, HRec improves the second best recommendation algorithm GeoBPR by 33.3%, 39% and 2.5%, 1.4% in terms of Pre@5, Rec@5 on Foursquare and Gowalla, respectively. Based on the performance comparison of non-ranking and ranking algorithms, the effectiveness and superiority of the proposed method HRec are proved. The reasons are two fold: (1) HRec makes full of social and geographical information by learning the embeddings of users and POIs in the heterogeneous

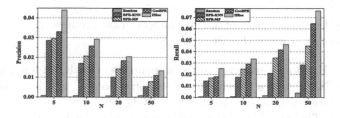

Fig. 2. Varying N on Foursquare

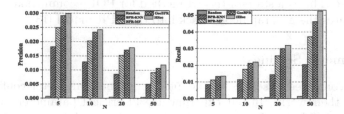

Fig. 3. Varying N on Gowalla

graph. (2) HRec effectively exploits a series of intermediate POIs learned from unvisited POIs and utilizes two pairwise feedback comparisons to greatly assist ranking.

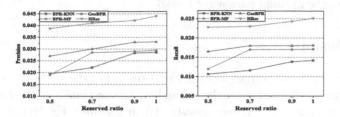

Fig. 4. Impact of data sparsity

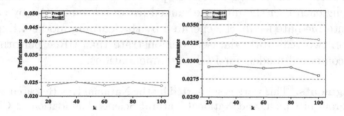

Fig. 5. Influence of latent factor dimensions k

Impact of Data Sparsity. Here, we study how HRec deals with the data sparsity problem. In order to produce user-POI check-in matrix with different sparsity, we randomly reserve $x\%$ ($x = 50,70,90,100$) of check-ins from each user's visited records. The smaller the reserved ratio x is, the sparser the user-POI check-in matrix is. Figure 4 reports Pre@5 and Rec@5 of all recommendation algorithms on Foursquare under different sparsity. Due to Random outputs poor performance, it is not added here for comparison. Based on the results, we can observe that the Pre@5 and Rec@5 of all algorithms increase with the increase of the reserved ratio x. One possible explanation is that, with the increase of the proportion of the training set, the number of positive examples increases, and then contributes to the improvement. We can further observe that our framework HRec consistently outperforms all ranking and non-ranking baselines under various data sparsity scenarios, which shows great strengths.

Parameter Sensitivity. In this study, we employ matrix factorization to predict the difference between the two scores of preference for users. Hence, in this section, we study the influence of variable k, which is the number of latent feature dimension. Due to limited space, we only show the performance of the recommendation on Foursquare dataset. In our experiment, k is set to 20, 40, 60, 80 and 100, respectively. Figure 5 reports the recommended quality for different values of k. Based on the results, we can observe that the performance in all evaluation metrics has similar behaviour with the varying value of k. The performance increases with the increase of the k at the beginning, then hits the highest recommended quality when $k = 40$, and eventually tends to decline. The above trend indicates that the performance achieves best at $k = 40$, and so we finally choose the optimal parameter $k = 40$.

6   Conclusions

This paper presents a novel personalized POI recommendation framework called the HRec, which can address the data sparsity issue and inefficiency of exploiting unobserved feedback. The HRec consists of two modules: the learning module and the ranking module. The learning module is designed for producing a series of intermediate feedback from unobserved feedback by learning the embeddings of users and POIs in the heterogeneous graph. The ranking module is devised for recommending each user the ultimate ranked list of relevant POIs by effectively exploiting intermediate feedback generated by the learning module. Experimental results on two real-world datasets demonstrate that HRec performs better than other compared models for POI recommendations.

Acknowledgments. This work is supported by the National Key Research and Development Program of China, and National Natural Science Foundation of China (No. U163620068).

References

1. Cheng, C., Yang, H., King, I., Lyu, M.R.: A unified point-of-interest recommendation framework in location-based social networks. ACM TIST **8**(1), 10:1–10:21 (2016)
2. Li, H., Ge, Y., Hong, R., Zhu, H.: Point-of-interest recommendations: learning potential check-ins from friends. In: ACM KDD, pp. 975–984 (2016)
3. Lian, D., et al.: Scalable content-aware collaborative filtering for location recommendation. IEEE TKDE **30**(6), 1122–1135 (2018)
4. Liu, Y., Pham, T.A.N., Cong, G., Yuan, Q.: An experimental evaluation of point-of-interest recommendation in location-based social networks. In: VLDB, pp. 1010–1021 (2017)
5. Ma, C., Zhang, Y., Wang, Q., Liu, X.: Point-of-interest recommendation: exploiting self-attentive autoencoders with neighbor-aware influence. In: ACM CIKM, pp. 697–706 (2018)
6. Manotumruksa, J., Macdonald, C., Ounis, I.: A personalised ranking framework with multiple sampling criteria for venue recommendation. In: ACM CIKM, pp. 1469–1478 (2017)
7. Mikolov, T., Sutskever, I., Chen, K., Corrado, G., Dean, J.: Distributed representations of words and phrases and their compositionality. In: NIPS, pp. 3111–3119 (2013)
8. Rendle, S., Freudenthaler, C., Gantner, Z., Schmidt-Thieme, L.: BPR: Bayesian personalized ranking from implicit feedback. In: UAI, pp. 452–461 (2009)

9. Tang, J., Qu, M., Mei, Q.: PTE: predictive text embedding through large-scale heterogeneous text networks. In: ACM KDD, pp. 1165–1174 (2015)
10. Wang, H., Shen, H., Ouyang, W., Cheng, X.: Exploiting poi-specific geographical influence for point-of-interest recommendation. In: IJCAI, pp. 3877–3883 (2018)
11. Xie, M., Yin, H., Wang, H., Xu, F., Chen, W., Wang, S.: Learning graph-based poi embedding for location-based recommendation. In: ACM CIKM, pp. 15–24 (2016)
12. Ye, M., Yin, P., Lee, W.C., Lee, D.L.: Exploiting geographical influence for collaborative point-of-interest recommendation. In: ACM SIGIR, pp. 325–334 (2011)
13. Yuan, F., Guo, G., Jose, J., Chen, L., Yu, H.: Joint geo-spatial preference and pairwise ranking for point-of-interest recommendation. In: IEEE ICTAI, pp. 46–53 (2016)
14. Zhang, J.D., Chow, C.Y.: iGSLR: personalized geo-social location recommendation: a kernel density estimation approach. In: ACM SIGSPATIAL, pp. 334–343 (2013)
15. Zhang, J.D., Chow, C.Y.: GeoSoCa: exploiting geographical, social and categorical correlations for point-of-interest recommendations. In: ACM SIGIR, pp. 443–452 (2015)
16. Zhang, J.D., Chow, C.Y., Li, Y.: Lore: exploiting sequential influence for location recommendations. In: ACM SIGSPATIAL, pp. 103–112 (2014)
17. Zhao, S., Zhao, T., King, I., Lyu, M.R.: Geo-teaser: geo-temporal sequential embedding rank for point-of-interest recommendation. In: WWW, pp. 153–162 (2017)

Embedding and Predicting Software Security Entity Relationships: A Knowledge Graph Based Approach

Hongbo Xiao[1], Zhenchang Xing[2], Xiaohong Li[1(✉)], and Hao Guo[1]

[1] Tianjin Key Laboratory of Advanced Networking (TANK), College of Intelligence and Computing, Tianjin University, Tianjin 300350, China
{xiaohongbo,xiaohongli,haoguo}@tju.edu.cn
[2] Research School of Computer Science, Australian National University, Canberra, ACT 2600, Australia
zhenchang.xing@anu.edu.au

Abstract. Software security knowledge involves heterogeneous security concepts (e.g., software weaknesses and attack patterns) and security instances (e.g., the vulnerabilities of a particular software product), which can be regarded as software security entities. Among software security entities, there are many within-type relationships as well as many across-type relationships. Predicting software security entity relationships helps to enrich software security knowledge (e.g., finding missing relationships among existing entities). Unfortunately, software security entities are currently documented in separate databases, such as Common Vulnerabilities and Exposures (CVE), Common Weakness Enumeration (CWE) and Common Attack Pattern Enumeration and Classification (CAPEC). This hyper-document representation cannot support effective reasoning of software entity relationships. In this paper, we propose to consolidate heterogeneous software security concepts and instances from separate databases into a coherent knowledge graph. We develop a knowledge graph embedding method which embeds the symbolic relational and descriptive information of software security entities into a continuous vector space. The resulting entity and relationship embeddings are predictive for software security entity relationships. Based on the Open World Assumption, we conduct extensive experiments to evaluate the effectiveness of our knowledge graph based approach for predicting various within-type and across-type relationships of software security entities.

Keywords: Software security entity relationship · Knowledge graph embedding · Link prediction

1 Introduction

Software weaknesses and vulnerabilities give malicious attacks a chance to compromise the system integrality, availability and confidentiality [14]. To facilitate security knowledge dissemination and to enhance software security defense,

T. Gedeon et al. (Eds.): ICONIP 2019, LNCS 11955, pp. 50–63, 2019.
https://doi.org/10.1007/978-3-030-36718-3_5

researchers invest a lot of efforts to document software weaknesses, vulnerabilities and attacks. For example, Common Weakness Enumeration (CWE) is a community-developed list of common software weakness patterns, such as *CWE-183: Permissive Whitelist*. Common Attack Pattern Enumeration and Classification (CAPEC) is a list of known attack patterns employed by adversaries to exploit known weaknesses, such as *CAPEC-182: Flash Injection*. Common Vulnerabilities and Exposures (CVE) is a database of publicly disclosed cybersecurity vulnerabilities and exposures of software products, such as *CVE-2018-1002200 is a directory traversal vulnerability of the plexus-archiver tool in Debian Linux*.

Entries in CWE, CAPEC and CVE databases can be considered as software security entities. CWEs and CAPECs represent abstract security concepts, while CVEs are specific security instances. Software security entities have a rich set of relationships within the same type of entities or across different types of entities. For example, *parentof* and *childof* relationships between CWEs (or CAPECs) give insights to similar weakness (or attack) patterns that may exist at higher and lower levels of abstraction, such as <*CWE-697: Incorrect Comparison, parentof, CWE-183: Permissive Whitelist*>. CWEs (or CAPECs) also have *peerof*, *canprecede* and *canfollow* relationships, for example, <*CAPEC-182: Flash Injection, peerof, CAPEC-248: Command Injection*>. Across-type relationships include those between security instances and concepts (e.g., <*CVE, instanceof, CWE*>) and those between weakness and attack patterns (i.e., <*CWE, targetof, CAPEC*>). For example, *CVE-2018-5390* is an instance of *CWE-20: Improper Input Validation*, and *CAPEC-136: LDAP Injection* can target *CWE-20*.

As seen in the above examples, software security entity relationships capture important security knowledge. Considering the complexity of software security knowledge, we generally make the Open World Assumption (OWA), which states that observed facts are true (as they are carefully curated by domain experts), and non-observed facts can be either false or just missing [4]. Under this assumption, predicting software security entity relationships becomes an important reasoning task. For example, the relationship <*CWE-128: Wrap-around Error, childof, CWE-682: Incorrect Calculation*> was not present in CWE version 1.0, but was added in CWE version 2.0. Finding such missing relationships among existing entities helps analysts enrich software security knowledge [5].

Although security databases (CWE, CAPEC, CVE) are an effective means of documenting software security entities, the underlying knowledge representation (i.e., hyperlinked documents) does not support the effective prediction of software security entity relationships. This is because software security entities and their relationships are implicit in document content and hyperlinks. In this paper, we propose to represent software security entities and relationships as first-class objects in a software security knowledge graph. As illustrated in Fig. 1, our knowledge graph contains CWEs and CAPECs as core concept knowledge and CVEs as peripheral instance knowledge. Each entity has a textual description and may have some relationships with other entities. A knowledge graph embedding approach is developed to learn predictive embeddings of entity descriptions and relationships in a continuous vector space by maximizing the total plausibility of observed facts [15]. A novel design of our embedding approach is to explicitly incorporate description-based and structure-based embeddings through joint training of translation-based knowledge graph embedding model [16], CNN text encoder [7] and word embeddings [11]. Entity and relationship embeddings are then used in link prediction task (i.e., given a head (or tail) entity and a relationship, predicting the likely tail (or head) entity) [3,16].

Our experiment results show that heterogeneous security entities result in more predictive embeddings than homogeneous entities. Furthermore, our advanced incorporation of description- and structure-based embeddings results in more predictive embeddings than concatenating these two types of embeddings.

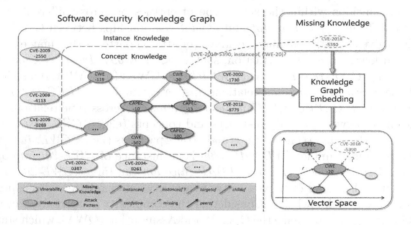

Fig. 1. An illustration of Software Security Knowledge Graph, Knowledge Graph Embedding, and prediction tasks.

The main contributions of this paper are as follows. (1) To our knowledge, our knowledge graph is the first software security knowledge graph that integrates heterogeneous security concepts and instances. This knowledge heterogeneity is beneficial for embedding software security entity relationships. (2) We develop an advanced knowledge graph embedding approach to embed the structural and descriptive knowledge of security concepts and instances into a continuous vector space to predict software security entity relationships. (3) Our extensive experiments show that our knowledge graph based embedding approach can accurately predict within-type and across-type relations of software security entities.

2   The Approach

2.1   Approach Overview

This paper aims to design a knowledge graph based approach for embedding and predicting software security entity relationships. As illustrated in Fig. 1, a knowledge graph is a multi-relational directed graph whose nodes and edges represent domain-specific entities and relationships. Each triple (or fact) is represented as *<head, relationship, tail>*, indicating that two entities are connected by a relationship. As shown in Fig. 2, our goal is to first construct a software security knowledge graph from heterogeneous security databases, and then use knowledge graph embedding method to learn an embedding model for embedding entity and relationship in a continuous vector space for link prediction task.

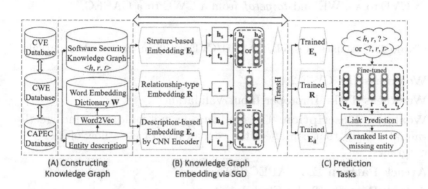

Fig. 2. Approach overview (SGD means stochastic gradient descent).

We denote the head entity, relationship and tail entity as h, r and t. The structure-based, description-based entity embedding and the relationship embedding are respectively denoted as $\mathbf{E_s}$, $\mathbf{E_d}$ and $\mathbf{R}$, which are of the same dimension. $\mathbf{E_s}$ and $\mathbf{R}$ are learned through an enhanced TransH [16] model, which captures relational knowledge in the knowledge graph. Word embeddings are obtained by training the word2vec [11] with the descriptions of CWE/CAPEC/CVE entities, and $\mathbf{E_d}$ is obtained by a CNN encoder jointly trained with the TransH model, which captures the descriptive knowledge of entities.

2.2 Constructing Software Security Knowledge Graph

We construct a software security knowledge graph from the CWE, CAPEC and CVE databases. Figure 1 shows an excerpt of the resulting knowledge graph.

Security Concepts and Instances as Entities. We extract software security entities from the CWE, CAPEC and CVE databases. These databases use a unique index to identify each security concept or instance, for example, CWE-20, CAPEC-182 and CVE-2018-1002200 in Table 1. Each concept or instance is considered as an entity in the knowledge graph. Each CWE and CAPEC entity has a title and a textual description, and each CVE entity has a textual description. This textual description is used as entity attribute to compute $\mathbf{E_d}$.

Relationship Extraction from Entry Cross-References. Relationships between CWE, CAPEC and CVE entries are documented as cross-reference of entry index in the databases. We parse these index cross-references to obtain entity relationships in the knowledge graph. As summarized in Table 2, CWE, CAPEC and CVE databases define seven categories of relationships for security concepts and instances. We have *parentof*, *childof*, *canprecede*, *canfollow* and *peerof* between CWE (or CAPEC) entities. These relationships are referred to as within-type relationships. We have two across-type relationships, i.e., *instanceof* from a CVE to a CWE and *targetof* from a CWE to a CAPEC.

Table 1. Examples of CWE/CAPEC/CVE entity in the knowledge graph.

Weakness ID: CWE-20
Weakness Title: Improper Input Validation
Weakness Description: The product does not validate or incorrectly validates input that can affect the control flow or data flow of a program
Attack Pattern ID: CAPEC-182
Attack Pattern Title: Flash Injection
Attack Pattern Description: An attacker tricks a victim to execute malicious flash content that executes commands or makes flash calls specified by
Vulnerability ID: CVE-2018-1002200
Vulnerability Description: plexus-archiver before 3.6.0 is vulnerable to directory traversal, allowing attackers to write to arbitrary via a ...

In addition to the seven pre-defined relationships, we also extract semantic relationship between a CWE and other CWEs mentioned in the document of this CWE. For example, the document of CWE-909 states that "...that might occur as a result of CWE-14.". From this description, we obtain a semantic relationship between CWE-909 and CWE-14. We treat this semantic relationship extracted from the CWE document as a category of general semantic relationship.

2.3   Translation-Based Knowledge Graph Embedding

We develop a translation-based, description-embodied knowledge graph embedding method to obtain $\mathbf{E_s}$, $\mathbf{E_d}$ and $\mathbf{R}$.

Basic TransH Model. Translation-based models [3,16] have been shown to be effective for embedding knowledge graph entities and relationships into a continuous vector space. Because our software security knowledge graph contains

Table 2. Relationships in our knowledge graph.

Relationship type	Head type	Tail type	Relationship property	Pre-defined	Relationship type	Head type	Tail type	Relationship property	Pre-defined
instanceof	CVE	CWE	many-to-1	✓	targetof	CWE	CAPEC	many-to-many	✓
childof	CWE	CWE	many-to-1	✓	childof	CAPEC	CAPEC	many-to-1	✓
parentof	CWE	CWE	1-to-many	✓	parentof	CAPEC	CAPEC	1-to-many	✓
peerof	CWE	CWE	1-to-1	✓	peerof	CAPEC	CAPEC	1-to-1	✓
canfollow	CWE	CWE	1-to-many	✓	canfollow	CAPEC	CAPEC	1-to-many	✓
canprecede	CWE	CWE	many-to-1	✓	canprecede	CAPEC	CAPEC	many-to-1	✓
semantic	CWE	CWE	many-to-many	✗					

1-to-many, many-to-1 and many-to-many relationships (see Table 2), we choose to use the TransH model [16] which is designed for such knowledge graphs.

To embed the 1-to-many, many-to-1 and many-to-many relationships, TransH introduces relation-specific hyperplanes that allow an entity to have distinct representations when involved in different relations. It regards a relation as a translating operation on a relation-specific hyperplane, which is characterized by a norm vector $\mathbf{a}_r$ and a translation vector $\mathbf{r}$. Given a triple $<h, r, t>$, the entity embeddings $\mathbf{h}$ and $\mathbf{t}$ are first projected onto the relation-specific hyperplane. The projection embeddings are assumed to be connected by $\mathbf{r}$ on the hyperplane. So the objective of the TransH model is to minimize the translation-based score function over all triples $<h, r, t>$ (i.e., observed facts) in a knowledge graph:

$$f_r(h,t) = \|\mathbf{h}_\perp + \mathbf{r} - \mathbf{t}_\perp\| \tag{1}$$

where $\mathbf{r}$ is the embedding of r. $\mathbf{h}_\perp$ and $\mathbf{t}_\perp$ are the projection embeddings of h and t on the hyperplane, respectively. By restricting $\|\mathbf{a}_r\| = 1$, $\mathbf{h}_\perp$ and $\mathbf{t}_\perp$ are calculated through $\mathbf{h}_\perp = \mathbf{h} - \mathbf{a}_r^\top \mathbf{h}\mathbf{a}_r$, $\mathbf{t}_\perp = \mathbf{t} - \mathbf{a}_r^\top \mathbf{t}\mathbf{a}_r$. Intuitively, if $<h, r, t>$ holds in the knowledge graph, then $\mathbf{h} + \mathbf{r} \approx \mathbf{t}$, i.e., the embedding obtained by element-wise addition of the embedding of the head entity and the relationship embedding should be close to the embedding of the tail entity in the continuous vector space.

Structure- and Description-Based Entity Embedding. The original TranH model considers only the structure-based entity embedding which captures the relational knowledge of entities in a knowledge graph. In our knowledge graph, each security entity has a textual description that documents the rich semantics of the entity. This textual description should also be embedded in order to obtain more predictive entity embedding [5,15]. Thus, we consider both structure-based and description-based entity embeddings when embedding our knowledge graph. The original TransH score function in Eq. (1) will be expanded as:

$$f_r(h,t) = f_r^{ss}(h,t) + f_r^{dd}(h,t) \tag{2}$$

where $f_r^{ss}(h,t) = \| \mathbf{h_s} + \mathbf{r} - \mathbf{t_s} \|$, $f_r^{dd}(h,t) = \| \mathbf{h_d} + \mathbf{r} - \mathbf{t_d} \|$, and $\mathbf{h_s}$ and $\mathbf{t_s}$ are structure-based entity embeddings, $\mathbf{h_d}$ and $\mathbf{t_d}$ are description-based entity embeddings.

To model the interaction between $\mathbf{E_s}$ and $\mathbf{E_d}$, we further expand Eq. (1) into

$$f_r(h,t) = f_r^{ss}(h,t) + f_r^{dd}(h,t) + f_r^{sd}(h,t) + f_r^{ds}(h,t) \tag{3}$$

where $f_r^{sd}(h,t) = \parallel \mathbf{h_s} + \mathbf{r} - \mathbf{t_d} \parallel, f_r^{ds}(h,t) = \parallel \mathbf{h_d} + \mathbf{r} - \mathbf{t_s} \parallel$. We refer Eqs. (2) and (3) as the basic individual and the interaction-enhanced score function, respectively. We investigate the effectiveness of these two score functions in our experiments.

Encoding Entity Description by Word Embedding and CNN. Entity description contains discrete words. To participate in the embedding process, entity descriptions have to be represented in sentence vectors. To represent sentences in vectors, we first need to represent words in word vectors. In this work, we represent words using the word2vec word embeddings [11], which are low-dimensional word vectors learned from a large text corpus. The word embeddings can encode rich semantic features of words in the general text [1,8] and domain-specific text [5,6]. In this work, we pre-train security-specific word embeddings using the text corpus of CWE/CAPEC/CVE entity descriptions.

Given the dictionary of pre-trained word embeddings, a naive way to obtain sentence embedding is to average the word embeddings of the words in the sentence (i.e., average pooling). However, studies [6,15] show that using a CNN encoder can extract more informative features for embedding sentences than average pooling. Therefore, we design a CNN encoder which takes as input a variable-length entity description and outputs a sentence embedding of the description. It has five layers, including the input layer, two convolution layers and two pooling layers. The input layer represents an input sentence as a sequence of n_w dimensional word embeddings. The convolution layers apply N filters to a sliding window of n-gram over the input sentence to extract features. The first pooling layer uses max-pooling to capture the most important feature. The second pooling layer uses mean-pooling to avoid information loss. We conduct hyperparameter optimization experiments on a validation set in the same way as existing works [5,6] on applying CNN to software-specific text. Based on the results, we set $n = 2$ and $N = 100$ for convolution layers, and set $n_w = 100$.

Given the description of an entity, the CNN encoder outputs a fixed-length vector as initial $\mathbf{E_d}$, which will be used in the score function Eqs. (2) or (3). During the embedding process, initial $\mathbf{E_d}$ will be adjusted to minimize the loss function Eq. (4) described in Sect. 2.3. The gradient will be back-propagated through the CNN layers to train the encoder model. The pre-trained word embeddings in the input layer can be optionally fine-tuned in this process.

Model Training and Optimization. We adopt margin-based ranking loss commonly used in translation-based knowledge graph embedding models [3,16]:

$$L = \sum_{<h,r,t> \in S} \sum_{<h',r',t'> \in S'} [\gamma + f_r(h,t) - f_{r'}(h',t')]_+ \tag{4}$$

where $[x]_+ = \max(0, x)$. γ is the margin separating positive and negative triples. The objective of the loss L is to make the score $f_r(h', t')$ of corrupted triples higher by at least γ than the score $f_r(h, t)$ of the positive triples, i.e., $f_r(h', t') - f_r(h, t) \geq \gamma$. We set $\gamma = 2.0$ as it results in the best prediction performance on a validation set in our hyperparameter optimization experiments. S is the set of observed triples $< h, r, t >$ (i.e., positive training samples). $S' = \{(h', r, t)|h' \in E\} \cup \{(h, r', t)|r' \in R\} \cup \{(h, r, t')|t' \in E\}$ denotes the set of corrupted triples (i.e., negative training samples) for the positive triples, which is produced by changing h, r or t of positive triples so that the resulting triples are not in S.

We minimize L by stochastic gradient descent. The entity and relationship embeddings will be updated when $f_r(h', t') - f_r(h, t) \geq \gamma$ does not hold. Gradient descent is back-propagated from $\mathbf{E_d}$ to the CNN kernel and the word embeddings. After embedding, we obtain trained $\mathbf{E_s}$ and trained $\mathbf{R}$ as well as a trained CNN encoder and the fine-tuned word embeddings $\mathbf{W}$ for obtaining trained $\mathbf{E_d}$.

2.4   Prediction Task

The entity and relationship embeddings support the link prediction task. Given h and r, link prediction predicts the most likely t. We represent the prediction task as a to-be-predicted triple $<h, r, ?t>$. Link prediction helps analysts find entities related to an entity by a particular relationship, for example, the likely CWE (i.e., abstract software weakness) for a CVE instance. Link prediction task can be solved by ranking all entities in the knowledge graph (other than h) by the similarity between embeddings of these entities and the resulting embedding of adding embeddings of h and r, i.e., $?t = argmin^k_{t \in E \setminus \{h\}} \|\mathbf{h} + \mathbf{r} - \mathbf{t}\|$. In practice, we return top-k most similar entities. The to-be-predicted triple $<?h, r, t>$ can be solved in the same way. Given an entity in a to-be-predicted triple, we use the element-wise addition of the entity's structure-based and description-based embeddings (i.e., $\mathbf{h_s} + \mathbf{h_d}$) as the entity embedding in the prediction task.

3   Experiment

3.1   Experiment Design

Method Variants. The solution space of knowledge graph embedding involves three aspects: score function, word embedding and description embedding. Score function has three ways to incorporate structure-based and description-based entity embeddings: concatenation $\| \mathbf{h_s} \oplus \mathbf{h_d} + \mathbf{r} - \mathbf{t_s} \oplus \mathbf{t_d} \|$ (used in Han et al. [5]), basic individual $\| \mathbf{h_s} + \mathbf{r} - \mathbf{t_s} \| + \| \mathbf{h_d} + \mathbf{r} - \mathbf{t_d} \|$ (i.e., Eq. (2)), and interaction-enhanced $\| \mathbf{h_s} + \mathbf{r} - \mathbf{t_s} \| + \| \mathbf{h_d} + \mathbf{r} - \mathbf{t_d} \| + \| \mathbf{h_s} + \mathbf{r} - \mathbf{t_d} \| + \| \mathbf{h_d} + \mathbf{r} - \mathbf{t_s} \|$ (i.e., Eq. (3)). Pre-trained word embeddings can be used as-is or fine-tuned during knowledge graph embedding. Description-based embeddings can be obtained by simple average pooling of word embeddings in the description or a CNN encoder (see Sect. 2.3).

Considering the variants of the three solution aspects, we design seven methods for the comparative experiments, as shown in Table 3. The M-1 is a replica of

Table 3. Variants of knowledge graph embedding method.

Model	M-1	M-2	M-3	M-4	M-5	M-6	M-7
Score function	Concatenation	Basic individual	Basic individual	Basic individual	Interaction enhanced	Interaction enhanced	Interaction enhanced
Word embedding	Pre-trained	Pre-trained	Pre-trained	Fine-tuned	Pre-trained	Pre-trained	Fine-tuned
Description embedding	Average pooling	Average pooling	CNN encoder	CNN encoder	Average pooling	CNN encoder	CNN encoder

the method proposed in Han et al. [5], while the other methods are variants of the approach proposed in this work. Note that using average pooling of word embeddings to compute description embeddings does not support fine-tuning of word embeddings. By comparing M-1 with M-2 and M-5, we can see the impact of different ways to incorporate structure- and description-based entity embeddings. By comparing M-2/3/4 (or M-5/6/7), we can understand the impact of different ways to compute word embeddings and description embeddings. By comparing M-2/5 (or M-3/6, M-4/7), we can understand the impact of explicitly modeling the interaction of structure-based and description-based entity embeddings.

Research Questions. Our experiments aim to answer two research questions:

RQ1: Can heterogeneous software security knowledge graph produce more predictive embeddings than homogeneous knowledge graph? Han et al. [5] construct a software weakness knowledge graph from CWEs only, but we construct a much broader software security knowledge graph from CWEs, CAPECs and CVEs. Heterogeneous security entities provide a more complete picture of security knowledge. We want to investigate if heterogeneous knowledge graph produces more predictive embeddings than considering CWEs only.

RQ2: How well can different knowledge graph embedding methods predict software security entity relationships? An important knowledge graph completion task is to find new relational facts among existing entities. We want to study the performance of different knowledge graph embedding methods in this task and investigate the impact of variations in score function, word embedding, and description embedding method on the performance.

Evaluation Metrics. We use three metrics: (1) **Top-k accuracy (Top-k Acc):** the proportion of prediction tasks for which the correct entity is in the top-k list. We report Top-5 Acc and Top-10 Acc. (2) **Mean Reciprocal Rank (MRR):** the mean of the reciprocal rank of the correct entity for each prediction task. (3) **Mean Average Precision (MAP):** the mean of average precision of all relevant entities for each prediction task. Notice that if a corrupted triplet exists in the knowledge graph, ranking it before the original triple is not wrong [3, 16]. So we also consider such a prediction as correct on Top-k Acc and MRR.

3.2   Software Security Knowledge Graph in Experiments

In this work, we use the latest CWE (version 3.2) and the latest CAPEC (version 3.0). All CWEs and CAPECs (except Category entries) are used as security concepts. We select CVEs of Linux system published by 1st October, 2018 as security instances and crawl them from the CVE details website. We construct a knowledge graph with 806 CWEs, 515 CAPECs, 2846 Linux CVEs and 8 relation types of 8067 triples. Data and statistical test result are available at https://github.com/kgembedding2019/Embedding-and-Predicting-Software-Security.

Table 4. Performance comparison: homogeneous KG versus (vs.) heterogeneous KG.

Metric	Top-5 Acc	Top-10 Acc	MRR	MAP
CWE-only KG	0.592	0.681	0.449	0.564
Full KG	**0.628**	**0.713**	**0.459**	**0.576**

3.3   Impact of Knowledge Heterogeneity (RQ1)

Method. We create a sub-knowledge graph with CWEs only (3021 triples) from the full knowledge graph. This sub-knowledge graph contains homogeneous security concepts (i.e., CWEs), as opposed to the full knowledge graph with heterogeneous security concepts and instances. We use M-7 in Table 3 for experiments.

We prepare link prediction task in the way described in Sect. 3.4. For CWE-only knowledge graph, we randomly select 85% triples of each relationship for training, 5% for model optimization, and 10% as testing triples. The partition result is duplicated on the full knowledge graph. All CAPEC and CVE entities in the full knowledge graph remain intact. The prediction will be done on the same testing set selected from CWE-only knowledge graph. We perform 10-fold cross-validation and report the average metrics. To determine if there is a statistically significant difference between the prediction performance of CWE-only and full knowledge graph, we perform Wilcoxon signed-rank test on all metrics.

Results. As reported in Table 4, the prediction performance of the full heterogeneous knowledge graph is always better than that of CWE-only homogeneous knowledge graph in all evaluation metrics. Wilcoxon signed-rank test confirms that all performance differences are statistically significant (at $p < 0.05$) [13].

> *Heterogeneous security concepts and instances produce more predictive knowledge graph embeddings than homogeneous security concepts.*

3.4   Predicting Software Security Entity Relationships (RQ2)

Method. In RQ2, we use our full software security knowledge graph. As the truly missing triples are unknown, we simulate the missing relational facts by randomly "remove" some triples in the knowledge graph. Specifically, we randomly select 85% triples of each relationship for training, 5% for optimization and 10% for testing. We remove the tail or head entity in each testing triple to make a predict-tail (or head) task $<h, r, ?t>$ (or $<?h, r, t>$). The tail or head entity of the testing triple is considered as the correct entity to be predicted. For each relationship, we compute the metrics listed in Sect. 3.1 for predict-tail and predict-head tasks respectively. We compute the weighted average of the performance metrics of all relationships as the overall performance. We report the average metrics of 10-fold cross-validation. We compare the prediction performance of embeddings learned by the seven methods listed in Table 3.

Results. *Overall Performance.* As shown in Table 5, the basic individual score function (M-2) performs worse than concatenation score function (M-1). But interaction-enhanced score function (M-5) outperforms concatenation score function (M-1) in all metrics. Under the same word embedding and description embedding method, interaction-enhanced score function always outperforms basic individual function (M-5 vs. M-2, M-6 vs. M-3, M-7 vs. M-4). Using the same score function, the more sophisticated text embedding technique is used, the better the model performs (M-4 vs. M-3 vs. M-2, M-7 vs. M-6 vs. M5). Combining interaction-based score function, fine-tuned word embedding and CNN encoder for description embedding lead to the best performing model (i.e., M-7). M-7 performs statistically significantly better than M-1 (i.e., existing model in [5]).

Table 5. Link prediction - overall performance.

	M-1	M-2	M-3	M-4	M-5	M-6	M-7
Top-5 Acc	0.503	0.474	0.528	0.542	0.529	0.573	**0.596**
Top-10 Acc	0.583	0.558	0.596	0.612	0.612	0.640	**0.661**
MRR	0.402	0.391	0.405	0.420	0.419	0.448	**0.464**
MAP	0.591	0.573	0.606	0.604	0.624	0.647	**0.688**

Performance by Relationship Type and Predict-Head/Tail. Due to the space limitation, we report the detailed performance for Top-5 Acc only in Table 6. We can see that M-7 achieves the best performance for all relationships and for both predict-head and predict-tail tasks (being statistically significantly better than M-1 in all cases). We can also observe a similar performance boost for each relationship by interaction-based score function, fine-tuned word embeddings, and CNN encoder for description embedding, as the overall performance.

The performance of a method varies across different relationships and across predict-head or predict-tail tasks. Take M-7 as an example. M-7 achieves high Top-5 Acc (0.689-0.878) for seven cases: *childof*, *parentof* and *canprecede* (predict-head/tail), *instanceof* (predict-tail). It achieves reasonable Top-5 Acc (0.466-0.523) for four cases: *targetof* (predict-head), *canfollow* (predict-head/tail) and *semantic* (predict-tail). It achieves below-0.4 Top-5 Acc for five cases: *instanceof* and *semantic* (predict-head), *targetof* (predict-tail), *peerof* (predict-head/tail).

Table 6. Link prediction - Top-5 Acc by relationship type and predict-head/tail.

	Model	instanceof	targetof	childof	parentof	peerof	canfollow	canprecede	semantic	overall
Predict head $<?h, r, t>$	M-1	0.024	0.396	0.572	0.792	0.111	0.286	0.571	0.193	0.378
	M-2	0.017	0.386	0.555	0.758	0.056	0.286	0.571	0.189	0.359
	M-3	0.047	0.409	0.578	0.811	0.111	0.307	0.653	0.204	0.383
	M-4	0.093	0.420	0.618	0.845	0.167	0.357	0.653	0.234	0.399
	M-5	0.065	0.420	0.630	0.831	0.167	0.429	0.643	0.259	0.396
	M-6	0.141	0.443	0.684	0.858	0.278	0.457	0.669	0.294	0.441
	M-7	**0.193**	**0.466**	**0.703**	**0.865**	**0.278**	**0.500**	**0.714**	**0.314**	**0.469**
Predict tail $<h, r, ?t>$	M-1	0.650	0.342	0.789	0.568	0.222	0.357	0.591	0.437	0.625
	M-2	0.595	0.330	0.760	0.557	0.167	0.357	0.571	0.429	0.588
	M-3	0.822	0.342	0.808	0.575	0.222	0.371	0.623	0.442	0.671
	M-4	0.831	0.352	0.851	0.604	0.222	0.428	0.714	0.465	0.684
	M-5	0.729	0.355	0.845	0.656	0.278	0.428	0.714	0.477	0.662
	M-6	0.838	0.386	0.862	0.656	0.278	0.457	0.757	0.500	0.704
	M-7	**0.848**	**0.398**	**0.878**	**0.689**	**0.278**	**0.500**	**0.766**	**0.523**	**0.720**

We identify three factors that affect the embedding performance. First, the more triples a relationship has, the more predictive embeddings it learns. Typical cases are *childof* and *parentof* relationships that have large numbers of triples, as opposed to *peerof* that has fewer instances. Second, the more diverse the semantics of a relationship are, the more difficult to learn predictive embeddings. A typical case is *semantic*. Unlike other relationships which have a unique semantic, *semantic* relationship is a general notion of different semantic relationships among CWEs. This semantic diversity will "dilute" the learning of predictive embeddings. Third, the more instances the "many" end of a relationship has, the less predictive the learned embeddings are for predicting the "many" end. A typical case is the CVE end of $<CVE, instanceof, CWE>$. One abstract software weakness (CWE) can have many instances of CVEs (up to 768). Predicting the CVE instances of a given CWE has the worst performance among all prediction tasks. However, the learned embeddings can still accurately predict the CWE given a CVE instance (0.848). linking the CVE instance to the corresponding weakness is more important than finding vulnerability examples for a weakness.

Interaction-enhanced score function, fine-tuned word embeddings and CNN encoder for description embedding can all boost the knowledge graph embedding performance. Three factors, i.e., the number of triples of relationships, the semantic diversity of relationships, and the number of instances at the "many" end of 1-to-many relationships, affect the performance of the learned embeddings.

4   Related Work

Software Security Databases and Research. CWE, CAPEC and CVE achieve rich software security knowledge. These knowledge bases have been exploited in some security analysis research [6,12]. Han et al. [6] propose a CNN based approach to predict severity level of software vulnerability using CVE descriptions. Ruohonen et al. [12] investigate information retrieval techniques for mapping CVE to CWE. Different from these text-mining based works, our work constructs a software security knowledge graph which allows us to exploit both relational and textual knowledge of security concepts and instances in security analysis.

Knowledge Graph Research in Software Engineering. Some general domain knowledge graphs (e.g., DBpedia [9] and Freebase [2]) have been built. In software engineering context, Li et al. [10] construct an API caveat knowledge graph from API reference documentation and support API-centric caveat search. The recent work by Han et al. [5] is the closest work to ours. The key differences are two folds. First, they consider only CWEs, while our knowledge graph contains CWEs, CAPECs and CVEs. Second, our knowledge graph embedding method uses more advanced score function to model structure- and description-based entity embeddings and adopts CNN encoder to compute description embeddings, which result in better performance in prediction task than the method in [5].

5   Conclusion and Future Work

This paper presents a novel knowledge graph based approach for embedding and predicting software security entity relationships. Our software security knowledge graph incorporates heterogeneous but complementary security concepts (i.e., weaknesses and attack patterns) and security instances (i.e., vulnerabilities). This heterogeneity results in more informative embeddings of software security entities and relationships. Our knowledge graph embedding method combines the recent advances in translation-based knowledge graph embedding model and the application of CNN encoder. Our experiments show that modeling the interaction between structure- and description-based entity embeddings, using a CNN encoder to compute sentence embeddings and fine-tuned word embeddings result in more predictive embeddings. The future work is to incorporate vulnerable code in the knowledge graph, which may enable new types of security analysis.

Acknowledgement. This work is supported in part by National Natural Science Foundation of China (Nos. 61572349, 61872262).

References

1. Abbes, M., Kechaou, Z., Alimi, A.M.: Enhanced deep learning models for sentiment analysis in Arab social media. In: Liu, D., Xie, S., Li, Y., Zhao, D., El-Alfy, E.-S.M. (eds.) ICONIP 2017. LNCS, vol. 10638, pp. 667–676. Springer, Cham (2017). https://doi.org/10.1007/978-3-319-70139-4_68
2. Bollacker, K., Evans, C., Paritosh, P., Sturge, T., Taylor, J.: Freebase: a collaboratively created graph database for structuring human knowledge. In: SIGMOD (2008)
3. Bordes, A., Usunier, N., Garcia-Duran, A., Weston, J., Yakhnenko, O.: Translating embeddings for modeling multi-relational data. In: NIPS, pp. 2787–2795 (2013)
4. Drumond, L., Rendle, S., Schmidt-Thieme, L.: Predicting RDF triples in incomplete knowledge bases with tensor factorization. In: SAC, pp. 326–331. ACM (2012)
5. Han, Z., Li, X., Liu, H., Xing, Z., Feng, Z.: DeepWeak: reasoning common software weaknesses via knowledge graph embedding. In: SANER, pp. 456–466. IEEE (2018)
6. Han, Z., Li, X., Xing, Z., Liu, H., Feng, Z.: Learning to predict severity of software vulnerability using only vulnerability description. In: ICSME, pp. 125–136 (2017)
7. Kalchbrenner, N., Grefenstette, E., Blunsom, P.: A convolutional neural network for modelling sentences. In: ACL, pp. 655–665 (2014)
8. Kim, Y.: Convolutional neural networks for sentence classification. In: EMNLP (2014)
9. Lehmann, J., Isele, R., Jakob, M., et al.: DBpedia-a large-scale, multilingual knowledge base extracted from Wikipedia. Semant. Web 6(2), 167–195 (2015)
10. Li, H., et al.: Improving API Caveats accessibility by mining API Caveats knowledge graph. In: ICSME. IEEE (2018)
11. Mikolov, T., Chen, K., Corrado, G., Dean, J.: Efficient estimation of word representations in vector space. In: ICLR (2013)
12. Ruohonen, J., Leppänen, V.: Toward validation of textual information retrieval techniques for software weaknesses. In: Elloumi, M., et al. (eds.) DEXA 2018. CCIS, vol. 903, pp. 265–277. Springer, Cham (2018). https://doi.org/10.1007/978-3-319-99133-7_22
13. Wilcoxon, F.: Individual comparisons by ranking methods. Biom. Bull. 1(6), 80–83 (1945)
14. Wu, Y., Gandhi, R.A., Siy, H.: Using semantic templates to study vulnerabilities recorded in large software repositories. In: ICSE, pp. 22–28. ACM (2010)
15. Xie, R., Liu, Z., Jia, J., Luan, H., Sun, M.: Representation learning of knowledge graphs with entity descriptions. In: AAAI, pp. 2659–2665 (2016)
16. Zhen, W., Zhang, J., Feng, J., Zheng, C.: Knowledge graph embedding by translating on hyperplanes. In: AAAI, pp. 1112–1119 (2014)

SACIC: A Semantics-Aware Convolutional Image Captioner Using Multi-level Pervasive Attention

Sandeep Narayan Parameswaran$^{(\boxtimes)}$ ⓘ and Sukhendu Das ⓘ

Visualization and Perception Lab, Department of Computer Science and Engineering, Indian Institute of Technology Madras, Chennai, India
sandeepn@cse.iitm.ac.in, sdas@iitm.ac.in

Abstract. Attention mechanisms alongside encoder-decoder architectures have become integral components for solving the image captioning problem. The attention mechanism recombines an encoding of the image depending on the state of the decoder, to generate the caption sequence. The decoder is predominantly recurrent in nature. In contrast, we propose a novel network possessing attention-like properties that are pervasive through its layers, by utilizing a convolutional neural network (CNN) to refine and combine representations at multiple levels of the architecture for captioning images. We also enable the model to use explicit higher-level semantic information obtained by performing panoptic segmentation on the image. The attention capability of the model is visually demonstrated, and an experimental evaluation is shown on the MS-COCO dataset. We exhibit that the approach is more robust, efficient, and yields better performance in comparison to the state-of-the-art architectures for image captioning.

Keywords: Image captioning · Convolutional neural networks · Deep learning · Computer vision

1 Introduction

Image captioning is a challenging problem that generates a sentence describing the contents of an image. This finds applications in aiding visually impaired users, improving human-machine communication, and organizing visual data, thereby attracting the attention of researchers in the fields of computer vision and machine learning communities. Among recently published work, an encoder-decoder framework modeled recurrently using LSTM networks [12,23] have been commonly employed for this task. Such frameworks are enhanced by associating the model with an attention mechanism [2,21,26,27,30]. Recently, the work by Aneja et al. [3] has shown that a convolutional neural network (CNN) based image captioning method coupled with an attention mechanism performs equally well for the captioning task in comparison to the recurrent approaches. Such

© Springer Nature Switzerland AG 2019
T. Gedeon et al. (Eds.): ICONIP 2019, LNCS 11955, pp. 64–76, 2019.
https://doi.org/10.1007/978-3-030-36718-3_6

models are not sequential and exploit parallelism better during training. In general, current attention mechanisms are a weighted sum of the encoded image representations and have limited modeling capabilities.

The work by Elbayad et al. [8] proposes an architecture for machine translation, based on a CNN by modeling an attention mechanism that is pervasive through its layers. Inspired by its success, we extend and adapt this architecture to solve the image captioning problem. Also, the use of attention at multiple levels of an architecture has benefited similar tasks [28,29]. Unlike the single-level attention model proposed in [8], we design a CNN based architecture which posses attention-like capabilities at multiple intermediate layers of a deep neural network to attain better performance for the task of image captioning.

Addition of explicit high-level semantic concepts of the input image can enhance captioning performance to a greater extent [6,30]. Semantic concepts are extracted either by modeling a multi-label classification problem [24] using a subset of the vocabulary, or learning them in an unsupervised nature [9], or using an object detection model [2,12,17].

Frameworks which resemble object detection allows the semantic concepts to be grounded in the image. The semantic concept can either refer to things (e.g., dog, airplane) with a well-defined shape or amorphous background regions (e.g., grass, road), referred to as objects and stuff respectively [5]. While some works [12,17] ignore the stuff classes, some other [2] tries to localize the stuff classes along with object classes. Panoptic segmentation [14] is a combination of semantic segmentation (every pixel is assigned a class label) and instance segmentation (detects each instance of an object and segments it) tasks, which considers both object and stuff classes. In this work, we perform panoptic segmentation [14] on the image for capturing the associated semantic concepts, allowing stuffs to be incorporated more naturally in addition to objects.

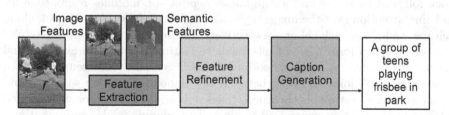

Fig. 1. Our model, where semantic and image features are combined and refined by using CNNs to generate the sentence describing the image.

This work proposes a CNN based image captioning method, modeling attention at multiple levels of the architecture that are pervasive. An overview of the complete framework is illustrated in Fig. 1. A feature representation for the image is obtained by passing it through a convolutional neural network (CNN). In addition, semantic features are obtained by performing panoptic segmentation [14] on the image. We combine both the extracted features and pass it to the feature refinement module, comprising of a CNN which possess attention capabilities across both dimensions of the image, to build an intermediate feature representation for the image. The product space of the intermediate feature representation and caption sequence defines the 2-dimensional grid over which a second attention modeling CNN is applied for generating the caption.

The major contributions of the work include:

- A novel approach which refines feature representations by modeling attention like capabilities at multiple levels of the architecture using a CNN.
- Introduction of higher-level semantic information based on a panoptic segmentation task to produce captions with better quality.
- Integrate the individual attention capability at multiple levels of the network to visualize the overall attention.

Experimental evaluation for the proposed method of describing images is performed on the MS-COCO dataset using established metrics. The standard image captioning and robust image captioning tasks are considered for evaluating the proposed framework. The ability of our proposed model to focus on salient regions in the image is also visually demonstrated.

2   Proposed Model

Our approach is based on the work proposed in [8], which follows a convolutional approach for the machine translation task. The proposed architecture is depicted in Fig. 2. It is composed of a feature refinement module and a caption generation module. We extract two sets of features from the image, namely the image and semantic features, which are then concatenated to form the input to the feature refinement module. The feature refinement module consists of a DenseBlock followed by a row and a column aggregator sub-modules responsible for modeling attention over the image regions as defined by the $M \times M$ grid, along each row and along each column respectively. The outputs of these sub-modules are then fused to form a set of intermediate features that captures the visual aspects of the image. A word embedding of size D is used to represent each word in the caption. A joint encoding between the embedded caption sequence and the intermediate features is then performed, forming a 3-D tensor which is fed as input to the caption generation module. This module is also composed of a DenseBlock followed by a column aggregator sub-module and a softmax operation. Attention over the intermediate features is modeled at this stage. Each module is described in detail in the subsequent sub-sections.

2.1   Feature Extraction

The image I (height H and width W) is passed through a standard CNN to extract features ($f_{img} \in \mathbb{R}^{M \times M \times D_{img}}$) corresponding to a uniform spatial grid ($M \times M$) of image regions, where D_{img} is the size of the feature vector for each image region. Besides, we also construct features capturing semantic information

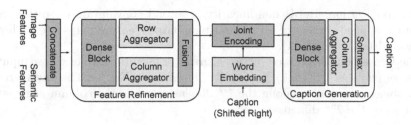

Fig. 2. Architecture block diagram of the proposed approach for captioning images. The processing modules in Fig. 1 are shown here as sub-modules.

using panoptic segmentation on the image, where a distinction is created between stuff and things. Each pixel in I is assigned a class label and the instance to which it belongs. A GLOVE [19] embedding of size D_{glv} is taken for each pixel, corresponding to the class label producing $f_{glv} \in \mathbb{R}^{H \times W \times D_{glv}}$. For each pixel, the instance number of the class it belongs is encoded by means of a one-hot vector of length D_{inst}, thereby generating $f_{inst} \in \mathbb{R}^{H \times W \times D_{inst}}$. Then, f_{glv} and f_{inst} are concatenated and a global average pooling is performed to obtain semantic features ($f_{sem} \in \mathbb{R}^{M \times M \times D_{sem}}$) with $D_{sem} = D_{glv} + D_{inst}$, corresponding to the uniform spatial grid of image regions in I. f_{img} and f_{sem} are further concatenated and passed to the feature refinement module.

2.2 Feature Refinement

This module consists of a DenseBlock [8] followed by 2 aggregators and a fusion sub-module. Each layer l of the DenseBlock [11] takes as input the activations of every preceding layer to produce g feature maps. The parameter g is called the "growth rate". The output of layer l has f_l output channels and is denoted as H^l. The DenseBlock has $f_0 = D_{img} + D_{sem}$ channels as input and f_L output channels, where L is the number of layers. A batch-normalization, ReLU non-linearity and a 1×1 convolution, is used to compute $4g$ channels from the $f_0 + (l-1)g$ input channels at each layer l. A sequence of operations as: another

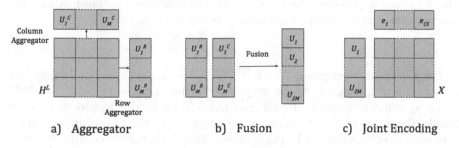

a) **Aggregator**   b) **Fusion**   c) **Joint Encoding**

Fig. 3. A visual illustration of the dimension changes of the tensor(s) (as H^L, U^R, U^C, U and e) upon passing through the sub-module present in the architecture.

batch-normalization, ReLU non-linearity, a second convolution operation, and dropout is applied thereafter for generating g output feature maps in each layer. For more details refer [8,11].

The DenseBlock is followed by two aggregator [8] sub-modules whose input is the tensor $(H^L \in \mathbb{R}^{M \times M \times f_L})$, as visually illustrated in Fig. 3a. The row aggregator combines information along the 1st dimension while the column aggregator does it along the 2nd dimension, as:

$$H_{id}^R = \max_{j \in \{1,\dots,M\}} H_{ijd}^L; \quad H_{jd}^C = \max_{i \in \{1,\dots,M\}} H_{ijd}^L \tag{1}$$

where $H^R \in \mathbb{R}^{M \times f_L}$ and $H^C \in \mathbb{R}^{M \times f_L}$. A linear projection to the word embedding size D is done as:

$$U_i^R = W^R H_i^R + b^R; \quad U_j^C = W^C H_j^C + b^C \tag{2}$$

where $W^R, W^C \in \mathbb{R}^{D \times f_L}$, $b^R, b^C \in \mathbb{R}^D$ are weight matrices and bias that are learned during training in the row and column aggregator sub-modules. $U^R \in \mathbb{R}^{M \times D}$ and $U^C \in \mathbb{R}^{M \times D}$ are the corresponding $2-D$ tensors that are computed.

The fusion sub-module interlaces U^R and U^C to form the intermediate feature $(U \in \mathbb{R}^{2M \times D})$ as shown in Fig. 3b. A fusion of the feature representations obtained by the row and column aggregator is necessary for implementing multi-level attention (details are given later in Sect. 2.4). This allows the network to adaptively focus attention on different image regions, based on the words seen in the caption generation module. For k in $\{1,\dots,2M\}$, the result of fusion is:

$$U_k = \begin{cases} U_{\lceil k/2 \rceil}^R & k \text{ is odd} \\ U_{k/2}^C & k \text{ is even} \end{cases} \tag{3}$$

2.3 Caption Generation

The caption of length CS represented as $y = \{y_1,\dots,y_{CS}\}$, where $y_t \in V$ and V is the vocabulary of words, is used to learn an embedding $E^{IN} \in \mathbb{R}^{|V| \times D}$ during training, transforming the caption y into a sequence $e = \{e_1,\dots,e_{CS}\}$, where $e_t \in \mathbb{R}^D$. The product space of the 2 sequences (U and e) defines the $2-D$ grid (Fig. 3c) which is processed by the CNN in the caption generation module. The sequences are concatenated to form a $3-D$ tensor X, as:

$$X_{kt} = [U_k \quad e_t] \tag{4}$$

The jointly encoded tensor $X \in \mathbb{R}^{2M \times CS \times 2D}$ is passed through a DenseBlock [8,11] having L layers, where the output of the final layer is $G^L \in \mathbb{R}^{2M \times CS \times s_L}$ having s_L output channels. Unlike the DenseBlock in the feature refinement module, the filters of the 2nd convolution operation in the DenseBlock needs to be masked here to suppress learning information from the succeeding words in the caption sequence [8]. The 1st dimension of the tensor obtained as the output of the DenseBlock (G^L) is collapsed by column aggregation to compute G^C, as:

$$G_{td}^C = \max_{k \in \{1,\dots,2M\}} G_{ktd}^L \tag{5}$$

The distribution over the words forming the output caption is modeled using the column aggregator module output ($G^C \in \mathbb{R}^{CS \times s_L}$) by learning a word embedding ($E \in \mathbb{R}^{|V| \times s_L}$). The probability for the occurrence of word y_t at position t in the output caption sequence, given all preceding words in the caption, is estimated using a softmax function as:

$$p(y_t|y_{1:t-1}) = softmax(E.G_t^C) \tag{6}$$

Consider the ground truth caption as $\{y_1^*, y_2^*, \dots, y_{CS}^*\}$ where $y_t^* \in V$. The cross-entropy loss ($\mathcal{L}_{XE}$) is used to train our model parameters (θ), as:

$$\mathcal{L}_{XE}(\theta) = - \sum_{t \in \{1,\dots,CS\}} \log(p(y_t^*|y_{1:t-1}^*)) \tag{7}$$

2.4 Multi-level Pervasive Attention

Each DenseBlock followed by either of the aggregators, models an attention mechanism that is pervasive [8] through its layers. There are three such instances in our architecture (see Fig. 2), twice in the feature refinement module (attention across the columns and rows of the concatenated image and semantic features) and once in the caption generation module (attention across the intermediate feature). This process is described below.

Consider the column aggregator function in the caption generation module as given in Eq. 5. At output caption position t, the s_L channels of the tensor $G^L \in \mathbb{R}^{2M \times CS \times s_L}$ are partitioned by assigning them across the intermediate feature positions k [8]. Considering the set of channels as $S = \{1, \dots, s_L\}$, the set of channels assigned to position k in the intermediate feature U for output caption position t, is obtained as:

$$\mathcal{B}_{kt} = \left\{ d \in S \mid k = \underset{k' \in \{1,\dots,2M\}}{\arg\max} \left(G_{k'td}^L \right) \right\} \tag{8}$$

The energy used for the softmax function (Eq. 6) to predict the word $w \in V$ for the output caption position at t, is:

$$\sum_{d \in S} E_{wd} G_{td}^C = \sum_{k \in \{1,\dots,2M\}} \sum_{d \in \mathcal{B}_{kt}} E_{wd} G_{ktd}^L \tag{9}$$

where $E \in \mathbb{R}^{|V| \times s_L}$ is the output word embedding matrix. The contribution of the intermediate feature at position k for generating the word at position t in the caption sequence is given by:

$$\alpha_{kt} = \sum_{d \in \mathcal{B}_{kt}} E_{wd} G_{ktd}^L \quad \text{where } \alpha \in \mathbb{R}^{2M \times CS} \tag{10}$$

The dependence on w is dropped here for simplicity, and the values α_{kt} corresponding to the word at position t in the output caption is used to visualize the attention experimentally.

Similarly, we consider the row and column aggregators in the feature refinement module as given in Eq. 1. The row aggregator partitions the f_L channels of the tensor $H^L \in \mathbb{R}^{M \times M \times f_L}$ by assigning them across the column position j for each row position i, whereas the column aggregator partitions them by assigning them across the row positions i for each column position j. Let F denote the set of channels $\{1, \ldots, f_L\}$, then the set of channels assigned to column position j and row position i by the row and column aggregators are :

$$\mathcal{B}_{ij}^R = \left\{ d \in F | j = \operatorname*{arg\,max}_{j' \in \{1,\ldots,M\}} \left(H_{ij'd}^L \right) \right\}; \quad \mathcal{B}_{ij}^C = \left\{ d \in F | i = \operatorname*{arg\,max}_{i' \in \{1,\ldots,M\}} \left(H_{i'jd}^L \right) \right\} \tag{11}$$

The sum of each tensor $H^R \in \mathbb{R}^{M \times f_L}$ and $H^C \in \mathbb{R}^{M \times f_L}$ (computed using Eq. 1) across the channels in F are expressed as (using Eq. 11):

$$\sum_{d \in F} H_{id}^R = \sum_{j \in \{1,\ldots,M\}} \sum_{d \in \mathcal{B}_{ij}^R} H_{ijd}^L; \quad \sum_{d \in F} H_{jd}^C = \sum_{i \in \{1,\ldots,M\}} \sum_{d \in \mathcal{B}_{ij}^C} H_{ijd}^L \tag{12}$$

The contribution of the regions along a column for each row (given by α^R) and the contribution of the regions along a row for each column (given by α^C), as computed in the feature refinement module, are:

$$\alpha_{ij}^R = \sum_{d \in \mathcal{B}_{ij}^R} H_{ijd}^L; \quad \alpha_{ij}^C = \sum_{d \in \mathcal{B}_{ij}^C} H_{ijd}^L \quad \text{where } \alpha^R, \alpha^C \in \mathbb{R}^{M \times M} \tag{13}$$

Since the row and column aggregations (U^R and U^C) are fused to obtain (U) (see Eq. 3), we split the attention weights ($\alpha \in \mathbb{R}^{2M \times CS}$) over the intermediate feature sequence of length $2M$ to obtain the corresponding attention weights over the row ($a^R \in \mathbb{R}^{CS \times M}$) and column ($a^C \in \mathbb{R}^{CS \times M}$) aggregated representations, obtained in the feature refinement module as:

$$a_{ti}^R = \alpha_{k_o t} \text{ where } k_o = 2i - 1; \quad a_{tj}^C = \alpha_{k_e t} \text{ where } k_e = 2j \tag{14}$$

where $i, j \in \{1, \ldots, M\}$. The overall attention ($\beta \in \mathbb{R}^{CS \times M \times M}$) over each region in the image grid, for predicting the word at caption position t is:

$$\beta_{tij} = a_{ti}^R \alpha_{ij}^R + a_{tj}^C \alpha_{ij}^C \tag{15}$$

The feature refinement module identifies specific salient image regions (using α^R and α^C) in the image, which are weighted differently (using a^R and a^C) for generating each word in the output caption. This helps to improve the performance of caption generation.

3   Experiments

We validate our approach on the MS-COCO 2014 captions dataset [16] by performing experimentation on two separate captioning tasks: Standard Image Captioning and Robust Image Captioning. Each image in the dataset is labeled with five captions. Each caption is converted to lower case while discarding non-alphanumeric characters. A vocabulary of size 9488 is built using words that occur at least five times in the training data. BLEU [18], METEOR [4], ROUGE-L [15], CIDEr [22], and SPICE [1] metrics are used for performance evaluation.

Table 1. Performance comparison for the standard captioning task on the MS-COCO [16] dataset. The evaluation metrics (all higher the better): BLEU-1 (B-1), BLEU-2 (B-2), BLEU-3 (B-3), BLEU-4 (B-4), METEOR (M), ROUGE (R), CIDEr (C) and Spice (S). $^+$ indicates that the results are reported by implementing the model [23] using ResNet-101 as the image encoder. * [2] uses better image features, and hence not proper to compare. Ours-GT indicates the usage of ground-truth class and instance labels for generating semantic features.

Method	B-1	B-2	B-3	B-4	M	R	C	S
NIC $^+$ [23]	0.701	0.531	0.396	0.299	0.243	0.519	0.908	0.171
LSTM [3,12]	0.724	0.552	0.405	0.294	0.251	0.532	0.961	–
CIC [3]	0.72	0.549	0.403	0.293	0.248	0.527	0.945	–
CompCap [6]	–	–	–	0.251	0.243	0.478	0.862	0.199
Up-Down [2]	0.745	–	–	0.334	0.261	0.544	1.054	0.192
NBT [17]	**0.755**	–	–	**0.347**	0.271	–	**1.072**	0.201
Up-Down * [2]	0.772	–	–	0.362	0.27	0.564	1.135	0.203
Baseline-Single	0.716	0.553	0.412	0.291	0.254	0.533	0.953	0.185
Baseline-Double	0.73	0.555	0.414	0.305	0.259	0.545	1.005	0.189
Baseline	0.736	0.563	0.422	0.316	0.263	0.544	1.034	0.193
Ours	0.74	**0.569**	**0.431**	0.326	**0.272**	**0.557**	1.072	**0.202**
Ours-GT	0.756	0.586	0.447	0.338	0.276	0.563	1.117	0.206

The ResNet-101 [10] architecture pre-trained on ImageNet [7] is used to encode the image. Similar to the work [2], the final convolutional layer output is resized to $M \times M \times D_{img}$, with $M = 7$ and $D_{img} = 2048$, using bilinear interpolation. The semantic feature is constructed using the segmented image obtained from the output of UPSNet [25], trained using a ResNet-101-FPN backbone, with 80 thing classes and 62 stuff classes on the MS-COCO dataset. A memory-efficient implementation [20] of the DenseNet architecture is used for experimentation. We found that setting the growth rate (g) and number of layers (L) for both DenseBlocks to 32 and 24 respectively gives optimum performance. We fix the encoding dimension (D) as 128 and filter kernel size to 3 as used in [8].

The splits detailed in the prior work of image captioning task [12], comprising of 113287 training images, and 5000 images for both validation and testing are used. The Adam optimizer [13] is used for training our model. The model that best performs on the validation data is selected for generating the captions using a beam search with width = 3. A performance comparison is tabulated in Table 1. The effectiveness of incorporating multi-level pervasive attention is demonstrated by evaluating three variants (as ablation studies) of our proposed architecture:

- Baseline: Models the architecture (see Fig. 2) by excluding the semantic features.
- Baseline-Double: The baseline architecture without the column aggregator and fusion sub-modules in the feature refinement module.
- Baseline-Single: A straight forward adaptation of the sequence to sequence framework [8] using single-level pervasive attention by linearizing the image features into a $M^2 \times D$ feature sequence.

Table 2. Computational efficiency on MS-COCO [16] dataset. The time is measured on a Nvidia GeForce GTX 1080 GPU with a batch size of 20.

Method	Training time per epoch	Parameters
NIC [23]	**0.1 h**	13 M
CIC [3]	1.26 h	20 M
NBT [17]	2.24 h	56 M
Up-Down [2]	0.22 h	20 M
Baseline	0.79 h	**9 M**
Ours	0.85 h	11 M

We see that modeling attention at different levels of the architecture can improve the performance consistently on all the metrics. The addition of the column aggregator in addition to the row aggregator gives the model enough flexibility to compute attention over regions in the image grid. The baseline registers a substantial performance boost in comparison to CIC [3] as seen in Table 1, which is a recently proposed convolutional framework for captioning images. The results obtained by our proposed model using the semantic features generated upon feeding the ground-truth class and instance labels for the panoptic segmentation task (Ours-GT) is also reported. The inclusion of semantic features alongside the image features, leads to a significant improvement in performance, as seen in the penultimate row of Table 1. We outperform other captioning models on all metrics except the BLEU-1 and BLEU-4 metrics.

In Table 2, we analyze the efficiency of the network in terms of the training time per epoch and the number of trainable parameters. Our baseline model has lesser number of parameters than all other compared models and needs

Table 3. Performance comparison for the robust image captioning task on MS-COCO [16] dataset. The metrics used are BLEU-4 (B-4), METEOR (M), ROUGE (R), CIDEr (C) and Spice (S). The results of other methods are obtained from [17]. Ours-GT indicates the usage of ground-truth class and instance labels for generating semantic features.

Method	B-4	M	C	S
Att2in [21]	0.315	0.246	0.906	0.177
Up-Down [2]	0.316	0.25	0.92	0.181
NBT [17]	**0.317**	0.252	0.941	0.183
Ours	0.312	**0.255**	**0.949**	**0.185**
Ours-GT	0.316	0.259	0.96	0.188

lesser time to train in comparison to CIC [3] which also follows a CNN based architectural framework, despite using a memory-efficient implementation [20].

We also perform experimentation on the Robust Image Captioning Task [17]. The dataset split [17] has 110234, 3915 and 9138 images for training, validation, and testing respectively. The split is devised such that there are sufficient examples having entity words that belong to the 80 MS-COCO object categories during training, whereas novel compositions (pairs) of the categories are encountered at test time. The results are tabulated in Table 3. We observe an improvement in performance in all metrics except BLEU-4.

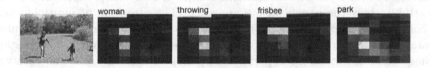

Fig. 4. Visualization of the attention over image regions while generating words "woman", "throwing", "frisbee" and "park". The predicted sentence is "A woman throwing a frisbee in a park."

The attention weights over the image regions for each word in the generated sentence is visualized using an example in Fig. 4. The attention weights are interpreted by combining individual attention weights obtained in the feature refinement and caption generation modules as given in Eq. 15.

An image and the generated panoptic segmentation map along with the generated captions using the baseline and the proposed architecture for 3 examples are shown in Fig. 5, to qualitatively highlight the role of semantic features in our model for caption generation. Semantic features guide caption generation process, by generating captions focusing on image regions belonging to the objects and stuff in the image. As seen in the 2nd example, our model is able to generate better captions for images depicting objects in an out-of-context environment.

a)

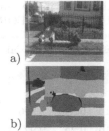
a)

a)

b)

b)

b)

Baseline: a dog sitting on a couch watching TV
Ours: a living room with a couch and a television
GT: a living room with a chair, couch, coffee table and television

Baseline: a dog sitting on a bench in front of a house
Ours: a couch sitting in the grass next to a fire hydrant
GT: a couch sitting next to a white fire hydrant

Baseline: a bus driving down a street next to a forest
Ours: a large truck is driving down the road
GT: a colorful truck is driving on a wet road

Fig. 5. Some qualitative results showing the role of semantic features in our proposed approach. (a) image, (b) the generated segmentation label map, with the captions obtained using the baseline, our approach and ground truth (GT).

4   Conclusion

A novel convolutional approach modeled using pervasive attention at multiple levels of the architecture is proposed, which exhibit substantial performance improvement over a recent convolutional framework for image captioning. Ablation studies show the benefit of our approach. The attention at multiple levels was combined. The proposed architecture is also efficient in terms of the number of parameters and training time. Moreover, an explicit semantic representation of image content formed upon performing panoptic segmentation was observed to improve the quality of generated captions.

References

1. Anderson, P., Fernando, B., Johnson, M., Gould, S.: SPICE: semantic propositional image caption evaluation. In: Leibe, B., Matas, J., Sebe, N., Welling, M. (eds.) ECCV 2016. LNCS, vol. 9909, pp. 382–398. Springer, Cham (2016). https://doi.org/10.1007/978-3-319-46454-1_24
2. Anderson, P., et al.: Bottom-up and top-down attention for image captioning and visual question answering. In: The IEEE Conference on Computer Vision and Pattern Recognition (CVPR) (2018)
3. Aneja, J., Deshpande, A., Schwing, A.G.: Convolutional image captioning. In: The IEEE Conference on Computer Vision and Pattern Recognition (CVPR) (2018)
4. Banerjee, S., Lavie, A.: METEOR: an automatic metric for MT evaluation with improved correlation with human judgments. In: The Association for Computational Linguistics (ACL) Workshop, vol. 29, pp. 65–72 (2005)

5. Caesar, H., Uijlings, J., Ferrari, V.: Coco-stuff: Thing and stuff classes in context. In: The IEEE Conference on Computer Vision and Pattern Recognition (CVPR), pp. 1209–1218 (2018)
6. Dai, B., Fidler, S., Lin, D.: A neural compositional paradigm for image captioning. In: Advances in Neural Information Processing Systems (NeurIPS), pp. 656–666. Curran Associates Inc., USA (2018)
7. Deng, J., Dong, W., Socher, R., Li, L.J., Li, K., Fei-Fei, L.: Imagenet: a large-scale hierarchical image database. In: The IEEE Conference on Computer Vision and Pattern Recognition (CVPR), pp. 248–255 (2009)
8. Elbayad, M., Besacier, L., Verbeek, J.: Pervasive attention: 2d convolutional neural networks for sequence-to-sequence prediction. In: The Conference on Computational Natural Language Learning (CoNLL), pp. 1–11 (2018)
9. Fang, H., et al.: From captions to visual concepts and back. In: The IEEE Conference on Computer Vision and Pattern Recognition (CVPR), pp. 1473–1482 (2015)
10. He, K., Zhang, X., Ren, S., Sun, J.: Deep residual learning for image recognition. In: The IEEE Conference on Computer Vision and Pattern Recognition (CVPR), pp. 770–778 (2016)
11. Huang, G., Liu, Z., Van Der Maaten, L., Weinberger, K.Q.: Densely connected convolutional networks. In: The IEEE Conference on Computer Vision and Pattern Recognition (CVPR), vol. 1, p. 3 (2017)
12. Karpathy, A., Fei-Fei, L.: Deep visual-semantic alignments for generating image descriptions. In: The IEEE Conference on Computer Vision and Pattern Recognition (CVPR), pp. 3128–3137 (2015)
13. Kingma, D.P., Ba, J.: Adam: A method for stochastic optimization. arXiv preprint arXiv:1412.6980 (2014)
14. Kirillov, A., He, K., Girshick, R., Rother, C., Dollar, P.: Panoptic segmentation. In: The IEEE Conference on Computer Vision and Pattern Recognition (CVPR) (2019)
15. Lin, C.Y.: Rouge: a package for automatic evaluation of summaries. In: The Association for Computational Linguistics (ACL) Workshop, vol. 8 (2004)
16. Lin, T.Y., et al.: Microsoft coco: common objects in context. In: The European Conference on Computer Vision (ECCV), pp. 740–755 (2014)
17. Lu, J., Yang, J., Batra, D., Parikh, D.: Neural baby talk. In: The IEEE Conference on Computer Vision and Pattern Recognition (CVPR), pp. 7219–7228 (2018)
18. Papineni, K., Roukos, S., Ward, T., Zhu, W.J.: BLEU: a method for automatic evaluation of machine translation. In: The Annual Meeting on Association for Computational Linguistics (ACL), pp. 311–318 (2002)
19. Pennington, J., Socher, R., Manning, C.: GloVe: global vectors for word representation. In: The Conference on Empirical Methods in Natural Language Processing (EMNLP), pp. 1532–1543 (2014)
20. Pleiss, G., Chen, D., Huang, G., Li, T., van der Maaten, L., Weinberger, K.Q.: Memory-efficient implementation of densenets. arXiv preprint arXiv:1707.06990 (2017)
21. Rennie, S.J., Marcheret, E., Mroueh, Y., Ross, J., Goel, V.: Self-critical sequence training for image captioning. In: The IEEE Conference on Computer Vision and Pattern Recognition (CVPR), pp. 1179–1195 (2017)
22. Vedantam, R., Lawrence Zitnick, C., Parikh, D.: Cider: consensus-based image description evaluation. In: The IEEE Conference on Computer Vision and Pattern Recognition (CVPR), pp. 4566–4575 (2015)

23. Vinyals, O., Toshev, A., Bengio, S., Erhan, D.: Show and tell: a neural image caption generator. In: The IEEE Conference on Computer Vision and Pattern Recognition (CVPR), pp. 3156–3164 (2015)
24. Wu, Q., Shen, C., Liu, L., Dick, A., Van Den Hengel, A.: What value do explicit high level concepts have in vision to language problems? In: The IEEE Conference on Computer Vision and Pattern Recognition (CVPR), pp. 203–212 (2016)
25. Xiong, Y., et al.: Upsnet: A unified panoptic segmentation network. In: The IEEE Conference on Computer Vision and Pattern Recognition (CVPR) (2019)
26. Xu, K., et al.: Show, attend and tell: Neural image caption generation with visual attention. In: The International Conference on International Conference on Machine Learning (ICML), pp. 2048–2057 (2015)
27. Yang, Z., Yuan, Y., Wu, Y., Cohen, W.W., Salakhutdinov, R.R.: Review networks for caption generation. In: Advances in Neural Information Processing Systems (NeurIPS), pp. 2361–2369 (2016)
28. Yang, Z., He, X., Gao, J., Deng, L., Smola, A.: Stacked attention networks for image question answering. In: The IEEE Conference on Computer Vision and Pattern Recognition (CVPR) (2016)
29. Yang, Z., Yang, D., Dyer, C., He, X., Smola, A., Hovy, E.: Hierarchical attention networks for document classification. In: The Conference of the North American Chapter of the Association for Computational Linguistics: Human Language Technologies (NAACL-HLT), pp. 1480–1489 (2016)
30. You, Q., Jin, H., Wang, Z., Fang, C., Luo, J.: Image captioning with semantic attention. In: The IEEE Conference on Computer Vision and Pattern Recognition (CVPR), pp. 4651–4659 (2016)

One Analog Neuron Cannot Recognize Deterministic Context-Free Languages

Jiří Šíma[✉] and Martin Plátek

Institute of Computer Science of the Czech Academy of Sciences,
P. O. Box 5, 18207 Prague 8, Czech Republic
sima@cs.cas.cz

Abstract. We analyze the computational power of discrete-time recurrent neural networks (NNs) with the saturated-linear activation function within the Chomsky hierarchy. This model restricted to integer weights coincides with binary-state NNs with the Heaviside activation function, which are equivalent to finite automata (Chomsky level 3), while rational weights make this model Turing complete even for three analog-state units (Chomsky level 0). For an intermediate model αANN of a binary-state NN that is extended with $\alpha \geq 0$ extra analog-state neurons with rational weights, we have established the analog neuron hierarchy 0ANNs $\subset$ 1ANNs $\subset$ 2ANNs $\subseteq$ 3ANNs. The separation 1ANNs $\subsetneq$ 2ANNs has been witnessed by the deterministic context-free language (DCFL) $L_\# = \{0^n 1^n \mid n \geq 1\}$ which cannot be recognized by any 1ANN even with real weights, while any DCFL (Chomsky level 2) is accepted by a 2ANN with rational weights. In this paper, we generalize this result by showing that any non-regular DCFL cannot be recognized by 1ANNs with real weights, which means (DCFLs \ REG) $\subset$ (2ANNs \ 1ANNs), implying 0ANNs = 1ANNs $\cap$ DCFLs. For this purpose, we show that $L_\#$ is the simplest non-regular DCFL by reducing $L_\#$ to any language in this class, which is by itself an interesting achievement in computability theory.

Keywords: Neural computing · Analog neuron hierarchy · Deterministic context-free language · Restart automaton · Chomsky hierarchy

1 The Analog Neuron Hierarchy

The computational power of discrete-time recurrent neural networks (NNs) with the saturated-linear activation function[1] depends on the descriptive complexity of their weight parameters [13,21]. NNs with *integer* weights, corresponding to

---

[1] The results are partially valid for more general classes of activation functions [8,12, 16,24] including the logistic function [7].

Research was done with institutional support RVO: 67985807 and partially supported by the grant of the Czech Science Foundation GA19-05704S.

T. Gedeon et al. (Eds.): ICONIP 2019, LNCS 11955, pp. 77–89, 2019.
https://doi.org/10.1007/978-3-030-36718-3_7

binary-state (shortly binary) networks (with Boolean outputs 0 or 1), coincide with finite automata (FAs) recognizing regular languages (REG) [1,3,4,9,17,23]. *Rational* weights make the analog-state (shortly analog) NNs (with real-valued outputs in the interval [0, 1]) computationally equivalent to Turing machines (TMs) [4,15], and thus (by a real-time simulation [15]) polynomial-time computations of such networks are characterized by the fundamental complexity class P. Moreover, NNs with arbitrary *real* weights can even derive "super-Turing" computational capabilities [13]. In particular, their polynomial-time computations correspond to the nonuniform complexity class P/poly while any input/output mapping (including undecidable problems) can be computed within exponential time [14]. In addition, a proper infinite hierarchy of nonuniform complexity classes between P and P/poly has been established for polynomial-time computations of NNs with increasing Kolmogorov complexity of real weights [2].

As can be seen, our understanding of the computational power of NNs is satisfactorily fine-grained when changing from rational to arbitrary real weights. In contrast, there is still a gap between integer and rational weights which results in a jump from regular languages capturing the lowest level 3 in the Chomsky hierarchy to recursively enumerable languages on the highest Chomsky level 0. In order to refine the classification of NNs which do not possess the full power of TMs (Chomsky level 0), we have initiated the study of binary-state NNs employing integer weights, that are extended with $\alpha \geq 0$ extra analog neurons having real weights, which are denoted as αANNs. Although this study has been inspired by theoretical issues, NNs with different types of units/layers are widely used in practical applications, e.g. in deep learning [11], and they thus require a detailed mathematical analysis.

In our previous work [20], we have characterized syntactically the class of languages that are accepted by 1ANNs with *one* extra analog unit, in terms of so-called *cut languages* [22] which are combined in a certain way by usual operations on languages. By using this syntactic characterization of 1ANNs we have proven a sufficient condition when a 1ANN recognizes only a regular language (Chomsky level 3), which is based on the *quasi-periodicity* [22] of some parameters derived from its real weights. In particular, a 1ANN with weights from the smallest field extension $\mathbb{Q}(\beta)$ over the rational numbers $\mathbb{Q}$ including a *Pisot number* $\beta > 1$, such that the self-loop weight w of its only analog neuron equals $1/\beta$, is computationally equivalent to a FA. For instance, since every integer $n > 1$ is a Pisot number, it follows that any 1ANN with rational weights such that $w = 1/n$, accepts a regular language. More complex examples of such neural FAs, are 1ANNs that have rational weights except for the irrational (algebraic) self-loop weight $w = 1/\rho \approx 0.754878$ or $w = 1/\varphi = \varphi - 1 \approx 0.618034$ for the *plastic constant* ρ or the *golden ratio* φ, respectively, which are Pisot numbers.

On the other hand, we have introduced examples of languages accepted by 1ANNs with rational weights that are not context-free (CFLs) [20], and they are thus above Chomsky level 2, while we have proven that any language accepted online[2] by this model is context-sensitive (CSL) at Chomsky level 1. For instance, the CSL $L_1 = \left\{ x_1 \ldots x_n \in \{0,1\}^* \,\middle|\, \sum_{k=1}^{n} x_{n-k+1} \left(\frac{216}{125} \right)^{-k} < 1 \right\}$ which is not in CFLs, can be recognized by a 1ANN. In other words, the computational power of binary-state networks having integer weights can increase from REG (Chomsky level 3) to that between CFLs (Chomsky level 2) and CSLs (Chomsky level 1), when an extra analog unit with rational weights is added, while a condition when this does not bring any additional power even for real weights, was formulated.

Furthermore, we have established an analog neuron hierarchy of classes of languages recognized by binary αANNs with α extra analog units having rational weights, for $\alpha = 0, 1, 2, 3, \ldots$, that is, 0ANNs $\subseteq$ 1ANNs $\subseteq$ 2ANNs $\subseteq$ 3ANNs $\subseteq \cdots$, respectively. Note that we use the notation αANNs also for the class of languages accepted by αANNs, which can clearly be distinguished by the context. Obviously, the 0ANNs are purely binary-state NNs which are equivalent to FAs and hence, 0ANNs $\subsetneq$ 1ANNs because we know there are non-context-free languages such as L_1 accepted by 1ANNs [20]. In contrast, we have proven that the deterministic context-free language (DCFL) $L_\# = \{0^n 1^n \,|\, n \geq 1\}$, which contains the words of n zeros followed by n ones, cannot be recognized even offline (see footnote 2) by any 1ANN with arbitrary real weights [19]. We thus know that 1ANNs are not Turing complete.

Nevertheless, we have shown that any DCFL included in Chomsky level 2 can be recognized by a 2ANN with two extra analog neurons having rational weights, by simulating a corresponding deterministic pushdown automaton (DPDA) [19]. This provides the separation 1ANNs $\subsetneq$ 2ANNs since the DCFL $L_\#$ is not accepted by any 1ANN. In addition, we have proven that any TM can be simulated by a 3ANN having rational weights with a linear-time overhead [18]. It follows that recursively enumerable languages at the highest Chomsky level 0 are accepted by 3ANNs with rational weights and thus this model including only three analog neurons is Turing complete. Since αANNs with rational weights can be simulated by TMs for any $\alpha \geq 0$, the analog neuron hierarchy collapses to 3ANNs:

$$\text{FAs} \equiv \text{0ANNs} \subsetneq \text{1ANNs} \subsetneq \text{2ANNs} \subseteq \text{3ANNs} = \text{4ANNs} = \ldots \equiv \text{TMs},$$

which is schematically depicted in Fig. 1. It appears that the analog neuron hierarchy is only partially comparable to that of Chomsky.

In this paper, we further study the relation between the analog neuron hierarchy and the Chomsky hierarchy. We show that any non-regular DCFL cannot be recognized online by 1ANNs with real weights, which provides the stronger separation (DCFLs \ REG) $\subset$ (2ANNs \ 1ANNs), implying REG = 0ANNs = 1ANNs $\cap$ DCFLs. Thus, the class of non-regular DCFLs is contained in 2ANNs

---

[2] In *online* input/output protocols, the time between reading two consecutive input symbols as well as the delay in outputting the result after an input has been read, is bounded by a constant, while in *offline* protocols these time intervals are not bounded.

with rational weights, having the empty intersection with 1ANNs, as depicted in Fig. 1. In order to prove this lower bound on the computational power of 1ANNs, we show that $L_\#$ is the simplest non-regular DCFL by reducing $L_\#$ to any language in DCFLs \ REG. Namely, for any non-regular DCFL L, we can recognize the language $L_\#$ by a FA that is allowed to call an online subroutine for solving L, which represents a kind of Turing reduction known in computability theory. Now if the language L is accepted by a 1ANN, then we could recognize $L_\#$ by a 1ANN, which is a contradiction, implying that L cannot be accepted by any 1ANN even with real weights. The proof exploits the technical representation of DCFLs by so-called deterministic monotonic restarting automata [5,6].

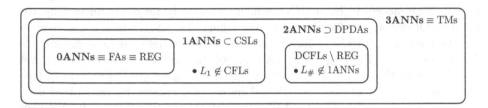

Fig. 1. The analog neuron hierarchy.

Note that the Turing-like reduction from $L_\#$ to any non-regular DCFL is by itself an interesting achievement in formal language theory, providing the simplest non-regular DCFL which any language in DCFLs \ REG must include. This is somewhat opposite to the usual hardness results in computational complexity theory where all problems in a class are usually reduced to its hardest problem such as in NP-completeness. Our result can thus open a new direction of research in computability theory aiming towards the existence of the simplest problems in traditional complexity classes and their mutual reductions.

The paper is organized as follows. In Sect. 2, we introduce basic definitions concerning the language acceptors based on 1ANNs. In Sect. 3, we present the theorem that reduces the languages $L_\#$ to any non-regular DCFL. For this purpose we use the formalism of deterministic monotonic restarting automata, which is shortly recalled. Section 4 shows that one extra analog neuron is not sufficient for recognizing any non-regular DCFL. Finally, we summarize the results and list some open problems in Sect. 5.

2   Neural Language Acceptors with One Analog Unit

We specify a computational model of a *discrete-time binary-state recurrent neural network with one extra analog unit* (shortly, 1ANN), $\mathcal{N}$, which will be used as a formal language acceptor. The network $\mathcal{N}$ consists of $s \geq 1$ *units (neurons)*, indexed as $V = \{1, \ldots, s\}$. All the units in $\mathcal{N}$ are assumed to be binary-state (shortly *binary*) neurons (i.e. *perceptrons, threshold gates*) except for the last sth neuron which is an analog-state (shortly *analog*) unit. The neurons are connected into a directed graph representing an *architecture* of $\mathcal{N}$, in which each edge $(i, j) \in V^2$ leading from unit i to j is labeled with a real *weight* $w(i, j) = w_{ji} \in \mathbb{R}$. The absence of a connection within the architecture corresponds to a zero weight between the respective neurons, and vice versa.

The *computational dynamics* of $\mathcal{N}$ determines for each unit $j \in V$ its *state (output)* $y_j^{(t)}$ at discrete time instants $t = 0, 1, 2, \ldots$. The states $y_j^{(t)}$ of the first $s - 1$ binary neurons $j \in V' = V \setminus \{s\}$ are Boolean values 0 or 1, whereas the output $y_s^{(t)}$ from analog unit s is a real number from the unit interval $\mathbb{I} = [0, 1]$. This establishes the *network state* $\mathbf{y}^{(t)} = \left(y_1^{(t)}, \ldots, y_{s-1}^{(t)}, y_s^{(t)} \right) \in \{0, 1\}^{s-1} \times \mathbb{I}$ at each discrete time instant $t \geq 0$.

For notational simplicity, we assume a synchronous fully parallel mode without loss of efficiency [10]. At the beginning of a computation, the 1ANN $\mathcal{N}$ is placed in an *initial state* $\mathbf{y}^{(0)} \in \{0, 1\}^s$. At discrete time instant $t \geq 0$, an *excitation* of any neuron $j \in V$ is defined as $\xi_j^{(t)} = \sum_{i=0}^s w_{ji} y_i^{(t)}$, including a real *bias* value $w_{j0} \in \mathbb{R}$ which can be viewed as the weight $w(0, j)$ from a formal constant unit input $y_0^{(t)} \equiv 1$ for every $t \geq 0$ (i.e. formally $0 \in V'$). At the next instant $t+1$, all the neurons $j \in V$ compute their new outputs $y_j^{(t+1)}$ in parallel by applying an *activation function* $\sigma_j : \mathbb{R} \longrightarrow \mathbb{I}$ to $\xi_j^{(t)}$, that is, $y_j^{(t+1)} = \sigma_j \left(\xi_j^{(t)} \right)$ for $j \in V$. For the neurons $j \in V'$ with binary states $y_j \in \{0, 1\}$, the *Heaviside* activation function $\sigma_j(\xi) = H(\xi)$ is used where $H(\xi) = 1$ for $\xi > 0$ and $H(\xi) = 0$ for $\xi < 0$, while the analog unit $s \in V$ with real output $y_s \in \mathbb{I}$ employs the *saturated-linear* function $\sigma_s(\xi) = \sigma(\xi)$ where $\sigma(\xi) = \xi$ for $0 \leq \xi \leq 1$, whereas $\sigma(\xi) = 1$ for $\xi > 1$, and $\sigma(\xi) = 0$ for $\xi < 0$. In this way, the new network state $\mathbf{y}^{(t+1)} \in \{0, 1\}^{s-1} \times \mathbb{I}$ is determined at time $t + 1$.

The computational power of NNs has been studied analogously to the traditional models of computations [21] so that the networks are exploited as acceptors of formal languages $L \subseteq \Sigma^*$ over a finite alphabet $\Sigma = \{\lambda_1, \ldots \lambda_p\}$ composed of p letters (symbols). For a finite 1ANN $\mathcal{N}$, we use the following *online* input/output protocol employing its special neurons nxt, out $\in V'$. An input word (string) $\mathbf{x} = x_1 \ldots x_n \in \Sigma^n$ of arbitrary length $n \geq 0$, is sequentially presented to the network, symbol after symbol, via the first $p < s$ so-called *input neurons* $X = \{1, \ldots, p\} \subset V'$, at the time instants $0 < \tau_1 < \tau_2 < \cdots < \tau_n$ when queried by $\mathcal{N}$, where $\tau_{k+1} - \tau_k$ is bounded by a constant for every $k = 1, \ldots, n$. Thus, once the prefix $x_1, \ldots, x_{k-1}$ of $\mathbf{x}$ for $1 \leq k \leq n$, has been read, the next input symbol $x_k \in \Sigma$ is presented to $\mathcal{N}$ one computational step after $\mathcal{N}$ activates the special neuron nxt $\in V'$. This means that $\mathcal{N}$ signals $y_{\text{nxt}}^{(t-1)} = 1$ if $t = \tau_k$ whereas $y_{\text{nxt}}^{(t-1)} = 0$ otherwise, for every $k = 1, \ldots, n$.

We employ the popular *one-hot encoding* of alphabet Σ where each letter $\lambda_i \in \Sigma$ is represented by one input neuron $i \in X$ which is activated when symbol λ_i is being read. The states of input neurons $i \in X$, which represent a current input symbol x_k at the time instant τ_k, are thus externally set as

$y_i^{(t)} = 1$ if $x_k = \lambda_i \in \Sigma$ and $t = \tau_k$, whereas $y_i^{(t)} = 0$ otherwise. At the same time, $\mathcal{N}$ carries its computation deciding about each prefix of the input word $\mathbf{x}$ whether it belongs to L, which is indicated by the output neuron out $\in V'$ when the neuron nxt is active, i.e. $y_{\text{out}}^{(\tau_{k+1}-1)} = 1$ if $x_1 \ldots x_k \in L$, and $y_{\text{out}}^{(\tau_{k+1}-1)} = 0$ if $x_1 \ldots x_k \notin L$, where $\tau_{n+1} > \tau_n$ is the time instant when the input word $\mathbf{x}$ is decided. We say that a language $L \subseteq \Sigma^*$ is *accepted (recognized)* by 1ANN $\mathcal{N}$, which is denoted as $L = \mathcal{L}(\mathcal{N})$, if for any input word $\mathbf{x} \in \Sigma^*$, $\mathcal{N}$ accepts $\mathbf{x}$ iff $\mathbf{x} \in L$.

3   The Simplest Non-regular Deterministic Language

In this section, we show that in some sense, any non-regular DCFL includes the language $L_\# = \{0^n 1^n \mid n \geq 1\}$ which is thus the simplest problem in the class DCFLs \ REG. This fact will be used in Sect. 4 for proving that any non-regular DCFL cannot be recognized by 1ANNs since we know that $L_\#$ is not accepted by 1ANNs [19]. For the proof, we employ *deterministic monotonic restarting automata* (shortly, *det-mon-R-automata*) which have been shown to recognize exactly the class of DCFLs [5,6].

Recall a det-mon-R-automaton $\mathcal{A} = (Q, \Sigma, k, I, q_0, Q_A, Q_R)$ has a finite-state control unit and one head moving on an input while possibly erasing some symbols. A finite set of its states, Q, includes the initial (start) state $q_0 \in Q$ and two disjoint subsets of accepting and rejecting states, $Q_A, Q_R \subseteq Q$, respectively. Moreover, the finite input alphabet Σ is extended with two new special symbols ¢, \$ (originally not contained in Σ), which always start and end any input to $\mathcal{A}$, respectively, and serve as sentinels which cannot be erased. The head of $\mathcal{A}$ scans a 'window' of $k \geq 1$ consecutive symbols of the input from its position to the right (or the remaining symbols to the end of the input if the distance of the head position to the right endmarker \$ is less than k).

For an input word $s \in \Sigma^*$, the det-mon-R-automaton $\mathcal{A}$ starts in the initial state q_0, while its head position is on the left endmarker ¢ of input ¢s\$. Then $\mathcal{A}$ carries out the computation by performing instructions from a finite set I, which are of the following two types:

1. the *move* instruction $(q, w) \longrightarrow q'$
2. the *restart* instruction $(q, w) \longrightarrow v$

The left-hand side (q, w) of an instruction determines when it is applicable, namely, the current state of $\mathcal{A}$ is $q \in Q$ and its head scans the string $w \in \Sigma^*$ composed of $k = |w|$ consecutive symbols of the input from the head position to the right (or $|w| < k$ if w ends with \$). We assume that $\mathcal{A}$ is *deterministic* which means there are no two instructions in I with the same left-hand side (q, w). The right-hand side of an instruction describes the activity to be performed. In a move instruction, $\mathcal{A}$ changes its current state to $q' \in Q$ and the head moves one symbol to the right. In a restart instruction, some of the symbols (excluding ¢,\$) in the string w are deleted which means the scanned part w of the input, is replaced with a shorter string $v \in \Sigma^*$ where $|v| < |w|$, which is a proper subsequence of w, and $\mathcal{A}$ restarts in the initial state q_0, while its head position is again on the left endmarker ¢ of this modified input. Moreover, we assume that $\mathcal{A}$ is *monotonic* which means that the whole string v which has replaced w, will be scanned by the head before the next restart instruction is applied. This ensures that the positions of deleted symbols do not increase their distances from the right endmarker $.

Furthermore, the subset of so-called halting states in which no instruction from I is applicable, coincide with $Q_A \cup Q_R \subseteq Q$. Thus, an input word $s \in \Sigma^*$ is accepted (recognized) by $\mathcal{A}$ if its computation on s (bounded by ¢, $) halts in an accepting state from Q_A. Such input words form the language $\mathcal{L}(\mathcal{A})$. For any $s_1, s_2 \in \Sigma^*$, the notation $s_1 \Rightarrow s_2$ means that if $\mathcal{A}$ starts in the initial states q_0 with the input s_1, then this input is rewritten to s_2 when $\mathcal{A}$ finds in q_0 for the next time, while $\Rightarrow^*$ denotes the reflexive and transitive closure of the relation $\Rightarrow$. In addition, the det-mon-R-automata satisfy the *correctness preserving property* [5,6] which guarantees that for every $s_1, s_2 \in \Sigma^*$ if $s_1 \Rightarrow^* s_2$, then $s_1 \in \mathcal{L}(\mathcal{A})$ iff $s_2 \in \mathcal{L}(\mathcal{A})$.

Theorem 1. *For any non-regular deterministic context-free language $L \subset \Sigma^*$ over a finite alphabet $\Sigma \neq \emptyset$, there exist words $u, w, z \in \Sigma^*$, nonempty strings $x, y \in \Sigma^+$, an integer $\kappa \geq 0$, and languages $L_k \in \{L, \overline{L}\}$ for $k \in K = \{-\kappa, \dots, -1, 0, 1, \dots, \kappa\}$, such that for every pair of integers, $m \geq 0$ and $n \geq \kappa$,*

$$\left(ux^m wy^{n+k}z \in L_k \text{ for all } k \in K\right) \quad iff \quad m = n. \tag{1}$$

Proof (Sketch). Let $L \subset \Sigma^*$ be a non-regular DCFL and assume $\mathcal{A} = (Q, \Sigma, k, I, q_0, Q_A, Q_R)$ is a det-mon-R-automaton that accepts $L = \mathcal{L}(\mathcal{A})$. It follows that $\mathcal{A}$ employs at least one restart instruction for some input since otherwise $\mathcal{A}$ would reduce to a finite automaton implying L is regular. Let $s \in \Sigma^*$ be an input presented to $\mathcal{A}$. We mark all the symbols in s (including ¢,$) that are scanned by the head at least once at a time instant when some restart instruction is applied in the course of computation of $\mathcal{A}$ on the input s. These marked symbols form contiguous segments in s called the *marked substrings* $\sigma_1, \dots, \sigma_\ell \in \Sigma^*$, which are separated by non-marked symbols and have length at least k since the head of $\mathcal{A}$ scans a window of length k. Observe that the number of marked strings in s' which is derived from $s \Rightarrow^* s'$ does not increases (i.e. is at most ℓ) because $\mathcal{A}$ is monotonic, which guarantees that the windows scanned by the head in the consecutive restarts, overlap when the distance of the restart head position to the left endmarker ¢ shortens.

Suppose that the length of marked substrings could be bounded by a constant, say $k \leq |\sigma_i| \leq c$ for every $i = 1, \dots, \ell$ and $s \in \Sigma^*$. In such a case, $\mathcal{A}$ could be modified to an equivalent $\mathcal{A}'$ recognizing the same language $L = \mathcal{L}(\mathcal{A}')$, which employs only the move instructions while the original restart operations of $\mathcal{A}$ are implemented by the finite-state control unit of $\mathcal{A}'$ when the length of the head window is extended to c symbols. This would imply that L is regular. Hence, there are inputs to $\mathcal{A}$ with marked substrings of unbounded length. In our analysis of input s, we can focus on only one marked substring σ of unbounded length since the other marked substrings in s can be eliminated by $\mathcal{A}$ through restart operations because $\mathcal{A}$ is monotonic and the marked substrings are separated by non-marked symbols.

It follows that there exists an infinite sequence of inputs $s_n \in \Sigma^*$ for $n \geq 1$, each with marked substring $\sigma_n \in \Sigma^*$, such that $s_{n+1} \Rightarrow^* s_n$ (i.e. $|s_{n+1}| > |s_n|$), and $(q, w') \longrightarrow v$ from I is the first restart instruction that is applicable when the input s_n is presented to $\mathcal{A}$, which can be assumed to be the same for every $n \geq 1$, since both the set of states Q and the set of instructions I are finite. This also ensures that the number of restart instructions that are applied in order to rewrite s_{n+1} to s_n, is bounded by a constant. Hence, $s_n = u'\sigma_n z'$ for some strings $u', z' \in \Sigma^*$ composed of symbols that are not marked in s_n, and $\sigma_n = x_n w' y_n$ for some $x_n, y_n \in \Sigma^*$ such that the head of $\mathcal{A}$ scans $w' \in \Sigma^*$ (following x_n) in state $q \in Q$, which implies $s_{n+1} = u' x_{n+1} w' y_{n+1} z' \Rightarrow u' x_{n+1} v y_{n+1} z' \Rightarrow^* u' x_n w' y_n z' = s_n$.

Since $\mathcal{A}$ is monotonic, we have $y_{n+1} = y'_n y_n$ for some $y'_n \in \Sigma^*$, while $x_{n+1} = \chi_n x'_n$ and $x_n = \chi_n \chi'_n$ for some $\chi_n, \chi'_n, x'_n \in \Sigma^*$. The length of x'_n and y'_n is bounded due to the number of restart operations rewriting s_{n+1} to s_n is bounded, which ensures the set $\{x'_n y'_n \mid n \geq 1\}$ is finite. Hence, there are $x', y \in \Sigma^*$ such that $x'_n = x'$ and $y'_n = y$ for infinitely many n. By pruning the sequence (s_n), we can assume without loss of generality that $x'_n = x'$ and $y'_n = y$ are the same for every $n \geq 1$. Thus, we have $s_{n+1} = u' \chi_n x' w' y y_n z' \Rightarrow^* u' \chi_n \chi'_n w' y_n z' = s_n = u' \chi_{n-1} x' w' y y_{n-1} z'$ where $|x'y| > |\chi'_n|$ due to any restart operation deletes at least one symbol.

Suppose that $\chi'_n = v_n x'$ where $v_n \in \Sigma^*$, for all but finitely many $n \geq 1$, which implies $y \neq \varepsilon$. In this case, the derivation $s_{n+1} = u' \chi_n x' w' y y_n z' \Rightarrow^* u' \chi_n v_n x' w' y_n z' = s_n$ only swaps the substrings $x'w'$ of bounded length and y, while rewriting y with v_n through a finite number of restart instructions, for every $n \geq 1$. If this is the only type of operations in any sequence (s_n) (apart from a finite number of n such that χ'_n is a suffix of x'), then $\mathcal{A}$ would accept only a regular language, which is a contradiction. Thus, by pruning the sequence (s_n), we can assume without loss of generality that for every $n \geq 1$, $x' = x\chi'_n$ for some nonempty $x \in \Sigma^+$, which means $\chi_n = \chi_{n-1} x = \chi_1 x^{n-1}$ due to χ'_n is the same for every $n \geq 1$, defining $u = u'\chi_1$ and $w = \chi'_n w'$. We obtain $s_{n+1} = u x^n w y y_n z' \Rightarrow^* u x^{n-1} w y_n z' = s_n$.

Furthermore, suppose that for any choice of considered (s_n), the string $y = \varepsilon$ is empty, which also ensure $y_n = \varepsilon$. Thus the derivation $s_{n+1} = u x^n w z' \Rightarrow^* u x^{n-1} w z' = s_n$ only deletes x, confirming that L is regular, which is a contradiction. Hence, $y \in \Sigma^+$ and we have $y_n = y y_{n-1} = y^{n-1} y_1$, defining $z = y_1 z'$. This results in $s_{n+1} = u x^n w y^n z \Rightarrow^* u x^{n-1} w y^{n-1} z = s_n$, for every $n \geq 1$.

It also follows that $u x^{n+k} w y^n z \Rightarrow^* u x^k w z$ and $u x^n w y^{n+k} z \Rightarrow^* u w y^k z$ for every $n \geq 1$ and $k \geq 0$. We show that $L_x = L \cap \{u x^k w z \mid k \geq 0\}$ is regular, while a similar argument proves $L_y = L \cap \{u w y^k z \mid k \geq 0\}$ to be regular. Consider the inputs $u x^k w z$ to $\mathcal{A}$ for any $k \geq 1$. If $\mathcal{A}$ applies only finitely many restart instructions to these inputs, then the restarts can be implemented by the finite-state control unit while the head possibly scans a wider window, which implies L_x is regular. Thus, suppose that the number of restarts that $\mathcal{A}$ applies to $u x^k w z$

is unbounded. We know the first restart instruction can possibly be applied first when the head scans w' in $ux^k wz = u'\chi_1 x^k \chi'_n w' y_1 z'$ where recall χ'_n is constant for every $n \geq 1$. According to the previous analysis, there is a repeated cycle of restart operations rewriting and shortening the sequence of substrings x^k from the right by a regular rule, since Q, k, and $|x|$ are finite. We conclude that L_x and L_y are regular languages.

Let $K_x = \{k \geq 0 \mid ux^k wz \in L_x\}$ which meets $K_x = \varrho_x \cup \{aq+r \mid a \geq 1, r \in R_x\}$ for some integer $q \geq 1$, and sets $\varrho_x, R_x \subseteq \{0, \ldots, q-1\}$, because L_x is regular. Note that we assume without loss of generality that the period q described by R_x equals the length of preperiodic part determined by ϱ_x, since we can align the preperiodic part to a multiple of the periods while shifting this new multiple period. Similarly, $K_y = \{k \geq 0 \mid uwy^k z \in L_y\} = \varrho_y \cup \{aq + r \mid a \geq 1, r \in R_y\}$ for $\varrho_y, R_y \subseteq \{0, \ldots, q - 1\}$. Without loss of generality, we employ the same periods q in K_x and K_y by taking their least common multiple. For simplicity, we consider only the case when $R_x \neq \emptyset$ and $R_y \neq \emptyset$. If $\varrho_x = \varrho_y$ and $R_x = R_y$ for any choice of sequence (s_n), then L would be regular. Hence, either $\varrho_x \neq \varrho_y$ or $R_x \neq R_y$.

Now set $\kappa = 2q - 1$, and for every $k = 0, 1, \ldots, \kappa$, define $K_{-k} = L$ if $k \in K_x$ and $K_{-k} = \overline{L}$ if $k \notin K_x$, while $K_k = L$ if $k \in K_y$ and $L_k = \overline{L}$ if $k \notin K_y$. It follows that $ux^k wz \in L_{-k}$ and $uwy^k z \in L_k$ for every $k = 0, \ldots, \kappa$. Let $m \geq 0$ and $n \geq \kappa$. First assume that $m = n$ which implies $ux^m wy^{n-k} z \Rightarrow^* ux^k wz$ for $0 \leq k \leq n$ and $ux^m wy^{n+k} z \Rightarrow^* uwy^k z$ for every $k \geq 0$. Hence, $ux^m wy^{n+k} z \in L_k$ for every $k \in K = \{-\kappa, \ldots, -1, 0, 1, \ldots, \kappa\}$, which proves the right-to-left implication in (1).

Further assume that $m > n$, while the argument for $m < n$ is analogous. In addition, we consider the special case without preperiodic parts, which means $\varrho_x = R_x$ and $\varrho_y = R_y$, whereas the general case can be handled similarly. On the contrary, suppose that $ux^m wy^{n+k} z \in L_k$ for all $k \in K$. Denote $\delta = m - n > 0$. Let $d \in \{0, \ldots, \kappa\}$ be the remainder after dividing δ by $2q$, and $b \geq 1$ be the greatest common divisor of d and $2q$. We have $ux^m wy^{n-k} z \Rightarrow^* ux^{\delta+k} wz$ which implies $ux^{\delta+k} wz \in L_{-k}$ for $0 \leq k \leq \kappa$. Hence, $L_k = L_{k-d}$ for $k = -\kappa + d, \ldots, 0$ whereas $L_k = L_{k-d+\kappa+1}$ for $k = -\kappa, \ldots, -\kappa + d - 1$, which is resolved as $L_i = L_{i-bj}$ for every $i = -b+1, \ldots, 0$ and $j = 1, \ldots, \frac{2q}{b} - 1$. Similarly, $ux^m wy^{n+k} z \Rightarrow^* ux^{\delta-k} wz \in L_k$ for $0 \leq k \leq \min(\delta, \kappa)$, and $ux^m wy^{n+k} z \Rightarrow^* uwy^{k-\delta} z \in L_k$ for $\delta + 1 \leq k \leq \kappa$. Hence, $L_k = L_{k-d}$ for every $k = 0, \ldots, \kappa$, which imposes $L_i = L_{i+bj}$ for every $i = 0, \ldots, b - 1$ and $j = 1, \ldots, \frac{2q}{b} - 1$. It follows that $R_x = R_y$ which is a contradiction, completing the proof of the left-to-right implication in (1). $\qquad \square$

Example 1. We illustrate Theorem 1 on a simple example of the non-regular deterministic context free language L over the binary alphabet $\Sigma = \{0, 1\}$ that is composed of words containing more zeros then ones. For this language L, Theorem 1 provides the empty words $u = w = z = \varepsilon$, the non-empty strings $x = 0 \in \Sigma^+$, $y = 1 \in \Sigma^+$, the integer $\kappa = 1$, and the languages $L_{-1} = L$ and $L_0 = L_1 = \overline{L}$ such that for every pair of integers, $m \geq 0$ and $n \geq 1$, condition (1) holds:

$$\left(0^m 1^{n-1} \in L_{-1} = L \ \& \ 0^m 1^n \in L_0 = \overline{L} \ \& \ 0^m 1^{n+1} \in L_1 = \overline{L}\right) \quad \text{iff}$$
$$(m > n - 1 \ \& \ m \le n \ \& \ m \le n + 1) \quad \text{iff} \ m = n.$$

4   One Analog Unit Doesn't Accept Non-regular DCFLs

In this section we show the main result that any non-regular DCFL cannot be recognized online by a binary-state 1ANN extended with one extra analog unit, which gives the stronger separation (DCFLs \ REG) $\subset$ (2ANNs \ 1ANNs) in the analog neuron hierarchy, implying REG = 0ANNs = 1ANNs $\cap$ DCFLs. For this purpose, we exploit the fact that the DCFL $L_\#$ is not accepted by any 1ANN:

Theorem 2 [19, Theorem 1]. *The deterministic context-free language* $L_\# = \{0^n 1^n \mid n \ge 1\}$ *cannot be recognized by any 1ANN with one extra analog unit having real weights.*

According to Theorem 1, the language $L_\#$ reduces to any non-regular DCFL, which can be implemented by a binary NN, providing the following theorem.

Theorem 3. *Any non-regular deterministic context-free language* L *cannot be recognized online by any 1ANN with one extra analog unit having real weights.*

Proof (Sketch). Let $L \subset \Sigma^*$ be a non-regular deterministic context-free language over a finite alphabet Σ including $p > 0$ symbols. On the contrary assume that there is a 1ANN $\mathcal{N}$ with the set of neurons V, that accepts $L = \mathcal{L}(\mathcal{N})$. We will outline a construction of a bigger 1ANN $\mathcal{N}_\#$ with the set of neurons $V_\# \supset V$, recognizing the language $L_\# = \{0^n 1^n \mid n \ge 1\}$ over the binary alphabet $\{0, 1\}$, which incorporates $\mathcal{N}$ as its subnetwork. Let $u, w, z \in \Sigma^*$ and $x, y \in \Sigma^+$ be the strings, $\kappa \ge 0$ be the integer, and L_k for $k \in K = \{-\kappa, \ldots, -1, 0, 1, \ldots, \kappa\}$ be the languages guaranteed by Theorem 1 for L. Since the class of languages accepted by 1ANNs is clearly closed under intersection with regular languages, we can confine ourselves only to strings $0^m 1^n$ for sufficiently large integers $m, n \ge \kappa$, which represent the inputs to $\mathcal{N}_\#$. Any such input $0^m 1^n$ is transformed to the strings $u x^m w y^{n+k} z \in \Sigma^*$ for all $k \in K$, which are presented as inputs to $\mathcal{N}$.

We first transform $\mathcal{N}$ to a 1ANN $\mathcal{N}'$ so that the output neuron out $\in V$ of $\mathcal{N}'$ decides about each prefix of an input string that has been read so far according to the input/output protocol (see Sect. 2), as if this prefix extended with the string z is presented to $\mathcal{N}$. The idea of building $\mathcal{N}'$ issues from the representation theorem [20, Theorem 4] characterizing syntactically the languages accepted by 1ANNs. According to this theorem, the state domain $\mathbb{I}$ of the only analog unit $s \in V$ can be partitioned into a finite number of subintervals so that the binary states $y_1^{(t+1)}, \ldots, y_{s-1}^{(t+1)} \in \{0, 1\}$ at the next time instant $t+1$ are uniquely determined by an index of the subinterval to which the real state $y_s^{(t)} \in \mathbb{I}$ belongs, apart from the current binary states $y_1^{(t)}, \ldots, y_{s-1}^{(t)} \in \{0, 1\}$. The partition of $\mathbb{I}$ can further be refined so that the membership in its subintervals, which can easily be tested by threshold gates, determines the output from out $\in V$ as if the tail z is already read. This refinement can be achieved by continuing the computation of $\mathcal{N}$ with the state of analog unit replaced by the end-points of the original subintervals until z is read which takes a constant number of computational steps in the online input/output protocol, producing a finite partition.

We introduce an input buffer $B_1 \subset V_\# \setminus V$ for the subnetwork $\mathcal{N}'$, which is implemented by p parallel oriented paths of binary neurons. These disjoint paths have the same length $b \geq |uw| + (\kappa + 1)|xy|$ and each p neurons in the same distance from the first units form a layer which encodes one symbol from Σ using the one-hot encoding. Thus, B_1 stores a string from Σ^* of length at most b, which is clamped by self-loop weights. Its last layer feeds the p input neurons $X \subset V$ encoding an input symbol from Σ, at the request of $\mathcal{N}'$ which is indicated by nxt $\in V$, according to the input protocol for $\mathcal{N}'$. At the same time, the neurons in each layer send their outputs to the subsequent layer so that the string is shifted in B_1 by one symbol forward after its last symbol is read by $\mathcal{N}'$.

On the other hand, B_1 is being filled so that it always contains an input symbol when queried by $\mathcal{N}'$. The initial states of $\mathcal{N}_\#$ ensures that B_1 contains $u \in \Sigma^*$ (and possibly some initial copies of $x \in \Sigma^+$). Furthermore, B_1 is being replenished by copies of x whose count m equals exactly the number of 0s which are being read by $\mathcal{N}_\#$ through its input neurons $X_\# \subset V_\#$ on request of nxt$_\# \in V_\#$ when there is a free space in B_1. If $\mathcal{N}_\#$ reads the first 1 following the input sequence 0^m, then the string $w \in \Sigma^*$ is pushed into B_1 which is further being filled by copies of $y \in \Sigma^+$ whose count n equals exactly the number of 1s being read by $\mathcal{N}_\#$, increased by κ.

Furthermore, the subnetwork $\mathcal{N}'$ has also its output buffer B_2 for storing the last $2\kappa + 1$ states of the output neuron out $\in V$ from $\mathcal{N}'$, which are recorded at the time instants when nxt $\in V$ fires, according to the output protocol for $\mathcal{N}'$. This is synchronized with the input string $0^m 1^n$ which has already been read by $\mathcal{N}_\#$ so that B_2 contains the results of whether $ux^m wy^{n+k}z$ belongs to L for every $k \in K$. The neural acceptor $\mathcal{N}_\#$ rejects the input $0^m 1^n$ for $n < \kappa$ through the output neuron out$_\# \in V_\#$ which is activated when nxt$_\# \in V_\#$ fires. For $n \geq \kappa$, the network $\mathcal{N}_\#$ accepts $0^m 1^n$ iff $ux^m wy^{n+k}z \in L_k$ for all $k \in K$, which can be determined from the contents of buffer B_2. According to Theorem 1, this happens if and only if $m = n$, which ensures $\mathcal{N}_\#$ recognizes $L_\#$. This contradicts Theorem 2 and completes the proof of Theorem 3.   □

5   Conclusion

In this paper, we have refined the analysis of the computational power of discrete-time binary-state recurrent neural networks αANNs extended with α analog-state neurons by proving a stronger separation 1ANNs $\subsetneq$ 2ANNs in the analog neuron hierarchy. Namely, we have shown that the class of non-regular deterministic context-free languages is contained in 2ANNs \ 1ANNs, which implies 0ANNs = 1ANNs ∩ DCFLs. For this purpose, we have reduced the deterministic language $L_\# = \{0^n 1^n \,|\, n \geq 1\}$, which is known to be not in 1ANNs [19], to any non-regular DCFL. This means that in some sense, $L_\#$ is the simplest problem in the class of non-regular DCFLs. This is by itself an interesting new achievement in computability theory, which can open a new direction of research aiming towards the existence of the simplest problems in traditional complexity classes as a counterpart to the hardest problems such as NP-complete problems. We conjecture that our result can be generalized to *nondeterministic* context-free languages. Another challenge for future research is an open question whether there is a non-context-sensitive language that can be accepted *offline* by a 1ANN or whether the separation 2ANNs $\subsetneq$ 3ANNs holds.

References

1. Alon, N., Dewdney, A.K., Ott, T.J.: Efficient simulation of finite automata by neural nets. J. ACM **38**(2), 495–514 (1991)
2. Balcázar, J.L., Gavaldà, R., Siegelmann, H.T.: Computational power of neural networks: A characterization in terms of Kolmogorov complexity. IEEE Trans. Inf. Theory **43**(4), 1175–1183 (1997)
3. Horne, B.G., Hush, D.R.: Bounds on the complexity of recurrent neural network implementations of finite state machines. Neural Netw. **9**(2), 243–252 (1996)
4. Indyk, P.: Optimal simulation of automata by neural nets. In: Mayr, E.W., Puech, C. (eds.) STACS 1995. LNCS, vol. 900, pp. 337–348. Springer, Heidelberg (1995). https://doi.org/10.1007/3-540-59042-0_85
5. Jančar, P., Mráz, F., Plátek, M., Vogel, J.: Restarting automata. In: Reichel, H. (ed.) FCT 1995. LNCS, vol. 965, pp. 283–292. Springer, Heidelberg (1995). https://doi.org/10.1007/3-540-60249-6_60
6. Jančar, P., Mráz, F., Plátek, M., Vogel, J.: On monotonic automata with a restart operation. J. Automata Lang. Comb. **4**(4), 287–311 (1999)
7. Kilian, J., Siegelmann, H.T.: The dynamic universality of sigmoidal neural networks. Inf. Comput. **128**(1), 48–56 (1996)
8. Koiran, P.: A family of universal recurrent networks. Theoret. Comput. Sci. **168**(2), 473–480 (1996)
9. Minsky, M.: Computations: Finite and Infinite Machines. Prentice-Hall, Englewood Cliffs (1967)
10. Orponen, P.: Computing with truly asynchronous threshold logic networks. Theoret. Comput. Sci. **174**(1–2), 123–136 (1997)
11. Schmidhuber, J.: Deep learning in neural networks: An overview. Neural Netw. **61**, 85–117 (2015)
12. Siegelmann, H.T.: Recurrent neural networks and finite automata. J. Comput. Intell. **12**(4), 567–574 (1996)
13. Siegelmann, H.T.: Neural Networks and Analog Computation: Beyond the Turing Limit. Birkhäuser, Boston (1999). https://doi.org/10.1007/978-1-4612-0707-8
14. Siegelmann, H.T., Sontag, E.D.: Analog computation via neural networks. Theoret. Comput. Sci. **131**(2), 331–360 (1994)
15. Siegelmann, H.T., Sontag, E.D.: On the computational power of neural nets. J. Comput. Syst. Sci. **50**(1), 132–150 (1995)
16. Šíma, J.: Analog stable simulation of discrete neural networks. Neural Netw. World **7**(6), 679–686 (1997)
17. Šíma, J.: Energy complexity of recurrent neural networks. Neural Comput. **26**(5), 953–973 (2014)

18. Šíma, J.: Three analog neurons are Turing universal. In: Fagan, D., Martín-Vide, C., O'Neill, M., Vega-Rodríguez, M.A. (eds.) TPNC 2018. LNCS, vol. 11324, pp. 460–472. Springer, Cham (2018). https://doi.org/10.1007/978-3-030-04070-3_36
19. Šíma, J.: Counting with analog neurons. In: Tetko, I.V., Kůrková, V., Karpov, P., Theis, F. (eds.) ICANN 2019. LNCS, vol. 11727, pp. 389–400. Springer, Cham (2019). https://doi.org/10.1007/978-3-030-30487-4_31
20. Šíma, J.: Subrecursive neural networks. Neural Netw. **116**, 208–223 (2019)
21. Šíma, J., Orponen, P.: General-purpose computation with neural networks: a survey of complexity theoretic results. Neural Comput. **15**(12), 2727–2778 (2003)
22. Šíma, J., Savický, P.: Quasi-periodic β-expansions and cut languages. Theoret. Comput. Sci. **720**, 1–23 (2018)
23. Šíma, J., Wiedermann, J.: Theory of neuromata. J. ACM **45**(1), 155–178 (1998)
24. Šorel, M., Šíma, J.: Robust RBF finite automata. Neurocomputing **62**, 93–110 (2004)

Tag-Based Semantic Features for Scene Image Classification

Chiranjibi Sitaula[1]([✉]), Yong Xiang[1], Anish Basnet[2], Sunil Aryal[1], and Xuequan Lu[1]

[1] School of Information Technology, Deakin University, Geelong, Australia
{csitaul,yong.xiang,sunil.aryal,xuequan.lu}@deakin.edu.au
[2] Ambition College, Kathmandu, Nepal
anishbasnetworld@gmail.com

Abstract. The existing image feature extraction methods are primarily based on the content and structure information of images, and rarely consider the contextual semantic information. Regarding some types of images such as scenes and objects, the annotations and descriptions of them available on the web may provide reliable contextual semantic information for feature extraction. In this paper, we introduce novel semantic features of an image based on the annotations and descriptions of its similar images available on the web. Specifically, we propose a new method which consists of two consecutive steps to extract our semantic features. For each image in the training set, we initially search the top k most similar images from the internet and extract their annotations/descriptions (e.g., tags or keywords). The annotation information is employed to design a filter bank for each image category and generate filter words (codebook). Finally, each image is represented by the histogram of the occurrences of filter words in all categories. We evaluate the performance of the proposed features in scene image classification on three commonly-used scene image datasets (i.e., MIT-67, Scene15 and Event8). Our method typically produces a lower feature dimension than existing feature extraction methods. Experimental results show that the proposed features generate better classification accuracies than vision based and tag based features, and comparable results to deep learning based features.

Keywords: Image features · Semantic features · Tags · Semantic similarity · Tag-based features · Search engine

1 Introduction

In computer vision, features of images are extracted primarily from the content and structure of images. They rely on information such as color, texture, shapes, and parts. Though these features are shown to work reasonably well in many image processing tasks [2,21,24,25,32,37–39], the involved information may be

© Springer Nature Switzerland AG 2019
T. Gedeon et al. (Eds.): ICONIP 2019, LNCS 11955, pp. 90–102, 2019.
https://doi.org/10.1007/978-3-030-36718-3_8

insufficient to distinguish ambiguous images, e.g., classifying images with inter-class similarity. Figure 1 shows two images which look very similar but they belong to two different categories (hospital room and bedroom).

Fig. 1. The images of bed room (left) and hospital room (right) look similar.

Contextual information is useful to distinguish such ambiguous images [18,33]. Contextual information about the image can be often obtained from its annotations or descriptions. Though it is impossible to have descriptions or annotations for all images, such information can be extracted from the web for certain types of images like objects and scenes. For the extraction of such contextual features, we use the well-known search engine Yandex[1] for two reasons: firstly, visually similar images of image categories such as wine cellar are not meaningful while using the Google search engine; secondly, we notice that the searched similar images of the input image usually belong to the same category.

Recently few prior works [35,40] have been proposed for scene image recognition using tag-based features. These methods suffer from the following major issues.

- The task-generic filter banks [35] lack context-based information for the images such as scene images, owing to their generality based on the help of pre-defined labels of ImageNet [3] and Places [41] dataset.
- The existing tag-based method [40] does not design filter banks, thus resulting in high dimensional features with noticeable outliers.

As such, these state-of-the-art techniques yield limited classification accuracy. In this paper, we introduce new semantic features of an image based on the annotation/description tags of similar images available on the web. We design two consecutive steps to extract our proposed features after we select top k most similar images of each image under the dataset using Yandex and extract annotation/description tags corresponding to those images. At first, we design filter banks based on such tags of training images of the dataset which yields filter words (codebook) corresponding to the dataset. Finally, for each input image which are represented by the tags, we design our proposed features as the histogram based on the codebook.

---

[1] https://www.yandex.com/images/.

We evaluate the performance of the proposed features in scene image classification on three popular scene image datasets: MIT-67 [30], Scene15 [4] and Event8 [17]. Our approach typically produces a smaller feature size than existing feature extraction methods. The experimental results suggest that the proposed features generate higher classification accuracies than vision-based and tag-based features and comparable classification to deep learning based features.

2   Related Works

Generally, there are three types of image features: (i) traditional vision-based features [2,21,24,25,37–39], (ii) deep learning based features [6,7,13,20,34], and (iii) tag-based features [35,40].

Traditional vision-based features are extracted based on the algorithms such as (SIFT) [39], Generalized Search Trees (GIST) [24,25], Histogram of Gradient (HOG) [2], GIST-color [25], SPM [16], CENsus TRansform hISTogram (CENTRIST) [37], multi-channel (mCENTRIST) [38], OTC [21], and so on. These features depend on the core information of the image such as colors, intensity, etc. Broadly, these features are computed in the local sense and are also called low-level features. These features are suitable for certain areas such as texture images. These features usually have high dimensions.

Similarly, deep learning based features, such as bilinear [20], Deep Unstructured Convolutional Activations (DUCA) [13], Bag of Surrogate Parts (BoSP) [7], Locally Supervised Deep Hybrid Model (LS-DHM) [6] and GMS2F [34], are extracted from the intermediate layers of deep learning models (pre-trained models or user-defined models). Different layers of deep learning models provide different semantics information related to the input image. Thus, they have the capability to extract discriminating features compared to traditional vision based features. Deep learning based features enjoy prominent successes in image classification.

Two prior works [35,40] have been recently presented for scene image recognition using tags-based features. Zhang et al. [40] used the search engine to extract the description/annotation tags and designed Bag of Words (BoW) straightly. Their method ignores the concepts of filter banks and creates high-dimensional features which yield limited classification accuracy. Similarly, Wang et al. [35] designed task-generic filters using pre-defined labels for the scene images but lacked task-specific filters to work in a specific domain. Also, because of the usage of pre-defined labels to design filter banks, the contextual information related to the images is hard to achieve. Moreover, due to the out of vocabulary (OOV) problem while constructing filter banks, their method discards the tags that are not present in the WordNet [23], and may contain insufficient vocabularies.

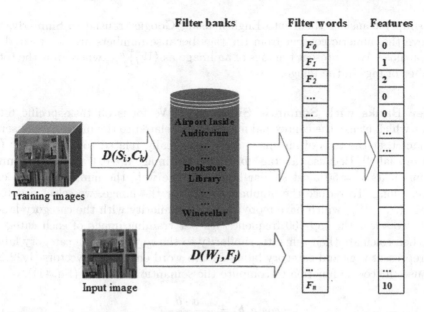

Fig. 2. Overview of the proposed method. $D(S_i, C_k)$ denotes averaged similarity for tags S_i and the category label C_k. $D(W_j, F_j)$ represents the semantic similarity of annotation/description tags W_j with the filter words F_j. The filter words are generated by concatenating the filtered tags from the filter banks. Finally, based on the filter words (codebook), we design the histogram and accumulate the histograms for each bin of the features. The resulting features can semantically represent the input image.

3 The Proposed Method

Before using an actual pipeline of our proposed method, we first extract annotation/description tags of each image on the dataset using Yandex search engine (see footnote 1) where we select only top k (i.e., $k = 50$) visually similar images ranked by the search engine. As suggested in [35,36], we use $k = 50$ for the extraction of the tags. Our method consists of two major steps: (1) design of filter banks (Sect. 3.1), and (2) feature extraction (Sect. 3.2). The overall flow of our proposed method is shown in Fig. 2.

3.1 Design of Filter Banks Using Training Images

In this section, we describe how to design filter banks using the training set of one dataset. We use training images to design the filter bank for each category. To extract the filter words using filter banks, we present the following two steps.

Pre-processing of Annotation/Description Tags. After the extraction of annotation/description tags of the images under various categories, we pre-process them by removing punctuation marks, numbers, tokenization and language translation. Some of the extracted tags are also in the Russian language.

We simply translate them into English using Google translator. Similarly, we remove the numeric content from the tags because numbers are not related to our purpose. We represent the tags of an image as $\{W_j\}_{j=1}^m$, where m is the total number of tags in the image.

Filter Banks with Semantic Similarity. We focus on task-specific filter banks which utilize the contextual information related to the image. We observe the fact that the tags of an image are semantically related to its category (or category label). Because raw tags for a training image are extracted from annotations of its $k = 50$ most similar images in the web, the number of tags can be very long. To reduce the number of tags for the image, we select a subset of tags ($S_i \subset W_j$) which have more semantic similarity with the category label. First, we select the top 500 frequent tags per training image of each category and then calculate their semantic similarity to the corresponding category label. We represent tags and category labels as two word embedding vectors [1,22,28] and use the cosine function to compute the semantic similarity (Eq. (1)).

$$cos(\boldsymbol{a}, \boldsymbol{b}) = \frac{\boldsymbol{a} \cdot \boldsymbol{b}}{||\boldsymbol{a}|| \cdot ||\boldsymbol{b}||}, \tag{1}$$

where $\boldsymbol{a}$ and $\boldsymbol{b}$ are the two embedding vectors. For word embeddings, we utilize three popular pre-trained words embedding models - Word2Vec [22], Glove [28] and fastText [1]. We find the final similarity by averaging the semantic similarity of tag and category label over the three types of word embedding vectors. The averaging strategy usually helps to mitigate the OOV problem. Also, it exploits the knowledge of three domains from three embedding models. To be efficient, we select only those tags whose averaged similarity (D) to the category label is greater than or equal to an empirical threshold of $\delta = 0.50$.

$$S_i = \begin{cases} 1 & \text{if } D(S_i, C_k) \geq \delta, \\ 0 & \text{otherwise.} \end{cases} \tag{2}$$

We extract the filter bank for each category C_k (the kth category) with the tags belonging to it. From Eq. (2), we determine whether the particular tag S_i is eligible to the filter bank for the corresponding category. The strategy to accept and reject the tags are represented by 1 and 0, respectively.

Table 1 lists the filter banks of the categories for the MIT-67 [30] dataset. We design three separate sets of filter banks for the MIT-67 [30], Scene15 [4] and Event8 [17] datasets in the experiments. We design filter banks for MIT-67 using the training images of the dataset. On MIT-67 dataset, the total number of filter banks is 67 where each contains filtered tags. We combine all those filter banks to obtain 1254-D filter words. Furthermore, for Scene15 and Event8, we design filter banks over 10 sets on the corresponding dataset. We utilize the corresponding training images of each set to separately design the filter banks and obtain filter words.

Table 1. Sample filter banks of some categories in the MIT-67 dataset.

Category	Filter banks
Airport inside	Airport, terminal, city, flight, hotel, flights, aviation
Library	Library, books, libraries, archives, collections
Winecellar	Wines, cellar, whiskey, winemaker, beverages, grapes, tastings
Subway	Metro, subway, train, railway, transit, tram

3.2 Extraction of Proposed Tag-Based Semantic Features for Input Image

We first utilize the annotation/description tags of each image to calculate the proposed features. These tags are preprocessed using Sect. 3.1. Then, all the filter banks are concatenated to form a list of filtered tags (or semantic tags), i.e., filter words (codebook). Inspired by the BoW approach [11], we design the histogram features of the input image using this codebook. Our codebook is functionally similar to the codebook obtained by the clustering algorithm [8]. However, our filter banks are based on contextual information and filter outliers significantly compared to the existing filter banks [35]. After that, we calculate the pairwise similarity of each filtered word with the pre-processed annotation/description tags of the input image. Denote the filter words by $\{F_j\}_{j=1}^n$. If we have n unique filter words and the input image contains m annotation/description tags, then the total similarity calculation is $n * m$. To calculate the similarity, we use the same scheme as that in designing the filter bank of each category.

$$H_j = \begin{cases} 1 & \text{if } D(W_j, F_j) \geq \text{T}, \\ 0 & \text{otherwise.} \end{cases} \tag{3}$$

H_j in Eq. (3) represents the histogram based on the filter words F_j. Here, 1 represents the tag accepts the similarity with the filter word, and 0 means the tag rejects similarity. We design the histogram by taking all the pre-processed tags of the input image. For the bin of features corresponding to that filter word F_j, we count the number of tags which have acceptable similarity with F_j.

4 Experimental Results

In this section, we discuss the experimental setup and present results of our evaluation of the proposed features against other existing feature extraction methods in scene image classification using Support Vector Machine (SVM) [10].

4.1 Implementation

We use Yandex as the search engine and implement the proposed method using Python. We use the python SVM implementation available in the sklearn machine learning package[2]. We utilize the default setting for the majority of the

---

[2] https://scikit-learn.org/stable/.

Fig. 3. Sample images from the MIT-67 dataset.

parameters. However, we tune three parameters in the experiments. The setting of two SVM parameters are: $kernel = rbf$ and $gamma = 10^{-5}$. And, we tune the cost parameter C in the range of 0 to 100 and tabulate only the setting that generates highest classification accuracy ($C = 9$ for MIT-67 and $C = 50$ for the remaining datasets). Furthermore, to take advantage of lightweight word-embedding vectors [1,22,28] of the tags, we use a popular Python package pymagnitude [27]. We fix a threshold of 0.50 (i.e., $\delta = 0.50$) to design the filter banks in Eq. (2) and empirically set a threshold of 0.40 (i.e., $T = 0.40$ in Eq. (3)) for the extraction of our features which produces best results compared to other thresholds. We will discuss about the threshold T for the extraction of our features in Sect. 4.4.

4.2   Datasets

We use three publicly available datasets in our experiments: MIT-67 [30], Scene15 [4], and Event8 [17]. The MIT-67 dataset contains pictures of 67 categories. This is a challenging dataset which has noticeable intra-class and inter-class barriers (e.g., Fig. 3). As defined in [30], the number of training and testing images per category are 80 and 20, respectively.

Scene15 includes both indoor and outdoor images. It has 15 categories. As with the previous works [14,16,19,21,25,34,35,37,40], we design 10 sets of train/test split, where each split randomly contains 100 images for training and remaining images for testing per category, and note the mean accuracy.

Event8 involves images of 8 sports categories. This dataset does not have pre-defined train/test splits, either. Like Scene15, we design 10 sets of train/test split as in previous works [9,14,15,18,19,29,31,35,40,41] and note the mean accuracy. For each split, we randomly select 130 images per category and divide 70 images for training and 60 images for testing.

Table 2. Comparisons of classification accuracy (%) for the existing methods and ours on the three datasets. The dash (-) symbol stands for no published accuracy on the specific dataset.

Method	MIT-67	Scene15	Event8
Traditional computer vision-based methods			
GIST-color [25]	-	69.5	-
ROI with GIST [30]	26.1	-	-
SPM [16]	-	81.4	-
MM-Scene [42]	28.3	-	-
CENTRIST [37]	-	83.9	-
Object Bank [18]	37.6	-	76.3
RBoW [26]	37.9	-	-
BOP [12]	46.1	-	-
OTC [21]	47.3	84.4	-
ISPR [19]	50.1	85.1	74.9
LscSPM [31]	-	-	85.3
IFV [29]	-	-	90.3
Deep learning-based methods			
EISR [40]	66.2	94.5	92.7
CNN-MOP [5]	68.0	-	-
BoSP [7]	78.2	-	-
G-MS2F [34]	79.6	92.9	-
CNN-sNBNL [15]	-	-	95.3
VGG [41]	-	-	95.6
ResNet152 [9]	-	-	96.9
Tag-based methods			
BoW [35]	52.5	70.1	83.5
CNN [14]	52.0	72.2	85.9
s-CNN(max)[35]	54.6	76.2	90.9
s-CNN(avg)[35]	55.1	76.7	91.2
s-CNNC(max)[35]	55.9	77.2	91.5
Ours	**76.5**	**81.3**	**94.4**

4.3   Comparison with Existing Methods

We compare the classification accuracy of our proposed features with the existing features which include traditional vision-based features, deep learning based features and tag-based features on the three datasets. The statistical accuracy numbers are listed in Table 2. To minimize the bias, we compare our accuracy with the existing published accuracy on the same dataset. We straightforwardly take the results of existing features from corresponding papers.

In the first column of Table 2, we see that BoW yields an accuracy of 52.5%, which is the lowest accuracy among the tag-based methods. Researchers improve the accuracy of tag-based features using Convolutional Neural Network (CNN) model up to 55.9% [35]. We suspect these methods still could not provide highly discriminable features of the images. By contrast, deep learning based features improve classification accuracy. For example, BoSP, the deep learning based features, has over 4000-D features size and its accuracy is higher than ours (78.2% versus 76.5%). Our semantic features, which are based on annotation tags, provide prominent accuracy in image classification. We notice that our proposed features generate the highest accuracy of **76.5%** among the tag-based methods. Despite that the accuracy looks slightly lower than some of the deep learning based methods that benefit from the high-dimensional features, our features still outperform some of them [5,13,40]. Our method soundly outperforms the traditional vision based methods [12,18,19,21,26,30,42]. Our method leads to a noticeably smaller size of features on this dataset compared to other features (e.g., 1254-D). The feature size differs, due to the number of categories and size of filter banks on different datasets.

The classification accuracies of different features on the Scene15 dataset are provided in the second column of Table 2. Since our method belongs to the tag-based methods, we first compare our features against existing tag-based features. The BoW method provides an accuracy of 70.1%, which is the lowest among the tag-based methods on this dataset. With the use of CNN on tag-based methods, the accuracy surges up to 77.2%. These methods, however, suffer from a large feature size. Since our features are dependent on the size of filter words (<100) on this dataset, our feature size is less than 100 which is significantly lower than other features. Despite that, we observe that the proposed features have a prominent accuracy of **81.3%** among the tag-based features.

In the third column of Table 2, we enlist the classification accuracies of different features on the Event8 dataset. In this dataset, the BoW method provides an accuracy of 83.5%, the lowest accuracy among the tag-based methods. Moreover, by using CNN on tag-based methods, the accuracy increases up to 91.5%. Similarly, our features have a very low size (<50) on this dataset and are remarkably lower than other features. We achieve the best accuracy of **94.4%** among the tag-based features.

4.4   Ablative Study of Threshold

We analyze the effects of different thresholds T in this section. To study the thresholds in depth, we use the Event8 dataset and follow the setup as above. We test thresholds between 0.30 and 0.80 with a step size of 0.10. We summarize the classification accuracy of the proposed features with the corresponding thresholds in Table 3. The best accuracy (94.41%) is obtained by $T = 0.40$, whereas the worst accuracy (60.4%) is produced by $T = 0.80$ on the dataset. We empirically observe that 0.40 is a suitable threshold for all datasets, so we use it in all experiments.

Table 3. Average accuracy over 10 sets corresponding to different thresholds (T in Eq. (3)) on the Event8 dataset.

Threshold	0.30	0.40	0.50	0.60	0.70	0.80
Accuracy (%)	93.7	**94.4**	93.0	89.4	87.5	60.4

4.5 Ablative Study of Individual Embedding

In this section, we study the proposed features based on individual word embedding and the averaged semantic similarity scheme. We set the threshold $T = 0.40$ and conduct experiments on the Event8 dataset and compute the mean accuracy over 10 sets.

Table 4 shows the accuracies generated by our proposed features based on the individual embedding and the averaged semantic similarity. It seems that the features induced by the averaged semantic similarity produce a higher accuracy (**94.4%**) than features of individual embeddings. This is because the features induced by the averaged semantic similarity act as the combined knowledge from three domains, which typically possess a higher separability than the individual embedding based features.

Table 4. Accuracy of the proposed features using the individual embedding and averaged semantic similarity on the Event8 dataset.

Embeddings	Word2Vec	Glove	fastText	Averaged
Accuracy (%)	94.3	93.5	93.1	**94.4**

5 Conclusion

In this paper, we propose a novel method to extract tag-based semantic features for the representation of scene images. We achieve this by performing two consecutive steps which are the design of filter banks and extraction of tag-based semantic features. We conduct experiments on three popular datasets and find that the proposed features produce better or comparable results to existing vision based, deep learning based and tag-based features, given a noticeably lower feature size of ours than those features. In the future, we would like to investigate the incorporation of the proposed features and deep features to further improve image classification accuracy.

References

1. Bojanowski, P., Grave, E., Joulin, A., Mikolov, T.: Enriching word vectors with subword information. Trans. Assoc. Comput. Linguist. **5**, 135–146 (2017)
2. Dalal, N., Triggs, B.: Histograms of oriented gradients for human detection. In: Proceedings of IEEE Computer Society Conference on Computer Vision and Pattern Recognition (CVPR), pp. 886–893 (2005)
3. Deng, J., Dong, W., Socher, R., Li, L.J., Li, K., Fei-Fei, L.: ImageNet: a large-scale hierarchical image database. In: Proceedings IEEE Conference Computer Vision and Pattern Recognition (CVPR) (2009)
4. Fei-Fei, L., Perona, P.: A Bayesian hierarchical model for learning natural scene categories. In: Proceedings of IEEE Computer Society Conference on Computer Vision and Pattern Recognition (CVPR), vol. 2, pp. 524–531, June 2005
5. Gong, Y., Wang, L., Guo, R., Lazebnik, S.: Multi-scale orderless pooling of deep convolutional activation features. In: Fleet, D., Pajdla, T., Schiele, B., Tuytelaars, T. (eds.) ECCV 2014. LNCS, vol. 8695, pp. 392–407. Springer, Cham (2014). https://doi.org/10.1007/978-3-319-10584-0_26
6. Guo, S., Huang, W., Wang, L., Qiao, Y.: Locally supervised deep hybrid model for scene recognition. IEEE Trans. Image Process. **26**(2), 808–820 (2017)
7. Guo, Y., Liu, Y., Lao, S., Bakker, E.M., Bai, L., Lew, M.S.: Bag of surrogate parts feature for visual recognition. IEEE Trans. Multimedia **20**(6), 1525–1536 (2018)
8. Hartigan, J.A.: Clustering Algorithms, 99th edn. Wiley, New York (1975)
9. He, K., Zhang, X., Ren, S., Sun, J.: Deep residual learning for image recognition. In: Proceedings of IEEE Conference on Computer Vision and Pattern Recognition (CVPR), pp. 770–778 (2016)
10. Hearst, M.A.: Support vector machines. IEEE Intell. Syst. **13**(4), 18–28 (1998)
11. Huang, A.: Similarity measures for text document clustering. In: Proceedings of Sixth New Zealand Computer Science Research Student Conference (NZCSRSC 2008), pp. 9–56 (2008)
12. Juneja, M., Vedaldi, A., Jawahar, C., Zisserman, A.: Blocks that shout: distinctive parts for scene classification. In: Proceedings of IEEE Conference Computer Vision Pattern Recognition (CVPR), pp. 923–930, June 2013
13. Khan, S.H., Hayat, M., Bennamoun, M., Togneri, R., Sohel, F.A.: A discriminative representation of convolutional features for indoor scene recognition. IEEE Trans. Image Process. **25**(7), 3372–3383 (2016)
14. Kim, Y.: Convolutional neural networks for sentence classification. arXiv preprint arXiv:1408.5882 (2014)
15. Kuzborskij, I., Maria Carlucci, F., Caputo, B.: When Naive Bayes nearest neighbors meet convolutional neural networks. In: Proceedings of IEEE Conference on Computer Vision and Pattern Recognition (CVPR), pp. 2100–2109 (2016)
16. Lazebnik, S., Schmid, C., Ponce, J.: Beyond bags of features: spatial pyramid matching for recognizing natural scene categories. In: Proceedings of IEEE Computer Society Conference on Computer Vision Pattern Recognition, pp. 2169–2178, June 2006
17. Li, L.J., Li, F.F.: What, where and who? Classifying events by scene and object recognition. In: ICCV, vol. 2, p. 6 (2007)
18. Li, L.J., Su, H., Fei-Fei, L., Xing, E.P.: Object bank: a high-level image representation for scene classification & semantic feature sparsification. In: Proceedings of Advance Neural Information Processing Systems (NIPS), pp. 1378–1386 (2010)

19. Lin, D., Lu, C., Liao, R., Jia, J.: Learning important spatial pooling regions for scene classification. In: Proceedings of IEEE Conference Computer Vision Pattern Recognition (CVPR), pp. 3726–3733, June 2014
20. Lin, T.Y., RoyChowdhury, A., Maji, S.: Bilinear convolutional neural networks for fine-grained visual recognition. IEEE Trans. Pattern Anal. Mach. Intell. 40(6), 1309–1322 (2018)
21. Margolin, R., Zelnik-Manor, L., Tal, A.: OTC: a novel local descriptor for scene classification. In: Fleet, D., Pajdla, T., Schiele, B., Tuytelaars, T. (eds.) ECCV 2014. LNCS, vol. 8695, pp. 377–391. Springer, Cham (2014). https://doi.org/10.1007/978-3-319-10584-0_25
22. Mikolov, T., Chen, K., Corrado, G., Dean, J.: Efficient estimation of word representations in vector space. arXiv preprint arXiv:1301.3781 (2013)
23. Miller, G.A.: WordNet: a lexical database for English. Commun. ACM 38(11), 39–41 (1995)
24. Oliva, A.: Gist of the scene. In: Neurobiology of Attention, pp. 251–256. Elsevier (2005)
25. Oliva, A., Torralba, A.: Modeling the shape of the scene: a holistic representation of the spatial envelope. Int. J. Comput. Vis. 42(3), 145–175 (2001)
26. Parizi, N., Oberlin, J.G., Felzenszwalb, P.F.: Reconfigurable models for scene recognition. In: Proceedings of Computer Vision Pattern Recognition (CVPR), pp. 2775–2782, June 2012
27. Patel, A., Sands, A., Callison-Burch, C., Apidianaki, M.: Magnitude: a fast, efficient universal vector embedding utility package. In: Proceedings Conference on Empirical Methods in Natural Language Processing: System Demonstrations, pp. 120–126 (2018)
28. Pennington, J., Socher, R., Manning, C.: Glove: global vectors for word representation. In: Proceedings of 2014 Conference on Empirical Methods in Natural Language Processing (EMNLP), pp. 1532–1543 (2014)
29. Perronnin, F., Sánchez, J., Mensink, T.: Improving the fisher kernel for large-scale image classification. In: Daniilidis, K., Maragos, P., Paragios, N. (eds.) ECCV 2010. LNCS, vol. 6314, pp. 143–156. Springer, Heidelberg (2010). https://doi.org/10.1007/978-3-642-15561-1_11
30. Quattoni, A., Torralba, A.: Recognizing indoor scenes. In: Proceedings of IEEE Conference Computer Vision Pattern Recognition (CVPR), pp. 413–420, June 2009
31. ShenghuaGao, I.H., Liang-TienChia, P.: Local features are not lonely-Laplacian sparse coding for image classification, pp. 3555–3561 (2010)
32. Sitaula, C., Xiang, Y., Aryal, S., Lu, X.: Unsupervised deep features for privacy image classification. arXiv preprint arXiv:1909.10708 (2019)
33. Sitaula, C., Xiang, Y., Zhang, Y., Lu, X., Aryal, S.: Indoor image representation by high-level semantic features. IEEE Access 7, 84967–84979 (2019)
34. Tang, P., Wang, H., Kwong, S.: G-MS2F: GoogLeNet based multi-stage feature fusion of deep CNN for scene recognition. Neurocomputing 225, 188–197 (2017)
35. Wang, D., Mao, K.: Task-generic semantic convolutional neural network for web text-aided image classification. Neurocomputing 329, 103–115 (2019)
36. Wang, D., Mao, K.: Learning semantic text features for web text aided image classification. IEEE Trans. Multimedia PP, 1 (2019)
37. Wu, J., Rehg, J.M.: CENTRIST: a visual descriptor for scene categorization. IEEE Trans. Pattern Anal. Mach. Intell. 33(8), 1489–1501 (2011)
38. Xiao, Y., Wu, J., Yuan, J.: mCENTRIST: a multi-channel feature generation mechanism for scene categorization. IEEE Trans. Image Process. 23(2), 823–836 (2014)

39. Zeglazi, O., Amine, A., Rziza, M.: Sift descriptors modeling and application in texture image classification. In: Proceedings of 13th International Conference Computer Graphics, Imaging and Visualization (CGiV), pp. 265–268, March 2016
40. Zhang, C., Zhu, G., Huang, Q., Tian, Q.: Image classification by search with explicitly and implicitly semantic representations. Inf. Sci. **376**, 125–135 (2017)
41. Zhou, B., Khosla, A., Lapedriza, A., Torralba, A., Oliva, A.: Places: An image database for deep scene understanding. arXiv preprint arXiv:1610.02055 (2016)
42. Zhu, J., Li, L.J., Fei-Fei, L., Xing, E.P.: Large margin learning of upstream scene understanding models. In: Proceedings of Advance Neural Information Processing Systems (NIPS), pp. 2586–2594 (2010)

Integrating TM Knowledge into NMT with Double Chain Graph

Qiuxiang He[1], Guoping Huang[2], and Li Li[1(✉)]

[1] School of Computer and Information Science,
Southwest University, Chongqing 400715, China
hqxiang@email.swu.edu.cn, lily@swu.edu.cn
[2] Tencent AI Lab, Tencent, Shenzhen 518000, China
donkeyhuang@tencent.com

Abstract. The approach based on translation pieces extracted from the translation memory (TM) knowledge is appealing for neural machine translation (NMT), owning to its efficiency in memory consumption and computation. However, the incapable of capturing sufficient contextual translation knowledge leading to a limited translation performance. This paper proposes a simple and effective structure to address this issue. The main idea is to employ the word chain and position chain knowledge from a TM as additional rewards to guide the decoding process of the neural machine translation. Experiments on six translation tasks show that the proposed Double Chain Graph yields consistent gains while achieving greater efficiency to the counterpart of translation pieces.

Keywords: Translation memory knowledge · Neural machine translation · Double Chain Graph

1 Introduction

Translation memory (TM) has been widely used to improve translation quality in machine translation (MT), such as statistical machine translation (SMT) and neural machine translation (NMT). TM provides the most similar source-target sentence pairs to the source sentence to be translated, and provides more reliable translation results than MT does for those matched segments. For example, a decade earlier, various research work has also been devoted to integrating TM into SMT [5,7,10,13]. Since the evolutional shift from SMT to the current mainstream NMT, there are increasingly interests in employing TM knowledge to help the NMT model to produce more reliable translation results for those matched segments.

In order to make full use of the TM knowledge, a fine tuning approach [3,6] was proposed to train a sentence-wise local neural model with the top of a retrieved TM, and the model was further used to test a particular sentence. In spite of its appealing performance, the fine-tuning for each testing sentence led to high latency in decoding process. On the contrary, in [4] and [14], the

© Springer Nature Switzerland AG 2019
T. Gedeon et al. (Eds.): ICONIP 2019, LNCS 11955, pp. 103–114, 2019.
https://doi.org/10.1007/978-3-030-36718-3_9

standard NMT model was augmented by additionally encoding a TM for each testing sentence, and the proposed model was trained to optimize for testing all source sentences. These approaches [4,14] are capable of capturing global context from a TM, but its encoding of a TM with neural networks requires intensive computation and considerable memory. The main reason is because a TM encodes much more words than those encoded by a standard NMT model, typically.

Gratefully, a simple approach was proposed in [15], which was efficient in both memory consumption and computation. For each sentence, they represented the TM as a collection of translation pieces consisting of weighted n-grams, whose weights were added into NMT as rewards. Unfortunately, because the translation pieces only capture very local context in a TM, this approach can not generate good enough translations even when a TM is very similar to the testing sentence: in particular, the translation quality is far away from perfect even if the reference translation of the source sentence is included in the training set as argued by [14].

To address the above issue, this paper proposes a novel and effective Double Chain Graph structure, with word chain and position chain from TM, to capture more contextual information in a TM while achieving greater efficiency to [15]. We apply our approach to Transformer, a strong NMT system [12]. Specifically, we make the following contributions in this paper:

- We present a simple but effective structure to construct the translation pieces collected from translation memory for integrating translation memory into neural machine translation.
- Our proposed structure achieves greater efficiency to the counterpart of translation pieces in terms of computation and memory consumption.
- Experiments on 6 translation tasks show that our proposed graph structure achieves substantial improvements over strong Transformer baseline and it further consistently and significantly outperforms the approach in [15].

2   Preliminary

2.1   Transformer-Based NMT

In this paper, our baseline model is the state-of-the-art NMT model, Transformer [12]. The Transformer is the most competitive neural sequence transduction model which has encoder and decoder stacks with attention. Suppose a source sentence is $\mathbf{x} = \langle x_1, \ldots, x_{|\mathbf{x}|} \rangle$ with length $|\mathbf{x}|$ and its corresponding target sentence is $\mathbf{y} = \langle y_1, \ldots, y_{|\mathbf{y}|} \rangle$ with length $|\mathbf{y}|$. Generally, for a given $\mathbf{x}$, the Transformer aims to generate its translation $\mathbf{y}$ according to the conditional probability $P(\mathbf{y}|\mathbf{x})$, which is defined by neural networks:

$$P(\mathbf{y}|\mathbf{x}) = \prod_{i=1}^{|\mathbf{y}|} P(y_i|\mathbf{y}_{<i}, \mathbf{x}) = \prod_{i=1}^{|\mathbf{y}|} \mathrm{softmax}\left(\phi(h_i^{D,L})\right) \tag{1}$$

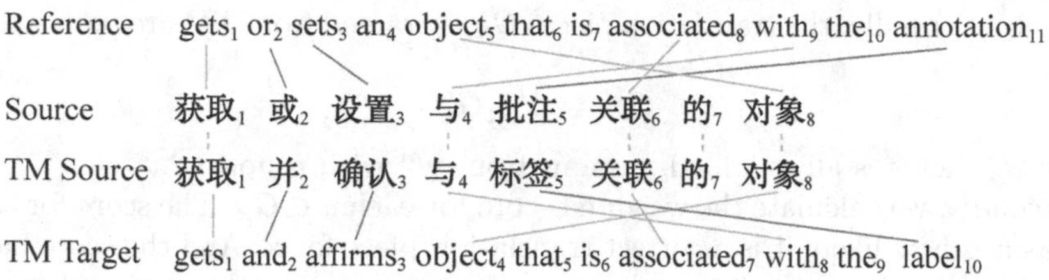

Reference   gets$_1$ or$_2$ sets$_3$ an$_4$ object$_5$ that$_6$ is$_7$ associated$_8$ with$_9$ the$_{10}$ annotation$_{11}$

Source   获取$_1$ 或$_2$ 设置$_3$ 与$_4$ 批注$_5$ 关联$_6$ 的$_7$ 对象$_8$

TM Source   获取$_1$ 并$_2$ 确认$_3$ 与$_4$ 标签$_5$ 关联$_6$ 的$_7$ 对象$_8$

TM Target   gets$_1$ and$_2$ affirms$_3$ object$_4$ that$_5$ is$_6$ associated$_7$ with$_8$ the$_9$ label$_{10}$

Fig. 1. An example of translation pieces in translation memory. The red part is employed to extract translation pieces, such as "gets", "object", "object that", "that", "that is", "is" and "is associated" etc. (Color figure online)

where $\mathbf{y}_{<i} = \langle y_1, \ldots, y_{i-1} \rangle$ denotes a prefix of $\mathbf{y}$ with length $i - 1$. And $h_i^{D,L}$ indicates the i_{th} hidden unit at L_{th} layer under the encoder-decoder framework, and ϕ is a linear network to project the hidden unit to a vector with the dimension of the target vocabulary size. To expand each factor $P(y_i|\mathbf{y}_{<i}, \mathbf{x})$, Transformer adopts the encoder-decoder framework similar to the standard sequence-to-sequence learning in [1].

During encoding $\mathbf{x}$, an encoder employs L identical layers of neural networks. And during decoding process, Transformer similarly employs L layers of neural networks. Finally, the factory $P(y_i|\mathbf{y}_{<i}, \mathbf{x})$ can be defined in Eq. 1.

In NMT decoding process, the standard decoding algorithm is beam search. The probability of a complete hypothesis is computed as:

$$\log P(\mathbf{y}|\mathbf{x}) = \sum_{i=1}^{|\mathbf{y}|} \log P(y_i|\mathbf{y}_{<i}, \mathbf{x}) \tag{2}$$

2.2 Translation Pieces Extracted from TM

For a source sentence $\mathbf{x}$ to be translated, we retrieve a set of source sentences along with corresponding translations from translation memory (TM) with an off-the-shelf search engine, so we get the TM list $\{(\mathbf{x}^m, \mathbf{y}^m)|m \in [1, M]\}$. Then, we calculate the similarity score between $\mathbf{x}$ and $\mathbf{x}^m$ as following [4]:

$$\text{sim}(\mathbf{x}, \mathbf{x}^m) = 1 - \frac{dist(\mathbf{x}, \mathbf{x}^m)}{\max(|\mathbf{x}|, |\mathbf{x}^m|)} \tag{3}$$

where $dist(\cdot)$ denotes the edit-distance. $|\mathbf{x}|$ denotes the word-based length of $\mathbf{x}$.

We firstly collect translation pieces from the TM list, which is similar to [15]. Specifically, translation pieces (1-gram and 2-grams) are collected from the target sentences $\mathbf{y}^m$, as the possible translation pieces $G_{\mathbf{x}}^m$ for $\mathbf{x}$, using word-level alignments information to select n-grams that are related to $\mathbf{x}$. For example, in Fig. 1, the red part in the retrieved TM target is employed to extracted translation pieces for the source sentence, such as "gets", "object", "that" and "object that" etc. Formally, the translation pieces $G_{\mathbf{x}}$ extracted from TM are represented as:

$$G_{\mathbf{x}} = \cup_{m=1}^{M} G_{\mathbf{x}}^{m} \tag{4}$$

where $G_{\mathbf{x}}^{m}$ denotes all weighted n-grams from $\mathbf{y}^{m}$ with n up to 2.

Secondly, we calculate the weighted score for each $u \in G_{\mathbf{x}}$. The score for each u measures how likely it is a correct translation piece for $\mathbf{x}$. And the score bases on sentence similarity between the input sentence $\mathbf{x}$ and the retrieved source sentences $\{\mathbf{x}^{m} | m \in [1, M]\}$ as following:

$$s_p(\mathbf{x}, u) = \max_{1 \le m \le M \wedge u \in G_{\mathbf{x}}^{m}} \mathrm{sim}(\mathbf{x}, \mathbf{x}^{m}) \tag{5}$$

In this section, we only provide a brief summary of how to collect translation pieces from TM. For more details, we refer readers to [15].

3 Double Chain Graph

How to use the collected translation pieces is a key challenge for integrating TM knowledge into NMT. Although the method in [15] has shown its effectiveness, it takes no account of the long-distance dependency words in translation memory. Hence, in order to achieve more reasonable word to reward, and more effective reward value to integrate TM knowledge into NMT, we design a novel Double Chain Graph (abbreviated as DCG), which consists of word chain and position chain. In this section, we will answer the following three questions: what is DCG, why we use DCG and how to construct the DCG.

3.1 Double Chain Graph Description

As shown in Fig. 2(iii), we first collect the translation pieces from TM target, then we construct the Double Chain Graph. The DCG consists of two chains: one is the word sequence chain, another is the position sequence chain. More specifically, we collect n-grams (n $\le$ 2) translation pieces of the top-5 TM instance $(\mathbf{x}^{m}, \mathbf{y}^{m})$, with $\mathbf{x}^{m}$ is similar to the input sentence $\mathbf{x}$. Using the TM target $\mathbf{y}^{m}$, we construct the word chain according to the order in which the words appear in the collected translation pieces. And the position chain is constructed by the corresponding position of the word in the TM target. We only use the top-1 TM instance $(\mathbf{x}^{1}, \mathbf{y}^{1})$ to construct the position chain.

3.2 The Effectiveness of Double Chain Graph

How to use the collected translation pieces is a key challenge in integrating TM knowledge into NMT. As we mentioned before, at each time step, the NMT decoder mechanism selects the best word as the output value according to the properties of words in NMT output layer. So, there are two key tasks, one is to decide which word should be given an additional reward at each decoding step,

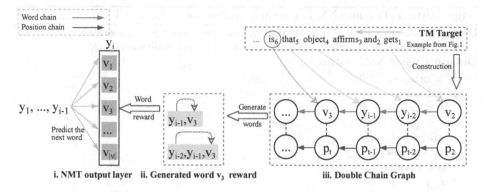

Fig. 2. Adding additional rewards into NMT output layer for words that are generated from Double Chain Graph. The red part in TM target is employed to extract translation pieces. In part (i), v refers to the word in the target vocabulary. In part (ii), we select the last word of the generated continuous pieces to reward according to current decoding step. In part (iii), v or y refers to a word in the translation pieces, and p refers to the position of word v or y according to TM. The orange chain in the first row is precedence links of the word in collected translation pieces. The blue chain in the second row is the position of the corresponding word v or y. For example, as the orange dot line shows, v_3 refers to "is", and p_t refers to "6". (Color figure online)

and another is how to compute the additional reward on the specific word at the current decoding time.

For which word to reward, in the paper [15], they collect continuous segment such as the red part of the retrieved target sentence shown in Fig. 1, and they only up-weights the words that match the retrieved translation pieces in the NMT output layer and has some drawbacks on capturing long patterns. For example, when the output sequence is "gets or sets an" at the previous decoding moment, they do not select the fragment "object" as the current word to reward at next decoding time. Namely, they do not give enough attention to the fragment "object" at next decoding time. Hence, in our proposed DCG model, we can give more attention to the discontinuous segment for we use the position chain to capture long distance dependency.

Considering how much additional reward to a word, in the paper [15], they don't give those words which are in the same collected translation piece, equal reward at different decoding step. For example, as shown in Fig. 1, at decoding step 7, the reward value for the word "associated" is four times than that of the word "object" at decoding step 4.

Hence, we propose a more reasonable and effective Double Chain Graph for integrating TM knowledge into NMT. The proposed DCG based on a translation fragment sequence is inspired by Coupled HMMs in [2]. While performing the experiments described in Sect. 4, we also perfect an algorithm with superior performance and lower complexity, based on the positive word reward and the feedback mechanism, as shown in Algorithm 1.

Algorithm 1. Guiding NMT decoding process using Double Chain Graph

---

Require: Double Chain Graph, decoding output sequence $\mathbf{y}_{<i}$, generated word-score pair U, transition probability matrix A, translation probability array B.
Output: Update NMT output layer

1: $U = \phi$; $s_u(y_x) = 0$.
2: **feedback:**
3:    **for** each $y_x \in B[:]$ **do**
4:        $s_u(y_x) = B[y_x]$; add $<y_x, s_u(y_x)>$ into U
5:    **end for**
6: **end feedback**
7: **main process:**
8: **for** $j = 0$; $j < 4$; $j{+}{+}$ **do**
9:    $y_a = y_{i-j-1}$ (note: $y_{i-j} \in \mathbf{y}_{<i}$)
10:    **for** each $y_x \in A[y_a, :]$ **do**
11:        $s_w(y_x) = A[y_a, y_x] \cdot B[y_x]$
12:        **if** $loc_{y_a} - loc_{y_x} == j$ **then**
13:            $s_w(y_x) = s_w(y_x) + \frac{1}{1+|loc_{y_a}-t|}$; $s_u(y_x)$ += $s_w(y_x)$
14:            **if** $j = 0$ **and** $y_x \notin P_{\mathbf{x}}^m$ **then**
15:                add $<y_x, s_u(y_x)>$ into U
16:            **else**
17:                update $<y_x, s_u(y_x)>$ in U
18:            **end if**
19:        **end if**
20:    **end for**
21:    **if** $j = 0$ **and** $y_x \notin A[y_a, :]$ **then**
22:        call **feedback; break**
23:    **end if**
24: **end for**
25: **if** $[\forall y_x \mid s_u(y_x) < 0.5]$ **then**
26:    call **feedback**
27: **end if**
28: $\log P(y_i | \mathbf{y}_{<i}, \mathbf{x})$ += $\lambda U(y_i)$
29: **end main process**

3.3   Guiding NMT Decoding with Double Chain Graph

This part describes how to guide the NMT decoding process using Double Chain Graph. Firstly, for the word chain in Double Chain Graph, we calculate the translation probability of each word using Eq. (3). The translation probability measures how likely it is a correct translation piece for the input sentence $\mathbf{x}$. Suppose $u = <w_a w_b w_c>$, we use p_b denotes the translation probability of word w_b. We also calculate the word-to-word (such as from w_a to w_b) transition probability p_{ab} as following:

$$p_{ab} = \frac{1}{N((w_a w_b) \in u)} \tag{6}$$

where $N(\cdot)$ denotes a statistic of all the cases that satisfy $(w_a w_b) \in u$.

Hence, the reward score of word w_b is defined by:

$$s_w(\mathbf{x}, w_b) = p_{ab} \cdot p_b \qquad (7)$$

Secondly, for the position chain in Double Chain Graph, at each decoding step, we will calculate the reward using Algorithm 1. Then, we calculate the updated score as following:

$$s'_w(\mathbf{x}, w_i) = s_w(\mathbf{x}, w_i) + \frac{1}{1 + |loc_{w_{i-n}} - t|}, (n \leq 4) \qquad (8)$$

where $loc_{w_{i-n}}$ denotes the word position in TM target and t denotes the current decoding step.

Thirdly, as shown in Fig. 2(i, ii), an additional word reward generated from Double Chain Graph will be added to NMT output layer according to:

$$S_u(y_i|\mathbf{y}_{<i}, \mathbf{x}) = \lambda \sum_{n=1}^{4} \delta\big(loc_{y_{i-n}} - loc_{y_i} == n, \ s_w(\mathbf{x}, y_i)\big) \qquad (9)$$

where λ can be tuned on the development set and $\delta(cond, val)$ is computed as: if $cond$ is true, then $\delta(\cdot)$ is val, otherwise 0. And the $loc_{y_{i-n}}$ denotes the position in TM target of word y_{i-n}.

Finally, based on Eqs. 1 and 9, the updated probability $P'(y_i|\mathbf{y}_{<i}, \mathbf{x})$ for the word y_i is calculated by:

$$P'(y_i|\mathbf{y}_{<i}, \mathbf{x}) = P(y_i|\mathbf{y}_{<i}, \mathbf{x}) \times e^{S_u(y_i|\mathbf{y}_{<i}, \mathbf{x})} \qquad (10)$$

And then, we use the Algorithm 1 to illustrate how to guide the NMT decoding process using our proposed DCG. We use a dictionary U to store the generated reward words and their scores for each decoding output sequence $\mathbf{y}_{<i}$. At each decoding step t, we update the output layer probabilities by traversing target words that belong to U and updating the corresponding probabilities in NMT output layer.

4   Experiments

In this section, we use experiments to demonstrate the advantages of the proposed approach: it yields better translation on the basis of Transformer and the method in [15] with the help of Double Chain Graph constructed from translation memory; and it still keep the low latency mainly because of the novel translation piece formulation in Double Chain Graph.

4.1   Settings

To explore the effectiveness of our proposed model fully, we conduct translation experiments on 6 language pairs: zh-en, fr-en, en-fr, es-en, en-es and en-de. We

Input	联合国 所有 人员 的 行动 自由 对本 组织 而言 属于 原则性 问题，也 是 联塞 部队 的 业务 需求 。
Reference	freedom of movement for all united nations personnel is a matter of principle for the organization and an operational requirement for unficyp .
TM Source	对本 组织 而言，联合国 所有 人员 的 行动 自由 属于 原则性 问题，也 是 联塞 部队 的 业务 需求 。
TM Target	freedom of movement for all united nations personnel is a matter of principle for the organization and an operational requirement for unficyp .
TFM	the freedom of movement of all united nations personnel is a matter of principle for the organization and of the operational requirements of unficyp .
TFM-P	the freedom of movement of all united nations personnel is a matter of principle for the organization and is a matter of principle for the operational needs of unficyp .
TFM-PG	freedom of movement for all united nations personnel is a matter of principle for the organization and an operational requirement for unficyp .

Fig. 3. An example of translation results generated by other methods and our model. **TM Source** denotes the sentence that is most similar to the input. **TM Target** denotes the target sentence of the TM source. Mis-translations in the **TFM*** are shown in red. (Color figure online)

use case-insensitive BLEU score on single references as the automatic metric [8] for translation quality evaluation. For zh-en experiments, we collect about 2 million news sentences from some online news websites. For other language pairs, we manage to obtain pre-processed JRC-Acquis corpus from [4]. The corpora are suitable for us to make evaluations. We randomly select 2000 samples to form the development and the test set respectively, for each language pair. The rest of the samples are used as the training set. We also employ Byte Pair Encoding [9] on the datasets. For each language pair, we maintain a source/target vocabulary of 35k tokens.

As the proposed model directly build upon the Transformer architecture [12], which is referred to as **TFM** in this paper. According to [15], we implement translation pieces method based on Transformer for fair comparison, and it is denoted by **TFM-P**. And the implemented system for the Double Chain Graph is denoted by **TFM-PG**.

For each source sentence, we retrieve 5 translation pairs from the training set using Apache Lucene, and score them with fuzzy matching value. Finally, we use those translation pairs as the TMs for the sentence **x** to be translated.

Furthermore, we tune the hyper-parameter λ carefully on the development set for all translation tasks as it is sensitive to the specific translation task for TFM-PG and TFM-P.

4.2   Results and Analysis

Some of the translation examples are shown in Fig. 3. As shown above, TFM and TFM-P have mis-translations while TFM-PG do not. Mis-translation refers

Table 1. Translation accuracy in terms of BLEU on 6 translation tasks. **Best** results are highlighted.

		zh-en	fr-en	en-fr	es-en	en-es	en-de
Dev	TFM	41.59	65.29	64.46	64.96	62.09	54.06
	TFM-P	48.87	70.74	68.94	67.10	67.35	60.86
	TFM-PG	**50.32**	**71.01**	**69.12**	**68.87**	**67.46**	**61.08**
Test	TFM	40.14	65.43	64.07	63.92	61.48	53.38
	TFM-P	46.65	70.95	69.12	67.32	66.95	60.06
	TFM-PG	**48.44**	**71.06**	**69.32**	**68.26**	**67.27**	**60.39**

Table 2. Similarity Analysis - Translation quality (BLEU score) on zh-en task for the divided subsets according to similarity. **Best** results are highlighted.

	Dev				Test			
Similarity	[0.0, 0.4)	[0.4, 0.7)	[0.7, 1.0]	[0.0, 1.0]	[0.0, 0.4)	[0.4, 0.7)	[0.7, 1.0]	[0.0, 1.0]
Ratio (%)	70.64	8.06	21.30	100.00	72.98	7.37	19.65	100.00
TFM	37.39	49.01	49.05	41.59	36.83	49.11	46.83	40.14
TFM-P	**37.60**	57.77	71.67	48.87	**37.53**	56.05	66.93	46.65
TFM-PG	37.38	**58.80**	**77.22**	**50.32**	37.20	**57.39**	**74.33**	**48.44**

to that some source words are not translated correctly. Our proposed model can make full use of the fragment knowledge in TM target, with the help of Double Chain Graph constructed from translation memory. And our method still achieves greater efficiency.

Translation Accuracy. The main experimental results are shown in Table 1. We can see that our model outperforms the state-of-the-art NMT model TFM 4.34–8.30 BLEU points, which varies as tasks from the overall perspective. And the method also outperforms the baseline TFM-P system 0.11–1.79 BLEU points, which varies as tasks. The zh-en translation task obtains the greatest promotion with the Double Chain Graph, while the fr-en translation task cannot make much benefit. The main reason is that the baseline TFM-P is extraordinarily strong with the score of 70.95, and this is still consistent with the discovery in [15].

Error Analysis. As shown in Table 2, compared to TFM-P, the low similarity subset, in the range of [0.0, 0.4), has an insignificant impact on the result. We learned from the TM knowledge: if there is a low similarity between the TM source sentence and the input sentence, the words in translation pieces are less helpful to guide the decoding process. Hence, the reason is that we still give some reward to those words which are in the matched translation pieces (actually, we shouldn't) during the decoding process, while the sentences in TM are not so similar to the input.

Table 3. Similarity Analysis - Translation quality (TER score) on zh-en task for the divided subsets according to similarity. **Best** results are highlighted.

	Dev				Test			
Similarity	[0.0, 0.4)	[0.4, 0.7)	[0.7, 1.0]	[0.0, 1.0]	[0.0, 0.4)	[0.4, 0.7)	[0.7, 1.0]	[0.0, 1.0]
Ratio (%)	70.64	8.06	21.30	100.00	72.98	7.37	19.65	100.00
TFM	50.85	40.74	40.08	47.20	50.68	40.86	42.59	48.07
TFM-P	**50.81**	36.20	25.41	43.00	**50.59**	35.32	30.77	45.00
TFM-PG	51.26	**35.61**	**20.40**	**41.77**	50.88	**34.90**	**23.39**	**43.20**

Table 4. Composition of dev and test sets based on similarity score on six translation tasks.

(Dev|Test) Ratio (%)	zh-en	fr-en	en-fr	es-en	en-es	en-de
[0, 0.1)	4.03|5.23	1.35|0.85	0.25|0.35	0.20|0.15	1.50|1.20	2.00|1.80
[0.1, 0.2)	43.74|42.81	9.85|11.3	4.85|6.55	5.45|4.95	10.00|11.20	12.45|13.25
[0.2, 0.3)	16.23|18.55	11.10|10.05	12.15|10.55	15.00|15.30	13.55|13.75	11.40|11.55
[0.3, 0.4)	6.64|6.38	10.00|10.40	10.90|10.50	13.25|11.90	10.15|8.45	10.35|9.20
[0.4, 0.5)	3.00|2.97	7.90|7.15	7.40|8.30	8.20|8.60	7.80|6.25	7.00|6.05
[0.5, 0.6)	2.89|2.37	8.65|8.10	11.55|10.05	8.60|10.45	6.50|9.40	8.30|8.85
[0.6, 0.7)	2.18|2.03	10.15|10.65	10.50|10.30	8.45|8.65	8.65|8.05	7.80|7.70
[0.7, 0.8)	2.89|2.70	13.00|12.90	12.75|14.10	9.00|9.30	8.80|9.35	8.55|9.85
[0.8, 0.9)	5.77|5.50	15.05|15.55	16.30|16.20	16.30|15.65	16.25|16.15	17.20|17.00
[0.9, 1)	12.58|11.45	12.95|13.05	13.25|13.10	15.65|15.05	16.80|16.20	14.95|14.75
[0, 1)	100|100	100|100	100|100	100|100	100|100	100|100

Table 5. Running time in terms of seconds/sentence on zh-en task.

	TFM	TFM-P	TFM-PG
Dev	0.31	0.76	0.58
Test	0.31	0.76	0.56

Table 6. Translation quality (BLEU score) among various values of λ on zh-en task.

λ	0.8	0.9	1.0	1.1
Dev	50.17	**50.32**	50.29	50.25
Test	48.18	48.44	**48.63**	48.35

Influence on Similarity. In order to dig on the influence of similarities deeply, we report the translation score on zh-en task for the divided subsets according to similarity, in terms of BLEU and TER [11] as shown in Tables 2 and 3, respectively.

The high similarity subset which is in the range of [0.7, 1.0], obtains significant improvements, up to 7.40 BLEU points and down to 7.38 TER (The lower the TER score, the better.) points for the test set, respectively, with the help of Double Chain Graph. Table 4 shows statistics datas of each dev and test set on six translation tasks where sentences are grouped by the similarity score. Generally speaking, we can conclude that the Double Chain Graph constructed from TM is efficient to improve the final translation results in most cases, especially for those source sentences which have high similarity sentences in TM.

Running Time. We eliminate the time of retrieving similar sentences from TM and directly compare running time for neural models as shown in Table 5. The average lengths of sentences in Dev and Test are 31.34 and 31.17 words/sentence, respectively. From Table 5, compared to the baseline TFM-P employing translation pieces, our proposed model can still keep the low latency, and our system TFM-PG achieves better translation performance with lesser time.

Hyper-parameter Robustness. We try to verify the robustness of the hyper-parameter λ among different translation tasks, and we show the search process on zh-en task. From Table 6, we can see that, to keep smaller translation quality volatility, there is enough parameter space for λ. In general, we can search a better value for λ on other translation tasks in the range of $[0.6, 1.2]$ according to our experience.

In summary, the extensive experimental results show that the proposed model achieves better translation results with the Double Chain Graph constructed from TM, especially for those source sentences that have high similarity sentences in TM. Furthermore, this model can keep the low latency in terms of running time.

5 Conclusion

The approach based on translation pieces, which are extracted from translation memory, is appealing for neural machine translation, owning to its efficiency in both memory consumption and computation. To capture sufficient contextual knowledge in translation pieces, in this paper, we propose a novel and effective Double Chain Graph that integrates word chain and position chain from translation memory. The extensive experimental results on 6 translation tasks demonstrate that the proposed approach further achieves better translation results by integrating translation memory knowledge into neural machine translation, especially for those source sentences that have high similarity sentences in translation memory. What's more, our method can still keep the low memory consumption, lower latency, and keep the system architecture as simple as possible.

Acknowledgments. This work is supported by NSFC (grant No. 61877051).

References

1. Bahdanau, D., Cho, K., Bengio, Y.: Neural machine translation by jointly learning to align and translate (2016). arXiv preprint arXiv:1409.0473
2. Brand, M., Oliver, N., Pentland, A.: Coupled hidden Markov models for complex action recognition. In: Proceedings of the 1997 Conference on Computer Vision and Pattern Recognition (CVPR 1997), pp. 994–999 (1997)
3. Farajian, M.A., Turchi, M., Negri, M., Federico, M.: Multi-domain neural machine translation through unsupervised adaptation. In: Proceedings of the Second Conference on Machine Translation, pp. 127–137 (2017)
4. Gu, J., Wang, Y., Cho, K., Li, V.O.: Search engine guided non-parametric neural machine translation. In: Proceedings of the Thirty-Second AAAI Conference on Artificial Intelligence (AAAI 2018), pp. 5133–5140 (2018)
5. Koehn, P., Senellart, J.: Convergence of translation memory and statistical machine translation. In: Proceedings of AMTA Workshop on MT Research and the Translation Industry, pp. 21–31 (2010)
6. Li, X., Zhang, J., Zong, C.: One sentence one model for neural machine translation (2016). arXiv preprint arXiv:1609.06490
7. Ma, Y., He, Y., Way, A., van Genabith, J.: Consistent translation using discriminative learning: a translation memory-inspired approach. In: Proceedings of the 49th Annual Meeting of the Association for Computational Linguistics (ACL 2011), pp. 1239–1248 (2011)
8. Papineni, K., Roukos, S., Ward, T., Zhu, W.: Bleu: a method for automatic evaluation of machine translation. In: Proceedings of the 40th Annual Meeting of the Association for Computational Linguistics ACL 2002, pp. 311–318. ACL (2002)
9. Sennrich, R., Haddow, B., Birch, A.: Neural machine translation of rare words with subword units. In: Proceedings of the 54th Annual Meeting of the Association for Computational Linguistics (ACL 2016), pp. 1715–1725 (2016)
10. Simard, M., Isabelle, P.: Phrase-based machine translation in a computer-assisted translation environment. In: Proceedings of the Twelfth Machine Translation Summit (MT Summit XII), pp. 120–127 (2009)
11. Snover, M., Dorr, B., Schwartz, R., Micciulla, L., Makhoul, J.: A study of translation edit rate with targeted human annotation. In: Proceedings of the 7th Conference of the Association for Machine Translation in the Americas, pp. 223–231 (2006)
12. Vaswani, A., et al.: Attention is all you need. In: Advances in Neural Information Processing Systems, vol. 30, pp. 5998–6008 (2017)
13. Wang, K., Zong, C., Su, K.Y.: Integrating translation memory into phrase-based machine translation during decoding. In: Proceedings of the 51th Annual Meeting of the Association for Computational Linguistics (ACL 2013), pp. 11–21 (2013)
14. Xia, M., Huang, G., Liu, L., Shi, S.: Graph based translation memory for neural machine translation. In: Proceedings of the Thirty-Third AAAI Conference on Artificial Intelligence (AAAI 2019) (2019)
15. Zhang, J., Utiyama, M., Sumita, E., Neubig, G., Nakamura, S.: Guiding neural machine translation with retrieved translation pieces. In: Proceedings of the 16th Annual Conference of the North American Chapter of the Association for Computational Linguistics: Human Language Technologies (NAACL-HLT 2018), pp. 1325–1335 (2018)

Learning Transferable Policies with Improved Graph Neural Networks on Serial Robotic Structure

Fengyi Zhang[1,2], Fangzhou Xiong[1,2], Xu Yang[1,3], and Zhiyong Liu[1,2,4($\boxtimes$)]

[1] The State Key Lab of Management and Control for Complex Systems,
Institute of Automation, Chinese Academy of Science, Beijing 100190, China
zhiyong.liu@ia.ac.cn
[2] School of Artificial Intelligence,
University of Chinese Academy of Sciences (UCAS), Beijing 100049, China
[3] Huizhou Advanced Manufacturing Technology Research Center Co., Ltd.,
Huizhou 516000, China
[4] Centre for Excellence in Brain Science and Intelligence Technology,
Chinese Academy of Sciences, Shanghai 200031, China

Abstract. Robotic control via reinforcement learning (RL) has made significant advances. However, a serious weakness with this method is that RL models are prone to overfitting and have poor transfer performance. Transfer in reinforcement learning means that only a few samples are needed to train policy networks for new tasks. In this paper we investigate the problem of learning transferable policies for robots with serial structures, such as robotic arms, with the help of graph neural networks (GNN). The GNN was previously employed to incorporate explicitly the robot structure into the policy network, and thus make the policy easier to be generalized or transferred. Based on a kinematics analysis particularly on the serial robotic structure, in this paper we further improve the policy network by proposing a weighted information aggregation strategy. The experiment is conducted in a few-shot policy learning setting on a robotic arm. The experimental results show that the new aggregation strategy significantly improves the performance not only on the learning speed, but also on the policy accuracy.

Keywords: Graph neural networks · Transferable policy · Serial robotic structure

This work is supported by National Key Research and Development Plan of China grant 2017YFB1300202, NSFC grants U1613213, 61375005, 61503383, 61210009, the Strategic Priority Research Program of Chinese Academy of Science under Grant XDB32050100, and Dongguan core technology research frontier project (2019622101001). The work is also supported by the Strategic Priority Research Program of the CAS (Grant XDB02080003).

T. Gedeon et al. (Eds.): ICONIP 2019, LNCS 11955, pp. 115–126, 2019.
https://doi.org/10.1007/978-3-030-36718-3_10

1   Introduction

Reinforcement learning (RL) based policy learning has received increasing attention on the grounds that RL enables autonomous robots to learn large repertoires of behavioral skills with minimal human intervention [10,16,18,27]. However, RL models tend to overfit with abundant data, especially for high dimensional data in the robot state space, and thus suffer from poor generalization performance, which is a significant challenge for transferring models. Therefore, transfer learning in particular has been considered to be an important direction in robotic control [23]. Some previous works have been proposed to establish the direct mapping between state spaces and transfer skills between robots [1,2,11]. However, most of these algorithms require specific domain knowledge to form the mapping, which makes these algorithms more complex. Besides, the policies learned by these methods lack clear structure information, making it difficult to utilize what was learned previously for a new robot with different structures [8].

Wang et al. [26] proposed learning structured policies by incorporating a prior on the structure via graph neural networks (GNN) [9]. Specifically, as the policy network of the agent, NerveNet [26] first propagates information through the structure of the agent and then outputs actions for different parts of the agent. To verify the transfer or generalization ability of NerveNet from one structure to another, with the goal of running as fast as possible along the y-direction, Wang et al. directly generalized the policy learned on a bilateral eight-leg centipede to a six-leg one, by just correspondingly dropping two leg modules in the NerveNet. It is intuitively easy to understand that when the agent loses its two bilateral legs, it does not affect the direction in which the agent runs. Hence, GNN model can not show its potential in transfer learning in the customized environment. NerveNet can directly achieve transfer learning for the customized task as most of the model weights are shared across the nodes. However, the model weights of some robots with serial structures are not transferable, in which case GNN model still needs to prove its potential in transfer learning.

In order to explore the performance of GNN on the tasks whose model weights are not transferable, we investigate the agent with a serial structure similar to the PR2 arms. The goal of the agent is to get the end of the PR2 arm to a fixed target point. Specifically, we consider the problem of transferring information across robots with different structures, including varying number of joints. Nevertheless, the discrepancy in the structure of the robots and the goals of the tasks prevent us from directly reusing policy parameters learned on different robots for a new combination. Instead of throwing away experience learned from past tasks, this work aims at learning structured policies from its past experience to obtain new skills more quickly via GNN model. We further explore the potential of the GNN model in transfer learning tasks. On the other hand, given that the joint information of the serial robotic structure has different importances at different positions, the average aggregation is inapplicable. Hence, a kinematic analysis of robotic arms with serial structures is performed. Based on the physical characteristics of robots with serial structures, we further propose a novel aggregation method of GNN model.

The main contributions of this paper are as follows: (1) We investigate that GNN model permits satisfactory transfer performance, and can achieve few-shot learning for PR2 arms. (2) For robotic arms with serial structures, we propose an improved propagation model to accelerate the convergence process and improve the control accuracy.

2 Related Work

Recently, researches on transfer learning have been receiving more and more attention [23] because of its potential for reducing the burden of data collection for learning complex policies. Ammar et al. [2] designed a common feature space between the states of two tasks, and learn a mapping between states by using the common feature space. Later research by Ammar et al. [1] applies unsupervised manifold alignment to assign pairings between states for transfer learning. In Gupta et al. [11], the authors tried to improve transfer performance via learning invariant visual features. Efforts have also been made by reusing policy parameters between environments [7,19] to transfer policies. Nevertheless, most of these methods need more domain knowledge to determine how to form the invariant features, making these algorithms more complex. The proposed method is extremely different from these policy transfer methods, since our aim is not to directly transfer a policy, which is typically impossible in the presence of structural differences. This paper adopts GNN model to learn structured policies.

This paper improves on policy network by utilizing graph neural networks [9]. A graph data structure consists of a finite set of vertices (objects) and edges (relationships). It is worth noting that graphs have complex structure with rich potential information [3]. Researches of graph with machine learning methods have been receiving more and more attention, given that graph structure data is ubiquitous in the real world. GNN was introduced in [9] as a generalization of recursive neural networks that can process graph structure data. Due to its good generalization performance and high interpretability, GNN has become a widely used graph analysis method in recent years. GNN [17,21] has been explored in a diverse range of problem domains, including supervised, semi-supervised, unsupervised, and reinforcement learning settings. GNN has been used to learn the dynamics of physical systems [6,20] and multi-agent systems [14,15]. These GNN models have also been used in both model-free [26] and model-based [13] continuous control. GNN models also have potential applications in model-free reinforcement learning [12], and for more classical approaches to planning [25].

In this paper, the work is based on the idea of representing a robot as a graph. Here, we define the graph structure of the robot as $G = (u, V, E)$. u is the global attribute of the graph. $V = \{v_i\}_{i=1:N_v}$ is the set of nodes(of cardinality N_v), where each v_i is the attribute of a node. $E = \{e_j, s_j, r_j\}_{j=1:N_e}$ is the set of edges (of cardinality N_e), where each e_j is the attribute of an edge, s_j is the index of the sender node and r_j is the index of the receiver node. In our tasks, the nodes correspond to the joints and the edges correspond to the bodies.

Battaglia et al. [4] presented the Graph Networks (GN) framework that unified and extended various graph neural networks. The GN framework defined a set of functions for relational reasoning on graphs and supported constructing complex structures from simple blocks. The main unit of the GN framework is the GN block which takes a graph as input and returns a graph as output. A GN block contains three "update" functions, ϕ, and three "aggregation" functions, ρ.

$$
\begin{aligned}
e_k' &= \phi^e(e_k, v_{s_k}, v_{r_k}, u) & \bar{e}_i' &= \rho^{e \to v}(E_i') \\
v_i' &= \phi^v(\bar{e}_i', v_i, u) & \bar{e}' &= \rho^{e \to u}(E') \\
u' &= \phi^u(\bar{e}', \bar{v}', u) & \bar{v}' &= \rho^{v \to u}(V')
\end{aligned}
\tag{1}
$$

where $E_i' = \{e_k', s_k, r_k\}_{r_k=i, k=1:N_e}$, $V' = \{v_i'\}_{i=1:N_v}$, and $E' = \cup_i E_i' = \{e_k', s_k, r_k\}_{k=1:N_e}$

As a graph, G, is the input value of a Graph Network, the computations propagate from the edge, to the node and the global level. Algorithm 1 shows the steps of computation for details.

Algorithm 1. Steps of computation in Graph Networks

Input: Graph, $G = (u, V, E)$
  for each edge $\{e_j, s_j, r_j\}$ **do**
    Compute updated edge attributes $e_k' \leftarrow \phi^e(e_k, v_{s_k}, v_{r_k}, u)$
  end for
  for each node$\{n_i\}$ **do**
    Aggregate edge attributes for each node $\bar{e}_i' \leftarrow \rho^{e \to v}(E_i')$
  end for
  Aggregate edge and node attributes globally $\bar{e}' \leftarrow \rho^{e \to u}(E'), \bar{v}' \leftarrow \rho^{v \to u}(V')$
  Compute updated global attribute $u' \leftarrow \phi^u(\bar{e}', \bar{v}', u)$
Output: Graph, $G' = (u', V', E')$

Recent work by Wang et al. [26] modelled the structure of the reinforcement learning agents using GNN model. Like in our method, they aim to transfer policies between robots by learning structured policies. The main difference from our work is that Wang et al. [26] uses the mean value of state information to do the aggregation. For the customized task in [26], the two legs the agent lost did not affect the direction in which it ran. Therefore, GNN model can not show its potential in transfer performance in the customized environment. The way of doing the aggregation by average functions is that the information of nodes in the neighborhood is considered without discrimination. However, for robotic arms with serial structures, the information of nodes in the neighborhood has different importance. The experiment (refer to Sect. 4.1) also witnesses the limitation of the way of average aggregation. Accordingly, a kinematic analysis of arms with serial structure needs to be done to obtain the physical characteristics of robots. The proposed method uses a new method of aggregation based on the analysis result.

3   Proposed Method

In the Graph Networks framework, the average function is a popular method for doing aggregation. This method of aggregation considers node information in the neighborhood to be equally important. Nevertheless, for robotic arms with serial structures, joints (nodes) at different positions have different effects on the end position. Here we derive the physical characteristics of a robotic arm by doing a kinematic analysis on the robotic arm, and then propose a novel aggregation method.

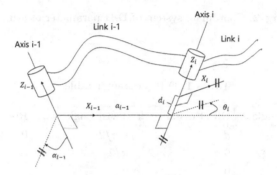

Fig. 1. Coordinate system of D-H parameter

Kinematics Analysis of a Robotic Arm. The forward kinematics of a robotic arm is to calculate the position and attitude of the end actuator relative to the base coordinate system according to the parameters of each joint. Figure 1 shows the D-H parameter coordinate system of two adjacent coordinate systems. Where α_{i-1} represents the angle from $\widehat{Z}_{i-1}$ to $\widehat{Z}_i$ measured about $\widehat{X}_{i-1}$; a_{i-1} is the distance from $\widehat{Z}_{i-1}$ to $\widehat{Z}_i$ measured along the $\widehat{X}_{i-1}$ direction($a_i > 0$); θ_i represents the angle from $\widehat{X}_{i-1}$ to $\widehat{X}_i$ measured about the $\widehat{Z}_i$; d_i is the distance from $\widehat{X}_{i-1}$ to $\widehat{X}_i$ measured along the $\widehat{Z}_i$ direction.

From Fig. 1, the transformation matrix of the joint coordinate system can be derived, as shown in (2).

$$
{}^{i-1}_{i}T = \begin{bmatrix} \cos(\theta_i) & -\sin(\theta_i) & 0 & a_{i-1} \\ \sin(\theta_i)\cos(\alpha_{i-1}) & \cos(\theta_i)\cos(\alpha_{i-1}) & -\sin(\alpha_{i-1}) & -\sin(\alpha_{i-1})d_i \\ \sin(\theta_i)\sin(\alpha_{i-1}) & \cos(\theta_i)\sin(\alpha_{i-1}) & \cos(\alpha_{i-1}) & \cos(\alpha_{i-1})d_i \\ 0 & 0 & 0 & 1 \end{bmatrix} \tag{2}
$$

Equation (2) is a general matrix representation of the D-H conversion. According to Fig. 2, the D-H parameters determined by the length and position of the connecting joint are shown in Table 1.

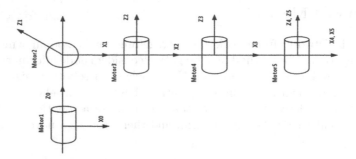

Fig. 2. Coordinate system of D-H parameter of arm

Table 1. D-H parameter table.

Joint	Joint angle θ_i	Offset distance d_i	Twist angle α_{i-1}	Rod length a_{i-1}
1	θ_1	d_1	$-\pi/2$	0
2	θ_2	0	$\pi/2$	a_1
3	θ_3	0	0	a_2
4	θ_4	0	0	a_3
5	θ_5	0	0	0

From Table 1 and Eq. (2), the forward kinematics formula can be expressed as:

$$T = {}_1^0T\,{}_2^1T\,{}_3^2T\,{}_4^3T\,{}_5^4T = \begin{bmatrix} & & & P_x \\ & R & & P_y \\ & & & P_z \\ 0 & 0 & 0 & 1 \end{bmatrix} \tag{3}$$

In (3), R is a matrix representing the spatial attitude of the endpoint of the robotic arm, and P_x, P_y, and P_z represent the position coordinates of the endpoint of the robotic arm.

$$P_x = a_3 \cos\theta_1 \cos\theta_2 \cos\theta_3 - a_3 \cos\theta_1 \sin\theta_2 \sin\theta_3$$
$$+ a_2 \cos\theta_1 \cos\theta_2 + a_1 \cos\theta_1 \tag{4}$$

$$P_y = a_3 \sin \theta_2 \cos \theta_3 + a_3 \cos \theta_2 \sin \theta_3 + a_2 \sin \theta_2 + d_1 \qquad (5)$$

$$P_z = -a_3 \sin \theta_1 \cos \theta_2 \cos \theta_3 + a_3 \sin \theta_1 \sin \theta_2 \sin \theta_3$$
$$- a_2 \sin \theta_1 \cos \theta_2 - a_1 \sin \theta_1 \qquad (6)$$

In (4), the partial derivative of P_y is constructed as follows,

$$\frac{\partial P_y}{\partial \theta_2} = a_3 \cos \theta_2 \cos \theta_3 - a_3 \sin \theta_2 \sin \theta_2 + a_2 \cos \theta_2 \qquad (7)$$

$$\frac{\partial P_y}{\partial \theta_3} = a_3 \cos \theta_2 \cos \theta_3 - a_3 \sin \theta_2 \sin \theta_3 \qquad (8)$$

$$\frac{\partial P_y}{\partial \theta_2} - \frac{\partial P_y}{\partial \theta_3} = a_2 \cos \theta_2 \qquad (9)$$

Given the actual physical structure, we have $\theta_2 \in [0, \frac{\pi}{2}]$. Then, we can obtain

$$\frac{\partial P_y}{\partial \theta_2} > \frac{\partial P_y}{\partial \theta_3}. \qquad (10)$$

$$P_y' - P_y = \Delta P_y = \frac{\partial P_y}{\partial \theta_2} \Delta \theta \qquad (11)$$

$$P_y'' - P_y' = \Delta P_y' = \frac{\partial \Gamma_y}{\partial \theta_3} \Delta \theta \qquad (12)$$

With the constraint of (10), we have,

$$\Delta P_y > \Delta P_y' \qquad (13)$$

The results, as shown in (13), indicate that θ_3 cause a smaller change in the end position of the robotic arm when joint angle θ_2 and θ_3 change the same angle $\Delta \theta$. As can be seen from Fig. 3, when the joint near the pedestal and the joint near the end are identically rotated by $\Delta \theta$, the former one will change the position of the end of the arm more. In other words, when the endpoint of the robotic arm is near to the target, we don't need to change θ_2 a lot, just adjust θ_3. Therefore, we consider the joint information at the end of the robotic arm to be more important. We propose a weighted aggregate function:

$$\rho_{ij} = softmax(f_{ij}) = \frac{exp(f_{ij})}{\sum_{k \in N_i} exp(f_{ik})} \qquad (14)$$

where f_{ij} is the serial number of the node in the graph. The closer to the end of the robotic arm, the larger the serial number of the node. N_i is the set of nodes adjacent to node i.

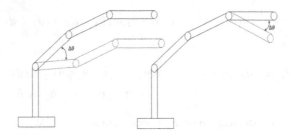

Fig. 3. Different joints with the same angle of rotation

4 Experiments

First, we evaluate the feasibility of GNN on a transfer learning task. In the second experiment, the improved GNN model is applied on a robotic arm with serial structure.

4.1 GNN Model

We run experiments on a simulated continuous control task from Gym, Brockman et al. [5], which is based on MuJoCo, Todorov et al. [24]. Particularly, we use a robotic arm task: PR2 arm. The maximum number of training steps is set to be 1 million for the PR2 arm task. In this paper, the proximal policy optimization (PPO) [22] is used to optimize the expected reward.

Two types of structural transfer learning tasks are investigated in this paper. The first type is to train a model with a robotic arm of small size (small graph) and apply the learned model to a robotic arm with a larger size. As increasing the size of the robotic arm, state and action space also increase which makes learning more difficult. In the second type of structural transfer task, we first learn a model for the robotic arm and then apply it to the robotic arm with a smaller size. Note that for both transfer tasks, none of the environmental factors change except the structure of the robotic arm.

Experimental Settings: The environment in which the agent has a similar structure to a PR2 arm is created in this paper. The goal of the agent is to get the end of the PR2 arm to the target point. By linking copies of arms, we create agents with different lengths. Specifically, the shorter arm consists of seven joints and the longer one is made up of eight joints. For each time step, the total reward is the negative value of the distance from the end of the arm to the target point.

Results: In the PR2 environment, we first run experiments of GNN models on PR2 with seven joints and PR2 with eight joints to get the pre-trained models for transfer learning.

This work then explores the transfer performance of GNN applied in PR2 environment in a zero-shot setting where zero-shot means directly applying the model trained with one structure to the other without any fine-tuning. The zero-shot transfer performance for PR2 arm is shown in Fig. 4. As we can see, GNN model does not achieve satisfactory transfer performance on PR2 tasks. On one hand, GNN has an average reward value of -135.02 when the policy learned from the PR2 arm with 8 joints is applied to the PR2 arm with 7 joints. On the other hand, GNN model has an average reward value of -266.13 when we apply the policy learned from the PR2 arm with 7 joints to the PR2 arm with 8 joints. Neither of them is a pretty good policy since the average reward value of -60 is considered as solved for the PR2 task. Consequently, GNN models can be used to learn structured policies. Furthermore, GNN model does not achieve good transfer performance for transfer learning tasks in a zero-shot setting.

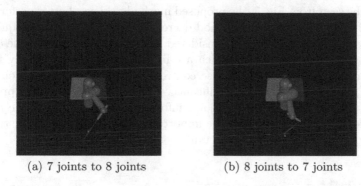

(a) 7 joints to 8 joints   (b) 8 joints to 7 joints

Fig. 4. Results on zero-shot transfer learning on the PR2 arm

4.2   The Proposed Method

In this section, we show that GNN model has excellent transfer performance for PR2 arms in a few-shot learning setting. And then it is experimentally shown that the proposed method has a better potential of transfer learning by incorporating physical structure prior into the network structure.

Experimental Settings: To show the better transfer performance of our proposed method, we compare our proposed method with the NerveNet [26]. More specifically, for the PR2 task, we use an equal number of time steps for each policy's update and calculate the information separately. For NerveNet, information is aggregated and the mean value of information is applied to update the network. While the proposed method adopts the weighted value of information to update the network.

Results: For the PR2 environment, we first run experiments of two models on PR2 with six joints and PR2 with seven joints to get the pre-trained models for transfer learning.

Table 2. Result of the proposed method

Model	Average reward	Solved time (number of iterations)
NerveNet	−30.26	264
Our proposed method	−27.57	192

We fine-tune for two kinds of transfer experiments and show the training curves in Fig. 5. From the figure, we can see that by using the pre-trained model, GNN model significantly decreases the number of episodes required to reach the level of reward which is considered as solved. In conclusion, GNN model can achieve satisfactory transfer performance in a few-shot learning setting.

As can be seen from Fig. 5, the proposed method achieves better performance in the PR2 task. The proposed method decreases about 27.3% time required to reach the level of reward which is considered as solved and increases the control accuracy by about 8.8% points, which are listed in Table 2. Especially for the robotic arm tasks that require precise control, the increase of 8.8% points has important practical application significance. The improvement of the proposed method is due to the fact that the joint information at the end of the robotic arm with serial structures to be more important, which accelerates the training process and improves the control accuracy.

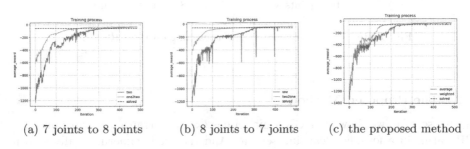

(a) 7 joints to 8 joints   (b) 8 joints to 7 joints   (c) the proposed method

Fig. 5. (a), (b): Results of fine-tuning for structural transfer learning tasks. (c): Results of the proposed method.

5   Conclusion

In this paper, we aim to explore whether applying GNN to a robotic arm with serial structure has good transfer performance. This work introduces an improved model that employs the weighted GNN model to represent the policy of the agent. The proposed model learns structured policies by aggregating and propagating information among joints. Aggregation is done by the proposed aggregation method which considers information of joint at the end of the robotic arm to be more important. The weighted aggregation method is proposed in this paper, which is specially designed for robotic arms with serial structures. The experiment in this work showed that the GNN model achieved good transfer performance on robotic arms in standard benchmark platform. Furthermore, we demonstrate that policies learned by the proposed model are significantly better than policies learned by traditional GNN models.

References

1. Ammar, H.B., Eaton, E., Ruvolo, P., Taylor, M.: Unsupervised cross-domain transfer for policy gradient reinforcement learning via manifold alignment. In: Twenty-Ninth AAAI Conference on Artificial Intelligence (2015)
2. Ammar, H.B., Taylor, M.E.: Reinforcement learning transfer via common subspaces. In: Vrancx, P., Knudson, M., Grześ, M. (eds.) ALA 2011. LNCS (LNAI), vol. 7113, pp. 21–36. Springer, Heidelberg (2012). https://doi.org/10.1007/978-3-642-28499-1_2
3. Barabási, A.L., et al.: Network Science. Cambridge University Press, Cambridge (2016)
4. Battaglia, P.W., et al.: Relational inductive biases, deep learning, and graph networks. arXiv preprint arXiv:1806.01261 (2018)
5. Brockman, G., et al.: OpenAI gym. arXiv preprint arXiv:1606.01540 (2016)
6. Chang, M.B., Ullman, T., Torralba, A., Tenenbaum, J.B.: A compositional object-based approach to learning physical dynamics. arXiv preprint arXiv:1612.00341 (2016)
7. Daftry, S., Bagnell, J.A., Hebert, M.: Learning transferable policies for monocular reactive MAV control. In: Kulić, D., Nakamura, Y., Khatib, O., Venture, G. (eds.) ISER 2016. SPAR, vol. 1, pp. 3–11. Springer, Cham (2017). https://doi.org/10.1007/978-3-319-50115-4_1
8. Devin, C., Gupta, A., Darrell, T., Abbeel, P., Levine, S.: Learning modular neural network policies for multi-task and multi-robot transfer. In: 2017 IEEE International Conference on Robotics and Automation (ICRA), pp. 2169–2176. IEEE (2017)
9. Franco, S., Marco, G., Ah Chung, T., Markus, H., Gabriele, M.: The graph neural network model. IEEE Trans. Neural Netw. **20**(1), 61 (2009)
10. Gu, S., Holly, E., Lillicrap, T., Levine, S.: Deep reinforcement learning for robotic manipulation with asynchronous off-policy updates. In: IEEE International Conference on Robotics and Automation (2017)
11. Gupta, A., Devin, C., Liu, Y., Abbeel, P., Levine, S.: Learning invariant feature spaces to transfer skills with reinforcement learning. arXiv preprint arXiv:1703.02949 (2017)
12. Hamrick, J.B., et al.: Relational inductive bias for physical construction in humans and machines. arXiv preprint arXiv:1806.01203 (2018)
13. Hamrick, J.B., Ballard, A.J., Pascanu, R., Vinyals, O., Heess, N., Battaglia, P.W.: Metacontrol for adaptive imagination-based optimization. arXiv preprint arXiv:1705.02670 (2017)
14. Hoshen, Y.: VAIN: attentional multi-agent predictive modeling. In: Advances in Neural Information Processing Systems, pp. 2701–2711 (2017)
15. Kipf, T., Fetaya, E., Wang, K.C., Welling, M., Zemel, R.: Neural relational inference for interacting systems. arXiv preprint arXiv:1802.04687 (2018)

16. Levine, S., Finn, C., Darrell, T., Abbeel, P.: End-to-end training of deep visuomotor policies. J. Mach. Learn. Res. **17**(1), 1334–1373 (2015)
17. Li, Y., Tarlow, D., Brockschmidt, M., Zemel, R.: Gated graph sequence neural networks. arXiv preprint arXiv:1511.05493 (2015)
18. Metz, L., Ibarz, J., Jaitly, N., Davidson, J.: Discrete sequential prediction of continuous actions for deep RL. arXiv preprint arXiv:1705.05035 (2017)
19. Rusu, A.A., et al.: Progressive neural networks. arXiv preprint arXiv:1606.04671 (2016)
20. Sanchez-Gonzalez, A., et al.: Graph networks as learnable physics engines for inference and control. arXiv preprint arXiv:1806.01242 (2018)
21. Scarselli, F., Gori, M., Tsoi, A.C., Hagenbuchner, M., Monfardini, G.: Computational capabilities of graph neural networks. IEEE Trans. Neural Netw. **20**(1), 81–102 (2008)
22. Schulman, J., Wolski, F., Dhariwal, P., Radford, A., Klimov, O.: Proximal policy optimization algorithms. arXiv preprint arXiv:1707.06347 (2017)
23. Taylor, M.E., Stone, P.: Transfer learning for reinforcement learning domains: a survey. J. Mach. Learn. Res. **10**(10), 1633–1685 (2009)
24. Todorov, E., Erez, T., Tassa, Y.: MuJoCo: a physics engine for model-based control. In: 2012 IEEE/RSJ International Conference on Intelligent Robots and Systems, pp. 5026–5033. IEEE (2012)
25. Toyer, S., Trevizan, F., Thiébaux, S., Xie, L.: Action schema networks: generalised policies with deep learning. In: Thirty-Second AAAI Conference on Artificial Intelligence (2018)
26. Wang, T., Liao, R., Ba, J., Fidler, S.: NerveNet: learning structured policy with graph neural networks (2018)
27. Wilson, M., Spong, M.W.: Robot modeling and control. Ind. Robot Int. J. **17**(5), 709–737 (2006)

Visualizing Readable Instance Graphs of Ontology with Memo Graph

Fatma Ghorbel[1,2]([⊠]), Wafa Wali[2]([⊠]), Fayçal Hamdi[1],
Elisabeth Métais[1], and Bilel Gargouri[2]

[1] CEDRIC Laboratory, Conservatoire National des Arts et Métiers (CNAM),
Paris, France
fatmaghorbel6@gmail.com,
{faycal.hamdi,metais}@cnam.fr
[2] MIRACL Laboratory, University of Sfax, Sfax, Tunisia
{wafa.wali,bilel.gargouri}@fsegs.rnu.tn

Abstract. In the context of the Captain Memo memory prosthesis for Alzheimer's patients, we want to generate the family/entourage tree of the user from data structured based on the PersonLink ontology. This graph ought to be accessible and readable to this particular user. In our previous work, we proposed an ontology visualization tool called Memo Graph. It aims to offer an accessible visualization to Alzheimer's patients. In this paper, we extend it to address the readability requirement based on the IKIEV approach. It extracts the most important instances (key-instances) from ontology and generates a "summary instance graph" (middle-out browsing method). The extraction and visualization processes are undertaken incrementally. First, an "initial summary instance graph" is generated, then permitting iteratively the visualization of supplementary key-instances as required. Key-instances' extraction is based on measures that take into account the semantic similarity between the ontological elements and the user's navigation history.

Keywords: Ontology visualization · Readable visualization · Ontology summarization · Key-instances · Alzheimer's patients

1 Introduction

In the context of the VIVA[1] project (*"Vivre à Paris avec Alzheimer en 2030 grâce aux nouvelles technologies"*), we are proposing a memory prosthesis, called Captain Memo [1], to help Alzheimer's patients to palliate mnesic problems. Patient's data are structured using PersonLink [2] which is a multilingual ontology for modeling and reasoning about interpersonal relationships and describing people. Among the services proposed by this prosthesis, one is devoted to "remember things about people" via the generation of the family/entourage tree of the patient from their stored data. Hence, there is a need to integrate in Captain Memo an ontology visualization tool.

---

[1] http://viva.cnam.fr/.

© Springer Nature Switzerland AG 2019
T. Gedeon et al. (Eds.): ICONIP 2019, LNCS 11955, pp. 127–139, 2019.
https://doi.org/10.1007/978-3-030-36718-3_11

Alzheimer's patients present own characteristics that are different from non-expert users. Some of these characteristics are related to Alzheimer's disease (e.g., concentration deficit) and the others are related to aging (e.g., sight loss). These characteristics impair this particular user to interact with graphs offered by standard ontology visualization tools targeting non-expert users e.g., Alzheimer's patients have difficulty to read small nodes; do not understand technical jargon and lose concentration when reading dense and crowded graphs. Hence, there is a need to integrate in Captain Memo an ontology visualization tool that generates an instance graph which has the particularity to be accessible and readable to Alzheimer's patients. Few ontology visualization tools have been proposed to be used by non-expert users.

However, to the best of our knowledge, there is no existing tool that is proposed to be used by Alzheimer's patients. In [3], we proposed a tool, called Memo Graph, which aims to offer accessible ontology visualizations to Alzheimer's patients.

In this paper, we propose an extension of Memo Graph that addresses the readability requirement based on the IKIEV approach (Incremental Key- Instances Extraction and Visualization). The aim is to alleviate the generated graph. It extracts and visualizes, in an incremental way, instance summarizations of a given ontology to offer concise and readable overviews and support a middle-out navigation method, starting from the most important instances (Key-instances). The extraction of the last ones is based measures that take into account the semantic similarity between the ontological elements and the user's navigation history.

The remainder of the present paper is structured as follows. In Sect. 2, we focus on related work. Section 3 presents our first version of Memo Graph. Section 4 presents the IKIEV approach. Section 5 details the evaluation results. In Sect. 6, we present the conclusions and some future research directions.

2 Related Work

The present work is closely related to the two following research areas: *(i)* ontology visualization and *(ii)* ontology summarization.

2.1 Ontology Visualization

Several ontology visualization tools have been proposed in the last two decades. Most of them target expert users. Only very few tools target non-expert users e.g., OWLeasyViz [4], WebVOWL [5] and ProtégéVOWL [5]. However, they are not designed to be used by Alzheimer's patients.

Most tools offer understandable visualizations only for expert users. ezOWL [6], OWLGrEd [7], and VOM[2] offer UML-based visualizations. A major drawback of these tools is that they require knowledge about UML. Thus, they are understandable only for expert users. In the same way, SOVA[3] and GrOWL [8] contain many abbreviations

---

[2] http://thematix.com/tools/vom.

[3] http://protegewiki.stanford.edu/wiki/SOVA.

and symbols from the Description Logic. Besides, almost all tools use technical jargon. For instance, WebVOWL and ProtégéVOWL, targeting users less familiar with ontologies, use some Semantic Web words.

Most tools overlook the importance of the readability requirement. According to [5], the current generated visualizations are hard to read for non-expert users. This problem becomes worse with Alzheimer's patients. For instance, SOVA, GrOWL, IsaViz[4] and RDF Gravity[5] require the loading of the entire graph in the limited space provided by the computer screen which generates an important number of nodes and a large number of crossing edges. Without applying any filter technique, the generated graphs appear crowded, which have a bad impact on their readability.

Only few tools aim for a comprehensive ontology visualization. For instance, OWLViz[6] and KC-Viz [9] visualize merely the class hierarchy of the ontology. OntoViz Tab [10], TGViz [11] and OntoRama [12] show only inheritance relationships between the graph nodes. Likewise, many visualization tools, like Jambalaya [13] and OWLPropViz[7], represent all types of property relations, but do not show datatype properties required to fully understand the data modeled in ontologies. Besides, most tools do not offer a clear visual distinction between the different ontology key-elements. For example, there is no visual distinction between datatype and object properties visualized by RDF Gravity. TGViz and NavigOWL [14] use a plain nodelink diagram where all links and nodes appear the same except for their color.

2.2 Ontology Summarization

Ontology summarization is the process of extracting knowledge from ontology to propose an abridged version for particular user(s) and task(s) [15]. It helps to quickly make sense of ontology. However, a "good" summary is a non-trivial task [16]. Several approaches have been proposed to identify important components in ontology.

Peroni et al. [17] propose an ontology summarization approach based on a number of measures, drawn from cognitive science (*Name Simplicity* and *Basic Level*), network topology (*Density* and *Coverage*) and lexical statistics (*Popularity*). *Name simplicity* favors classes labeled with simple names and penalizes compounds. *Basic Level* measures how "central" a class is in the taxonomy of the ontology. *Density* is computed on the basis of the number of direct instances, sub-classes and properties.

Coverage aims to show how well the selected classes are spread over the whole class hierarchy. The *Popularity* measure is introduced to indentify classes that are commonly visited based on the Yahoo search history.

Pires et al. [18] propose an approach to summarize ontologies based on two measures. The *Degree Centrality* measure is based on the number of properties of the class. The *Frequency* is used as a distinguishing criterion if the ontologies to be summarized are merged ontologies. The combination of two measures is defined as a

---

[4] https://www.w3.org/2001/11/IsaViz/overview.html.

[5] http://semweb.salzburgresearch.at/apps/rdf-gravity/.

[6] http://protegewiki.stanford.edu/wiki/OWLViz.

[7] http://protegewiki.stanford.edu/wiki/OWLPropViz.

Relevance score. This score needs to be greater than or equal to a given threshold to consider the class as a good candidate for the summary.

Queiroz-Sousa et al. [19] propose an algorithm to summarize ontology in two ways: automatically, using the Relevance measure and semi-automatically, using the users' opinion. For the first step, they introduce the Relevance measure which is inspired from the Degree Centrality measure. It is determined through the sum of the properties that class has. However, this algorithm produces summaries which include nodes that are already represented by other nodes.

Troullinou et al. [16] propose an approach to summarize RDF schemas. In the first step, the importance of each property is determined through the Relative Cardinality. This measure is based on the number of corresponding instances of the property. In the next step, the importance of each node is estimated by combining the Relative Cardinality and number of the edges (In/Out Degree Centrality). Compared to other approaches that estimate the importance of a class based on the number of its associated properties, they take into account not only the number of these properties, but their importance. The final step in this approach is generating valid sub-schema graphs that cover more relevant nodes by minimizing their overlaps.

We note that the majority of the measures are common to more than one approach. For instance, three approaches estimate the importance of a concept from its associated properties (Degree Centrality [18], Relevance [19] and In/Out Degree Centrality [16]). Furthermore, we criticize the fact that none of the mentioned measures allows estimating the importance of the ontological components based on their "semantics" (semantic similarity). For instance, in the context of PersonLink, it is obvious that the object property "doctor" related to the instance representing the "patient" is more important than the object property "butcher". Finally, these approaches focus only on summarizing the schema. They do not define measures to identify important instance in ontology.

3   Background: The Memo Graph Ontology Visualization Tool

Memo Graph is a tool that visualizes ontology. It aims to offer an accessible graph to Alzheimer's patients. The graph design is based on our 146 guidelines for designing user interfaces dedicated to Alzheimer's patients, presented in [20]. The generated graph has the adequate size of nodes and text. An auditory background is added to help users in their interactions. For instance, if they position the cursor on the keyword search field, they are informed that they can search a given element in the graph via an input field. We provide the traditional and speech-to-text modalities. We use easy-to-understand wording. For instance, we do not use Semantic Web vocabulary. Graph nodes are identified using both photos and labels. The photo facilitates the comprehension. It can be automatically added from Google if it is not given by the user. Nodes representing classes are slightly larger than nodes representing instances. Memo Graph offers the interaction techniques detailed by Shneiderman [21]: zoom, overview, details-on-demand, filter, history, relate and extract.

We evaluated the accessibility of the generated graph with 22 Alzheimer's patients. We noticed that they lose concentration when reading dense entourage/family graph. Thus, we extend Memo Graph based on the IKIEV approach.

4 Extending Memo Graph: The IKIEV Approach

In this paper, we extend Memo Graph. Its second version is based on the IKIEV approach. It tends to avoid problems related to dense and non-legible instance graph by limiting the number of visible nodes and preserving the most important ones. It allows an incremental extraction and visualization of instance summaries of the ontology – *incremental* being the operative word. Initially, it generates an "initial summary instance graph" of N_0 key-instances with the associated properties, then allowing iteratively the visualization of supplementary key-instances as required (key-instances are visualized as nodes and properties are visualized as labeled edges). For each iteration i, it extracts and visualizes $N_i = N_{i-1} + A_i$ key-instances; where A_i represents the number of additional key-instances compared to the previous iteration. N_0 and A_i are set by the user. Figure 1 summarizes the IKIEV approach.

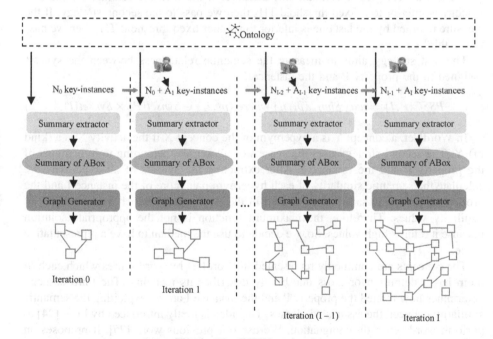

Fig. 1. The IKIEV approach.

4.1 Measures Determining Key-Instances

We present the properties that a sub-graph of the initial instance graph is required to have in order to be considered a high-quality summary. Compared to related work, the

generated summary is determined takes into account the "semantic" dimension as it favors properties which are semantically related to the associated instance. Besides, the generated summary is "personalized" as it depends on the user's navigation history when navigating the generated graph. Initially, we determine how important the properties are (*Property Centrality*). Based on the importance of the last ones, we estimate the centrality of the instances (*Instance Centrality*).

Estimating the Importance of a Property. We introduce the *Property Centrality* measure to estimate the importance of a given property. It is estimated based on the *Property Semantic Similarity Centrality* and *Property History Centrality* measures.

Property Semantic Similarity Centrality (PSSC). It aims to estimate the semantic similarity between a property P and an instance I. We exploit the WordNet features ("is a" taxonomy) coupled with the Lin formula [22].

$$Sim_{Lin}(P, I) = (2 \times IC(MSCA(P, I))/(IC(P) + IC(I)) \tag{1}$$

MSCA is the Most Specific Common Abstraction. In our approach, we use the Information Content (IC) metric proposed by [23].

We use 3 strategies to estimate this measure. If the measure returned by the first strategy is inferior to a fixed threshold TH_1 then we pass to the second strategy. If the measure returned by the last one is inferior to another fixed threshold TH_2 then we pass to the third strategy.

The first strategy aims to measure the semantic relatedness between the synsets assigned to the property P and the instance I.

$$PSSC(P, I) = max\ Sim_{Lin}(p_k, i_k)\ where\ (p_k, i_k) \in Synset(P) \times Synset(I) \tag{2}$$

In WordNet, a concept Y is a hypernym of the concept X if the activity X is a (kind of) Y. The second strategy uses the synsets of all synsets belonging to hypernyms of the property P and the instance I. After extracting the synsets of all hypernym, we calculate the semantic similarity of each hypernym pair score of the instance I and the property P using the same measure used in the first strategy which give a variety of similarity values. Therefore, the maximum function is not the appropriate solution because it returns high values. So, we decide to use the median to have a representative value.

The concepts are commonly represented in WordNet by word senses which each of them has a definition or gloss that briefly describes its meaning. The third strategy determines how related the property P and the instance I are by exploiting the semantic similarity between the associated glosses. This idea is firstly introduced by Lesk [24] to perform word sense disambiguation. We use our previous work [25]. It proposes an approach that estimates the semantic similarity between sentences (glosses are considered as sentences) based on three similarity scores: lexical, semantic and syntactico-semantic similarity scores.

The lexical similarity score exploits the shared words (overlaps) in the word senses of the glosses using Jaccard similarity [26].

$$Sim_L(G_P, G_I) = W_C/(W_{GP} + W_{GI} - W_C) \tag{3}$$

Where W_C is the number of common words between the two glosses; W_{GP} is the number of words contained in the gloss W_{GP} associated to the property P and W_{GI} is the number of words contained in the gloss W_{GI} associated to the instance I.

To determine the semantic similarity score, we associate the Semantic Vectors to each gloss. The number of entries of each vector is equal to the number of distinct words in the associated gloss. We associate the synonymy set of each word. After that, we calculate the degree of similarity between them using the Jaccard coefficient. On the basis of the calculated semantic vectors, the semantic similarity degree, is computed between the two glosses by applying the Cosine similarity

$$Sim_S(G_P, G_I) = V_{GP} \times V_{GI}/(||V_{GP}|| \times ||V_{GI}||) \tag{4}$$

The syntactico-semantic similarity score takes into account the common semantic arguments between the definitions notably the semantic class and the thematic role. It uses the Jaccard similarity.

$$Sim_{SS}(G_P, G_I) = AS_C/(AS_{GP} + AS_{GI} - AS_C) \tag{5}$$

Where AS_C is the number of common semantic arguments between the two glosses; AS_{GP} is the number of semantic arguments contained in the gloss G_P and AS_{GI} is the number of semantic arguments contained in the gloss G_I.

Finally, we estimate the semantic similarity between the property and the instance using a weighted sum of the mentioned scores.

$$PSSC(P, I) = Sim_L(G_P, G_I) \times W_L + Sim_S(G_P, G_I) \times W_S + Sim_{SS}(G_P, G_I) \times W_{SS} \tag{6}$$

Property History Centrality (PHC). This measure identifies the properties that are commonly visited by the users based on user's navigation history.

$$PHC(P) = MGH(P) \times W_H + MGS(P) \times W_S \tag{7}$$

MGH(P) returns the number of hits of P recorded in previous sessions by the user in Memo Graph (We use the click-tracking tool). *MGS(P)* returns the number of searches when querying the ontology with the name of P as a keyword.

Instance History Centrality. This measure identifies the instances that are commonly visited by the user. Compared to the *Popularity* measure, based on the Yahoo search history, this measure makes the generated summary "Personalized" in the sense that it is based on user's navigation history when navigating the generated graph.

$$PHC(I) = MGH(I) * W_H + MGS(I) * W_S \tag{8}$$

Property Centrality (PC). The mentioned measures are used as a weighted sum in an overall value to estimate the importance of a property P.

$$PC(P) = PSSC(P) * W_{SS} + PHC(P) * W_H \tag{9}$$

Estimating the Importance of an Instance. We introduce the *Instance Centrality* measure to estimate the importance of a given instance. It is estimated based on the *Instance Properties Centrality* and *Instance History Centrality* measures.

Instance Properties Centrality (IPC). This measure is based on the structure of the instance graph. It is an adaptation of the In/Out Centrality [16] measure. The Instance Properties Centrality of an instance is the sum of the Property Centrality of the associated object and datatype properties.

$$IPC(I) = \sum_{i=1}^{m} PC(Pi) \tag{10}$$

M is the number of incoming/outgoing object properties and datatype properties.

Instance History Centrality (IHC). This measure identifies the instances that are commonly visited by the user. Compared to the Popularity measure, based on the Yahoo search history, this measure makes the generated summary "Personalized" in the sense that it is based on user's navigation history when navigating the generated graph.

$$IHC(I) = MGH(I) * W_H + MGS(I) * W_S \tag{11}$$

Instance Centrality (IC). We rank instances based on their Instance Centrality. A higher score for an instance means that it is more adequate for the summary.

$$IC(I) = PHC(I) * W_H + PHC(I) * W_P \tag{12}$$

4.2   General Algorithm

The general algorithm of our IKIEV approach is given below.

Inputs: *Ontology O (N is the number of instances), Initial number of key-instances N0*
Outputs: *"Summary instance graphs"*
For each instance $n_i \in N$
    Calculate the Importance Score (n_i);
Extract N_0 key-instances having the highest score and enrich the last ones with properties;
Generate an "initial summary instance graph" (N_0 nodes);
While (The user needs to display Ai further nodes AND [$N_{i-1} + A_i$] $\leq |N|$) do
    Extract the [$N_{i-1} + A_i$] key-instances having the highest importance score and enrich
    the last ones with properties; Update the "summary instance graph" ; i := i + 1;

Algorithm 1. The general algorithm of the proposed IKIEV approach.

5   Experimentation

The IKIEV approach is implemented using the J2EE platform. We use the JENA[8] API
for managing ontology and the JWNL[9] API to connect to WorldNet.

5.1   Integration of Memo Graph in Captain Memo

We integrated Memo Graph in Captain Memo to generate the patient family/entourage
tree from data structured using PersonLink. Figure 2 shows a summary instance graph
generated using Memo Graph. It shows 10 key-instances. The total of instances is 217.
As PersonLink manage interpersonal relationships, the Hits Centrality measure takes
into account the history of the user hits when using social networks.

Fig. 2.   A family/entourage tree created based on Memo Graph.

5.2   Other Applications

Memo Graph can be used by expert and non-expert users to offer readable graphs not
only of small-scale inputs, but also for large-scale ones thanks to the IKIEV approach.

Visualization of a Large-Scale Dataset for Ontology Expert Users.   Memo Graph is
tested on the large-scale DBpedia dataset which is a semantic knowledge base built
from structured and extracted information from Wikipedia. Memo Graph tends to avoid
the problems of scalability by limiting the number of visible nodes. It extracts the key-
instances, while hiding away the "less important" ones. Figure 3 shows that Memo is
used for visualizing $N_1 = 30$ key-instances of the "Sport" class.

---

[8] https://jena.apache.org/.

[9] http://jwordnet.sourceforge.net/handbook.html.

Fig. 3. Visualizing 30 key-instances of the "Sport" class (DBpedia) with Memo Graph.

Visualization of LingOnto for Ontology Non-expert Users (Linguistic Experts).
Neji et al. [27] proposed a semantic approach that aims to identify valid linguistic web services composition scenarios and targets both linguistic experts (non-ontology expert). It is based on a multilingual ontology, called LingOnto, which models and reasons about linguistic knowledge. It consists of three steps. The first step consists in generating, from LingOnto, a dynamic ontological view that aims to highlight the components that correspond to the user's need. In the second step, the ontological view is used to identify an initial composition scenario by selecting a sequence of linguistic processing. The final step helps discover linguistic web services corresponding to each selected linguistic processing. The kernel of Memo Graph is integrated in the prototype of this approach. We select the "Lemmatization" class node to display the associated datatype property (description) (Fig. 4).

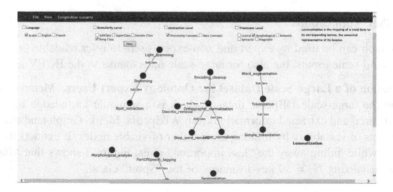

Fig. 4. Visualizing LingOnto with Memo Graph.

5.3   Evaluation

We evaluate the usability of our approach IKIEV in determining the key-instances. This evaluation is done in the context of Captain Memo. A total of 12 Alzheimer's patients $\{P_1 \ldots P_{12}\}$ and their associated caregivers $\{C_1 \ldots C_{12}\}$ were recruited. All caregivers are first-degree relatives. Let us consider $\{KB_1 \ldots KB_{12}\}$, where KB_i represents knowledge base associated to P_i and structured using PersonLink. The number of the key-instances is set as 10. Three scenarios are proposed:

- "Golden standard scenario": Each caregiver C_i is requested to identify the 10 closest relatives of the patient P_i. The last ones formed the "gold standard" GS_i.
- "IKIEV scenario @ 2 weeks": For each KB_i, we associate a summary Si@2 based on our IKIEV approach. The summaries are generated after 2 weeks of using and interacting with the resulting graph.
- "IKIEV scenario @ 10 weeks": For each KB_i, we associate a summary Si@10 based on our IKIEV approach. The summaries are generated after 10 weeks of using and interacting with the resulting graph.

We compare the generated summaries against the golden standard ones. PRi@2 $(|Si@2 \cap GSi|/|Si@2|)$ and PRi@10 represent respectively, the Precision associated to "IKIEV scenario @ 2 weeks" and "IKIEV scenario @ 10 weeks" (Fig. 5).

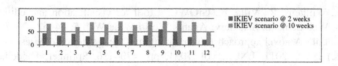

Fig. 5. Evaluation's results.

All entities of KBi are instances of the same class (Person). Thus, the *Class Centrality* measure has no influence on determining key-instances.

The overall mean of the precision associated to "IKIEV scenario @ 10 weeks" is better than the overall mean of the precision associated to "IKIEV scenario @ 2 weeks". This difference is explained by the fact that the *Hits Centrality* measure is improved from one navigation session to another.

6 Conclusion

This paper introduced an extension of Memo Graph to offer readable instance visualizations. It is based on our IKIEV approach. It allows an incremental extraction and visualization of instance summaries of the ontology. To determinate the relevance of a given instance, we are based on the relevance of its associated class and properties as well as the history of its user hits. The proposed tool is integrated in the prototype of Captain Memo to generate the family/entourage tree of the Alzheimer's patient from their personal data structured using the PersonLink ontology. We evaluated the usability of our IKIEV approach in determining key-instances. The results are promising.

Future work will be devoted to extend our IKIEV approach to allow an incremental extraction and visualization of summaries of the ontology's schema.

References

1. Herradi, N., Hamdi, F., Métais, E., Ghorbel, F., Soukane, A.: PersonLink: an ontology representing family relationships for the CAPTAIN MEMO memory prosthesis. In: Jeusfeld, M.A., Karlapalem, K. (eds.) ER 2015. LNCS, vol. 9382, pp. 3–13. Springer, Cham (2015). https://doi.org/10.1007/978-3-319-25747-1_1
2. Ghorbel, F., Ellouze, N., Métais, E., Hamdi, F., Gargouri, F., Herradi, N.: MEMO GRAPH: an ontology visualization tool for everyone. In: KES 2016, York, United Kingdom, pp. 265–274 (2016). Procedia Comput. Sci.
3. Catenazzi, N., Sommaruga, L., Mazza, R.: User-friendly ontology editing and visualization tools: the OWLeasyViz approach. In: International Conference Information Visualisation (2013)
4. Lohmann, S., Negru, S., Haag, F., Ertl, T.: Visualizing ontologies with VOWL. Semant. Web 7, 399–419 (2016)
5. Chung, M., Oh, S., Kim, K., Cho, H., Cho, H.K.: Visualizing and authoring OWL in ezOWL. In: International Conference on Advanced Communication Technology (2005)
6. Bārzdiņš, J., Bārzdiņš, G., Čerāns, K., Liepiņš, R., Sproģis, A.: OWLGrEd: a UML style graphical notation and editor for OWL 2. In: OWL: Experiences and Directions Workshop (2010)
7. Krivov, S., Williams, R., Villa, F.: GrOWL: a tool for visualization and editing of OWL ontologies. Web Semant.: Sci. Serv. Agents World Wide Web 5, 54–57 (2007)
8. Motta, E., et al.: A novel approach to visualizing and navigating ontologies. In: Aroyo, L., et al. (eds.) ISWC 2011. LNCS, vol. 7031, pp. 470–486. Springer, Heidelberg (2011). https://doi.org/10.1007/978-3-642-25073-6_30
9. Singh, G., Prabhakar, T.V., Chatterjee, J., Patil, V.C., Ninomiya, S.: OntoViz: visualizing ontologies and thesauri using layout algorithms. In: Fifth International Conference of the Asian Federation for Information Technology in Agriculture (2006)
10. Harith, A.: TGVizTab: an ontology visualisation extension for Protégé. In: Knowledge Capture (2003)
11. Eklund, P., Nataliya, R., Green, S.: OntoRama: browsing RDF ontologies using aperbolic-style browser. In: First International Symposium on Cyber Worlds (2002)
12. Storey, M.A., et al.: Jambalaya: interactive visualization to enhance ontology authoring and knowledge acquisition in Protégé. In: Workshop on Interactive Tools for Knowledge Capture (K-CAP-2001) (2001)
13. Hussain, A., Latif, K., Rextin, A.T., Hayat, A., Alam, M.: Scalable visualization of semantic nets using power-law graph. In: Applied Mathematics and Information Sciences (2014)
14. Zhang, X., Cheng, G., Qu, Y.: Ontology summarization based on RDF sentence graph, pp. 707–716 (2007)
15. Troullinou, G., Kondylakis, H., Daskalaki, E., Plexousakis, D.: Ontology understanding without tears: the summarization approach. Semant. Web J. 8, 797–815 (2017)
16. Peroni, S., Motta, E., d'Aquin, M.: Identifying key concepts in an ontology, through the integration of cognitive principles with statistical and topological measures. In: Domingue, J., Anutariya, C. (eds.) ASWC 2008. LNCS, vol. 5367, pp. 242–256. Springer, Heidelberg (2008). https://doi.org/10.1007/978-3-540-89704-0_17
17. Pires, C.E., Sousa, P., Kedad, Z., Salgado, A.C.: Summarizing ontology-based schemas in PDMS. In: Data Engineering Workshops (ICDEW), pp. 239–244 (2010)
18. Queiroz-Sousa, P.O., Salgado, A.C., Pires, C.E.: A method for building personalized ontology summaries. J. Inf. Data Manag. 4, 236–250 (2013)

19. Ghorbel, F., Métais, E., Ellouze, N., Hamdi, F., Gargouri, F.: Towards accessibility guidelines of interaction and user interface design for Alzheimer's disease patients. In: Tenth International Conference on Advances in Computer-Human Interactions (2017)
20. Shneiderman, B.: The eyes have it: a task by data type taxonomy for information visualizations. In: Proceedings of the 1996 IEEE Symposium on Visual Languages (1996)
21. Lin, D.: An information-theoretic definition of similarity. In: International Conference on Machine Learning (1998)
22. Hadj Taieb, M.A., Ben Hamadou, A.: A new semantic relatedness measurement using WordNet features. Knowl. Inf. Syst. **41**(2), 467–497 (2014)
23. Lesk, M.: Automatic sense disambiguation using machine readable dictionaries: how to tell a pine cone from an ice cream cone. In: Proceedings of the 5th Annual International Conference on Systems Documentation (1986)
24. Wali, W., Gargouri, B., Ben Hamadou, A.: Using standardized lexical semantic knowledge to measure similarity. In: Buchmann, R., Kifor, C.V., Yu, J. (eds.) KSEM 2014. LNCS (LNAI), vol. 8793, pp. 93–104. Springer, Cham (2014). https://doi.org/10.1007/978-3-319-12096-6_9
25. Jaccard, P.: Etude comparative de la distribution orale dans une portion des Alpes et du Jura. In: Impr. Corbaz (1901)
26. Neji, M., Gargouri, B., Jmaiel, M.: A semantic approach for constructing valid composition scenarios of linguistic web services. In: KES (2017)

Spiking Neuron and Related Models

Hippocampus Segmentation in MRI Using Side U-Net Model

Wenbin Yao[✉], Shan Wang, and Huiyuan Fu

Beijing Key Laboratory of Intelligent Telecommunications Software and Multimedia,
Beijing University of Posts and Telecommunications, Beijing, China
yaowenbin_cdc@163.com

Abstract. Convolutional neural networks (CNN) have been applied in medical image analysis over the past few years. U-Net architecture is one of the most well-known CNN architectures in many different medical image segmentation tasks. However, it is hard to capture subtle local features because of its limitations in standard convolution layers and one output prediction. In addition, some objects like hippocampus in the biomedical image occupies an only small area which increases the difficulty of segmentation. In this manuscript, we present an architecture, called Side U-Net, which addresses these challenging problems. In the condition of giving unbalanced class images, Side U-Net outperforms the U-Net by upgrading loss function and capturing more important local features using multiple side outputs. And the experimental results verified our method and demonstrated that our method outperformed the U Net model over 0.75% in terms of dice score and in the same threshold of classification, our model has a higher TPR (True Positive Rate) when evaluated in ADNI dataset.

Keywords: Hippocampus segmentation · Cross entropy · Side U-Net architecture

1 Introduction

A medical image such as magnetic resonance imaging (MRI) can depict the different anatomical structures throughout the human body. The result from which are used to diagnose and treat disease. One of the significant processes is image segmentation which is often a prerequisite to further interventions in many different types of clinical applications.

In this manuscript, we focus on the segmentation of the hippocampus from MRI. The hippocampus is located in the medial temporal lobe. Changes in the size and shape of the hippocampus are closely related to Alzheimer's and other diseases. Hippocampus segmentation can facilitate possible biomarker identification, prognosis and diagnosis of diseases, and optimum treatment identification [7,10].

The manual segmentation of hippocampus is tedious, time-consuming. Some traditional automatic segmentation methods are almost based on atlas-based

© Springer Nature Switzerland AG 2019
T. Gedeon et al. (Eds.): ICONIP 2019, LNCS 11955, pp. 143–150, 2019.
https://doi.org/10.1007/978-3-030-36718-3_12

methods [19]. Multiple atlases are separately registered to the new target image to avoid biased registration [11,16]. A few pieces of research showed that multi-atlas segmentation approaches significantly have a better performance than a single atlas [4,19]. Other researches have proposed a patch-based segmentation (PBS) framework [1,15], because of the challenge in significant intersubject variability, only some of the subset of atlases are used to improve performance in both frameworks, which raises a new difficulty in atlases selection.

In recent year, deep learning has revolutionized computer vision with many excellent examples compared with prior state-of-the-art, especially the convolutional neural network (CNN) studies on image classification [6]. Gradually many researchers have started applying deep CNN to medical image filed like MRI segmentation lately [2,12,14], and significant progress has been achieved because of the advent of CNNs [5].

Among the different approaches that use CNNs for medical image segmentation, the U-Net [13] is trained in an end-to-end fashion yielding good segmentation results and this architecture is widely used as their flexible architectures. However, first, the only one output can not update the weights from multi-scale feature maps respectively which maybe result in gradient vanishing with the network deepening. Second, in MRI, the number of negative examples is far more than positive ones, and the latter is also hard to classify accurately, the cross-entropy loss function can not meet the requirement of accurate segmentation. In order to address these challenges and apply it into hippocampus segmentation, we proposed a Side U-Net model with a updated version of class balanced cross-entropy loss function. More specifically, our major contributions include the following:

- First, we extended the standard U-Net model for hippocampus segmentation by introducing multiple side outputs in the expanding path.
- Second, we combined all side outputs to update the weights in multi-scale feature maps in training phase.
- Third, we proposed a new version of the cross-entropy loss function to solve the unbalanced class images.

2   Related Works

U-Net Model. The basic image-to-image CNN architecture for many semantic segmentation problems is the fully convolutional network (FCN) [17], which consists of cascaded convolution, pooling, and deconvolution layers. The U-Net consists of a contracting path and an expanding path. In addition it proposed a skip connection between symmetrical layers in contracting and expanding path. This connection improves the network performance for remaining some local features in contracting path and combining them with corresponding upsampling layers.

Loss Function. Cross-entropy (CE) loss is for classification (shown in Eq. 1), where $y \in \{1, -1\}$ specifies the ground truth class and $p \in [0, 1]$ is the model's estimated probability for class with label $y = 1$.

$$CE(p, y) = \begin{cases} -log(p), & if \quad y = 1 \\ -log(1 - p), & otherwise. \end{cases} \tag{1}$$

Class-balanced cross entropy (BCE) loss function (shown in Eq. 2) performs well with unbalanced-class image [20] in multi-scale side outputs.

$$l_{side}^{(m)}(W, w^m) = -\beta \sum_{j \in Y_+} log Pr(y_i = 1 | X; W, w^{(m)})$$

$$- (1 - \beta) \sum_{j \in Y_-} log Pr(y_i = 0 | X; W, w^{(m)}) \tag{2}$$

Focal loss [8] was a reshaped cross entropy loss function to down-weight easy examples and focused on hard ones. The Eq. 3 is the Focal Loss that the implementation of the loss layer combines the sigmoid operation for computing p with the loss computation.

$$FL_{p_t} = -\alpha_t (1 - p_t)^\gamma log(p_t) \tag{3}$$

3   Proposed Method

3.1   Side U-Net Model

Figure 1 demonstrates our proposed Side U-Net model architecture. Like the U-Net, our model has a contracting path and an expanding path, five layers for contracting and four layers for expanding.

In the contracting phase, two convolution and one pool operations are included in every layer, the output of the second convolution operation in every layer was connected to the corresponding upsampling layers. For expanding, every step of upsampling is followed with a side output by deconvoluting to the same shape as the ground truth, all of four side outputs are fused then convoluted one more time so that the final output is a coalition which can take features in muti-scale maps into account. The weights from different layers can update by both the final output and side outputs to capture crucial features according to the corresponding reception field (RF) during training phase.

3.2   Loss Function

The main obstacle of small object segmentation is caused by imbalanced data distribution and difficulty of classification, because the pixel-wise labeling is required and small-area organs contribute less to the loss function. In our case, the area of hippocampus only takes about 0.6% of the whole MRI. The dice loss can be used to partly solve the issue by transporting pixel-wise labeling issue into

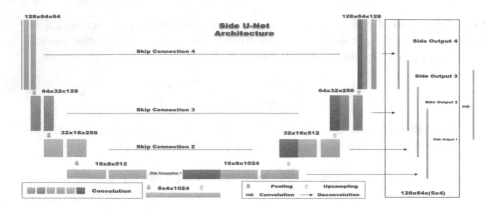

Fig. 1. There are nine layers in Side U-Net which are separated into two phases, encoding phase and decoding phase. Encoding phase capture the features by convolutional layer (in different colors) and pooling layers (orange arrows stand for pooling process). Decoding phase generates the prediction by four different side outputs from different layers. (Color figure online)

minimizing class-level distribution distance [9]. But it makes the optimization unstable in the extremely unbalanced segmentation [18]. The focal loss function we mentioned above in Eq. 3 introduced a multiplier $\alpha_t(1 - p_t)^\gamma$ to increase the importance of hard samples. But the multiplier α_t was fixed and classed-balance cross-entropy in Eq. 2 only worked with sigmoid operation in two-classification problem.

In terms of segmentation there are four types of pixel or four classes of sample on pixel according to a prediction compared with the ground-truth, true positive (TP), true negative (TN), false positive (FP) and false negative (FN). In our Side U-Net model, we employed a hybrid loss function consisting of contributions from both dice loss and the updated version of class-balanced cross entropy loss we proposed. The dice loss learns the class distribution alleviating the imbalanced pixel issue while the new cross entropy loss forces the model to learn poorly classified pixel better which also maintains crucial features. The total loss function is show as following.

$$TP_{p(c)} = \sum_{n=1,i=1}^{N} p_n(c_i)g_n(c_i) \tag{4}$$

$$FN_{p(c)} = \sum_{n=1,i=1}^{N} (1 - p_n(c_i))g_n(c_i) \tag{5}$$

$$FP_{p(c)} = \sum_{n=1,i=1}^{N} p_n(c_i)(1 - g_n(c_i)) \tag{6}$$

$$L = L_{dice} + L_{NCE}$$
$$= D + \lambda\mu(1 - p_n(c_i))^\gamma \sum_i g_n(c_i)log(p_n(c_i)) \tag{7}$$

Where $TP_{p(c)}$ is the true positives which is a vector keeping the prediction probabilities for class c_i, $FN_{p(c)}$ is the probabilities for false negatives and $FP_{p(c)}$ is the probabilities for false positives. $g_n(c)$ is the ground truth for pixel n being class c_i. $D = 2TP_p(c)/(FN_p(c) + TP_p(c) + FP_p(c))$, λ is the trade-off between dice loss L_{dice} and the new cross entropy loss L_{NCE}, μ is the dynamic multiplier whose function like the α_t in Focal Loss, $\mu = -(1 - TP_{mean}(c))$. And $TP_{mean}(c)$ is an average value of $TP_p(c)$.

4   Experiments and Results

4.1   Dataset and Setting

We used the publicly available dataset of T1-weighted MRI brain scans in ADNI [10]. There are different ages subjects in total dataset and we randomly selected 206 subjects. The segmentation was based on 2D images that resampled the brain slices to 256×128 pixels, and affinely align and crop the images to 128×64. We obtained anatomical segmentation maps and labels for all scans using Free-Surfer [3] and transformed them into 2D images. Using one-hot method to generate ground-truth. The ratio between training and testing set was 0.75, and in training set we divided it into two parts, training and validation. During every iteration we shuffled the images for each mini-patch in training set.

We implemented our Side U-Net model with updated cross entropy loss function using the TensorFlow framework with Python API and used the gradient descent method to train model. The learning ratio was set to 0.0001, number of iterations was 500 and batch was 20. We ran all experiments on NVIDIA-SMI 418.39. And augmented the training data by rotating and flipping.

4.2   Baseline and Comparison Result

Baseline and Evaluation Metrics. We trained and tested the 256 subjects in various methods including U-Net with cross-entropy (CE), class-balanced cross-entropy (BCE) and updated class-balanced cross-entropy (UBCE) respectively and Side U-Net with three types of cross-entropy loss function. In addition, we fine-tune the size of original U-Net to adjust our dataset.

Dice Similarity Coefficient (dice score) is used to evaluate the accuracy which is an overlapping coefficient between prediction and ground-truth. The evaluation was based on the whole hippocampus region (left and right), the choroid fissure region (left and right) and the temporal horn region (left and right), instead of individual hippocampus structure.

Comparison Result and Analysis. We list dice scores in three iterations, 100, 300 and 500 in Fig. 2. We can see that:

- only use UBCE (shown in Fig. 3(left)), the result is better than CE and BCE in three iterations.
- only use Side U-Net architecture (shown in Fig. 3(right)), the result is also better than the original U-Net architecture. Especially in the last iteration, the comparison is more obvious.
- use both Side U-Net and UBCE, the dice score is the highest in the all methods.

and the Fig. 4 shows the dice score in five iterations between 100 and 500 iterations in four parts in MRI, right parts keep increasing iteration by iteration, while left parts are unstable, but the last results both are better than the others.

Organ	Iteration	Dice(%)					
		CE		BCE		UBCE	
		Side U-Net	U-Net	Side U-Net	U-Net	Side U-Net	U-Net
Hippocampus (left)	100	45.127	51.208	84.927	54.874	86.721	83.221
	300	77.12	66.744	87.31	77.01	87.355	86.996
	500	77.552	66.932	89.69	79.974	**89.834**	87.504
Choroid Fissuerand TemporalHorn (left)	100	45.736	56.362	85.77	46.606	87.127	87.198
	300	75.601	67.692	87.1	74.575	87.243	87.195
	500	74.682	67.784	87.222	81.393	**89.825**	89.394
Hippocampus (right)	100	46.801	47.721	82.78	46.841	84.284	83.443
	300	73.772	63.43	87.248	77.392	87.311	87.169
	500	73.258	67.935	89.658	83.375	**89.814**	89.935
Choroid Fissuerand TemporalHorn (right)	100	45.051	54.727	86.565	57.387	84.25	82.338
	300	75.258	61.083	86.329	67.403	87.051	87.477
	500	77.894	64.546	87.249	84.415	**89.783**	89.41

Fig. 2. U-Net and Side U-Net with three loss functions.

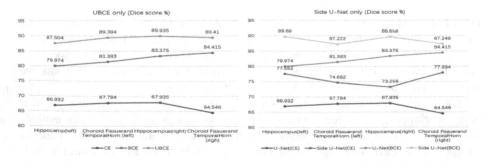

Fig. 3. The left graph shows dice score only UBCE applied in the U-Net and right graph shows the result only Side U-Net architecture applied.

In addition, we test different thresholds (0.6, 0.7, 0.8) of the classification in pixels and find when threshold is more than 0.8 our model has a better performance.

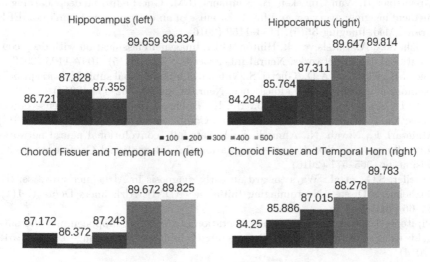

Fig. 4. This graph shows the dice score in four parts from 100th to 500th iteration as the interval of 100. The dice score fluctuates till about 400th iteration and remains stable and high in 500th iteration.

5 Discussion and Conclusion

In this manuscript, we proposed a novel model Side U-Net model based on U-Net. And got the average dice score 89.814% which was 0.75% more than U-Net model in our experiment condition. When enlarge the threshold of classification in pixels our model are more reliable.

References

1. Coupe, P., Manjon, J.V., Fonov, V., Pruessner, J.C., Robles, M., Collins, D.L.: Patch-based segmentation using expert priors: application to hippocampus and ventricle segmentation. NeuroImage **54**(2), 940–954 (2011)
2. Dhungel, N., Carneiro, G., Bradley, A.P.: Deep learning and structured prediction for the segmentation of mass in mammograms. In: Navab, N., Hornegger, J., Wells, W.M., Frangi, A.F. (eds.) MICCAI 2015. LNCS, vol. 9349, pp. 605–612. Springer, Cham (2015). https://doi.org/10.1007/978-3-319-24553-9_74
3. Fischl, B.: Freesurfer. NeuroImage **62**(2), 774–781 (2012). https://doi.org/10.1016/j.neuroimage.2012.01.021

4. Fritscher, K.D., Peroni, M., Zaffino, P., Spadea, M.F., Schubert, R., Sharp, G.: Automatic segmentation of head and neck CT images for radiotherapy treatment planning using multiple atlases, statistical appearance models, and geodesic active contours. Med. Phys. **41**(5), 051910 (2014)

5. Greenspan, H., Van Ginneken, B., Summers, R.M.: Guest editorial deep learning in medical imaging: overview and future promise of an exciting new technique. IEEE Trans. Med. Imaging **35**(5), 1153–1159 (2016)

6. Krizhevsky, A., Sutskever, I., Hinton, G.E.: Imagenet classification with deep convolutional neural networks. Neural Inf. Process. Syst. **141**(5), 1097–1105 (2012)

7. Lee, J.K., Ekstrom, A.D., Ghetti, S.: Volume of hippocampal subfields and episodic memory in childhood and adolescence. NeuroImage **94**, 162–171 (2014)

8. Lin, T., Goyal, P., Girshick, R.B., He, K., Dollar, P.: Focal loss for dense object detection. In: International Conference on Computer Vision, pp. 2999–3007 (2017)

9. Milletari, F., Navab, N., Ahmadi, S.: V-Net: fully convolutional neural networks for volumetric medical image segmentation. In: International Conference on 3D Vision, pp. 565–571 (2016)

10. Mueller, S.G., et al.: Ways toward an early diagnosis in Alzheimer's disease: the Alzheimer's Disease Neuroimaging Initiative (ADNI). Alzheimers Dement. **1**(1), 55–66 (2005)

11. Pipitone, J., et al.: Multi-atlas segmentation of the whole hippocampus and subfields using multiple automatically generated templates. NeuroImage **101**, 494–512 (2014)

12. Prasoon, A., Petersen, K., Igel, C., Lauze, F., Dam, E., Nielsen, M.: Deep feature learning for knee cartilage segmentation using a triplanar convolutional neural network. In: Mori, K., Sakuma, I., Sato, Y., Barillot, C., Navab, N. (eds.) MICCAI 2013. LNCS, vol. 8150, pp. 246–253. Springer, Heidelberg (2013). https://doi.org/10.1007/978-3-642-40763-5_31

13. Ronneberger, O., Fischer, P., Brox, T.: U-Net: convolutional networks for biomedical image segmentation. In: Navab, N., Hornegger, J., Wells, W.M., Frangi, A.F. (eds.) MICCAI 2015. LNCS, vol. 9351, pp. 234–241. Springer, Cham (2015). https://doi.org/10.1007/978-3-319-24574-4_28

14. Roth, H.R., et al.: DeepOrgan: multi-level deep convolutional networks for automated pancreas segmentation. In: Navab, N., Hornegger, J., Wells, W.M., Frangi, A.F. (eds.) MICCAI 2015. LNCS, vol. 9349, pp. 556–564. Springer, Cham (2015). https://doi.org/10.1007/978-3-319-24553-9_68

15. Rousseau, F., Habas, P.A., Studholme, C.: A supervised patch-based approach for human brain labeling. IEEE Trans. Med. Imaging **30**(10), 1852–1862 (2011)

16. Sharp, G., et al.: Vision 20/20: perspectives on automated image segmentation for radiotherapy. Med. Phys. **41**(5), 050902–050902 (2014)

17. Shelhamer, E., Long, J., Darrell, T.: Fully convolutional networks for semantic segmentation. IEEE Trans. Pattern Anal. Mach. Intell. **39**(4), 640–651 (2017)

18. Sudre, C.H., Li, W., Vercauteren, T., Ourselin, S., Cardoso, M.J.: Generalised dice overlap as a deep learning loss function for highly unbalanced segmentations. arXiv Computer Vision and Pattern Recognition, pp. 240–248 (2017)

19. Wu, G., Wang, Q., Zhang, D., Nie, F., Huang, H., Shen, D.: A generative probability model of joint label fusion for multi-atlas based brain segmentation. Med. Image Anal. **18**(6), 881–890 (2014)

20. Xie, S., Tu, Z.: Holistically-nested edge detection. In: International Conference on Computer Vision, pp. 1395–1403 (2015)

AutoML for DenseNet Compression

Wencong Jiao, Tao Li, Guoqiang Zhong$^{(\boxtimes)}$, and Li-Na Wang

Department of Computer Science and Technology, Ocean University of China,
Qingdao 266100, China
939843754@qq.com, 1403371024@qq.com, gqzhong@ouc.edu.cn, alinagq@163.com

Abstract. DenseNet, which connects each convolutional layer to all preceding layers, is a classic model of utilizing skip connections to improve the performance and learning efficiency of deep convolutional neural networks. However, many of the skip connections in DenseNet are redundant, which may lead to huge consumption of computational resources and computing time. In this paper, we propose an automatic model compression method based on reinforcement learning to prune redundant skip connections in DenseNet and improve its performance. We call the proposed method automatic DenseNet sparsification (ADS). ADS can be implemented with remarkable efficiency, for a 40-layer DenseNet, only running on 1 single GPU and taking less than 1 day. Experimental results on image classification tasks show that, the sparsified DenseNet outperforms not only the original DenseNet, but also related state-of-the-art deep architectures. Moreover, the sparsified DenseNet has strong transferability to new image classification tasks.

Keywords: Automatic model compression · Reinforcement learning · Sparsified DenseNet · Transferability

1 Introduction

In recent years, deep convolutional neural networks (CNNs) have been increasingly used in many pattern recognition and computer vision applications, such as image classification, object recognition and semantic segmentation [14]. Specifically, DenseNet is a classic CNNs model of utilizing skip connections by directly connecting each layer to all preceding layers (with matching feature map sizes) [12]. For an L-layer DenseNet, the lth layer has l inputs (consisting of the feature maps from all preceding dense blocks), and passes on its own feature maps to the rest $L - l$ layers. This dense connectivity induces $O(L^2)$ run-time complexity, which is excessively expensive. We hypothesize that much of the $O(L^2)$ computation is redundant, in that early features are not necessary to be useful for all the later layers. Moreover, DenseNet with this dense connectivity is usually restricted by its latency and model size budget in many real-world applications, e.g., in robotics, self-driving cars and mobile devices [8]. Therefore, it is crucial to remove redundant skip connections in DenseNet, so as to make it more efficient and accurate.

W. Jiao and T. Li—The authors have equal contributions.

© Springer Nature Switzerland AG 2019
T. Gedeon et al. (Eds.): ICONIP 2019, LNCS 11955, pp. 151–161, 2019.
https://doi.org/10.1007/978-3-030-36718-3_13

In this paper, we propose an automatic model compression method, called automatic DenseNet sparsification (ADS), to prune redundant skip connections in DenseNet and improve its efficiency. The target of ADS is to leverage reinforcement learning (RL) to find a well-performing sparsified DenseNet. In contrast to many existing network compression approaches [3,5,6,9], ADS can be implemented efficiently without specialized accelerator requirements. For a 40-layer DenseNet, it can run on 1 single GPU only with less than 1 day. Figure 1(a) illustrates the RL process of ADS. The RL agent takes actions to prune skip connections in DenseNet according to a certain compression ratio c, and then sample candidate sparsified models. The sampled models are then validated to obtain their prediction accuracies. The reward R, as a function with respect to the validation accuracies of the sparsified models, is used to update the parameters of the RL agent with policy gradient method. This RL process is iterated to learn better and better compression policies. Therefore, compared with other compression techniques on DenseNet [11,16], which mainly consider the channel pruning between adjacent layers, ADS focuses on reducing the redundant skip connections in DenseNet.

We have conducted extensive experiments to demonstrate the effectiveness and efficiency of ADS. Experimental results show that the automatically sparsified DenseNet can outperform not only the original DenseNet, but also related state-of-the-art networks. Besides, it has strong transferability to new image classification tasks.

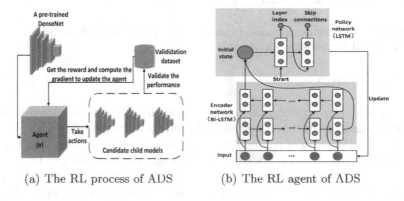

(a) The RL process of ADS   (b) The RL agent of ADS

Fig. 1. (a) shows the RL process of ADS; (b) shows the RL agent of ADS.

2 Related Work

In this section, we review some work related to model compression and DenseNet.

2.1 Model Compression

Deep neural networks usually have a substantial number of redundant parameters [6,15]. Many network compression methods has been proposed to reduce redundancies and computational costs in the networks, e.g., low-rank decomposition, weight quantization, knowledge distillation and weight pruning [3,5,6,9,15]. However, these conventional network compression methods usually require hand-crafted heuristics and domain expertise to explore the compression strategies for each layer, which is time-consuming. Recently, with the development of network architecture search (NAS) [2,19,20], there has arisen a growing interest in automatic model compression [1,8]. In [1], the authors implemented network compression by leveraging reinforcement learning (RL) and knowledge distillation. Additionally, He et al. proposed an automatic model compression (AMC) approach to compress deep CNNs with an RL algorithm in a layer-by-layer manner [8]. Both of these two methods mainly focus on layer removal or layer shrinkage, but neither of them can be directly used to remove skip connections in Densenet.

2.2 DenseNet

DenseNet concatenates feature maps from all previous layers of each layer as its inputs [12]. Although DenseNet has relatively better parameter efficiency compared with other networks including skip connections [7,17], there still exist redundancies. Some study has been conducted to alleviate the redundancies in DenseNet. [10] presented the Log-DenseNet, where each layer i was connected to $1 + log(i)$ previous layers in terms of human-designed principle. [16] proposed a network slimming method by employing $L1$ regularization on the scaling factors γ in the batch normalization (BN) layers to prune unimportant channels. [11] introduced the CondenseNet by learning group convolutions to remove superfluous connections between adjacent layers. Due to utilizing the concatenation operation, the redundancies in DenseNet are mostly resulted from the skip connections, but the network slimming and CondenseNet methods do not explicitly perform pruning operations on the skip connections.

3   RL-Based AutoML for DenseNet Compression

In this section, we first formulate skip connections pruning in DenseNet as a reinforcement learning (RL) problem. Then, we introduce the automatic DenseNet sparsification (ADS) framework, which is an RL-based AutoML method for DenseNet compression. Last but not the least, we describe how to optimize the policy network during the RL process.

3.1   RL Formulation of DenseNet Sparsification

In an RL problem, an *agent* transits from the initial *state* to the final target *state* by performing a sequence of *actions*, and it is updated when receiving a *reward*. The goal of the agent is to learn an optimal *policy* to maximize the expected reward. The RL process for searching the sparsified DenseNet can be modeled as a Markov decision process (MDP), $\mathcal{M} = \{\mathcal{S}, \mathcal{A}, T, R\}$. We define $\mathcal{S}, \mathcal{A}, T, R$ as follows.

State Space $\mathcal{S}$. The state space $\mathcal{S}$ consists of all possible sparsified DenseNet architectures. That is, by pruning some skip connections, we can obtain a sparsified DenseNet s' from the original DenseNet s ($s, s' \in \mathcal{S}$).

Action Space $\mathcal{A}$. The action space $\mathcal{A}$ contains a finite set of actions that can transform the original DenseNet into a sparsified network architecture. Here, the actions refer to the operations pruning the skip connections.

State Transition Function $F : \mathcal{S} \times \mathcal{A} \rightarrow \mathcal{S}$. Concretely, for the original DenseNet represented by the state $s \in \mathcal{S}$, there is always a set of actions $\mathcal{A}(s) \subseteq \mathcal{A}$ that the agent can take from to transit s to a new state s', which represents a sparsified DenseNet.

Reward Function $R : \mathcal{S} \rightarrow \mathbb{R}$. The reward function R is used to measure the performance of a sparsified DenseNet architecture s' and update the RL agent. To find the optimal compression policy $\pi : \mathcal{S} \rightarrow \mathcal{A}$, the agent should maximize its expected total reward over all possible action sequences $q_{a_{1:T}}$:

$$R_\pi = \max \mathbb{E}_{P(q_{a_{1:T}})}[R], \tag{1}$$

where $P(q_{a_{1:T}})$ is the probability of the action sequence taking actions $\{a_1, \ldots, a_T\}$ and T is the length of the sequence.

3.2 Automatic DenseNet Sparsification

From a graph theory perspective, the DenseNet architecture can be formulated as a direct acyclic graph (DAG), and all possible candidate sparsified models can be obtained by taking subgraphs of the DAG. Hence, we first pre-train a DenseNet as baseline, and then in the RL process of ADS we force all the sampled models to directly reuse weights from the pre-trained DenseNet to validate their performances instead of training thousands of individual candidate models from scratch. By utilizing this weight sharing mechanism, the RL process of ADS can be implemented efficiently and save a lot of computational resources. Figure 1(a) shows the RL process of ADS, and Fig. 1(b) illustrates the RL agent that includes an encoder network for encoding the architecture and a policy network for taking actions to prune the skip connections.

The encoder network with an input embedding layer is to learn the architecture state representations of the original DenseNet and the sparsified DenseNet. For an L-layer DenseNet, we use an $L \times L$ binary matrix to represent the skip connection states between the layers. Each column in the matrix represents the connection state of a layer. In each iteration, the encoder network takes columns of the matrix as inputs and learns the representations of the network, which are then fed into the policy network. We utilize a bidirectional long short-term memory (Bi-LSTM) to implement the encoder network, which can accurately learn the network structure information.

Alternatively, the policy network is implemented by an LSTM, whose initial hidden state is the final hidden state of the encoder network. The policy network is to make necessary decisions for taking actions to prune skip connections in

DenseNet. For concreteness, given the initial DenseNet state s, the policy network iteratively determines to (1) select which layer index; (2) prune which skip connections of this layer. The state encoding is updated iteratively with these two action steps, and the repeated number of these two action decision steps in a round is determined according to the compression ratio c. In our work, the maximum compression ratio c is set to 50%. After taking a round of actions, we obtain a sparsified DenseNet s', and its validation accuracy is used to update the whole encoder and policy network.

3.3   Optimization for the Policy Network

By performing an action sequence $q_{a_{1:T}}$, we can obtain a candidate sparsified DenseNet. It is noted that we compute the reward for the final state after obtaining the sparsified DenseNet in each iteration of the RL process, not for the intermediate pruning steps. For computing the reward function R, we perform a non-linear transformation on the validation accuracy acc of the sparsified DenseNet:

$$R = \tan(\frac{\pi}{2} \times acc). \tag{2}$$

Suppose that the policy network is parameterized by θ, which needs to be optimized for the purpose of maximizing the expected total reward. Here, the expected total reward over all possible action sequences $q_{a_{1:T}}$ is specified as the objective function with respect to θ:

$$J(\theta) = \mathbb{E}_{P(q_{a_{1:T};\theta})}[R]. \tag{3}$$

We iteratively update θ to train the policy network by utilizing the REINFORCEMENT policy gradient method [18]:

$$\nabla_\theta J(\theta) = \nabla_\theta \mathbb{E}_{P(q_{a_{1:T};\theta})}[R]$$
$$= \sum_{t=1}^{T} \mathbb{E}_{P(q_{a_{1:T};\theta})}[\nabla_\theta \log P(a_t|a_{1:(t-1)};\theta)R]$$
$$\approx \frac{1}{m}\sum_{i=1}^{m}\sum_{t=1}^{T}[\nabla_\theta \log P(a_t|a_{1:(t-1)};\theta)R_i], \tag{4}$$

where m is the number of sparsified architectures that the agent samples in one batch, T is the length of the action sequences $q_{a_{1:T}}$, $P(a_t|a_{1:(t-1)};\theta)$ is the probability of selecting actions a_t given $a_{1:(t-1)}$ and θ, and R_i is the reward for the i-th sparsified DenseNet after validating.

Equation (4) is an unbiased estimate of the gradient, which generally has a high variance. Following the common practice [2,19], we reduce the variance by employing an exponential moving average of the previous rewards, as the state-independent baseline function f:

$$\nabla_\theta J(\theta) \approx \frac{1}{m}\sum_{i=1}^{m}\sum_{t=1}^{T}[\nabla_\theta \log P(a_t|a_{1:(t-1)};\theta)(R_i - f)]. \tag{5}$$

Algorithm 1 describes the main pipeline of the proposed automatic DenseNet sparsification algorithm.

Algorithm 1. Automatic DenseNet Sparsification

Input: A pre-trained DenseNet D, Maximum iteration step N, Batch size b and Compression ratio c

Output: The best-performing sparsified DenseNet under compression ratio

1: Compute the number of the agent's actions, T, according to the compression ratio c
2: **for** iteration step=1 to N **do**
3:     Given a set of matrices, $M = \{M_{01}, M_{02}, \dots, M_{0b}\}$, which represents b uncompressed DenseNets D
4:     **for** t=1 to T **do**
5:         The encoder network encodes the initial state of M as $S = \{S_{t1}, S_{t2}, \dots, S_{tb}\}$
6:         The policy network takes the state S as input, and zeroes a path in M to get new $M = \{M_{t1}, M_{t2}, \dots, M_{tb}\}$
7:         The sparsified networks represented by M are tested on the validation set to obtain the reward R
8:         The encoder network and the policy network are updated according to R
9:     **end for**
10: **end for**

---

4   Experiments

To test the proposed ADS method, we conducted extensive experiments on the CIFAR-10 and CINIC-10 datasets. In the following, we describe the implementation details and report the experimental results on the used datasets.

4.1   Implementation Details

Pre-training of DenseNet. Before performing the RL process of ADS, we pre-trained a 40-layer DenseNet [12] with growth rate $k = 12$ on the CIFAR-10 dataset. We trained this DenseNet for 600 epochs using stochastic gradient descent (SGD) with Momentum optimizer, setting the batch size to 64 and momentum to 0.9. The learning rate was initialized to 0.1, and was reduced to 0.01, 0.001 and 0.0005 in the 300-th, 475-th and 540-th epoch, respectively.

Since we enforced the sparsified architectures to reuse corresponding weights of the original network in the RL process of ADS, pruning skip connections from the original DenseNet had a large possibility to result in severe degradation of the network performance. In order to ensure the sparsified architectures to be robust to such changes, we incorporated the path dropout technique [20] into the training of the original DenseNet. Specifically, we disabled path dropout at the beginning of the training, and gradually increased the rate p of path dropout over time in a linear scheme. The maximum of p was 0.6.

Implementation Details of ADS. In ADS, the encoder network was a Bi-LSTM with 50 hidden units, and its embedding size was 16. The policy network was an LSTM with 100 units. They were trained using the Adam optimizer [13] with an initial learning rate of 0.002. At each iteration, the RL agent sampled 10 sparsified architectures at compression ratio 10%, 20%, 30%, 40%, and 50%. We ran 300 iterations in total (sampling 15,000 sparsified architectures). Since the sampled networks directly reuse the weights from the pre-trained DenseNet rather than training from scratch, ADS is implemented with remarkable efficiency. For a 40-layer DenseNet, running on 1 single NVIDIA 1080Ti GPU within less than 1 day.

After the RL process of ADS, we selected the best-performing sparsified models under each compression ratio of 10%–50% to do further training. We trained these sparsified architectures for 300 epochs without pushing path dropout. We employed the Momentum optimizer with momentum 0.9, and set the batch size to 64. The learning rate was initialized to 0.1, and was reduced to 0.01, 0.001 in the 150-th and 225-th epoch, respectively.

4.2 Experimental Results Obtained on the CIFAR-10 Dataset

The CIFAR-10 dataset consists of 50,000 training images and 10,000 test images, belonging to 10 classes. Each RGB image has a size of $32 \times 32 \times 3$ pixels. We randomly held out 45,000 training samples for pre-training the original DenseNet, and used the remaining 5,000 samples for validating the performance of the sparsified architectures in the RL process of ADS. For preprocessing data augmentation, we normalized each image using channel means and standard deviations. And more, we followed the standard scheme to zero-pad the images with 4 pixels on each side, then randomly crop them to produce 32×32 images, and horizontally mirror them with probability 0.5 for data augmentation [12]. After the RL process of ADS, we used all the training images including the validation set to do further training on the best-performing sparsified model and tested the network performance on the test set.

Table 1. Error rate (%) obtained on the CIFAR-10 dataset. RL-err refers to the validation error in the RL process of ADS, and FT-err refers to the test error after the further training process.

Compression ratio	RL-err	FT-err	#Params (M)
10%	5.89	5.86	0.91
20%	5.70	5.66	0.82
30%	5.74	5.67	0.74
40%	5.99	5.83	0.65
50%	6.63	6.32	0.56
Baseline	–	6.43	1.0

The pre-trained DenseNet achieved an accuracy of 93.57% (our baseline). In Table 1, we listed the best results under each compression ratio of 10%–50% in the RL process of ADS and after the further training process. We can see that, the results after further training are all better than the baseline, which demonstrates that the skip connections in the original DenseNet are redundant and pruning them can improve the performance. Furthermore, the results in the RL process and that after further training only differ slightly, which shows the effectiveness of both the parameter sharing strategy and the proposed ADS method.

RL *vs* RS. We compared the RL-based ADS and random search based (RS-based) ADS, which are visualized in Fig. 2(a) and (b), respectively. We can clearly see that RL-based ADS gradually improves its performance and maintains its stability, but RS-based ADS performs worse than RL-based ADS and is not stable.

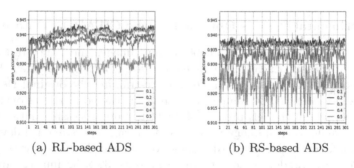

(a) RL-based ADS   (b) RS-based ADS

Fig. 2. Mean accuracy against the iterative steps. (a) RL-based ADS, where we sampled the sparsified architectures under compression ratio $c = 10\%, 20\%, 30\%, 40\%$ and 50%, respectively. (b) RS-based ADS, with the same compression ratio.

Extension. In order to further compress DenseNet and improve its performance, we consider to apply $L1$-norm regularization (please refer to Sect. 2.2) on the sparsified DenseNet to do channel-level pruning in each layer, and widen the layers by a width factor ω to improve its performance. Towards a size-accuracy trade-off, we used the best-performing sparsified DenseNet ($L = 40, k = 12$) with compression ratio $c = 40\%$ to conduct experiments on the CIFAR-10 dataset. For the application of the $L1$-norm regularization, the experimental settings followed that of [16]. The scaling factors γ of all the BN layers were initialized to 0.5, and the sparsity hyper-parameter λ to 10^{-5}. We used a global pruning ratio to prune unimportant channels. For example, "$L1$-70%" means the global pruning ratio is 70%. For the width factor ω, it was used to increase the number of filters in each dense block by increasing the growth rate k. We set two schemes: (1) A: $k = \omega \cdot k_0$; (2) B: $k = \omega^{b-1} \cdot k_0$, where k_0 refers to the initial growth rate (i.e. $k_0 = 12$) and $b = 1, 2, 3$ denotes the index of the dense block. For instance, "Sparsified DenseNet (A)" stands for using network widening scheme A; "Sparsified DenseNet $(B + L1\text{-}70\%)$" refers to using network widening scheme B and $L1$ regularization with pruning 70% unimportant channels. In the comparison experiments, we set global pruning ratio to 70%, and $\omega = 2$.

In Table 2, we show the comparison results between the sparsified DenseNet and the state-of-the-art deep architectures, including that obtained by compressing DenseNet and by other compression techniques on the VGGNet and ResNet, on the CIFAR-10 dataset. Note that, a Log-DenseNet [10] is noted by a pair (n, k), where n refers to the number of layers in each of the 3 dense blocks, and k denotes the growth rate. The layers and growth rate of Log-DenseNet-40 (12, 24) is the same with the sparsified DenseNet using widening scheme A with $\omega = 2$. From Table 2, we can easily see that the automatically sparsified DenseNet achieves the highest classification accuracy among all the compared deep architectures, which also indicates the effectiveness of the proposed ADS method.

Table 2. Comparison results between the sparsified DenseNet and the state-of-the-art methods on the CIFAR-10 dataset.

Model	Test error (%)	#Params (M)
DenseNet-40 ($L1$-70% in [16])	5.65	0.35
CondenseNet-94 [11]	5.19	0.66
Log-DenseNet-40 V1 (12, 24) [10]	5.98	–
Log-DenseNet-40 V2 (12, 24) [10]	5.12	–
VGGNet-16 [15]	6.60	5.40
VGGNet-19 [16]	6.20	2.30
ResNet-34 (N2N learning) [1]	7.65	2.07
ResNet-50 (AMC) [8]	6.45	–
ResNet-56 [15]	6.94	0.73
ResNet-164 [16]	5.27	1.21
Sparsified DenseNet	5.83	0.65
Sparsified DenseNet ($L1$-70%)	5.66	**0.25**
Sparsified DenseNet (A) (12, 24)	**4.50**	–
Sparsified DenseNet ($A + L1$-70%)	4.66	0.96
Sparsified DenseNet ($B + L1$-70%)	5.12	1.01

4.3 Experimental Results Obtained on the CINIC-10 Dataset

The CINIC-10 dataset contains 270,000 images in total, 60,000 images from the entirety of the original CIFAR-10 dataset and the remaining 210,000 images from the down-sampled ImageNet dataset [4]. Each image consists of $32 \times 32 \times 3$ pixels, belonging to 10 classes. This dataset has been split into 3 equal-sized training, validation, and test subsets (9,000 images per class within each subset). The preprocessing and data augmentation applied on this dataset were the same as that on CIFAR-10. In this experiment, we transferred the sparsified DenseNet ($c = 40\%$) learned on the CIFAR-10 dataset to the CINIC-10 application. We trained the sparsified DenseNet for 300 epochs with the Momentum optimizer, with batch size 64 and momentum 0.9. The initial learning rate was set to 0.1, and was reduced to 0.01, 0.001 in the 150-th and 225-th epoch, respectively.

We compared the sparsified DenseNet with MobileNet [4], and listed the results in Table 3, where the column "Train" and "Train+Val" refers to the *test error* (%) when training the sparsified DenseNet on the training set and the training and validation sets, respectively. From Table 3, we can see that the sparsified DenseNet outperforms MobileNet on this task in terms of both classification accuracy and the number of parameters. These results also provide evidence for that the sparsified DenseNet learned with the proposed ADS method on the CIFAR-10 can generalize well to other image classification problems.

Table 3. Results obtained on the CINIC-10 dataset.

Model	Train	Train+Val	#Params(M)
MobileNet [4]	18.00	19.55	3.20
Sparsified DenseNet	13.12	–	0.65
Sparsified DenseNet (L1-70%)	**13.11**	–	**0.25**
Sparsified DenseNet (A)	–	**18.40**	2.57
Sparsified DenseNet ($A + L$1-70%)	–	18.60	0.96

5   Conclusion

In this paper, we propose an RL-based automatic DenseNet sparsification (ADS) method to automatically prune redundant skip connections in DenseNet. The sparsified DenseNet can outperform not only the original DenseNet, but also related state-of-the-art deep architectures. Moreover, ADS can be implemented with remarkable efficiency, for a 40-layer DenseNet, only running on 1 single GPU with less than 1 day. In addiction, the sparsified DenseNet learned by ADS has strong transferability to new image classification applications.

Acknowledgments. This work was supported by the National Key R&D Program of China under Grant 2016YFC1401004, the National Natural Science Foundation of China (NSFC) under Grant No. 41706010, the Science and Technology Program of Qingdao under Grant No. 17-3-3-20-nsh, the CERNET Innovation Project under Grant No. NGII20170416, the Joint Fund of the Equipments Pre-Research and Ministry of Education of China under Grand No. 6141A020337, and the Fundamental Research Funds for the Central Universities of China.

References

1. Ashok, A., Rhinehart, N., Beainy, F., Kitani, K.M.: N2N learning: network to network compression via policy gradient reinforcement learning. In: ICLR (2018)
2. Cai, H., Chen, T., Zhang, W., Yu, Y., Wang, J.: Efficient architecture search by network transformation. In: AAAI (2018)
3. Chen, W., Wilson, J.T., Tyree, S., Weinberger, K.Q., Chen, Y.: Compressing neural networks with the hashing trick. In: ICML (2015)
4. Darlow, L.N., Crowley, E.J., Antoniou, A., Storkey, A.J.: CINIC-10 is not ImageNet or CIFAR-10. CoRR abs/1810.03505 (2018)
5. Denton, E.L., Zaremba, W., Bruna, J., LeCun, Y., Fergus, R.: Exploiting linear structure within convolutional networks for efficient evaluation. In: NeurIPS (2014)
6. Han, S., Pool, J., Tran, J., Dally, W.J.: Learning both weights and connections for efficient neural network. In: NeurIPS (2015)
7. He, K., Zhang, X., Ren, S., Sun, J.: Deep residual learning for image recognition. In: CVPR (2016)
8. He, Y., Lin, J., Liu, Z., Wang, H., Li, L.-J., Han, S.: AMC: AutoML for model compression and acceleration on mobile devices. In: Ferrari, V., Hebert, M., Sminchisescu, C., Weiss, Y. (eds.) ECCV 2018. LNCS, vol. 11211, pp. 815–832. Springer, Cham (2018). https://doi.org/10.1007/978-3-030-01234-2_48
9. Hinton, G.E., Vinyals, O., Dean, J.: Distilling the knowledge in a neural network. CoRR abs/1503.02531 (2015)
10. Hu, H., Dey, D., Giorno, A.D., Hebert, M., Bagnell, J.A.: Log-DenseNet: how to sparsify a DenseNet. In: ICLR (2018)
11. Huang, G., Liu, S., van der Maaten, L., Weinberger, K.Q.: CondenseNet: an efficient DenseNet using learned group convolutions. In: CVPR (2018)
12. Huang, G., Liu, Z., van der Maaten, L., Weinberger, K.Q.: Densely connected convolutional networks. In: CVPR (2017)
13. Kingma, D.P., Ba, J.: Adam: a method for stochastic optimization. In: ICLR (2015)
14. Krizhevsky, A., Sutskever, I., Hinton, G.E.: ImageNet classification with deep convolutional neural networks. In: NeurIPS (2012)
15. Li, H., Kadav, A., Durdanovic, I., Samet, H., Graf, H.P.: Pruning filters for efficient ConvNets. In: ICLR (2017)
16. Liu, Z., Li, J., Shen, Z., Huang, G., Yan, S., Zhang, C.: Learning efficient convolutional networks through network slimming. In: ICCV (2017)
17. Srivastava, R.K., Greff, K., Schmidhuber, J.: Training very deep networks. In: NeurIPS (2015)
18. Williams, R.J.: Simple statistical gradient-following algorithms for connectionist reinforcement learning. Mach. Learn. 8, 229–256 (1992)
19. Zoph, B., Le, Q.V.: Neural architecture search with reinforcement learning. In: ICLR (2017)
20. Zoph, B., Vasudevan, V., Shlens, J., Le, Q.V.: Learning transferable architectures for scalable image recognition. In: CVPR (2018)

Mechanisms of Reward-Modulated STDP and Winner-Take-All in Bayesian Spiking Decision-Making Circuit

Hui Yan[1,2], Xinle Liu[1,2], Hong Huo[1,2], and Tao Fang[1,2(✉)]

[1] Department of Automation, Shanghai Jiao Tong University,
Shanghai 200240, China
{yanhuinina, tfang}@sjtu.edu.cn
[2] Key Laboratory of System Control and Information Processing,
Ministry of Education, Shanghai 200240, China

Abstract. Decision making, as one of the most essential functions of the human brain, is the key neural process from sensory stimuli to neuropsychological choices till actions. More recently, numerous growing neurophysiology and neuroscience experimental evidence has indicated that the human brain performs near-optimal Bayesian inference in various tasks, such as perception, learning and decision making. In order to further understand the computational mechanism of decision-making circuit, particularly from the perspective of biological plausibility and interpretability, this paper proposes a novel brain-inspired decision-making circuit based on spiking neural networks for perceptual decision-making tasks. The proposed model employs a winner-take-all (WTA) mechanism and reward-modulated spike-timing-dependent plasticity (STDP) related with Bayesian computation to simulate the neural representation of decision-making. Experiments in the random-dot motion discrimination task demonstrate that the proposed spiking decision-making circuit exhibits WTA property and has a better performance compared with unsupervised STDP.

Keywords: Spiking decision-making circuit · Reward-modulated spike-timing-dependent plasticity · Winner-take-all · Bayesian computation

1 Introduction

Due to the high complexity of the human brain, exploring and revealing how the brain works has become one of the major challenges in neuroscience research. Decision-making is one of the basic functions of central nervous systems, ranging from simple perceptual decisions to advanced cognitive functions. When making a decision, our brain first extracts the useful information from the complex environments full of uncertainty and then integrates a low-level stimulus with evidence accumulation, finally makes a higher-level decision. Recently, increasing psychological and behavioral experiments have shown that our brain performs near-optimal probabilistic inference [1, 2] - more akin to a Bayesian machine, that is, Bayesian computation of perceptual decision making provides a probabilistic relationship between noisy sensory input and the accumulating sensory evidence [3] to make a final and optimal decision.

© Springer Nature Switzerland AG 2019
T. Gedeon et al. (Eds.): ICONIP 2019, LNCS 11955, pp. 162–172, 2019.
https://doi.org/10.1007/978-3-030-36718-3_14

In the last few years, spiking neural networks (SNNs) with Bayesian inference have been widely used in perceptual decision-making circuit due to its known neuronal properties. For instance, in [4, 5] a two-level recurrent spiking neural network was proposed to carry out Bayesian computation for a visual motion detection task. Beck et al. [6] presented a hierarchical network of decision making with middle temporal (MT) and lateral intraparietal (LIP) layer. In their work, the firing rates of MT neurons encode the external stimulus, while LIP neurons only need to integrate the activity of MT neurons so as to infer the posterior of the stimulus. More specifically, Nessler et al. [6–8] showed that Bayesian computation also emerges in the winner-take-all (WTA) circuit through a variant of the spike-timing-dependent plasticity (STDP) rule.

To better understand the computational mechanism of decision-making circuit, a brain-inspired SNN is presented to analog actual decision-making circuit corresponding to specific regions of the cerebral cortex. The network has recurrent excitation and WTA competition mediated by lateral inhibition. In addition, a dopamine system is incorporated into the circuit. A reward modulated STDP (R-STDP), which combines unsupervised STDP with a reinforcement signal used for modulating the synaptic weights, is employed to train the SNNs model. Besides, this paper provides a Bayesian insight into the role that how such a WTA decision-making circuit of spiking neurons infers the posterior probability distribution over hidden causes given external input patterns through the firing probabilities of excitatory neurons and synaptic learning rule. Experimental results in a random-dot motion discrimination task indicate that decision-making circuit equipped with R-STDP learning rule exhibits WTA competition and outperforms that with STDP learning rule.

The remainder of this paper is organized as follows. Section 2 introduces the spiking neuron model and synaptic learning rule that we adopted in our work. Then a novel decision-making circuit model is proposed in Sect. 3. After that, we evaluate the performance of the proposed model in a perceptual decision task in Sect. 4. Finally, we conclude our work in Sect. 5.

2 Spiking Neural Network

SNNs, as the third generation of neural networks, are used to simulate the decision-making circuit in the human brain due to its biological plausibility. The spiking decision-making circuit used in our model is inspired by Wang's work [9, 10]. In this section, we introduce the single spiking neuron model and synaptic learning rule of the proposed model, respectively.

2.1 Spiking Neuron Model

Each neuron in the decision-making neural circuit is simulated by the interconnected conductance-based leaky integrate-and-fire model [11], which contains N_E pyramidal neurons (excitatory) and N_I interneurons (inhibitory) (normally, $N_E{:}N_I = 4{:}1$) for network balance. The membrane potential $V(t)$ obeys the following dynamics

$$C_m \frac{dV(t)}{dt} = -g_L(V(t) - V_{rest}) - I_{syn}(t) \tag{1}$$

where C_m is the membrane capacitance, g_L is the leak conductance, V_{rest} is the resting potential. When the membrane potential reaches a threshold, i.e., $V(t) > V_{th} = -50$ mV, an action potential occurs, that is a neuron fires, and then $V(t)$ is set to its reset potential $V_{reset} = -55$ mV for a refractory period τ_{ref}, during which time the $V(t)$ remains as V_{reset}. The total synaptic current I_{syn} to excitatory and inhibitory neurons are as follows

$$I_{i,syn}^E(t) = (I_{i,AMPA}^{E \to E} + I_{i,NMDA}^{E \to E} + I_{i,GABA}^{I \to E}) + I_{i,AMPA}^{ext \to E} + I_{i,AMPA}^{noise \to E} \tag{2}$$

$$I_{i,syn}^I(t) = (I_{i,AMPA}^{E \to I} + I_{i,NMDA}^{E \to I} + I_{i,GABA}^{I \to I}) + I_{i,AMPA}^{noise \to I} \tag{3}$$

where the first three terms represent excitatory postsynaptic currents (EPSCs) mediated by AMPA and NMDA receptors, and inhibitory postsynaptic currents (IPSCs) mediated by GABA receptors. $I_{i,AMPA}^{ext \to E}$ represents external AMPA-mediated input signals (visual stimulus) applied to the excitatory populations. $I_{i,AMPA}^{noise}$ represents that all neuronal populations receive a background noise mediated by AMPA, which is modeled as uncorrelated Poisson spike trains. Three types of receptors for synaptic currents, AMPA, NMDA and GABA are described by

$$I_{i,AMPA}(t) = g_{AMPA}(V_i(t) - V_E)\bar{s}_{i,AMPA}(t) \tag{4}$$

$$I_{i,NMDA}(t) = \frac{g_{NMDA}(V_i(t) - V_E)}{1 + [Mg^{2+}]e^{-0.062V_i(t)/3.57}} \bar{s}_{i,NMDA}(t) \tag{5}$$

$$I_{i,GABA}(t) = g_{GABA}(V_i(t) - V_I)\bar{s}_{i,GABA}(t) \tag{6}$$

where reversal potentials $V_E = 0$ mV for excitatory synapses and $V_I = -70$ mV for inhibitory synapses. $g_{AMPA/NMDA/GABA}$ is the synaptic efficacy, $[Mg^{2+}] = 1$ mM is the extracellular magnesium concentration. The synaptic gating variable $\bar{s}_i(t)$ is the fraction of open channels and $\bar{s}_i(t) = \sum_j w_{ij}s_j(t)$ for the recurrent connections, where w_{ij} is the synaptic weight between presynaptic j and postsynaptic i neuron, s_j depends on the spikes of the presynaptic neuron j, where j runs over all the presynaptic neurons. For AMPA and GABA receptor, the gating variable is given by

$$\dot{s} = -\frac{s}{\tau_s} + \sum_k \delta(t - t^k) \tag{7}$$

for NMDA receptor-mediated currents, the gating variable follows

$$\dot{s} = -\frac{s}{\tau_s} + \alpha x(1 - s) \tag{8}$$

$$\dot{x} = -\frac{x}{\tau_x} + \sum_k \delta(t - t^k) \qquad (9)$$

where δ is the Dirac delta function, and t^k is the firing time of the kth presynaptic neuron. $\alpha = 0.5$ kHz, τ_s is the decay time constant, 2 ms for AMPA, 100 ms for NMDA, and 10 ms for GABA, $\tau_x = 2$ ms regulates the rise time of NMDA channels.

2.2 Reward-Modulated Synaptic Plasticity

Numerous studies show that different human behaviors are driven by changes in the number of synaptic connections and synaptic strengths (weights) between presynaptic neurons and postsynaptic neurons, which is called neural plasticity [12]. So far, STDP is a widely used an unsupervised learning rule, and it mainly depends on the spike time interval between pre- and post-synaptic neuron. One kind of the original STDP formula is described as

$$STDP(\Delta t) = \begin{cases} A_+ exp(\Delta t/\tau_+), & if \ \Delta t < 0 \\ -A_- exp(-\Delta t/\tau_-), & if \ \Delta t \geq 0 \end{cases} \qquad (10)$$

As can be seen from Eq. (10), the changes of synaptic weights are exponentially related to the time interval Δt of pairs of pre- and post-synaptic spikes. Briefly, if the presynaptic spike arrives before the postsynaptic spike, long-term potentiation (LTP) occurs, otherwise long-term depression (LTD) occurs. Where τ_+ and τ_- are time constant to determine temporal window for synaptic modifications. A_+ and A_- are learning rates, both representing the maximum amounts of synaptic modification.

Moreover, reward system of our brain plays a critical role in decision-making process. What has increasingly been found in physiological experiments is that a kind of neuromodulator, namely dopamine (DA), is one of the important chemical substances involved in the reward system [13]. Dopaminergic neurons could encode some behaviors related to rewards (reward signals) by modulating synaptic plasticity at corticostriatal synapses [14, 15], including simple decisions based on perceptual stimulus or advanced decisions involving working memory. This reward mechanism relies on the dopamine modulation of synaptic modification created by STDP. R-STDP adopted in our work for training SNNs collects the weight changes in an eligibility trace, instead of instantaneously applying these weight changes to synapses as mentioned in the classic STDP, it can be written as

$$\dot{w} = e \times (d - b) \qquad (11)$$

According to the Eq. (11), the synaptic weight changes are proportional to the product of eligibility trace e with a reward signal d, where e denotes the eligibility trace of synapse j-i at time t which collecting weight changes given by $STDP(\Delta t)$ mentioned as Eq. (10) and reward function d describes the extracellular concentration of DA. $d - b$ signals a deviation of the reward d from a baseline b [16]. The baseline ensures that the synaptic weight does not encounter significant modification unless a reward is issued. The eligibility trace and reward function can be defined as

$$\dot{e} = -\frac{e}{\tau_e} + STDP(\Delta t)\delta(t - t_{pre/post}) \tag{12}$$

$$\dot{d} = -\frac{d}{\tau_d} + \frac{\delta(t - t_n)}{\tau_d} \tag{13}$$

where τ_e is the time constant of the synaptic eligibility trace indicating the exponential decay rate of the eligibility trace function, δ is the Dirac delta function, τ_d is the time constant of neuromodulator concentration, t_n represents the spike times of the neuromodulator (dopaminergic neurons).

In short, triggered by dopaminergic neurons, effects of STDP events are collected in an eligibility trace and synaptic weight changes are induced by a reward signal, see Fig. 1 for an illustration of the R-STDP learning rule. Each pre- and post-synaptic spike pair contributes to the eligibility trace. LTP and LTD can be promoted by a reward that is issued within the time of an active eligibility trail.

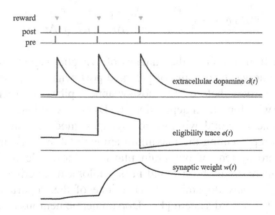

Fig. 1. Illustration of a reward-modulated STDP learning rule.

3 Spiking Decision-Making Circuit Model

In this section, we introduce a spiking decision-making model arranged in a WTA circuit and discuss how our model can be implemented with biologically realistic mechanisms. Particularly, we will show how Bayesian computation occur in the synaptic plasticity.

3.1 The Neural Circuit of Decision Making

Here, we develop a computational model of perceptual decision-making circuit of spiking neurons and synaptic plasticity to execute a two-alternative forced-choice motion discrimination task. Specifically, we use a simplified SNN to perform perceptual decision making, which consists of input encoded layer and output decoded layer (namely decision-making layer) with recurrent connections between all these neurons. Two selective subpopulations of excitatory neurons in the decision-making layer compete against each other via lateral inhibition from a group of inhibitory neurons. Lateral inhibition is generally considered to stabilize the activity of excitatory populations [17].

The decision-making process can be divided into the following stages: (1) After the external sensory stimulus onset, two signals are encoded to population firing activity and can be represented by probability distributions over the stimulus. (2) These two signals then project to the excitatory populations that compete with each other through the inhibitory interneurons, respectively. The dopamine system brings about dopaminergic plasticity at corticostriatal synapses that impacting the evidence accumulation process during decision-making. Such synaptic learning process will modify the synapses from input signals to the excitatory pool. (3) Consequently, the activity in one excitatory population increases, and the other population suppresses. The final decision of the circuit depends on which neural population has a higher population firing rate. In a word, the cortical network model of perceptual decision-making trained through a reward-based STDP learning rule can discriminate external input patterns which are encoded into spiking activity to ensure that definitive decision is made between alternatives.

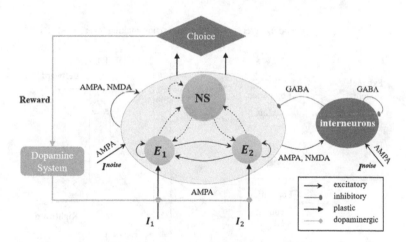

Fig. 2. The cortical neural circuit model of decision-making with two alternatives.

As illustrated in Fig. 2, the connections from pyramidal neurons to other pyramidal neurons and interneurons are mediated by AMPA and NMDA receptors. The connections from interneurons to pyramidal neurons and other interneurons are GABAergic. The circuit receives external input and background noise mediated exclusively by AMPA receptors. According to the selectivity of excitatory neurons in WTA circuit, the network can be divided into N subpopulations ($N = 2$ here). And NS represents the non-selective neuronal group. The choice of the decision in trials determines the reward and thereby influences the DA system. The dopamine activity modulates the decision process by changing the synaptic weights through R-STDP learning rule.

In reality, we map the simplified network model of spiking neurons into a sensory area and its associative decision cortical area in visual cortex, such as MT and LIP. A large body of evidence indicates that neurons in the sensory area MT encode the motion stimulus, and neurons in a possible decision area LIP integrate the accumulated sensory evidence downstream from MT [18, 19]. Therefore, we divide the decision-making circuit into a sensory circuit (MT) and an integration circuit (LIP). In order to make a final decision, the circuit employs WTA competition between two decision populations through the same lateral inhibition. Furthermore, the accumulated evidence is transmitted to the downstream areas for further computation.

3.2 Underlying Bayesian Computation

Previous works have shown that a network with STDP and lateral inhibition can produce directional selectivity similar to the visual cortex in the brain. STDP learning rule has been proved to approximate Bayesian computation using expectation-maximization algorithm [7, 8]. In the Bayesian framework, a *posterior* probability distribution over hidden causes is obtained by the product of the *prior* knowledge distribution and the *likelihood* of the sensory observation for each possible cause.

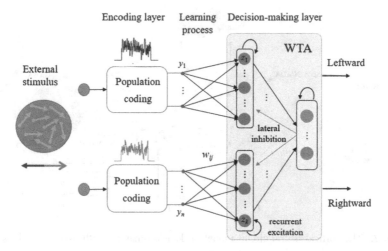

Fig. 3. Architecture of spiking decision-making circuit

The spiking decision-making circuit architecture is sketched in Fig. 3. Since external inputs are encoded through population coding represented by spiking input neurons $y_1, \ldots, y_n$, we define that, when the output layer emits an output spike at time t, as in Eq. (14), the firing probability p_k^t of the kth output neuron z_k in a WTA circuit is equivalent to the posterior distribution over the hidden cause k, given the current evidence encoded in the input activations $y(t)$. The posterior probability of hidden cause k as $p(z_k = 1|y(t), w)$ is given by Bayesian inference:

$$p(z_k = 1|y(t), w) \propto \overbrace{p(z_k = 1|w)}^{prior} \cdot \overbrace{p(y(t)|z_k = 1, w)}^{likelihood} \tag{14}$$

We assume that the membrane potential of each neuron z_k is calculated as a summation of excitatory inputs from the presynaptic neurons through synaptic weights w_{ij}. In the WTA circuit, the instantaneous firing rate of each excitatory output neuron depends exponentially on the membrane potential and lateral inhibition. Based on the theoretical work on spike-based Bayesian inference [6, 8], the firing probability of each excitatory output neuron k at time t can be written as

$$p_k^t = \frac{e^{u_i(t)}}{\sum\limits_{l=1}^{k} e^{u_l(t)}} = \frac{\overbrace{e^{w_{i0}}}^{prior} \cdot \overbrace{e^{\sum_{j=1}^{n} w_{ij}y_j(t)}}^{likelihood}}{\underbrace{p(y(t)|w)}_{normalization}} = p(z_k = 1|y(t), w) \tag{15}$$

The synaptic weights w_{ij} in feed-forward synapses from presynaptic input neurons to postsynaptic output neurons of the network can be explained as an implicit neural encoding of likelihood distributions $p(y(t)|z_k = 1, w)$. w_{k0} represents the intrinsic excitability of the neuron z_k. The inference process of the Bayesian model is performed through the dynamic activities of the proposed WTA circuits. The learning purpose of the network is to ensure that the marginal distribution of the Bayesian model approximates the actual distribution of external inputs as closely as possible, by continuously updating synaptic weights through the synaptic learning rule.

4 Experiments and Results

To verify the WTA property and R-STDP performance of the proposed decision-making circuit, we test our model in a random-dot visual direction discrimination task [18], which is widely used in perceptual decision-making experiments.

4.1 Random-Dot Motion Discrimination

In the experiment, the model is required to make a two-alternative forced choice (2AFC) about the coherent direction, which is assumed to be either rightward or leftward in our simulation. Neurons in area MT receive external visual inputs modeled as time-varying currents induced by random-dot motion stimuli (leftward and rightward). Then the encoded motion information is transmitted to two competing populations of excitatory neurons in the decision-making layer like LIP, respectively.

During stimulation, both excitatory units receive stochastic Poisson input trains. Two signals, representing external sensory inputs induced by the leftward and rightward moving dots, are projected into left- and right-preferring cortical areas E1 and E2, respectively. The distributions of time-varying stimuli are Gaussian with a mean rate μ and a standard deviation σ. The mean firing rate μ of each input neuron linearly depends on the coherence level c or motion strength which is the percentage of dots that move coherently, $\mu = \mu_0 + \mu_A \times c$ for the preferred direction and $\mu = \mu_0 - \mu_B \times c$ for non-preferred direction. μ_0 (20 Hz) is the baseline input for the random motion, μ_A (60 Hz) and μ_B (20 Hz) are factors of proportionality [20].

4.2   Simulation of the Visual Discrimination Experiment

In the visual random-dot motion discrimination task, after repeating the experiment for hundreds of times, we obtain the average performance. Note that the two selective excitatory populations compete with each other over the simulation periods. It will eventually lead to the situation that the activity in one excitatory population continuously increases, whereas the other is inhibited through lateral inhibition. When the mean population firing rate of one decision population reaches a decision threshold of population firing activity, a decision is finally made.

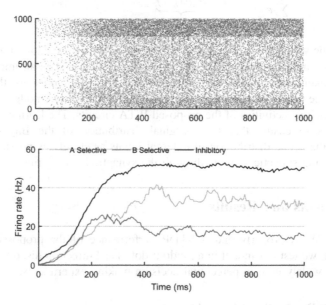

Fig. 4. Neural activity of two selective populations and interneurons in the decision-making circuit. Top: raster plot. Bottom: population firing rates. $N_E = 800$, $N_I = 200$.

As shown in Fig. 4, raster plot shows the spiking activity of neurons in the two selective populations E1, E2 and inhibitory pool. The choice of the decision-making circuit depends on the mean firing rate of selective populations. Although not receiving external inputs, the interneurons also exhibit stable ramping activity. Furthermore, we test several different levels of motion strength c in trials. The results show that it is easier to make a decision in trials with a strong motion strength, compared to a weak condition.

4.3 Simulation of Learning with Reward-Modulated STDP

In our decision-making circuit, R-STDP occurred during the learning process at corticostriatal synapses from external inputs to the selective pyramidal neuronal groups. If a decision is made, the dopamine neurons release a reward signal, then the synaptic weights between the pre- and post-neurons are modified by setting the extracellular concentration of DA. The selected frequency of decision A and B are calculated in n trials with and without reward signals, where $n = 100$ in our experiment. As shown in Fig. 5, after training with R-STDP, the selected frequency of decision A increased significantly to 87%. Obviously, R-STDP has better performance than STDP. The results indicate that dopaminergic plasticity can influence the evidence accumulation process and change the competitive behavior in the decision-making process.

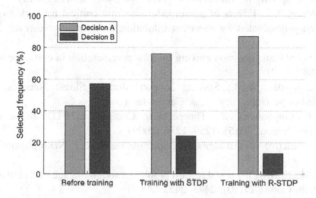

Fig. 5. The selected frequency of decision A and B. The network is trained through R-STDP compared with STDP.

5 Conclusion

In this paper, we have proposed a biologically inspired decision-making circuit model which can perform Bayesian inference through R-STDP. The experimental results in the random-dot motion discrimination task have demonstrated that the proposed spiking decision-making circuit trained by R-STDP learning rule exhibits a kind of WTA competition and outperforms STDP rule, which indicates the superiority of the proposed model in perceptual decision making. Our future work will focus on hierarchical SNNs equipped with R-STDP, which has already shown a potential computational ability for modeling cortical processing.

References

1. Knill, D.C., Pouget, A.: The Bayesian brain: the role of uncertainty in neural coding and computation. Trends Neurosci. **27**(12), 712–719 (2004)
2. Ma, W.J., Beck, J.M., Pouget, A.: Bayesian inference with probabilistic population codes. Nat. Neurosci. **9**(11), 1432–1438 (2006)

3. Beck, J.M., Ma, W.J., Pouget, A.: Probabilistic population codes for Bayesian decision making. Neuron **60**(6), 1142–1152 (2008)
4. Rao, R.P.: Hierarchical Bayesian inference in networks of spiking neurons. In: Advances in Neural Information Processing Systems, pp. 1113–1120 (2004)
5. Rao, R.P.: Bayesian computation in recurrent neural circuits. Neural Comput. **16**(1), 1–38 (2004)
6. Nessler, B., Pfeiffer, M., Buesing, L., Maass, W.: Bayesian computation emerges in generic cortical microcircuits through spike-timing-dependent plasticity. PLoS Comput. Biol. **9**(4), e1003037 (2013)
7. Kappel, D., Nessler, B., Maass, W.: STDP installs in winner-take-all circuits an online approximation to hidden Markov model learning. PLoS Comput. Biol. **10**(3), e1003511 (2014)
8. Bill, J., Legenstein, R.: A compound memristive synapse model for statistical learning through STDP in spiking neural networks. Front. Neurosci. **8**, 412 (2014)
9. Brunel, N., Wang, X.J.: Effects of neuromodulation in a cortical network model of object working memory dominated by recurrent inhibition. J. Comput. Neurosci. **11**(1), 63–85 (2001)
10. Wang, X.J.: Probabilistic decision making by slow reverberation in cortical circuits. Neuron **36**(5), 955–968 (2002)
11. Gerstner, W., Kistler, W.M.: Spiking Neuron Models: Single Neurons, Populations, Plasticity. Cambridge University Press, Cambridge (2002)
12. Masquelier, T., Guyonneau, R., Thorpe, S.J.: Competitive STDP-based spike pattern learning. Neural Comput. **21**(5), 1259–1276 (2009)
13. Schultz, W.: Predictive reward signal of dopamine neurons. J. Neurophysiol. **80**(1), 1–27 (1998)
14. Izhikevich, E.M.: Solving the distal reward problem through linkage of STDP and dopamine signaling. Cereb. Cortex **17**(10), 2443–2452 (2007)
15. Legenstein, R., Pecevski, D., Maass, W.: A learning theory for reward-modulated spike-timing-dependent plasticity with application to biofeedback. PLoS Comput. Biol. **4**(10), e1000180 (2008)
16. Frémaux, N., Gerstner, W.: Neuromodulated spike-timing-dependent plasticity, and theory of three-factor learning rules. Front. Neural Circ. **9**, 85 (2016)
17. Douglas, R.J., Martin, K.A.: Neuronal circuits of the neocortex. Annu. Rev. Neurosci. **27**, 419–451 (2004)
18. Roitman, J.D., Shadlen, M.N.: Response of neurons in the lateral intraparietal area during a combined visual discrimination reaction time task. J. Neurosci. **22**(21), 9475–9489 (2002)
19. Shadlen, M.N., Newsome, W.T.: Neural basis of a perceptual decision in the parietal cortex (area LIP) of the rhesus monkey. J. Neurophysiol. **86**(4), 1916–1936 (2001)
20. Lo, C.C., Wang, X.J.: Cortico-basal ganglia circuit mechanism for a decision threshold in reaction time tasks. Nat. Neurosci. **9**(7), 956–963 (2006)

Homeostasis-Based CNN-to-SNN Conversion of Inception and Residual Architectures

Fu Xing, Ye Yuan, Hong Huo, and Tao Fang[✉]

Department of Automation, Shanghai Jiao Tong University, Shanghai, China
{xingfu,tfang}@sjtu.edu.cn

Abstract. Event-driven mode of computation provides SNNs with potential to bridge the gap between excellent performance and computational load of deep neural networks. However, SNNs are difficult to train because of the discontinuity of spike signals. This paper proposes an efficient framework for CNN-to-SNN conversion, which converts pre-trained convolution neural networks (CNNs) into corresponding spiking equivalents. Different from previous work, this paper focuses on the conversion of deep CNN architectures, such as Inception and ResNet. As networks in conversion are rate-encoding, a novel weight normalization method is employed to approximate the spiking rates of SNNs to the activations of CNNs. And, inspired from homeostatic plasticity in neural system, a compensation approach is introduced to reduce the deterioration of spiking rates at deep layers and accelerate the inference of SNNs. Experimental results on CIFAR dataset show that the SNNs built by the conversion framework achieve better performance than those trained with spike-based algorithms. In particular, the accuracy gap between converted SNNs and original CNNs is further reduced, which is helpful for large-scale employment of spiking networks.

Keywords: Spiking neural network · Homeostatic plasticity · Brain-inspired computing · Object classification

1 Introduction

Spiking neural networks (SNNs) have gained great attentions recently as they are more brain-inspired and biologically plausible. Signals in SNNs are transmitted as discrete spikes between layers, and neurons are sparsely and asynchronously activated by afferent spikes [1]. This event-based mode of operation enables SNNs more powerful in mobile and embedded applications where real-time computing and low computational cost is necessary [2]. Studies show that SNNs with tens of thousands of neurons can be emulated on large-scale neuromorphic spiking platforms such as TrueNorth [3] and SpiNNaker [4], with orders of magnitude less energy consumption than on contemporary computing hardware. Meanwhile, deep neural networks require substantial computational costs to do inference

© Springer Nature Switzerland AG 2019
T. Gedeon et al. (Eds.): ICONIP 2019, LNCS 11955, pp. 173–184, 2019.
https://doi.org/10.1007/978-3-030-36718-3_15

although they have achieved great success on many challenging tasks. Thus, it would be advantageous if deep network architectures can be implemented into efficient spiking forms while still producing the excellent performance.

SNNs are not suitable for training with backpropagation due to the discontinuity of spike signals, and the spike-based learning algorithms, such as Spiking-Timing-Dependent Plasticity (STDP) [5], are still ineffective in training deep networks. Driven by this, a particular category of conversion methods are developed, which train a convolution neural network (CNN) using standard training schemes and subsequently map the parameters to an SNN of same structure. Early studies on conversion began with the work of Perez-Carrasco et al. [6], where CNN units were translated into spiking units with leaks and refractory periods. Cao et al. presented the relation between firing rates of spiking neurons and the activations of rectified linear units (ReLUs) in network conversion [7]. Diehl et al. significantly improved the performance of converted SNNs by introducing weight normalization, which optimize the ratio of synaptic weights to spiking threshold [8]. Lately, Rueckauer et al. analyzed the approximation of the firing rate of spiking neuron to the corresponding activation of ReLU unit in theory, and derived a measure of approximation errors [9]. In addition, they improved the implementation of spiking max-pooling, softmax and neuron biases in SNNs and the performance loss arising from CNN-to-SNN conversion is reduced. Recently, Hu et al. presented a shortcut connection normalization for ResNet and achieved high accuracy on CIFAR dataset with spiking ResNet [10].

In order to enable deeper and more powerful SNNs, this paper proposes a framework for conversion of Inception [11–13] and ResNet [14] which have achieved the state-of-the-art performance in many benchmarks. In particular, Inception and Residual architectures are composed of parallel computing branches, and hundreds of layers are stacked in networks. As SNNs in the conversion scheme are rate-encoding, the firing rates of spiking neurons should approximate to the corresponding activations of CNN for the purpose of maintaining the network performance. On one hand, a novel weight normalization method, as an extension of the work by Diehl et al. [8], is proposed to normalize the CNN activations. This method considers the characteristics of parallel branches and can avoid distorting the feature maps at concatenation stage. On the other hand, a compensation approach, inspired from homeostatic plasticity in neural system [15], is introduced to reduce the deterioration of firing rates at deep layers of SNN through adapting the spiking threshold. The proposed methods are evaluated with several efficient CNN architectures, such as Inception-v4 and Inception-ResNet-v2 [13], on CIFAR benchmark [16]. Results show that the performance of converted SNNs is nearly comparable to the original CNNs, and much higher than SNNs trained with spike-based methods.

2 Methods for Conversion of CNN into SNN

The main differences between SNNs and CNNs are the forms of input and neural activation. SNNs operate on dynamic binary spike trains as a function of time, while the input and activation of CNNs are static analog values without the notion of time. In our framework for CNN-to-SNN conversion (Fig. 1), two neural networks have the same architecture, and the network parameters (weights and biases) of CNN are trained with backpropagation and then mapped into an equivalent SNN. Static inputs of CNN are rate-encoded as Poisson spike trains into the first hidden layer of SNN. Firing rates of spiking neurons correspond to the static activation of CNN neurons and the approximation errors between them are the main source of performance loss in conversion [9]. Weight normalization (Sect. 2.2) is aimed at reducing the approximation errors through rescaling the network parameters and normalizing the activations. Compensation approach (Sect. 2.3) adapts the spiking threshold of neurons to modulate the firing rates of each layer. Here, we start with the overview of conversion as following in Sect. 2.1.

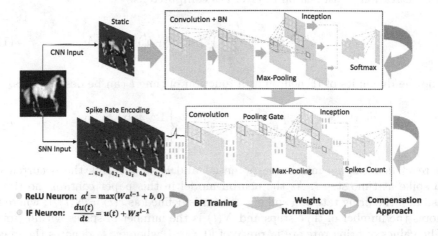

Fig. 1. Scheme of CNN-to-SNN conversion for Inception and Residual architectures

2.1 Spiking Implementation of CNN Operations

Input and Output Representation. Neurons in SNNs receive and transmit binary spikes at each time step, while in CNNs, inputs and outputs of neurons are both analog values. In this paper, networks are evaluated on image datasets and an rate-encoding operation is utilized to encode the static pixel intensity into spike trains. Pixel values of an image are normalized and considered as probabilities in a Poisson event-generation process where at each time step, spikes of input neurons are triggered based on their individual probability. This process ensures that the average number of input spikes in SNN is proportional to the intensity of corresponding image pixel of CNN. Meanwhile, with Poisson-generated spike trains being fed into SNN, spikes will be produced at the network output. Inference is implemented based on the cumulative spike count of neurons at the output layer over a given time-window. Generally, the accuracy of SNN goes higher as the time-window becomes larger. This characteristic of SNN is inherent and known as accuracy-latency trade-off.

Neuron Operations. CNN-to-SNN conversion methods generally consider Rectified Linear Unit (ReLU) as the activation function of CNN. Not only are ReLU neurons computationally cheaper and not subject to gradient saturation, but also they bear functional equivalence to an Integrate-Fire (IF) spiking neuron without any leak and refractory period [7]. IF neuron keeps track of a membrane potential, which integrates presynaptic spikes at each time step. Once the membrane potential accumulates beyond the spiking threshold, the neuron fires a spike and the membrane potential is reset to zero.

For a neural network, let W^l and b^l denote the synaptic weights and biases of layer $l, l \in \{1, \ldots, L\}$ respectively. $|l|$ is the number of neurons in layer l. The ReLU activation of ith neuron in layer l is computed as:

$$a_i^l := \max(0, \sum_{j=1}^{|l-1|} W_{ij}^l a_j^{l-1} + b_i^l) \tag{1}$$

While the dynamics of IF neuron as a function of time t can be described as:

$$\frac{dv_i^l(t)}{dt} = \sum_{j=1}^{|l-1|} W_{ij}^l \theta_{t,j}^{l-1} + b_i^l, \quad \theta_{t,i}^l = \begin{cases} 1, & v_i^l(t) > V_{\text{thr}} \\ 0, & \text{else.} \end{cases} \tag{2}$$

Where v_i^l denotes the membrane potential and $\theta_{t,i}^l$ represents the occurrence of a spike at time step t. As the neuron model in this paper contains no time constants, the firing rate of a spiking neuron is defined as $r(t) = N(t)/t$, where t denotes the number of time steps and $N(t)$ is the number of spikes within time t. The values of firing rate are in range of $[0, r_{\text{max}}]$, where r_{max} denotes the max firing rate, i.e. spike at every time step and therefore $r_{\text{max}} = 1$.

Since the inputs of CNN are rate-encoded into spike trains, the firing rates of input spikes can be considered as an approximation of analog values of CNN inputs, i.e. $r_i^0 = x_i$. By replacing the input spikes $\theta_{t,i}^0$ with the average firing rate x_i and associating Eqs. 1 and 2, the dynamics of membrane potential in the first hidden layer can be presented as:

$$v_i^1(t) := v_i^1(t-1) + a_i^1 - v_{\text{thr}} \theta_{t,i}^1 \tag{3}$$

By averaging the membrane potential in Eq. 3 over the simulation time t, the firing rate of IF neurons can be derived as [9]:

$$l = 1 \quad r_i^1(t) = a_i^1 r_{\text{max}} - \frac{v_i^1(t)}{t \cdot v_{\text{thr}}} \tag{4}$$

$$l \geq 2 \quad r_i^l(t) = \sum_{j=1}^{|l-1|} W_{ij}^l r_j^{l-1}(t) + r_{\text{max}} b_i^l - \frac{v_i^l(t)}{t \cdot v_{\text{thr}}} \tag{5}$$

Equations 4 and 5 state that the firing rates of IF neurons are convergent to the ReLU activations, reduced by a time-decaying approximation error. With enough time duration, the activations of CNN can be approximated by the firing rates of SNN, which is consistent with the foundation of rate-encoding networks.

Conversion of CNN Operations. The convolution operation in CNNs is to compute the weighted sum of output activations of previous layer and it is kept unchanged in SNNs. Notably, in order to accelerate the training of CNNs, the convolution operation is usually followed by a batch-normalization (BN) operation [17] and after training, the parameters of BN can be integrated into the weight vectors of the preceding convolution layer.

Nonlinear pooling operations (such as max-pooling and average-pooling) are widely used in CNNs as the basis of feature selectivity and invariance. Average pooling can be considered as an specialization of convolution operation and realized in the same way. However, since the signals between layers of SNN are transmitted as dynamic binary spikes, the max pooling cannot be implemented by simply selecting maximum value of spikes. Here, a pooling gate is introduced, which evaluates the firing rates of input neurons every time step and transmit the signal of the neuron whose firing rate is maximum at that time [9].

2.2 Weight Normalization Method

In time-stepped simulation of SNNs, the firing rates of spiking neurons are restricted to the range of $[0, r_{max}]$, whereas the ReLU activations have no such limits. In order to ensure the approximation of the firing rates to the activations, a weight normalization method is proposed to normalize the ReLU activations from $[0, a_{max}^l]$ to $[0, r_{max}]$ through rescaling the weights of convolutional layers. Denote λ^l as the max activation of layer l in training process, then the weight normalization can be described as [8]:

$$\overline{W^l} = \frac{\lambda^{l-1}}{\lambda^l} W^l, \quad \overline{b^l} = \frac{1}{\lambda^l} b^l \tag{6}$$

However, this method is focused on simple CNN architectures, such as LeNet and VGG [18], and can not be directly applied to Inception and ResNet. Inception and Residual architectures consist of more than one computing branches, which must be taken into consideration when normalizing the weights. Taking 16×16 grid module of Inception-ResNet architecture (Fig. 2) as example, three branches of Inception have different numbers of convolutional layers. If the normalizing factor of one branch, i.e. the product of normalizing factors of stacked convolutional layers is different from the other branches, the outputs of branches will be scaled disproportionately and the feature maps at concatenation layer will be distorted. Thus the three branches of Inception architecture should have the same normalizing factor. Similarly, the shortcut connection of Residual architecture should be scaled equally as the stacked convolutional layers, in order to keep the inputs of sum layer are valid.

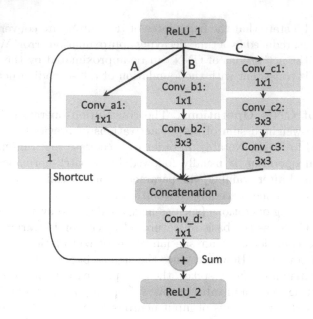

Fig. 2. Schema for 16×16 grid module of Inception-ResNet-v2

Since branch A, B and C receive the same input from ReLU_1 layer and output to Concatenation layer, the normalizing factors of three branches are computed as $\frac{\lambda_{\text{ReLU\_1}}}{\lambda_{\text{Concat}}}$. Then the normalizing factor of Conv_a1, Conv_b2 and Conv_c3 which are the inputs of Concatenation layer, should be $\frac{\lambda_{\text{ReLU\_1}}}{\lambda_{\text{Concat}}}$, $\frac{\lambda_{\text{Conv\_b1}}}{\lambda_{\text{Concat}}}$, $\frac{\lambda_{\text{Conv\_c2}}}{\lambda_{\text{Concat}}}$ instead of $\frac{\lambda_{\text{ReLU\_1}}}{\lambda_{\text{Conv\_a1}}}$, $\frac{\lambda_{\text{Conv\_b1}}}{\lambda_{\text{Conv\_b2}}}$, $\frac{\lambda_{\text{Conv\_c2}}}{\lambda_{\text{Conv\_c3}}}$ derived from Eq. 6. Similarly, as the inputs of Sum layer, Conv_d and shortcut connection should be normalized by $\frac{\lambda_{\text{Concat}}}{\lambda_{\text{Sum}}}$ and $\frac{\lambda_{\text{ReLU\_1}}}{\lambda_{\text{Sum}}}$ respectively. Through the analysis above, weight normalization for networks of Inception and Residual architectures could be concluded as the following Algorithm 1.

2.3 Homeostasis-Based Compensation Approach

The relationship described by Eqs. 4 and 5 demonstrates that the firing rate of a neuron in layer l is given by the weighted sum of the firing rates of previous layer, minus a time-decaying approximation error. By inserting the expression for the firing rates of previous layers and starting with the known firing rates of the first layer in Eq. 4, the recursive expression in Eq. 5 can be solved iteratively as follows [9]:

Algorithm 1. Weight Normalization for Inception and Residual architectures

Input: Max activations of training set λ^l, Weights and Biases $W^l, b^l, l = 1, \ldots, L$.
Output: Normalized weights and biases $\overline{W^l}, \overline{b^l}$.

1: /* l is index of *layer*, i is index of input of *layer*. */
2: **for** *layer* in *Conv.layers* **do**
3:    **if** *layer* in *Concat.Inputs* **then**
4:       $\overline{W^l} = W^l \cdot \lambda^i / \lambda^{cat}, \overline{b^l} = b^l \cdot 1/\lambda^{cat}$
5:    **else if** *layer* in *Sum.Inputs* **then**
6:       $\overline{W^l} = W^l \cdot \lambda^i / \lambda^{sum}, \overline{b^l} = b^l \cdot 1/\lambda^{sum}$
7:    **else**
8:       $\overline{W^l} = W^l \cdot \lambda^i / \lambda^l, \overline{b^l} = b^l \cdot 1/\lambda^l$

Note: *Conv.layers* includes convolutional layers, fully-connected layers and identity mapping (shortcut connection). The max activations λ^l are recorded on training set and weight normalization rescales the parameters after training.

$$
r_i^l = a_i^l r_{\max} - \frac{v_{i_l}^l(t)}{t \cdot V_{thr}} - \sum_{i_{l-1}=1}^{n^{l-1}} W_{i_l i_{l-1}}^l \frac{v_{i_{l-1}}^{l-1}(t)}{t \cdot V_{thr}} - \cdots
$$

$$
- \sum_{i_{l-1}=1}^{n^{l-1}} W_{i_l i_{l-1}}^l \cdots \sum_{i_1=1}^{n^1} W_{i_2 i_1}^2 \frac{v_{i_1}^1(t)}{t \cdot V_{thr}} \tag{7}
$$

Equation 7 implies that each layer computes a weighted sum of the approximation errors of earlier layers, and adds its own approximation error. These errors accumulate layer by layer, which explains why firing rates of SNN deteriorate at deep layers and why it takes longer to achieve convergence of firing rates to corresponding ReLU activations. Since the inference is operated on the cumulative spike count of neurons of output layer, time required for inference will be greatly increased if the firing rates at deep layers are too low. For deep SNNs such as spiking ResNet composed of hundreds of layers, the problem is more prominent.

Inspired from the homeostatic plasticity in neural system, a compensation approach is proposed to reduce the deterioration of firing rates. Neuroscience researches show that homeostasis is an important neural mechanism which balances Hebbian plasticity and stabilizes the neural activity [19]. Among methods of homeostatic plasticity, adapting spiking threshold is widely used in SNNs to keep stable firing rates of spiking neurons [20]. As the inputs of IF neuron are binary spikes, the firing rate mainly depends on the relative scale of synaptic weights to the spiking threshold. Thus, the deterioration of firing rates can be reduced by modulating the spiking threshold. For CNN-to-SNN conversion, the max activation of each layer in CNN is scaled to $r_{\max}$ through weight normalization and accordingly, the max firing rate of each layer is supposed to be $r_{\max}$. However, the actual max firing rates declines with the network depth due to the accumulated approximation errors presented in Eq. 7. The compensation approach takes the ratio of actual max firing rates to the expected $r_{\max}$ as compensation factors to scale down the spiking threshold for each layer. Here the max firing rates of layers are recorded in the simulation of SNN on training sets, and denoted as $\tau^l, l \in \{1, \dots, L\}$. As the max firing rate τ^l generally increases with time and converge to $r_{\max}$, it is available to consider only the firing rates at the end of simulation for simplicity.

$$\tau^l = \max_{t,i} r_i^l(t), \quad i = 1, \dots, |l|, t \in [0, T] \tag{8}$$

$$\overline{Vl}_{\mathrm{thr}} = V_{\mathrm{thr}}^l \tau^l, \quad l = 1, \dots, L \tag{9}$$

Here T denotes the duration of simulation on training set and is an hyperparameter to tune on the validation set.

3   Experiment and Analysis

The proposed methods are evaluated on CIFAR-10 and CIFAR-100 datasets. CIFAR-10 consist of 50k training images and 10k testing images, and are classified into 10 classes with 6000 images per class. The original size of each image is 32 × 32. CIFAR-100 is similar to CIFAR-10, except that it has 100 classes with 600 images per class. Networks built in experiment include Inception-v4, Inception-ResNet-v2 and ResNet. In order to adapt for the image size (original designed for ImageNet 256 × 256 [21]), Inception-v4 and Inception-ResNet-v2 in this paper are composed of 16 × 16 and 8 × 8 grid modules (Fig. 3), and the dimensionality of filters is accordingly scaled down, while the basic structures from original papers [13] are unchanged. ResNets for CIFAR-10 in this paper are the same as that proposed by He et al. [14]. For inference of SNNs, the classification accuracy is obtained with simulation of 3000 time steps. The details of network architectures and the parameters for training are accessible online[1].

3.1   Comparison with Other SNNs

Table 1 shows that the spiking Inception-v4 achieves the state-of-the-art performance of SNNs, with classification error rates of 7.51% and 29.60% on CIFAR-10 and CIFAR-100 respectively. Further, the error rates of converted SNNs are nearly comparable to original CNNs, with very low accuracy loss in conversion. This result demonstrates that the advantages of deep CNN architectures are available for spiking networks and the conversion framework is effective in training deep SNNs. Additionally, comparisons of spiking ResNets show that the accuracy loss caused by conversion increases with the network depth, and the high performance of deep SNNs is gradually compromised, as in the case of ResNet-44 and ResNet-56. Here the main reason for accuracy loss is that the firing rates of SNN is not absolutely convergent to the CNN activations due to inherent differences of neuron operations and time-decaying approximation

---

[1] https://github.com/Xingfush/ANN-to-SNN-for-Inception-ResNet.

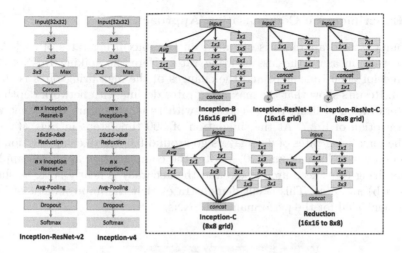

Fig. 3. Network architectures of Inception-v4 and Inception-ResNet-v2 for CIFAR-10

Table 1. Classification error rates on CIFAR-10 and CIFAR-100 for our converted spiking models, in comparison with other SNNs. The Accuracy loss in conversion is defined as the error rate gap between original CNN and the converted SNN. In Inception-v4 and Inception-ResNet-v2, m, n denote the number of 16×16 and 8×8 grid modules (Fig. 3), respectively.

Dataset [architecture]	Depth	CNN err.	SNN err.	Acc loss.
CIFAR-10 [Inception-v4, **ours**]	$m = 4, n = 1$	6.69	**7.51**	0.82
CIFAR-10 [Inception-ResNet-v2, **ours**]	$m = 4, n = 1$	7.28	8.42	1.14
CIFAR-10 [ResNet-20, **ours**]	20	8.89	9.06	0.17
CIFAR-10 [ResNet-32, **ours**]	32	7.48	8.10	0.62
CIFAR-10 [ResNet-44, **ours**]	44	7.09	7.94	0.85
CIFAR-10 [ResNet-56, **ours**]	56	6.97	8.12	1.15
CIFAR-10 [ResNet-44, Hu et al. [10]]	44	7.15	8.02	0.87
CIFAR-10 [VGG, Rueckauer et al. [9]]	16	8.09	9.15	1.06
CIFAR-10 [Esser et al. [22]]	16	NA	12.50	NA
CIFAR-100 [Inception-v4, **ours**]	$m = 4, n = 1$	28.18	**29.60**	1.42
CIFAR-100 [ResNet-44, Hu et al. [10]]	44	29.82	31.44	1.62
CIFAR-100 [Esser et al. [22]]	16	NA	34.52	NA

errors. Deep SNNs are likely to accumulate more approximation errors and thus suffer more accuracy loss. Despite this, the deep SNNs built by the conversion methods still outperform those by other training algorithms, including unsupervised STDP learning and SNNs of VGG architecture.

3.2 Experiment on Compensation Approach

The compensation approach is operated on the max firing rates of each layer because they measure the loss of firing rates. Here the spiking ResNet-56 is simulated for 3000 time steps and the changes of the max firing rates is shown in Fig. 4. Results show that the max firing rates decline with network depth and the deterioration of firing rates decreases with time, which are consistent with the description of Eq. 7. At the simulation of 500 time steps in Figs. 4(a) and 5(a), the max firing rates of deep layers go around 0.6 before compensation and the accuracy of SNN is around 70%. After the compensation approach applied, the max firing rates keep around 0.8 and the accuracy is nearly 90%, as shown in Figs. 4(b) and 5(a). This result demonstrates that the improvement of firing rates is beneficial for the performance of SNNs.

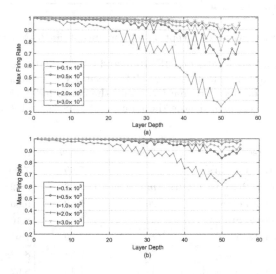

Fig. 4. Changes of max firing rates with layer depth and simulation time, of spiking ResNet-56 on CIFAR-10 before compensation (a) and after compensation (b).

The tendency of curves in Fig. 5 presents the accuracy-latency trade-off of SNNs, i.e. the error rates decrease as the simulation goes. Notably the time steps required for convergence of SNNs is distinct. The comparison between four spiking ResNets in Fig. 5(a) shows that deeper networks need more time to converge, while they can achieve higher accuracy finally. Further, the compensation approach obviously accelerates the convergence of SNNs, and the time steps for inference are nearly halved while the accuracies are not compromised, for both spiking ResNet and spiking Inception.

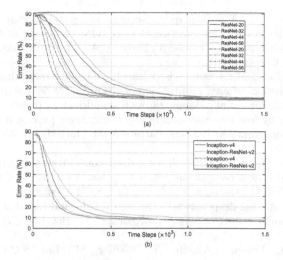

Fig. 5. Simulation of converted SNNs on CIFAR-10. Bold lines denote results before compensation and dashed lines denote results after compensation. (a) spiking ResNets of depth 20, 32, 44, 56. (b) spiking Inception-v4 and Inception-ResNet-v2 of depth $m = 4, n = 1$.

4   Conclusion

This paper proposes a homeostasis-based CNN-to-SNN conversion framework for Inception and Residual architectures. A novel weight normalization method and a bio-inspired compensation approach are developed. Deep networks, including Inception-v4, Inception-ResNet-v2 and ResNets, are successfully implemented in SNNs, with nearly comparable performance to original CNNs. Experimental results show that the spiking Inception-v4 achieves the state-of-the-art performance of SNNs on CIFAR-10 and CIFAR-100 datasets. It is verified that training deep SNNs by conversion methods is promising and the advantage of deep neural networks is available for SNNs. This work is helpful for large-scale employment of spiking networks on efficient neuromorphic spiking platforms.

Acknowledgments. This study was partly supported by the National Natural Science Foundation of China (No. 41571402), the Science Fund for Creative Research Groups of the National Natural Science Foundation of China (No. 61221003), and National Key R&D Program of China (No. 2018YF-B0505000).

References

1. Neil, D., Liu, S.C.: Minitaur, an event-driven FPGA-based spiking network accelerator. IEEE Trans. Very Large Scale Integr. (VLSI) Syst. **22**(12), 2621–2628 (2014)
2. Liu, S.C., Delbruck, T., Indiveri, G., Douglas, R., Whatley, A.: Event-Based Neuromorphic Systems. Wiley, Hoboken (2015)

3. Merolla, P.A., et al.: A million spiking-neuron integrated circuit with a scalable communication network and interface. Science **345**(6197), 668–673 (2014)
4. Furber, S.B., Galluppi, F., Temple, S., Plana, L.A.: The SpiNNaker project. Proc. IEEE **102**(5), 652–665 (2014)
5. Diehl, P.U., Cook, M.: Unsupervised learning of digit recognition using spike-timing-dependent plasticity. Front. Comput. Neurosci. **9**, 99 (2015)
6. Pérez-Carrasco, J.A., et al.: Mapping from frame-driven to frame-free event-driven vision systems by low-rate rate coding and coincidence processing–application to feedforward ConvNets. IEEE Trans. Pattern Anal. Mach. Intell. **35**(11), 2706–2719 (2013)
7. Cao, Y., Chen, Y., Khosla, D.: Spiking deep convolutional neural networks for energy-efficient object recognition. Int. J. Comput. Vis. **113**(1), 54–66 (2015)
8. Diehl, P.U., Neil, D., Binas, J., Cook, M., Liu, S.C., Pfeiffer, M.: Fast-classifying, high-accuracy spiking deep networks through weight and threshold balancing. In: 2015 International Joint Conference on Neural Networks (IJCNN), pp. 1–8. IEEE (2015)
9. Rueckauer, B., Lungu, I.A., Hu, Y., Pfeiffer, M., Liu, S.C.: Conversion of continuous-valued deep networks to efficient event-driven networks for image classification. Front. Neurosci. **11**, 682 (2017)
10. Hu, Y., Tang, H., Wang, Y., Pan, G.: Spiking deep residual network. arXiv preprint arXiv:1805.01352 (2018)
11. Szegedy, C., et al.: Going deeper with convolutions. In: Proceedings of the IEEE Conference on Computer Vision and Pattern Recognition, pp. 1–9 (2015)
12. Szegedy, C., Vanhoucke, V., Ioffe, S., Shlens, J., Wojna, Z.: Rethinking the inception architecture for computer vision. In: Proceedings of the IEEE Conference on Computer Vision and Pattern Recognition, pp. 2818–2826 (2016)
13. Szegedy, C., Ioffe, S., Vanhoucke, V., Alemi, A.A.: Inception-v4, Inception-ResNet and the impact of residual connections on learning. In: AAAI, vol. 4, p. 12 (2017)
14. He, K., Zhang, X., Ren, S., Sun, J.: Deep residual learning for image recognition. In: Proceedings of the IEEE Conference on Computer Vision and Pattern Recognition, pp. 770–778 (2016)
15. Fernandes, D., Carvalho, A.L.: Mechanisms of homeostatic plasticity in the excitatory synapse. J. Neurochem. **139**(6), 973–996 (2016)
16. Krizhevsky, A., Hinton, G.: Learning multiple layers of features from tiny images. Technical report, Citeseer (2009)
17. Salimans, T., Kingma, D.P.: Weight normalization: a simple reparameterization to accelerate training of deep neural networks. In: Advances in Neural Information Processing Systems, pp. 901–909 (2016)
18. Simonyan, K., Zisserman, A.: Very deep convolutional networks for large-scale image recognition. arXiv preprint arXiv:1409.1556 (2014)
19. Turrigiano, G.G., Nelson, S.B.: Homeostatic plasticity in the developing nervous system. Nat. Rev. Neurosci. **5**(2), 97 (2004)
20. Miner, D., Triesch, J.: Plasticity-driven self-organization under topological constraints accounts for non-random features of cortical synaptic wiring. PLoS Comput. Biol. **12**(2), e1004759 (2016)
21. Deng, J., Dong, W., Socher, R., Li, L.J., Li, K., Fei-Fei, L.: ImageNet: a large-scale hierarchical image database. In: 2009 IEEE Conference on Computer Vision and Pattern Recognition, pp. 248–255. IEEE (2009)
22. Esser, S., et al.: Convolutional networks for fast, energy-efficient neuromorphic computing. Preprint on ArXiv http://arxiv.org/abs/1603.08270 (2016). Accessed 27 2016

Training Large-Scale Spiking Neural Networks on Multi-core Neuromorphic System Using Backpropagation

Megumi Ito[1]($\boxtimes$), Malte Rasch[2], Masatoshi Ishii[1], Atsuya Okazaki[1],
Sangbum Kim[3], Junka Okazawa[1], Akiyo Nomura[1], Kohji Hosokawa[1],
and Wilfried Haensch[2]

[1] IBM Research - Tokyo, Tokyo, Japan
megumii@jp.ibm.com
[2] IBM Research, Yorktown Heights, NY, USA
[3] Seoul National University, Seoul, Korea

Abstract. Neuromorphic circuits with nonvolatile memory crossbar arrays can train and inference neural networks in a highly power-efficient manner, which can be a solution to overcome the von Neumann bottleneck. This paper proposes a scalable multi-core spiking neuromorphic system architecture that can support a large-scale multi-layer neural network larger than a network supported by a computing system with a single neuromorphic circuit core. To simplify the inter-core communication, neuromorphic cores communicate only by sending and receiving spikes. Deep networks can be easily formed on this architecture by connecting multiple cores. The neuromorphic cores are trained on-chip by backpropagation, which is a well-known and sophisticated algorithm for training neural networks in software. We made modifications to the traditional backpropagation algorithm to propagate errors and update weights by spikes on the spiking neuromorphic cores of a computing system using our architecture. The proposed algorithm was evaluated by an spike event-based neuromorphic circuit simulator using three datasets. Cancer1 and Thyroid1 were used for a small network evaluation, which results showed better test error than previous studies, and MNIST was used to evaluate a large realistic neural network.

Keywords: Neuromorphic · Backpropagation · Spiking neural network

1 Introduction

Neuromorphic computing systems have a great potential to offer huge computing power in a highly energy efficient manner, which can be a solution to overcome the von Neumann bottleneck [1]. Spiking neural networks, which mimic the human brain, can reduce the energy consumption of the neuromorphic circuits by consuming energy only when required to process spike events [2,3]. Nonvolatile memories (NVMs), such as resistive random-access memories and phase change

© Springer Nature Switzerland AG 2019
T. Gedeon et al. (Eds.): ICONIP 2019, LNCS 11955, pp. 185–194, 2019.
https://doi.org/10.1007/978-3-030-36718-3_16

memories, have been explored as synaptic devices for neuromorphic circuits, where conductance represents a synaptic weight [4,5]. NVM crossbar arrays well represent a neural network connection and offer scalable and low-power weighted sum operation in parallel, which is extensively used in training and inferencing neural networks.

Backpropagation is a well-known and established algorithm for training neural networks in software [6]. There are algorithms for training multi-layered spiking neural networks on neuromorphic circuits using backpropagation [7–9]. They calculate the error of every output neuron in every layer and have a training circuit per layer to generate signals to increase or decrease synaptic weights of the NVM crossbar arrays based on the combinations of errors and inputs. Those by Hasan and Tarek [7] and Zamanidoost et al. [8] update weights in 4 steps based on the sign of the input and error, and that by Hassan et al. [9] reduces this into 2 steps. These authors simulated their training algorithms with some small networks that can be easily implemented within a single neuromorphic core.

To solve real-world problems by using the increasing huge amount of data, we need large and deep neural networks, whose size cannot be fit into a single neuromorphic core. We need multiple neuromorphic cores to construct deep multi-layered neural networks. Moreover, the cores need to be flexibly coupled to support neural networks whose sizes differ depending on the application.

The main contributions of this paper are as follows.

- Proposing a scalable multi-core spiking neuromorphic system architecture for large-scale multi-layer neural networks.
- Proposing a backpropagation algorithm for training multi-core spiking neuromorphic circuits.
- Showing experiment results using a large real-world dataset, MNIST [13].

The rest of the paper is organized as follows. Section 2 introduces our flexible and scalable multi-core spiking neuromorphic system architecture for large-scale multi-layer neural networks. Section 3 introduces the proposed backpropagation training algorithm. We first explain the mathematical model then the implementation of our algorithm in a 2-core neuromorphic system using our architecture. Section 4 evaluates the proposed algorithm with Cancer1 and Thyroid1 from the Proben1 benchmark and the MNIST dataset, and Sect. 5 summarizes the paper.

2   Multi-core Neuromorphic System Architecture

We propose a flexible and scalable multi-core spiking neuromorphic system architecture that can support a large multi-layer neural network. Figure 1 illustrates a neuromorphic core composed of an NVM crossbar array as synapses and leaky Integrate and Fire (LIF) neuron circuits ($N_{*,*}$) [10]. Since synaptic weights can be both positive and negative, a pair of NVM cells forms a synapse, where each of the pair represents a positive and negative weight [11]. In the forward phase of backpropagation, the input neurons issue spikes, and the output neurons generate output spikes when the accumulated weighted-sum exceeds a threshold. In the backward and weight update phases, spikes for propagating the errors and updating the weights are issued from the output neurons.

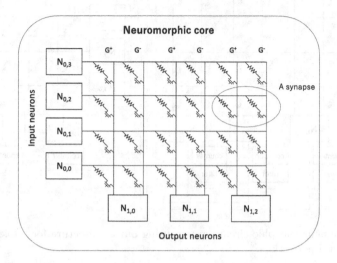

Fig. 1. Single neuromorphic core. Each synapse is composed of two NVM devices, where one contributes positive weight G+ and the other contributes negative weight G−.

Figure 2 shows a 2-core neuromorphic circuit system using our architecture for implementing a $4 \times 3 \times 2$ network. The first layer of the network is mapped to core 1 and the second layer is mapped to core 2. The middle layer with three neurons is physically duplicated in both cores 1 and 2, and its neurons are connected one by one. The connected neurons communicate only by sending spikes to each other to simplify the inter-core communication. The upper layers in each core ($N_{1,*}$ and $N_{2,*}$) have spike counters associated with each output neuron to maintain the generated spike count of the neuron. The upper layer in core 1 ($N_{1,*}$) also has spike filters to drop unnecessary spikes in backward operation, which is explained in detail in Sect. 3.

This system enables the mapping of a larger and deeper neural network by connecting more cores. It can also easily support the different network sizes depending on the application by changing the connections between cores.

3 Backpropagation Training Algorithm

In this section, we introduce how to train a multi-layer neural network mapped on the multi-core neuromorphic system shown in Fig. 2 by backpropagation. We first describe the proposed algorithm in the mathematical model in Sect. 3.1, then show its implementation in the multi-core neuromorphic system in Sect. 3.2.

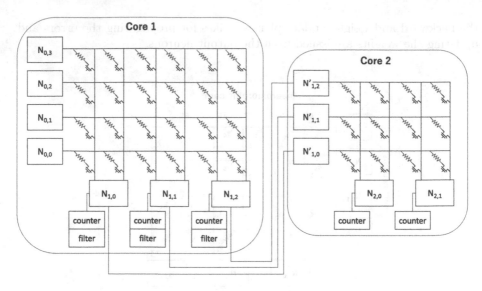

Fig. 2. 2-core neuromorphic circuit system using our architecture for implementing a $4 \times 3 \times 2$ neural network.

3.1   Mathematical Model

To train multi-layer neural networks by backpropagation, we follow the traditional backward algorithm, but modify the backward and weight update phases specifically for the spiking neuromorphic circuit of our multi-core neuromorphic system architecture.

In the mathematical derivation, we assume that an activation value of a neuron x is a continuous number. In the spiking circuit, it will be approximated by the rate of the spikes of the neuron.

Forward Pass. First, in a forward pass, training data is fed to the network and the forward activations are propagated through the layers. The weighted sum of the jth output neuron $z_j^{(l)}$ of the lth layer is given by

$$z_j^{(l)} = \sum_i w_{ji}^{(l)} x_i^{(l-1)} \tag{1}$$

where $x_i^{(l-1)}$ is the input spike rate (output of the previous layer) and $w_{ji}^{(l)}$ is the weight of the synapse connecting the input neuron i and output neuron j in layer l. We call $z_j^{(l)}$ the sub-threshold potential, since this is, in the spiking neuron analogy, roughly proportional to the membrane voltage of the neuron when averaged over a given time window of constant stimulation with the same input spiking rate.

The neuron output y_j is given by (omitting the layer index l)

$$y_j = f(z_j) \tag{2}$$

where we assume the activation function $f(\cdot)$ to be the rectified linear unit (ReLU) activation, which can be implemented approximately by the threshold mechanism of the noisy Integrate and Fire neuron circuit in our system (see [10] for similar discussion). Note that in this case, if $z_j < 0$, it is $y_j = 0$ (assuming the threshold is arbitrarily at zero), and if $z_j \geq 0$, it is at least roughly $z_j \propto y_j$ for the neural implementation (or even identical $z_j = y_j$ in our mathematical formulation).

Backward and Update Pass. The gradient of the error function at the output layer L at the jth output neuron δ_j is calculated by taking the difference between the target output t_j and actual output $y_j^{(L)}$;

$$\delta_j^{(L)} = t_j - y_j^{(L)} \tag{3}$$

Note that since $y_j^{(L)} \geq 0$ and t_j are either 1 (or some set target rate) or 0; thus $\delta_j^{(L)}$ can be in principle be represented by spike rates, which are necessarily positive.

However, in the traditional form of backpropagation, the errors are now propagated backwards through the other hidden layers in the following manner. For the hidden layer l, the error is propagated back from the layer $l+1$ such that

$$\delta_j^{(l)} = f'(z_j^{(l)}) \sum_k \delta_k^{(l+1)} w_{kj}^{(l+1)} \tag{4}$$

where $f'(z)$ is either 0 if $z \leq 0$ or 1 if $z > 0$ for ReLU; thus, equaling the Heaviside function H. However, the value $\delta_j^{(l)}$ can in principle be positive or negative, even if the previous deltas $\delta_k^{(l+1)}$ were all positive, because the weights might be both positive or negative. Thus, representing the deltas in spike rates is problematic.

Inspired by the formulation of the spiking Boltzmann machines of Neftci et al. [10], we solve this problem by representing positive and negative deltas separately by two backward phases. Note that when having individual positive and negative deltas, the update pass can be conveniently represented in two phases as well, i.e., computing (in sequence)

$$w_{ji} \leftarrow w_{ji} + \eta\ ^\oplus\delta_j x_i$$
$$w_{ji} \leftarrow w_{ji} - \eta\ ^\ominus\delta_j x_i \tag{5}$$

where η is the learning rate and $^\oplus\delta_j$ and $^\ominus\delta_j$ are the (all positive) deltas of the positive and negative phases, respectively.

To use two phases on the backward pass, we first assign $^\oplus\delta_j^{(L)} \equiv t_j$ and $^\ominus\delta_j^{(L)} \equiv y_j$ in the output layer L, which is identical to Eq. 3.

To compute the other layers' backward pass (Eq. 4) in a manner applicable to spiking neural networks, modifications have to be made. There are various possibilities. We found that one good solution is to add the sub-threshold activity z_j to the deltas then apply an activation function,

$$^{\oplus}\delta_j^{(l)} = f\left(z_j + \sum_k {}^{\oplus}\delta_k^{(l+1)} w_{kj}^{(l+1)}\right) \tag{6}$$

and do this analogously for the negative phase. This form is implementable in spiking neurons since it has the same form as the forward pass, except that an additional input is given.

Note that if the neuron did not fire during the forward pass, z_j is negative (below the threshold), inhibiting the neuron's activity when the delta "synaptic" input $I_j \equiv \sum_k {}^{\oplus}\delta_k^{(l+1)} w_{kj}^{(l+1)}$ is positive. Together, this mechanism thus implements the $f'(z_j^{(l)}) \equiv H(z_j^{(l)})$ term in Eq. 4. Moreover, if the delta synaptic input I_j is negative (and $y_k > 0$ during forward), z_j provides an additive offset, so that the neuron representing the output firing rate is likely to be positive. Although this additional offset adds to the amount of update in one phase, the same offset is used for both negative and positive phases; therefore, it will be subtracted out in the differential update phase (see Eq. 5).

We found that this mixing of forward and backward synaptic inputs signals of Eq. 6 is an effective and elegant solution for a backward pass applicable to spiking neurons, and seems to be a good approximation of traditional backpropagation. We found that the test error was not significantly impacted, when comparing against the traditional backpropagation algorithm on the same 3-layer fully-connected network on MNIST (in the rate formulation presented here, both algorithms reach test errors of 2–3%).

However, in the 2-core neuromorphic system (Fig. 2), when crossing the core boundaries of a multi-core system, sub-threshold activities z_j from one core cannot be mixed directly with synaptic inputs from another core because only spikes can cross core-boundaries.

Thus, we used an alternative, approximate backward pass. In other words, we add neuron output spikes y_j to the neuron's input, i.e.,

$$^{\oplus}\delta_j^{(l)} = H(y_j)f(y_j + \sum_k {}^{\oplus}\delta_k^{(l+1)} w_{kj}^{(l+1)}) \tag{7}$$

and do this analogously for the negative phase. Since y_j is the spiking activity (rate); thus, cannot be negative, it provides a similar offset to potentially negative delta synaptic inputs I_j as before, which again is corrected during the differential update. However, because y_j cannot be negative, it needs to be ensured explicitly that the deltas are set to zero when the neuron was not active during forward, thus the $H(y_j) \equiv H(z_j)$.

The implementation of this modified backward process in our multi-core spiking neuromorphic system is explained in the next section.

3.2   Hardware Implementation

The backpropagation mathematical model described in Sect. 3.1. was implemented in the 2-core neuromorphic system in Fig. 2.

The forward processes Eqs. 1 and 2 are naturally mapped to the circuit by the NVM crossbar arrays and LIF neurons. The input training data are converted to spike trains based on the Poisson distribution. When an input neuron circuit receives a spike, the signal flows through the NVM crossbar array, which performs a weighted sum operation in Eq. 1. The result of the weighted sum is delivered to an output neuron and accumulated to the neuron's potential. If the accumulated potential exceeds a certain threshold, the output neuron generates a spike, which works as a nonlinear activation function in Eq. 2. The generated spike in core 1 is transferred to a corresponding input neuron in core 2 as an input spike to the next layer. A spike counter associated with each output neuron in every layer counts the number of spikes generated during the forward process for the backward process.

The backward process is combined with the weight update process to propagate errors for updating weight. A weight update process of a layer is divided into two phases, positive and negative update phases, as in Eq. 5. Propagated errors are used to update synaptic weights by each layer, from top to bottom. First, as in Fig. 2(b), the synaptic weights of the last output layer are updated to a negative direction based on the negative error, which is the output spikes counted in the forward process. Then, the layer is updated to a positive direction based on the target output, as in Fig. 2(c). In the both phases, core 1 runs a forward process to generate input spikes for core 2.

The procedure is more complex for the other hidden layers. To propagate positive and negative errors from the last output layer, the layers between the last layer and the layer updating its weight performs a backward process. During the process, we add neuron output y_i, which is collected by the spike counters in the forward process, to the visible neurons of the next layer. This is done by increasing the corresponding visible neuron's potential by a constant amount based on y_i. The generated backward spikes are dropped by a spike filter when y_i was not positive. This operation implements the inner-product with $f'(z_i)$. The filtered backward spike trains represent the propagated positive and negative errors. As in the similar procedure in the last layer, the target layer is updated to the negative and positive directions. The backward and weight update process is repeated by each layer until the first layer in core 1 is updated.

Figure 3 illustrates the whole entire training procedure for a 2-core neuromorphic system. There are a total of five phases, i.e., a forward phase and positive and negative weight update phases per each core. In the forward phase in (a), both cores perform a forward process to generate the current output of the network. The output spikes are counted in both cores for the later phases. From (b) to (e), back-ward and weight update processes are performed by each core. First, in (b), the negative weight update of the core 2 is performed by applying the outputs generated in (a) to the output neurons of core 2. Then, in (c), the target outputs are applied to the output neurons to perform the positive weight update of core 2. We repeat applying the forward and target outputs in (d) and (e) to update the weights of core 1. In (d) and (e), core 2 performs a backward process along with the forward outputs of core 1 generated in (a) to propagate errors. The propagated error spikes transferred to core 1 are dropped if the output neuron in that core did not spike during (a). In all phases, training data are provided to the input neurons of core 1.

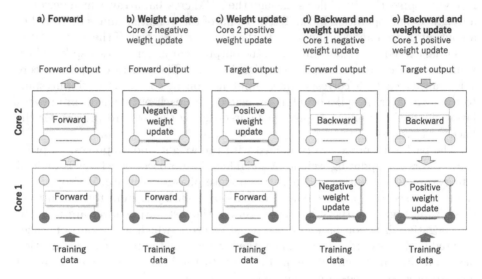

Fig. 3. Training procedure of 2-core neuromorphic system. There is one forward step and four weight update phases, which performs positive and negative weight updates per each core.

4   Experimental Results

We evaluated our proposed backpropagation algorithm through simulation using an spike event-based C++ simulator for neuromorphic circuits that implements the proposed architecture described in the Sects. 2 and 3. Three datasets were used for the evaluation. Cancer1 and Thyroid1 from the Proben1 benchmark [12] were used to evaluate small networks and the MNIST handwritten dataset [13] was used to evaluate a realistic learning problem. The network size and number of training sets in Cancer1 and Thyroid1 are shown in Table 1. For MNIST, we randomly selected 4,000 images (400 images per label) every epoch from the 60,000 training image set to training a $784 \times 500 \times 40$ network, where each pixel of the 28×28 MNIST images was mapped to one input neuron of the first layer. In the output layer, four sets of ten labels (0–9) were mapped to the label neurons. All networks of the three datasets were mapped on a 2-core neuromorphic system. Spike trains of the training data and labels were generated based on the Poisson distribution. The training time of each image was 50 ms. The NVM synapses were simulated as ideal devices in which conductance increases by a constant amount by each weight update pulse.

Figure 4 shows the best training and test error rates of Cancer1, Thyroid1, and MNIST which are simulated for 30 epochs of training. Table 1 compares the results of Cancer1 and Thyroid1 with those of previous studies. It shows that our training algorithm achieved the better results than those algorithms. The MNIST results in Fig. 4 shows that our backpropagation algorithm successfully trained a large network which requires multiple neuromorphic cores. Some of the NVM devices hits the maximum weight in the later epochs, which does not make it possible to update the synaptic weight further to the positive or negative direction. This can be solved by introducing the NVM conductance refresh [14], which periodically resets the weight of the each NVM device while maintaining the total synaptic weight.

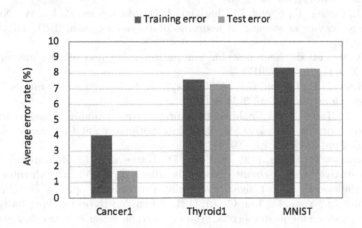

Fig. 4. Simulated best training and test error rates for Cancer1, Thyroid1, and MNIST, trained for 30 epochs.

Table 1. Comparison of the simulation conditions and of results of Cancer1 and Thyroid1 from different studies.

Study	Cancer1			Thyroid1		
	Network	Training set	Error	Network	Training set	Error
[8]	$9 \times 4 \times 2$	350	2.9%	$21 \times 4 \times 3$	3,600	7.7%
[9]	$9 \times 10 \times 2$	600	≒6.2%	$21 \times 15 \times 3$	6,120	≒9.2%
This study	$9 \times 6 \times 2$	350	1.7%	$21 \times 15 \times 3$	3,600	7.3%

5   Conclusion

We proposed an NVM-based scalable multi-core spiking neuromorphic system architecture and its training algorithm by backpropagation. We demonstrated that the proposed algorithm trained both small and large networks on a 2-core neuromorphic system through simulation. For future work, we plan to improve our backpropagation algorithm to further reduce the error rate and the training cost. Also, the impact of variations in the NVM devices is one of the items to be investigated in the future.

References

1. Taha, T.M., Hasan, R., Yakopcic, C., McLean, M.R.: Exploring the design space of specialized multicore neural processors. In: The 2013 International Joint Conference on Neural Networks, pp. 1–8. IEEE (2013)
2. Merolla, P.A., et al.: A million spiking neuron integrated circuit with a scalable communication network and interface. Science 345(6197), 668–673 (2014)
3. Davies, M., et al.: Loihi: a neuromorphic manycore processor with on-chip learning. IEEE Micro 38(1), 82–99 (2018)
4. Jo, S.H., Chang, T., Ebong, I., Bhadviya, B.B., Mazumder, P., Lu, W.: Nanoscale memristor device as synapse in neuromorphic systems. Nano Lett. 10(4), 1297–1301 (2010)
5. Burr, G.W., et al.: Neuromorphic computing using non-volatile memory. Adv. Phys.: X 2(1), 89–124 (2017)
6. Rumelhart, D.E., Hinton, G.E., Williams, R.J.: Learning representations by back-propagating errors. Nature 5(3), 1 (1988)
7. Hasan, R., Tarek M.T.: Enabling back propagation training of memristor cross-bar neuromorphic processors. In: 2014 International Joint Conference on Neural Networks, pp. 21–28. IEEE (2014)
8. Zamanidoost, E., Bayat, F.M., Strukov, D., Kataeva, I.: Manhattan rule training for memristive crossbar circuit pattern classifiers. In: 2015 IEEE 9th International Symposium on Intelligent Signal Processing Proceedings, pp. 1–6. IEEE (2015)
9. Hassan, A.M., Yang, C., Liu, C., Li, H.H., Chen, Y.: Hybrid spiking-based multi-layered self-learning neuromorphic system based on memristor crossbar arrays. In: Design, Automation and Test in Europe Conference and Exhibition, pp. 776–781. IEEE (2017)
10. Neftci, E., Das, S., Pedroni, B., Kreutz-Delgado, K., Cauwenberghs, G.: Event-driven contrastive divergence for spiking neuromorphic systems. Front. Neurosci. 7, 272 (2014)
11. Bichler, O., Suri, M., Querlioz, D., Vuillaume, D., DeSalvo, B., Gamrat, C.: Visual pattern extraction using energy-efficient "2-PCM synapse" neuromorphic architecture. IEEE Trans. Electron Dev. 59(8), 2206–2214 (2012)
12. Prechelt, L.: PROBEN 1: a set of benchmarks and benchmarking rules for neural network training algorithms. Technical report, Fakultät für Informatik, Universität Karlsruhe (1994)
13. LeCun, Y., Bottou, L., Bengio, Y., Haffner, P.: Gradient-based learning applied to document recognition. Proc. IEEE 86, 2278–2324 (1998)
14. Ito, M., et al.: Lightweight refresh method for PCM-based neuromorphic circuits. In: 2018 IEEE 18th International Conference on Nanotechnology, pp. 1–4. IEEE (2018)

Deep Learning of EEG Data in the NeuCube Brain-Inspired Spiking Neural Network Architecture for a Better Understanding of Depression

Dhvani Shah[1]($\boxtimes$), Grace Y. Wang[2], Maryam Doborjeh[3],
Zohreh Doborjeh[1], and Nikola Kasabov[1,3]

[1] Knowledge Engineering and Discovery Research Institute,
Auckland University of Technology, Auckland, New Zealand
dshah@aut.ac.nz
[2] Department of Psychology, Auckland University of Technology,
Auckland, New Zealand
[3] Department of Computer Science, Auckland University of Technology,
Auckland, New Zealand

Abstract. In the recent years, machine learning and deep learning techniques are being applied on brain data to study mental health. The activation of neurons in these models is static and continuous-valued. However, a biological neuron processes the information in the form of discrete spikes based on the spike time and the firing rate. Understanding brain activities is vital to understand the mechanisms underlying mental health. Spiking Neural Networks are offering a computational modelling solution to understand complex dynamic brain processes related to mental disorders, including depression. The objective of this research is modeling and visualizing brain activity of people experiencing symptoms of depression using the SNN NeuCube architecture. Resting EEG data was collected from 22 participants and further divided into groups as healthy and mild-depressed. NeuCube models have been developed along with the connections across different brain regions using Synaptic Time Dependent plasticity (STDP) learning rule for healthy and depressed individuals. This unsupervised learning revealed some distinguishable patterns in the models related to the frontal, central and parietal areas of the depressed versus the control subjects that suggests potential markers for early depression prediction. Traditional machine learning techniques, including MLP methods have been also employed for classification and prediction tasks on the same data, but with lower accuracy and fewer new information gained.

Keywords: Spiking Neural Networks (SNN) · Electroencephalogram (EEG) · Depression · NeuCube

1 Introduction

In the recent years, deep learning models have been successful in achieving high accuracy in various applications like speech recognition [1], image recognition [2], biomedicine and bioinformatics [3, 4], temporal data processing etc. [5], assisting

© Springer Nature Switzerland AG 2019
T. Gedeon et al. (Eds.): ICONIP 2019, LNCS 11955, pp. 195–206, 2019.
https://doi.org/10.1007/978-3-030-36718-3_17

humans and challenging the other traditional machine learning models. In all the standard deep neural architectures (supervised learning), the input data in the form of vectors are passed into multiple hidden layers with numerous neurons in each layer (depending on the size of the input data) and activation functions are applied to produce an outcome. The actual aim is to minimize the error by hyperparameter optimization methods. All these methods used a scalar, vector-based information representation.

In the human brain, spikes (represented by the spiking neurons – spiking neural network (SNN) models as binary units) are generated when a neuron's activation crosses a threshold value during changes in the membrane potential based on the stimulation. Here, the time of spiking, the location of the neuron, the firing rate of neurons and the temporal patterns carry information about external stimuli and the various internal calculations. Extracting knowledge and learning patterns from them helps in understanding the various brain states and processes modelled with the use of brain data. SNN are more biologically realistic [6] as compared with the deep neural network (DNN). Spiking neurons work with spatial-temporal data using pulse coding strategies to send information to many other neurons and receive the same from others. Based on the membrane potentials, these neurons can be excitatory or inhibitory. In this research, the NeuCube SNN architecture [7] is employed on depression case study data for extracting knowledge from the EEG signals in order to understand the brain processes in the healthy and the depressed individuals.

By 2030, World Health Organization reported that around 322 million people worldwide will be affected by depression and this will lead to some other physiological issues in the near future [8]. Depression is a major contributor to the overall global burden of disease wherein it is more prevalent in females than males. Depression affects the physical and mental well-being of a person in various aspects, such as lack of memory power, heart attacks, suicidal thoughts, lack of motivation and interest, high fatigue, erratic sleep patterns etc. It is very important to identify and treat depression before depression is manifested for a better treatment outcome.

There are many techniques to detect depression like laboratory methods, non-laboratory methods, genomics etc. [9]. One of them is using EEG data recordings. After capturing EEG data, processes like Pearson correlation coefficient (PCC), phase locking value (PLV) and phase lag index [10], detrended fluctuation analysis and power spectral analysis [11, 12], etc. can be applied to the EEG data for identifying the detectors of the underlying brain condition. Deep learning architectures [13–19] have been recently applied in addition to the classical machine learning models [14, 20–24].

Some researchers first acquire features from the raw data and then feed them into machine learning (ML) and artificial neural networks (ANN) for classifying the depressed individuals from the healthy ones using various algorithms, such as: logistic regression [25]; artificial feedforward network [26]; support vector machine (SVM) [27]. Convolutional Neural Network have been used extensively for classifying raw EEG signals [28, 29]. In [30], the authors implemented a deep learning approach varying the number of hidden units (100 and 50) outperforming SVM and naïve Bayes classifiers. In [31] and [32] authors used a hybrid model of CNN and LSTM for categorizing EEG signals. In recent studies of depression detection, Acharya and team

[33] developed a 13-layer CNN achieving 93.54% and 95.96% from EEG signals of left and right hemisphere respectively. To overcome the drawback of CNN (poor sequential learning) in [16] authors employed hybrid CNN-LSTM model for depression detection, reaching classification accuracy of 97.66% (L.H.) and 99.12% (R.H.).

Despite the high accuracy of classification results of EEG data, none of the papers reviewed above reported the actual brain patterns that can be used to distinguish the groups, and there are gaps related to application of brain features underlying depression into ML.

Brain inspired SNN have been used in variety of applications like forecasting [34], modelling the effect of mindfulness on depressed individuals [35], real world data classification, image recognition, odour recognition, motor control and trajectory tracking, etc. SNN aid in providing unique brain patterns and also models of brain functions and brain connectivity. A SNN NeuCube model [36] reached 90.91% accuracy whereas traditional methods achieved just 50.55% accuracy in classifying opiate addicts from the healthy controls. This is a result of a deeper modelling insight into neural circuitry, information processing and plasticity in the brain areas to build a relation between the depression symptoms at the neural level and the resulting mental disorders of a subject.

Following the successful usage of the NeuCube SNN architecture for EEG data modelling and understanding, here we apply this architecture on EEG data related to depressed and control individuals in an attempt to better understand and predict depression.

2 Methods and Procedures

Ethics: Auckland University of Technology (AUT) Ethics Committee (AUTEC), New Zealand granted the ethics approval.

2.1 Dataset Description

The EEG data was collected under strict monitoring with 2 min eyes opening state and 2 min eyes closing state. Recordings were carried out using a SynAmps amplifier and 61-channels (FP1, FPZ, FP2, AF3, AF4, F7, F5, F3, F1, FZ, F2, F4, F6, F8, FT7, FC5, FC3, FC1, FCZ, FC2, FC4, FC6, FT8, T7, C5, C3, C1, CZ, C2, C4, C6, T8, TP7, CP5, CP3, CP1, CPZ, CP2, CP4, CP6, TP8, P7, P5, P3, P1, PZ, P2, P4, P6, P8, PO7, PO3, POZ, PO4, PO8, O1, OZ, O2, PO1, PO2, OI1) with electrode placements based on standard 10–20 international system. The data was recorded at a sampling rate of 1000 Hz. After EEG recording, 2 s epoch was extracted. Off-line ICA computerized artefact correction was used to remove detectable eye movement or muscles potentials. The dataset consists of participants with BDI score ranging from 0 to 3. Participants having BDI score 0-10 are considered as healthy subjects (12) and those having BDI score > 10 are considered as mild-depressed subjects (10) for this experiment. After data pre-processing techniques, each participant's data consists of 16383 time points.

2.2   Proposed NeuCube Model for Classifying and Analyzing the Brain Regions Using EEG Data of Healthy and Depressed Individuals

The NeuCube computational model as shown in Fig. 1 consists of various algorithms for encoding input data into spike trains, for unsupervised and supervised learning and for optimization [7]. For this research, we have performed experiments differently for two cases: Eyes Open and Eyes Closed state for each of the groups (healthy and depressed) to understand their brain conditions.

The following procedures are applied in the modelling part.

- Encoding (Threshold Based method): Spikes are generated based on the threshold from the EEG spatio-temporal data (continuous real values) using the threshold-based method [37, 39]. If the signal changes above the spike threshold (0.5), then a positive spike is generated, if the signal changes below the threshold value, a negative spike is generated or else no spikes are generated.
- Mapping spike input data into the SNNr reservoir: The SNNr (mapping inputs into high dimensional space for pattern analysis) holds the structural and functional spatial connections following the Talairach brain template [38]. A leaky-integrate and fire model of spiking neurons with recurrent connections have been implemented in the SNNr module [7].
- Unsupervised Learning: In our experiments, STDP [40] learning method is used in the SNNr to learn spike sequences from the input data. After the learning, new connections are generated in the SNNr reservoir that represent spatio-temporal interactions between the input variables distributed in the SNNr.
- Visualisation of learned patterns: Our results include visualization for the various connectivity in the brain regions in the depressed and healthy group
- Pattern Classification: This module maps the learned SNN connectivity and temporal activity to known class labels for a classification task. The output layer classifier is trained using the dynamic evolving Spiking Neural Network method (deSNN) [41].

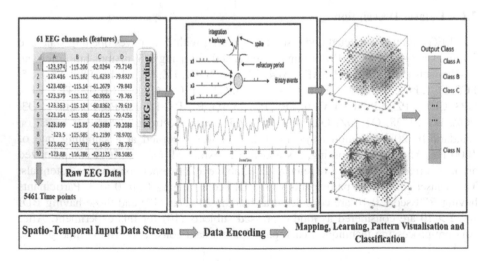

Fig. 1. NeuCube computational model [7]

3 Results

This study is structured in a two-step analysis as follows:

- NeuCube SNN model learning and visualization of the EEG data to investigate brain connectivity of depressed and healthy individuals for both the Eyes Closed and the Eyes Opened states
- Using MLP (Multilayer perceptron) machine learning techniques for a comparative analysis.

3.1 Experiment Design

The original dataset consists of 16383 rows (temporal features) with 61 columns (spatial features) for each participant (10 depressed, 12 healthy). But for experimentation purposes, we formulated the dataset to suit our requirements according to the architecture:

- NeuCube: Each participant is termed as a 'sample' which consists spatio-temporal dataset ('.csv'). Each sample is a matrix consisting of 16383 rows and 61 columns. To have more samples, we divided each sample into three more samples generating 66 samples altogether (30 depressed, 36 healthy) with 5461 time points (rows) in each sample keeping number of columns consistent (61).
- MLP and machine learning algorithms: Here, we performed averaging on each sample (5461 rows) to obtain one frame for each participant keeping number of columns consistent (61).

3.2 Classification Accuracy

NeuCube, being a stochastic model, classification accuracy depends on the parameters' settings [39, 42] as described below:

- Spike threshold was set to 0.5 for converting the input data to sequences of spikes. The spike rate depends on this threshold value.
- The threshold of firing, the refractory time and the potential leak rate were set to 0.5, 6 ms and 0.002 respectively after optimization.
- The STPD learning rate parameter was set to 0.01 which cause changes in the connection weights (increase or decrease) of two connected neurons depending on the order of firing.
- For unsupervised learning, the training iteration was set to one which is considered optimal for incremental, on-line adaptive learning.
- For supervised learning, the parameters 'mod' and 'drift' of deSNN classifier were set to 0.4 and 0.25 respectively. Also, we set k = 3 in K-NN classifier for mapping the input data to the labelled outcome in the training procedure.

For a comparative analysis, we implemented 2-layer MLP network after using grid search optimization with 100- neurons in each layer. 'relu' was used as an activation function for hidden layers, 'softmax' was used for output layer activation, 'adam' was used for weight optimization, learning rate was set to 0.001, alpha was set to 0.001 (L2 regularization parameter).

After applying cross-validating techniques (5 folds), the accuracy of the NeuCube model for classifying depressed versus healthy subjects EEG data was 68.18% (EC) and 72.13% (EO). The MLP NN models for both eyes opened, and eyes closed EEG data achieved slightly higher than 50% accuracy which was inferior to the NeuCube model classification.

The reason for reporting only the MLP results and parameters is that all other traditional machine learning algorithms, such as SVM, decision tree and logistic regression obtained worse results than MLP. The NeuCube models not only obtained much higher classification accuracy, but here they have been used to reveal patterns of brain activities related to each of the two classes of subjects, facilitating a better interpretation and understanding of the depression phenomenon as explained in the following section.

3.3   Pattern Discovery of Dynamic Brain Activities of Depressed Versus Healthy Individuals Through Visualization of the NeuCube Models

This section discusses the functional connectivity inside the brain through the analysis of the learned NeuCube models using visualization of the feature interaction network (FIN) [7, 46] graphs and the SNN connectivity graphs.

3.3.1   Eyes Closed State

This section explains the similarities and differences in the eyes closed state byanalysing the Feature Interaction Networks (FIN) and SNNr connectivity models,as presented in Figs. 2 and 3 across 61 EEG channels (features).

In terms of similarity between groups there are feature input interactions in the frontal, parietal and temporal regions suggested by a great number of lines observed in these areas. Also, the interactions are stronger in the frontal and lower part of the brain as these areas have thick black lines like channels F8, F6, FC6, FT8, T8, TP8, PO3, PO7. Interaction between PO7 and FT8 is evident in both groups.

Some noticeable differences between groups include interaction between channels F5, FT8 and CP5In contrast to the healthy group, depressed group failed to exhibit any interaction between F5 and FT8 channels. The lack of connection between frontal and frontotemporal regions may be reflective of dysfunction within corticolimbic connections in individuals vulnerable to depression [42]. There is a continuous long-range communication between F4 and T8 indicating cross-hemispheric communication in the depressed group. By analyzing the SNN connectivity network (Fig. 2 b and d), there is complete absence of interaction in the parietal region in the depressed group. By observing the FIN of the depressed group, it is seen that P4 plays no role in the change of the network. It may be speculated that the relative reduction in right parietal activity may reflect a reduction in arousal in those at risk of depression. Previous research has demonstrated the decreased right parietal activity in resting state EEG data in those with major depressive disorder in females [43] and within males [44]. More positive

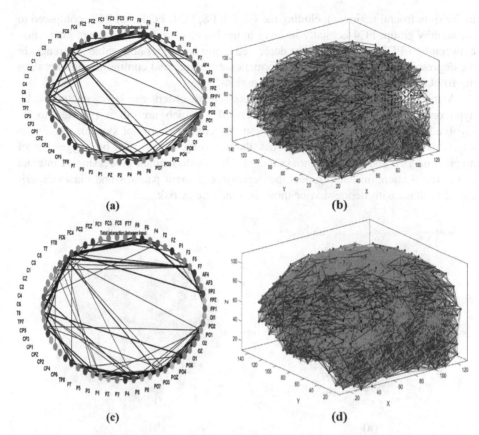

Fig. 2. Visualization for eyes closed state of individual: (a) Depressed FIN; (b) Depressed SNN connectivity; (c) Healthy FIN; (d) Healthy SNN connectivity. (Here FIN stands for feature interaction network, the features being the 61 EEG channels).

connections (blue color) are seen in the healthy group whereas there is lot of saturation of positive (excitatory) and negative (inhibitory) connections in the depressed group across the scalp. There is a combination of positive and negative connections in the lower occipital region for both the groups.

3.3.2 Eyes Open State

Both groups have strong connections in the frontal, parietal-occipital and parietal brain regions of the FIN models (PO3, PO7, PO8, PO4, F4, FP2, T8), but the interaction in the parietal region of the depressed group is greater than those in the healthy group as shown in Fig. 3.

The evident difference is the strong triangular connection between F4-T8-PO8 across the right hemisphere in the healthy group which is completely absent in the depressed group (less interaction between PO8 and T8). There are greater connections in the right frontal regions, including the F4, F6, F8, FC4, FC6, and FC8, compared to the healthy group. FC4 is totally inactive in the healthy group. Long-range interaction between FT8-PO7 and F8-P1 in the depressed group is another noticeable difference. In the depressed group, there is more information exchange and communication between the frontal-parietal and parietal-occipital regions.

A meta-analysis [45] suggests that depressive disorders can be characterized by hypoconnectivity within frontoparietal networks, which are often reported to be involved with attention, emotion regulation and cognitive control systems. Additionally, this abnormal connectivity across these resting states may be suggestive of atypical internal and self-referential thought. This dysfunctional processing of internal and external attention could reflect the depressive thought patterns and biases experienced in those with depression or those that may be at risk.

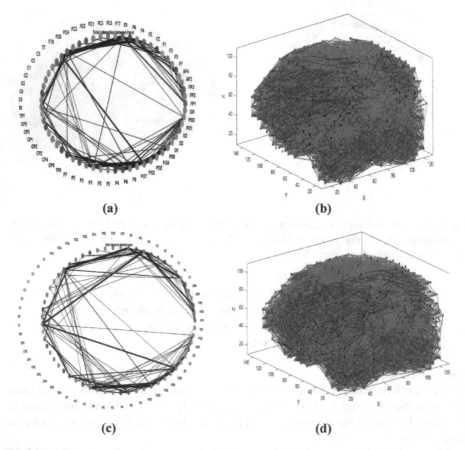

Fig. 3. Visualization for eyes open state: (a) Depressed FIN;(b) Depressed SNN connectivity; (c) Healthy FIN; (d) Healthy SNN connectivity.

4 Conclusion

In this research, we performed EEG data analysis for groups of depressed and control subjects using the NeuCube SNN framework. There were significant differences discovered and reported in the paper that can potentially be used as markers for an early prediction and a possible prevention of depression. The study also applied a comparative analysis using other machine learning techniques such as MLP to demonstrate the advantage of using the SNN approach of time-space brain data modelling. The NeuCube SNN models not only achieved a much better accuracy of classifying samples from the two subject groups but revealed informative patters of brain activities that can be further interpreted for a better understanding of depression.

Future work is planned in terms of detecting not only the dynamic patterns that can be used to predict depression but representing them as deep spatio-temporal rules for a better understanding of the related brain processes [46]. Research papers claim that SNNs are still unable to outperform ANNs with regard to accuracy as ANNs employ backpropagation for reducing the error, however, the learning concept inside the brain is diverse and still not explored fully. Spiking neurons emit spikes carrying most of the information to be transferred across all the neurons, replicating the behavior of the biological neurons [47]. NeuCube is a complex SNN architecture that proved to be useful for knowledge extraction and pattern recognition from spatio-temporal brain data [7]. Conversion of deep networks into SNN [55], deep spiking networks [48, 49], spiking variants of backpropagation [50–52], biologically variants of STDP [53] and hybrid CNN-SNN models [54] are some of the current techniques employed for SNN. In the future we aim to develop a more complex brain inspired SNN models, for example such that use convolution layers/ Gabor filter deriving the features from the EEG signals, feeding them into SNN, using better learning strategies to adapt the model connection weights. Finally, using evolutionary algorithms and in particular quantum-inspired evolutionary algorithms, we can optimize the parameters of SNN to improve the classification accuracy [46, 56].

Acknowledgements. We would like to show our gratitude to Thekkekara Joel Philip (PhD student, AUT) and Mark Crook-RumSey (PhD student, NTU) for sharing their knowledge with us during the course of this research.

References

1. Hinton, G., et al.: Deep neural networks for acoustic modeling in speech recognition: the shared views of four research groups. IEEE Signal Process. Mag. **29**(6), 82–97 (2012)
2. Krizhevsky, A., Sutskever, I., Hinton, G.E.: Imagenet classification with deep convolutional neural networks. In: Advances in Neural Information Processing Systems, pp. 1097–1105 (2012)
3. Mamoshina, P., Vieira, A., Putin, E., Zhavoronkov, A.: Applications of deep learning in biomedicine. Mol. Pharm. **13**(5), 1445–1454 (2016)
4. Min, S., Lee, B., Yoon, S.: Deep learning in bioinformatics. Brief. Bioinform. **18**(5), 851–869 (2017)

5. Venna, S.R., Tavanaei, A., Gottumukkala, R.N., Ragha-van, V.V., Maida, A., Nichols, S.: A novel data-driven model for real-time influenza forecasting. bioRxiv (2017)
6. Maass, W.: Networks of spiking neurons: the third generation of neural network models. Neural Netw. **9**, 1659–1971 (1997)
7. Kasabov, N.: NeuCube: a spiking neural network architecture for mapping, learning and understanding of spatio-temporal brain data. Neural Netw. **52**, 62–76 (2014)
8. World Health Organization. Depression. Who.int. https://www.who.int/news-room/factsheets/detail/depression. Accessed 12 May 2019
9. Smitha, K.M., Renshawb, P.F., Bilello, J.: The diagnosis of depression: current and emerging methods. Compr. Psychiatry **54**, 1–6 (2013)
10. Moon, S.-E., Jang, S., Lee, J.-S.: Convolutional Neural Network Approach for EEG-based Emotion Recognition using Brain Connectivity and its Spatial Information. https://arxiv.org/abs/1809.04208 (2018)
11. Abasolo, D., Hornero, R., Escudero, J., Espino, P.: A study on the possible usefulness of detrended fluctuation analysis of the electroencephalogram background activity in Alzheimer's disease. IEEE Trans. Biomed. Eng. **55**, 2171–2179 (2008). https://doi.org/10.1109/tbme.2008.923145
12. Bachmann, M., Lass, J., Hinrikus, H.: Electroencephalographic spectral asymmetry index for detection of depression. Med. Biol. Eng. Comput. **47**, 1291–1299 (2009)
13. Yıldırım, O., Plawiak, P., Tan, R.S., Acharya, U.R.: Arrhythmia detection using deep convolutional neural network with long duration ECG signals. Comput. Biol. Med. **102**, 411–420 (2018)
14. Bairy, G.M., et al.: Automated diagnosis of depression electroencephalograph signals using linear prediction coding and higher order spectra features. J. Med. Imaging Health Inform. **7**(8), 1857–1862 (2017)
15. Acharya, U.R., Oh, S.L., Hagiwara, Y., Tan, J.H., Adeli, H., Subha, D.P.: Automated EEG-based screening of depression using deep convolutional neural network. Comput. Methods Prog. Biomed. **161**, 103–113 (2018)
16. Martinez-Murcia, F.J., Górriz, J.M., Ramírez, J., Ortiz, A.: Convolutional neural networks for neuroimaging in Parkinson's disease: is preprocessing needed? Int. J. Neural Syst. **28**(10), 1850035 (2018)
17. Yildirim, O., Tan, R.S., Acharya, U.R.: An efficient compression of ECG signals using deep convolutional autoencoders. Cogn. Syst. Res. **52**, 198–211 (2018)
18. Antoniades, A., et al.: Deep neural architectures for mapping scalp to intracranial EEG. Int. J. Neural Syst. **28**(08), 1850009 (2018)
19. Książek, W., Abdar, M., Acharya, U.R., Pławiak, P.: A novel machine learning approach for early detection of hepatocellular carcinoma patients. Cogn. Syst. Res. **54**, 116–127 (2018)
20. Abdar, M., et al.: A new nested ensemble technique for automated diagnosis of breast cancer. Pattern Recogn. Lett. (2018)
21. Abdar, M.: Using decision trees in data mining for predicting factors influencing of heart disease. Carpathian J. Electron. Comput. Eng. **8**(2), 31–36 (2015)
22. Mumtaz, W., et al.: Electroencephalogram (EEG)-based computer-aided technique to diagnose major depressive disorder (MDD). Biomed. Signal Process. Control **31**, 108–115 (2017)
23. Bachmann, M., et al.: Methods for classifying depression in single channel EEG using linear and nonlinear signal analysis. Comput. Methods Prog. Biomed. **155**, 11–17 (2018)
24. Puthankattil, S.D., Joseph, P.K.: Classification of EEG signals in normal and depression conditions by ANN using RWE and signal entropy. J. Mech. Med. Biol. **12**(04), 1240019 (2012)

25. Puthankattil, S., Joseph, P.: Classification of EEG signals in normal and depression conditions by ANN using RWE and signal entropy. J. Mech. Med. Biol. **12**(4), 1240019 (2012)
26. Hosseinifard, B., Moradi, M.H., Rostami, R.: Classifying depression patients and normal subjects using machine learning techniques and nonlinear features from EEG signal. Comput. Methods Prog. Biomed. **109**(3), 339–345 (2013)
27. Acharya, U.R., et al.: A novel depression diagnosis index using nonlinear features in EEG signals. Eur. Neurol. **74**, 79–83 (2015)
28. Schirrmeister, R.T., et al.: Deep learning with convolutional neural networks for brain mapping and decoding of movement-related information from the human EEG. arXiv: 170305051. March 2017
29. Bashivan, P., Rish, I., Yeasin, M., Codella, N.: Learning representations from EEG with deep recurrent-convolutional neural networks. presented at ICLR, San Juan, Puerto Rico, May 2016
30. Jirayucharoensak, S., Pan-Ngum, S., Israsena, P.: EEG-based emotion recognition using deep learning network with principal component based covariate shift adaptation. Sci. World J. (2014)
31. Oh, S.L., Ng, E.Y.K., Tan, R.S., Acharya, U.R.: Automated diagnosis of arrhythmia using combination of CNN and LSTM techniques with variable length heart beats. Comput. Biol. Med. **102**, 278–287 (2018)
32. Yildirim, O.: A novel wavelet sequence based on deep bidirectional LSTM network model for ECG signal classification. Comput. Biol. Med. **96**, 189–202 (2018)
33. Ay, B., et al.: Automated depression detection using deep representation and sequence learning with EEG signals. J. Med. Syst. **43**(7), 205 (2019)
34. Mohanty, R., Priyadarshini, A., Desai, V.S., Sirisha, G.: Applications of spiking neural network to predict software reliability. In: Bhateja, V., Coello Coello, C.A., Satapathy, S.C., Pattnaik, P.K. (eds.) Intelligent Engineering Informatics. AISC, vol. 695, pp. 149–157. Springer, Singapore (2018). https://doi.org/10.1007/978-981-10-7566-7_16
35. Doborjeh, Z., Kasabov, N., Doborjeh, M., Sumich, A.: Spiking neural network modelling approach reveals how mindfulness training rewires the brain. Sci. Rep. **9**(1), 6367 (2019)
36. Doborjeh, M., Wang, G., Kasabov, N., Kydd, R., Russell, B.: A spiking neural network methodology and system for learning and comparative analysis of EEG data from healthy versus addiction treated versus addiction not treated subjects. IEEE Trans. Biomed. Eng. **63** (9), 1830–1841 (2016)
37. Chan, V., Liu, S.-C., van Schaik, A.: AER EAR: a matched silicon cochlea pair with address event representation interface. IEEE Trans. Circ. Syst.: Regul. Pap. **54**, 48–59 (2007)
38. Talairach, J., Tournoux, P.: Co-planar stereotaxic atlas of the human brain: 3-dimensional proportional system: an approach to cerebral imaging (1988)
39. Petro, B., Kasabov, N., Kiss, R.M.: Selection and optimization of temporal spike encoding methods for spiking neural networks. IEEE Trans. Neural Netw. Learn. Syst. (2019). https://doi.org/10.1109/TNNLS.2019.2906158
40. Natalia, C., Yang, D.: Spike timing–dependent plasticity: a hebbian learning rule. Ann. Rev. Neurosci. **31**, 25–46 (2008)
41. Kasabov, N., Dhoble, K., Nuntalid, N., Indiveri, G.: Dynamic evolving spiking neural networks for on-line spatio and spectro temporal pattern recognition. Neural Netw. **41**, 188–201 (2013)
42. Goulden, N., et al.: Reversed frontotemporal connectivity during emotional face processing in remitted depression. Biol. Psychiatry **72**(7), 604–611 (2012)
43. Stewart, J., Towers, D., Coan, J., Allen, J.: The oft-neglected role of parietal EEG asymmetry and risk for major depressive disorder. Psychophysiology **48**(1), 82–95 (2011)

44. Flor-Henry, P., Lind, J., Koles, Z.: A source-imaging (low-resolution electromagnetic tomography) study of the EEGs from unmedicated males with depression. Psychiatry Res.: Neuroimag. **130**(2), 191–207 (2004)
45. Kaiser, R., Andrews-Hanna, J., Wager, T.D., Pizzagalli, D.A.: Large-Scale network dysfunction in major depressive disorder: a meta-analysis of resting-state functional connectivity. JAMA Psychiatry **72**(6), 603–611 (2015)
46. Kasabov, N.: Time-Space, Spiking Neural Networks and Brain-Inspired Artificial Intelligence. Springer, Heidelberg (2019)
47. Illing, B., Gerstner, W., Brea, J.: Biologically plausible deep learning - but how far can we go with shallow networks? Neural Netw.: Official J. Int. Neural Netw. Soc. **118**, 90–101 (2019)
48. Connor, P., Welling, M.: Deep Spiking Networks. arXiv:1602.08323. 2016
49. Tavanaei, A., Ghodrati, M., Kheradpisheh, S.R., Masquelier, T., Maida, A.: Deep learning in spiking neural networks. Neural Netw. **111**, 47–63 (2019)
50. Lee, C., Srinivasan, G., Panda, P., Roy, K.: Deep spiking convolutional neural network trained with unsupervised spike-timing-dependent plasticity. IEEE Trans. Cogn. Dev. Syst. **11**(3), 384–394 (2009)
51. Tavanaei, A., Maida, A.: BP-STDP: approximating backpropagation using spike timing dependent plasticity. Neurocomputing **330**, 39–47 (2017)
52. Bellec, G., Scherr, F., Hajek, E., Salaj, D., Legenstein, R., Maass, W.: Biologically inspired alternatives to backpropagation through time for learning in recurrent neural nets (2019)
53. Jun Haeng, L., Tobi, D., Michael, P.: Training deep spiking neural networks using backpropagation. Front. Neurosci. **10**, 508 (2016)
54. Tavanaei, A., Maida, A.: Bio-Inspired Spiking Convolutional Neural Network using Layer-wise Sparse Coding and STDP Learning, June 2017
55. Rueckauer, B., Lungu, I., Hu, Y., Pfeiffer, M.: Theory and tools for the conversion of analog to spiking convolutional neural networks. In: 29th Conference on Neural Information Processing Systems (NIPS) (2016)
56. Silva, M., Koshiyama, A., Vellasco, M., Cataldo, E.: Evolutionary features and parameter optimization of spiking neural networks for unsupervised learning. In: 2014 International Joint Conference on Neural Networks (IJCNN), pp. 2391–2398 (2014)

Text Computing Using Neural Techniques

Watch and Ask: Video Question Generation

Shenglei Huang[1]([✉]), Shaohan Hu[2], and Bencheng Yan[2]

[1] Department of Computer Science and Engineering,
Shanghai Jiao Tong University, Shanghai, China
shengleihuang@sjtu.edu.cn
[2] School of Software, Tsinghua University, Beijing, China
{hush17,ybc17}@mails.tsinghua.edu.cn

Abstract. Question generation (QG) has been well studied in text and image but never been studied in video, which is popular multimedia in practice. In this paper, we propose a new task, video question generation. We adopt the encoder-decoder based framework to deal with this task. With the consideration that each video can be asked with more than one questions, and each question can belong to different types, we involve question type to guide the generation process. Specifically, a novel type-conditional temporal-spatial attention is proposed, which could capture required information of different types from video content at different time steps. Experiments show that our models outperform baseline and our type-conditional attention module captures the required information precisely. To best of our knowledge, we are the first to apply the end-to-end model on video question generation.

Keywords: Video question generation · Type conditional · Spatial attention

1 Introduction

Asking questions is a way to understand the surroundings. For example, kids ask questions to get knowledge of the world, and teachers use questions to assess students' comprehension. In this paper, we focus on video question generation, which is a brand new task and has never been studied yet.

Video question generation is a significant task and can be applied in many fields. As a popular material for kids education, video-QG can be applied to generate questions automatically to promote children's understanding. As mainstream multimedia in the social network, video-QG can help to filter out spam, since only users who understand the video content could comment. As a question generation model, video-QG can also be used to augment Question-and-Answering data, which requires manual annotation currently.

Instead of summarizing video content as what video caption does, video-QG is required to select necessary information to ask detailed questions about.

© Springer Nature Switzerland AG 2019
T. Gedeon et al. (Eds.): ICONIP 2019, LNCS 11955, pp. 209–221, 2019.
https://doi.org/10.1007/978-3-030-36718-3_18

Q1: What does the man do before get hit in head with log?

Q1: What does the girl do 8 times ?

Q2: How many times does the girl clap her hand ?

Q3: What does the woman who is clapping do after bow head ?

Fig. 1. Video-questions pairs sampled from TGIF-QA dataset

For example, in Fig. 1, a video question generator asks questions about a specific moving action. To make use of the sequential information in the video, we adopt an encoder-decoder based framework with Recurrent Neural Network as the encoder. To capture temporal information in the video, we used the attentive decoder [18]. There is one limitation of this model that it can only output one question per video. However, we argue that different questions should be asked based on different focuses in one video. The focused region in one video depends on the information required. In terms of required information, the questions are pre-classified into 7 different types, namely *Repetitive-Count, Repeating-Action, State-Transition, Frame-Object, Frame-Count, Frame-Color* and *Frame-Location*. In conclusion, there are two main points in this task: (1) Each video could be asked questions with different types. (2) Questions with different types require different information from the video.

For the first main point, we frame the task as a type-guided video question generation. For the second main point, we propose a novel type-conditional temporal-spatial attention to guide the model to obtain the required information. Specifically, after extracting frame feature maps and type features, the type-conditional temporal-spatial attention module will calculate weights which represent the focuses on this frame feature map under this type. Then the type-fused frame feature is obtained by weighted average pooling. Through this mechanism, irrelevant information will be filtered out, and the required information will be preserved, which improves the performance of the model.

In summary, the contributions of this paper are:

1. We present a new task, video-QG, to generate questions from video automatically.
2. We propose a novel model to generate diverse questions considering the temporal structure of video under the guidance of question types on each video.

3. A novel type-conditional temporal-spatial attention is proposed to guide model to focus on main information in the video.

2   Related Work

In recent years, researchers pay more attention on the inter-discipline of computer vision and natural language processing, such as image question generation [4,17,21] and visual question answering [7,19,22].

2.1   Question Generation

Text question generation (text-QG) has attracted the attention of researchers in natural language processing again after the work of Du et al. [3], who is the first to use deep learning model to do text-QG. After that, text related question generation has been studied in depth in NLP. At the meantime, image question generation (image-QG) are also understudying. Different from text-QG, the input is an image instead of text. Li et al. [9] framed image-QG as the dual task of image-QA, and the results showed this model improved answering performance. Both Zhang et al. [21] and Fan et al. [4] generated diverse questions from one image. Zhang et al. used additional information from image caption to help to generate questions. Fan et al. proposed a VAE-based model that only relies on the image. Uehara et al. [17] proposed to use question generation to ask about unknown objects in images. Image question generation has attracted much attention in computer vision and several public datasets, such as VQG-MS COCO and VQG-Flickr [12] have been published to promote the research in this task. Different to the image, the sequential property makes the video more difficult to analyze.

Video-only question generation hasn't been studied yet. Skalban [15] studied to generate factoid question from video subtitles, and one frame will be extracted from the video as an auxiliary, which is actually the text-based question generation process. Besides, these questions are generated from templates which are labor-consuming to collect. Our model generates questions from video without the help of any additional text information, and the model is trained end-to-end without question templates.

2.2   Video Question Answering

Video question answering (Video-QA) is a new and difficult task. Video-QA requires an understanding of both text and video temporal structure [5]. Recently, Video-QA attracts more attention, and there are several public datasets being released. MovieFIB [11] is a dataset with fill-in-the-blank questions collected automatically by removing a phrase from the video's grounded description. MovieQA [16] is another dataset consisting of questions collected manually by referring to plot synopses (movie summaries). Mun et al. released MarioQA dataset [13] in which the videos are collected from Super Mario Bros.

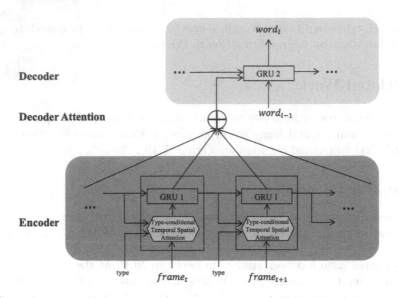

Fig. 2. This is the overall model architecture. The encoder and decoder has been rolled out to better represent time series.

gameplay videos and questions are about the events occurring in videos. Poro-roQA dataset [8] is another dataset containing unrealistic videos, collected from children's cartoon videos.

Recently, Jang et al. [7] released TGIF-QA dataset, which is a large-scale dataset for video-QA. The videos in this dataset are GIF, which could be regarded as short but content-focused videos. Questions in this dataset are divided into 7 types, namely Repetitive-Count, Repeating-Action, State-Transition, Frame-Object, Frame-Count, Frame-Color and Frame-Location (details in Sect. 3.2). We use TGIF-QA in our work since videos in TGIF-QA is short and content-focused, it is a suitable dataset to start on video-QG.

3   Task Definition

Given a video V_i, a question type C_j, our goal is to generate a related question Q_{ij}. This task is to find $\hat{Q}_{ij}$ that satisfies:

$$\hat{Q}_{ij} = \arg\max_{Q_{ij}} P(Q_{ij}|V_i, C_j) \tag{1}$$

Q_{ij} is a sequence of words with arbitrary length: $Q_{ij} = [w_1, w_2, ..., w_L]$, L is the length of Q_{ij}. The conditional probability $P(Q_{ij}|V_i, C_j)$ is factorized approximately to the product of each word conditional probability in the question:

$$P(Q_{ij}|V_i, C_j) = \prod_{l=1}^{L} P(w_i|V_i, C_j, w_{<l}) \tag{2}$$

V_i is a sequence of frames with fixed length T after sampling.

4   Model

The overall model is based on the encoder-decoder framework, as shown in Fig. 2. First, frame encoder encodes frame with type. Then video encoder extracts video features from frame sequences. Finally, a decoder generates questions based on these video features.

4.1   Type-Fused Frame Encoder

Video is a sequence of frames, which is similar to the sentence in natural language processing. Therefore, in this work, we first need to encode each frame.

Frame Encoding: We apply ResNet-152 [6], pre-trained by ImageNet dataset [1] to process frames and use the *stage-5* outputs as frame feature maps m_t. The normal approach to extract frame feature is applying average pooling on each feature map. However, with the intuition that the extracted frame feature should be varied with different types at a different time step, we propose to use weighted average pooling, and the weights are calculated by "type-conditional temporal-spatial attention" module, which will be discussed later in this section. Before the discussion of novel attention mechanism, we introduce the question types used in our work and how to encode these types.

Question Type Encoding: Question type decides how the question should be asked and what to ask. In TGIF-QA dataset, there are 7 pre-defined question types. (1) Repeating-Action questions ask the action that repeats several times; (2) Repetition-Count questions ask the times one action repeats; (3) State-Transition questions ask the action after an action; (4) Frame questions do not require temporal information and could be asked by a single frame, divided into 4 types: (a) Frame-Object questions ask about object description question; (b) Frame-Count questions ask counting question; (c) Frame-Color questions ask about color and (d) Frame-Location questions ask location of the object. These questions, except Frame questions, are unique to video question generation considering the temporal structure and different focuses between different types, which makes this work challenge and novel.

A type embedding layer is added to map each type to a type feature, with the intuition that related types should be mapped closely, for example, both Repetition-Count questions and Repeating-Action questions concentrate on repeated actions in videos, therefore these two type features should be similar to some extent. Specifically, each question type will be represented as a one-hot vector $c_{onehot} \in \mathbb{R}^{n_c \times 1}$, where n_c is the number of types. To get the type feature, a type look-up table $W_{type} \in \mathbb{R}^{D_c \times n_c}$ is provided, then the type feature c is obtained by $c = W_{type} \cdot c_{onehot}$, and $c \in \mathbb{R}^{D_c \times 1}$. W_{type} is learned when training.

Type-Conditional Temporal Spatial Attention: This attention mechanism is the approach to make model focus on main information required by the observed type, and is inspired by spatial attention [20] with type and temporal information as constraints.

Given frame feature map $\mathbf{m}_t \in \mathbb{R}^{C \times H \times W}$ at time step t, type feature $\mathbf{c} \in \mathbb{R}^{D_c \times 1}$ and temporal feature $\mathbf{h}_{t-1} \in \mathbb{R}^{D_h \times 1}$, which is the previous hidden state in GRU video encoder (Sect. 4.2). First, we broadcast type feature and hidden state to $\mathbf{c} \in \mathbb{R}^{D_c \times H \times W}$ and $\mathbf{h}_{t-1} \in \mathbb{R}^{D_h \times H \times W}$. Then the attention is calculated on each grid location as follows, and the idea is that the model should focus on some locations in this frame, instead of treating each location equally:

$$
\begin{aligned}
\mathbf{H}_t &= \tanh(\mathbf{W}_m \cdot \mathbf{m}_t + \mathbf{W}_c \cdot \mathbf{c} + \mathbf{W}_h \cdot \mathbf{h}_{t-1}) \\
\mathbf{a}_t &= \mathrm{softmax}(\mathbf{w}^T \cdot \mathbf{H}_t)
\end{aligned}
\tag{3}
$$

The type-fused frame feature is obtained by weighted average pooling as follows:

$$
\mathbf{z}_t = \sum_{i=1}^{H} \sum_{j=1}^{W} (\mathbf{a}_t)_{ij} (\mathbf{m}_t)_{ij}
\tag{4}
$$

$\mathbf{W}_m \in \mathbb{R}^{D_a \times C}$, $\mathbf{W}_c \in \mathbb{R}^{D_a \times D_c}$ $\mathbf{W}_h \in \mathbb{R}^{D_a \times D_h}$ and $\mathbf{w} \in \mathbb{R}^{D_a \times 1}$ are all learned parameters, and $\mathbf{a}_t \in \mathbb{R}^{H \times W}$. Each score in $\mathbf{a}_t$ represents how much attention should the model paid on in this region at this time.

After type-fused frame encoding, a fully connected layer is applied to compress this feature and outputs the feature $\mathbf{f}_t \in \mathbb{R}^{D_f \times 1}$. With the consideration that spatial attention may lose some type information, we also attempt to concatenate the fused feature $\mathbf{f}_t$ with type features $\mathbf{c}$ to stress the guidance of type, which makes $\mathbf{f}_t \in \mathbb{R}^{(D_f + D_c) \times 1}$.

4.2 Video Encoding and Question Generation

After applying frame encoder (Sect. 4.1) on each frame, we obtain $V_i = [\mathbf{f}_1, \mathbf{f}_2, ..., \mathbf{f}_T]$ which represents the video content. Then, we use a Gated Recurrent Neural Networks (GRU) to encode video content V_i and outputs a sequence of hidden states $\mathbf{h}_1, ..., \mathbf{h}_T$ as video features. Next, another GRU is used to decode video features into a sequence of words to form a question $Q_i = [w_1, ..., w_L]$. When decoding, the attention mechanism [18] is used to make the model focus on different frames at different decoding time step.

The loss function for question generation is the cross-entropy loss between ground-truth question and the generated question.

5 Experiments

We study our proposed task on existing VQA dataset TGIF-QA [7]. In this section, firstly, we describe the composition of the dataset and the reason to use it. Then we give implementation details of our proposed model and baselines. Finally, we analyze the experiments and their results.

5.1   Dataset

The dataset we used to evaluate our model is TGIF-QA. It contains 72420 GIFs with the various number of questions for each. Questions in this dataset are pre-classified into 7 types based on the information required to ask (Sect. 4.1). To fix the length of each GIF, we use a fixed frame sampling, that is, the frame duration length is a fixed constant, and we obtain 35 frames per GIF. For GIFs whose length is shorter than 35 frames, we pad empty frames at the beginning.

5.2   Comparative Models

Since we are the first to do this task, we compare our model with the basic encoder-decoder model without type-conditional temporal-spatial attention module. To study our "type-conditional temporal-spatial attention" (See Sect. 4.1 for details), we do ablation test on this module and to study the importance of temporal information, we first extract keyframe from video and then apply our attention module on image question generation model proposed in [12] to generation questions from this frame.

Video2Seq: This is the video-to-question model without type as guidance. First, ResNet-152 is applied on each frame, and the output of last average pooling layer is used as a frame feature. Then a GRU model is applied on frame features to encode video. Finally, a decoder with the attention mechanism is used to generate questions.

Video2Seq+concat: This is the video-to-question model with type as guidance by concatenation. Each frame feature is extracted from the last average pooling layer from ResNet-152. Type feature is obtained from type embedding layer. Then a GRU model is applied to obtain the video feature. Finally, a decoder with the attention mechanism is used to generate questions.

Video2Seq+concat+spatial: This is the model we mentioned in Sect. 4. Different to the first two models, frame features in this model are extracted from the stage-5 layer in ResNet-152 in order to compute type-conditional attention map. In this model, as mentioned in Sect. 4.1, type information is added by both concatenation and using our novel attention in frame encoding.

KFrame2Seq+concat: This is the key-frame-to-question model with type as guidance by concatenation. Comparing with this model is to prove the importance of temporal information in video-QG. This is an image-QG model which is similar to the model in [12], but involves the type information. We extract keyframes from video based on the sum of absolute differences in LUV color space. Then we extract frame feature from the last average pooling layer in ResNet-152, concatenated with type feature from type embedding layer. Finally, a GRU decoder is used to generate questions.

KFrame2Seq+concat+spatial: Addition to "KFrame2Seq+concat", the type information is also added by using our type-conditional attention module. Different to applying this module in the video, here we do not have temporal infor-

Table 1. Overall results of different models. V2S = Video2Seq, KF2S = KeyFrame2Seq, c = concat, s = spatial, BL = BLEU, M = Meteor, R = Rouge.

	BL-1	BL-2	BL-3	BL-4	M	R-L
V2S	45.35	36.85	30.52	25.30	22.76	45.90
KF2S+c	58.23	50.96	44.99	39.45	30.75	61.65
KF2S+c+s	61.04	53.81	47.79	42.17	30.61	62.14
V2S+c	60.43	53.02	47.00	41.47	31.31	62.75
V2S+c+s	**61.31**	**54.19**	**48.28**	**42.76**	**31.40**	**63.04**

mation in type conditional attention module. In order to compute the attention map, the frame feature is extracted from the stage-5 layer in ResNet-152.

5.3 Implementation Details

We replace the word whose frequency is 1 with UNK symbol, and finally, the size of the vocabulary is 5846. The dimensions of type and word embedding are both set to 512, and both of them are randomly initialized. We set the GRU hidden unit size to 512, and the number of layers is set to 1 in both encoder and decoder. Dropout with probability 0.2 is applied after frame encoding and word embedding. Dropout with probability 0.5 is applied in both encoder GRU and decoder GRU. When training, we optimize models with Adam, and the batch size is fixed to 32. Learning rate was initially set to 0.0004 and halved at every 10 epochs.

5.4 Evaluation Methods

In automatic evaluation, considering our goal is to generate high-quality questions with the guidance of question type, we evaluate our models on the performance of overall question quality and type-aware question quality. For overall question quality, we adopt metrics which are regularly used in machine translation and text summarization, in terms of BLUE scores [14], METEOR scores [2] and ROUGE-L scores [10], on all generated questions, each with one ground-truth question. For type-aware question quality, first, we group questions with the same type, and then apply the same evaluation methods on each type separately.

6 Results and Analysis

In this section, we analyze the results of our models and visualize the "type conditional temporal-spatial attention" module. We also do error analysis to demonstrate the limitation of our models.

Table 2. Results on each type. Each score is calculated in one-to-one manner with ground-truth and generated question pairs. V2S = Video2Seq, KF2S = KeyFrame2Seq, c = concat, s = spatial, M = Meteor, R = Rouge.

Type	V2S		KF2S+c+s		V2S+c+s	
	M	R-L	M	R-L	M	R-L
Repeating-Action	26.37	53.45	37.23	75.53	**38.53**	**76.77**
Repetition-Count	12.72	28.36	36.31	63.41	**36.63**	**63.82**
State-Transition	28.41	55.80	29.21	58.04	**29.43**	**59.12**
Frame-Object	10.79	28.92	13.48	37.81	**14.40**	**38.95**
Frame-Count	8.08	6.58	20.32	39.43	**21.20**	**41.12**
Frame-Color	15.52	35.00	45.23	84.48	**45.59**	**84.78**
Frame-Location	9.15	17.15	19.10	39.93	**20.28**	**42.54**

Table 1 shows the overall results of different models. Our model, which uses both type-conditional temporal-spatial attention and type concatenation, achieves the best performance over all metrics.

V2S vs. V2S+c: As expected, type information brings a large improvement, and all scores have been improved a lot, such as ROUGE-L has been improved from 45.90 to 62.75. This is because, in our dataset, there are more than one questions can be asked in one video, and these questions belong to different types, which is also the case in reality.

V2S+c/KF2S+c vs. V2S+c+s/KF2S+c+s: After adding "type conditional spatial attention" module, both Video2Seq model and KeyFrame2Seq model improve. But the improvement between KeyFrame2Seq (from 61.65 to 62.14) models is larger than that between Video2Seq models (from 62.75 to 63.04). The explanation is that the additional temporal information in Video2Seq models have made up the type information loss since we stress the type information by concatenating type feature with each frame feature.

KF2S+c/KF2S+c+s vs. V2S+c/V2S+c+s: Temporal information is important to video question generation task. It improves the performance of the model by around 1.0 ROUGE-L. Compared with models both using type concatenation and "type conditional attention" module, the performance improvement between models only using type concatenation is greater. One explanation is that in this dataset, the influence of type information is larger than temporal information.

Table 2 shows the scores in each question type among different models. And we analyze the results by comparing with different models and by comparing across each type in one model.

Model Comparison Across All Types: With the guidance of type, Video2Seq model achieves significant improvements for all types (V2S+c+s vs. V2S), which proves the importance of type information when more than

Generated question: What does the man do after jump ?

Generated question: What is the cat biting ?

Fig. 3. "Type-conditional temporal spatial attention" visualization. The type for first example is State-Transition and the type for second example is Frame-QA.

one question should be asked from one video. With the temporal information, Video2Seq outperforms KeyFrame2Seq model (V2S+c+s vs. KF2S+c+s) in all types, even on "Frame-based" questions, which demonstrates that temporal information is essential to video question generation.

Type Results Comparison in One Model: Without type information, V2S performs best in State-Transition type. This is because most samples in our training data belong to this type. Therefore without the guidance of type, it is easier for the model to learn this type questions. When type information is added, the situation is different. Both KF2S+c+s and V2S+c+s performs best on Frame-Color questions with the type as guidance because the template of this question type is very easy to learn, which is "What is the color of [object]?" or other templates similar to it.

6.1   Attention Visualization

Figure 3 shows the visualization result of "type-conditional temporal-spatial attention". The attention mechanism should be able to focus on the regions related to the question type at this time step. In the first example, the question type is State-Transition, therefore the model is always focusing on the man, and the attention varies on the different time step. In the second example, the question type is Frame-Object, therefore, with the changing of the main object in different frames, the model firstly focuses on the cat and then focus on the lizard. From these examples, our "type-conditional temporal-spatial attention" captures required information effectively in each frame.

Generated:

Q1: how many women are dancing in the park ?

Ground-Truth:

Q1: how many women exercise in front of the water ?

Generated:

Q1: what does the woman do 2 times ?

Q2: how many times does the woman wave her hand ?

Q3: what is the color of the dress ?

Ground-Truth:

Q1: what does the woman do 2 times ?

Q2: how many times does the woman skip ?

Q3: what is the color of the dress ?

Generated:

Q1: what does the man do after jump ?

Q2: what does the man do after jump ?

Ground-Truth:

Q1: what does the woman do after jump on tall box ?

Q2: what does the woman do before sit on small box ?

Fig. 4. Samples of generated questions by our best model "V2S+c+s"

6.2   Case Study and Error Analysis

Figure 4 shows some examples generated by our best model "V2S+c+s". We see that the generated questions have good quality, which captures moving actions in the video. For example, in the first video, our model captures the action "dance", which is very similar to the ground-truth action "exercise". In the second video, the model captures another action "wave hand" which is different to the annotated action "skip" but is also right even better. And in the third video, our model captures the action "jump" precisely. Besides, our model could also capture counting information, such as Q1 in the second video. For static information, our model also performs well, such as Q3 in the second video.

However, there are still remains some problems. The first problem is that action recognition accuracy needs to be improved. For example, in the first video of Fig. 4, our model recognizes the action as "dance" which is very similar to ground-truth action "exercise" but still not precise. The second problem is that there is more than one question that could be asked with the same type. For example, in the third video of Fig. 4, both Q1 and Q2 have State-Transition type, but our model could only generate one question with observed type.

7   Conclusion and Future Works

In this paper, we presented a new task - video question generation (video-QG) to automatically generate questions from the video. And we proposed the first model to generate questions from video content with the observed question type. Specifically, a novel type-aware temporal-spatial attention module was proposed to capture the required information for that question type at different time steps. For future works, as mentioned in error analysis of Sect. 6.2, we will study how to improve the action recognition performance and how to generate diverse high-quality questions with the same question type.

References

1. Deng, J., Dong, W., Socher, R., Li, L., Li, K., Li, F.: Imagenet: a large-scale hierarchical image database. In: CVPR, pp. 248–255 (2009)
2. Denkowski, M.J., Lavie, A.: Meteor universal: language specific translation evaluation for any target language. In: WMT@ACL, pp. 376–380 (2014)
3. Du, X., Shao, J., Cardie, C.: Learning to ask: neural question generation for reading comprehension. In: ACL, vol. 1, pp.1342–1352 (2017)
4. Fan, Z., Wei, Z., Li, P., Lan, Y., Huang, X.: A question type driven framework to diversify visual question generation. In: IJCAI, pp. 4048–4054 (2018)
5. Gao, J., Ge, R., Chen, K., Nevatia, R.: Motion-appearance co-memory networks for video question answering. In: CVPR, pp. 6576–6585 (2018)
6. He, K., Zhang, X., Ren, S., Sun, J.: Deep residual learning for image recognition. In: CVPR, pp. 770–778 (2016)
7. Jang, Y., Song, Y., Yu, Y., Kim, Y., Kim, G.: TGIF-QA: toward spatio-temporal reasoning in visual question answering. In: CVPR, pp. 1359–1367 (2017)
8. Kim, K., Heo, M., Choi, S., Zhang, B.: Deepstory: video story QA by deep embedded memory networks. In: IJCAI, pp. 2016–2022 (2017)
9. Li, Y., et al.: Visual question generation as dual task of visual question answering. In: CVPR, pp. 6116–6124 (2018)
10. Lin, C.Y.: Rouge: a package for automatic evaluation of summaries. In: Text Summarization Branches Out (2004)
11. Maharaj, T., Ballas, N., Rohrbach, A., Courville, A.C., Pal, C.J.: A dataset and exploration of models for understanding video data through fill-in-the-blank question-answering. In: CVPR, pp. 7359–7368 (2017)
12. Mostafazadeh, N., Misra, I., Devlin, J., Mitchell, M., He, X., Vanderwende, L.: Generating natural questions about an image. In: ACL (2016)
13. Mun, J., Seo, P.H., Jung, I., Han, B.: Marioqa: answering questions by watching gameplay videos. In: ICCV, pp. 2886–2894 (2017)
14. Papineni, K., Roukos, S., Ward, T., Zhu, W.J.: Bleu: a method for automatic evaluation of machine translation. In: ACL, pp. 311–318. Association for Computational Linguistics (2002)
15. Skalban, Y.: Automatic generation of factual questions from video documentaries. Ph.D. thesis, University of Wolverhampton, UK (2013)
16. Tapaswi, M., Zhu, Y., Stiefelhagen, R., Torralba, A., Urtasun, R., Fidler, S.: Movieqa: understanding stories in movies through question-answering. In: CVPR, pp. 4631–4640 (2016)

17. Uehara, K., Tejero-de-Pablos, A., Ushiku, Y., Harada, T.: Visual question generation for class acquisition of unknown objects. In: ECCV, pp. 492–507 (2018)
18. Vaswani, A., et al.: Attention is all you need. In: NIPS, pp. 6000–6010 (2017)
19. Xiong, C., Merity, S., Socher, R.: Dynamic memory networks for visual and textual question answering. In: ICML, pp. 2397–2406 (2016)
20. Yu, L., et al.: Mattnet: modular attention network for referring expression comprehension. In: CVPR, pp. 1307–1315 (2018)
21. Zhang, S., Qu, L., You, S., Yang, Z., Zhang, J.: Automatic generation of grounded visual questions. In: IJCAI, pp. 4235–4243 (2017)
22. Zhu, Y., Groth, O., Bernstein, M.S., Fei-Fei, L.: Visual7w: grounded question answering in images. In: CVPR, pp. 4995–5004 (2016)

Multi-perspective Denoising Reader for Multi-paragraph Reading Comprehension

Fengcheng Yuan[1,2], Yanfu Xu[1,2], Zheng Lin[2(✉)], Weiping Wang[2], and Gang Shi[1,2]

[1] School of Cyber Security, University of Chinese Academy of Sciences, Beijing, China
[2] Institute of Information Engineering, Chinese Academy of Sciences, Beijing, China
{yuanfengcheng,xuyanfu,linzheng,wangweiping,shigang}@iie.ac.cn

Abstract. Multi-paragraph reading comprehension (MPRC) aims to answer questions based on a number of paragraphs. The background paragraphs in MPRC are usually collected by information retrieval (IR) systems. Most of the MPRC models indiscriminately read all the background paragraphs, and regard paragraphs which contain the answer string as ground truths. Among these paragraphs, some are not semantically related to the question, therefore, the noisy data will distract the model from finding the right answer. Besides, most of the MPRC methods only use the paragraph-question relevance to predict the answer span. However, the utilization of the paragraph-paragraph relevance that provides enhanced and complementary evidence has only been explored in limited methods. To address these issues, we propose a hierarchical model with a multi-level attention mechanism, which can leverage both the inter-relation (paragraph-question relevance) and the intra-relation (paragraph-paragraph relevance), to filter out noisy data and extract the final answer. We conduct experiments on two challenging public datasets Quasar-T and SearchQA. The results demonstrate that our model outperforms recent MPRC baselines.

Keywords: Reading comprehension · Multi-paragraph · Multi-perspective

1 Introduction

Reading comprehension (RC), which aims to answer a question based on a pre-selected paragraph, has made great progress with the development of neural networks and attention mechanisms. Different from the traditional RC task, MPRC is designed to answer a question based on multiple paragraphs. For example, given a pre-prepared question as shown in Fig. 1, an MPRC system predicts the final answer by aggregating the evidence from some related paragraphs. Some studies simply treat MPRC as a RC task and directly apply recent RC models to the MPRC problem, but the performance of these RC models drops a lot. The reasons are summarized below:

© Springer Nature Switzerland AG 2019
T. Gedeon et al. (Eds.): ICONIP 2019, LNCS 11955, pp. 222–234, 2019.
https://doi.org/10.1007/978-3-030-36718-3_19

> **Question:** Which physicist, mathematician and astronomer discovered the first 4 moons of Jupiter ?
> **Answer:** Galileo Galilei
> **Paragraph1:** Galileo Galilei was an Italian physicist, mathematician, astronomer, and philosopher who played a major role in the Scientific Revolution .
> **Paragraph2:** Sir Isaac Newton was an English physicist, mathematician, astronomer, natural philosopher , alchemist and theologian ...
> **Paragraph3:** Galileo Galilei is credited with discovering the first four moons of Jupiter.
> **Paragraph4:** Galileo Galilei discovered sunspots, craters and peaks in the moon.

Fig. 1. An example of MPRC. The answer string is marked in green. The key information is marked in red and blue. (Color figure online)

First, MPRC usually uses an IR system to coarsely select paragraphs that are relevant to a question. As seen in Fig. 1, some of the paragraphs may not contain the answer string, e.g. Paragraph2, and some of them are wrong labeled samples, e.g. Paragraph4. We consider these two kinds of paragraphs as noisy paragraphs. In general, the IR system will find paragraphs that are similar but not relevant to the question. Therefore, the returned paragraphs may not contain the answer. Besides, according to the distant supervision assumption [8], paragraphs that contain the answer string are considered as ground truths. In this way, wrong labeled samples will be inevitably introduced. Neglecting these noisy paragraphs will degrade the performance of MPRC models.

Second, an ideal MPRC model should have the ability of comprehending and reasoning based on multi-perspective evidence, i.e. the inter-relation between paragraphs and questions and the intra-relation among paragraphs. As shown in Fig. 1, the answer "Galileo Galilei" appears in Paragraph1 and Paragraph3, both of which only contain a part of the information of the question. Through combining them together, the model is more likely to predict the right answer "Galileo Galilei".

To address the noise problem in MPRC, Lin et al. [7] propose a coarse-to-fine denoising model. At first, a paragraph selector is adopted to produce a confidence score for each paragraph based on its plausible correlation with the question. After that, a paragraph reader is used to extract the answer based on the confidence score. However, in both selection and extraction processes, they deal with every paragraph independently. This model only considers the inter-relation between paragraphs and questions, but it ignores the mutual information among paragraphs. As a result, it does not support iterative reasoning, where the evidence aggregation from multiple paragraphs is needed.

In order to aggregate evidence from multiple paragraphs and provide a more accurate answer, Wang et al. [13] and Wang et al. [14] first use an MPRC model to extract answer candidates from each paragraph, and then they re-rank the answer candidates to select the final answer. However, these answer re-ranking approaches still rely on the performance of the MPRC model and ignore the problem of noisy data.

In order to address the noise problem and make full use of the multi-perspective information in MPRC, we propose a hierarchical model with a multi-level attention mechanism. Similar to the framework of Lin et al. [7], our model consists of a paragraph selector and a paragraph reader. The paragraph selector is used to select the relevant paragraphs. After that, these paragraphs are passed to the paragraph reader to predict the final answer. Furthermore, by utilizing the multi-level attention mechanism, our selector is capable of effectively utilizing the inter-relation and intra-relation to select more relevant paragraphs. For the reader, the selected paragraphs will be concatenated to provide enhanced and complementary evidence and better predict the correct answer.

To sum up, our work makes the following contributions:

(1) We propose a hierarchical model for MPRC, which can simultaneously make full use of the multi-perspective information and solve the noise problem.
(2) To better model the inter-relation and intra-relation, we adopt the multi-level attention mechanism to select question-related paragraphs and extract the answer. Furthermore, we find that utilizing the relevance among all paragraphs can further improve the performance of MPRC.
(3) We conduct experiments on two public datasets Quasar-T and SearchQA. The experimental results demonstrate that our model achieves significant improvement as compared to all baseline methods.

2   Related Work

Recent approaches on MPRC extract the answer by focusing on paragraphs retrieved from the web [1,2,6,12,15]. Generally, there are two basic approaches to addressing this task, pipeline and answer re-ranking approaches. Most existing methods applied pipeline approaches, which selected some related paragraphs from all background paragraphs and then extracted answers by passing the paragraphs to a RC model. Answer re-ranking approaches adopted an extra submodule to re-rank the answer candidates.

For pipeline methods, Chen et al. [1] proposed a two-step method which consisted of a retriever and a reader. They used an IR system to retrieve a collection of paragraphs and utilized a RC model to extract the answer. However, these paragraphs were only relevant to the question and many of them did not contain the answer string. As a result, the effectiveness of the RC model was reduced. Therefore, to avoid the influence of noisy paragraphs, Wang et al. [12] proposed another pipeline model, R3. They utilized a paragraph-selection model to select the most relevant paragraph from the paragraphs and then used a RC model to extract the answer. But this method ignored the fact that some other paragraphs might also contain the answer. Subsequently, Lin et al. [7] proposed a selector to produce a confidence score for each paragraph to filter out the noisy ones. However, they dealt with these paragraphs separately and ignored the information among the paragraphs. As a result, they do not support iterative reasoning, where the evidence aggregated from multiple paragraphs is needed.

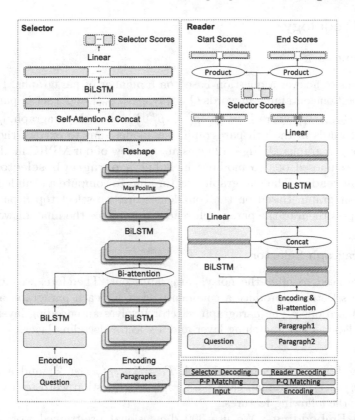

Fig. 2. The framework of our model. Our model consists of a paragraph selector (left) and a paragraph reader (right). The selector first chooses top k ($k = 2$) paragraphs. The reader concatenates the selected paragraphs (paragraph1 and paragraph2) together and computes the start score and the end score for each word in the concatenated paragraph.

For answer re-ranking methods, Wang et al. [13] proposed a re-ranking based framework for further utilizing the information of all paragraphs. Firstly, a pipeline model R3 [12] was used to extract answer candidates from all the paragraphs and then a re-ranking model was used to select the final answer by aggregating evidence from multiple paragraphs. But this method still relied heavily on the result of the first process and would cause the accumulation of errors if the answer extractor was not accurate enough.

After analyzing the characteristics of the MPRC task, we propose a hierarchical multi-level attention based model, Multi-perspective Denoising Reader, which utilizes not only the inter-relation but also the intra-relation to predict the answer. Our system consists of a paragraph selector which computes a confidence score for each paragraph and a paragraph reader that takes full advantage of the information of all paragraphs to predict the final answer.

3 Methodology

3.1 Framework

MPRC aims to answer a question based on a number of paragraphs. Formally, given a question containing m words $Q = \{q_1, q_2, ..., q_m\}$ and a set of paragraphs $D = \{P_1, P_2, ..., P_n\}$ where $P_i = \{p_i^1, p_i^2, ..., p_i^{|p_i|}\}$ is the i-th paragraph, $|p_i|$ is the number of words in the i-th paragraph, our model aims to extract the answer from these paragraphs D. Figure 2 gives an overview of our MPRC model which is mainly composed of two modules including a **paragraph selector** and a **paragraph reader**. The paragraph selector aims to compute a confidence score for each paragraph. Based on the confident score, we select top k paragraphs and then pass them to the paragraph reader to produce the final answer.

3.2 Paragraph Selector

Firstly, we need to filter the noisy paragraphs out. Therefore, we utilize the paragraph selector to produce a confidence score for each paragraph and keep the top-ranked ones. The paragraph selector involves an encoding layer, a P-Q matching layer, a P-P matching layer and a selector decoding layer.

Encoding Layer. Given a paragraph $P_i = \{p_i^1, p_i^2, ..., p_i^{|p_i|}\}$ and a question $Q = \{q_1, q_2, ..., q_m\}$, we map each paragraph and question word to a vector by combining the following features:

  Word Embeddings: We use 300 dimensional pre-trained word vectors, GloVe [9], to obtain the fixed embedding of each word.

  Char Embeddings: We map each character in a word to a 20-dimensional vector which is then passed to a convolutional layer and a max pooling layer to obtain the fixed-size vector of each word.

  Common word: The feature is set to 1 if the word appears in both the question and paragraph, otherwise 0. Then the feature is mapped to a vector of fixed size.

  By concatenating the above features, we obtain the encoding sequence of a paragraph $\mathbf{P}_i^{emb} = \{\mathbf{p}_i^t\}_{t=1}^{|p_i|} \in \mathbb{R}^{d_{emb} \times |p_i|}$ and the question $\mathbf{Q}^{emb} = \{\mathbf{q}^t\}_{t=1}^{m} \in \mathbb{R}^{d_{emb} \times m}$. Here $|p_i|$ is the number of words in the i-th paragraph. After that, we use a bi-directional LSTM to obtain a contextual encoding for each word in the paragraph and question respectively.

$$\mathbf{P}_i^{enc} = BiLSTM(\mathbf{P}_i^{emb}) \in \mathbb{R}^{d_{hid} \times |p_i|}, \mathbf{Q}^{enc} = BiLSTM(\mathbf{Q}^{emb}) \in \mathbb{R}^{d_{hid} \times m} \quad (1)$$

P-Q Matching Layer. The P-Q matching layer takes $\mathbf{P}_i^{enc}$ and $\mathbf{Q}^{enc}$ as inputs and produce a question-aware representation $\mathbf{C}_i$ for each paragraph. We use the bi-directional attention, which is introduced by BIDAF [10], to obtain the hidden states $\mathbf{H}_i$ for $\mathbf{P}_i^{enc}$, where $\mathbf{H}_i \in \mathbb{R}^{d_{hid} \times |p_i|}$. After that, we use a bi-directional

LSTM to obtain a question-aware paragraph embedding $\mathbf{C}_i$ for the paragraph P_i.

$$\mathbf{C}_i = BiLSTM(\mathbf{H}_i) \in \mathbb{R}^{d_{hid} \times |p_i|} \tag{2}$$

P-P Matching Layer. Given $\mathbf{D}_c = \{\mathbf{C}_1, \mathbf{C}_2, ..., \mathbf{C}_n\}$, the P-P matching layer aims to produce a new representation $\mathbf{Z}_i$ for each paragraph by effectively aggregating evidence from all paragraphs. Firstly, we use max pooling to obtain a fixed-size vector for the question-aware paragraph embedding.

$$\mathbf{C}_i^{pool} = max(\mathbf{C}_i) \in \mathbb{R}^{d_{hid}}, \mathbf{C}^{pool} = \{\mathbf{C}_i^{pool}\}_{i=1}^n \in \mathbb{R}^{d_{hid} \times n} \tag{3}$$

where $\mathbf{C}^{pool}$ represents the sequence of summary vectors for all paragraphs. Next, in order to make full use of the intro-relation among paragraphs, a self attention layer and a bi-directional LSTM are utilized to produce a final paragraph representation for each paragraph.

$$\mathbf{A} = softmax(\mathbf{C}^{pool^T}\mathbf{C}^{pool}) \in \mathbb{R}^{n \times n}, \mathbf{U} = \mathbf{C}^{pool}\mathbf{A} \in \mathbb{R}^{d_{hid} \times n} \tag{4}$$

Here, $\mathbf{A}$ is the similarity matrix and A_{ij} indicates the similarity between $\mathbf{C}_{:i}^{pool}$ and $\mathbf{C}_{:j}^{pool}$. $\mathbf{U}_{:i}$ is the i-th column of $\mathbf{U}$ which is the representation of the i-th paragraph and this representation contains the information of all paragraphs. The $\mathbf{U}$ and $\mathbf{C}^{pool}$ are concatenated together to yield $\mathbf{G}$. We define G by

$$\mathbf{G}_{:i} = [\mathbf{C}_{:i}^{pool}; \mathbf{U}_{:i}; \mathbf{C}_{:i}^{pool} \circ \mathbf{U}_{:i}; \mathbf{C}_{:i}^{pool} - \mathbf{U}_{:i}] \in \mathbb{R}^{4d_{hid}} \tag{5}$$

where $\circ$ is element-wise multiplication, $-$ is element-wise subtraction, and $[;]$ is vector concatenation across row. After that, a bi-directional LSTM is used to obtain the final paragraph representation $\mathbf{Z}$.

$$\mathbf{Z} = BiLSTM(\mathbf{G}) \in \mathbb{R}^{d_{hid} \times n} \tag{6}$$

Selector Decoding Layer. The selector decoding layer aims to compute a confidence score for each paragraph. A linear layer and a sotfmax function are used to produce a normalized score for each paragraph.

$$\mathbf{Pr}^{sen} = softmax(W_1^T\mathbf{Z}) \in \mathbb{R}^n \tag{7}$$

where $W_1 \in \mathbb{R}^{d_{hid}}$ is a trainable weight vector. $\mathbf{Pr}_i^{sen}$ is the i-th element of $\mathbf{Pr}^{sen}$ which represents the probability that the i-th paragraph contains the answer.

3.3 Paragraph Reader

The inputs of the paragraph reader are the k top-ranked paragraphs $D^{top} = \{P_1, P_2, ..., P_k\}$ which are selected by the selector. Note that k is a hyperparameter. After that, we concatenate these paragraphs together to obtain $\hat{P} = [P_1; P_2; ...; P_k]$ which aggregates the evidence from the selected paragraphs in word level. Given $\hat{P}$ and Q, the output of the reader is the probability distribution of the start index and end index over the concatenated paragraph. The paragraph reader consists of an encoding layer, a P-Q matching layer and a reader decoding layer.

The reader and the selector have the same encoding and P-Q matching layers. After converting $\hat{P}$ and Q to these two layers, we obtain the hidden states $\hat{\mathbf{H}} \in \mathbb{R}^{d_{hid} \times |\hat{P}|}$ where $|\hat{P}|$ is the number of words in the concatenated paragraphs.

Reader Decoding Layer. The input of reader decoding layer is $\hat{\mathbf{H}}$. After that, we use a bi-directional LSTM to obtain a matrix $\mathbf{M}$. Next, a linear layer and a sotfmax function are used to produce the start probabilities.

$$\mathbf{M} = BiLSTM(\hat{\mathbf{H}}) \in \mathbb{R}^{d_{hid} \times |\hat{P}|}, \mathbf{Pr^s} = softmax(\mathbf{W}_4\mathbf{M}) \in \mathbb{R}^{|\hat{P}|} \qquad (8)$$

The concatenation of $\hat{\mathbf{H}}$ and $\mathbf{M}$ is passed to a second bi-directional LSTM to obtain $\mathbf{M}^2$. Hence, We compute the end probabilities by

$$\mathbf{M}^2 = BiLSTM([\hat{\mathbf{H}}; \mathbf{M}]) \in \mathbb{R}^{d_{hid} \times |\hat{P}|}, \mathbf{Pr^e} = softmax(\mathbf{W}_5\mathbf{M}^2) \in \mathbb{R}^{|\hat{P}|} \qquad (9)$$

After that, we split $\mathbf{Pr^s}$ and $\mathbf{Pr^e}$ into k vectors according to the length of each paragraph and obtain $\{\mathbf{Pr}_1^s, \mathbf{Pr}_2^s, ..., \mathbf{Pr}_k^s\}$ and $\{\mathbf{Pr}_1^e, \mathbf{Pr}_2^e, ..., \mathbf{Pr}_k^e\}$. We hope that the final score of a word in each paragraph contains the output probabilities of the selector and the reader, so we multiply these two probabilities to get the final scores.

$$\mathbf{score_i^s} = \mathbf{Pr}_i^{sen}\mathbf{Pr}_i^s, \ \mathbf{score_i^e} = \mathbf{Pr}_i^{sen}\mathbf{Pr}_i^e \qquad (10)$$

where $\mathbf{Pr}_i^{sen} \in \mathbb{R}$, produced by the selector, represents the probability that the i-th paragraph contains the answer, $\mathbf{score_i^s} \in \mathbb{R}^{|P_i|}$ is a vector representing the start scores of the i-th paragraph.

3.4 Training and Prediction

We train our model in two stages and regard all paragraphs that contain the answer string as ground truths following the distantly supervised setup.

For the paragraph selector, every paragraph in set $\{P_i\}_{i=1}^n$ is associated with a label $y_i \in \{0, 1\}$. The label is 1 if the paragraph contains the answer string. Given the paragraph probabilities $\mathbf{Pr}^{sen} \in \mathbb{R}^n$, the selector is trained by minimizing the loss :

$$\mathcal{L}_s = -\sum_{i=1}^n \mathbf{y}_i log(\mathbf{Pr}_i^{sen}) \qquad (11)$$

For the paragraph reader, we first select k top-ranked paragraphs and obtain the final scores $\mathbf{score_i^s}, \mathbf{score_i^e}$ for each paragraph where $\mathbf{score_i^s}(t)$ represents the start score of the t-th word in the i-th paragraph. As described above, the answer string can appear multiple times in a paragraph. Therefore, let $\{(x_i^t, z_i^t)\}_{t=1}^{|a_i|}$ be the set of the start and end positions of the answer strings that appear in the paragraph P_i. The reader is trained using a summed objective function that maximizes the probability of selecting any correct answer span.

$$\mathcal{L}_r = -(log(\sum_{i=1}^{k} \sum_{t=1}^{|a_i|}(\textbf{score}_\textbf{i}^\textbf{s}(x_i^t))) + log(\sum_{i=1}^{k} \sum_{t=1}^{|a_i|}(\textbf{score}_\textbf{i}^\textbf{e}(z_i^t)))) \qquad (12)$$

During testing, we first utilize the selector to predict a confidence score for each paragraph and select top k paragraphs. Next, the reader calculates the start and the end score of each word in all selected paragraphs. After that, we extract an answer candidate A_i that has maximum span score for each paragraph. This span score is the product of the start score of the first word and the end score of the last word in the candidate span. Next, if the answer candidates from different paragraphs have the same characters, we will add the scores of these answer candidates together and choose the answer candidate with the maximum score as our final prediction.

4   Experiments

4.1   Datasets and Baselines

We evaluate our model on two MPRC datasets, Quasar-T [3] and SearchQA [4]. The background paragraphs of these datasets are retrieved from webpages by IR systems.

Quasar-T. It consists of 43K open-domain trivia question-answer pairs, and about 100 relevant paragraphs are provided for each question-answer pair by using the Solr search engine.

SearchQA. It consists of more than 140K question-answer pairs, and about 50 webpage snippets are provided as background paragraphs for each question-answer pair by using the Google search engine.

To better evaluate the effectiveness of our model, we carefully select some recent approaches as baselines, including traditional RC models (GA [2], BIDAF [10]), answer re-ranking models (Re-Ranker [13], Joint [14]) and pipeline models (DrQA [1], R3 [12], DS-QA [7]).

4.2   Implementation Details

In the experiments, we adopt the same data preprocessing scheme mentioned in [13]. Our model is tuned on the development set and then the model achieving best results is used to the predict answer on the test set. We use 300-dimensional word embeddings pre-trained by GloVe [9] and the word embeddings are not updated during training. Additionally, 20-dimensional character embeddings are randomly initialized and updated during training. The common word feature is

Table 1. Experimental results on Quasar-T and SearchQA.

Models	Quasar-T		SearchQA		Average	
	EM	F1	EM	F1	EM	F1
GA [2]	26.4	26.4	–	–	–	–
BIDAF [10]	25.9	28.5	28.6	34.6	27.2	31.5
Re-Ranker [13]	42.3	49.6	57.0	63.2	49.6	56.4
Joint [14]	45.9	53.9	58.3	64.2	52.1	59.0
DrQA [1]	37.7	44.5	41.9	48.7	39.8	46.6
R3 [12]	35.3	41.7	40.9	55.3	38.1	48.5
DS-QA [7]	42.2	49.3	58.5	64.5	50.3	56.9
Our model	**46.7**	**55.6**	**61.1**	**67.3**	**53.9**	**61.4**

Table 2. The performance of our selector on the Quasar-T test set.

Models	Quasar-T			SearchQA		
	Hit@1	Hit@3	Hit@5	Hit@1	Hit@3	Hit@5
IR	6.3	10.9	15.2	13.7	24.1	32.7
R3	40.3	51.3	54.5	–	–	–
DS-QA	27.7	36.8	42.6	59.2	70.0	75.7
Our model	**48.2**	**57.3**	**61.4**	**72.3**	**84.0**	**87.9**

mapped to a 4-dimensional vector and it is updated during training. For the selector, we set the hidden size of LSTM as 150 and the number of LSTM layers as 1. We use Adam [5] to optimize the model and set batch size as 8, learning rate as 5e-4. Dropout [11] is adopted to the outputs of all LSTM layers at a rate of 0.2. For the reader, the parameters of the selector are fixed. We utilize the selector to produce the confidence score for every paragraph and select the 30, 25 top-ranked paragraphs for Quasar-T, SearchQA respectively. Different from the settings of the selector, we set the batch size as 16 and learning rate as 1e-3. The other settings of parameters of the reader are the same as the selector.

4.3 Results and Analysis

In this section, we focus on the performance of the whole model. Table 1 presents the F1 and Exact Match (EM) scores of our model and the baseline models. The evaluation metrics is widely-adopted for MPRC. We can observe that our model outperforms the baselines. Compared with the answer re-ranking models, the performance of our model is better. The main reason is that these baselines deal with each paragraph indiscriminately. They ignore the influence of noisy paragraphs. However, by utilizing the inter-relation between paragraphs and questions, our model could effectively filter out the noisy data and promote the overall performance. Compared with the pipeline models, our model also achieves a better result. The main reason is that our model can use the intra-relation

Table 3. The upper bound of the Top 1,3,5 answer candidates on the Quasar-T development set.

Models	R3		DS-QA		Our model	
Quasar-T	EM	F1	EM	F1	EM	F1
Top1	35.3	41.6	42.2	49.3	**47.6**	**56.5**
Top3	46.2	53.5	53.1	62.0	**55.8**	**65.0**
Top5	51.0	58.9	56.4	66.4	**57.9**	**67.9**

among all paragraphs to select relevant paragraphs and answer questions, while these baselines always handle each paragraph independently.

The experimental results demonstrate our assumption that making full use of the inter-relation and intra-relation among paragraphs and questions can further help us to solve the MPRC problem. The following three parts are used to further analyze the submodule, the potentiality and the case study of our system.

Performance of the Selector. Table 2 shows the performance of our selector and the baselines including an IR model[1] and some neural network models (DS-QA [7], R3 [12]). Since we do not know which paragraph actually answers the question in the distantly supervised setup, we follow the previous work to regard the paragraph which contains the answer string as ground truth. We adopt Hit@K as evaluation metrics which measures the probability that the answer string appears in the K top-ranked paragraphs. As shown in the table, our selector significantly outperforms the baselines which only utilize the inter-relation between the paragraph and the question. The result proves that the intra-relation among paragraphs can be used to further improve the performance of the selector. By simultaneously employing the inter-relation and intra-relation, we can effectively solve the noisy problem in MPRC.

Potential Improvement. This part is the analysis of the potential of our model. The scores in the Table 3 could be viewed as the upper bounds of our model after it is equipped with the answer re-ranking submodule. Specifically, for each question, we choose the top k predictions and record the best EM/F1 score among them. From the table, we can observe that the scores of the top 3 and top 5 are much higher than those of the top 1. It means that we can find the correct answer in a small range of k and our model still has a great potential to be improved by the answer re-ranking submodule. Moreover, the scores of our model are both higher than those of the DS-QA and R3. This means that our model has a higher potential to be improved by the answer re-ranking strategy.

Case Study. Table 4 shows two examples of our models, which indicates that our model can make full use of the multi-perspective information and solve the

---

[1] The IR model ranks the paragraph with BM25.

Table 4. An example from Quasar-T.

Question: The Latin phrase "Citius Altius Fortius" is the motto for which sporting event?	Label	
Answer: The Olympic Games	Distant	Select
The motto of the Olympic Games is the hendiatris "Citius, Altius, Fortius", which is Latin for "Faster, Higher, Stronger"	1	1
As the official motto of the Olympic Games, Coubertin adopted "Citius, altius, fortius", Latin for "Faster, higher, stronger"	1	1
The Olympic Games is a sporting event that takes place in a different city every four years	1	0
Question: Where, in 1955, was one of the worst accidents in motor racing history, when 82 spectators were killed?	Label	
Answer: Le Mans	Distant	Select
The worst accident in motor racing history happened at the 1955 24 hours of Le Mans	1	1
In 1955, Hawthorn was the winner of the 24 hours of Le Mans race, despite being involved in the terrible crash that killed 82 spectators	1	1
His skills were just as highly valued when he was testing for and racing at Le Mans	1	0

noise problem. "Distant" means the distantly supervised label. "Select" means the label produced by the paragraph selector. We can observe from the table:

(1) On both examples, all three paragraphs contain the answer string while the third paragraph is noisy. Because the third one is not relevant to the question. In the distant supervision setup, we consider the noisy paragraph as the ground truth and this will affect the performance of the reader. The table shows that the paragraph selector can effectively filter out the noisy paragraphs by jointly utilizing the inter-relation and intra-relation.

(2) On the first example, the first two paragraphs are relevant to the question and both of them support "The Olympic Games" as the answer. These paragraphs provide enhanced evidence for the correct answer. On the second example, the first two paragraphs contain the answer string while both of them only contain a part of the information of the question. These paragraphs provide complementary evidence for the correct answer. By concatenating the selected paragraphs together, we can provide more useful information for the reader.

5   Conclusion

In this paper, we propose a hierarchical model with a multi-level attention mechanism which can make full use of the multi-perspective information and solve the noise problem simultaneously. Experiments on two challenging public MPRC datasets, Quasar-T and SearchQA, show that our model outperforms recent MPRC baselines. In the future, we will explore the utilizing of structured knowledge in solving the MPRC problem. We believe that the performance of our model will be further improved by effectively exploiting the commonsense knowledge.

Acknowledgement. This work was supported by National Natural Science Foundation of China (No. 61976207, No. 61906187).

References

1. Chen, D., Fisch, A., Weston, J., Bordes, A.: Reading wikipedia to answer open-domain questions. In: Proceedings of the 55th Annual Meeting of the Association for Computational Linguistics, (Volume 1: Long Papers), pp. 1870–1879. Association for Computational Linguistics (2017)
2. Dhingra, B., Liu, H., Yang, Z., Cohen, W.W., Salakhutdinov, R.: Gated-attention readers for text comprehension. In: Proceedings of the 55th Annual Meeting of the Association for Computational Linguistics (Volume 1: Long Papers), pp. 1832–1846. Association for Computational Linguistics (2017)
3. Dhingra, B., Mazaitis, K., Cohen, W.W.: Quasar: Datasets for question answering by search and reading. Computing Research Repository. arXiv:1707.03904 (2017)
4. Dunn, M., Sagun, L., Higgins, M., Güney, V.U., Cirik, V., Cho, K.: SearchQA: a new Q&A dataset augmented with context from a search engine. Computing Research Repository. arXiv:1704.05179 (2017)
5. Kingma, D.P., Ba, J.: Adam: A method for stochastic optimization. In: International Conference on Learning Representations (2014)
6. Lee, J., Yun, S., Kim, H., Ko, M., Kang, J.: Ranking paragraphs for improving answer recall in open-domain question answering. In: Proceedings of the 2018 Conference on Empirical Methods in Natural Language Processing, pp. 565–569. Association for Computational Linguistics (2018)
7. Lin, Y., Ji, H., Liu, Z., Sun, M.: Denoising distantly supervised open-domain question answering. In: Proceedings of the 56th Annual Meeting of the Association for Computational Linguistics (Volume 1: Long Papers), pp. 1736–1745. Association for Computational Linguistics (2018)
8. Mintz, M., Bills, S., Snow, R., Jurafsky, D.: Distant supervision for relation extraction without labeled data. In: Proceedings of the 47th Annual Meeting of the Association for Computational Linguistics (Volume 1: Long Papers), pp. 1003–1011. Association for Computational Linguistics (2009)
9. Pennington, J., Socher, R., Manning, C.D.: Glove: global vectors for word representation. In: Proceedings of the 2014 Conference on Empirical Methods in Natural Language Processing, pp. 1532–1543. Association for Computational Linguistics (2014)
10. Seo, M.J., Kembhavi, A., Farhadi, A., Hajishirzi, H.: Bidirectional attention flow for machine comprehension. In: International Conference on Learning Representations (2016)
11. Srivastava, N., Hinton, G.E., Krizhevsky, A., Sutskever, I., Salakhutdinov, R.: Dropout: a simple way to prevent neural networks from overfitting. J. Mach. Learn. Res. **15**(1), 1929–1958 (2014). http://dl.acm.org/citation.cfm?id=2670313
12. Wang, S., et al.: R3: reinforced ranker-reader for open-domain question answering. In: Association for the Advancement of Artificial Intelligence (2018)

13. Wang, S., et al.: Evidence aggregation for answer re-ranking in open-domain question answering. In: Proceedings of International Conference on Learning Representations (2018)
14. Wang, Z., Liu, J., Xiao, X., Lyu, Y., Wu, T.: Joint training of candidate extraction and answer selection for reading comprehension. In: Proceedings of the 56th Annual Meeting of the Association for Computational Linguistics (Volume 1: Long Papers), pp. 1715–1724. Association for Computational Linguistics (2018)
15. Zhang, C., Zhang, X., Wang, H.: A machine reading comprehension-based approach for featured snippet extraction. In: IEEE International Conference on Data Mining, pp. 1416–1421 (2018)

Models in the Wild: On Corruption Robustness of Neural NLP Systems

Barbara Rychalska[1(✉)], Dominika Basaj[1,2], Alicja Gosiewska[1], and Przemysław Biecek[1]

[1] Warsaw University of Technology, Warsaw, Poland
{b.rychalska,d.basaj,a.gosiewska,p.biecek}@mini.pw.edu.pl
[2] Tooploox, Wrocław, Poland

Abstract. Natural Language Processing models lack a unified approach to robustness testing. In this paper we introduce WildNLP - a framework for testing model stability in a natural setting where text corruptions such as keyboard errors or misspelling occur. We compare robustness of deep learning models from 4 popular NLP tasks: Q&A, NLI, NER and Sentiment Analysis by testing their performance on aspects introduced in the framework. In particular, we focus on a comparison between recent state-of-the-art text representations and non-contextualized word embeddings. In order to improve robustness, we perform adversarial training on selected aspects and check its transferability to the improvement of models with various corruption types. We find that the high performance of models does not ensure sufficient robustness, although modern embedding techniques help to improve it. We release the code of WildNLP framework for the community.

Keywords: Natural Language Processing · Robustness · Adversarial examples · Deep learning

1 Introduction

Adversarial examples have been shown to severely degrade performance of deep learning models [11,15]. Natural Language Processing systems are no different in this respect. Multiple areas of NLP, such as machine translation [2], question answering [13], or text classification [14] have been studied to assess the impact of adversaries generated with various methods. However, these works tend to focus on one area only, often with attacks designed just for the selected problem. It makes comparisons between models, datasets, and NLP areas impossible. In particular, the robustness of modern contextualized word embedding systems - such as ELMo [18], Flair [1] and language model based BERT [6] remains unstudied.

B. Rychalska and D. Basaj—Equal contribution.

T. Gedeon et al. (Eds.): ICONIP 2019, LNCS 11955, pp. 235–247, 2019.
https://doi.org/10.1007/978-3-030-36718-3_20

In this article, we evaluate the behavior of natural language models in the wild. We propose WildNLP - a comprehensive robustness testing framework which can be used for any NLP model. Instead of focusing on elaborate attacks, which are unlikely to originate by accident, we simulate the quality of models in a natural setting, where input data is poisoned with errors involuntarily generated by actual users.

We put these notions into a set of tests called *aspects*. Moreover, we introduce the concept of corruption severity and prove that it is critical to model improvement via adversarial training. The framework is aimed at any NLP problem irrespective of its form of input and output.

In summary, our contributions are the following:

1. **We offer a systematic framework for testing corruption robustness - the WildNLP.** In total, we introduce 11 aspects of robustness testing, with multiple severity levels. We release the WildNLP code for the community[1]. The framework is easy to extend. New aspects can be defined by the community.
2. **We test corruption robustness of a number of NLP tasks: question answering (Q&A), natural language inference (NLI), named entity recognition (NER), and sentiment analysis (SA).** We verify stability of neural models trained on contextualized embeddings like ELMo and

Table 1. Examples of text corruptions introduced by WildNLP aspects.

Aspect	Example sentence
Original	Warsaw was believed to be one of the most beautiful cities in the world
Article	Warsaw was believed to be one of **a** most beautiful cities in world
Swap	Warsaw **aws** believed to be one **fo teh** most beautiful cities in the world
Qwerty	Wadsaw was bdlieved to be one of the most beautiful citiee in the world
Remove_char	Warsaw was believed to be one **o th** most **eautiful** cities in the world
Remove_space	Warsaw was believed **tobe** one of the most beautiful cities in the world
Original	You cannot accidentally commit vandalism. It used to be a rare occurrence
Misspelling	You can not **accidentaly** commit vandalism. It used to be a rare **occurrence**
Original	Bus Stops for Route 6, 6.1
Digits2words	Bus Stops for Route **six, six point one**
Original	Choosing between affect and effect can be scary
Homophones	Choosing between **effect** and effect can **bee** scary
Original	Laughably foolish or false: an absurd explanation
Negatives	**Laughab*y fo*lish** or **fal*e**: an **a*surd** explanation
Original	Sometimes it is good to be first, and sometimes it is good to be last
Positives	Sometimes it is **go*d** to be first, and sometimes it is **goo*** to be last
Marks	Sometimes, it is good to be first and sometimes, it, is good to be last

---

[1] https://github.com/MI2DataLab/WildNLP/.

Flair in contrast to non-contextualized FastText [3] and GloVe [17]. We also analyze BERT in the task of Q&A. We find that new forms of text representation, despite greater contextual awareness, do not offer a sufficient increase in robustness.
3. **We find that model training on one aspect does improve performance on another aspect, contrary to previous studies** [2]. For this to be true, two corruption types must be similar to some extent.

In Sect. 2 we present related literature in the domain of NLP robustness. In Sect. 3 we present WildNLP framework, describing in detail each introduced aspect. In Sect. 4 we compare robustness of NER, Q&A, NLI and Sentiment Analysis. In Sect. 5 we perform adversarial training on `Qwerty` aspect with different severities and test these models on other aspects. We conclude in Sect. 6.

2   Related Work

The problem of natural noise in textual data has been studied by [2], however exclusively in the context of character-based machine translation models. They find that errors such as typos and misspelling cause significant drops in BLEU scores. Other recent approaches to generating textual adversaries include the work of [14], who exploit important word manipulations for text classification models from 2014 and 2015. [8] identify important words and apply 4 kinds of character perturbations: swap, substitution, deletion and insertion. They test on vanilla LSTM and CNN model, applying them to 8 datasets. Among others, they aim for the character swaps to map a word vector to an 'unknown' vector in traditional word embeddings. [20] create rules of substitutions between texts which produce correct and semantically identical samples in Q&A domain. [10] design adversaries for NLI systems, swapping words which share a relation such as antonymy or co-hyponymy.

3   WildNLP: Corruption Robustness Testing Approach

We postulate that performance of each model should be tested on three levels:

1. **Performance measures** - established metrics such as F1 score, accuracy, BLEU score should indicate to what extent the model performs correctly on the testset.
2. **Corruption robustness** - robustness towards corruptions which can occur naturally in the model deployment setting. They reflect involuntary perturbations introduced to text by users, resulting from misspelling, haste or varied writing habits. As such, these are black box attacks as no knowledge of underlying models is exploited. WildNLP, presented in this paper, is an example of this attack method.
3. **Targeted robustness** - attacks designed for a specific problem and/or dataset, or demanding access to model internals. An example is the whole class of white box attacks [7] as well as highly specialized attacks [13].

3.1   Corruption Aspects

The WildNLP aspects define classes of common disturbances found in natural text. These corruptions can be produced naturally due to haste, lacking space, individual writing habits or imperfect command of English.

Articles. Randomly removes or swaps articles into wrong ones.

Swap. Randomly shuffles two characters within a word.

Qwerty. Simulates errors made while writing on a QWERTY-type keyboard. Characters are swapped for their neighbors on the keyboard.

Remove_char. Randomly removes characters from words.

Remove_space. Removes a space from text, merging two words.

Misspelling. Misspells words appearing in the Wikipedia list of commonly misspelled English words[2].

Digits2words. Rewrites digit numbers into words.

Homophones. Changes words into their homophones from the Wikipedia list of common misspellings/homophones[3]. The list contains around 500 pairs or triples of homophonic words.

Negatives. This aspect reflects attempts made by some Internet users to mask profanity or hate speech in online forums to evade moderation. We perform masking of negative words from Opinion Lexicon[4]. The lexicon contains a list of English positive and negative opinion words or sentiment words, in total around 6800 words.

Positives. Masks positive words from Opinion Lexicon, similarly as in the case of Negatives (described above).

Marks. Randomly removes and insert punctuation marks. Marks are inserted between last letter of a word and space.

Table 2. Exemplary context, question and answer from SQuAD dataset.

Question&Answer	Context
Q: How many provinces did the Ottoman empire contain in the 17th century? A: 32	(...) At the beginning of the 17th century the empire contained 32 provinces and numerous vassal states. (...)

---

[2] https://en.wikipedia.org/wiki/Commonly_misspelled_English_words.
[3] https://en.wikipedia.org/wiki/Wikipedia:Lists_of_common_misspellings/ Homophones.
[4] https://www.cs.uic.edu/~liub/FBS/sentiment-analysis.html.

Table 3. Exemplary hypotheses, questions and answers from SNLI dataset.

Premise	Hypothesis	Type
A woman with a green headscarf, blue shirt and a very big grin	The woman is young	Neutral
An old man with a package poses in front of an advertisement	A man poses in front of an ad	Entailment
A couple walk hand in hand down a street	A couple is sitting on a bench	Contradiction

Table 4. Exemplary tagged sentence fron CoNLL dataset.

Token	SOCCER	-	JAPAN	GET	LUCKY	WIN	CHINA	IN	DEFEAT	.
Class	O	O	I-LOC	O	O	O	I-PER	O	O	O

Table 5. Excerpts from exemplary reviews from IMDB dataset.

Review	Sentiment
Kutcher played the character of Jake Fischer very well, and Kevin Costner played Ben Randall with such professionalism. The sign of a good movie is that it can toy with our emotions. (...)	Positive
Once again Mr. Costner has dragged out a movie for far longer than necessary. Aside from the terrific sea rescue sequences, of which there are very few I just did not care about any of the characters. (...)	Negative

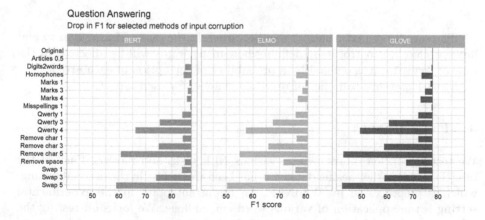

Fig. 1. Robustness testing results for Q&A models. Each bar starts in the F1 score for the original data and ends in F1 score for data after selected method of corruption is applied. The shorter the bar the more robust is a given method.

Table 6. Influence of the severity of corruption of training data on results of corrupted testsets in Q&A BiDAF ELMo model.

Tested on	Trainset		
	Original EM	Qwerty_1 EM	Qwerty_5 EM
Original	**71.6**	70.7	69.0
Qwerty_1	66.4	**68.2**	67.8
Qwerty_5	46.2	58.2	**63.8**

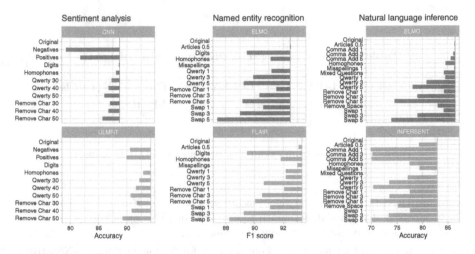

Fig. 2. Robustness testing results for NLI, NER, and SA models. Corruptions of smaller severities (1–5) are not evaluated on SA models due to greater length of IMDB dataset sequences. Each bar starts in the performance for the original data and ends in performance for data after selected method of corruption is applied.

The severity of perturbations can be varied. In the case of Swap, Qwerty and Remove_char we control it by defining how many words will be affected. In the case of Article, it is defined by a probability of corruption of each article.

Table 1 presents examples of resulting changes for each aspect.

4   Experiments

We test corruption robustness on various NLP tasks and models. Each of the models is run on the specific dataset it has been trained on in the original setting, which is preprocessed by WildNLP. An important point in the experimental setting is the application of various word embeddings. We focus on testing the robustness of models trained with newly introduced context-aware embeddings: ELMo, Flair and language model based BERT. We compare their performance on corrupted data to older embedding systems - GloVe, FastText (within InferSent) and in the case of one of sentiment analysis models, even one-hot encoded words.

We do so to verify the assumption that greater context awareness and lack of problems with out-of-vocabulary (OOV) words in ELMo, Flair and BERT would increase robustness of models.

4.1 Experimental Setting

We use our framework on the selection of well known models that are widely used in NLP community. For training ELMo-based models we use open-source implementations available in AllenNLP [9], for BERT we follow implementation of HuggingFace[5] and for the rest of the models we use original author research code. In particular, following models and datasets are used in experiments:

– **Q&A task**
  Models. We test BiDAF and BERT trained on the SQuAD dataset [19]. We analyze two versions of BiDAF - with ELMo (BiDAF-E) and GloVe (BiDAF-G) embeddings. BiDAF uses character and word embeddings with a bidirectional attention flow to obtain a query-aware context representation. It is one of the popular models listed on the SQuAD leaderboard. BERT, on the other hand, applies a bidirectional Transformer to language modeling task and is currently used with great success in various NLP tasks, achieving the current state-of-the-art. We evaluate the models with the common performance scores in Q&A task, which are Exact Match (EM) and F1 score.
  Dataset. SQuAD dataset comprises around 100,000 question-answer pairs prepared by crowdworkers. The dataset is based on Wikipedia articles. Table 2 displays examples of the question-answer pairs.
– **NLI task**
  Models. We analyze decomposable attention model [16] trained on ELMo embeddings and InferSent model [5]. The aim of InferSent embeddings is to create the universal sentence representations. They are initialized with FastText embeddings and trained using SNLI dataset.
  Dataset. The Stanford Natural Language Inference (SNLI) Corpus [4] is a collection of 570,000 manually created and labeled English sentence pairs. Table 3 contains an example of the three possible entailment relations.
– **NER task**
  Models. We use two sequence tagging models with ELMo implementation (CRF-E) [18] and Flair [1]. Flair comprises new word embeddings an a BiLSTM-CRF sequence labeling system. It models words as sequences of characters, which allows to effectively eliminate the notion of separate tokens. Flair is currently the state-of-the-art model in NER task.
  Dataset. The CoNLL 2003 dataset is a standard training dataset used in NER sequence tagging. It is a collection of news articles from Reuters corpus annotated as Person, Organization, Location, Miscellaneous, or Other for non-named entities. Due to licensing agreement this is the only corrupted dataset that we cannot release.

---

[5] https://github.com/huggingface/pytorch-pretrained-BERT.

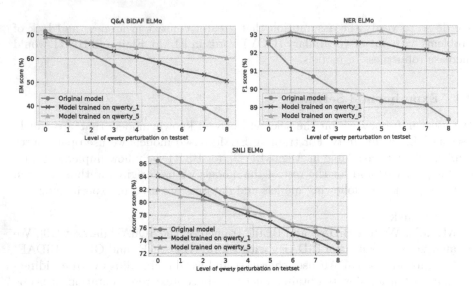

Fig. 3. Performance of models trained on varied levels of `Qwerty` aspect tested on varied levels of `Qwerty` aspects applied to testset.

- **SA task**

    Models. We use the current state-of-the-art ULMFiT model [12] that consists of language model pretrained on Wikipedia and fine-tuned on the specific text corpus that is used in classification task. In adversarial training scenario, we pretrain this language model on corrupted data. We compare ULMFiT with CNN based classification model, which uses one-hot encoding of words.

    Dataset. We train and test described models on IMDB dataset that consists of 25000 positive and 25000 negative reviews of movies (Tables 4 and 5).

4.2   Model Robustness

Figure 1 (Q&A models) and Fig. 2 (other models) present aggregate results of testing on all models and all corruption aspects.

Robustness Measure. To comprehensively measure model robustness to corruptions, we calculate an overall mean of drops across all aspects (Av-Drop). We use this aggregated metric to compare robustness between models.

Q&A. The robustness of Q&A models was the lowest of all tested tasks. The corruptions which proved most damaging to the performance and in result to Av-Drop were the following: `Swap_5` (32–37 EM drop), `Remove_char_5` (29–37 EM drop), `Qwerty_5` (25–30 EM drop).

BERT and ELMo-based systems were found to mitigate performance loss to some degree compared to GloVe. However, their performance loss pattern across corruptions was similar to GloVe, and the difference of Av-Drop between BERT (most robust model) and BiDAF GloVe (least robust model) was 2.8 pp, despite huge performance differences reflected in F1 and EM (1).

We observe that severity of aspects plays an important role in drop of performance metrics across all Q&A models. For aspects that corrupt individual words like Qwerty, Remove_char or Swap, drop in performance of GloVe-based models is intuitive - we substitute words from out of vocabulary (OOV) with *unknown token*. However, in the case of ELMo and BERT the problem of OOV tokens is not that severe - they are character or subword-based, which means that they can reconstruct word embeddings for unknown words. Still, we observe an average drop of F1 metric on these three aspects (severity 5) at the level of 23.04 (BiDAF-E) and 24.46 (BERT) in comparison to drop of BiDAF-G at 32.9. Lower severities of word corruptions induce much lower drops - in case of severity 1 it is still a noticeable difference of 4.48 (BiDAF-E), 3.44 (BERT) and 5.63 (BiDAF-G).

WildNLP also tests on aspects that do not alter words but sentences. As previously, we state that context-aware models should be indifferent to such changes as they do not alter sentence meaning. However, we observe that aspects such as Remove_space and Marks decrease F1 values among all Q&A even by 8.89 in case of Remove_space tested with BiDAF-E, whereas BERT proves to be more robust to this sentence-level corruption with drop of F1 at 2.47.

NLI. Natural Language Inference task tested by WildNLP framework is more robust when trained with decomposable attention model with ELMo embeddings (Dec-E) rather than simple MLP classifier that uses sentence embeddings created by InferSent method (InferSent). The Av-Drop for Dec-E is half the value of Av-Drop for InferSent, being at the level of 4.19. On all sets of aspects, Dec-E model has lower drops of performance metric. However, it still has relatively high drops when it comes to word corruption aspects like Qwerty, Remove_char or Swap, with average drop of 10.92 at severity 5 and 2.09 at severity 1. InferSent performs worse by around 3 pp (5.56 and 12.82 respectively).

However, when we consider sentence level aspects like adding extra commas to the sentence, Dec-E model is very robust, having only 0.85 of drop in accuracy on highest possible severity.

NER. Both NER models seems to be robust, having the Av-Drop measure at the level of 2.37 (CRF-E) and 2.14 (Flair). However, in the case of state-of-the-art NER models, differences in performance are so small, that such relatively small values of Av-Drop must be seen as meaningful.

SA. ULMFiT model was found to be slightly less robust than CNN using one-hot encodings (2.36 vs 2.28 of Av-Drop). Drop in performance of the CNN model was mainly caused by Positives and Negatives corruptions (7.22 and 9.7 Av-Drop). Presumably this behavior is caused by the model's focus on detecting sentiment-carrying words, which were on average rarely affected by other corruptions. On the other hand, ULMFiT was less affected by Positives and Negatives corruptions (3.6 and 4.2 Av-Drop) probably because of its reliance on context and more subtle expressions of sentiment. In spite of the fact that

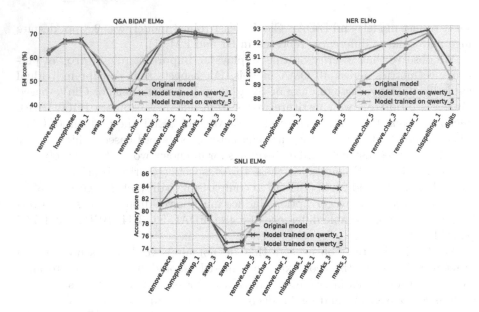

Fig. 4. Influence of training on data corrupted with `Qwerty` aspects on testing on other aspects.

the CNN model suffered from out-of-vocabulary words problem (corrupted words were simply unrecognized) while ULMFiT did not, the CNN proved more robust to most deformations in WildNLP framework.

5   Robustness Enhancements

We use adversarial training to research the potential of overcoming corruption errors. We validate two hypotheses:

1. **Adversarial training on data corrupted with aspects of greater severity should help to resolve problems with data corrupted with lesser severity.** For example, training on `Qwerty_5`-corrupted data should increase performance of data corrupted with `Qwerty_1` up to `Qwerty_5` severities.
2. **Adversarial training on one corruption type should increase model robustness to other corruptions.** [2] suggest that this might not be the case. They find that models trained on one type of noise do not perform well on others in character-based translation models. However, this analysis includes a very limited set of corruptions. We hope to prove that robustness can be improved between aspects which are related.

Corruption Severity. In agreement with our hypothesis we find that increased severity of corruption during training does increase performance on data corrupted with the same aspect type but lesser severity. Table 6 presents numeric scores for the training setting in Q&A BiDAF ELMo models, while Fig. 3 shows plots for multiple models. In all scenarios, we test on `Qwerty_1` and `Qwerty_5` corruptions.

Interestingly, in the case of NER models, results obtained on models trained on both corruption types are even better than for the original model (for `Qwerty_5` model, this behavior is consistent across levels of severity of test data perturbations).

Empirically, the severity of `Qwerty` perturbation (and others) does make the text unintelligible for humans at some point. For example, this boundary was found to be level 5 for Q&A questions. However, the Q&A BiDAF ELMo model trained on `Qwerty_5` performs reasonably well even at severity level 8. This suggests that the model learned to decode this corruption even beyond human ability.

Relation Between Corruption Types. To verify relations between performance of models trained and tested on various corruption types, we test models trained on `Qwerty` corruption with severity 1 and 5. `Qwerty` exhibits similarities to `Swap` and `Remove_char` types, since all of them imply manipulations of word characters. We find our hypothesis to be true - the performance on related aspects is improved by training a model adversarially on one of them. We observe that BiDAF ELMo and NER ELMo models trained on `Qwerty` and tested on similar aspects perform better than original models not trained in adversarial setting. Results are depicted in Fig. 4.

6 Conclusions

We have presented the WildNLP framework for corruption robustness testing. We have introduced 11 text corruption types (at various severity levels) which can occur naturally in model deployment setting: misspellings, keyboard errors, attempts at masking emotional language, and others. We test on four NLP areas and multiple deep learning models, verifying corruption robustness of state-of-the-art BERT system and new LM-based embeddings: ELMo and Flair, contrasted with GloVe and Fasttext. We find that the problem of lacking corruption robustness is not solved by these recent systems. However, we find that the issue can be partially alleviated by adversarial training, even across aspects. Without doubt, more work is needed to make models robust to noise.

Acknowledgements. Barbara Rychalska and Dominika Basaj were financially supported by grant no. 2018/31/N/ST6/02273 funded by National Science Centre, Poland. Our research was partially supported as a part of RENOIR Project by the European Union's Horizon 2020 Research and Innovation Programme under the Marie Skodłowska-Curie grant agreement No. 691152 and by the Ministry of Science and Higher Education (Poland), grant No. W34/H2020/2016.

References

1. Akbik, A., Blythe, D., Vollgraf, R.: Contextual string embeddings for sequence labeling. In: COLING 2018, 27th International Conference on Computational Linguistics, pp. 1638–1649 (2018)
2. Belinkov, Y., Bisk, Y.: Synthetic and natural noise both break neural machine translation. CoRR abs/1711.02173 (2017). http://arxiv.org/abs/1711.02173
3. Bojanowski, P., Grave, E., Joulin, A., Mikolov, T.: Enriching word vectors with subword information. Trans. Assoc. Comput. Linguist. **5**, 135–146 (2017)
4. Bowman, S.R., Angeli, G., Potts, C., Manning, C.D.: A large annotated corpus for learning natural language inference. In: Proceedings of the 2015 Conference on Empirical Methods in Natural Language Processing (EMNLP). Association for Computational Linguistics (2015)
5. Conneau, A., Kiela, D., Schwenk, H., Barrault, L., Bordes, A.: Supervised learning of universal sentence representations from natural language inference data. In: Proceedings of the 2017 Conference on Empirical Methods in Natural Language Processing, pp. 670–680. Association for Computational Linguistics, Copenhagen, September 2017. https://www.aclweb.org/anthology/D17-1070
6. Devlin, J., Chang, M.W., Lee, K., Toutanova, K.: Bert: pre-training of deep bidirectional transformers for language understanding. arXiv preprint arXiv:1810.04805 (2018)
7. Ebrahimi, J., Rao, A., Lowd, D., Dou, D.: HotFlip: white-box adversarial examples for NLP. CoRR abs/1712.06751 (2017). http://arxiv.org/abs/1712.06751
8. Gao, J., Lanchantin, J., Soffa, M.L., Qi, Y.: Black-box generation of adversarial text sequences to evade deep learning classifiers. CoRR abs/1801.04354 (2018). http://arxiv.org/abs/1801.04354
9. Gardner, M., et al.: AllenNLP: a deep semantic natural language processing platform (2017)
10. Glockner, M., Shwartz, V., Goldberg, Y.: Breaking NLI systems with sentences that require simple lexical inferences. CoRR abs/1805.02266 (2018). http://arxiv.org/abs/1805.02266
11. Goodfellow, I., Shlens, J., Szegedy, C.: Explaining and harnessing adversarial examples. In: International Conference on Learning Representations (2015). http://arxiv.org/abs/1412.6572
12. Howard, J., Ruder, S.: Fine-tuned language models for text classification. CoRR abs/1801.06146 (2018). http://arxiv.org/abs/1801.06146
13. Jia, R., Liang, P.: Adversarial examples for evaluating reading comprehension systems. CoRR abs/1707.07328 (2017). http://arxiv.org/abs/1707.07328
14. Liang, B., Li, H., Su, M., Bian, P., Li, X., Shi, W.: Deep text classification can be fooled. CoRR abs/1704.08006 (2017). http://arxiv.org/abs/1704.08006
15. Papernot, N., McDaniel, P.D., Goodfellow, I.J.: Transferability in machine learning: from phenomena to black-box attacks using adversarial samples. CoRR abs/1605.07277 (2016). http://arxiv.org/abs/1605.07277
16. Parikh, A.P., Täckström, O., Das, D., Uszkoreit, J.: A decomposable attention model for natural language inference. In: EMNLP (2016)
17. Pennington, J., Socher, R., Manning, C.D.: Glove: global vectors for word representation. In: Empirical Methods in Natural Language Processing (EMNLP), pp. 1532–1543 (2014). http://www.aclweb.org/anthology/D14-1162
18. Peters, M.E., et al.: Deep contextualized word representations. In: Proceedings of NAACL (2018)

19. Rajpurkar, P., Zhang, J., Lopyrev, K., Liang, P.: Squad: 100,000+ questions for machine comprehension of text. In: Proceedings of the 2016 Conference on Empirical Methods in Natural Language Processing, pp. 2383–2392. Association for Computational Linguistics (2016). https://doi.org/10.18653/v1/D16-1264. http://aclweb.org/anthology/D16-1264
20. Ribeiro, M.T., Singh, S., Guestrin, C.: Semantically equivalent adversarial rules for debugging NLP models. In: Proceedings of the 56th Annual Meeting of the Association for Computational Linguistics, Long Papers, vol. 1, pp. 856–865. Association for Computational Linguistics (2018). http://aclweb.org/anthology/P18-1079

Hie-Transformer: A Hierarchical Hybrid Transformer for Abstractive Article Summarization

Xuewen Zhang, Kui Meng, and Gongshen Liu[(✉)]

Shanghai Jiao Tong University, Shanghai 200240, China
{zxwtony,mengkui,lgshen}@sjtu.edu.cn

Abstract. Abstractive summarization methods based on neural network models can generate more human-written and higher qualities summaries than extractive methods. However, there are three main problems for these abstractive models: inability to deal with long article inputs, out-of-vocabulary (OOV) words and repetition words in generated summaries. To tackle these problems, we proposes a hierarchical hybrid Transformer model for abstractive article summarization in this work. First, the proposed model is based on a hierarchical Transformer with selective mechanism. The Transformer has outperformed traditional sequence-to-sequence models in many natural language processing (NLP) tasks and the hierarchical structure can handle the very long article inputs. Second, the pointer-generator mechanism is applied to combine generating novel words with copying words from article inputs, which can reduce the probability of the OOV words. Additionally, we use the coverage mechanism to reduce the repetitions in summaries. The proposed model is applied to CNN-Daily Mail summarization task. The evaluation results and analyses can demonstrate that our proposed model has a competitively performance compared with the baselines.

Keywords: Abstractive summarization · Hierarchical transformer · Selective mechanism · Pointer-generator · Coverage mechanism

1 Introduction

Text summarization can be considered as a process to compress the main information and generate a short summary from a original longer text. There are two main approaches to achieve text summarization: extractive and abstractive [11]. Extractive methods simply copy same words and phrases from the source text to assemble summaries. While abstractive methods usually get more human-written sentences since it is based on semantic representation and may generate novel words and phrases. Abstractive framework have sophisticated abilities to paraphrase, generalize and incorporate real-world knowledge [14], as a result, more and more researches have been focused on abstractive text summarization. Since abstractive summarization aims to map long input documents into brief

© Springer Nature Switzerland AG 2019
T. Gedeon et al. (Eds.): ICONIP 2019, LNCS 11955, pp. 248–258, 2019.
https://doi.org/10.1007/978-3-030-36718-3_21

output summaries, it is usually based on a encoder-decoder framework to achieve this task.

The fundamental challenge of abstractive summarization is that the original sentences to be summarized is too long and have multiple sentences with redundant information. It causes that the summaries generated by abstractive framework have out-of-vocabulary (OOV) words and repeated words. Many recent researches have made progress in sequence-to-sequence models to tackle these problems. Some abstractive frameworks combine the extractive method to reduce OOV words with a pointer-generator models, which considers both copying probabilities and generating probabilities to get the summaries [5,14]. Gehrmann et al. [4] develop a bottom-up model with coverage penalty and length penalty to get summaries with fewer repeated words. Besides the OOV and repeated problems, when the original article contains too many sentences and words, the simple neural network encoder can not receive all words from the inputs and have huge numbers of parameters. As a result, the encoder can not get high quality semantic information and the huge numbers of parameters cost too much time and too many memory resources for training. The hierarchical framework is used to deal with the training issues in the encoder [18].

In this paper, we focus on article summarization rather than headline generation tasks in abstractive summarization. The document summarization has longer text and multiple sentences which requires higher levels of abstraction and more effective encoder to get the core semantic information. Motivated by the recent researches, we propose a hierarchical hybrid framework to address the OOV, repeated words and long article inputs in abstractive article summarization. And the proposed model is based the Transformer [16], which outperforms Recurrent Neural Network (RNN) and Convolutional Neural Network (CNN) in many natural language processing (NLP) tasks [8,15,19]. The proposed model (Hie-Transformer) contains a hierarchical encoder (words to sentences, sentences to an article) based on the Transformer with selective layer to obtain semantic information and long-range dependencies between sentences more effectively. To deal with OOV word issues, we apply the pointer-generator mechanism in the decoder stack. This method combines getting novel words by generating with copying same word from article inputs by pointing. Besides, the coverage mechanism which keeps track of the words already generated to reduce the repetition probability when getting the next new word. We evaluate the proposed model on CNN-Daily Mail dataset [6,12] and it achieves improvements compared with the baseline models. The analyses on the summary results show the model facilitates reducing OOV and repeated words.

2   Related Work

Most of abstractive text summarization methods are based on sequence-to-sequence model [1]. It can be divided into headline generation task [13] and article summarization task [12].

The headline generation task is more concerted with the sentence level summarization. It gets semantic information from one or two sentences and compress to a single headline. Rush et al. [13] are first to use sequence-to-sequence framework on this task with a CNN encoder and a language model decoder. Chopra et al. [3] extend their work with a RNN decoder and get a better performance. Nallapati et al. apply a full RNN sequence-to-sequence framework with attention mechanism to get headline summarization. And recent researches on this task apply a selective mechanism to filter out the secondary information in the input sentences to improve the performance [10,20].

On the other hand, the article summarization task usually has a much longer input with multiple sentences, and it is document or paragraph level summarization. Nallapati et al. [12] also apply their model on the article summarization task and provide the baseline on CNN-Daily Mail dataset. See et al. [14] apply extractive method in abstractive model. They combine the copying mechanism [5] with attention mechanism and get a pointer-generator method to reduce the OOV words in output summaries. Many recent researches are motivated by this pointer-generator framework. Celikyilmaz et al. [2] propose a similar model with communicating agents to deal with the long input text. Gehrmann et al. [4] add a content selector to mask some words in the input text before the neural network model. And the bottom-up attention model improves the performance on article summarization.

When it comes to long text inputs with many words or tokens in NLP tasks, hierarchical structures are usually applied to the neural network models. These hierarchical structures obtain whole semantic representation from sentence-level to document level. Yang et al. [18] propose a hierarchical attention networks for document classification task. The model has a better performance than those without a hierarchical structure. Xing et al. [17] use a hierarchical network in response generation task. The communicating agents structure in Celikyilmaz's work can also considered as a hierarchical framework for abstractive summarization.

3   Proposed Model

As show in Fig. 1, we extend the original Transformer model with a hierarchical hybrid structure. The encoder stack has a word level encoder and a sentence level encoder, which gets sentence level semantic vector and document level semantic vector respectively. A selective layer is added after each encoder to filter out the secondary information. The pointer-generator mechanism is applied in the summary decoder, which combines vocabulary distribution with attention distribution to get the final distribution to predict the generated words. We introduce the details of different components in the following sections.

3.1   Problem Formulation

For article summarization, given a dataset $\mathcal{D}$ which contains L article-summary pairs $(\boldsymbol{x}, \boldsymbol{y})$, each source article has M sentences $\boldsymbol{x} = (s_1, \cdots, s_M)$ and each sentence consists of n words $s_m = (w_{m1}, \cdots, w_{mn})$. The corresponding target

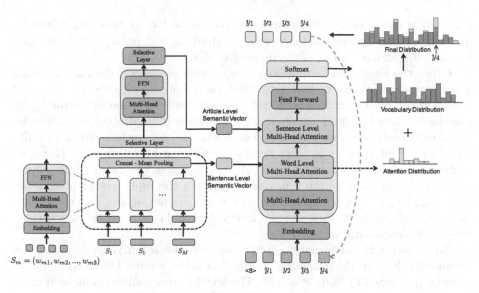

Fig. 1. The overview of the proposed model.

summary has T words $\boldsymbol{y} = (y_1, \cdots, y_T)$. The abstractive article summarization can be considered as a sequence-to-sequence task. As a result, the problem can be given by:

$$p(\boldsymbol{y}|\boldsymbol{x}; \boldsymbol{\theta}) = \prod_{t=1}^{T} p(y_t|\boldsymbol{y}_{<t}, \boldsymbol{x}; \boldsymbol{\theta}) \qquad (1)$$

where $\boldsymbol{\theta}$ is a set of model parameters and $\boldsymbol{y}_{<t}$ is a partial target summary; y_t is the t_{th} word in generated summary and we call t as time step t in this paper.

3.2 Hierarchical Encoder

The proposed model contains a encoder stack and a decoder stack similar with the original Transformer, which use multi-head attention instead of RNN structure. Given a list of queries $Q = (q_1, \cdots, q_t)$ and key-value pairs (K, V), multi-head attention maps the query and key-value pairs to an output h times as follows:

$$\text{MultiHead}(Q, K, V) = \text{Concat}(head_1, \cdots, head_h) \qquad (2)$$

$$head_i = \text{Attention}(QW_i^Q, KW_i^K, VW_i^V) \qquad (3)$$

$$\text{Attention}(Q, K, V) = attn V \qquad (4)$$

$$attn = softmax(\frac{QK^T}{\sqrt{d_k}}) = \text{Concat}(a_0, \cdots, a_n) \qquad (5)$$

$$a_t = softmax(\frac{q_t K^T}{\sqrt{d_k}}) \qquad (6)$$

where a_t is the attention distribution between q_t and K at time step t (the t_{th} query in Q); $attn$ is the total attention distribution matrix; W_i^Q, W_i^K, W_i^V are parameter matrices and d_k is the dimension of K.

Given the input article $x = (s_1, \cdots, s_M)$ with sentences, the encoder stack gets the semantic vector by two steps. First, each sentence $s_m = (w_{m1}, \cdots, w_{mn})$ is sent to the word level encoder to get the sentence level semantic vector h_m^s by calculating the multi-head attention in one sentence. It obtains the semantic relationship between word and word, and each sentence semantic vector isn't influenced by the information in other sentence in this word level encoder. Then, the sentence level semantic vector $h^s = (h_1^s, \cdots, h_M^s)$ gets the mean pooling operation at the sentence length dimension to obtain the input vector of sentence level encoder. The sentence level encoder works similar as vanilla Transformer encoder. Differently, it takes sentence level vector and calculates the article (document) level semantic vector h^a.

To obtain a better semantic vector, we add the selective layer after each encoder to filter out the secondary information in the vector. The selective mechanism is motivated by Zhou et al. [20]. The selective mechanism combines n-gram features and whole semantic information. We use a CNN structure with three 1-dimension convolutions to obtain the n-gram features c. The kernel size is set to 1, 3, 3 respectively and the output is concatenated into a dense vector. And the whole semantic information is the vector itself. For each time step t, the selective layer calculates the gate vector $gate_t$ as follows:

$$gate_t = \delta(i_t W_g + c_t U_g + b_g) \tag{7}$$

$$i_t' = i_t \odot gate_t \tag{8}$$

where W_g and U_g are weight matrices; b_g is bias vector; δ denotes sigmoid activation function and $\odot$ is element-wise multiplication; i_t is the input semantic vector and i_t' is the tailored vector. The gate vector $gate_t$ contains values between 0 and 1 at each dimension. If the value is close to 0, the semantic vector at corresponding dimension be considered as secondary information.

3.3   Summary Decoder

We also extend the vanilla Transformer decoder with multiple mechanisms. Given the generated summary $y = (y_1, \cdots, y_{t-1}, y_t)$ at time step t, the decoder stack aims to generate the word y_{t+1}. The decoder stack contains four sub-layer to calculate the probability distribution of y_{t+1} (the vanilla Transformer decoder only has three sub-layer). As shown in Fig. 1, the multi-head attention layer calculates the self attention distribution between word and word in y and get the semantic vector s_t of the target sentence. The word level multi-head attention sub-layer calculates the word attention distribution matrix $attn^w$ between summary tokens y and every word w_{mi} in source article x. The summary tokens are queries and words in the article are key-value pairs and this layer outputs the sentence level context vector h_s^*. Similarly, the sentence level multi-head attention layer gets the sentence attention distribution $attn^s$ and article level context vector h_a^*. Finally, the feed forward and softmax layer get the vocabulary probability distribution P_{vocab} and generate the word y_{t+1} at highest score dimension.

To tackle the OOV problem, we apply the pointer-generator mechanism in the decoder stack. The basic idea is to combine the vocabulary distribution with the word attention distribution $attn^w$. It first calculates a scalar p_{gen} as follows:

$$p_{gen} = \delta(y W_y + s_t W_s + h_w^* W_w + h_a^* W_a + b_p) \tag{9}$$

where W_y, W_s, W_w and W_a are weight matrices; b_p is bias vector; δ is the sigmoid activation function. Each article has a extended vocabulary which contains the words in the article but not in the vocabulary and let these words denote *oov-in-article* sets. This p_{gen} works as a weight to calculate the final probability distribution P_{final}:

$$P_{final} = p_{gen} P_{vocab} + (1 - p_{gen}) \sum_{i:w_i=w} attn_i^w \tag{10}$$

The P_{final} combines generating a word from vocabulary with copying a word from the article by sampling from the word attention distribution $attn^w$. If the P_{vocab} gets a highest value at the OOV word dimension, the pointer-generator mechanism may get a word from *oov-in-article* sets, which helps to reduce the probability of generating a OOV word.

The coverage mechanism is applied in the word level multi-head attention sub-layer to deal with the repetition problem. Let cov_t denote the coverage vector at time step t and it is calculated by attention distribution a_t between query and keys as follows:

$$cov_t = \sum_{i=0}^{t-1} a_{t,i} \tag{11}$$

The coverage vector keeps track the information of the total attention distributions before time step t. It is added to the multi-head attention to reduce the probability of focusing on the same words at adjacent time steps:

$$\text{Attention}(Q, K, V) = \text{Concat}(a_0, \cdots, a_t)V \tag{12}$$

$$a_t = softmax(e_t) \tag{13}$$

$$e_{t,i} = v^T tanh(K W_k + q_t W_q + cov_{t,i} W_{cov} + b_{attn}) \tag{14}$$

where v, W_k, W_q and W_{cov} are parameter matrices; b_{attn} is bias vectors and $a_{t,i}$ denotes the attention value between the query at time step t and i_{th} key in K. In this word level multi-head attention sub-layer, the dot-product attention in formulation 6 is replaced by the additive attention. This calculating method is not calculated by using highly optimized matrix multiplication code as the dot-product method, but it is necessary in the coverage mechanism. Because the coverage vector cov_t is calculated by the attention distributions before time step t, and at the next time step $t + 1$, the attention distribution a_{t+1} is calculated by the cov_t. That means the attention distribution and coverage vector influence each other at each time step, which can not be calculated paralleling.

3.4 Overall Loss Function

The training process is to minimize the negative log-likelihood loss function:

$$L = \frac{1}{T} \sum_{t=1}^{T} (-log P_{final}(w_t^*) + \lambda \sum_i min(a_{t,i}, cov_{t,i})) \tag{15}$$

where T is the length of target sentence; w_t^* is the predicted words at time step t; λ is a hyperparameter. The second part of the loss function is the coverage loss to fit the coverage mechanism.

4 Experiments

In this section, we introduce the datasets and baseline models we use; the experiment details and performance of the proposed Hie-Transformer model. And some analyses are provided to show the performance of each proposed mechanism.

4.1 Datasets and Baselines

The CNN-Daily Mail [6,12] dataset is the standard corpora for article summarization, which consists of online news articles and corresponding multi-sentences summaries. We pre-process the anonymized version of dataset by the scripts provided by Nallapati et al. [12]. The dataset contains more than 287k training pairs, 13k validation pairs and 11k test pairs. There are 781 words in articles and 56 tokens in summaries on average.

The performance of our proposed model is compared with some recent researches', which reported in their original papers. *Abstractive Model* is a full RNN based model with attention mechanism proposed by Nallapati et al. [12]. *PG-Original* [14] is a RNN based sequence-to-sequence model with pointer-generator mechanism. *CopyTransformer* [4] and *PG-BRNN* [4] are both implements of copying mechanism based on a 4-layer Transformer and a sequence-to-sequence model with bidirectional RNN encoder respectively.

4.2 Experiment Settings

We implement our experiment in Tensorflow on an NVIDIA 1080Ti GPU. The encoder stack has a 4-layer word level encoder and a 4-layer sentence level encoder both with 512 hidden dimension size. The num of decoder stack layer is set to 6 just like the vanilla Transformer. The word embeddings dimension is also 512 and the vocabulary size is set to 50k. The source articles are truncated to 20 sentences with 40 words each at most for the hierarchical structure and the target summaries are truncated to 100 words at training stage. We use Adam optimizer [7] with $\beta_1 = 0.9$, $\beta_2 = 0.98$ and $\epsilon = 10^{-9}$ and the learning rate is varied over the course of training as Vaswani et al. [16] mentioned. We use beam search to generate summaries and the beam size is set to 5 in our experiments.

Table 1. ROUGE scores on CNN-Daily Mail test set.

Model	R-1	R-2	R-L
Abstractive Model	35.46	13.30	32.65
PG-Original	36.44	15.66	33.42
PG-Original + Coverage	39.53	17.28	36.38
PG-BRNN	39.12	17.35	36.12
Copy-Transformer	39.25	17.54	36.45
transformer	36.34	14.95	33.53
transformer + h	37.16	15.25	34.41
transformer + h + s	37.74	15.71	34.86
transformer + h + pg	38.63	16.80	35.87
transformer + h + coverage	38.77	16.97	35.93
Hie-Transformer	**39.96**	**17.61**	**37.26**

The coverage mechanism is not always used during the training stage. The model is supposed to focus on learning to get a better semantic information first, and at the end of training, the coverage mechanism is turned on to help the decoder to reduce repetitions. The hyperparameter λ is set to 1 and the coverage model is trained about 5000 iterations.

We employ ROUGE [9] to evaluate the qualities of generated summaries. ROUGE score calculates the overlapping between output summary and reference. We use the F1 scores of ROUGE-1, ROUGE-2 and ROUGE-L metrics to evaluate the performance at CNN-Daily Mail works [14].

4.3   Results and Discussion

The evaluation results of our proposed model and the baselines are shown in Table 1. The first section of the table shows the results of the recent abstractive baselines. And the second section presents the performance of our implement baselines in this work. In detail, *transformer* is the original Transformer model we implement, it contains a 6-layer encoder and decoder stack with 512 hidden dimension. *transformer+h* is the basic hierarchical transformer introduced in this work and it doesn't contain any other mechanisms except hierarchical encoder structures. *transformer+h+s* is the hierarchical model with selective mechanism in the encoder stack. *transformer+h+pg* and *transformer+h+coverage* are the basic hierarchical model with pointer-generator mechanism and coverage mechanism respectively. And *Hie-Transformer* is the proposed model with all mechanisms described in this work.

The proposed Hie-Transformer model achieves 39.96 ROUGE-1 scores, 17.61 ROUGE-2 scores and 37.26 ROUGE-L scores, which outperforms the baseline models in Table 1. The basic *transformer* model gets a litter higher results than the RNN based *Abstractive Model*, which proves that the Transformer framework

Table 2. The percentage (%) of repetitions and OOV words on CNN-Daily Mail test sets.

Model	Repetitions			OOV words
	2-gram	3-gram	4-gram	
reference	17.95	1.91	0.44	–
transformer	39.76	24.51	19.10	54.01
transformer + h	39.51	24.24	18.88	53.26
transformer + h + pg	31.74	23.47	16.69	**1.27**
transformer +vh + coverage	24.31	18.87	**3.56**	16.69
Hie-Transformer	23.48	18.01	**2.83**	**1.17**

outperforms the RNN based framework in abstractive summarization. And our hierarchical baseline models get a competitively results, which all achieve a gain in ROUGE scores compared with the basic *transformer*. It demonstrates that the hierarchical structure with selective layer, pointer-generator mechanism and coverage mechanism help the basic *transformer* model get higher quality summaries.

We also provide some analyses on each mechanisms described in this work. First, the hierarchical structure can reduce the calculating resources and use less memory for training. For example, if the input article has 400 words to feed into the encoder stack, the multi-head attention layer will compute a matrix with $400 * 400 = 160,000$ size of self attention weights. However, the hierarchical structure receives the article with 10 sentences with 40 words each at most and the size of attention weights matrix is $40 * 40 * 10 + 10 * 10 = 16,100$, which is much smaller. The gap will be more obvious with longer input article. Additionally, Table 2 presents the percentage of repetitions and OOV words in the generated summaries. We compute the percentage at summary level, which means if one repeated word or one unknown token appears in summary *sum*, this summary will be counted as one number of summary with repetitions and OOV words. There are many named entities in the CNN-Daily Mail and they are easily duplicated in the summaries, so we don't compute the 1-gram repetitions. As shown in Table 2, the percentage of OOV words declines a lot by pointer-generator mechanism and the coverage mechanism helps the model reduce repetitions in the summaries.

5   Conclusion

This work presents a hierarchical hybrid Transformer model for abstractive article summarization. The hierarchical structure encoder stack with selective mechanism makes the model train long article inputs easier, the pointer-generator mechanism and the coverage mechanism can reduce OOV words and repeated words effectively. The evaluation results on CNN-Daily Mail test set show the proposed model has a competitively performance compared with the recent article summarization models. We plan to apply a extractive method to select which sentences are sent into the abstractive model in the future work.

Acknowledgements. This research work has been funded by the National Natural Science Foundation of China (Grant No. 61772337, U1736207), and the National Key Research and Development Program of China NO. 2018YFC0830703 and 2016QY03D0604.

References

1. Bahdanau, D., Cho, K., Bengio, Y.: Neural machine translation by jointly learning to align and translate. arXiv preprint arXiv:1409.0473 (2014)
2. Celikyilmaz, A., Bosselut, A., He, X., Choi, Y.: Deep communicating agents for abstractive summarization. In: Proceedings of the 2018 Conference of the North American Chapter of the Association for Computational Linguistics: Human Language Technologies, Long Papers, vol. 1, pp. 1662–1675 (2018)
3. Chopra, S., Auli, M., Rush, A.M.: Abstractive sentence summarization with attentive recurrent neural networks. In: Proceedings of the 2016 Conference of the NAACL: Human Language Technologies, pp. 93–98 (2016)
4. Gehrmann, S., Deng, Y., Rush, A.: Bottom-up abstractive summarization. In: Proceedings of the 2018 Conference on Empirical Methods in Natural Language Processing, pp. 4098–4109 (2018)
5. Gu, J., Lu, Z., Li, H., Li, V.O.: Incorporating copying mechanism in sequence-to-sequence learning. In: ACL, vol. 1, pp. 1631–1640 (2016)
6. Hermann, K.M., et al.: Teaching machines to read and comprehend. In: Advances in Neural Information Processing Systems, pp. 1693–1701 (2015)
7. Kingma, D.P., Ba, J.: Adam: a method for stochastic optimization. CoRR abs/1412.6980 (2014)
8. Letarte, G., Paradis, F., Giguère, P., Laviolette, F.: Importance of self-attention for sentiment analysis. In: Proceedings of the 2018 EMNLP Workshop BlackboxNLP: Analyzing and Interpreting Neural Networks for NLP, pp. 267–275 (2018)
9. Lin, C.Y., Hovy, E.: Automatic evaluation of summaries using n-gram co-occurrence statistics. In: Proceedings of the 2003 Conference of the NAACL on Human Language Technology, vol. 1, pp. 71–78. ACL (2003)
10. Lin, J., Xu, S., Ma, S., Su, Q.: Global encoding for abstractive summarization. In: ACL, vol. 2, pp. 163–169 (2018)
11. Mani, I.: Advances in Automatic Text Summarization. MIT Press, Cambridge (1999)
12. Nallapati, R., Zhou, B., dos Santos, C., Gulçehre, Ç., Xiang, B.: Abstractive text summarization using sequence-to-sequence RNNs and beyond. In: CoNLL 2016, p. 280 (2016)
13. Rush, A.M., Chopra, S., Weston, J.: A neural attention model for abstractive sentence summarization. In: EMNLP, pp. 379–389 (2015)
14. See, A., Liu, P.J., Manning, C.D.: Get to the point: summarization with pointer-generator networks. In: ACL, vol. 1, pp. 1073–1083 (2017)
15. Tao, C., Gao, S., Shang, M., Wu, W., Zhao, D., Yan, R.: Get the point of my utterance! learning towards effective responses with multi-head attention mechanism. In: IJCAI, pp. 4418–4424 (2018)

16. Vaswani, A., et al.: Attention is all you need. In: Advances in Neural Information Processing Systems, pp. 5998–6008 (2017)
17. Xing, C., Wu, Y., Wu, W., Huang, Y., Zhou, M.: Hierarchical recurrent attention network for response generation. In: Thirty-Second AAAI Conference on Artificial Intelligence (2018)
18. Yang, Z., Yang, D., Dyer, C., He, X., Smola, A., Hovy, E.: Hierarchical attention networks for document classification. In: Proceedings of the 2016 Conference of the North American Chapter of the Association for Computational Linguistics: Human Language Technologies, pp. 1480–1489 (2016)
19. Zhang, J., et al.: Improving the transformer translation model with document-level context. In: EMNLP, pp. 533–542 (2018)
20. Zhou, Q., Yang, N., Wei, F., Zhou, M.: Selective encoding for abstractive sentence summarization. In: ACL, Long Papers, vol. 1, pp. 1095–1104 (2017)

Target-Based Attention Model for Aspect-Level Sentiment Analysis

Wei Chen[1], Wenxin Yu[1(✉)], Zhiqiang Zhang[1], Yunye Zhang[1], Kepeng Xu[1], Fengwei Zhang[1], Yibo Fan[2], Gang He[3], and Zhuo Yang[4]

[1] Southwest University of Science and Technology, Mianyang, China
1868126834@163.com, yuwenxin@swust.edu.cn, star_yuwenxin27@163.com
[2] State Key Laboratory of ASIC and System, Fudan University, Shanghai, China
[3] Xidian University, Xi'an, China
[4] Guangdong University of Technology, Guangzhou, China

Abstract. Aspect-level sentiment classification, which aims to determine the sentiment polarity of the specific target word or phrase of a sentence, is a crucial task in natural language processing (NLP). Previous works have proposed various attention methods to capture the important part of the context for the desired target. However, these methods have less interaction between aspects and contexts and can not accurately quantify the importance of context words with the information of aspect. To address these issues, we firstly proposed a novel target-based attention model (TBAM) for aspect-level sentiment analysis, which employs an attention mechanism between the position-aware context representation matrix. TBAM can generate more accurate attention scores between aspects and contexts at the word level in a joint way, and generate more discriminative features for classification. Experimental results show that our model achieves a state-of-the-art performance on three public datasets compared to other architectures.

Keywords: Natural language processing · Sentiment analysis · LSTM · Attention mechanism

1 Introduction

Aspect based sentiment analysis aims to determine the sentiment polarity (negative, neutral, or positive) of the specific target or aspect of a sentence. For example, given a sentence "Dreadful food but the service was good" the sentiment polarity of aspect "food" is negative while the polarity of aspect "service" is positive. There are some different sentiment polarities in the same sentence for different aspects.

In recent years, neural networks have played an increasingly important role in the field of aspect-level sentiment analysis. In these methods, aspect words are usually regarded with equal importance across the context words, the aspect information is not fully considered into the context in the neural network model.

© Springer Nature Switzerland AG 2019
T. Gedeon et al. (Eds.): ICONIP 2019, LNCS 11955, pp. 259–269, 2019.
https://doi.org/10.1007/978-3-030-36718-3_22

Later, some neural attention mechanisms have applied to this task, although performance has improved through these methods, according to our empirical study, there are still some common problems shared by these previous models. For example, given the sentence "The local sweet food is delicious, but the service is dreadful.", the aspect words are "local sweet food". Suppose these words become one-dimensional vectors after word embedding, and the specific value of each word is '1', '3' and '5'. If we directly average these vectors with the same importance in previous methods, so the average result is '3', which is same to the value of the word 'sweet'. In other words, the semantic information of "local sweet food" is similar to the word "sweet", obviously, it is not correct and the key word for this sentence is 'food'. They only consider unilateral information and do not consider the impact of each context word on the aspect word.

To solve the above issues, in this paper, a target-based attention model (TBAM) is induced for aspect-level sentiment analysis. TBAM can better detect the most important textual information in the given aspect of a sentence. Aspect information plays a key role in its sentence. In our datasets, the number of words containing more than one word in the aspect account for approximately 25%, 38% and 70% respectively. The previous processing methods treated the word vectors average as a word vector, and often ignore the important relationship between the aspect words, TBAM uses the attention information to assign the corresponding weights to each aspect word, which compute the attention scores between content and aspect at the word level in a joint way, and effectively quantify the representations. Moreover, TBAM can observe the position information between the context and aspect at the sentence level, which is important for capturing the key words. The model is evaluated on three datasets: Restaurant and Laptop are from SemEval 2014 [12], and the third one is Twitter dataset. The experimental results show that TBAM can effectively predict the polarity of the given aspect sentence and reach the highest level.

The remainder of this paper is structured as follows: Sect. 2 discusses the overview of related work, Sect. 3 gives a detailed description of TBAM, Sect. 4 presents extensive experiments to justify the effectiveness of TBAM, and Sect. 5 provides some conclusions and the future direction.

2   Related Work

Aspect-level sentiment analysis is designed to determine the sentiment polarity of the sentence for a given aspect or target. Traditional approaches to solve the problem are to manually design set of features and most of them focus on building sentiment classifiers with feature [10,11]. However, the results highly depend on the quality of these features and the feature engineering is labor intensive.

Recursive neural networks (RecNNs) were firstly introduced into this field by Dong et al. [1], and their proposed algorithm can adaptively propagate the sentiment of contexts to the aspect, but they often make mistakes in the face of some grammatical errors that are common in practice. Later, the recurrent neural networks (RNNs) have been demonstrated to be more effective for the tasks of sentence sequence [13,14]. Tang et al. [2] introduced the TD-LSTM approach which learns the feature representation from the leftmost and rightmost sides of the sentence. Vo and Zhang [3] used neural pooling functions to extract features from word embeddings.

Most of the neural network models often suffer from the semantic mismatching problems. Hence, attention mechanism has been successfully applied to the aspect-level sentiment analysis. Wang et al. [9] proposed the attention based LSTM with aspect embedding (ATAE-LSTM), which firstly applied attention mechanism to aspect level sentiment analysis by simply concatenating the aspect vector into the sentence hidden representations and achieving a good performance. Tang et al. [5] developed a deep memory network based on a multi-hop attention mechanism (Mem-Net), which introduced the position information into the hidden layer. Ma et al. [4] proposed an interactive attention mechanism (IAN), which interactively learns attentions from the aspect and context, their approach is similar ours. However, the semantic information between context and aspect and the relation between aspects in the same sentence are not well exploited, they only consider unilateral information and do not consider the impact of each context word on the aspect word. For example, given the sentence "The sweet food is delicious, but the service is dreadful.", the aspect information is "sweet food", it's easy to know the word "good" is more important to the aspect information than the word "dreadful" according to the position information. In addition, based on our Linguistic habit, we know the word good" is more to describe the word "food" than the word "sweet", however, in the previous work, they only qualitatively described the importance and did not materialize it.

Compared with the above models, TBAM captures the attention scores to assign the corresponding weights for each aspect word and can also observe the location information between the aspect and context, which is the first work to explore the aspect-level interactions.

3 Model Overview

Our target-based attention modeling framework consists of four components: Input Embedding Layer, Contextual Layer, Target-Based Attention Layer and Output Layer. As the Fig. 1 has shown, TBAM takes a sentence $w = [w_1, w_2, ..., w_n]$ and an aspect $t = [t_1, t_2, ..., t_n]$ as input, and the goal of its process is to predict the sentiment polarity of the sentence over the aspect.

3.1 Input Embedding Layer

The input embeddings layer contains two components: context word embeddings and aspect word embeddings. Given a sentence $w = [w_1, w_2, ...w_i..., w_n]$ and an aspect $t = [t_i, t_{i+1}, ..., t_{i+m-1}]$ where n is the sentence length and m is the aspect length. They would be mapped from two one-hot matrixes

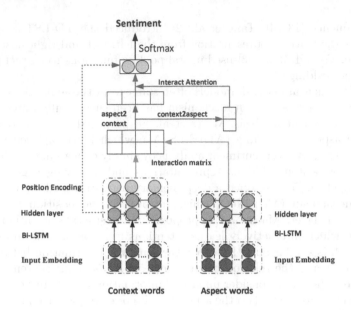

Fig. 1. The framework of target-based attention model.

into two matrixes M^{V*d} make up with vector $v_1; v_2; ...; v_n] \in R^{n*d}$ and vector $[v_i; v_{i+1}; ...; v_{i+m-1}] \in R^{m*d}$ from both context and aspect where d is the dimension of word embedding and V is the vocabulary size.

3.2   Contextual Layer

The contextual layer with Bi-LSTM architecture is used for learning the more abstract representation of sentence and aspect, which can obtain richer semantic information from both ends of the sentence and avoid vanishing-gradient and over-fitting in the same time.

The output $h = [\overrightarrow{h}, \overleftarrow{h}]$ of Bi-LSTM encoder is the concatenation of forward hidden state $h = [\overrightarrow{h_1}, \overrightarrow{h_2}, ..., \overrightarrow{h_n}]$ and backward hidden state $h = [\overleftarrow{h_1}, \overleftarrow{h_2}, ..., \overleftarrow{h_n}]$ where n is the length of the sentence.

In addition, considering that the context words with closer distance to an aspect may have higher influence to the aspect, and the hidden layer neurons have the same weight in one sentence, which is not flexible enough for predicting respective sentiments of these aspects. We utilize the position encoding mechanism to simulate the observation. Based upon this understanding, the position encoding is defined as follows:

$$dis(i) = \begin{cases} i - m_0, & i < m_0 \\ i - m_0 - m, & n \geq i > m_0 + m \\ 0, & m_0 + m \geq i \geq m_0 \end{cases} \quad (1)$$

$$l_i = 1 - \frac{|dis(i)|}{n} \quad (2)$$

where i is the current word index and m_0 is the first word index of the aspect, $dis(i)$ indicates the relative distance of the i-th word. m is the length of the aspect and n is the length of the context. The l_i is used to as the weight of the hidden layer neuron to measure the relative position between each word and the first aspect word. As a result, there are new hidden layer neurons $\overline{v} = [v_1, v_2, ..., v_i, ..., v_n] \in R^{2d}$.

$$v_i = l_i \cdot \overline{v_i} \tag{3}$$

where the $\overline{v_i}$ is the i-th original hidden layer neuron.

3.3 Target-Based Attention Layer

Attention mechanism is a common way to capture the interactions between the aspect and context words. When getting the hidden semantic representations of the context and the aspect, the dot product is used for obtain the pairwise matching matrix. Unlike previous works on introducing complex architectures or many untrainable hyperparameters into models, our operational mechanism is much simpler, but better than the advanced systems. The matching matrix as follow:

$$M(i, j) = h_s(i) \cdot h_t(j)^T \tag{4}$$

where $M(i, j)$ is the similarity between the i-th word in the sentence and the j-th word in aspect. The attention mechanism is used to automatically determine the importance of each word, rather than using simple heuristics (such as summation or averaging) to focus these words' attention on the final attention. The attention mechanism consists of two parts. Firstly, with the portrait normalization, we obtain the attention score of each aspect word to the context. Then, with the portrait normalization, we can also obtain the attention score of each context word to the aspect, which is inspired by the AOA module in question answering [15]. The attention score is calculated as:

$$\alpha_{i,j} = \frac{exp(M_{i,j})}{\sum_i exp(M_{i,j})} \tag{5}$$

$$\beta_{i,j} = \frac{exp(M_{i,j})}{\sum_i exp(M_{i,j})} \tag{6}$$

In order to consider the differences between the aspect words, and make full use of the information of the aspect term, the attention score β is used to them as weights. We interact two attention α and β scores and get the final attention weight $\overline{\alpha}$. h is the representation of the entire sentence, which obtains sentence representation r. And the interacting formula is as follows:

$$\overline{\alpha} = \varphi(\alpha_{i,j} \odot \beta_{i,j}) \tag{7}$$

$$r = h^T \cdot \overline{\alpha} \tag{8}$$

where the function represents the matrix summing by row, the range of values of i is $0 \leq j \leq n - 1$ and j is $0 \leq j \leq m - 1$. The $\odot$ means the matrix is multiplied by the element and $r \in R^{2d}$.

3.4   Output Layer

At last, we get the final classification feature vector r, and feed it into a linear layer, the length of whose output equals to the number of class. Finally, we add a softmax layer to compute the probability distribution for judging the sentiment polarities as positive, negative or neutral:

$$y = softmax(W \cdot r + b) \tag{9}$$

where W and b are the weight matrix and bias respectively, y is the estimated probability. TBAM is trained to use end-to-end back propagation and minimize the cross-entropy loss with L_2 regularization. p is the distribution for sentence, $\widehat{p}$ is the predicted sentiment distribution, the loss objective is defined as follows:

$$loss = -\sum_i \sum_j p_i^j \log \widehat{p}_i^j + \lambda \parallel \theta \parallel^2 \tag{10}$$

where i stands for the index of the sentence, j stands for the category index, and there are three categories, λ indicates L_2 regularization parameter, θ is the parameter of setting weights in Bi-LSTM networks and liner classifier.

4   Experiment

4.1   Dataset and Settings

Our algorithm is evaluated on SemEval 2014 dataset (PontiKi et al. 2014), which includes the review data for Restaurant and Laptop and the other one is Twitter. They were widely used in previous work. The first two reviews are labeled with four sentiment polarities: positive, neutral, negative and conflict, we remove conflict category as the number of conflict samples is very small and make the dataset extremely unbalanced. Table 1 shows the training and test sample numbers in each sentiment polarity. Taking into account the differences between aspect words, the number of aspect words of each dataset is listed in Table 2.

Table 1. Details of the experimental datasets.

Dataset	Positive	Neutral	Negative
Restaurant-train	2164	637	807
Restaurant-test	728	196	196
Laptop-train	994	464	870
Laptop-test	341	169	128
Twitter-train	1561	3217	1560
Twitter-test	173	346	173

Table 2. Statistics on the number of aspect words.

Dataset	Num(word) = 1	Num(word) > 1
Restaurant	0.7447	0.2553
Laptop	0.6110	0.3840
Twitter	0.2999	0.7001

The pre-trained 300-dimensional Glove word vectors are initialized for our experiments. The dimensions of hidden layer are set to 300. Model training through 128 samples in each batch, Set the learning rate to 0.001, dropout rate to 0.5 and L_2 regularization to 0.001. The model runs on the ubuntu16.04 system, operating environment are pytorch and NVIDIA GTX 1080ti.

4.2 Results and Discussions

To verify the validity of our model, we compare it to several baseline methods. In the experiments, the classification accuracy and macro-F1 score are used as the evaluation metrics. The performances of these baselines are cited from their original papers (Table 3).

Table 3. Classification results of different methods on three datasets. The result of '*' are retrieved from Li et al. [18], '−' means this result is not available, the '[]' stand for their original papers index.

Method	Laptop (%)		Restaurant (%)		Twitter (%)	
	Acc	Macro-F1	Acc	Macro-F1	Acc	Macro-F1
Feature-SVM [15]	70.49	–	80.16	–	63.4	63.3
TD-LSTM [4]	68.13	68.43	75.63	66.73	70.8	69
ATAE-LSTM [2]	68.7	62.45	77.2	64.95	–	–
IAN [13]	72.1	67.48	78.6	67.9	–	–
MemNet [7]	72.37	64.09	80.32	65.83	68.5	66.91
RAM [16]	74.49	71.35	80.23	70.8	69.36	67.3
TBAM	**74.66**	**71.39**	**80.99**	**71.59**	**73.12**	**71.24**

The performance fluctuates with different random initialization, which is a common issue in training neural networks, so the model is run 5 times, and report the best average performance. We can observe that TBAM achieves the best performance among all these methods, it learns the attention weights between content and aspect at the word level in a joint way, which is helpful for aspect sentiment analysis. This indicates that exploiting the clues of target and position effectively can improve the performances.

In addition, The TD-LSTM model, which gets the worst performance, the main reason is the semantics of the divided sentences are already incomplete. Further, the LSTM based model ATAE-LSTM and IAN perform better than TD-LSTM on three datasets. One main reason maybe the introduction of an attention mechanism that can make the models notice the important parts of the sentence for a given aspect. This result also shows that introducing aspect clues only by splitting the sentence according to position of aspect is not enough.

4.3   Effects of Position Encoding

Obviously, the closer the word is to aspect, the higher weight the word would be assigned. In this experiment, we use absolute values to measure the distance between them, which is most effective. In order to verify the validity of the position encoding, we conducted two sets of comparative experiments, which were tested on two public datasets.

Table 4. Effects of position encoding on three datasets

Models	Laptop (%)		Twitter (%)	
	Acc	Macro-F1	Acc	Macro-F1
No-Position	72.57	68.19	72.39	70.86
TBAM	**74.66**	**71.39**	**73.12**	**71.24**

In Table 4, we report the performance of the two models. The No-Position represents the model that removes location information in the TBAM. After inducing the position embeddings, the performance has an increase of about 3% and 1% on two datasets, which indicates that exploiting the position clues effectively can improve the performance of TBAM in this task.

4.4   Effects of Attention Interaction

In TBAM, with the portrait normalization, we obtain the attention score β of each context word to the aspect, which is used to the aspect words as weights. Then we interact two attention α and β scores and get the final attention. In order to verify the validity of the method of attention interaction, we test the following three sets of experiments and the results are shown in Table 5.

No-Inter-mean refers to directly calculate attention α by average, in other words, it only calculates the attention weights of the aspect words for the context words. Similarly, No-Inter-max refers to calculate attention by maximum pooling. Inter-mean refers to calculate two attentions and interact them, but removing the influence of location information. We can be observed that Inter-mean performs mostly better than other models, which verifies that interacting two attentions weights according to context words for the aspect is ineffective

Table 5. Effects of information interaction on three datasets.

Models	Laptop (%)		Restaurant (%)		Twitter (%)	
	Acc	Macro-F1	Acc	Macro-F1	Acc	Macro-F1
No-Inter-mean	71.92	67.13	80.61	71.27	71.38	69.12
No-Inter-max	71.64	**69.27**	**80.64**	71.32	71.56	69.94
Inter-mean	**72.57**	68.19	80.44	**72.11**	**72.39**	**70.86**

in this task. We also found that the accuracy on Restaurant is lower than No-Inter-max. On the one hand, because the proportion of more than two words in aspect is relatively small, on the other hand, it is mostly about food in Restaurant, which is relatively easy to find the main semantic information of the aspect information.

4.5 Case Study

In order to better understand TBAM, the sample of the restaurant dataset is extracted and visualized the weight of the context words in the sentence in Fig. 2. The aspect of context a is "food" while the aspect of context b is "service". The color depth represents the level of weight $\overline{\alpha}$. The sentence is "**good food but the service was dreadful!**", when the current aspect term is food, obviously, its neighboring words such as "good" should play a great role for judging sentiment polarity of **food**. For aspect term **service**, it is obvious that the word "dreadful" is more important to express the aspect term than the word "**service**. In addition, given the sentence "The sweet food is good, but the service is dreadful.", based on our Linguistic rules, we know the word "good" is more to describe the word food" than the word "sweet", TBAM captures the attention information to assign the corresponding weights for each aspect word and help it find out the sentiment.

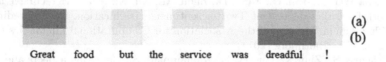

Fig. 2. Visualization of specific context aspect.

5 Conclusion

In this paper, we proposed the target-based attention model (TBAM) for aspect-level sentiment analysis. The main proposal is to compute the attention scores between contents and aspects at the word level in a joint way, and effectively quantify the representations. Moreover, the position encoding is induced into the model which makes TBAM more robust to against irrelevant information and achieves the best results on SemEval 2014 Datasets and Twitter.

Before the popularity of deep learning, the predecessors summarized a lot of knowledge bases, which could be a huge treasure in the field of natural language processing. Now many scholars are trying to use these knowledge bases. In the future, we would like to explore how to fuse linguistic rules into the neural network models.

Acknowledgement. This research was supported by 2018GZ0517, 2019YFS0146, 2019YFS0155, which supported by Sichuan Provincial Science and Technology Department, 2018KF003 Supported by State Key Laboratory of ASIC & System. No. 61907009 Supported by National Natural Science Foundation of China, No. 2018A030313802 Supported by Natural Science Foundation of Guangdong Province, No. 2017B010110007 and 2017B010110015 Supported by Science and Technology Planning Project of Guangdong Province.

References

1. Dong, L., Wei, F., Tan, C., Tang, D., Zhou, M., Xu, K.: Adaptive recursive neural network for target-dependent Twitter sentiment classification. In: Proceedings of the 52nd Annual Meeting of the Association for Computational Linguistics (Short Papers). ACL, Baltimore (2014)
2. Tang, D., Qin, B., Feng, X., Liu, T.: Effective LSTMs for target-dependent sentiment classification. In: Proceedings of COLING (2016)
3. Vo, D.-T., Zhang, Y.: Target-dependent Twitter sentiment classificaiton with rich automatic features. In: Proceedings of the 24th International Joint Conference on Artificial Intelligence, Buenos Aires, Argentina, pp. 1347–1353 (2015)
4. Ma, D., Li, S., Zhang, X., Wang, H.: Interactive attention networks for aspect-level sentiment classification. In: Proceedings of 26th IJCAI, Melbourne, Australia, pp. 4068–4074 (2017)
5. Tang, D., Qin, B., Liu, T.: Aspect level sentiment classification with deep memory network. In: Proceedings of EMNLP (2016)
6. Dong, L., Wei, F., Tan, C., Tang, D., Zhou, M., Xu, K.: Adaptive recursive neural network for target-dependent Twitter sentiment classification. In: Proceedings of the 52nd Annual Meeting of the Association for Computational Linguistics (Short Papers). ACL, Baltimore (2014)
7. Kiritchenko, S., Zhu, X., Cherry, C., Mohammad, S.: Detecting aspects and sentiment in customer reviews. In: Proceedings of the 8th International Workshop on Semantic Evaluation, pp. 437–442 (2014)
8. Chen, P., Sun, Z., Bing, L., Yang, W.: Recurrent attention network on memory for aspect sentiment analysis. In: Proceedings of the 2017 Conference on Empirical Methods in Natural Language Processing, pp. 452–461 (2017)
9. Wang, Y., Huang, M., Zhao, L.: Attention-based LSTM for aspect-level sentiment classification. In: EMNLP, pp. 606–615 (2016)
10. Jiang, L., Yu, M., Zhou, M., Liu, X., Zhao, T.: Target-dependent twitter sentiment classification. In: Proceedings of the 49th Annual Meeting of the Association for Computational Linguistics: Human Language Technologies, vol. 1, pp. 151–160 (2011)

11. Wagner, J., et al.: DCU: aspect-based polarity classification for semeva task 4 (2014)
12. Pontiki, M., et al.: Semeval 2016 task 5: aspect based sentiment analysis. In: ProWorkshop on Semantic Evaluation (SemEval-2016), pp. 19–30 (2016)
13. Lai, S., Xu, L., Liu, K., Zhao, J.: Recurrent convolutional neural networks for text classification. In: Proceedings of the 29th AAAI Conference on Artificial Intelligence, vol. 333, pp. 2267–2273 (2015)
14. Tang, D., Qin, B., Liu, T.: Document modeling with gated recurrent neural network for sentiment classification. In: Proceedings of the 2015 Conference on Empirical Methods in Natural Language Processing, pp. 1422–1432 (2015)
15. Cui, Y., Chen, Z., Wei, S., Wang, S., Liu, T., Hu, G.: Attention-over-attention neural networks for reading comprehension. In: Proceedings of the 55th Annual Meeting of the Association for Computational Linguistics, pp. 593–602 (2017)

Keyphrase Generation with Word Attention

Hai Huang, Tianshuo Huang[✉], Longxuan Ma, and Lei Zhang

Beijing University of Posts and Telecommunications, Beijing, China
{hhuang,huangtianshuo,malongxuan,zlei}@bupt.edu.cn

Abstract. Keyphrase generation aims to generate several words that can simply summarize the semantics of the article, which is the basis of many natural language processing tasks. Although most previous approaches have achieved good results, they neglect the independent word information in the source text. Previous models use attention mechanism to calculate the relationship between the encoder RNN hidden states and the target side. However hidden state h_t is the summarization of the first t words as a subsequence in the source sentence. We, in this paper, propose a novel sequence-to-sequence model called WordRNN, which can capture word level representations in the source text. Our model can enrich the expression of the source text by directly promoting the pure word level information. Moreover, we use fuse gate and simply concat operation to combine the subsequence level and word level contextual information. Experiment results demonstrate that our approach achieves higher performance than the state-of-the-art methods.

Keywords: Keyphrase generation · Sequence-to-sequence · Attention

1 Introduction

Keyphrases are a set of words used to highly summarize the semantics of an article [9]. They can often be used to retrieve, summarize, query articles. Before reading an essay, we can use the keyphrases to get an overview of it. The keyphrase with higher quality can make it easier for us to understand, organize and access the content of the document. Due to the necessity and accuracy of keyphrase, keyphrase tasks have been used extensively for information retrieval [12], text summarization [23], text categorization [11] and opinion mining [2].

Keyphrase-related tasks can be divided into two categories: extractive tasks [10,15,24] and generative tasks [4,5,18,26]. The conventional extractive task extracts the keyphrase candidate set from the source article and ranks each keyphrase in the set to select the final result. The first generation task is proposed by Meng *et al.* [18]. This model employs a sequence-to-sequence model [21] which generates keyphrases from a predefined vocabulary and a copy mechanism [8] which computes the distribution of copy probability for keyphrase generation.

In the previous sequence-to-sequence model, the encoder first converts the source text into a hidden state vector representation. Then the target RNN make

© Springer Nature Switzerland AG 2019
T. Gedeon et al. (Eds.): ICONIP 2019, LNCS 11955, pp. 270–281, 2019.
https://doi.org/10.1007/978-3-030-36718-3_23

use of the hidden state vector representation to generate the distribution over the hidden state. The hidden state representation of the source text is linearly weighted into a context vector of the source text based on the current distribution. The target keyphrases are then generated through this context vector step by step. However, they only consider the connection between the target side and the hidden state representation h_t of the source text which representing the summary of the first t words, and do not take into account the association between the target side and each individual word in the source text. We use a word-attention to weight each individual word in the source text to help generate target keyphrases more comprehensively. Within each decoding step, word-attention can take care of different individual words in the original text, resulting in a word-context that only focuses on the expression of the clean source text. Then we use the word-context and the hidden-context which is generated by the association between the hidden state representation and the target side to generate the keyphrases. In order to make the representation combined with the two contexts more effective acting on the target side, we experiment with a variety of methods such as fuse gate [7] and simply concat.

In summary, our contribution includes the following three aspects:

- A new keyphrase generation model which named WordRNN that can simultaneously notice the hidden layer state of the source text and individual independent words in the source text;
- Using fuse gate and concat methods which could better combine the hidden context and word context to further improve the performance;
- The new state-of-the-art performance on several real-world benchmarks. A detailed analysis of the experimental results and explain why the algorithm and model have better results.

2 Related Work

Keyphrase-related tasks have been studied for a long time, but currently the task can be divided into two categories: extraction based and generation based.

Extractive tasks have been proposed in a variety of ways, the most typical extraction method can be broken down into two steps: generating candidate sets and ranking choices for candidate sets. In the first step, when generate candidate sets, we usually get a larger candidate set, so that the probability that the candidate set contains the target keyphrase will increase accordingly. The methods of extracting the candidate set include extracting important n-grams [10], selecting text chunks with certain postags [14,15,24] and sequence match [14,24]. The second step is to rank the candidate set according to the original text and obtain the top keyphrases as the result. Some studies use supervised tasks to treat it as a classification task [6,10,17,25], while others employ unsupervised approaches [3,16,27] to solve this task. In addition, Liu et al. [15] solved the problem of inconsistent vocabulary between source text and target keyphrases through an alignment model. Zhang et al. [28] use a joint recurrent neural network to extract keypharses from small dataset such as tweets.

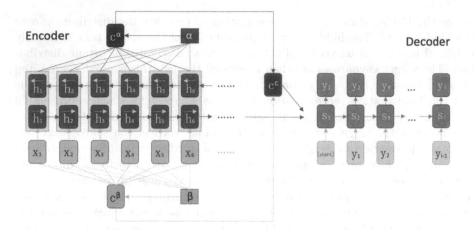

Fig. 1. The overall architecture of our model. Note that α and β indicates the conventional attention and word attention respectively, c^α and c^β indicates the hidden-context and word-context respectively, c^c is a combination of the two contexts.

Generating tasks can predict keyphrases when they are in subtle different order or synonymous. It aims to predict absent keyphrases in the original article. Meng *et al.* [18] first raised a generative model named CopyRNN with an Encoder-Decoder [1] and a copy mechanism [8]. Chen *et al.* [4] consider the correlation among keyphrases and propose CorrRNN which is an improvement of CopyRNN. Later, Ye and Wang [26] and Chen *et al.* [5] have effectively utilized the title of the source text as additional information to enhance the ability to generate. Ye and Wang [26] first used a semi-supervised method to generate keyphrases.

The model we proposed is based on the generative method. The main difference between our model and the previous generative model is that we consider the connection between the generated keyphrases and each of the independent words in the source text, and make the representation of the source text more comprehensive through combining the word-context and the hidden-context. This allows for more accurate keyphrase generation.

3   Model

In this section, we introduce the implementation details of our model. We describe the traditional sequence-to-sequence model first, and then introduce our special word-attention and combination methods. The overall framework of our model is illustrated in Fig. 1.

3.1   Seq2seq Model with Coverage and Copying Mechanism

In this paper, our contributions are based on the sequence-to-sequence encoder-decoder model. The sequence-to-sequence model first converts the input sequence

$\mathbf{x} = (x_1, x_2, ..., x_N)$ into a hidden layer vector representation $\mathbf{h} = (h_1, h_2, ..., h_N)$ via the encoder which is a bidirectional Long Short-Term Memory. N denote the length of word sequence x. In the following equation f is a non-linear function.

$$h_t = f(x_t, h_{t-1}) \tag{1}$$

Then the weighted vector α is calculated through a conventional attention mechanism.

$$\alpha_{tj} = \frac{exp(e_{tj}^\alpha)}{\sum_{k=1}^{T} exp(e_{tk}^\alpha)} \tag{2}$$

$$e_{tj}^\alpha = v_\alpha^T tanh(W_h^\alpha h_j + W_s^\alpha s_{t-1} + b_{attn}^\alpha) \tag{3}$$

where α_{tj} represents the degree of matching between the output target y_t and the hidden state h_j. The weighted representation is redistributed back into h to get the context vector c^α.

$$c_t^\alpha = \sum_{j=1}^{T} \alpha_{tj} h_j \tag{4}$$

Decoder uses this context vector c^α to generate target words step by step.

$$s_t = f(y_{t-1}, s_{t-1}, c^\alpha) \tag{5}$$

$$p(y_t | y_{<t}, x) = g(y_{t-1}, s_t, c^\alpha) \tag{6}$$

where s_t is the hidden layer state at time t of decoder, and y_t is the word selected from the vocabulary with a higher probability after the g function.

However, the traditional generation method can not generate keyphrases which are not in the vocabulary. At this time, we need a copy mechanism to predict out-of-vocabulary words by copying the appropriate words from the source text into the target. The copy mechanism differs from the predictive process in that it performs weighting operations on the source text representation by calculating positional attention. We give different proportions to generate and copy mechanism to combine copy and generate methods.

$$p(y_t | y_{<t}, x) = p_g(y_t | y_{<t}, x) + p_c(y_t | y_{<t}, x) \tag{7}$$

$$p_c(y_t | y_{<t}, x) = \frac{1}{Z} \sum_{j:x_j=y_t} exp(\psi_c(x_j)), y \in \mathcal{X} \tag{8}$$

$$\psi_c(x_j) = \sigma(h_j^T W_c) [y_{t-1}; s_t; c_t] \tag{9}$$

In the above formula, p_g and p_c denote the generating and copying probability respectively. $\mathcal{X}$ is the set of unique words in source text x, σ is a non-linear function and W_c is a learned parameter matrix. Z is the sum of all the scores and is used for normalization. You can see more details in Gu $et\ al.$ [8].

Redundant issues arise with the generated target keyphrases. Different target keyphrases should focus on different aspects, and the keyphrases that have been summarized should not continue to receive attention. To overcome this problem, we combine the coverage mechanism in our model. The mechanism can notice the connection between the different keyphrases generated.

In our model, we maintain a coverage vector c^t to record all the original text information that has been noticed before the t step. It is the weighted sum of the attention at the previous t moments, which is derived from the following formula:

$$c^t = \sum_{i=0}^{t-1} \alpha^i \tag{10}$$

Due to this vector is equivalent to a summary vector, and our goal is to make different keyphrases focus on different aspects of the text, the connection between the keyphrases should be as small as possible. We use this coverage vector c^t as an additional input to improve the effect of attention. $\mathbf{w_c}$ is a learnable parameter vector, and its length is the same as v_α.

$$e_{tj}^\alpha = v_\alpha^T tanh(W_h^\alpha h_j + W_s^\alpha s_t + \mathbf{w_c}\mathbf{c_j^t} + b_{attn}^\alpha) \tag{11}$$

By combining a coverage mechanism, the attention mechanism can pay less attention to the previous results. The generated keyphrases can be reduced in the same way.

3.2   Word Attention

From the previous formula we can see that the attention in the model only considers the hidden layer state of LSTM. This makes the target word focus on h_t which represents the summary of the first t words. And it does not pay attention to the individual words in the original text. So we use a more intuitive way to pay attention to the original text representation, and we consider it would be more effective in helping the decoder generate keyphrases. We represent word-attention by calculating the input vector and the target output hidden vector at each moment. We use β_{tj} to represent the relationship between the output hidden vector s_{t-1} and the input vector x_j. We obtain a word-based context vector by weighting the input vector x with β and the context vector is denoted as c^β. The following is the implementation details of the word-attention.

When the decoder decodes the target word y_t, we first calculate the energy vector e_{tj} which is computed by the target hidden layer representation s_{t-1} and the source input representation x_j (the j-th word embedding of the source text). Then we get β_{tj} which is obtained by performing a softmax operation on e_{tj}. The attention weight β_{tj} represents the connection between the t-th target word and the j-th word in the original text.

$$\beta_{tj} = \frac{exp(e_{tj}^\beta)}{\sum_{k=1}^{T} exp(e_{tk}^\beta)} \tag{12}$$

$$e_{tj}^{\beta} = v_{\beta}^{T} tanh(W_h^{\beta} x_j + W_s^{\beta} s_{t-1} + b_{attn}^{\beta}) \tag{13}$$

Since we only consider x_j when calculating this attention weight β_{tj}, the difference between this attention weight and the traditional attention weight is whether using the words before position j in the source text as extra input. The above attention weight β_{tj} can be simply treated as the probability that target word y_t directly align to an individual source word x_j. After we calculate the weight of the original text input, the word-context c^{β} is the weighted sum of all the source word embedding vectors.

$$c_t^{\beta} = \sum_{j=1}^{T} \beta_{tj} x_j \tag{14}$$

3.3   Combine Hidden Context and Word Context

The word-context is regarded as an extra input to get the target hidden state s_t. In order to better combine word-context and hidden-context, we experiment in a variety of ways. For example, the first method we used is called fuse gate which is proposed by Gong et al. [7] and another is a simply concat operation. The implementation of fuse gate is as follows, where W^1, W^2, W^3, W^4 and b^1, b^2, b^3 are trainable weights, σ is sigmoid nonlinear operation:

$$r_1 = tanh(W^1[c^{\alpha}; c^{\beta}] + b^1) \tag{15}$$

$$r_2 = \sigma(W^2[c^{\alpha}; c^{\beta}] + b^2) \tag{16}$$

$$r_3 = \sigma(W^3[c^{\alpha}; c^{\beta}] + b^3) \tag{17}$$

$$c^c = r_2 \otimes (W^4[c^{\alpha}; c^{\beta}]) + r_1 \otimes r_3 \tag{18}$$

However, a simple concat has fewer parameters than a fuse gate, and it can also combine two contexts well. W^c in the following formula is a learnable parameter vector.

$$c^c = W^c[c^{\alpha}; c^{\beta}] \tag{19}$$

Then, we use the combined context c^c as an additional input to generate target word.

$$s_t = f(y_{t-1}, s_{t-1}, c^c) \tag{20}$$

The decoding hidden state s_t now consider both word-context and hidden-context and it can benefit from both contexts. They can help to generate words under different situations. We denote our model with concat method and fuse gate as WordRNN$_C$ and WordRNN$_F$ respectively.

4 Experiment

In this section, we would introduce our experimental details, including datasets, baseline models and evaluation metrics, implementation details and results analysis.

4.1 Datasets

Similar to Meng *et al.* [18], we also train our model on the dataset **KP20k** [18]. This dataset contains 529,816 articles for training, 20,000 for validation, and 20,000 for testing. After removing the duplicated data in the dataset, we get 503,614 articles for training. We employ several testing datasets which often be used in the previous works. The testing datasets we used include **Inspec** [10], **NUS** [20], **SemEval** [13], and **KP20k**. Each dataset is described in detail below.

- **Inspec**: This dataset includes 2,000 paper abstracts. We randomly selected 500 papers as our testing dataset from the whole papers.
- **NUS**: This dataset contains 211 papers with author-assigned keyphrases and we use all of them as our testing dataset.
- **SemEval**: This dataset includes 288 papers from the ACM Digital Library. We use 100 papers among them as our testing dataset.
- **KP20k**: This dataset contains titles, abstracts and keyphrases in computer science. Due to the memory limits of implementation, we were not able to train the supervised baselines on the whole training set. Thus we randomly selected about 20k articles as our testing dataset.

4.2 Baseline Models and Evaluation Metrics

To measure the effectiveness of our model in a more comprehensive way. We compare our model with traditional extractive baselines and generative baselines. The extractive methods includes unsupervised methods which are Tf-idf, TextRank [19], SingleRank [22] and ExpandRank [22], supervised methods which are TopicRank [3], KEA [25] and Maui [17]. The generative baselines consist of RNN, CopyRNN [18] and CorrRNN [4].

In order to fairly measure the gap between our model and other models, we adopt *F-measure* score based on the exact match for keyphrases while predicting top-5 and top-10 keyphrases (F_1@5, F_1@10) as our evaluation metrics. Note that, when we judge whether two keyphrases are the same, we use Porter Stemmer for preprocessing.

4.3 Implementation Details

Similar to Meng *et al.* [18] in the preprocessing procedures, we process the origin text with lowercasing, tokenizing and changing digits into ⟨*digit*⟩ symbol. In the origin **KP20k** dataset, each has an abstract, a title and several target

Table 1. The performance of total keyphrase prediction on all testing datasets. The best results are bold.

Method	Inspec		NUS		SemEval		KP20k	
	F_1@5	F_1@10	F_1@5	F_1@10	F_1@5	F_1@10	F_1@5	F_1@10
Tf-Idf	0.171	0.243	0.112	0.150	0.096	0.144	0.085	0.117
TextRank	0.209	0.253	0.152	0.156	0.131	0.138	0.151	0.124
SingleRank	0.172	0.247	0.132	0.169	0.133	0.176	0.096	0.119
ExpandRank	0.177	0.252	0.132	0.162	0.139	0.170	N/A	N/A
TopicRank	0.201	0.268	0.115	0.123	0.083	0.102	0.101	0.103
KEA	0.093	0.124	0.069	0.084	0.025	0.026	0.154	0.152
Maui	0.040	0.042	0.249	0.263	0.045	0.039	0.257	0.230
RNN	0.085	0.064	0.169	0.127	0.157	0.124	0.176	0.189
CopyRNN	0.240	0.272	0.263	0.268	0.186	0.197	0.270	0.256
CorrRNN	0.243	0.276	0.267	0.269	0.188	0.199	0.276	0.260
WordRNN$_C$	0.247	0.281	0.268	0.272	**0.191**	**0.210**	0.279	0.261
WordRNN$_F$	**0.250**	**0.283**	**0.274**	**0.273**	0.187	0.189	**0.288**	**0.263**

keyphrases. We stitch the title and abstract together as input to the source text. Our vocabulary has 50000 words which are frequently occurred. The text after 200 words are cutted. In the training procedures, we use a bidirectional Long Short-Term Memory Network as the encoder and another forward Long Short-Term Memory Network as the decoder. Two seq2seq models are trained by us. One model has the word-attention mechanism and the word-context and hidden-context are concated, another has both word-attention mechanism and Fuse Gate to combine the two contexts. For both models, the embedding dimension is set to 150, the dimension of hidden layers is set to 300, and the word embeddings are randomly initialized with uniform distribution in $[-0.1, 0.1]$. The optimizer is set to Adam with learning rate 10^{-4}, gradient clipping $= 0.1$, and dropout rate $= 0.5$. We use early-stopping strategy to control model's training process, that is the training would be stopped once the cross-entropy loss stops dropping for several iterations. In the generation procedures, we set the max depth of beam search to 6, and set the beam size to 200.

4.4 Results Analysis

In order to evaluate our model more comprehensively, we do not filter out the keyphrases in the evaluation. Instead, we consider both the present keyphrases and absent keyphrases in the evaluation. The F_1 scores for our model and other baseline models are listed in Table 1. From the table we can see that our model is much better in terms of performance and accuracy than other baseline models in most cases. Especially in terms of F_1@5 scores, our model is more prominent. This indicates the strength of our combination with the word level information.

Table 2. MAP@10 scores of total keyphrase predictions. The best results are bold.

Method	Inspec	NUS	SemEval	KP20k
Tf-Idf	0.142	0.067	0.041	0.066
TextRank	0.156	0.088	0.159	0.112
SingleRank	0.134	0.091	0.109	0.086
ExpandRank	0.129	0.103	0.112	N/A
TopicRank	0.157	0.074	0.038	0.065
KEA	0.052	0.173	0.017	0.126
Maui	0.024	0.147	0.019	0.193
RNN	0.043	0.077	0.035	0.131
CopyRNN	0.194	0.216	0.118	0.275
CorrRNN	0.196	0.218	0.119	0.277
WordRNN$_C$	0.190	0.218	**0.127**	0.278
WordRNN$_F$	**0.200**	**0.224**	0.124	**0.284**

Notably, WordRNN$_C$ outperforms WordRNN$_F$ for SemEval dataset because of the gold keyphrases of SemEval testing dataset have already been stemmed. For mean average precision (MAP) metric which considers prediction orders, we obtain similar conclusions as shown in Table 2.

Then we analyze the performance of present and absent keyphrase prediction. We use F_1@5 metric for present predictions and R@10 which denote the recall score for absent predictions. We compare with the neural-based baselines since they are the state-of-the-art models. We can see that our model outperform baselines in Fig. 2.

In addition, we also pay attention to the performance of the model which only use word-attention, and found that the result is not particularly good. This proves that the individual word-level features are not particularly suitable for this task.

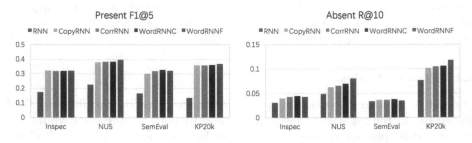

Fig. 2. The present and absent keyphrase prediction performance.

5   Conclusion

In this paper, we propose a new keyphrase generation model named WordRNN which consider both hidden state and specific word in the input sequence. We use a word-attention to leverage pure source word level information to make the semantic representation of source text more comprehensive. We also use several methods to combine word-context and hidden-context. Comprehensive empirical studies demonstrate that our model can generate keypharses more accurately and effectively. Compared to other state-of-the-art models, our model achieves significant improvements as a result of the word-attention. To the best of our knowledge, we are the first to use word-attention for keyphrases generation models and the model is able to generate target keyphrases better.

References

1. Bahdanau, D., Cho, K., Bengio, Y.: Neural machine translation by jointly learning to align and translate. In: 3rd International Conference on Learning Representations, ICLR 2015. Conference Track Proceedings, San Diego, CA, USA, 7–9 May 2015 (2015). http://arxiv.org/abs/1409.0473
2. Berend, G.: Opinion expression mining by exploiting keyphrase extraction. In: Fifth International Joint Conference on Natural Language Processing, IJCNLP 2011, Chiang Mai, Thailand, 8–13 November 2011, pp. 1162–1170 (2011). http://aclweb.org/anthology/I/I11/I11-1130.pdf
3. Bougouin, A., Boudin, F., Daille, B.: TopicRank: graph-based topic ranking for keyphrase extraction. In: Sixth International Joint Conference on Natural Language Processing, IJCNLP 2013, Nagoya, Japan, 14–18 October 2013, pp. 543–551 (2013). http://aclweb.org/anthology/I/I13/I13-1062.pdf
4. Chen, J., Zhang, X., Wu, Y., Yan, Z., Li, Z.: Keyphrase generation with correlation constraints. In: Proceedings of the 2018 Conference on Empirical Methods in Natural Language Processing, Brussels, Belgium, 31 October–4 November 2018, pp. 4057–4066 (2018). https://aclanthology.info/papers/D18-1439/d18-1439
5. Chen, W., Gao, Y., Zhang, J., King, I., Lyu, M.R.: Title-guided encoding for keyphrase generation. CoRR abs/1808.08575 (2018). http://arxiv.org/abs/1808.08575
6. Frank, E., Paynter, G.W., Witten, I.H., Gutwin, C., Nevill-Manning, C.G.: Domain-specific keyphrase extraction. In: Proceedings of the Sixteenth International Joint Conference on Artificial Intelligence, IJCAI 1999, Stockholm, Sweden, 31 July–6 August 1999, vol. 2, 1450 p, pp. 668–673 (1999). http://ijcai.org/Proceedings/99-2/Papers/002.pdf
7. Gong, Y., Luo, H., Zhang, J.: Natural language inference over interaction space. In: 6th International Conference on Learning Representations, ICLR 2018. Conference Track Proceedings, Vancouver, BC, Canada, 30 April–3 May 2018 (2018). https://openreview.net/forum?id=r1dHXnH6-
8. Gu, J., Lu, Z., Li, H., Li, V.O.K.: Incorporating copying mechanism in sequence-to-sequence learning. In: Proceedings of the 54th Annual Meeting of the Association for Computational Linguistics, ACL 2016, Berlin, Germany, 7–12 August 2016, Long Papers, vol. 1 (2016). http://aclweb.org/anthology/P/P16/P16-1154.pdf

9. Hasan, K.S., Ng, V.: Automatic keyphrase extraction: a survey of the state of the art. In: Proceedings of the 52nd Annual Meeting of the Association for Computational Linguistics, ACL 2014, Baltimore, MD, USA, 22–27 June 2014, Long Papers, vol. 1, pp. 1262–1273 (2014). http://aclweb.org/anthology/P/P14/P14-1119.pdf

10. Hulth, A.: Improved automatic keyword extraction given more linguistic knowledge. In: Proceedings of the Conference on Empirical Methods in Natural Language Processing, EMNLP 2003, Sapporo, Japan, 11–12 July 2003 (2003). https://aclanthology.info/papers/W03-1028/w03-1028

11. Hulth, A., Megyesi, B.: A study on automatically extracted keywords in text categorization. In: ACL 2006, Proceedings of the Conference 21st International Conference on Computational Linguistics and 44th Annual Meeting of the Association for Computational Linguistics, Sydney, Australia, 17–21 July 2006 (2006). http://aclweb.org/anthology/P06-1068

12. Jones, S., Staveley, M.S.: Phrasier: a system for interactive document retrieval using keyphrases. In: SIGIR 1999: Proceedings of the 22nd Annual International ACM SIGIR Conference on Research and Development in Information Retrieval, Berkeley, CA, USA, 15–19 August 1999, pp. 160–167 (1999). https://doi.org/10.1145/312624.312671

13. Kim, S.N., Medelyan, O., Kan, M., Baldwin, T.: SemEval-2010 task 5: automatic keyphrase extraction from scientific articles. In: Proceedings of the 5th International Workshop on Semantic Evaluation, SemEval@ACL 2010, Uppsala University, Uppsala, Sweden, 15–16 July 2010, pp. 21–26 (2010). http://aclweb.org/anthology/S/S10/S10-1004.pdf

14. Le, T.T.N., Nguyen, M.L., Shimazu, A.: Unsupervised keyphrase extraction: introducing new kinds of words to keyphrases. In: AI 2016: Advances in Artificial Intelligence - Proceedings of the 29th Australasian Joint Conference, Hobart, TAS, Australia, 5–8 December 2016, pp. 665–671 (2016). https://doi.org/10.1007/978-3-319-50127-7_58

15. Liu, Z., Chen, X., Zheng, Y., Sun, M.: Automatic keyphrase extraction by bridging vocabulary gap. In: Proceedings of the Fifteenth Conference on Computational Natural Language Learning, CoNLL 2011, Portland, Oregon, USA, 23–24 June 2011, pp. 135–144 (2011). http://aclweb.org/anthology/W/W11/W11-0316.pdf

16. Liu, Z., Li, P., Zheng, Y., Sun, M.: Clustering to find exemplar terms for keyphrase extraction. In: Proceedings of the 2009 Conference on Empirical Methods in Natural Language Processing, EMNLP 2009, A Meeting of SIGDAT, a Special Interest Group of the ACL, Singapore, 6–7 August 2009, pp. 257–266 (2009). http://www.aclweb.org/anthology/D09-1027

17. Medelyan, O., Frank, E., Witten, I.H.: Human-competitive tagging using automatic keyphrase extraction. In: Proceedings of the 2009 Conference on Empirical Methods in Natural Language Processing, EMNLP 2009, A Meeting of SIGDAT, a Special Interest Group of the ACL, Singapore, 6–7 August 2009, pp. 1318–1327 (2009). http://www.aclweb.org/anthology/D09-1137

18. Meng, R., Zhao, S., Han, S., He, D., Brusilovsky, P., Chi, Y.: Deep keyphrase generation. In: Proceedings of the 55th Annual Meeting of the Association for Computational Linguistics, ACL 2017, Vancouver, Canada, 30 July–4 August, Long Papers, vol. 1, pp. 582–592 (2017). https://doi.org/10.18653/v1/P17-1054

19. Mihalcea, R., Tarau, P.: TextRank: bringing order into text. In: Proceedings of the 2004 Conference on Empirical Methods in Natural Language Processing, EMNLP 2004, A Meeting of SIGDAT, a Special Interest Group of the ACL, held in

conjunction with ACL 2004, Barcelona, Spain, 25–26 July 2004, pp. 404–411 (2004). http://www.aclweb.org/anthology/W04-3252

20. Nguyen, T.D., Kan, M.: Keyphrase extraction in scientific publications. In: Asian Digital Libraries. Looking Back 10 Years and Forging New Frontiers, Proceedings of the 10th International Conference on Asian Digital Libraries, ICADL 2007, Hanoi, Vietnam, 10–13 December 2007, pp. 317–326 (2007). https://doi.org/10.1007/978-3-540-77094-7_41

21. Sutskever, I., Vinyals, O., Le, Q.V.: Sequence to sequence learning with neural networks. In: Advances in Neural Information Processing Systems 27: Annual Conference on Neural Information Processing Systems 2014, Montreal, Quebec, Canada, 8–13 December 2014, pp. 3104–3112 (2014). http://papers.nips.cc/paper/5346-sequence-to-sequence-learning-with-neural-networks

22. Wan, X., Xiao, J.: Single document keyphrase extraction using neighborhood knowledge. In: Proceedings of the Twenty-Third AAAI Conference on Artificial Intelligence, AAAI 2008, Chicago, Illinois, USA, 13–17 July 2008, pp. 855–860 (2008). http://www.aaai.org/Library/AAAI/2008/aaai08-136.php

23. Wang, L., Cardie, C.: Domain-independent abstract generation for focused meeting summarization. In: Proceedings of the 51st Annual Meeting of the Association for Computational Linguistics, ACL 2013, Sofia, Bulgaria, 4–9 August 2013, Long Papers, vol. 1, pp. 1395–1405 (2013). http://aclweb.org/anthology/P/P13/P13-1137.pdf

24. Wang, M., Zhao, B., Huang, Y.: PTR: phrase-based topical ranking for automatic keyphrase extraction in scientific publications. In: Neural Information Processing - Proceedings of the 23rd International Conference, ICONIP 2016, Kyoto, Japan, 16–21 October 2016, Part IV, pp. 120–128 (2016). https://doi.org/10.1007/978-3-319-46681-1_15

25. Witten, I.H., Paynter, G.W., Frank, E., Gutwin, C., Nevill-Manning, C.G.: KEA: practical automatic keyphrase extraction. In: Proceedings of the Fourth ACM Conference on Digital Libraries, Berkeley, CA, USA, 11–14 August 1999, pp. 254–255 (1999). https://doi.org/10.1145/313238.313437

26. Ye, H., Wang, L.: Semi-supervised learning for neural keyphrase generation. In: Proceedings of the 2018 Conference on Empirical Methods in Natural Language Processing, Brussels, Belgium, 31 October–4 November 2018, pp. 4142–4153 (2018). https://aclanthology.info/papers/D18-1447/d18-1447

27. Zhang, F., Huang, L., Peng, B.: WordTopic-multirank: a new method for automatic keyphrase extraction. In: Sixth International Joint Conference on Natural Language Processing, IJCNLP 2013, Nagoya, Japan, 14–18 October 2013, pp. 10–18 (2013). http://aclweb.org/anthology/I/I13/I13-1002.pdf

28. Zhang, Q., Wang, Y., Gong, Y., Huang, X.: Keyphrase extraction using deep recurrent neural networks on Twitter. In: Proceedings of the 2016 Conference on Empirical Methods in Natural Language Processing, EMNLP 2016, Austin, Texas, USA, 1–4 November 2016, pp. 836–845 (2016). http://aclweb.org/anthology/D/D16/D16-1080.pdf

Dynamic Neural Language Models

Edouard Delasalles$^{(\boxtimes)}$, Sylvain Lamprier, and Ludovic Denoyer

Sorbonne Université, CNRS, LIP6, 75005 Paris, France
{edouard.delasalles,sylvain.lamprier,ludovic.denoyer}@lip6.fr

Abstract. Language evolves over time with trends and shifts in technological, political, or cultural contexts. Capturing these variations is important to develop better language models. While recent works tackle temporal drifts by learning diachronic embeddings, we instead propose to integrate a temporal component into a recurrent language model. It takes the form of global latent variables, which are structured in time by a learned non-linear transition function. We perform experiments on three time-annotated corpora. Experimental results on language modeling and classification tasks show that our model performs consistently better than temporal word embedding methods in two temporal evaluation settings: prediction and modeling. Moreover, we empirically show that the system is able to predict informative latent representations in the future.

Keywords: Temporal modelling · Language model · RNN

1 Introduction

Language modeling with deep neural networks is a very active research field [13,21–23]. It is a central task in Natural Language Processing (NLP) as it plays a major role in various text-related tasks such as speech recognition [5], image captioning [35], or text generation [8]. LSTM networks for language modeling [12, 25] are still the state of the art in language modeling [21,23], although research on new architectures is very active [1,6,26,34]. However, most recurrent language models are static and do not consider the various shifts that affect language; the meaning of words can shift, new words appear as other vanish, and yesterday's topics are different from tomorrow's.

To handle temporal variations in texts, recent research mainly focuses on learning distinct word embeddings per timestep [11,17,20], and smoothing them in time [2,39]. Word embeddings are powerful tools to capture and analyze semantic relations between word pairs [24]. However, learning different embeddings for each timestep leads to learning algorithms with high time and memory complexity. Moreover, to our knowledge, no proper neural language models taking into account publication date have been proposed yet.

This work has been partially supported by the ANR (French National Research Agency) LOCUST project (ANR-15-CE23-0027).

T. Gedeon et al. (Eds.): ICONIP 2019, LNCS 11955, pp. 282–294, 2019.
https://doi.org/10.1007/978-3-030-36718-3_24

In this paper, we propose a state-based dynamic neural language model, that learns transitions between global states through time, rather than focusing on distinct word embeddings. Our contribution is threefold:

- We empirically show that temporal word embeddings models are not well suited for language modeling.
- We propose a dynamic neural language model in the form of an LSTM conditioned on global latent variables structured in time.
- We evaluate the proposed model on three datasets for language modeling and downstream classifications tasks.

2   Related Work

Studying language evolution has been of interest for a long time in machine learning and information retrieval communities. Topics detection and tracking were among the firsts approaches to study language evolution. In 2002, [16] proposed a Hidden Markov Model (HMM) to visualize the temporal evolution of topics in a textual stream. In 2006, [37] and [3] proposed non-Markovian models based on Latent Dirichlet Allocations (LDA). While [37] learns distributions of topics through time, [3] learns word distributions conditioned on latent topics that evolve through time with a State Space Model. However, these methods require to manually tune the number of latent topics, and language models are limited to simple word occurrence distributions. Moreover, these models are usually limited to specific conjugate distributions on the latent variables to allow tractable Variational Inference. Note that [3] led to several extensions, e.g. with multi-scale temporal variables [14], or continuous time dependencies [36].

After the introduction of the Word2Vec model [24], numerous papers proposed derivations of the famous skip-gram algorithm for time annotated corpora [10]. All these approaches attempt to acquire a better understanding of language evolution by studying shifts in words semantic through time. Among them, [7] learns linear temporal dependencies between word representations. [39] learns diachronic word representations by matrix factorization with temporal alignment constraints. [2] proposed a temporal probabilistic skip-gram model with a diffusion prior. [29] also proposes a probabilistic framework that uses exponential embeddings. However, all these temporal word embeddings approaches suffer from a major drawback: complete sets of embeddings must be learned for each timestep. This leads to learning algorithms, with high time and memory complexity, requiring several approximations, like alternate optimization that breaks gradient flow through time in [39], or gradient approximations in [2]. An exception is [28] that combines a static word representation to a scalar timestep in a deep neural network that produces a temporal embedding.

An alternative to these various models is to leverage RNNs for language modeling. A recurrent language model takes a sequence of words of arbitrary size as input and outputs a probability distribution of the next word. Such models are often parameterized by LSTM networks [12]. Compared to the skip-gram algorithm that uses a limited context window, recurrent language models operate on sequences of arbitrary length and can capture long-term dependencies.

In this paper, we propose a dynamic language model based on RNNs. The aim is to capture the language evolution through time *via* an end-to-end framework, where a standard RNN is conditioned by a latent representation of temporal drifts in language. Incorporating latent random variables in RNNs is not new [9] and have been applied to textual data [31,40]. However, to the best of our knowledge, no RNN LMs methods have been proposed for the extraction of temporal dynamics in text. Moreover, the cited methods learn local latent variables, that must be inferred for each word or each sentence. We propose to learn latent variables that are global to all documents published during the same time period.

3   Model

We propose a dynamic recurrent neural network for language modeling in document corpora, where each document is annotated with a discrete timestep. The model is a State Space Model (SSM) with one global latent state per timestep used to condition an LSTM Language Model. Unlike most current methods that learn complete word embedding matrices for each timestep, we only learn one embedding per word which is augmented with a state of the SSM. The LSTM captures general language dynamics, and uses the temporal states to adapt its dynamics depending on language bias specific to each timestep. We also learn a transition function between states that enables prediction of future states.

3.1   Notations and Task

We consider textual documents defined over a vocabulary of size V and annotated by discrete timesteps $t \in \{1, 2, \ldots, T\}$. Let $\mathcal{D} = (\mathbf{d}^{(i)}, \mathrm{t}^{(i)})_{i=1..N}$ be a corpus composed of N documents associated with their publication timestep. A document $\mathbf{d}^{(i)}$ is a word sequence of size $n^{(i)}$ of the form $\mathbf{d}^{(i)} = \{\mathrm{w}_1^{(i)}, \mathrm{w}_2^{(i)}, \ldots, \mathrm{w}_{n^{(i)}}^{(i)}\}$. We denote by N_t the number of documents in $\mathcal{D}$ published at timestep t.

In standard language modeling task, the objective is to find parameters $\boldsymbol{\theta}^*$ maximizing the likelihood of words given previous ones in documents:

$$\boldsymbol{\theta}^* = \arg\max_{\boldsymbol{\theta}} \prod_{i=1}^{N} \prod_{k=0}^{n^{(i)}-1} p_{\boldsymbol{\theta}}(\mathrm{w}_{k+1}^{(i)} | \mathbf{w}_{0:k}^{(i)}), \tag{1}$$

where $\mathrm{w}_0^{(i)}$ is always the start token, and $\mathrm{w}_{n^{(i)}}^{(i)}$ the end of sentence token. $\mathbf{w}_{0:k}^{(i)}$ is the sequence of the first $k+1$ tokens in document $\mathbf{d}^{(i)}$, and $p_{\boldsymbol{\theta}}$ is parametrized by an RNN with parameters $\boldsymbol{\theta}$ that outputs next token probabilities. Specifically, we have $p_{\boldsymbol{\theta}}(\mathrm{w}_{k+1}^{(i)} | \mathbf{w}_{0:k}^{(i)}) = \mathrm{softmax}(\boldsymbol{W} h_k^{(i)} + \boldsymbol{b})$ where $\boldsymbol{W} \in \mathbb{R}^{V \times d_h}$ and $\boldsymbol{b} \in \mathbb{R}^V$ are parameters to learn, $h_k^{(i)} = f(\mathbf{w}_k^{(i)}, h_{k-1}^{(i)}; \boldsymbol{v})$ is a hidden vector of size d^h for all $k \in \{1, \ldots, n^{(i)} - 1\}$ ($h_0^{(i)}$ being the null vector for all i), and f is the LSTM's recurrent function with parameters $\boldsymbol{v}$. We thus have $\boldsymbol{\theta} = \{\boldsymbol{U}, \boldsymbol{W}, \boldsymbol{b}, \boldsymbol{v}\}$ where $\boldsymbol{U}$ is the word embeddings matrix.

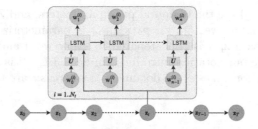

Fig. 1. Schematic representation of our model.

3.2 Dynamic Recurrent Language Model

Our goal is to extend classic recurrent language models with a dynamic component in order to adapt it to language shifts through time. To that aim, we condition an LSTM LM with temporal latent variables. We learn global latent variables structured in time with a transition function learned jointly with the LSTM. The latent variables are global because documents published at the same timestep all share the same latent variable. This allows the LSTM to capture language structures common to the entire dataset, while global latent variables are able to factorize language elements specific to their timestep. A schematic overview of the model is presented on Fig. 1.

Let $\mathbf{z}_t \in \mathbb{R}^{d_z}$ be the latent variable corresponding to timestep t. The sequence probability of a document $\mathbf{d}^{(i)}$ published at timestep $\mathrm{t}^{(i)}$ is now computed as

$$p_{\theta}(\mathbf{d}^{(i)}|\mathrm{t}^{(i)}) = p_{\theta}(\mathbf{d}^{(i)}|\mathbf{z}_{\mathrm{t}^{(i)}}) = \prod_{k=0}^{n^{(i)}-1} p_{\theta}(\mathrm{w}_{k+1}^{(i)}|\mathbf{w}_{0:k}^{(i)}, \mathbf{z}_{\mathrm{t}^{(i)}}).$$

Note that $\mathbf{z}_{\mathrm{t}^{(i)}}$ depends only on the *timestep* at which $\mathbf{d}^{(i)}$ has been published, and not specifically on $\mathbf{d}^{(i)}$ itself. In our architecture, we concatenate $\mathbf{z}_{\mathrm{t}^{(i)}}$ to the embeddings of each word $\mathbf{w}_k^{(i)}$ as we have found it to work best empirically.

The latent states $\mathbf{z}_t$ are Gaussian random variables structured in time *via* a dynamic component taking the form of a Gaussian model. Its mean is a function g of the previous state and its covariance is a learned diagonal matrix σ^2:

$$\mathbf{z}_{t+1}|\mathbf{z}_t \sim \mathcal{N}(g(\mathbf{z}_t; \boldsymbol{w}), \sigma^2),$$

where $\boldsymbol{w}$ are the parameters of g. Learning a transition model gives the system more freedom for learning useful trajectories. Moreover, it gives us the possibility to estimate future states of the system, where data is not available during training. The prior's mean on the first timestep is a learned vector $\boldsymbol{z}^0$ acting as the initial conditions of the system. The joint distribution factorizes as follows:

$$p_{\theta,\psi}(\mathcal{D}, \mathbf{Z}) = \prod_{i=1}^{N} p_{\theta}(\mathbf{d}^{(i)}|\mathbf{z}_{\mathrm{t}^{(i)}}) \prod_{t=0}^{T-1} p_{\psi}(\mathbf{z}_{t+1}|\mathbf{z}_t), \tag{2}$$

where $\psi = (\boldsymbol{w}, \sigma^2, \mathbf{z}_0)$ are the temporal prior parameters, and $\mathbf{Z} \in \mathbb{R}^{T \times d_z}$ is the matrix containing latent vectors $\mathbf{z}_t$. $p_\theta(\mathbf{x}|\mathbf{z}_{t^{(i)}})$ is parameterized by an LSTM where the latent state $\mathbf{z}_{t^{(i)}}$ is concatenated to every word embedding vectors. Note that, following our notation introduced in Sect. 3.1, $t^{(i)}$ is a variable representing the publication timestep of document i, whereas t are timestep values.

3.3   Inference

Learning the generative model in Eq. 2 requires to infer the latent variables $\mathbf{z}^t$. In Bayesian inference, it is done by estimating their posterior $p_{\theta,\psi}(\mathbf{Z}|\mathcal{D}) = \frac{p_{\theta,\psi}(\mathcal{D},\mathbf{Z})}{\int p_{\theta,\psi}(\mathcal{D},\mathbf{Z})d\mathbf{Z}}$. Unfortunately, the marginalization on $\mathbf{Z}$ requires to compute an intractable normalizing integral. We therefore use Variational Inference (VI), and consider a variational distribution $q_\phi(\mathbf{Z})$ that factorizes across all timesteps:

$$q_\phi(\mathbf{Z}) = \prod_{t=1}^{T} q_\phi^t(\mathbf{z}_t),$$

where q_ϕ^t are independent Gaussian distributions $\mathcal{N}(\mu_t, \sigma_t^2)$ with diagonal covariance matrices σ_t^2, and ϕ is the total set of variational parameters.

This factorization is possible because recurrent language modeling is an autoregressive task (c.f. Eq. 1) that does not require an auto-encoding scheme. We are thus able to learn a model with fewer parameters while avoiding common pitfalls associated with variational text auto-encoders, e.g. KL vanishing [4]. A particularity of our approach is that we have several documents published at the same timestep. So, to obtain an Evidence Lower Bound (ELBO) $\mathcal{L}(\boldsymbol{\theta}, \boldsymbol{\psi}, \boldsymbol{\phi})$, we adapt the derivation in [19] as follows:

$$\log p_{\theta,\phi}(\mathcal{D}) = \log \int_{\mathbf{Z}} p_\psi(\mathbf{Z}) \prod_{t=1}^{T} p_\theta(\mathcal{D}_t|\mathbf{z}_t)d\mathbf{Z} \geq \int_{\mathbf{Z}} q_\phi(\mathbf{Z}) \log \left(p_\psi(\mathbf{Z}) \frac{\prod_{t=1}^{T} p_\theta(\mathcal{D}_t|\mathbf{z}_t)}{q_\phi(\mathbf{Z})} \right) d\mathbf{Z}$$

$$= \sum_{t=1}^{T} \int_{\mathbf{z}_t} q_\phi^t(\mathbf{z}_t) \log p_\theta(\mathcal{D}_t|\mathbf{z}_t)d\mathbf{z}_t + \int_{\mathbf{z}_{t-1}} q_\phi^{t-1}(\mathbf{z}_{t-1}) \log \frac{p_\psi(\mathbf{z}_t|\mathbf{z}_{t-1})}{q_\phi^t(\mathbf{z}_t)} d\mathbf{z}_{t-1}d\mathbf{z}_t$$

$$= \sum_{t=1}^{T} \mathbb{E}_{q_\phi^t(\mathbf{z}_t)} [\log p_\theta(\mathcal{D}_t|\mathbf{z}_t)] - \mathbb{E}_{q_\phi^{t-1}(\mathbf{z}_{t-1})} \left[D_{\mathrm{KL}}(q_\phi^t(\mathbf{z}_t)\|p_\psi(\mathbf{z}_t|\mathbf{z}_{t-1})) \right], \quad (3)$$

where $\mathcal{D}_t$ is the set of all documents published at timestep t, and the inequality is obtained thanks to the Jensen theorem on concave functions.

This ELBO exhibits two expectation terms. The first one corresponds to a conditional log-likelihood of the observations at t given the state z_t. The second one is the Kullback-Leibler divergence of the variational distribution from its Gaussian prior given the previous state z_{t-1}, which owns an analytically closed form (as given in the supplementary material[1]). This ELBO can be classically optimized via stochastic gradient ascent using the re-parametrization trick [18,27].

---

[1] Supplementary material available at https://github.com/edouardelasalles/drlm/raw/master/supplementary.pdf.

Global temporal states coupled with variational distributions independent in time offer several learning and computation advantages. This allows the system to deal with strong disruptions in language shifts, for which regularities observed on other steps could not hold. Rather than considerably upsetting the transition function, and thus highly impacting consecutive states, the learning algorithm can choose to ignore such difficult transitions, at a cost depending on the variance σ^2. This variance σ^2, learned jointly with the model, allows the learning algorithm to adapt the stochastic transition according to the regularity level of the data. Moreover, since temporal dependency is broken, optimization over all timesteps can be done in parallel using mini-batches containing texts published at t.

4   Experiments

4.1   Models and Baselines

In our experiments, we compare the following models[2]:

- **LSTM:** a standard regularized LSTM. This baseline has no temporal component but is currently the state-of-the-art in language modeling.
- **DT:** the DiffTime model presented in [28] is a deep model which learns only one embedding vector per word. It combines those word embeddings with a temporal prior obtained by scaling a learned vector with a scalar timestep.
- **DWE:** the Dynamic Word Embedding model [2] learns Gaussian word embeddings with a probabilistic version of the skip-gram algorithm. It learns a different set of word embeddings per timestep, that are smoothed in time with a diffusion prior.
- **DRLM-Id:** the Dynamic Recurrent Language Model proposed in this paper, where the transition function is replaced by the identity matrix so that $\mathbf{z}^{t+1} \sim \mathcal{N}(\mathbf{z}^t, \sigma^2)$.
- **DRLM:** the Dynamic Recurrent Language Model proposed in this paper with learned transition function.

For comparison purposes, we adapted the temporal word embedding models DT and DWE for language modeling, by replacing the skip-gram component with an LSTM. More details can be found in the supplementary material.

4.2   Temporal Settings

We propose to evaluate the models in the two following temporal settings:

- **Prediction:** The first T_p timesteps are used to train the model. Timesteps $T_p + 1$ to T, with T the total number of timesteps, are used for evaluation. For DRLM, we use the transition model g to predict future states $\mathbf{z}_t$ in time. For DT and DWE we use the embeddings from the last training timestep T_p. Timestep $T_p + 1$ is used for hyperparameters tuning.

---

[2] Code of the models available at https://github.com/edouardelasalles/drlm.

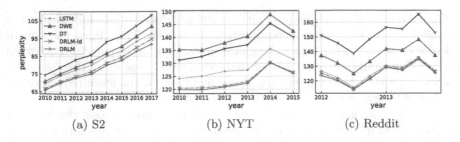

(a) S2   (b) NYT   (c) Reddit

Fig. 2. Perplexity through time for the *prediction* setting.

– **Modeling:** In this configuration, corpora are randomly split into training (60%), validation (10%) and test (30%) sets for each timestep.

We evaluate the models on language modeling and downstream classification tasks. For language modeling, the evaluation metric is the token level perplexity on the respective test sets. For classification, we report F1 scores for multi-label classification, and top1 scores for multi-class classification.

4.3 Datasets

We use three different corpora for our experiments:

– The **Semantic Scholar**[3] corpus (S2) contains 50K titles published in machine learning venues from 1985 to 2017, split by years (33 timesteps).
– The **New York Times** [39] corpus (NYT) contains 50K newspaper headlines (500K words) spanning from 1990 to 2015, split by years (26 timesteps).
– The **Reddit** corpus contains a sample of 3% of the social network's posts presented in [33]. It is composed of 100K posts sampled from January 2006 to December 2013 split by quarters (32 timesteps).

For each corpus, the vocabulary is constructed with words appearing at least 5 times in training sets (3 times for S2). The resulting vocabulary sizes are 5K tokens for S2, 8K for NYT and 13K for Reddit. All baselines and models are based on 2 layers AWD-LSTM [23] with hidden units and word embeddings of size 400. We use weight dropout, variational dropout, embedding dropout, and embeddings weight-tying (except for DWE that learns distinct word embeddings per timestep).

4.4 Language Modeling Results

Prediction. Figure 2 shows perplexity evolution for the prediction setup (numerical results are provided in the supplementary material). On the three corpora, both DRLM-Id and DRLM beat all baselines. The standard LSTM always

---
[3] http://labs.semanticscholar.org/corpus/.

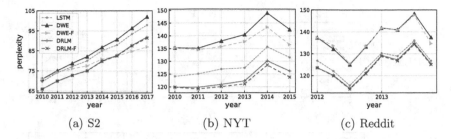

Fig. 3. Perplexity through time with *recursive inference*. DRLM-F and DWE-F are trained on T_p timesteps, and then their variational parameters are recursively inferred on data at timestep $T_p + \tau$ and evaluated at $T_p + \tau + 1$.

performs better than the DWE and DT baselines that systematically overfit. This shows that LSTMs language models are powerful, even without temporal components, and conditioning them is not trivial. Results on Reddit (Fig. 2c) tend to confirm this observation: performances of LSTM, DRLM-Id, and DRLM are quasi-equivalent, with a gain of 2 points of perplexity for DRLM compared to LSTM. It is a corpus twice larger than the others, with longer sequences. Our analysis is that with sufficient data, and due to the auto-regressive nature of textual data, LSTM, even without explicit temporal prior, manages to capture temporal biases implicitly.

In the S2 corpus, we can see in Fig. 2a that, while the perplexity of DRLM-Id tends to converge to LSTM's perplexity, DRLM presents consistent improvement through time. On the NYT corpus, while DRLM-Id and DRLM have significant performance gain compared to LSTM (more than 5 points), the difference between the two models is small and vanishes with time. This is explained by the fact that news headlines from NYT are mostly induced by external factors, while scientific publications from S2 are influenced by one another through time.

Recursive Inference. To validate this hypothesis, we recursively infer the latent states of DRLM. We optimize the variational parameters of every $\mathbf{z}_t$ for $t > T_p$ by maximizing Eq. 3 according to data from $\mathcal{D}^t$ and states inferred form previous steps. All other parameters remain unchanged. Specifically, we infer $\mathbf{z}_t$ according to $\mathcal{D}^t$ and $\mathbf{z}_{t-1}$. We then evaluate the resulting model at $t+1$, and next we infer $\mathbf{z}^{t+1}$ according to $\mathcal{D}^{t+1}$ and $\mathbf{z}_t$, evaluate at $t + 2$ and so on. The same process is performed for the variational parameters of DWE. The two resulting models are respectively referred to as DRLM-F and DWE-F in Fig. 3.

We first observe that the DWE baseline benefits a lot more from recursive inference than DMLR. This is expected since it can adapt each word embedding at each timestep, whereas DRLM-F only infers the distribution of a single vector per timestep. This thus makes DWE-F a good baseline for assessing temporal drift. DRLM-F improves performances on the last timesteps of NYT, meaning that the trained language model is able to interpret latent states $\mathbf{z}^t$ never seen during training. This is not trivial, given the difficulties and various tricks present

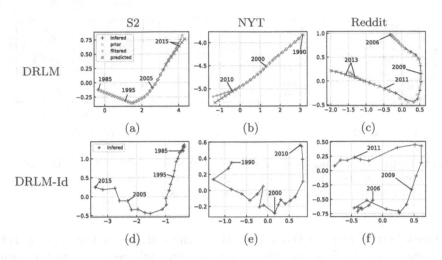

Fig. 4. Latent trajectories through time of the two most varying components of z_t for the prediction task on the three datasets, for DRLM and DRLM-Id.

in the literature to condition LSTM language models [4,30,38]. We also see that recursive inference does not improve DRLM results on S2, while DWE results are greatly improved. This shows that there is a temporal drift in S2, which is less clear on Reddit since recursive inference improves performances neither on DMLR nor on DWE. It then follows that DLRM predicts accurate latent states on the S2 corpus, since there is a temporal drift, and latent states inferred with future data yield performances similar to those with predicted states.

To confirm these hypotheses, we plot on Fig. 4 the latent trajectories of the two components of z that vary the most through time for DRLM (first row) and DRLM-Id (second row). For DRLM, the inferred points correspond to the means of $q(\mathbf{z}_t)$, and the prior points correspond to the means of $p(\mathbf{z}_t|\mathbf{z}_{t-1})$ for train timesteps. The predicted points for test timesteps are obtained by recursively applying the transition function g from the last training $\mathbf{z}_t$, and the filtered points are those obtained by recursive inference. For DRLM-Id, we only report the inferred points, as there is no transition function to apply (and the prior at each timestep is the state inferred at the previous one).

By comparing the first and second row of Fig. 4, we first observe that learning a transition function allows the model to learn smoother latent states in time compared to DRLM-Id. This confirms the relevance of our end-to-end learning process, compared to an approach that would extract trajectories from DRLM-Id *a posteriori*. DRLM automatically organizes states in a smooth fashion, from which extrapolation is easier. On Fig. 4a, we see that the predicted latent states are very close to the filtered ones, confirming the ability of the transition model to capture and predict global tendencies in the data. On the NYT corpus (Fig. 4b), we observe that the predicted latent states diverge slightly from the filtered states, which is coherent with the gain in perplexity observed on Fig. 3b by

Table 1. Modeling perplexity.

	S2	NYT	Reddit
LSTM	62.8	109.9	116.7
DT	70.7	125.6	136.8
DWE	65.9	119.9	129.4
DRLM-Id	60.6	104.0	115.5
DRLM	**60.2**	**103.5**	**114.7**

Table 2. Classification results.

Task	Prediction			Modeling		
Corpus	S2	NYT	Reddit	S2	NYT	Reddit
Metric	F1	top1	top1	F1	top1	top1
LSTM	0.19	35.1	32.0	0.22	41.4	44.0
DT	0.15	19.1	12.5	0.11	17.3	40.9
DWE	0.18	33.4	34.3	0.17	24.8	44.5
DRLM	**0.21**	**41.2**	**38.0**	**0.23**	**44.8**	**45.2**

DRLM-F. On the Reddit corpus, we see that the filtered states are close in time, indicating a slow temporal drift. This is also coherent with the perplexities observed on Fig. 3c.

Modeling. Table 1 presents results for the modeling setup. As for prediction, temporal word embeddings baselines also fail to beat the LSTM baseline. All perplexities are lower since the task is easier, but our models DRLM and DRLM-Id keep their perplexity gain over LSTM.

4.5 Text Classification Results

To further evaluate the representations learned by DRLM, we extract its word embeddings augmented with temporal states and use them for text classification. For the DT and DWE baselines, we learned temporal embeddings exactly as described in their respective papers. For every classification task, we learn a linear classifier that takes as inputs the average of the embeddings of each sequence, as done in [15] and [32]. Labels are articles' keywords for S2 (multi-label with 400 classes), articles' sections for NYT (mono-label with 28 labels) and subreddits in which posts were submitted for Reddit (mono-label with 60 labels). Classification results for prediction and modeling settings are presented in Table 2. DRLM outperforms all baselines. This shows that the representations it learns contain useful information that can be used for downstream tasks such as classification.

4.6 Text Generation Through Time

We present here texts samples generated by beam search with DRLM trained with the modeling setting. We use starting word triplets that most often appear in the S2 test set as a seed, and we change the latent state through time. Table 3 presents generated samples where the latent state evolves from 1985 to 2017. We can see a smooth evolution in vocabulary. Around the 90s, we can see that the language model evolves slowly, as the exact same sequences are generated 5

Table 3. Texts generated with DRLM for different timesteps on the S2 corpus.

Year	A framework for...	Unsupervised learning of...	A comparison of...
1985	Shape recovery from images	Hidden markov models	Smoothing techniques for statistical machine translation
1995	Shape recovery from images	Gaussian graphical models	Smoothing techniques for word sense disambiguation
2005	Automatic evaluation of statistical machine translation	Named entity recognizers	Smoothing techniques for statistical machine translation
2015	Unsupervised feature selection	Deep convolutional neural networks	Convolutional neural networks for action recognition
2016	Unsupervised learning of deep neural networks	Convolutional neural networks	Convolutional neural networks for action recognition
2017	Training deep convolutional neural networks	Generative adversarial networks	Convolutional neural networks for action recognition

years apart in the first set of samples. And we see that the language model start to evolve quickly from 2015, where references to deep learning begin to appear. In the second set, we even see a reference to GAN on the 2017 sample.

5   Conclusion

We proposed a Dynamic Recurrent Language Model (DRLM) for handling temporal drifts in language. Language evolution dynamics are captured via a learned transition function, which defines trajectories of temporal states through time. Experiments on three corpora showed that our approach beats temporal embeddings baselines in various settings and on downstream classification tasks.

References

1. Bai, S., Kolter, J.Z., Koltun, V.: An empirical evaluation of generic convolutional and recurrent networks for sequence modeling. arXiv:1803.01271 (2018)
2. Bamler, R., Mandt, S.: Dynamic word embeddings. In: ICML (2017)
3. Blei, D.M., Lafferty, J.D.: Dynamic topic models. In: ICML (2006)
4. Bowman, S.R., Vilnis, L., Vinyals, O., Dai, A., Jozefowicz, R., Bengio, S.: Generating sentences from a continuous space. In: SIGNLL (2016)
5. Chiu, C.C., et al.: State-of-the-art speech recognition with sequence-to-sequence models. arXiv:1712.01769 (2017)

6. Devlin, J., Chang, M.W., Lee, K., Toutanova, K.: BERT: pre-training of deep bidirectional transformers for language understanding. arXiv:1810.04805 (2018)

7. Eger, S., Mehler, A.: On the linearity of semantic change: investigating meaning variation via dynamic graph models. In: ACL (2016)

8. Fedus, W., Goodfellow, I., Dai, A.M.: MaskGAN: better text generation via filling in the _. In: ICLR (2018)

9. Fraccaro, M., Sønderby, S.K., Paquet, U., Winther, O.: Sequential neural models with stochastic layers. In: NeurIPS (2016)

10. Frermann, L., Lapata, M.: A Bayesian model of diachronic meaning change. ACL (2016)

11. Hamilton, W.L., Leskovec, J., Jurafsky, D.: Diachronic word embeddings reveal statistical laws of semantic change. In: ACL, vol. 1 (2016)

12. Hochreiter, S., Schmidhuber, J.: Long short-term memory. Neural Comput. **9**, 1735–1780 (1997)

13. Howard, J., Ruder, S.: Universal language model fine-tuning for text classification. In: ACL (2018)

14. Iwata, T., Yamada, T., Sakurai, Y., Ueda, N.: Sequential modeling of topic dynamics with multiple timescales. ACM Trans. KDD **5**, 19 (2012)

15. Joulin, A., Grave, E., Bojanowski, P., Mikolov, T.: Bag of tricks for efficient text classification. arXiv:1607.01759 (2016)

16. Kabán, A., Girolami, M.A.: A dynamic probabilistic model to visualise topic evolution in text streams. J. Intell. Inf. Syst. **18**, 107–125 (2002)

17. Kim, Y., Chiu, Y.I., Hanaki, K., Hegde, D., Petrov, S.: Temporal analysis of language through neural language models. In: ACL Workshop on Language Technologies and Computational Social Science (2014)

18. Kingma, D.P., Welling, M.: Auto-encoding variational Bayes. In: ICLR (2014)

19. Krishnan, R.G., Shalit, U., Sontag, D.: Structured inference networks for nonlinear state space models. In: AAAI (2017)

20. Kulkarni, V., Al-Rfou, R., Perozzi, B., Skiena, S.: Statistically significant detection of linguistic change. In: WWW (2015)

21. Melis, G., Dyer, C., Blunsom, P.: On the state of the art of evaluation in neural language models. In: ICLR (2018)

22. Merity, S., Keskar, N.S., Socher, R.: An analysis of neural language modeling at multiple scales. arXiv:1803.08240 (2018)

23. Merity, S., Keskar, N.S., Socher, R.: Regularizing and optimizing LSTM language models. In: ICRL (2018)

24. Mikolov, T., Chen, K., Corrado, G., Dean, J.: Efficient estimation of word representations in vector space. arXiv:1301.3781 (2013)

25. Mikolov, T., Karafiát, M., Burget, L., Černocký, J., Khudanpur, S.: Recurrent neural network based language model. In: ISCA (2010)

26. Radford, A., Wu, J., Child, R., Luan, D., Amodei, D., Sutskever, I.: Language models are unsupervised multitask learners (2019)

27. Rezende, D.J., Mohamed, S., Wierstra, D.: Stochastic backpropagation and approximate inference in deep generative models. In: ICML (2014)

28. Rosenfeld, A., Erk, K.: Deep neural models of semantic shift. In: NAACL (2018)

29. Rudolph, M., Blei, D.: Dynamic Bernoulli embeddings for language evolution. arXiv:1703.08052 (2017)

30. Semeniuta, S., Severyn, A., Barth, E.: A hybrid convolutional variational autoencoder for text generation. In: EMNLP (2017)

31. Serban, I.V., Ororbia, A.G., Pineau, J., Courville, A.: Piecewise latent variables for neural variational text processing. In: EMNLP (2017)

32. Shen, D., et al.: Baseline needs more love: on simple word-embedding-based models and associated pooling mechanisms. arXiv:1805.09843 (2018)
33. Tan, C., Lee, L.: All who wander: on the prevalence and characteristics of multi-community engagement. In: WWW (2015)
34. Vaswani, A., et al.: Attention is all you need. In: NeurIPS (2017)
35. Vinyals, O., Toshev, A., Bengio, S., Erhan, D.: Show and tell: lessons learned from the 2015 MSCOCO image captioning challenge. PAMI **39**, 652–663 (2017)
36. Wang, C., Blei, D., Heckerman, D.: Continuous time dynamic topic models. arXiv:1206.3298 (2012)
37. Wang, X., McCallum, A.: Topics over time: a non-Markov continuous-time model of topical trends. In: ACM SIGKDD (2006)
38. Yang, Z., Hu, Z., Salakhutdinov, R., Berg-Kirkpatrick, T.: Improved variational autoencoders for text modeling using dilated convolutions. In: ICML (2017)
39. Yao, Z., Sun, Y., Ding, W., Rao, N., Xiong, H.: Dynamic word embeddings for evolving semantic discovery. In: WSDM (2018)
40. Zaheer, M., Ahmed, A., Smola, A.J.: Latent LSTM allocation joint clustering and non-linear dynamic modeling of sequential data. In: ICML (2017)

A Fast Convolutional Self-attention Based Speech Dereverberation Method for Robust Speech Recognition

Nan Li[1,2], Meng Ge[1], Longbiao Wang[1(✉)], and Jianwu Dang[1,2]

[1] Tianjin Key Laboratory of Cognitive Computing and Application,
College of Intelligence and Computing, Tianjin University, Tianjin, China
{tju_linan,gemeng,longbiao_wang}@tju.edu.com
[2] Japan Advanced Institute of Science and Technology, Nomi, Ishikawa, Japan
jdang@jaist.ac.jp

Abstract. Speech dereverberation based on deep learning has recently gained a remarkable success with the substantial improvement of speech recognition for the accuracy in the distant speech recognition task. However, environmental mismatches due to noise and reverberation may result in performance degradation when the features (e.g. MFCCs) are simply fed into a speech recognition system without feature enhancement. To address the problem, we propose a new speech dereverberation approach based on the deep convolution and self-attention mechanisms to enhance the MFCC-based feature in distant signals. The deep convolutional component used in this approach can efficiently exploit the frequency-temporal context patterns, and the multi-head self-attention mechanism can obtain the complete time-domain cues to enhance the temporal context. Meanwhile, the bottleneck features trained on a clean corpus are utilized as teacher signals, because they contain relevant cues to phoneme classification and the mapping is performed with the objective of suppressing noise and reverberation. Extensive experimental results on the REVERB challenge corpus demonstrate that our proposed approach outperforms all the competitors, reducing about 17% relative word error rate (WER) compared with the deep neural network (DNN) baseline method.

Keywords: Speech dereverberation · Speech recognition · Multi-head self-attention · Bottleneck feature · DNN

1 Introduction

With the development of speech processing techniques, hands-free speech techniques for various applications are increasingly popular, such as chat robots and smart speakers. However, automatic speech recognition from distant microphones remains a challenge because the speech signals to be recognized are degraded by the presence of interfering signals and reverberation due to a long

© Springer Nature Switzerland AG 2019
T. Gedeon et al. (Eds.): ICONIP 2019, LNCS 11955, pp. 295–305, 2019.
https://doi.org/10.1007/978-3-030-36718-3_25

speaker-to-microphone distance. To overcome such a challenging task, speech dereverberation algorithms often function as a preprocessing module that to help suppress the reverberation in observed speech signals before they are fed into the following stage of speech recognition systems.

Recently, speech dereverberation methods based on deep neural networks have been shown to significantly improve speech recognition performance due to the strong regression capability. The general solution is to view the speech dereverberation problem as a multivariate regression problem, where the nonlinear regression function is parametrized by various deep neural networks, such as deep neural networks (DNNs) [1–3], convolutional neural networks (CNNs) [4,5], recurrent neural networks (RNNs) [6–8] and generative adversarial networks (GANs) [9–11]. Based on how the enhanced target is achieved, the techniques can be categorized into the mapping-based methods [1,4,12] and masking-based methods [13,14]. The former aims to learn a non-linear mapping function from the observed noisy speech into the desired clean speech, while the latter focuses on learning a time-frequency mask from the observed noisy speech to desired clean speech. Despite the success of these existing methods, they often fail to meet the realistic complex scenarios for the following two drawbacks. First, the mismatch between the training and testing environments degrades significantly the performance of speech recognition. Second, high computing costs make it difficult to apply to real-world applications.

To address the above problems, we propose a fast single-channel speech dereverberation approach for distant speech recognition. Specifically, in order to solve the first mismatch problem, we make efforts to the exploration of input cues and enhancement of target prediction. In terms of the input cues, 2D deep convolution operations are adopted to exploit the frequency-temporal context patterns, and a self-attention mechanism [15] is incorporated into our approach to preserving the complete time-domain context patterns. Complete signal preservation on the time-frequency domain is conducive to better target prediction, and we call this as deep convolutional self-attention neural network (DCANN). As regard to the target prediction, the conventional log-power spectral representation or time-frequency mask prediction only focuses on the front-end speech dereverberation, ignoring the back-end speech recognition task. Motivated by the strong discriminative ability of the bottleneck feature [16], we first extract the phoneme-based bottleneck features based on the close-talking corpus from the DNN-HMM speech recognition system [17], and then use them as another teacher signals besides the traditional ones (P-DCANN). The discriminatory bottleneck features do not only enhance the robust of speech dereverberation but also provide more feature choices for an back-end speech recognition system in real cases. Benefited from the proposed network structure without recursive operations, the speed has been significantly improved compared with the traditional LSTM and CNN-based frameworks. Lastly, the results obtained from various experiments demonstrate that our approach achieves better performance than all other competitors based on the REVERB challenge database [18].

The paper is organized as follows. Section 2 discusses detailed mapping based speech enhancement studies. We then describe our approach in detail in Sect. 3. The experiment and its results are shown in Sect. 4. We discuss related issues and conclude the paper in the last section.

2 Related Work

It has been reported that the DNN mapping method [1] is useful to improve the speech dereverberation system performance. In this method, the DNN is used for a regression task to learn a nonlinear function between acoustic features of reverberant speech and clean speech. The used features before inputting to the network need a mean normalization. In the dereverberation stage, the reverberant speech acoustic features are fed into the DNN model to generate the corresponding enhanced acoustic features. After obtaining the dereverberated speech acoustic features, these features are used to train the DNN or the other acoustic model and the dereverberated test data features are used to do a decoding process. Finally, a higher accuracy rate compared with the model of dereverberation without the DNN will be obtained.

Furthermore, the CNN [4] and LSTM [6] based methods can be used as a speech enhancement method as well. The utility of CNN as the feature extraction part is the capability of overviewing broader features, and its use will attain a better learning performance on speech in the frequency-temporal context domain. Although the LSTM will bring good performance in the sequence learning, it requires a higher cost for the training. In the end-to-end automatic speech recognition (ASR) [19,20], some researchers use a structure called the transformer [15] that does not to use the CNN, and the LSTM obtains a high accuracy rate. The core of the transformer is for a multi-head self-attention application. We expect that the efficient and effective combination of these neural networks finally achieves a good performance in speech dereverberation for robust speech recognition in the real condition.

3 Proposed Method

3.1 DCANN Based Speech Dereverberation Model

In this section, a detailed introduction to our proposed DCANN model is described. As shown in Fig. 1, the system contains three modules: the CNN module, multi-head self-attention module, and post-mapping module.

In the CNN module, a 4-layer CNN is used to extract deep level features, which learns several different filters simultaneously. The CNN filters with multiple sizes capture valuable features of different scales, it helps learn MFCC features for robust frequency-temporal patterns. Then the multi-head self-attention will facilitate feature learning in the time-domain context patterns, and compared with LSTM, it will also save much time. In the post-mapping module, a

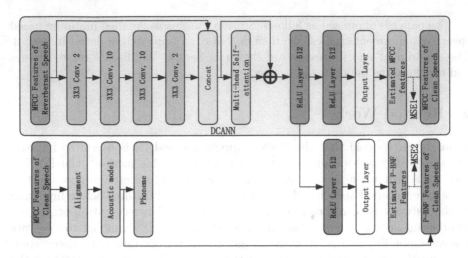

Fig. 1. P-DCANN structure for robust speech recognition. The upper part is the DCANN method.

2-layer DNN is used to learn the detail of the MFCC features. To further suppress the problem of data mismatch between the training and testing set, some *concat* and *resnet* structures are used. Specifically, we concatenate the output of the CNN features and the input of the MFCC features, and use the concatenated features combined with multi-head self-attention output features. The DCANN architecture combines different strengths for the three modules, which does not only gain a better result but also will save training and decoding time. We also detail the multi-head self-attention in the subsection.

Multi-head Self-attention. Many tasks have successfully applied the attention mechanism, including ASR, machine translation [15] and language understanding [21]. It is expected that the attention mechanism used in speech dereverberation tasks resembles the human auditory mechanism, which focuses on the frames that contain more useful information, and gives low attention for the reverberant speech frames.

In this paper, we adopt the multi-head self-attention proposed by [15]. The core of multi-head self-attention is the scaled dot-product attention being improved from the dot-product attention. Because of the utilization of highly optimized matrix multiplication code, the dot-product attention could do a faster computation compared with the standard additive attention mechanism [22]. The scaled dot-product attention computes the attention value based on the following equation:

$$Attention\left(\boldsymbol{Q}, \boldsymbol{K}, \boldsymbol{V}\right) = softmax\left(\frac{\mathbf{Q}\mathbf{K}^T}{\sqrt{d}}\right) V \tag{1}$$

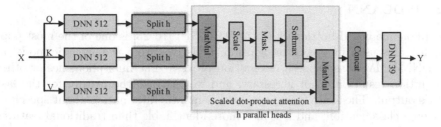

Fig. 2. The computation flow of multi-head self-attention mechanism. All the heads can be computed in parallel for scaled dot-product attention.

where the query vectors $\mathbf{Q} \in \mathbb{R}^{n \times d}$, keys $\mathbf{K} \in \mathbb{R}^{n \times d}$, and values $\mathbf{V} \in \mathbb{R}^{n \times d}$ is the same matrix, d is the number of hidden units of our network.

Figure 2 shows the computational flow of the multi-head self-attention mechanism. In the first step, it uses three different linear projection maps for the input vectors queries $\mathbf{Q}$, keys $\mathbf{K}$, and values $\mathbf{V}$ matrices. $\mathbf{Q}$, $\mathbf{K}$, and $\mathbf{V}$ are the same as the input matrix $\mathbf{X}$. In the next step, the mapped queries, keys, and values are respectively split into h parallel head channels. If i is the i-th head, we use $\mathbf{W}_i^Q \in \mathbb{R}^{n \times d/h}$, $\mathbf{W}_i^K \in \mathbb{R}^{n \times d/h}$, $\mathbf{W}_i^V \in \mathbb{R}^{n \times d/h}$ respectively as the queries, keys and values that pass through the DNN layer and split expressing. Then the scaled dot-product attention is used to compute the relationship between queries and keys, and a mask matrix in this part will be learned. By multiplying the mask matrix of the last step by the value matrix, we will obtain the attention matrix. The mathematical formulation is shown in the following equation:

$$Head_i = Attention\left(\mathbf{W}_i^Q, \mathbf{W}_i^K, \mathbf{W}_i^V\right) \tag{2}$$

After obtaining every head attention, we concatenate all parallel head together to form a single vector:

$$Multihead\left(\mathbf{Q}, \mathbf{K}, \mathbf{V}\right) = Concat\left(head_1 \ldots head_h\right) \tag{3}$$

Lastly, by a DNN layer, the final vector $\mathbf{Y}$ will be computed. In this paper, the parallel head is set to $h = 8$.

The use of the multi-head self-attention mechanism has many merits compared with the LSTM. It is highly parallel, compare with LSTM without recursive computation.

DCANN Loss Function. In the training stage of DCANN speech dereverberation system, the mean square error (MSE) is applied as a loss function:

$$L_{mse} = \frac{1}{N} \sum_{i=0}^{N} (y_i - x_i)^2 \tag{4}$$

where y_i represents the features generated from the DCANN model, x_i is the clean speech MFCC features. N is the length for the dimension from one frame.

3.2 P-DCANN

The phoneme-based bottleneck feature (P-BNF) [16,23] is one of the most popular features used in speech recognition. It derives from the acoustic model in the DNN-HMM-based speech recognition process. The final phonemes or other recognition results are not necessary, and we just use the feature for the last layer's output. The P-BNF contains some semantic information about speech to phoneme classification, and it is also more identifiable than traditional features (e.g. MFCCs) in the real environment.

In this paper, based on the DCANN we further propose a P-DCANN model, as shown in Fig. 1. It is expected that the clean MFCC features would better perform in a speech recognition task with a P-BNF constraint imposed at another output layer as a teacher signal. It will bring stronger discriminant power for the clean speech MFCC features learning, and this treatment especially useful in the training set and testing set for the environmental mismatch case.

One similar work in [24] showed that the use of the multi-target learning with both input and output layers could improve the performance of DNN-based speech enhancement. However, the motivation of our work is using the multi-target learning to learn some discriminant cases in the MFCC feature generating process, since these features are effective for the back-end speech recognition in the real condition.

For the P-DCANN training stage, the loss function is:

$$L = L_{mse1} + \alpha L_{mse2} \tag{5}$$

where L_{mse1} is the MFCC features MSE loss, and L_{mse2} is the P-BNF features MSE loss. The MSE loss of the P-BNF is controlled by a hyper-parameter α. Finally, the P-DCANN by coordinating the DCANN and multi-target learning could efficiently work in the real condition.

4 Experiments

4.1 Datasets

To verify the effectiveness of our approach, we evaluate it experimentally on the single channel official data of the REVERB challenge [18]. The training set used in our experiment contains about 7861 reverberant utterances (about 17.5 h) and 7861 corresponding clean utterances from the WSJCAM0 corpus [25]. The reverberant utterances are generated from the clean WSJCAM0 training data by convolving the clean utterances with measured room impulse responses and adding recorded background noise with an SNR of 20 dB. The reverberation times of the measured impulse responses in the dataset range from 0.2 s to 0.8 s. In addition, the evaluation test set consists of two different parts, namely simulated data (SimData) and real recordings (RealData). The SimData contains 2176 reverberant speech utterances (about 4.8 h) that are artificially simulated in the same way as the training set. It simulates six different reverberation

Table 1. WERs (%) comparisons by previous mapping based networks and our proposed method. "Avg" means the average.

Method	Simulated data							Real data		
	Room1		Room2		Room3		Avg	Room1		Avg
	Far	Near	Far	Near	Far	Near		Far	Near	
No process	8.18	7.47	13.58	9.11	16.33	10.85	10.92	27.95	28.07	28.01
DNN	8.44	7.45	12.22	8.07	14.23	10.13	10.09	25.02	24.43	24.73
R-CED	7.39	7.17	11.81	7.76	13.31	8.94	9.40	24.81	23.76	24.29
LSTM	8.42	7.20	11.94	7.86	14.40	9.88	9.95	24.44	24.05	24.25
DCNN	7.72	7.32	11.62	8.34	14.53	10.15	9.95	23.16	21.72	22.44
DCANN	7.20	6.34	11.01	7.83	13.43	8.82	9.11	22.18	20.44	21.31
P-DCANN	7.47	6.78	10.61	7.33	13.25	9.11	**9.09**	21.54	19.51	**20.52**

conditions: three rooms with different volumes (small, medium and large) and two different speaker-to-microphone distances (near = 50 cm and far = 200 cm). Meanwhile, the RealData from the MC-WSJ-AV corpus [26] contains 372 real recordings (about 0.6 h) made in a reverberant meeting room, which includes two different speaker-to-microphone distances (near = 100 cm and far = 250 cm). The reverberation time in the RealData is about 0.7 s.

4.2 Experimental Setup

Our speech dereverberation front-end is used to enhance the MFCC features for speech recognition experiments. The Kaldi [27] toolkit is used to train our back-end ASR system with a DNN acoustic model and the enhanced the MFCC features. For the speech dereverberation front-end, the ReLU is used as the activation function of each hidden layer, and the *Adam* algorithm is used to ensure a stationary solution [28]. In practice, the learning rate is set to 0.01, and the batch size is set to 256. For the back-end ASR, it is mainly divided into two stages: training and decoding. In the training stage, 13-dimensional MFCC features of each frame are extracted from reverberant and clean speech with a frame length of 512 and a frame shift of 256. To enhance context information of input features, each frame is combined with 10 frames in the context to form the final MFCC features. The MFCC features of reverberant and clean speech are both used as input into the DNN acoustic model. During the decoding stage, the tri-gram language model with explicit pronunciation and silence probability modeling is utilized. All the experiments are listed as follows:

No Process: A speech recognition system without speech dereverberation front-end processing.

DNN [1]: A speech recognition system with DNN-based speech dereverberation front-end processing. The structure of DNN model consists of 3 hidden layers with 512 units per hidden layer.

Table 2. The training time compared with previous speech dereverberation method and proposed method.

Metric	DNN	R-CED	LSTM	DCANN	P-DCANN
Time epoch/h	0.05	0.42	0.62	0.11	0.13

R-CED [4]: A speech recognition system with R-CED speech dereverberation processing. The 2D CNN component contains 9 convolutional layers, where the number of filters for each convolution layer is 12, 16, 20, 24, 32, 24, 20, 16, and 12 respectively.

LSTM [7]: A speech recognition system with the speech dereverberation processing based on an LSTM model. The LSTM model has 3 hidden layers and 512 units in each hidden layer.

DCNN: A speech recognition system using our proposed DCANN model without multi-head self-attention mechanism.

DCANN: A speech recognition system with our proposed DCANN as shown in DCANN block of Fig. 1.

P-DCANN: A speech recognition system with our proposed P-DCANN as shown in Fig. 1. After the fine tune, hyper-parameter α is set to 3.

4.3   Experimental Results and Discussion

The experimental results are summarized in Table 1, with summaries detailed below: (1) The ASR system with DNN front-end processing significantly outperformed the system without speech dereverberation processing by respectively 7.6% and 11.7% relative error reduction in terms of simulated and real condition WER, proving that speech dereverberation processing based on the deep learning can effectively suppress the interference of reverberation and significantly improve the performance of back-end ASR system. (2) The R-CED and LSTM systems have better performance than the DNN system. To be specific, compared with the conventional independent modeling of temporal context in a DNN system, the frequency-temporal context can be exploited by using the convolution operations in the R-CED, and the dynamic temporal context can be obtained by adopting the sequential operations in the LSTM. (3) Our proposed DCNN system achieves better results than the R-CED system with about 7.6% relative error reduction in terms of WER on the real data. One possible explanation is that the DCNN not only effectively acquires deep frequency-temporal context patterns by using deep convolution operations, but also preserves the original shallow speech information by using the *concat* structure, instead of only deep information in the R-CED. (4) Our proposed DCANN system with an attention mechanism achieves better performance compared with the DCNN system, indicating that the attention block preserves the real signal of target speech well and removes the disturbing noise from various environments. This fact enables our approach to better enhances the temporal context. (5) Our P-DCANN achieves the best performance than all the competitors, reducing WER from 10.09 to 9.09 with 10% relative WER reduction on the simulated data and from 24.73 to 20.52 with 17% relative WER reduction on the real data compared with the DNN baseline. It proves that the additional phoneme-based bottleneck objective function brings the stronger discriminant power for the back-end speech recognition. The bottleneck features are extracted from the DNN-HMM speech recognition system with the close-talking corpus as inputs, which make the final MFCC from the P-DCANN model more suitable for the back-end speech recognition task.

To verify the efficiency of our proposed P-DCANN approach, the training time of each of the above methods in a single TITAN X GPU is listed in Table 2. As we can see in Table 2, our P-DCANN approach is faster than other competitors. Specifically, the training time of the LSTM is about five times that of our P-DCANN. The reason is that our approach does not have recursive operations used in the LSTM, thus achieving fewer training parameters and shorter training time. Besides, the R-CED system is slower than our P-DCNN and DCNN systems due to numerous convolution layers in the R-CED. To summarize, the proposed P-DCANN is more effective and efficient compared with the existing methods.

5 Conclusion

In this paper, we proposed a DCANN-based single-channel speech dereverberation system with multi-head self-attention that learns the time domain information. We also propose a P-DCANN structure to further improve DCANN performance. The use of our proposed dereverberation methods achieves impressive performance improvement compared with the DNN-based speech dereverberation methods. Our approach also attain a faster training and decoding speed compared with use for CNN and LSTM to do speech dereverberation in a single TITAN X GPU. We also note that the proposed method has the great potential for further improvement. The bidirectional self-attention structure is also proposed in the BERT. We believe that using it will further improve our system performance.

Acknowledgements. This work was supported in part by the National Natural Science Foundation of China under Grant 61771333 and the Tianjin Municipal Science and Technology Project under Grant 18ZXZNGX00330.

References

1. Xu, Y., Du, J., Dai, L.R., Lee, C.: An experimental study on speech enhancement based on deep neural networks. IEEE Signal Process. Lett. **21**, 65–68 (2013)
2. Han, K., Wang, Y., Wang, D.: Learning spectral mapping for speech dereverberation. In: IEEE International Conference on Acoustics, Speech and Signal Processing (ICASSP), pp. 4628–4632 (2014)

3. Oo, Z., Wang, L., Phapatanaburi, K., Nakagawa, S., Iwahashi, M., Dang, J.: Phase and reverberation aware DNN for distant-talking speech enhancement. Multimed. Tools Appl. **77**(14), 18865–18880 (2018)
4. Park, S.R., Lee, J.: A fully convolutional neural network for speech enhancement. In: Interspeech 2017, pp. 1993–1997 (2017)
5. Fu, S.W., Tsao, Y., Lu, X., Kawai, H.: Raw waveform-based speech enhancement by fully convolutional networks. In: Asia-Pacific Signal and Information Processing Association Annual Summit and Conference (APSIPA ASC), pp. 006–012 (2017)
6. Weninger, F., Watanabe, S., Tachioka, Y., Schuller, B.: Deep recurrent de-noising auto-encoder and blind de-reverberation for reverberated speech recognition. In: IEEE International Conference on Acoustics, Speech and Signal Processing (ICASSP), pp. 4623–4627 (2014)
7. Weninger, F., et al.: Speech enhancement with LSTM recurrent neural networks and its application to noise-robust ASR. In: Vincent, E., Yeredor, A., Koldovský, Z., Tichavský, P. (eds.) LVA/ICA 2015. LNCS, vol. 9237, pp. 91–99. Springer, Cham (2015). https://doi.org/10.1007/978-3-319-22482-4_11
8. Ge, M., Wang, L., Li, N., Shi, H., Dang, J., Li, X.: Environment-dependent attention-driven recurrent convolutional neural network for robust speech enhancement. In: Interspeech 2019, pp. 3153–3157 (2019)
9. Pascual, S., Bonafonte, A., Serrà, J.: SEGAN: speech enhancement generative adversarial network. In: Interspeech 2017, pp. 3642–3646 (2017)
10. Wang, K., Zhang, J., Sun, S.: Investigating generative adversarial networks based speech dereverberation for robust speech recognition. In: Interspeech 2018, pp. 1581–1585 (2018)
11. Li, C., Wang, T., Xu, S., Xu, B.: Single-channel speech dereverberation via generative adversarial training. In: Interspeech 2018, pp. 1309–1313 (2018)
12. Ueda, Y., Wang, L., Kai, A., Ren, B.: Environment-dependent denoising autoencoder for distant-talking speech recognition. EURASIP J. Adv. Signal Process. **2015**(1), 1–11 (2015)
13. Narayanan, A., Wang, D.: Ideal ratio mask estimation using deep neural networks for robust speech recognition. In: IEEE International Conference on Acoustics, Speech and Signal Processing, pp. 7092–7096 (2013)
14. Williamson, D.S., Wang, Y., Wang, D.: Complex ratio masking for monaural speech separation. IEEE/ACM Trans. Audio Speech Lang. Process. **24**, 483–492 (2016)
15. Vaswani, A., Shazeer, N., Parmar, N.: Attention is all you need. In: Advances in Neural Information Processing Systems, pp. 5998–6008 (2017)
16. Paulik, M.: Lattice-based training of bottleneck feature extraction neural networks. In: Interspeech 2013, pp. 89–93 (2013)
17. Hinton, G., Deng, L., Yu, D.: Deep neural networks for acoustic modeling in speech recognition: the shared views of four research groups. IEEE Signal Process. Mag. **29**, 82–97 (2012)
18. Kinoshita, K., Delcroix, M., Yoshioka, T.: The REVERB challenge: a common evaluation framework for dereverberation and recognition of reverberant speech. In: IEEE Workshop on Applications of Signal Processing to Audio and Acoustics (2014)
19. Zhou, S., Dong, L., Xu, S., Xu, B.: Syllable-based sequence-to-sequence speech recognition with the transformer in Mandarin Chinese. In: Interspeech 2018, pp. 791–795 (2018)
20. Chiu, C.C., Sainath, T.N., Wu, Y.: State-of-the-art speech recognition with sequence-to-sequence models. In: IEEE International Conference on Acoustics, Speech and Signal Processing (ICASSP), pp. 4774–4778 (2018)

21. Devlin, J., Chang, M.W., Lee, K.: Pre-training of deep bidirectional transformers for language understanding. arXiv preprint arXiv:1810.04805 (2018)
22. Bahdanau, D., Cho, K., Bengio, Y.: Neural machine translation by jointly learning to align and translate. arXiv preprint arXiv:1409.0473 (2014)
23. Ren, B., Wang, L., Lu, L., Ueda, Y., Kai, A.: Combination of bottleneck feature extraction and dereverberation for distant-talking speech recognition. Multimed. Tools Appl. **75**(9), 5093–5108 (2016)
24. Xu, Y., Du, J., Huang, Z.: Multi-objective learning and mask-based post-processing for deep neural network based speech enhancement (2017)
25. Graff, D., Kong, J., Chen, K.: English gigaword. Linguist. Data Consortium Philadelphia
26. Lincoln, M., McCowan, I., Vepa, J.: The multi-channel Wall Street Journal audio visual corpus (MC-WSJ-AV): specification and initial experiments. In: IEEE Workshop on Automatic Speech Recognition and Understanding, pp. 357–362 (2005)
27. Povey, D., Ghoshal, A., Boulianne, G.: The Kaldi speech recognition toolkit. In: IEEE Signal Processing Society (2011)
28. Kingma, D.P., Ba, J.: Adam: a method for stochastic optimization. arXiv preprint arXiv:1412.6980 (2014)

Option Attentive Capsule Network for Multi-choice Reading Comprehension

Hang Miao$^{(\boxtimes)}$, Ruifang Liu, and Sheng Gao

School of Information and Communication,
Beijing University of Posts and Telecommunications, Beijing, China
{miaohang123,lrf,gaosheng}@bupt.edu.cn

Abstract. In this paper, we study the problem of multi-choice reading comprehension, which requires a machine to select the correct answer from a set of candidates based on the given passage and question. Most existing approaches focus on designing sophisticated attention to model the interactions of the sequence triplets (passage, question and candidate options), which aims to extract the answer clues from the passage. After this matching stage, a simple pooling operation is usually applied to aggregate the matching results to make final decisions. However, a bottom-up max or average pooling may loss essential information of the evidence clues and ignore the inter relationships of the sentences, especially dealing with complex questions when there are multiple evidence clues. To this end, we propose an option attentive capsule network with dynamic routing to overcome this issue. Instead of pooling, we introduce a capsule aggregating layer to dynamically fuse the information from multiple evidence clues and iteratively refine the matching representation. Furthermore, we design an option attention-based routing policy to focus more on each candidate option when clustering the features of low-level capsules. Experimental results demonstrate that our proposed model achieves state-of-the-art performance on RACE dataset.

Keywords: Multi-choice reading · Capsule network · Attention

1 Introduction

Machine reading comprehension (MRC) is a fundamental and crucial topic in the field of natural language understanding and question answer (QA), and has attracted an increasing number of attentions in recent years. In this paper, we mainly focus on the problem of MRC with multiple-choice questions, which requires a machine to choose the correct answer based on the given passage, question and several candidate options. Compared with extractive MRC whose expected answer is a short text span in the passage, multi-choice MRC is more challenging because most of the answers do not appear in the passage, which means more complex reasoning and inferences are required to tackle this task. Owning to the release of a relatively large-scale dataset called RACE, many neural network based models have been proposed to solve this task, though there are still a significant gap between humans and AI systems.

© Springer Nature Switzerland AG 2019
T. Gedeon et al. (Eds.): ICONIP 2019, LNCS 11955, pp. 306–318, 2019.
https://doi.org/10.1007/978-3-030-36718-3_26

Typically, most deep learning based models for MRC task contain three main stages: encoding, matching and aggregating. To be more specific, a compositional encoder is firstly applied to encode the given texts into context-aware representations after the word embedding layer. Subsequently, a word-level attention mechanism is employed to model the interactions between text sequences, which matches the information of a sequence to specific parts of another sequence, then we could get the matching representation. Finally, a aggregating layer is added to project the matching representation into a fix-size encoding vector and we reason over it to select the correct answer. Most recent works involving multi-choice MRC concentrate on matching stage and many sophisticated matching mechanisms have been proposed to model the relationships of text sequence triplets (passage, question and candidate options). However, few works pay attention to how to aggregate information from the matching representation. Most previous works apply a pooling operation (max pooling or average pooling) to aggregate the matching information, which may loss essential information of the evidence clues and it lack the guide of task information [5].

In order to handle the aforementioned problems, we regard the aggregation as a routing problem, and employ an attentive capsule network to iteratively aggregate information from the matching representation to make final decisions. A capsule is a small group of neurons to represent features. Here we treat the matching representation obtained from matching stage as capsules which capture the low-level semantic information of evidence clues. By leveraging dynamic routing policy [12], we could decide which parts and how much of the information should be transferred from each state of the matching representation (low-level capsules) to the final output representation (high-level capsules). Noticing that traditional dynamic routing algorithm does not focus on the candidate option in the routing process, we introduce an option attention-based routing policy to our capsule network. This could help to better fuse the information from multiple evidence clues and reason over them to make decisions. This strategy is similar to the method used by humans when doing reading examinations. When we humans are doing multi-choice reading, we firstly match the key information of the question and each candidate option against the passage to extract evidence snippets. For some complex questions, we tend to get multiple evidence snippets based on the question and options. Then we need to jointly consider the relationships of the snippets, and fuse the essential information with respect to each candidate option to make final decisions. To the best of our knowledge, we are the first to investigate capsule network for multi-choice MRC task.

2   Related Works

Multi-choice Reading Comprehension. Multi-choice MRC is a task which aims to select a certain answer from several candidate options given a passage and a question. [7] adopted and modified two deep learning based models used in cloze-style MRC task: Stanford Attentive Reader (SAR) and Gated-Attention Readers (GA) as baselines for this dataset. After that, a rich line of studies have attempted to design sophisticated attention mechanism to model the relationship of the input triples. Xu et al. [21] designed a dynamic multiple matching method to fuse the information of the input triples into attention vectors and utilized a multi-step reasoning strategy for answer selection. [14] was the first to propose a triple sequences matching strategy to jointly match the passage against the question and candidate options and performed a hierarchical LSTM aggregation to capture sentence-level information. [3] proposed a Convolutional Spatial Attention (CSA) which leveraged a modified attention mechanism to extract the enriched representation of the input triples and then used a CNN to summarize the attention values.

Capsule Network. Capsule network was firstly introduced by [6] at 2011 to tackle the representational limitation issues of CNN. Basically, a capsule is a group of neurons whose activity vector denotes the instantiation parameters of a specific type of entity [12]. Combining with an iterative dynamic routing mechanism, capsule network achieved state-of-the-art performance on MNIST dataset. Recently, several works began to investigate the performance of capsule network in NLP tasks such as text classification and relation extraction. [20] employed capsule network with dynamic routing for text classification. [5] introduced two dynamic routing mechanisms to aggregate the representation of CNN or RNN into a fixed-size vector, and validated the effectiveness of this aggregation method on document and sentence level text classification tasks. [18] proposed a capsule network with attention mechanism for relation extraction, which performed better on multiple entity pairs. [19] devised an attention-based routing policy in the capsule network for multi-labeled relation extraction, which improved the capability of clustering relation features. Apart from that, capsule network has also been explored in recommendation system. [8] made use of capsule routing mechanism to learn users' diverse interest representations and achieved superior performance on public benchmarks. To our best knowledge, there are no work that employs capsule network in the field of multi-choice MRC task.

3   Our Proposed Model

In this section, we describe the overall structure of our proposed Option Attentive Capsule Network for multi-choice MRC. Our model expects three inputs: question, passage and four candidate options, denoted as Q, P and $\{O_i\}_{i=1}^4$, respectively. The objective of our model is to infer the correct answer based on the interaction between the question, passage and candidate options. Our model consists of four main components: context encoding layer, sequence matching layer, capsule aggregating layer and option selecting layer. The overall structure is depicted in Fig. 1.

3.1   Content Encoding Layer

The input triplet of sample is: $\left(Q, P, \{O_i\}_{i=1}^4\right)$, where $Q = \{w_t\}_{t=1}^{|Q|}$, $P = \{w_t\}_{t=1}^{|P|}$, $O_i = \{w_t\}_{t=1}^{|O|}$; w_t is the t-th word of each text sequence; $|Q|$, $|P|$ and

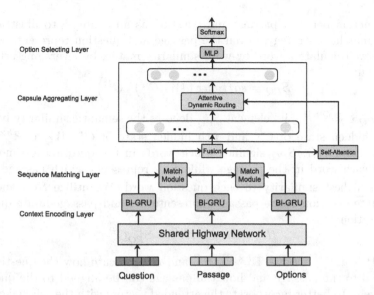

Fig. 1. Overall neural structure of the attentive capsule model for multi-choice MRC.

$|O|$ are the max sequence length of the question, passage and each candidate option respectively. Firstly, we map each word into a continuous representation space by leveraging a pre-trained word embedding and obtain the word representations: $Q^{emb} \in \mathbb{R}^{d \times |Q|}$, $P^{emb} \in \mathbb{R}^{d \times |P|}$ and $O_i^{emb} \subset \mathbb{R}^{d \times |O|}$, d is the embedding size. In order to control the information flow and alleviate over fitting, we use a two-layer highway network following a *ReLU* activation to process the word representations as follows:

$$E^Q = \text{ReLU}\left(\text{Highway}\left(Q^{emb}\right)\right), E^P = \text{ReLU}\left(\text{Highway}\left(P^{emb}\right)\right)$$
$$E^{o_i} = \text{ReLU}\left(\text{Highway}\left(O_i^{emb}\right)\right) \tag{1}$$

where $E^Q \in \mathbb{R}^{d \times |Q|}$, $E^P \in \mathbb{R}^{d \times |P|}$ and $E^{O_i} \in \mathbb{R}^{d \times |O|}$. After that, we feed them into a bidirectional Gated Recurrent Unit (BiGRU) to process the text sequences from both sides and capture the contextual information of each sequence:

$$C^Q = \text{BiGRU}\left(E^Q\right), C^P = BiGRU\left(E^P\right), C^{o_i} = BiGRU(E^{o_i}) \tag{2}$$

where $C^Q \in \mathbb{R}^{h \times |Q|}$, $C^P \in \mathbb{R}^{h \times |P|}$ and $C^{O_i} \in \mathbb{R}^{h \times |O|}$, h denotes the hidden size of BiGRU encoder. Unlike the shared highway network, we use three separated BiGRU without sharing weights for the sequence triplets and concatenate the forward and backward hidden states to form the final contextual representations.

3.2 Sequence Matching Layer

The sequence matching layer is responsible for modeling the interactions between passage, question and each candidate option, producing the matching representation which captures the evidence clues in the original passage. We take the interaction between passage and question as an example to illustrate the detailed matching strategy. Given the passage and question representation C^P and C^Q, we calculate a word-by-word similarity matrix by leveraging attention mechanism:

$$S_{PQ} = softmax\left(\left(W_Q C^Q\right)^T C^P \right) \qquad (3)$$

where $S_{PQ} \in \mathbb{R}^{|Q| \times |P|}$, its element S_{PQ}^{ij} denotes the semantic similarity between the i-th hidden state of C^Q and j-th hidden state of C^P; $W_Q \in \mathbb{R}^{h \times h}$ is a trainable parameter. S_{PQ} signifies which words in the question are most relevant to each word in the passage while S_{PQ}^T represents which passage words have the highest similarity to each question word. We utilize S_{PQ} and S_{PQ}^T to calculate question-aware passage representation and passage-aware question representation:

$$H^P = S_{PQ}C^Q, H^Q = S_{PQ}^T C^P \qquad (4)$$

where $H^P \in \mathbb{R}^{h \times |P|}$, $H^Q \in \mathbb{R}^{h \times |Q|}$. H^P and H^Q indicate how the question can be aligned to the passage and how the passage can be aligned to the question, respectively. To better incorporate the attended vectors with the original contextual representation, we leverage an effective matching tricks [2,14–16] to obtain the fusion representation:

$$M^P = ReLU \left(W_M^P \begin{bmatrix} H^P - C^P \\ H^P \cdot C^P \\ H^P \end{bmatrix} + b_M^P \right) \qquad (5)$$

where $M^P \in \mathbb{R}^{h \times |P|}$, $M^Q \in \mathbb{R}^{h \times |Q|}$; $W_M^P, W_M^Q \in \mathbb{R}^{h \times 3h}$ and $b_M^P, b_M^Q \in \mathbb{R}^h$ are the learnable weights and biases. $\begin{bmatrix} \cdot \\ \cdot \\ \cdot \end{bmatrix}$ denotes the column-wise concatenation. After that, we conduct a row-wise concatenation to form a enriched representation:

$$M^{PQ} = [M^P; M^Q] \qquad (6)$$

where $M^{PQ} \in \mathbb{R}^{h \times (|P|+|Q|)}$, $[;]$ is the raw-wise concatenation. In the same method, we obtain the enriched representation $M^{PO} \in \mathbb{R}^{h \times (|P|+|O|)}$ based on the passage and candidate option. Finally, we use a BiGRU layer to project the concatenation of M^{PQ} and M^{PO} and produce the final matching representation:

$$U = \text{BiGRU} \left(W_U \begin{bmatrix} M^{PQ} \\ M^{PO} \end{bmatrix} + b_U \right) \qquad (7)$$

where $U \in \mathbb{R}^{h \times (|P|+|Q|)}$, $W_U \in \mathbb{R}^{h \times 2h}$ and $b_U \in \mathbb{R}^h$ are parameters to learn. To concatenate M^{PQ} and M^{PO} across column, we keep $|Q|$ and $|O|$ equal by setting the max sequence length of question and each option to the same value.

Algorithm 1. Attentive Dynamic Routing Algorithm

Input: the matching representation $U = \{u_1, u_2, \ldots, u_N\}$, iteration times T,
number of high-level capsules K
Output: $V = \{v_1, v_2, \ldots, v_K\}$
1 Initialize: $b_{ij} \leftarrow 0$
2 **for** T iterations **do**
3 $\quad$ for all low-level capsules u_i and high-level capsules v_j:
4 $\quad\quad$ $c_{ij} = softmax(b_{ij})$
5 $\quad$ for all high-level capsules v_j:
6 $\quad\quad$ $s_j = \sum_{i=1}^{N} c_{ij}\alpha_i W_{ij} u_i$, $v_j = squash(s_j)$
7 $\quad$ for all low-level capsules u_i and high-level capsules v_j:
8 $\quad\quad$ $b_{ij} = b_{ij} + v_j^T \alpha_i W_{ij} u_i$
9 **end**
10 **return** $V = \{v_1, v_2, \ldots, v_K\}$;

3.3 Capsule Aggregating Layer

Given the input capsule vectors $U = \{u_1, u_2, \ldots, u_N\}$, $u_i \in \mathbb{R}^{h \times 1}$, N denotes the number of low-level capsules, we compute the total input candidate vector of each high-level capsule by a weight sum operation as follows:

$$s_j = \sum_{i=1}^{N} c_{ij}\widehat{u}_{j|i} \qquad (8)$$

where $\widehat{u}_{j|i}$ is the prediction vector produced by capsule u_i; c_{ij} is coupling coefficient determined by the dynamic routing process. It represents how much information need to be transformed from low-level capsule u_i to high-level capsule v_j, computed by:

$$c_{ij} = softmax(b_{ij}) = \frac{\exp(b_{ij})}{\sum_k \exp(b_{ik})} \qquad (9)$$

where b_{ij} denotes the logits which are the log probabilities of capsule u_i being coupled to capsule v_j. After that, we could obtain the final high-level output capsule vectors by applying a non-linear "squash" function:

$$v_j = squash(s_j) = \frac{\|s_j\|^2}{1 + \|s_j\|^2} \frac{s_j}{\|s_j\|} \qquad (10)$$

In the traditional dynamic routing algorithm, $\widehat{u}_{j|i}$ is produced by multiplying u_i by a mapping matrix, computed as:

$$\widehat{u}_{j|i} = W_{ij} u_i \qquad (11)$$

where $W_{ij} \in \mathbb{R}^{h \times l}$ is a mapping matrix to be learned, l denotes the hidden size of each output capsule unit; Inspired by [19], we propose an option attentive dynamic routing policy to focus more on the candidate options when aggregating the low-level capsules. To be more specific, we apply an attention weight to each low-level capsule and then obtain the prediction vector:

$$\hat{u}_{j|i} = \alpha_i W_{ij} u_i \tag{12}$$

where α_i is relevance of the i-th low-level capsule and the option representation, computed by:

$$\alpha_i = softmax\left(C_{self-O} u_i\right) \tag{13}$$

C_{self-O} is the self-attended option representation, which could better capture the whole semantic meaning of the option sentence. The details of the self-attention mechanism are as follows:

$$A = softmax\left(W_{s2} \tanh\left(W_{s1} C^O\right)\right) \tag{14}$$

where $A \in \mathbb{R}^{1 \times h}$ represents the self attention vectors, $W_{s_1} \in \mathbb{R}^{h \times h}$ and $W_{s_2} \in \mathbb{R}^{1 \times h}$ are weight matrices. Then we sum up the hidden state of C^O according to the self attention vectors:

$$C_{self-O} = A C^O \tag{15}$$

The initial logits b_{ij} and each output capsule v_j are iteratively updated in the routing process. The detailed option attentive dynamic routing policy is demonstrated in Algorithm 1.

3.4   Option Selection Layer

For each candidate option O_i, we flatten its corresponding output capsule vectors V^i and feed them into a fully connected layer to get the matching score. Then we add a softmax layer to get the final probability distributions over all the candidate options:

$$Pr(O_i|P, Q, O) = \frac{exp(W_v V^i)}{\sum_{k=1}^{4} exp(W_v V^k)} \tag{16}$$

where W_v is a trainable parameter. The whole model is trained by minimize the cross entropy loss function.

4   Experiments

4.1   Dataset and Experimental Setups

We evaluate the empirical performance of our proposed model on the RACE dataset. RACE is a recently proposed large-scale dataset collected from English reading comprehension tests for Chinese students. In RACE, each passage is associated with several questions and for each given question, we need to select only one correct answer from the candidate options. This dataset is composed of two subsets: high school subset and middle school subset, denoted as RACE-H and RACE-M respectively. The main difference between RACE-M and RACE-H

Table 1. Performance comparison of published single models.

Single models	RACE-M	RACE-H	RACE
Random	24.6	25.0	24.9
Sliding Window [11]	37.3	30.4	32.2
Stanford AR [1]	44.2	43.0	43.3
GA Reader [4]	43.7	44.2	44.1
ElimiNet [9]	44.5	44.5	44.5
Hierarchical Attention Flow [21]	45.3	44.2	44.1
Dynamic Fusion Network [17]	51.5	45.7	47.4
Hierarchical Co-Matching [14]	55.8	48.2	50.4
BiAttention + Simple MRU [13]	57.7	47.5	50.4
Convolutional Spatial Attention [3]	52.2	**50.3**	50.9
Attentive-Capsule (Our model)	**59.7**	50.1	**52.9**
Turkers [7]	85.1	69.4	73.3
Ceiling [7]	95.4	94.2	94.5

lies on that RACE-H is associated with more complex questions which require sentence reasoning and inference.

In the experiment, we set the maximum words of the question and each candidate option to 30. The pre-trained 300-dim Glove embeddings [10] is used as the embedding initialization. To mitigate over-fitting, we apply a recurrent dropout of 0.25 to each BiGRU cell and a dropout of 0.5 to each fully-connected layer. Additionally, the hidden size of BiGRU is fixed to 128. We use Adam optimizer with an initial learning rate of 10^{-3} for weight optimization.

4.2   Overall Results and Ablation Study

We use accuracy to evaluate the performance of our model. Experimental results are shown in Table 1. We report the results of all the compared baselines from respective papers. Here we just include the performances of single models, without ensemble models. As we can see, our model outperforms all the compared single models on RACE and its' subset RACE-H, which demonstrates the effectiveness of our model. On the RACE-H dataset with more complicated questions involving sentence reasoning and summarizing, our model outperforms Hierarchical Co-Matching and BiAttention with Simple MRU by 2.1% and 2.8%, respectively. When compared to the recent published work Convolutional Spatial Attention Model (CSA), our model achieves a comparable result on RACE-H, and gets a much higher accuracy on RACE-M. That indicates our model is capable of handling relatively complicated questions. However, there is still a gap between human ability and deep learning based models, as the performance of Amazon Tuckers and human ceilings are 73.3% and 94.5% on RACE.

We carry out an ablation study to further determine the contributions of each component of our model, the results are illustrated in Table 2. We mainly

Table 2. Results of ablation study.

Model	RACE-M	RACE-H	RACE
Full-model	**59.7**	**50.1**	**52.9**
- Capsule aggregating	57.7	47.8	50.7
- Option attentive routing	58.1	49.2	51.8
- Highway	59.5	49.9	52.7

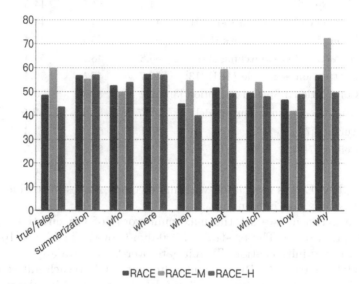

Fig. 2. Performance on different type of questions on RACE test set.

focus on investigating the influence of the capsule aggregating layer. We firstly remove the capsule aggregating layer and replace with a max-pooling layer to aggregate the information based on the matching representation. It could be observed that the accuracy decreases significantly by 2.2% on RACE, which indicates that utilizing capsule network to dynamically aggregate information from the matching representation is much more efficient compared with simple pooling operation. Then we remove the option attention in the routing process and use the traditional dynamic routing algorithm instead. We can see that the performance drops by 1.1%. That suggests it is useful to incorporate the option attention routing policy. We also removed the highway network in the contextual encoding layer. The result decreases by 0.2%, indicating that adding highway to control the information flow in the encoding stage is moderately effective.

4.3   Analysis and Discussion

Performance w.r.t. Question Type. We carry out an analysis with respect to different question types to evaluate the performance of our model. Firstly, we

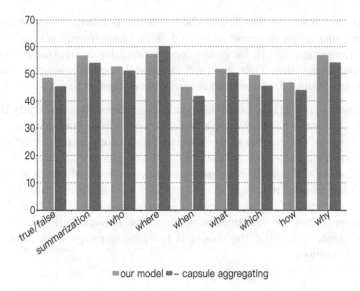

●our model ■- capsule aggregating

Fig. 3. Comparison results on RACE test set.

divide the test examples into nine categories according to the key words that appear in the question: six 'wh' types, 'how' type, judgement type and summarization type. Specifically, judgement type questions require to select the true or false option, symbolized by key words 'true', 'not true' or 'false'. Summarization type questions usually involve the 'purpose', 'title' or 'main idea', which require high-level information summarizing capability. Relatively speaking, 'why', 'how' and summarization types are more complex compared with other types. The results are as shown in Fig. 2. As we can observe, our model achieves a better performance on 'why' questions and summarization questions. Especially, our model achieves an accuracy of over 70% on RACE-M subset when dealing with 'why' questions. That suggests that our model could handle relatively complicated questions involving sentence reasoning. However, there is a significantly drop on RACE-H subset, indicating that more efforts need to be made to tackle with difficult reasoning questions.

To fairly validate the effect of our proposed capsule aggregating layer, we compare the performance between our full model and that discarding capsule aggregating layer. Figure 3 shows the comparison results. When we remove the capsule aggregating layer, performance on most type of questions decreases. On the question type 'why' and summarization, the accuracy drops by 2.7% and 2.6%, respectively. This indicates that utilizing capsule network as an aggregating method is effective in handling relatively sophisticated questions.

Performance w.r.t. Routing Iteration. We conduct experiments to investigate how the iteration number of the routing affect the overall performance of our model. We train our model with different number of routing iteration from 1 to 5, as Table 3 shows. We can see from the table that as the number of iteration increase, the accuracy on RACE and the two subsets increases and achieves the best performance when iteration is set to 3. This phenomenon is consistent with the original capsule network for image recognition, demonstrating the effectiveness of dynamic routing. Then the performance decreases when the number of iteration is large than 3, we assume it may due to over fitting.

Performance w.r.t. High-Level Capsule Numbers. We also study the effect of different number of high-level capsules in the capsule aggregating layer. In the experiment, we fix the number of iteration to 3 and train the model with different high-level capsule numbers $(4, 8, 12, 16, 20)$. The results are illustrated in Table 4. We could observe the performance increase as we increase the high-level capsule numbers. That means relatively larger number of high-level capsules tend to increase the capacity of high-level feature information contained in each capsule unit. However, when we continue to enlarge the capsule numbers, there is a substantial drop, indicating the model is hard to converge with relatively too large capsule numbers.

Table 3. Performance w.r.t. routing iteration

Dataset	RACE-M	RACE-H	RACE
Iteration = 1	59.2	49.2	52.1
Iteration = 2	59.4	49.7	52.5
Iteration = 3	59.7	50.1	52.9
Iteration = 4	58.4	48.5	52.4
Iteration = 5	57.6	48.7	52.3

Table 4. Performance w.r.t. capsule nums

Dataset	RACE-M	RACE-H	RACE
K = 4	58.4	49.0	51.8
K = 8	59.0	49.4	52.2
K = 12	59.7	50.1	52.9
K = 16	59.0	49.1	52.0
K = 20	57.7	48.1	50.9

5   Conclusion

In this paper, we introduce an option attentive capsule network for multi-choice machine reading comprehension. Our model firstly extracts the contextual information from the passage, question and candidate answers, then matches the passage against the question and option to extract specific evidence clues in the passage, obtaining a matching representation. Instead of using a simple pooling operation to aggregate the matching vectors, we introduce a capsule aggregating layer to dynamically fuse the information from multiple evidence clues and iteratively refine the matching representation. Furthermore, we design an option attention-based routing policy to focus more on the candidate options when clustering the features of low-level capsules. Experimental results demonstrate that our model outperforms all the compared baselines and achieves the state-of-the-art performance on RACE and RACE-M for single models.

References

1. Chen, D., Bolton, J., Manning, C.D.: A thorough examination of the CNN/daily mail reading comprehension task. In: Meeting of the Association for Computational Linguistics, vol. 1, pp. 2358–2367 (2016)
2. Chen, Q., Zhu, X., Ling, Z.H., Inkpen, D.: Natural language inference with external knowledge (2018)
3. Chen, Z., Cui, Y., Ma, W., Wang, S., Hu, G.: Convolutional spatial attention model for reading comprehension with multiple-choice questions. arXiv preprint arXiv:1811.08610 (2018)
4. Dhingra, B., Liu, H., Yang, Z., Cohen, W.W., Salakhutdinov, R.: Gated-attention readers for text comprehension. In: Meeting of the Association for Computational Linguistics, pp. 1832–1846 (2017)
5. Gong, J., Qiu, X., Wang, S., Huang, X.: Information aggregation via dynamic routing for sequence encoding. arXiv preprint arXiv:1806.01501 (2018)
6. Hinton, G.E., Krizhevsky, A., Wang, S.D.: Transforming auto-encoders. In: Honkela, T., Duch, W., Girolami, M., Kaski, S. (eds.) ICANN 2011. LNCS, vol. 6791, pp. 44–51. Springer, Heidelberg (2011). https://doi.org/10.1007/978-3-642-21735-7_6
7. Lai, G., Xie, Q., Liu, H., Yang, Y., Hovy, E.H.: RACE: large-scale reading comprehension dataset from examinations. In: Empirical Methods in Natural Language Processing, pp. 785–794 (2017)
8. Li, C., et al.: Multi-interest network with dynamic routing for recommendation at Tmall. arXiv preprint arXiv:1904.08030 (2019)
9. Parikh, S., Sai, A., Nema, P., Khapra, M.M.: ElimiNet: a model for eliminating options for reading comprehension with multiple choice questions, pp. 4272–4278 (2018)
10. Pennington, J., Socher, R., Manning, C.D.: GloVe: global vectors for word representation, pp. 1532–1543 (2014)
11. Richardson, M., Burges, C.J.C., Renshaw, E.: MCTest: a challenge dataset for the open-domain machine comprehension of text, pp. 193–203 (2013)
12. Sabour, S., Frosst, N., Hinton, G.E.: Dynamic routing between capsules. In: Advances in Neural Information Processing Systems, pp. 3856–3866 (2017)
13. Tay, Y., Tuan, L.A., Hui, S.C.: Multi-range reasoning for machine comprehension. arXiv Computation and Language (2018)
14. Wang, S., Yu, M., Jiang, J., Chang, S.: A co-matching model for multi-choice reading comprehension. In: Meeting of the Association for Computational Linguistics, vol. 2, pp. 746–751 (2018)
15. Wang, S., et al.: Evidence aggregation for answer re-ranking in open-domain question answering. In: International Conference on Learning Representations, p. 1 (2018)
16. Wang, W., Yan, M., Wu, C.: Multi-granularity hierarchical attention fusion networks for reading comprehension and question answering. In: Meeting of the Association for Computational Linguistics, vol. 1, pp. 1705–1714 (2018)
17. Xu, Y., Liu, J., Gao, J., Shen, Y., Liu, X.: Dynamic fusion networks for machine reading comprehension. arXiv preprint arXiv:1711.04964 (2017)
18. Zhang, N., Deng, S., Sun, Z., Chen, X., Zhang, W., Chen, H.: Attention-based capsule networks with dynamic routing for relation extraction. arXiv preprint arXiv:1812.11321 (2018)

19. Zhang, X., Li, P., Jia, W., Zhao, H.: Multi-labeled relation extraction with attentive capsule network. arXiv preprint arXiv:1811.04354 (2018)
20. Zhao, W., Ye, J., Yang, M., Lei, Z., Zhang, S., Zhao, Z.: Investigating capsule networks with dynamic routing for text classification. arXiv preprint arXiv:1804.00538 (2018)
21. Zhu, H., Wei, F., Qin, B., Liu, T.: Hierarchical attention flow for multiple-choice reading comprehension, pp. 6077–6085 (2018)

Exploring and Identifying Malicious Sites in Dark Web Using Machine Learning

Yuki Kawaguchi[1] and Seiichi Ozawa[2](✉)

[1] Graduate School of Engineering, Kobe University, Kobe, Japan
[2] Center for Mathematical and Data Sciences, Kobe University, Kobe, Japan
ozawasei@kobe-u.ac.jp

Abstract. In recent years, various web-based attacks such as Drive-by-Download attacks are becoming serious. To protect legitimate users, it is important to collect information on malicious sites that could provide a blacklist-based detection software. In our study, we propose a system to collect URLs of malicious sites in the dark web. The proposed system automatically crawls dark web sites and collects malicious URLs that are judged by using VirusTotal and the Gred engine. We also predict dangerous categories of collected web sites that are potentially malicious using a document embedding with a gradient boosting decision tree model. In the experiments, we demonstrate that the proposed system can predict dangerous site categories with 0.82 accuracy in F1-score.

Keywords: Cybersecurity · Tor · Dark web · Document classification · Machine learning

1 Introduction

Recently, web-based cyberattacks such as Drive-by-Download attacks, phishing and social engineering attacks have become serious. One of the countermeasures against such cyberattacks is to introduce a mechanism into a web browser so that it deters a user from guiding to so-called malicious sites. A famous security function of web browsers is Google Safe Browsing (GSB), which has been introduced in Chrome browser. In GSB, when a user tries to access a malicious site, an alert is appeared on a browser and it blocks the user's access to dangerous sites. However, it is known that GSB alone cannot completely block, and there are not a few malicious sites not detected by GSB. Therefore, it makes sense to develop a function that complements the GSB protection mechanism. For this purpose, a browser sensor has been developed to collect users' web browsing histories through the construction of a user participation type observation network, and a research project called WarpDrive has been conducting a proof-of-concept to stop users from accessing malicious URLs since 2018.

The purpose of this paper is to develop a mechanism to find unknown malicious sites through dark web crawling. Specifically, we propose a system that

© Springer Nature Switzerland AG 2019
T. Gedeon et al. (Eds.): ICONIP 2019, LNCS 11955, pp. 319–327, 2019.
https://doi.org/10.1007/978-3-030-36718-3_27

crawls the Tor network [1] and find malicious URLs from collected HTML contents. The Tor network is one of the highly anonymized and popular web areas called the dark web, which is not allowed to browse and search with ordinary browsers. In the dark web, tools used for cyberattacks such as Exploit Kit are traded, and there is also a community of crackers. Generally, Dark Web is considered to be used by persons with high computer skills, such as attackers, but in fact links to malicious sites targeting dark web users and places where attackers exchange malicious site information are found. There is no doubt that crawling the dark web to get information on malicious sites is effective.

There are several researches obtain information related to cyberattacks from the Tor network. Nunes et al. [2] crawled forums and markets on the dark web, and classified whether they obtained product information related to cyberattacks using classifiers such as ensemble random trees and label propagation. They also show that classification was carried out with high accuracy and that the collected information was useful for discovering unknown cyberattacks. Tavabi et al. [3] predicted the possibility of exploiting the vulnerability by monitoring discussions in the dark web. Specifically, they proposed Darkembed, which obtains document vectors using neural networks for unstructured documents, and showed that it is actually useful for prediction. Our research differs from the previous researches in that we collect information related to malicious sites, and also differ in that we target Web-based attacks targeting general dark web users.

Section 2 explains the developed Tor crawler and a system to collect malicious URLs in Dark Web. In Sect. 3, we construct a classification system to find suspicious site using a document analysis for collected HTML contents. Finally, we show our conclusions and future work in Sect. 4.

2   A Study on Malicious Sites in Dark Web

2.1   Collection System of Malicious URLs in Tor Network

Using seed URLs in the link collection, we crawled the website in the Tor network [1] and developed a crawler for collecting HTML content in Python 3.6. In addition, we used Python library AIOHTTP [12] to generate HTML request. AIOHTTP is a library designed to work with ASYNCIO, an asynchronous I/O library introduced in Python 3.4. Considering the purpose of our research that a broad area of dark web space must be crawled, it is desirable to introduce parallel processing in our Tor crawler so that multiple requests are requested in parallel at high speed. Also, SQLite [13] is used as a database to manage collected URLs and HTML contents.

We adopt VirusTotal [11] and Gred engines as a mechanism to predict the maliciousness of extracted URLs from collected HTML contents. VirusTotal is a web service that can perform 66 detection engines consisting of anti-virus software and blacklist based classifiers for files and URLs. The Gred engine is also a Web service developed by SecureBrain Corporation, and can be used to determine the degree of malignancy such as tampering and phishing sites for HTML contents. The HTML obtained by the Tor crawler is stored in the dark

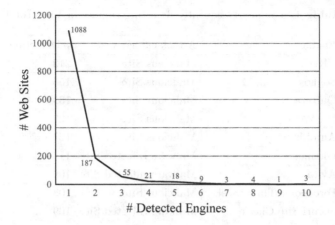

Fig. 1. Distribution of malicious sites for the number of detected engines.

web database, from which the links to the surface (including not only the links of the 'href' attribute but also the format of the URL in the text) are extracted and the surface URLs are saved in the link database. Then, the degree of malignancy of the website registered in this database is judged using external engines where an URL is posted to VirusTotal and a collected HTML is posted to the Gred engine. Note that crawling Tor network and evaluating maliciousness of collected HTML contents are performed independently once a month.

2.2 Exploration of Malicious Sites in Dark Web

The developed malicious-site collection system was operated from April 1, 2018 to January 23, 2019. With the developed Tor crawler, we collected HTML contents from a total of 8,910 domains, but only 5,101 domains were accessible on the last day of collection. Then, 569,138 URLs to the surface web (65,869 unique domains) were extracted from the collected HTML contents.

Using VirusTotal API, 1,444 sites on the surface web were judged malicious by one or several engines. Figure 1 illustrates the distribution of malicious sites that are detected by a different number of engines. As seen in Fig. 1, many malicious web sites are detected by a single engine, and almost all malicious web sites are detected only by one or a few engines.

Table 1 shows the major VirusTotal engines that frequently detect maliciousness and their decisions on attacks. As seen in Table 1, *Malicious Sites* are detected most frequently by the CRDF engine, while many web sites are also judged maliciousness by other engines. Since Fig. 1 shows that only one or a few engines detect maliciousness at the same time, it is assumed that the judgement by each engine was distinctively varied; that is, the engines seem to have strong and weak points for different types of web-based attacks. Therefore, even if there

Table 1. The most frequently detecting engines in VirusTotal

Engine	Attack category	#Detection
CRDF	Malicious Site	212
Sophos	Malicious Site	156
Quttera	Malicious Site	139
Dr. Web	Malicious Site	127
AutoShun	Malicious Site	121
Fortinet	Malware Infected Site	118
Avira	Malware Infected Site	109
Forcepoint ThreatSeeker	Malicious Site	108
Sucuri Site Check	Malware Infected Site	109

Table 2. Detection results in Gred engine.

Detection results	#Detection
Phishing site	10
Fraud attack	3

is only one active engine judging maliciousness, it is better to consider that such a web site is danger. Therefore, we need more evidence about the maliciousness of collected web sites so that we can make sure to be safe or danger with more confidence.

On the other hand, as seen in Table 2, the Gred engine judges 13 cases as malicious sites. It is worth mentioning that such 13 sites were not judged maliciousness by VirusTotal; that is, they might be unknown malicious sites. Although the number of malicious judgements by the Gred engine is much smaller than that by VirusTotal, note that the Gred engine is good at detailed analysis of HTML contents with less false detection.

2.3   Discussions

As seen in Table 1, only a small number of web sites were detected maliciousness with 5 or more engines in VirusTotal and such web sites are highly suspected to be malicious. We collected 71 web pages from such malicious sites (31 domains). To understand the features of such malicious sites, we looked at the pages individually and categorized them into several groups. Table 3 summarizes the categories of such highly suspected web sites.

The Scams category in Table 3 mainly consists of sites for buying and selling credit card information. Hacking/Programming/Software includes web pages on technical topics for cyberattacks (e.g., virtual environments) and descriptions of attack codes causing a browser to crash. The Libraries/Wikis category includes wiki pages that contain useful information and mail services when

Table 3. Categorization of collected dark web pages with malicious links.

Category	#Domain	#Pages
Forums	7	11
Scams	6	19
Hacking/Programming/Software	6	15
Libraries/Wikis	5	12
Adult/Porn	1	2
Other	2	9
Empty/Error/Unknown	3	3

using the Tor service. In Forums, bulletin board sites are classified. Some bulletin board sites introduce links to malicious sites and attract users to be dangerous links. The Adult/Porn category contains links to adult contents and pages that summarize sexual preferences. The other categories include miscellaneous sites, mentioning biographies about certain US military personnel, and the Empty/Error/Unknown consists of pages with meaningless texts.

Among highly suspected web sites in Table 3, there is only one URL that was explicitly mentioned to be malicious at the bulletin board site. For other sites, there was no explicit warning for malicious URLs. Therefore, it is very likely that most of malicious URLs in dark web is targeting dark web users. For example, at a credit card trading site, the link to the marketplace itself was a malicious URL that promptly drives users to a malicious site. On the other hand, as seen in Table 3, the pages containing malicious URLs are distributed over specific categories. Therefore, if such category information is combined with the above-mentioned less confident detection result given by one or a few engines in VirusTotal, it might effectively work to keep users away from dangerous malicious sites. Then, let us see if we can identify web sites whose HTML contents are categorized into the 8 groups in Table 3.

3 Categorization of HTML Contents in Dark Web

In the previous section, we found that the categories of web pages that contain malicious URLs have some bias. Therefore, let us verify whether the category of a web page can be predicted accurately from HTML contents. If certain accuracy is expected, it is possible to give an alert to users based on the category of a web page being browsed even when one or a small number of VirusTotal engines detected maliciousness.

3.1   Feature Embedding and Classification Method

In this paper, we use FastText [4] and Sparse Composite Document Vector (SCDV) [5] for feature transformation of HTML contents, and LightGBM [6] where ensemble learning and random tree are combined for classification. In the following, let us give a brief explanation about each method.

FastText is one of the methods to convert words into distributed representation, and is one of the derivatives of Word2Vec [7]. Word2Vec learns a word embedding space with a neural network under the assumption that words that can be exchangeable each other in a sentence are located close to each other in the embedding space. It has been proved that such feature embedding gives high performance in document analysis. However, Word2Vec makes it difficult to learn words that appear infrequently and requires a huge amount of documents to obtain effective features. To alleviate this, FastText has been proposed. In FastText, we focus on the fact that the word itself contains morphological meaning, and a word can be decomposed into meaningful parts of word (i.e., sub words). Considering the co-occurrence of decomposed sub words, we can obtain an embedded vector space that introduces similarity between words with the same sub words. In this way, even with words that have a low frequency of occurrence, linguistic feature can be obtained by using sub words, and the amount of documents required for learning can be reduced.

FastText is a method to obtain word embedding vectors, not a feature representation for a document. Therefore, we adopt Sparse Composite Document Vectors (SCDV) that can generate document embedding vectors from the word embedding vector obtained by FastText. In SCDV, words are clustered, and the weighted average of word embedding vectors in a document is calculated using the probability of belonging to a cluster and Inverse Document Frequency (IDF) [8], and this is used as a document embedding vector.

Gradient Boosting Decision Tree (GBDT) [10], which combines gradient boosting with RandomForest [9]. More concretely, LGBM is composed of Gradient-based One-side Sampling (GOSS) for an active learning purpose and Exclusive Feature Bundling (EFB) for automatic feature selection. In GOSS, data with small gradients in each iteration are removed from training data as being well-trained. EFB finds sparse effective features that are often found in large-scale data by combining multiple exclusive features with non-zero elements into a single bundle. It also contributes to reducing the number of features and achieving faster computation.

3.2   Experiments

Experimental Setup. HTML contents used for evaluation were collected from web sites in the Tor network that were accessible as of January 10, 2019. In addition to the categories including malicious URLs shown in Table 3, 'Communication/Social category' dealing with anonymous mail service, encrypted chat service, etc., 'Cryptocurrencies' category dealing with wallet of bitcoin and

Table 4. Evaluated Web Site Categories.

Category	#Web pages
Adult/Porn	1246
Communication/Social	1753
Cryptocurrencies	1493
Empty/Error/Unknown	9527
Forums	2148
Hacking/Programming/Software	2063
Hosting	303
Libraries/Wikis	228
Market/Shops/Store	2157
Other	2108
Personal Sites/Blogs	2727
Scams	9085
Search	777
Security/Privacy/Encryption	2464
Whistle-blowing	342

mixing (a method to enhance the anonymity by mixing transactions of 'Cryptocurrencies'), and whistle-blowing dealing with underground information from journalists are added. The number of web pages in each category is shown in Table 4. In addition, categories with high risk including malicious URLs are considered as positive data which are categorized into 'Forums', 'Scams', 'Hacking/Programming/Software', and 'Libraries/Wikis'.

Experimental Results and Discussions. The developed system has the performance of 0.9523 in AUC, which means the classification of dangerous web pages is accurately conducted with less false positives. Table 5 shows the classification results for the dangerous prediction with the four performance scales (i.e., accuracy, precision, recall and F1-score). As seen from Table 5, the accuracy is relatively stable for different thresholds, which differentiate the LGBM prediction between positive (dangerous) and negative (safe). In contrast, the precision and recall have a trade-off property and the F1-score, a harmonic mean of precision and recall, is highest when the threshold value is 0.35.

Considering the actual operation, instead of F1-score, it might be appropriate to adopt the threshold as the key performance indicator (KPI), since security operators want to reduce the number of false-positives and do not want to miss dangerous sites significantly. An optimal threshold can be found by looking at the values of precision and recall. In this experiment, we can say that an optimal threshold would be 0.5.

Table 5. Performance of Dangerous web page classification.

	Threshold				
	0.30	0.35	0.40	0.45	0.50
Accuracy	0.8603	0.8647	0.8674	0.8720	0.8770
Precision	0.7557	0.7767	0.7996	0.8397	0.8605
Recall	0.8910	0.8640	0.8319	0.7992	0.7664
F1-score	0.8178	0.8180	0.8154	0.8146	0.8163

4   Conclusions

In this paper, under the WarpDrive project where a browser sensor of Chrome is developed to protect internet users from serious web-based attacks, the crawling of the dark web was performed in order to obtain information on malicious sites. The developed system automatically collects malicious URLs from the dark web and we evaluate the risk allowance of such sites based on the number of active detectors in the VirusTotal and Gred engines. In addition, in order to determine the category of malicious sites, we developed a system where FastText and SCDV are adopted to have document embedding vectors of the collected web pages and such embedding vectors are used for identifying dangerous sites with LightGBM. The experimental results show that the developed system attains the performance of 0.9523 in AUC, 0.8770 in accuracy, 0.7664 in recall, and 0.8664 in F1-score.

Here, we used external detection engines (i.e., VirusTotal and Gred engine) to judge the maliciousness of websites. However, it is known that there are quite a few malicious sites that are not even detected by state-of-the-art security engines. Therefore, it might be promising to judge the maliciousness of web sites not only by relying on the detection engine results but also by considering the malicious prediction using other information such as HTML contents and JavaScripts. This is left as our future work.

Acknowledgement. This research was supported by the Commissioned Research of National Institute of Information and Communications Technology (NICT) No. 190 and the Ministry of Education, Science, Sports and Culture, Grant-in-Aid for Scientific Research (B) 16H02874.

References

1. Syverson, P., Dingledine, R., Mathewson, N.: Tor: the second generation onion router. In: Usenix Security, pp. 303–320 (2004)
2. Nunes, E., et al.: Darknet and deepnet mining for proactive cybersecurity threat intelligence. In: IEEE Conference on Intelligence and Security Informatics, pp. 7–12 (2016)

3. Tavabi, N., Goyal, P., Almukaynizi, M., Shakarian, P., Lerman, K.: DarkEmbed: exploit prediction with neural language models. In: Thirty-Second AAAI Conference on Artificial Intelligence, pp. 7849–7854 (2018)
4. Bojanowski, P., Grave, E., Joulin, A., Mikolov, T.: Enriching word vectors with sub word information. Trans. Assoc. Comput. Linguist. **5**, 135–146 (2017)
5. Mekala, D., Gupta, V., Paranjape, B., Karnick, H.: SCDV: Sparse Composite Document Vectors using soft clustering over distributional representations. In: Proceedings of 2017 Conference on Empirical Methods in Natural Language Processing, pp. 659–669 (2017)
6. Ke, G., et al.: LightGBM: a highly efficient gradient boosting decision tree. In: Advances in Neural Information Processing Systems, pp. 3146–3154 (2017)
7. Mikolov, T., Sutskever, T., Chen, K., Corrado, G.S., Dean, J.: Distributed representations of words and phrases and their compositionality. In: Advances in Neural Information Processing Systems, pp. 3111–3119 (2013)
8. Robertson, S.: Understanding inverse document frequency: on theoretical arguments for IDF. J. Doc. **60**(5), 503–520 (2004)
9. Breiman, L.: Random forests. Mach. Learn. **45**(1), 5–32 (2001)
10. Friedman, J.H.: Greedy function approximation: a gradient boosting machine. Ann. Stat. **29**, 1189–1232 (2001)
11. Hispasec Sistemas S.L.: @miscvt, VirusTotal Public API v2.0 (2018). https://www.virustotal.com/en/documentation/public-api/
12. Bateman, A., Arcand, J.: Asynchronous I/O tricks and tips (2009)
13. Owens, M., Allen, G.: SQLite. Springer, Heidelberg (2010)
14. Mowery, K., Bogenreif, D., Yilek, S., Shacham, H.: Fingerprinting information in JavaScript implementations. Hydrol. Earth Syst. Sci. **19**(1), 137–157 (2015)

Paragraph-Level Hierarchical Neural Machine Translation

Yuqi Zhang(iD), Kui Meng, and Gongshen Liu(✉)(iD)

Shanghai Jiao Tong University, No. 800 Dongchuan Rood, Shanghai, China
{cici--q,mengkui,lgshen}@sjtu.edu.cn

Abstract. Neural Machine Translation (NMT) has achieved great developments in recent years, but we still have to face two challenges: establishing a high-quality corpus and exploring optimal parameters of models for long text translation. In this paper, we first attempt to set up a paragraph-parallel corpus based on English and Chinese versions of the novels and then design a hierarchical model for it to handle these two challenges. Our encoder and decoder take all the sentences of a paragraph as input to process the words, sentences, paragraphs at different levels, particularly with a two-layer transformer. The bottom transformer of encoder and decoder is used as another level of abstraction, conditioning on its own previous hidden states. Experimental results show that our hierarchical model significantly outperforms seven competitive baselines, including ensembles.

Keywords: Neural Machine Translation · Hierarchical structure · Paragraph parallel corpus · Natural language processing

1 Introduction

In the past few years, Neural Machine Translation (NMT) has seen great progress, especially in short-single-sentence translation. NMT model is mainly based on the encoder-decoder framework: the encoder compresses the input sentences of the source language into an abstraction from which the decoder generates target sentences. Since [20] introduced Multi-Head attention mechanisms to capture contexts in different semantic spaces, the transformer has become a dominant NMT architecture.

However, we still have to face two big challenges. First, the quality of machine translation mainly depends on the quantity and quality of the used corpus. Recently, many corpora that have been well studied are mostly based on TED Talks, Open Subtitles, news and so on. However, it seems that all of the open-source corpora employed in these studies are sentence-aligned even for document-level translation. But in the translation of paragraphs (from novels in our case), though the paragraphs are aligned between source and target languages, there are no strict alignments at sentence-level, which renders the models based the above open source corpora less applicable in this situation. Second, the performance of NMT for long text is still not ideal due to the reasons mentioned in [4].

© Springer Nature Switzerland AG 2019
T. Gedeon et al. (Eds.): ICONIP 2019, LNCS 11955, pp. 328–339, 2019.
https://doi.org/10.1007/978-3-030-36718-3_28

Recently, hierarchical structures used by some researchers [12,14] have shown a clear advantage in modeling paragraphs and documents. Unfortunately, these models cannot be directly used in paragraph parallel corpus since the numbers and orders of sentences in paragraph pairs are different.

To the best of our knowledge, this study is the first attempt to explore end-to-end paragraph level NMT based on the paragraph-parallel corpus. Our corpus is established on translated novels, which contributes to addressing the problem of data scarcity in NMT to some extent. To model our corpus, we propose a hierarchical model to get context from word-level and sentence-level abstractions in a structured manner. Specifically, we first segment the input paragraphs into a sequence of sentences. Second, we use hierarchical models based on transformers to capture the context from target and source languages. When encoding a paragraph, the sentence-level abstraction generated by the bottom encoder which will be further used as the input of the top encoder to generate paragraph-level abstraction. Correspondingly, in decoding, we use two layers of decoders, with the given paragraph abstraction as input, the paragraph-level decoder first generates the sequence of sentence-level abstraction. Second, the sentence-level decoder translates these sentences individually. In addition, the above two layers encoder and decoder can directly solve the problem of not aligned sentences in source and target language. In other aspects, the hierarchical encoder can effectively disambiguate the expression of source words, while the hierarchical decoder improves the cohesion and coherence of target words. In this way, our model will jointly optimize the translation of paragraphs, overcoming the difficulties in modeling paragraph-parallel corpus.

Our main contributions are summarized as follows:

1. We are the first to introduce paragraph-level corpus based on literary works (novels) into NMT. The corpus and code will be shared in GitHub.
2. Based on the two layers hierarchical encoder and decoder structure, we compress a whole paragraph to abstraction by two steps and then also decode it by two steps, from paragraph to sentences, then from sentences to words, which considering the whole paragraph for prediction.
3. According to the experimental results, our model significantly outperforms seven strong baselines, in translation tasks.

2   Related Work

In recent years, many researchers have tried to use models with a hierarchical structure in some of different NLP tasks, such as the auto-encoder in paragraph and document [12], translation for long sentences [8], query suggestion [17], dialogue modeling [16], and document classification [22]. Among these, based on our paragraph-parallel corpus, we introduce a two layers hierarchy transformer model, which is beneficial in parameter learning and context modeling in paragraph-translation.

Our work is related to the studies on segmenting long sentences into short ones, and [2] first explored dividing a sentence into a set of parts. Later, many criteria are proposed, such as N-gram, edit distance clues [5], and word alignment [21]. For the translation of long sentences, [8] adopt a two-level encoder model at word and clause levels. In order to build sentence alignments, [19] uses a distributed system to reliably mine parallel text from large corpora.

Nowadays, all the existing translation works of long texts are intended to capture contexts from either the source or target side. For document-level translation, in statistical machine translation (SMT), [18] provide a novel method for long distance, sentence-level reordering, and [7] translate with cross-sentential context. The cache-based approach is also introduced in document-level translation [6]. In NMT, [9] uses a hierarchical attention model to dynamically introduce document-level context into the NMT structure. And [13] takes both source and target contexts into account using memory networks.

In contrast, to the best of our knowledge, the paragraph-parallel corpus based on literary translations has never been investigated before in NMT. Although, in SMT, [19] use e-books as sources for machine translation data sets, while it is based on not end-to-end learning model. The most relevant models could be found include [9] and [8]. But these are always based on sentence aligned corpus, which is not that suitable for the translation of paragraph parallel corpus.

3   The Proposed Approach

Essentially, NMT is to maximize the likelihood of a sentence in the target language as sequence of words $\mathbf{y} = (y_1, y_2, \ldots, y_t)$ when given a sentence in source language in sequence $\mathbf{x} = (x_1, x_2, \ldots, x_n)$, i.e.:

$$\max_{\Theta} \frac{1}{N} \sum_{n=1}^{N} \log\left(P_\Theta\left(\mathbf{y}^n|\mathbf{x}^n\right)\right). \tag{1}$$

Thus, paragraph PARA translation is the combination of translating each individual sentences. Specially in this paper, we take into consideration the co-relations among all the sentences within a paragraph from both source and target languages.

$$\max_{\Theta} \frac{1}{N} \sum_{n=1}^{N} \log\left(P_\Theta\left(\mathbf{y}^n|\mathbf{x}^n, \mathbf{PARA}_{\mathbf{y}^T}, \mathbf{PARA}_{\mathbf{x}^n}\right)\right), \tag{2}$$

where $\mathbf{PARA}_{\mathbf{x}^n} = \left(\mathbf{x}^1, \ldots, \mathbf{x}^n\right)$ and $\mathbf{PARA}_{\mathbf{y}^T} = \left(\mathbf{y}^1, \ldots, \mathbf{y}^T\right)$ represent the sentences from source and target sides respectively. The contexts of $\mathbf{PARA}_{\mathbf{y}^n}$ and $\mathbf{PARA}_{\mathbf{y}^T}$ are constructed by the hierarchical encoder and decoder.

3.1   Corpus

In order to establish the corpus, we need to convert the formats of the bilingual e-books from pdf, mobi, epub, and azw3 to text, remove invalid words and scrambles, divide the bilingual texts into two separate single-language files, and

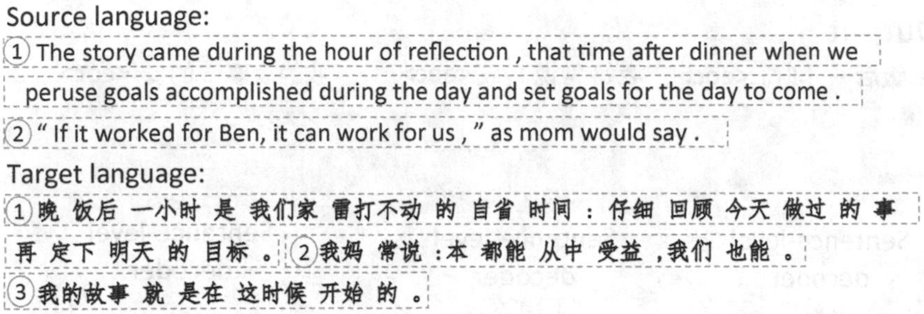

Source language:

① The story came during the hour of reflection , that time after dinner when we peruse goals accomplished during the day and set goals for the day to come .

② " If it worked for Ben, it can work for us , " as mom would say .

Target language:

① 晚 饭后 一小时 是 我们家 雷打不动 的 自省 时间 ： 仔细 回顾 今天 做过 的 事 再 定下 明天 的 目标 。 ② 我妈 常说 ：本 都能 从中 受益 ，我们 也能 。 ③ 我的故事 就 是在 这时候 开始 的 。

Fig. 1. An example of parallel paragraph in source language and target language. The dotted line frames represent the boundary of segmented sentences.

finally manually check and rearrange the sentence order within paragraphs to form the one-to-one correspondences between paragraph pairs.

Based on the proposed corpus, we segment the paragraphs to sentences in source and target language, as shown in Fig. 1, to fit the word-sentence-paragraph structure. The number and order of sentences in source and target language are different. It needs to be noted that we choose to divide the paragraphs into natural sentences rather than clauses, because sentences are usually single semantic blocks that could be easily matched between the original text and the translation, whereas clauses are more semantically complex with a little less poor performance than the one with sentences.

3.2 Hierarchical Transformer Encoder

The input paragraph $PARA$ is divided into T sentences, $PARA = (s_1, s_2, ...s_T)$, and s_j is made up of certain number of words. Specifically, $<eoc>$ is appended at the end of each sentence. As shown at the bottom of Fig. 2, we use the hierarchical encoder to model the input paragraph by two steps to a low-dimensional vector from which the two-layer decoders generate target sequences from paragraph to sentences, then from sentence to words.

We build our model based on the transformer model [20] for its high efficiency and accuracy in translation tasks. First, the bottom layer of our model operates at the word level, and generates abstraction of each sentence j into a vector s_j.

$$Q_w = F_w (h_t), \tag{3}$$

$$s_j = \text{MultiHead} \left(Q_w, h_i^j \right), \tag{4}$$

where h_t is the last hidden state of the word to be encoded or decoded at time t, h_i^j is the last hidden state of word i of sentence j. Function Fw is a linear transformation to get query Qw. The MultiHead attention function [20] can obtain of different semantic information within the sentence. The hidden representations h_i^j is used as value V and key K for this attention.

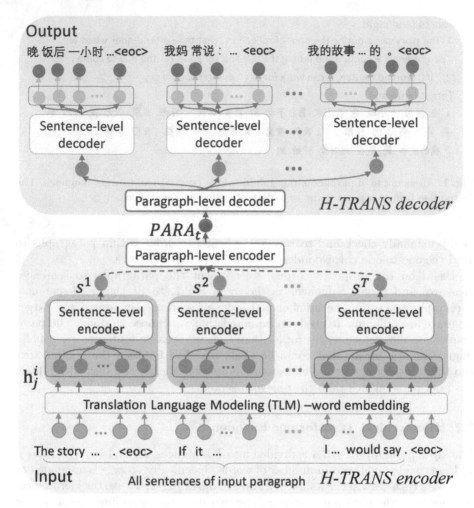

Fig. 2. Hierarchical NMT model at time step t. $\widetilde{h}_t$ is the hidden state for the word x_t.

And then the top layer of the model takes these sentences abstraction as input and works at the sentence level to obtain the abstraction of the entire input paragraph as $PARA_t$ at time t. The context $PARA_t$ that pays attention to all source sentences of the input paragraph.

$$Q_s = F_s\left(h_t\right), \tag{5}$$

$$PARA_t = \text{FFN}\left(\text{MultiHead}\left(Q_s, s_j\right)\right), \tag{6}$$

where F_s is a linear transformation, Q_s is the query, FFN is a position-wise feed-forward layer [20]. Each layer is followed by a normalization layer in the transformer. During the encoding and decoding, when the $<eoc>$ is detected at the end of a sentence, the translation process of this sentence terminates, and it moves on to the next sentence with a new h_{t+1}.

3.3   Hierarchical Transformer Decoder

Similar to conventional NMT [20], our decoder is based on two layers of transformers and trained to predict next word context representation sequentially with the considering of all the words of given paragraph $PARA_t$. As illustrated in Fig. 2, the translated paragraph contains M sentences, and with the given paragraph abstraction $PARA_t$, the paragraph-level decoder first generates the sequence of sentence-level abstraction $(s'_1, s'_2, ... s'_M)$. Second, the sentence-level decoder translate these sentences individually. For example, given s'_j, the sentence-level decoder then generates an output sequence $(y_1, y_2, ... y_m)$ of symbols one element at a time. In each step, the model is auto-regressive, containing the previously generated symbols as additional inputs when generating the next one.

3.4   Synthesis Model

When encoding or decoding a word, we can take the contexts from different scopes. The contexts are distinguished by the input *query Q* and *value V* of the function. In this study, five kinds of context are experimented: one in encoding, three in decoding, one combining both. In the process of encoding, *query* is the function of the hidden state h_{x_t} of the word x_t currently being encoded in the source side, and *values* are the states of all the encoded sentences in the same paragraph $h^j_{x_t}$ (*H-TRANS encoder*). In the process of decoding, *query* is the function of h_{y_t} of the currently decoded word y_t in target side, while the *values* can be of three states: the encoded states of $h^j_{x_t}$ (*H-TRANS decoder source*); the decoded states of sentences in target language $h^j_{y_t}$ (*H-TRANS decoder*); the alignment vectors [1] h^j_i (*H-TRANS decoder alignment*). Finally, our model (referred to as **H-TRANS-joint**) with the combination of hierarchical encoder and decoder is used to capture contexts from both target and source sides.

Notably, the non-segmented paragraphs can also be better translated with only one hidden state in the top transformer layer, as the overall parameters of our model have been optimized by training segmented paragraphs (as proved in Sect. 4.4). Thus, our model is suitable for all paragraph pairs.

4   Experiments

4.1   Corpus Establishing

We establish our paragraph-parallel corpus based on more than one hundred translated novels from English to Chinese, such as *The Wonderful Wizard of Oz, Robinson Crusoe, Little Women* etc., with a total of 114k bilingual paragraph pairs of 19.4M Chinese words and 20.2M English words. The building of the

Table 1. The Statistics of our proposed corpus (English-Chinese).

Language pairs (English-Chinese)	Training	Validation	Test
Number of parallel paragraph pairs	91.2K	11.4K	11.4K
Number of sentences in source language	186.1K	26.5K	24.3K
Kept parallel pairs (≤ 250) %	99.5%	99.1%	98.7%
Segmented paragraphs %	67.5%	74.6%	66.2%
Average number of sentences/paragraph	4.08	4.64	4.27

corpus involves a series of seemingly trivial tasks including converting the formats of the e-books, separating English and Chinese texts from the original bilingual contents, and wiping out the garbles generated during the process. The most troublesome is to manually rearrange the paragraph-pairs of the original texts and their translations as they are not strictly aligned at paragraph-level. With our great effort, the paragraph-parallel corpus based on more than one hundred novels are built and it will be shared in GitHub.

In order to better evaluate our model, we use MT track from TED Talks of IWSLT 2017 [3] which contains transcripts of TED talks aligned at sentence-level. Each talk is considered to be a paragraph here. We take *tst2016-2017 (En-Zh)* for testing and the rest for development.

4.2 Setup

We randomly set the ratio of training, verification, and test to 8:1:1 as shown in Table 1. We use the case insensitive 4-gram BLEU score [15] to evaluate the results and the script from Moses [11] to test the BLEU scores. The vocabulary size of Chinese and English is 90,000, and the words outside the vocabulary are marked as "unk". In addition, we keep the paragraph pairs with less than 250 words, covering 99.5% of our corpus, where the max sentence-number of paragraphs is six. And 81.8% of the input paragraph has less than 80 words of each.

We used the Open NMT [10] implementation of the transformer. The encoder and decoder are each made up of 6 hidden layers. All hidden states have a dimension of 512, dropout of 0.1 and heads of 8 for MultiHead attention. The optimization and regularization methods were the same as proposed by [20]. We trained the models in two steps: first, the network parameters are optimized without considering the whole paragraph, and then the parameters of the whole network are optimized.

4.3 Overall Performance

Our model referred to as **H-TRANS-joint**, is based on H-TRANS encoder and H-TRANS decoder to translate sentences considering the context information from source and target sides. It is compared to the following systems.

Table 2. BLEU scores for the different model based on our paragraph parallel English-Chinese corpus and English-Chinese TED Talks.

Models	Our corpus	TED Talks
TRANS (paragraph as input)	17.12 (baseline)	–
TRANS (sentence as input)	–	16.87 (baseline)
Bi-LSTM (attention)	16.02 (− 1.10)	16.01 (− 0.86)
Deep Conv+LSTM [23]	16.15 (− 0.97)	16.13 (− 0.74)
H-TRANS - encoder	18.30 (+ 1.18)	17.92 (+ 1.05)
H-TRANS - decoder	18.21 (+ 1.09)	17.73 (+ 0.86)
H-TRANS - decoder (source)	18.24 (+ 1.12)	17.86 (+ 0.99)
H-TRANS - decoder (alignment)	18.18 (+ 1.06)	17.67 (+ 0.80)
H-TRANS-joint	**19.44** (**+ 2.32**)	**18.21** (+ 1.34)

1. TRANS (paragraph as input): based on the normal transformer with the whole paragraphs as inputs to train the model.
2. Bi-LSTM (attention): base on the bidirectional LSTM model with input as whole paragraphs.
3. Deep Conv+LSTM [23] is made up of a deep convolutional network as an encoder and LSTM decoder with input as whole paragraphs.
4. H-TRANS encoder: based on two layers transformers as the encoder and one layer decoder to translate sentences sequentially.
5. H-TRANS decoder: based on the whole paragraph as input, one layer encoder and two layers transformer as the decoder. Three kinds of decoders have similar performance.

The overall experimental results of different models are evaluated by the BLEU score, based on our paragraph-parallel corpus and the document-level corpus from TED Talks. As shown in Table 2, *H-TRANS-joint* significantly outperforms *TRANS (paragraph as input)*, *Bi-LSTM (attention)* and *Deep Conv +LSTM*, by **2.32**, **3.42** and **3.29** BLEU scores on our corpus, respectively. In addition, our model also has better performance over the other seven baselines based on TED talks. Furthermore, the transformer performs better than the bidirectional LSTM and deep convolutional model.

Next, the test sets are divided into different groups according to the number of the sentence as shown in Fig. 3. We found that our model always outperforms other baselines when the input contains more than three sentences. Particularly, compared with *TRANS (paragraph as input)*, our model gains **2.33** BLEU points with no less than six sentences.

These results strongly prove that our model can better handle paragraph translation, while remains effective in dealing with sentences and non-segmented paragraphs. Because many long paragraphs have been divided into sentences, the parameters of the model are fine-tuned by these training data.

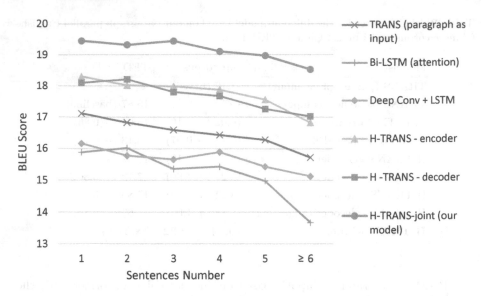

Fig. 3. BLEU scores on translation groups of different sentence-number of the input paragraph in source language based on our corpus.

4.4   Analysis on the Effect of Attention Mechanism

As shown in Table 2, we try to compare the influence of different contexts as mentioned in Sect. 3.4. Obviously, the model with a joint hierarchical encoder and decoder gets the best scores, which is significantly higher than the others. An important improvement comes from *H-TRANS-encoder* because the source language always contains the correct information, while the target language may have incorrect predictions. Using inter-clause context in decoder also improves the performance in translation. In addition, combining *H-TRANS-encoder* and *H-TRANS-decoder* can further improve the translation performance, which proves that we can get more information in a complementary way. The above-mentioned three kinds of contexts in decoder perform in a similar way.

4.5   Case Study

To better understand the advantages of our model, we compared the translation results of different models on our corpus, as shown in Table 3. In this case, the *TRANS (paragraph as input)*, *Bi-LSTM (attention)* and *Deep Conv+LSTM* often produce incorrect translation, incoherently translated sentences and some mistakes as well as repetitions in the translations, with the latter two models *Bi-LSTM (attention)* and *Deep Conv+LSTM* incorrectly overlooking some contexts. In *H-TRANS - encoder*, we also find some incorrect translations. And *H-TRANS - decoder* results in some incoherently translated sentences. In contrast, *H-TRANS-joint* is able to solve all these problems in translation to some extent.

Table 3. A translation example based on our corpus. Texts in red are incorrectly translated, in yellow are incoherently translated, in blue are correctly translated.

Source	And her insinuation that I was somehow abnormal because I hadn't yet been kissed infuriated me. None of my friends had boyfriends yet. The only girl at the Seattle Academy of Academic Excellence with any dating experience was Wendy Stupacker, who discovered boys in sixth grade—which certainly hadn't helped her procrastination any. Photographic memory and photogenic looks—tough life.
Reference	还有她含沙射影的说我不正常，就因为没接过吻。气死我了。我的朋友们也没男朋友呢。整个西雅图英才预科学校里，唯独一个女孩子有过约会经历：温迪司徒派克。她从六年级就开始接触男孩子了——竟然没影响成绩。她有过目不忘的记性，和一张让人过目不忘的脸——老天不公啊。
TRANS (paragraph as input)	她暗示我有点不正常，因为我还没有被吻unk。我的朋友还没有朋友。西雅图优秀学院唯一有约会经历的女孩是温迪UNK，她发现六年级的男生对她的拖延毫无帮助。摄影记忆和上镜看起来很艰难。
Bi-LSTM (attention)	而她批评说我很不寻常，因为我从来没有吻过UNK。我的朋友们都没有幽灵。只有浪漫的女孩在西雅图的UNK UNK大学经历学习成绩优秀时开眼睛，他 UNK UNK六年级的男性，是不是真的有助于避免。镜像和生活回忆的样子UNK。
Deep Conv+LSTM	而且她暗示我有些不正常，这是因为我还没有亲吻。我的朋友们都没有男朋友。任何约会经历都是温迪UNK，她是西雅图UNK学院唯一一位学术卓越的女性，谁在UNK找到男性，它并没有帮助任何迫害。照片记忆和上镜看起来很难的生活
+ H-TRANS-encoder	她暗示我有点不正常，因为我还没有被吻，这让我很生气。我的朋友都还没有男朋友。在西雅unk学院，唯一有过约会经历的女孩是温迪UNK，她在六年级时发现了男孩——这对她的拖延症毫无帮助。照片散的记忆和上镜的样子——艰难的生活
+ H-TRANS-decoder	而她的暗示，我有点不正常，因为我尚未被亲吻激怒了我。 我的朋友们都没有男朋友。 西雅图学术卓越学院唯一一位任何约会经历的女孩是温迪UNK，她在六年级时发现了男孩unk - 这当然没有帮助她拖延。 摄影记忆和上镜看起来坚韧的生活。
+ H-TRANS-joint	她含沙射影地说我有点不正常，因为我还没有被吻过，这激怒了我。我的朋友都没有男朋友。西雅图学术卓越学院唯一有约会经验的女孩是温迪UNK，她在六年级就发现了男孩-这对她的拖延毫无帮助。摄影记忆和照片相貌-艰难的生活。

5 Conclusion

To improve the performance of NMT in paragraph-level translation, we are the first to establish a paragraph parallel corpus and propose a hierarchical model. What distinguishes this study from previous ones is that a two-layer transformer model is applied in the encoder-decoder system to modify the input paragraph in a word-sentences-paragraph structure. As shown in the experimental results, our model significantly outperforms seven competitive baselines on our model and TED Talks. The study shows that the context from source and target can work in a complementary way to further improve translation performance. From the case study, it is found that our model can address most of the problems in paragraph translation to some extent.

In future work, we intend to explore the possibility of integrating an auto-encoder into our model to get a better abstraction of the sentences.

Acknowledgements. This research work has been funded by the National Natural Science Foundation of China (Grant No. 61772337, U1736207), and the National Key Research and Development Program of China No. 2016QY03D0604 and 2018YFC0830703.

References

1. Bahdanau, D., Cho, K., Bengio, Y.: Neural machine translation by jointly learning to align and translate. arXiv preprint arXiv:1409.0473 (2014)
2. Brown, P.F., Della Pietra, S.A., Della Pietra, V.J., Mercer, R.L., Mohanty, S.: Dividing and conquering long sentences in a translation system. In: Proceedings of the Workshop on Speech and Natural Language, pp. 267–271. Association for Computational Linguistics (1992)
3. Cettolo, M., Girardi, C., Federico, M.: WIT3: web inventory of transcribed and translated talks. In: Conference of European Association for Machine Translation, pp. 261–268 (2012)
4. Cho, K., Van Merriënboer, B., Bahdanau, D., Bengio, Y.: On the properties of neural machine translation: encoder-decoder approaches. arXiv preprint arXiv:1409.1259 (2014)
5. Doi, T., Sumita, E.: Splitting input sentence for machine translation using language model with sentence similarity. In: COLING 2004: Proceedings of the 20th International Conference on Computational Linguistics, pp. 113–119 (2004)
6. Gong, Z., Zhang, M., Zhou, G.: Cache-based document-level statistical machine translation. In: Proceedings of the Conference on Empirical Methods in Natural Language Processing, pp. 909–919. Association for Computational Linguistics (2011)
7. Hardmeier, C., Federico, M.: Modelling pronominal anaphora in statistical machine translation. In: IWSLT (International Workshop on Spoken Language Translation), Paris, France, 2nd–3rd December 2010, pp. 283–289 (2010)
8. Su, J., Zeng, J., Xiong, D., Liu, Y.: A hierarchy-to-sequence attentional neural machine translation model. IEEE/ACM Trans. Audio Speech Lang. Process. **26**(3), 623–632 (2018)
9. Li, J., Luong, M.T., Jurafsky, D.: Document-level neural machine translation with hierarchical attention networks. In: EMNLP 2018 (2018). arXiv preprint arXiv:1809.01576. version 2
10. Klein, G., Kim, Y., Deng, Y., Senellart, J., Rush, A.M.: OpenNMT: open-source toolkit for neural machine translation. arXiv preprint arXiv:1701.02810 (2017)
11. Koehn, P., Hoang, H., Birch, A., Callison-Burch, C.: Moses: open source toolkit for statistical machine translation. In: Proceedings of the 45th Annual Meeting of the Association for Computational Linguistics Companion Volume Proceedings of the Demo and Poster Sessions, pp. 177–180 (2007)
12. Li, J., Luong, M.T., Jurafsky, D.: A hierarchical neural autoencoder for paragraphs and documents. arXiv preprint arXiv:1506.01057 (2015)
13. Maruf, S., Haffari, G.: Document context neural machine translation with memory networks. arXiv preprint arXiv:1711.03688 (2017)

14. Miculicich, L., Ram, D., Pappas, N.: Document-level neural machine translation with hierarchical attention networks. arXiv preprint arXiv:1809.01576 (2018)
15. Papineni, K., Roukos, S., Ward, T., Zhu, W.J.: BLEU: a method for automatic evaluation of machine translation. In: Proceedings of the 40th Annual Meeting on Association for Computational Linguistics, pp. 311–318. Association for Computational Linguistics (2002)
16. Serban, I.V., Sordoni, A., Bengio, Y., Courville, A., Pineau, J.: Building end-to-end dialogue systems using generative hierarchical neural network models. In: Thirtieth AAAI Conference on Artificial Intelligence (2016)
17. Sordoni, A., Bengio, Y., Vahabi, H., Lioma, C., Grue Simonsen, J., Nie, J.Y.: A hierarchical recurrent encoder-decoder for generative context-aware query suggestion. In: Proceedings of the 24th ACM International on Conference on Information and Knowledge Management, pp. 553–562. ACM (2015)
18. Sudoh, K., Duh, K., Tsukada, H., Hirao, T., Nagata, M.: Divide and translate: improving long distance reordering in statistical machine translation. In: Proceedings of the Joint Fifth Workshop on Statistical Machine Translation and Metrics-MATR, pp. 418–427. Association for Computational Linguistics (2010)
19. Uszkoreit, J., Ponte, J.M., Popat, A.C., Dubiner, M.: Large scale parallel document mining for machine translation. In: Proceedings of the 23rd International Conference on Computational Linguistics, pp. 1101–1109. Association for Computational Linguistics (2010)
20. Vaswani, A., et al.: Attention is all you need, pp. 5998–6008 (2017)
21. Xu, J., Zens, R., Ney, H.: Sentence segmentation using IBM word alignment model 1. In: Proceedings of EAMT, pp. 280–287 (2005)
22. Yang, Z., Yang, D., Dyer, C., He, X., Smola, A., Hovy, E.: Hierarchical attention networks for document classification. In: Proceedings of the 2016 Conference of the North American Chapter of the Association for Computational Linguistics: Human Language Technologies, pp. 1480–1489 (2016)
23. Zhou, J., Cao, Y., Wang, X., Li, P., Xu, W.: Deep recurrent models with fast-forward connections for neural machine translation. Trans. Assoc. Comput. Linguist. 4, 371–383 (2016)

Residual Connection-Based Multi-step Reasoning via Commonsense Knowledge for Multiple Choice Machine Reading Comprehension

Yixuan Sheng and Man Lan[✉]

School of Computer Science and Technology, East China Normal University,
Shanghai 200062, People's Republic of China
51164500026@stu.ecnu.edu.cn, mlan@cs.ecnu.edu.cn

Abstract. Generally, the candidate options for multiple choice machine reading comprehension (MRC) are not explicitly present in the document and need to be inferred from text or even from the world's knowledge. Previous work endeavored to improve performance with the aid of commonsense knowledge or using multi-step reasoning strategy. However, there is no model adopt multi-step reasoning with external commonsense knowledge information to solve multiple choice MRC, and two shortcomings still remain unsolved, i.e., external knowledge may involve undesirable noise and only the latest reasoning step makes contribution to the next reasoning. To address the above issues, we propose a multi-step reasoning neural network based on the strong Co-Matching model with the aid of commonsense knowledge. Firstly, we present a sentence-level knowledge interaction (SKI) module to integrate commonsense knowledge with corresponding sentence rather than the whole MRC instance. Secondly, we present a residual connection-based multi-step reasoning (RCMR) answer module, which makes the next reasoning depending on the integration of several early reasoning steps rather than only the latest reasoning step. The comparative experimental results on MCScript show that our single model achieves a promising result comparable to SOTA single model with extra samples and specifically achieves the best result for commonsense type questions.

Keywords: Machine reading comprehension · Question answering · Attention · Multi-step reasoning · Commonsense knowledge

1 Introduction

Unlike span-based or cloze-style machine reading comprehension (MRC) tasks (e.g., SQuAD [1], CNN/DailyMail [2]) locating the span of answer in given document, multiple choice MRC selects the right answer from multiple candidate choices (i.e. options). Thus for the first two MRC tasks, their answers must appear in the given document. However, for multiple choice MRC most options

© Springer Nature Switzerland AG 2019
T. Gedeon et al. (Eds.): ICONIP 2019, LNCS 11955, pp. 340–352, 2019.
https://doi.org/10.1007/978-3-030-36718-3_29

are not explicitly present in the document and need to be inferred from the given document or even from the world's knowledge. Thus the questions of multiple choice MRC can be divided into two types according to the source from which their answers can be inferred: (1) "text" type questions which can be answered or inferred from the given document and (2) "commonsense" type questions which need to be reasoned with the aid of external knowledge.

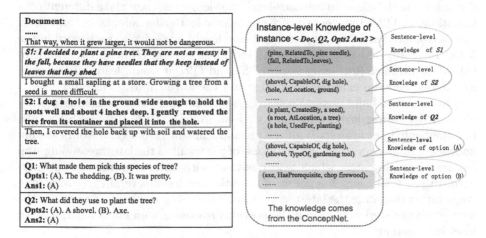

Fig. 1. Two types of questions and one MRC instance <**Doc, Q2, Opts2, Ans2**> from MCScript dataset with two types of related knowledge, i.e., sentence-level knowledge is external knowledge relevant to one specific sentence, and instance-level knowledge is relevant to one given MRC instance, which includes all sentence-level knowledge.

Figure 1 shows one "text" type question **Q1** and one "commonsense" type question **Q2** from the MCScript dataset [3]. **Q1** can be easily answered by sentence $S1$ (in green) in document. But the answer to **Q2** is not mentioned in given document. We need to both use the information of $S2$ (in blue) (i.e., the author digs a hole during planting tree) and the external knowledge (i.e., **a shovel is used to dig holes**) together to reason out that they plant the tree with a **shovel**.

On the one hand, most existing multiple choices MRC models focus on solving the "text" type questions [4–8] through attention mechanism to enrich the text representations for answer prediction. Among them, Co-Matching [6] is a strong model, which concurrently makes the interaction in between document and question and the interaction in between document and option, in order to obtain strong integrated representation among document, question and option. These studies have insufficient reasoning ability when answering "commonsense" type questions due to lack of assistance of external knowledge. More recently, several studies explore the ways of external knowledge usage. One line of research implicitly transfer external knowledge (i.e., ConceptNet [9]) in word embedding (e.g., TriAN [10], GCN [11]) or even augment training dataset with extra samples from similar domain (TriAN [10]). Another line explicitly transfer additional knowledge to each word in MRC instance after context encoding to solve the cloze-style MRC task (e.g., Knowledgeable Reader [12]). However, one shortcoming of these work using external knowledge is that external commonsense knowledge may bring in undesirable noise as well. This can be observed in Fig. 1, given the MRC instance <**Doc, Q2, Opts2, Ans2**>, the related knowledge of $S1$ (e.g., "(pine, RelatedTo, pine needle)") and of $S2$ (e.g., "(shovel, CapableOf, dig hole)") both belong to instance-level knowledge but they make different contributions to **Q2**. However, since Knowledgeable Reader adopts instance-level knowledge interaction (i.e. interact instance-level knowledge to each word in the MRC instance) and combines the related knowledge of $S1$ with each word in this MRC instance (including words of $S2$ and **Q2**), it would lead to inaccurate interaction between external knowledge and the words in MRC instance.

On the other hand, several researchers explore multi-step reasoning mechanism in the answer layer of MRC (e.g., ReasoNet [7], DFN [13] and SAN [14]) but they only infer answers from the given document rather than from external knowledge. Moreover, they only make use of the result of the latest reasoning step for next reasoning step, which is inconsistent with human experience for inference. In practical cases, human would use the results of several early reasoning steps rather than only the latest step to make next step reasoning. Otherwise the next reasoning step would fail if the previous reasoning step infers incorrectly or loses information.

In this paper, to address the above two issues, we propose a novel residual connection-based multi-step reasoning neural networks with the aid of commonsense knowledge to solve the multiple-choice MRC. Specifically, we design a sentence-level knowledge interaction module (SKI) to interact sentence-level external knowledge with each word in corresponding sentence, then a residual connection-based multi-step reasoning module (RCMR) to improve the reasoning ability of the model in dealing with "commonsense" type questions. Meanwhile, in order to solve the "text" type questions, we implement our model based on the strong Co-Matching model [6]. The main contributions of our work are summarized as follows:

- **Knowledge.** To our knowledge, this is the first work to treat external commonsense knowledge beyond instance-level alone but leverage its relevance to individual sentence and interaction with words in the corresponding sentence.
- **Reasoning.** To our knowledge, this is the first work to adopt multi-step reasoning with external commonsense knowledge model to address multiple choice MRC task. And we add residual connections to multi-step reasoning module to integrate several early reasoning results, rather than only the latest result, for the next reasoning step.

2   Related Work

Most existing multiple choice MRC models [4–8] still struggle with the "text" type questions by designing various attentions for semantic matching between the given texts and enriching representation of the given texts. For example, Co-Matching [6] matches the document with the question and an option concurrently to get a strong representation of the Furthermore, several works explore the multi-step reasoning in MRC models [7,13–15]. For example, GA Reader [15] integrates question and document multiple times by an attention mechanism. SAN [14] applies a stochastic prediction dropout on multi-step reasoning answering layer. ReasoNet [7] and DFN [13] use reinforcement learning to determine how many reasoning steps to take. These models rely on the latest reasoning result to make the next reasoning, not make use of results from previous steps to reason in the next step. And they only use the given texts information to reasoning without external commonsense knowledge help.

Although the models above achieve promising results on "text" type questions, the ability of these models is still limited when answering the "commonsense" type questions. In order to solve the "commonsense" type questions, one research line is implicitly transfer external knowledge by enhancing the word embeddings [10,11] or training model parameters with extra datasets [10]. Another study line is explicitly transfer external knowledge into the model. For example, Knowledgeable Reader [12] explicitly fuses external instance-level knowledge to each word in the MRC instance after context encoding to solve the cloze-style MRC task.

3   Problem Statement

3.1   Task Definition

In multiple choice MRC, given an MRC instance $<D, Q, OP>$, the task outputs an option from the candidate options set OP as correct answer, where the document $D = \{w_{i,j}^D\}_{j=1}^m$, the question $Q = \{w_j^Q\}_{j=1}^n$, the candidate options set OP contains y options $op = \{w_j^{op}\}_{j=1}^l$, $w_{i,j}^D$ represents the j-th word of the i-th sentence in the document, the document has p sentences, w_j^Q and w_j^{op} represents the j-th word of the question and the candidate option, respectively. Since the questions and options are short, we treat each of them as a sentence.

3.2   Commonsense Knowledge

Knowledge is usually stored in the graphical structure and represented by a knowledge triple $k = (subj, rel, obj)$, where $subj$ and obj are terms that contain at least one word, and rel is the relationship between $subj$ and obj defined by the knowledge graph. In our work, we use ConceptNet[1][9] as an external commonsense knowledge source, which is a large graph-structured commonsense knowledge base built from OMCS[2], Open Multilingual WordNet [16],

---

[1]   http://www.conceptnet.io/.
[2]   http://www.openmind.org/commonsese.

OpenCyc[3], DBPedia[4], JMDict[5], Wiktionary[6], and "Games with a purpose" [17–19]. An example from ConceptNet is: $(shovel, CapableOf, dig\ hole)$.

3.3 Sentence-Level Knowledge Construction

Since there are a lot of commonsense knowledge triples in ConceptNet, we use four steps to build sentence-level knowledge sets associated with each sentence of the MRC instance. We first retrieve the triples whose $subj$ or obj contain at least one word (except stopwords) in the MRC instance. Second, we heuristically score these triples via Eqs. (1) and (2) to evaluate relevance between triples and instance, and then rank them via their scores to select top T triples:

$$score_k = (score_{subj} + score_{obj}) * weight \tag{1}$$

$$weight = \frac{count((subj \cup obj) \cap (D \cup Q \cup OP))}{count(sub) + count(obj)}, \tag{2}$$

where $score_k$ is the score of a triple k, $score_{subj}$ is the score of the $subj$ in the k, $score_{subj}$ has four values, i.e., 4: if $OP \cap subj \neq \emptyset$; 3: else if $Q \cap subj \neq \emptyset$, 2: else if $D \cap subj \neq \emptyset$. 0: else if $(D \cup Q \cup OP) \cap subj = \emptyset$. Same for $score_{obj}$. In Eq. (2), $count()$ means the number of words. We think that if more words in $subj$ and obj appear in the MRC instance means the triple is more relevant to MRC instance, so this triple has a higher weight. Third, we set the amount of triples per options to be the same in order to avoid knowledge frequency bias [12], and the remaining triples are grouped into instance-level knowledge set K'. Finally, we use the same method in the first step to retrieve the triples from the set K' to construct the sentence-level knowledge set $K_i^D = \{k_{i,1}, k_{i,2}..., k_{i,km}\}$, $K^Q = \{k_1, k_2, ..., k_{kn}\}$ and $K^{op_o} = \{k_1, k_2, ..., k_{kl}\}$ for each sentence in D, Q or $op_o(o \in [1, y])$, respectively. Where K_i^D is the knowledge set of the i-th sentence of D, km means the number of triples, kn and kl means the number of triples of the question and the o-th candidate option in OP, respectively.

4 Our Model

In this section, we introduce the base model Co-Matching and two proposed modules of our model, i.e. SKI and RCMR.

4.1 The Co-Matching Model

The Co-Matching model reads an MRC instance $<D, Q, OP>$ as the input. For each candidate option $op_o(o \in [1, y])$ in OP, the model get a co-matching state by jointly matching the Q and op_o to the D concurrently. Then, the model use

---

[3] https://www.cyc.com/opencyc/.
[4] https://wiki.dbpedia.org/.
[5] http://www.edrdg.org/jmdict/.
[6] https://www.wiktionary.org.

the co-matching states to predict answer. Co-Matching model consists of five layers, i.e. Embedding Layer, Encoding Layer, Interaction Layer, Modeling layer and Answer Layer.

Embedding Layer. Embedding Layer converts each word of the input to the vector space. Co-Matching model use the pre-trained GloVe embedding [20]. Differently, we concatenate GloVe embedding with the binary match features, which can be described as: if the word appears in D, in Q, in $op_o (o \in [1, y])$, in both Q and op_o, and in Q or op_o. So we get $\mathbf{E}_i^D = \{e_{i,j}^D\}_{j=1}^m$, $\mathbf{E}^Q = \{e_j^Q\}_{j=1}^n$, $\mathbf{E}^{op_o} = \{e_j^{op_o}\}_{j=1}^l$, where $e = [e_{glove}, e_{feature}]$, "[,]" means concatenate.

Encoding Layer. A bi-directional LSTM (biLSTM) is used to encode context information for all words in the each sentence of D, the Q and each option, respectively. Then we get $\mathbf{H}_i^D = \{h_{i,j}^D\}_{j=1}^m$, $\mathbf{H}^Q = \{h_j^Q\}_{j=1}^n$, $\mathbf{H}^{op_o} = \{h_j^{op_o}\}_{j=1}^l$. Where $h_{i,j}^D, h_j^Q$ and $h_j^{op_o} \in \mathbb{R}^{1 \times 2hdim}$, $hdim$ is the hidden size of the biLSTM.

Interaction Layer. This layer enables the model to focus on the relevant parts of the document, questions and an option by attention mechanism. The Co-Matching model plays attention on each sentence of the document with both the question and the candidate option concurrently.

$$\widetilde{\mathbf{H}}_i^Q = Attmodule(\mathbf{H}_i^D, \mathbf{H}^Q, \mathbf{H}^Q), \widetilde{\mathbf{H}}_i^{op_o} = Attmodule(\mathbf{H}_i^D, \mathbf{H}^{op_o}, \mathbf{H}^{op_o}) \quad (3)$$

Then, $\widetilde{\mathbf{H}}_i^Q$ and $\widetilde{\mathbf{H}}_i^{op_o}$ are concatenated to get a co-matching state of $C_{i,o}^D = [\widetilde{\mathbf{H}}_i^Q, \widetilde{\mathbf{H}}_i^{op_o}]$. And for all sentences in D, we have a co-matching states set $\{C_{1,o}^D, C_{2,o}^D, ..., C_{p,o}^D\}$.

Modeling Layer. The base model uses the hierarchical LSTM [21] to modeling the $\{C_{1,o}^D, C_{2,o}^D, ..., C_{p,o}^D\}$ into a vector d^{op_o}.

Answer Layer. For each candidate option, Co-Matching build a co-matching states set through above layers. The probability of each option to be the answer is computed as follows:

$$pro(op_o|D, Q) = \frac{exp(w_1 d^{op_o} + b_1)}{\sum_{x=1}^y exp(w_1 d^{op_x} + b_1)} \quad (4)$$

where op_o means o-th option in the candidate options set $\mathbf{OP}$, y is the number of candidate options, w_1 and b_1 are trainable parameters.

4.2 Attention Mechanism

The $Attmodule(Query, Key, Value)$ above refers to the attention mechanism calculated with specific $Query$, Key and $Value$ inputs, which can be summarize as mapping a query and a key-value pair to an output [6, 22, 23] and calculated as follow:

$$V_{att} = softmax(QueryKey^T)Value \quad (5)$$

$$Att(Query, Key, Value) = ReLU(W[V_{att} - Query, V_{att} * Query] + b) \quad (6)$$

where $Query \in \mathbb{R}^{u \times dim}$ is u dim-dimensional vector, Key and $Values \in \mathbb{R}^{v \times dim}$ are both v dim-dimensional vectors, $V_{att} \in \mathbb{R}^{u \times dim}$. W and b are trainable parameters, "$-$" and "$*$" are element-wise operation. ReLU is a non-linear activation function. The attention mechanism is very important in MRC, because it allows the model to selectively focus on the relevant parts of the document, the question and the option.

4.3   Sentence-Level Knowledge Interaction Module (SKI Module)

In order to solve the "commonsense" type questions, we decide to enrich the representations of the given texts with their related commonsense knowledge. Figure 2 provides an overview of our proposed model architecture.

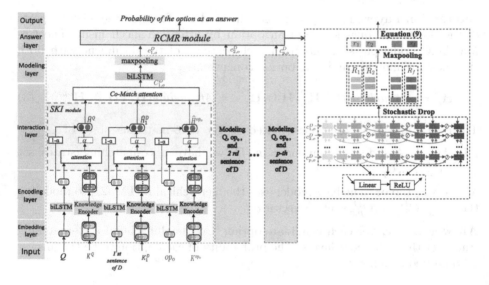

Fig. 2. An overview of our model that modeling the D, the Q and the op_o, and their corresponding sentence-level knowledge K_i^D, K^Q and K^{op_o}.

We design a sentence-level knowledge interaction module (SKI module) in interaction layer before calculating co-matching states.

Input: Different from the Co-Matching, the input of our model add the sentence-level knowledge sets build in Sect. 3.3. For each knowledge triple in the sets, we map each word into embedding as descript above. To ensure the representation vector of each knowledge triple in the same vector space as D, Q, OP, we encode each knowledge triple by the method in Mihaylov et al. [12] that use biLSTM to encode $subj$, rel and obj in each triple respectively. Hence, we get h^{subj}, h^{rel}, and h^{obj} for each triple. Example with K_i^D, we have $H_i^{Dsubj} = \{h_{i,j}^{subj}\}_{j=1}^{km}$, $H_i^{Drel} = \{h_{i,j}^{rel}\}_{j=1}^{km}$ and $H_i^{Dobj} = \{h_{i,j}^{obj}\}_{j=1}^{km}$. Where $h_{i,j}^{subj}$, $h_{i,j}^{rel}$ and $h_{i,j}^{obj}$ are represents $subj$, *rel* and *obj* of j-th triple in K_i^D, respectively. Same for the K^Q and K^{op}. Then, we send encoded triples and encoded text in to SKI module.

SKI Module: The SKI module employs attention mechanism to calculate the sum of weighted sentence-level related knowledge triples to represents each word in the corresponding sentence. Example with j-th word $h_{i,j}^D$ in i-th sentence of document, we use Eq. (7) to calculate the sum of weighted knowledge triples representation $\bar{h}_{i,j}^D$:

$$\bar{h}_{i,j}^D = Attmodule(h_{i,j}^D, H_i^{Dsubj}, H_i^{Dobj}) \tag{7}$$

Then, we use context encoded representation $h_{i,j}^D$ and the sum of weighted knowledge triples representation $\bar{h}_{i,j}^D$ to obtain $\widehat{h}_{i,j}^D$ (Eq. (8)). So $\widehat{h}_{i,j}^D$ contains information of the word in the context that encoded by biLSTM and information from related sentence-level external commonsense knowledge.

$$\widehat{h}_{i,j}^D = \alpha * \bar{h}_{i,j}^D + (1 - \alpha) * h_{i,j}^D \tag{8}$$

where $\alpha \in \mathbb{R}^{1 \times hdim}$ is a trainable vector that randomly initialized.

We do the same operations for the words in the Q and each option. Hence, we can get $\widehat{\mathbf{H}}_i^D = \{\widehat{h}_{i,j}^D\}_{j=1}^m$, $\widehat{\mathbf{H}}^Q = \{\widehat{h}_j^Q\}_{j=1}^n$ and a candidate option $\widehat{\mathbf{H}}^{op_o} = \{\widehat{h}_j^{op_o}\}_{j=1}^l$. Thus, we can use $\widehat{\mathbf{H}}_i^D$, $\widehat{\mathbf{H}}^Q$ and $\widehat{\mathbf{H}}^{op_o}$ to calculate co-matching states instand of using $\mathbf{H}_i^D$, $\mathbf{H}^Q$ and $\mathbf{H}^{op_o}$.

4.4 Residual Connection-Based Multi-step Reasoning Module (RCMR Module)

To improve the reasoning ability of the model and make full use of reasoning results for next reasoning, we propose a residual connection-based multi-step reasoning module (RCMR) to replace the answer layer.

Input: The input of the RCMR module is also different from the original Co-Matching, at the modeling layer, we only use a layer biLSTM followed by a maxpooling layer to model matrix $C_{i,o}^D$ into a sentence vector $c_{i,o}$, all the sentence vectors in the D consist of matrix $\{c_{i,o}^D\}_{i=1}^p$.

RCMR Module: As shown in Fig. 2, we use multi-layer biLSTMs to infer the information from $\{c_{i,o}^D\}_{i=1}^p$. In the multi-layer biLSTMs, we add residual connections to some reasoning steps (The arcs with an arrow in Fig. 2, which represents a linear layer followed by ReLU). "⊘" in Fig. 2 means the element-wise average of two vectors. We obtain the N-steps reasoning results through the N layers biLSTM. To avoid a "step bias problem" [14] , we use the stochastic prediction dropout [14] on the N-steps reasoning results. Thus, we get f reasoning results $\{R_1, R_2, ...R_f\}$ after the stochastic prediction dropout. We perform maxpooling on these results respectively to make each reasoning result into a vector

$\{r_1, r_2, ..., r_f\}$. Then we calculate the probability of each option to be the correct answer according to the formula below:

$$pro(op_o|D, Q) = Avg(\sum_{t=1}^{f} \frac{exp(w_2 r_t^{op_o} + b_2)}{\sum_{x=1}^{y} exp(w_2 r_t^{op_x} + b_2)}) \tag{9}$$

Equation (9) means that we use the inference results in $\{r_1, r_2, ..., r_f\}$ to calculates the probability of op_o as the answer respectively, and then averages these probabilities to get the final probability of op_o.

5   Experiments

5.1   Dataset

We evaluate on the MCScript [3]. According to the dataset paper, about 70% of the questions in MCScript can be answered or inferred from the given documents, and about 30% of the questions require commonsense inference. Therefore, we apply this dataset to verify the effectiveness of the proposed model. Table 1 shows the statistics of MCScript. We use accuracy to evaluate the model performance. "#" represent the number of questions.

Table 1. Statistics of train, dev and test data.

Dataset	Documents	Questions		
		#text	#commonsense	#all
train	1,470	7,032	2,699	9,731
dev	219	1,006	405	1,411
test	430	2,074	723	2,797

5.2   Preprocessing and Training Details

For data preprocessing, we use Stanford CoreNLP[7] to perform tokenization, lowercase, and lemmatization. And we adjust the following hyper-parameters according to the performance on the MCScript development set. For each instance, we select the top 50 knowledge triples from the ranking results. We use 300-dims pre-trained GloVe [20] word vectors concatenate with 8-dims features as initial word embedding, which is fixed during training. Each question in the MCScript has 2 options, so the features are 8-dims, i.e., if the word in D, Q, op_1, op_2, $Q\&op_1$, $Q\&op_2$, $Q\|op_1$, $Q\|op_2$. The relationships (rel) of triples from ConceptNet are represented by 308-dimensional random initialization vectors. The hidden size of biLSTMs in encoding layer and answering layer is 150-dims. The objective function is Cross Entropy. We use Adamax [24] with an initial

---
[7]   https://stanfordnlp.github.io/CoreNLP/.

learning rate of 0.002 to update parameters and a minibatch size is 10 for each update. We run all the models up to 50 epochs. To avoid overfitting, dropout with probability 0.4 is adopted for embedding layer and encoding layer. We use 8-steps reasoning answer layer, residual connect every three steps, and the probability of stochastic dropout is 0.4. Our model is implemented with PyTorch[8].

5.3   Results

Table 2 shows the results of our model and other models on MCScript. We achieve 81.73%(accuracy) on the test dataset, which is competitive compared to the SOTA single model (TriAN) with extra training samples and the ensemble model (MITRE). The accuracy on "text" and "commonsense" types questions are 82.11% and 80.64%, respectively. Obviously, our model achieves the best result of the "commonsense" question compared to the other models.

Table 2. Results on the MCScript test set. "–" indicates not available. † is our run on source code provided by author.

Models	Extra training samples	Ensemble	Test		
			text(%)	commonsense(%)	all(%)
Human Performance [3]	–	–	–	–	98.20
Random [3]	No	No	50.00	50.00	50.00
Sliding Window [3]	No	No	55.70	53.10	55.00
Bilinear Model [3]	No	No	69.80	71.40	70.20
Attentive Reader [3]	No	No	70.90	75.20	72.00
GCN [11]	No	No	–	–	78.97
Co-Matching† [6]	No	No	81.21†	77.03†	80.01†
HMA [25]	No	No	–	–	80.94
TriAN w/o extra training samples [10]	No	No	80.61†	80.05†	80.44†
TriAN [10]	**Yes**	No	–	–	81.94
MITRE [26]	No	**Yes**	**83.00**	79.00	**82.27**
MITRE(NN-T) [26]	No	No	–	–	80.23
MITRE(NN-GN) [26]	No	No	–	–	80.12
MITRE(LR) [26]	No	No	–	–	79.66
Our model	No	No	**82.11**	**80.64**	**81.73**

The first four models are the experimental benchmark models on MCScript [3]. Co-Matching is our base model.[9] HMA [25], TriAN [10] and MITRE [26] are the top three models in SemEval-2018 Task 11 [10]. Compared with MITRE, the accuracy of our model is 0.54% lower than MITRE for "all" questions, maybe MITRE ensemble three kinds of different submodels. The accuracy of our single

---

[8] https://github.com/pytorch/pytorch.

[9] We use the code on https://github.com/shuohangwang/comatch to implement Co-Matching model. But one difference is that we add binary features to the word embedding.

[10] The ensemble results of the HMA and the TriAN were 84.13% and 83.95% in SemEval-2018 Task 11, respectively. Table 2 shows the results of their single models.

model is higher than MITRE submodels (i.e., NN-T, NN-GN and LR). Furthermore, the accuracy of our model is 1.64% higher than MITRE for "commonsense" type questions[11]. Compared with TriAN, the accuracy of our model is 0.21% lower than TriAN. The reason maybe TriAN not only uses ConceptNet as an external knowledge source but also uses extra training samples (RACE [28]). However, our model only uses ConceptNet. And the accuracy of our model is 1.29% higher than TriAN without extra training samples. As for "commonsense" type questions, the accuracy of our model is 0.59% higher than TriAN without extra training samples[12].

5.4 Analysis

We perform ablation experiments to verify the SKI and RCMR modules are positively contributed to our model, the results are shown in Table 3. Compare the results of "Our model" and "Our model w/o SKI&RCMR", we observe the accuracy decrease by 1.02%, 3.47%, 1.64% on "text", "commonsense", and "all" types questions, respectively. These results show that the two proposed modules are useful, and our model achieves a comfortable margin on the "commonsense" type questions than the baseline model.

Table 3. Our model ablation experiments on the MCScript test set.

Models	text(%)	commonsense(%)	all(%)
Our model	**82.11**	**80.64**	**81.73**
Our model replace SKI with IKI	81.67	79.52	81.12
Our model w/o SKI	81.43	78.83	80.76
Our model replace RCMR with MR	81.73	79.81	81.23
Our model w/o RCMR	81.29	78.99	80.70
Our model w/o SKIR&RCMR	81.09	77.17	80.09

The Impact of SKI Module. Removing SKI results in 0.68%, 1.81% and 0.97% point accuracy drop on "text", "commonsense", and "all" questions, respectively. The results reveal that external commonsense knowledge plays an important character in answer reasoning. To show the effectiveness of SKI, we compared the SKI with the IKI (i.e. we implemented instance-level knowledge interaction method in Knowledgeable Reader). Compare the results of "Our model" and "Our model replace SKI with IKI" on the "commonsense" type of question, SKI module leads to an improvement of 1.12%over the IKI module. This result illustrates the SKI module contributes towards the model's performance since it interacts words with more relevant external knowledge.

---

[11] The "commonsense" type questions accuracy of MITRE is reported in reference [27].

[12] We use the code on https://github.com/intfloat/commonsense-rc to implement TriAN model.

The Impact of RCMR Module. Removing the RCMR module perform with 0.82%, 1.65%, and 1.03% decrease on the accuracy of "text", "commonsense", and "all" questions, respectively. This illustrates the RCMR module is useful. And in order to check whether the residual connections are valid in multi-step reasoning, we remove the residual connections in the RCMR module and retain the remaining multi-step reasoning (MR) module for experimentation (i.e. "Our model replace RCMR with MR"). The result on "all" types questions shows that MR leads to a reduction of 0.5% over the RCMR module, which indicates that making each step of reasoning not only rely on the latest reasoning results by adding residual connections on multi-step reasoning is helpful.

6 Conclusion and Future Work

In this paper, we propose an residual connection-based multi-step reasoning MRC model that using commonsense knowledge to solve multiple choice MRC task. The proposed SKI and RCMR modules improve the accuracy of "commonsense" type questions. However, compared with human performance, there is still a lot of room for improvement. In future work, we would explore more on how to infer using external knowledge for MRC tasks.

References

1. Rajpurkar, P., Zhang, J., Lopyrev, K., Liang, P.: SQuAD: 100,000+ questions for machine comprehension of text. In: EMNLP, pp. 2383–2392 (2016)
2. Hermann, K.M., et al.: Teaching machines to read and comprehend. In: NIPS, pp. 1693–1701 (2015)
3. Ostermann, S., Modi, A., Roth, M., Thater, S., Pinkal, M.: MCScript: a novel dataset for assessing machine comprehension using script knowledge. In: LREC (2018)
4. Zhu, H., Wei, F., Qin, B., Liu, T.: Hierarchical attention flow for multiple-choice reading comprehension. In: AAAI (2018)
5. Parikh, S., Sai, A.B., Nema, P., Khapra, M.M.: ElimiNet: a model for eliminating options for reading comprehension with multiple choice questions. In: IJCAI, pp. 4272–4278 (2018)
6. Wang, S., Yu, M., Jiang, J., Chang, S.: A co-matching model for multi-choice reading comprehension. In: ACL, pp. 746–751 (2018)
7. Shen, Y., Huang, P.-S., Gao, J., Chen, W.: ReasoNet: learning to stop reading in machine comprehension. In: SIGKDD, pp. 1047–1055 (2017)
8. Tang, M., Cai, J., Zhuo, H.H.: Multi-matching network for multiple choice reading comprehension. In: AAAI (2019)
9. Speer, R., Chin, J., Havasi, C.: ConceptNet 5.5: an open multilingual graph of general knowledge. In: AAAI, pp. 4444–4451 (2017)
10. Wang, L., Sun, M., Zhao, W., Shen, K., Liu, J.: Yuanfudao at SemEval-2018 task 11: three-way attention and relational knowledge for commonsense machine comprehension. In: SemEval, pp. 758–762 (2018)

11. Chen, W., Quan, X., Chen, C.: Gated convolutional networks for commonsense machine comprehension. In: Cheng, L., Leung, A.C.S., Ozawa, S. (eds.) ICONIP 2018. LNCS, vol. 11301, pp. 297–306. Springer, Cham (2018). https://doi.org/10.1007/978-3-030-04167-0_27

12. Mihaylov, T., Frank, A.: Knowledgeable reader: enhancing cloze-style reading comprehension with external commonsense knowledge. In: ACL, pp. 821–832 (2018)

13. Xu, Y., Liu, J., Gao, J., Shen, Y., Liu, X.: Dynamic fusion networks for machine reading comprehension. arXiv preprint arXiv:1711.04964 (2017)

14. Liu, X., Shen, Y., Duh, K., Gao, J.: Stochastic answer networks for machine reading comprehension. In: ACL, pp. 1694–1704 (2018)

15. Dhingra, B., Liu, H., Yang, Z., Cohen, W., Salakhutdinov, R.: Gated-attention readers for text comprehension. In: ACL, pp. 1832–1846 (2017)

16. Bond, F., Foster, R.: Linking and extending an open multilingual wordNet. In: ACL, pp. 1352–1362 (2013)

17. Kuo, Y.-L., et al.: Community-based game design: experiments on social games for commonsense data collection. In: Proceedings of the ACM SIGKDD Workshop on Human Computation, pp. 15–22. ACM (2009)

18. Nakahara, K., Yamada, S.: Development and evaluation of a web-based game for common-sense knowledge acquisition in Japan. Unisys Technol. Rev. 30(4), 295–305 (2011)

19. Von Ahn, L., Kedia, M., Blum, M.: Verbosity: a game for collecting common-sense facts. In: Proceedings of the SIGCHI Conference on Human Factors in Computing Systems, pp. 75–78. ACM (2006)

20. Pennington, J., Socher, R., Manning, C.D.: Glove: global vectors for word representation. In: EMNLP, pp. 1532–1543 (2014)

21. Tang, D., Qin, B., Liu, T.: Document modeling with gated recurrent neural network for sentiment classification. In: EMNLP, pp. 1422–1432 (2015)

22. Vaswani, A., et al.: Attention is all you need. In: NIPS, pp. 5998–6008 (2017)

23. Tai, K.S., Socher, R., Manning, C.D.: Improved semantic representations from tree-structured long short-term memory networks. In: ACL, pp. 1556–1566 (2015)

24. Kingma, D.P., Ba, J.: Adam: a method for stochastic optimization. arXiv preprint arXiv:1412.6980 (2014)

25. Chen, Z., Cui, Y., Ma, W., Wang, S., Liu, T., Hu, G.: HFL-RC system at SemEval-2018 task 11: hybrid multi-aspects model for commonsense reading comprehension. arXiv preprint arXiv:1803.05655 (2018)

26. Merkhofer, E., Henderson, J., Bloom, D., Strickhart, L., Zarrella, G.: MITRE at SemEval-2018 task 11: commonsense reasoning without commonsense knowledge. In: SemEval, pp. 1078–1082 (2018)

27. Ostermann, S., Roth, M., Modi, A., Thater, S., Pinkal, M.: SemEval-2018 task 11: Machine comprehension using commonsense knowledge. In: SemEval, pp. 747–757 (2018)

28. Lai, G., Xie, Q., Liu, H., Yang, Y., Hovy, E.: Race: large-scale reading comprehension dataset from examinations. arXiv preprint arXiv:1704.04683 (2017)

Zero-Shot Transfer Learning Based on Visual and Textual Resemblance

Gang Yang[✉] and Jieping Xu

Key Lab of Data Engineering and Knowledge Engineering,
Renmin University of China, Beijing, China
{yanggang,xjieping}@ruc.edu.cn

Abstract. Existing image search engines, whose ranking functions are built based on labeled images or wrap texts, have poor results on queries in new, or low-frequency keywords. In this paper, we put forward the zero-shot transfer learning (ZSTL), which aims to transfer networks from given classifiers to new zero-shot classifiers with little cost, and helps image searching perform better on new or low-frequency words. Content-based queries (i.e., ranking images was not only based on their visual looks but also depended on their contents) can also be enhanced by ZSTL. ZSTL was proposed after we found the resemblance between photographic composition and the description of objects in natural language. Both composition and description highlight the object by stressing the particularity, so we consider that there exists a resemblance between visual and textual space. We provide several ways to transfer from visual features into textual ones. The method of applying deep learning and Word2Vec models to Wikipedia yielded impressive results. Our experiments present evidence to support the existence of resemblance between composition and description and show the feasibility and effectiveness of transferring zero-shot classifiers. With these transferred zero-shot classifiers, problems of image ranking query with low-frequency or new words can be solved. The image search engine proposed adopts cosine distance ranking as the ranking algorithm. Experiments on image searching show the superior performance of ZSTL.

Keywords: Transfer learning · Zero-shot learning · Deep learning

1 Introduction

In natural languages, people distinguish one object from another by identifying the differences between them. As a result, these differences become features, which are set up for distinguishing objects [1]. Features in natural languages

G. Yang—This work was supported by the Beijing Natural Science Foundation (No. 4192029), and the National Natural Science Foundation of China (61773385, 61672523). We gratefully acknowledge the support of NVIDIA Corporation with the donation of the Titan Xp used for this research.

T. Gedeon et al. (Eds.): ICONIP 2019, LNCS 11955, pp. 353–362, 2019.
https://doi.org/10.1007/978-3-030-36718-3_30

usually exist in definitions or descriptions of objects, e.g. "the cat is probably a Persian cat, because of its long white fur". These visual features in natural language play a constructive role in how humans learn to classify objects.

As for the object recognition in machine learning, the usual method is to train a model with training data, which should satisfy the following requirements: (1) each sample should include an expert labeled image; (2) its size should be big enough to make the model be able to converge [2]. However, the limitations are: (1) expert labeling is expensive; (2) Some classes have few training data, it is too hard for classifiers to recognize it. Under these limitations, zero-shot learning and transfer learning show their talents: zero-shot learning can automatically label the unlabeled data in the neighborhood, while transfer learning can transfer the known information to different fields, thus it can scale down the necessary training data and shorten the training time [3].

Zero-shot learning has received a growing amount of attention recently [4]. Zero-shot learning is inherently a two stage process: training and inference. In the training stage, knowledge about the attributes is captured, and in the inference stage, this knowledge is used to categorize instances among a new set of classes [5]. The key to zero-shot learning is the use of a set of semantic embedding vectors associated with the class labels. These semantic embedding vectors might be obtained from human-labeled object attributes, or they might be learned from a text corpus in an unsupervised fashion, based on an independent natural language modeling task [6].

Zero-shot learning has succeeded in labeling the data without training data set on all classes. According to Lampert's research [7], zero-shot learning can label the unlabeled data based on humans concluded features. They find out that humans concluded features play a constructive role in the object conjecture in zero-shot learning. So far, Norouzi and Li's research [6,8] has made some achievements: they used natural language model to widen the label field of the model, thus labelling the unlabeled data which is similar to the labeled data in semantic. Also, it showed the efficiency of using natural language model for zero-shot learning.

Zero-shot learning resembles the use of human knowledge scattered in semantic space to widen the existing classifier's recognition range within the same category: e.g. make a dog breed classifier able to recognize more breeds of dog without more training data. Moreover, the information in the language model is more than the neighborhood information, e.g. the information among similar various categories [9,10].

For these various categories, we make an assumption that there exists some categories sharing similar distribution in semantic space. The assumption is based on the human regularity that people use similar features to classify similar categories. For example, in the classification of cat breeds, the somatotype, the coat color and the fur length are all important indexes, which are also used in dog classifications. Based on this assumption, we conjecture that language model can help us transfer classifying knowledge between categories, which makes transfer classifier become possible. Simultaneously, considering the continuity of semantic space, we can obtain a multi-category classifier with the efficiency of zero-shot learning and broader applicable scope at a very low cost. We name the method as zero-shot transfer learning (ZSTL).

In the image retrieval area, ZSTL can improve the image retrieval of the categories with few image samples, the low frequency or unlabeled words and new words. Like humans describe objects by features, photographers tend to emphasis subjects in picture composition, that is: (1) the subject shows in the salient position. (2) The subject has salient feature [11]. The common composition method makes it possible to transfer visual feature to semantic feature [12]. In this paper, we first utilize the common composition method to form a zero-shot transfer learning module, which will bridge the visual space and textual space.

2 Zero-Shot Transfer Learning

2.1 Problem Statement

The methods used to search images on the Internet are based on the similarity of visual content. However, it is difficult to rank images just according to their similarity of content in semantic space. Moreover, if there are rarely tags, or even no exact tags, relative to some images, searching them will be extra difficult. In order to accomplish image searching based on visual content, a neat idea is to transform from visual features into semantic features to simplify the searching process, which has performed well in natural language processing.

Here our research focuses on converting visual features to textual features, which can improve the quality of image ranking according to content similarity. What's more, it can help transfer a classifier into another zero-shot one by a few target labels. In image searching, when users submit an image to search for the information it contains, such as the name of the object in the image, it will be a very difficult job, if this image was not used to train the classifier. Similarly, quite a few zero-shot learning methods are not fit for large visual space. Thus, we not only focus on the thought of zero-shot learning, but also highlight the key of transfer learning in large expression domain.

In this paper, we propose the zero-shot transfer learning to solve the problems above. The target of zero-shot transfer learning is to build a classifier containing few or no training data through applying another known similar classifier (e.g. building a classifier of tiger based on a classifier of cat). To meet this aim, we convert the known image classifier into a textual feature extractor, and transform its output space into somewhere near target labels' textual space.

Base on our observations of images, we make an assumption that the structure of source and the target labels are similar in natural language, which means it is possible that their semantic feature space share the similar distribution with the textual feature space through non-linear transformation.

More formally, let x denotes a image, y denotes a label, and $p(y-x)$ denotes a classifier. Given a known classifier p_{train} on data set $D_{train} = \{(x_i, y_i)\}_{i=1}^{n_{train}}$ where n_{train} stands for the size of train data set, we aim to build a classifier p_T

on test set $D_T = \{(x_i, y_i)\}_{i=1}^{n_T}$, and give a label set $L_{target} \subset \{y_i | (x_i, y_i) \in D_T\}$ as target, where $\{y_i | (x_i, y_i) \in D_{train}\} \cap \{y_i | (x_i, y_i) \in D_T\} = \emptyset$ and n_T stands for the size of test set. In Sect. 2.2, we transform p_{train} into p_T using the similarity in semantic space, and introduce a way to improve it by a fine tuning net described in Sect. 2.3.

2.2   The Transfer Model

Our target is to transfer a classifier into another one which is in a new semantic space. The similarity of semantic space would help our model transfer. That is to say, we expect $\{y_i | (x_i, y_i) \in D_T\}$ and $\{y_i | (x_i, y_i) \in D_{train}\}$ to have similar distribution in different semantic space. The semantic transfer part [13] embedded in our transfer model assumes that each label $y \in \{y_i | (x_i, y_i) \in D_{train}\} \cup \{y_i | (x_i, y_i) \in D_T\}$ can be presented with a semantic vector $s(y)$, $S \in R^k$, where k denotes the dimensions of semantic feature space. The semantic space is continuous, which helps transfer extensively. In the semantic space, two words are similar only if they have short distance corresponding to semantic features. To reach the target transferring p to p_T, there are three problems needed be handled: 1. Find a way to transform visual features into semantic features. 2. Find a method of shifting semantic features into a specified space. 3. Find a strategy of ranking labels based on similarity.

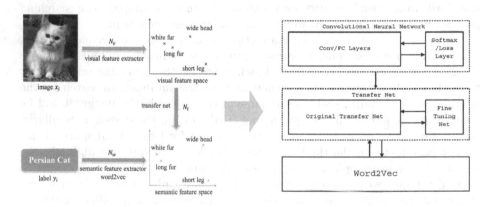

Fig. 1. Zero-Shot transfer learning model.

Transfer Net. For problem 1, we designed a transfer neural network to transform visual features, as shown in Fig. 1. The transfer net has four layers: 1 inputting layer, 2 hidden layers and 1 outputting layer. Nodes of the hidden layer constructed a 1024-1024 architecture. We denote the transfer net as N_t, denote convolutional neural network (CNN) based visual feature extractor as N_v, and denote semantic feature extractor word2vec as N_w. Let $x'_i = N_t(N_v(x_i)), y'_i = N_w(y_i), (x_i, y_i) \in D_{train}, n = |D_{train}|$, the loss function is defined as

$$loss_t(i) = -\frac{1}{k} \sum_{j=1}^{k} [y'_{i,j} ln x'_{i,j} + (1 - y'_{i,j}) ln(1 - x'_{i,j})] \tag{1}$$

Feature Shifting. The problem 2 is how to shift features into target semantic space. An obvious way is to shift the source center into target center. Equation 2 evaluates the shifting effect.

$$V_s = \frac{1}{|L_{target}|} \sum_{l \in L_{target}} N_w(l) - \frac{1}{|L_o|} \sum_{l \in L_o} N_w(l) \tag{2}$$

Here $L_o = \{y_i | (x_i, y_i) \in D_{train}\}$, and we denote $N_t(N_v(x)) + V_s$ as shifted semantic feature.

Word2Vec. As for an image x to be labeled, our method is to rank word vectors in word2vec model according to cosine distances of $N_t(N_v(x)) + V_s$, and export Top-10 words as potential labels.

2.3 Transfer Model with Fine-Tuning

If a small data set $D_{tuning} \neq \emptyset$ ($D_{tuning} \subset D_T$) is used, the fine tuning net can enhance feature transformation. The previous work has strict requirement for semantic space, which makes the model perform inefficiently. The strict requirement is: the source label space and the target space should share an exactly same distribution, with only the concept center being different. Obviously, as it is hard to find the concept matches in the semantic space, a fine tuning net is applied to fit the source space for the target space. Using the method of transferring model with fine tuning, the problem is redefined as follows: let $x'_i = mN_t(N_v(x_i)) + b, y'_i = N_w(y_i)$ and $(x_i, y_i) \in D_{tuning}$; defining loss function

$$loss_f(i) = -\frac{1}{k} \sum_{j=1}^{k} [y'_{i,j} ln(x'_{i,j}) + (1 - y'_{i,j}) ln(1 - x'_{i,j})] \tag{3}$$

and minimizing $loss_f$ to build the fine tuning net, with $m \in R^{k \times k}, b \in R^k$. In our model, we use gradient descent to optimize.

3 Empirical Evaluation

3.1 Dataset

Our visual data set was obtained from *image.google.com*, which contained 9,336 images in 31 classes with plenty of noisy images. The data set can be retrieved at *http://bit.ly/1Rv0NVA*. In order to study how training data set affects our transfer model, we used two different training datasets to study our visual feature extractor. One data set was about 80% animals images (7,468 images in 31 classes), and the other one included 80% of dog images (4,034 images in 13 breeds). The feature extractor trained by the first data set was used to extract common features of animals, and specially, the feature extractor formed by the second dog data set focused on producing the features of different dog breeds. Meanwhile, we used the second data set to train our transfer net to build different breed mappings. Furthermore, as English Wikipedia is one of the largest encyclopedia and it has much analogous expression space with human being, it was selected to train our word2vec model. In the experiment, Wikipedia helped word2vec build a comprehensive semantic space, and it was comprehensive enough to build a global express space, in which the visual feature can be transferred reasonably.

3.2 Platform Setup

We chose two outstanding convolutional neural networks, AlexNet [14] and GoogleNet [15], to demonstrate the influence of visual feature extractor upon our transfer model. We trained our model on Caffe with GPU. We used Theanets, based on Theano, to train our transfer net and fine tuning net.

3.3 Experiments

We studied three problems through lots of the experiments to reveal the regularity of zero-shot transfer learning: (1) Verify the resemblance between visual space and semantic space. (2) Verify the effectiveness of feature transfer. (3) Check the result of transfer model, and make comparisons between different settings.

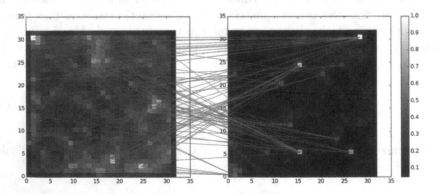

Fig. 2. Self organizing feature map (SOM) of visual feature (left) and semantic feature (right), with lines showing 100 samples. (Color figure online)

To verify the resemblance between visual space and semantic space, we utilized the self-organizing feature map (SOM) to build the mapping relationship between image visual feature and tagging semantic feature. Through summarizing the statistics of a large number of training data, we formed some interesting mappings that clearly revealed the resemblance among different spaces. In our experiment, we built two coordinate systems. one represented the visual feature space, and the other represented the semantic feature space. From D_{train}, we randomly selected 100 samples, each one of which had two attributes(the visual features and the semantic features). For example, assume that one of the 100 samples is "Persian cat" and one of its attributes is the visual features, like "white fur", "long fur", "wide head" and "short leg", which are depicted in pictures. The other attribute of this sample is semantic features, like "white fur", "long fur", "wide head" and "short leg", which are depicted through words and phrases. After the 100 samples were selected, we mapped their attributes into the two coordinate systems we built in the beginning. Therefore, each sample was represented by a point in the coordinate systems. For each sample, we matched its two attributes in two coordinate systems by drawing a red line to connect the two points. So far, we had 100 red lines, as shown in Fig. 2, revealing the correlative objects between visual space and semantic space. It showed that the clustering results of visual features and semantic features were similar, which means it is quite possible that resemblance exists between visual and semantic space. In addition, the distance relationships are also included in two different spaces, which is helpful in assisting image searching by similarity computation.

Table 1. Top-5 labels (the correct label is shown in **bold**)

Test image	Feature shifting	Fine-tuning
	american_shorthair	**british_shorthair**
	maine_coon	american_shorthair
	japanese_bobtail	exotic_shorthair
	devon_rex	devon_rex
	british_shorthair	cornish_rex
	devon_rex	british_shorthair
	british_shorthair	**exotic_shorthair**
	american_shorthair	american_shorthair
	egyptian_mau	devon_rex
	cornish_rex	japanese_bobtail
	american_shorthair	british_shorthair
	devon_rex	**exotic_shorthair**
	japanese_bobtail	american_shorthair
	maine_coon	devon_rex
	exotic_shorthair	cornish_rex

Feature transfer relies on mapping the relationship between different spaces. To achieve feature transfer, a transfer network, as shown in Fig. 1, is proposed to reveal the mapping according to the resemblance of visual and semantic space. The transfer network are constructed with multiple full-connection layers. We trained the transfer network by the dog breeds training data set. After conducting a series of experiments, we gladly found out that the result turned out to be impressive. The mean-squared error in the results was less than 0.185%. Then we tested feature shifting and fine tuning models, and we chose three representative results, as shown in Table 1, to demonstrate the quality of our models. In the first column of Table 1, three pictures of three different-breed cats are shown, which served as the test image of our model. On the right, we listed the top-5 results for each sample picture, and the two columns are results produced by applying the feature shifting model and the fine tuning method. Compared with the results of feature shifting model, the results of fine tuning model are more accurate, so it shows: (1) The visual feature strongly affects the results of transfer learning, because complex visual features like the second cat example in Table 1 produce worse feature shifting results. (2) The fine tuning net can enhance our model greatly, as the correct label of the second cat was ranked at the second position through applying the fine tuning model.

Table 2. Performance of different models (best results are shown in **bold**)

CNN Model	CNN training set	Transfer model	Fine tuning set size	Top-k(accuracy%)		
				1	5	10
AlexNet	80% of whole data	Feature shifting	–	7.66	32.74	71.26
AlexNet	80% of dog breeds	Feature shifting	–	6.60	33.21	70.01
AlexNet	80% of whole data	Fine-tuning net	100 in 3 labels	8.51	37.62	75.85
AlexNet	80% of dog breeds	Fine-tuning net	100 in 3 labels	**9.19**	**40.27**	**76.88**
AlexNet	80% of whole data	Fine-tuning net	500 in 5 labels	5.64	33.97	71.37
AlexNet	80% of dog breeds	Fine-tuning net	500 in 5 labels	6.73	35.99	71.40
GoogLeNet	80% of whole data	Feature shifting	–	8.12	36.83	71.89
GoogLeNet	80% of dog breeds	Feature shifting	–	9.05	31.92	68.89
GoogLeNet	80% of whole data	Fine-tuning net	100 in 3 labels	8.59	**39.53**	**78.60**
GoogLeNet	80% of dog breeds	Fine-tuning net	100 in 3 labels	8.78	38.90	77.21
GoogLeNet	80% of whole data	Fine-tuning net	500 in 5 labels	4.12	32.22	36.65
GoogLeNet	80% of dog breeds	Fine-tuning net	500 in 5 labels	**10.01**	33.45	69.66

Meanwhile, we would like to find out the performance of our transfer network under different circumstances. In the beginning, we set up various conditions, including different CNN networks, CNN training set, transfer model, and the size of fine tuning set (if we chose the fine tuning as the transfer model). These conditions were carefully designed to control variables, as shown in Table 2, which assured that the results are helpful when we compared one to another to find out the influence of the single variable. The variables could be divided into the internal factors and the external ones. On one hand, the transfer model and the size of fine tuning set was the internal factor, because it was set up before we started training. On the other hand, various visual features and sensitivity of the training data set are the external cause, as they could affect the robustness and accuracy of the transfer net.

In Table 2, the three columns on the right demonstrate the results of those 12 models, with the best ones labeled in bold, revealing the influence of numerous properties upon the zero-shot transfer learning. The results of fine tuning net are better averagely than the ones of feature shifting, which verifies the conclusion of the previous experiment. Moreover, the results of choosing dog breeds as training data set mostly outperform the ones of using the whole data to train our models, which indicate that the semantic feature space should be transformed to fit for specific breeds. Because the visual space is more complex than semantic space, the fine tuning net is sensitive to the data set, and we should utilize a preferable image data set to fit for specific image searchings. As for the size of fine tuning set, 100 in 3 labels have averagely better results.

4   Conclusions

This paper reveals the resemblance between visual and textual features and proposes the zero-shot transfer learning model (ZSTL). Differ from zero-shot learning and transfer learning, ZSTL has an advantage that it is able to convert visual features to semantic features, which further helps the feature transformation in semantic space. Our model is capable of transferring a classifier into a new classifier with zero-shot samples. Meanwhile, the transformed semantic feature can be used to help labels rank by computing similarity on cosine distance. This property solves the problem of image querying with rare images or new low-frequency keywords. Through conducting numerous experiments, ZSTL has been validated to be effective on the image querying. We believe ZSTL provides an inspired way for the semantic space transformation and image querying. In the near future, we will extend our approach to research how to adapt the domain shift problems which is widely existing in zero-shot learning.

References

1. Farhadi, A., Endres, I., Hoiem, D., Forsyth, D.: Describing objects by their attributes. In: IEEE Conference on Computer Vision and Pattern Recognition, CVPR 2009, pp. 1778–1785. IEEE (2009)
2. Mitchell, T.M., et al.: Machine learning, vol. 45, no. 37, pp. 870–877. McGraw Hill, Burr Ridge (1997)
3. Larochelle, H., Erhan, D., Bengio, Y.: Zero-data learning of new tasks. In: AAAI, vol. 1, p. 3 (2008)
4. Rohrbach, M., Stark, M., Schiele, B.: Evaluating knowledge transfer and zero-shot learning in a large-scale setting. In: 2011 IEEE Conference on Computer Vision and Pattern Recognition (CVPR), pp. 1641–1648. IEEE (2011)
5. Romera-Paredes, B., Torr, P.: An embarrassingly simple approach to zero-shot learning. In: International Conference on Machine Learning, pp. 2152–2161 (2015)
6. Norouzi, M., et al.: Zero-shot learning by convex combination of semantic embeddings. arXiv preprint arXiv:1312.5650 (2013)
7. Lampert, C.H., Nickisch, H., Harmeling, S.: Learning to detect unseen object classes by between-class attribute transfer. In: IEEE Conference on Computer Vision and Pattern Recognition, CVPR 2009, pp. 951–958. IEEE (2009)

8. Li, X., Liao, S., Lan, W., Du, X., Yang, G.: Zero-shot image tagging by hierarchical semantic embedding. In: Proceedings of the 38th International ACM SIGIR Conference on Research and Development in Information Retrieval, pp. 879–882 (2015)

9. Socher, R., Ganjoo, M., Manning, C.D., Ng, A.: Zero-shot learning through cross-modal transfer. In: Advances in Neural Information Processing Systems, pp. 935–943 (2013)

10. Palatucci, M., Pomerleau, D., Hinton, G.E., Mitchell, T.M.: Zero-shot learning with semantic output codes. In: Advances in Neural Information Processing Systems, pp. 1410–1418 (2009)

11. Torralba, A., Murphy, K.P., Freeman, W.T.: Sharing visual features for multiclass and multiview object detection. IEEE Trans. Pattern Anal. Mach. Intell. **29**(5), 854–869 (2007)

12. Feng, Y., Lapata, M.: Visual information in semantic representation. In: Human Language Technologies: The 2010 Annual Conference of the North American Chapter of the Association for Computational Linguistics, Association for Computational Linguistics, pp. 91–99 (2010)

13. Mikolov, T., Chen, K., Corrado, G., Dean, J.: Efficient estimation of word representations in vector space. arXiv preprint arXiv:1301.3781 (2013)

14. Krizhevsky, A., Sutskever, I., Hinton, G.E.: ImageNet classification with deep convolutional neural networks. In: Pereira, F., Burges, C., Bottou, L., Weinberger, K. (eds.) Advances in Neural Information Processing Systems 25, pp. 1097–1105. Curran Associates, Inc., New York (2012)

15. Szegedy, C., et al.: Going deeper with convolutions. In: Proceedings of the IEEE Conference on Computer Vision and Pattern Recognition, pp. 1–9 (2015)

Morphological Knowledge Guided Mongolian Constituent Parsing

Na Liu[1,2,3], Xiangdong Su[1,2(✉)], Guanglai Gao[1,2],
Feilong Bao[1,2], and Min Lu[1,2]

[1] Inner Mongolia Key Laboratory of Mongolian Information Processing
Technology, Hohhot, China
[2] College of Computer Science, Inner Mongolia University, Hohhot, China
cssxd@imu.edu.cn
[3] Department of Science, Hetao University, Bayannur, China

Abstract. Mongolian constituent parsing is a challenging task due to lack of hand-annotated corpus and rich morphological varying. This paper takes a self-attention neural network to deal with Mongolian constituent parsing, which follows an encoder-decoder architecture. Concerning the syntactic functions of morphemes in Mongolian words, we make morphological analysis on each word and learn a novel word representation on such basis. To fully utilize the morphological knowledge, we adopt the last suffix tag of each word in the input embedding instead of its POS. The input embedding is the accumulation of word representation, the last suffix tag and the word position. The test experiment demonstrates that our model significantly outperforms the previous Mongolian constituent parsers. We achieve 87.16% $F1$ on the development set and 86.23% $F1$ on the test set.

Keywords: Mongolian constituent parsing · Morphological analysis · Word representation

1 Introduction

Constituent parsing is a fundamental task in natural language processing (NLP), such as machine translation and question answering. The goal of constituent parsing is to obtain the syntactic structure of sentences expressed as a phrase structure tree [1]. For example, given the sentence in Fig. 1, a parser maps it into a parenthesized version of the constituent parse tree.

Mongolian is an agglutinative language which words are formed by attaching suffixes to stem. There are two kinds of scripts Mongolian: traditional Mongolian and an Cyrillic Mongolian. In this work, we address the constituent parsing of traditional Mongolian. This kind of script and its Latinize letters are shown in Fig. 1. The internal morphological of Mongolian words, relatively fixed position of the central word and sentence form provide the theoretical basis for building traditional constituent parsers. Therefore, a lot of morphological rules [2–6] are annotated manually, which require a lot of domain knowledge and consume a lot of time. However, even so, comparing its performance with the Chinese or English, there is still a very big promotion space.

© Springer Nature Switzerland AG 2019
T. Gedeon et al. (Eds.): ICONIP 2019, LNCS 11955, pp. 363–375, 2019.
https://doi.org/10.1007/978-3-030-36718-3_31

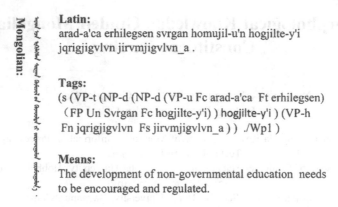

Fig. 1. Example of Mongolian, Latin trans literature, constituent parsing tags and the sentence meanings.

In recent years, deep learning based constituent parsers have shown excellent performance without handcraft features [1, 7–10]. Recently, Kitaev et al. [9] presented a new state-of-the-art parsing approach which relies on a self-attentive encoder and a chart decoder. However, it is extremely hard for training a neural parser with large scale parameters only dependent on a small size of Mongolian annotated corpus. Therefore, parameter learning instructed by the external knowledge is very significant, such as the word distributed representation ELMO and BERT. Nevertheless, those works of Mongolian constituent parsing have not been well studied. That is not just only because lack of hand-annotated corpus, but also due to its nature of rich morphological varying.

In this paper, we propose a solution to this problem by using a self-attention neural network, which follows an encoder-decoder architecture. Our method is inspired by Hall et al. [11] who found it effective to replace words with frequently-occurring morphemes (suffixes). By learning word embeddings from morphemes, we try to get more syntactic representations. Moreover, we use the last suffix tag to replace the POS (Part-of-Speech) in input embedding. Then an accumulation embedding of word representation, word position and the last suffix tag of each word, as the input embedding feed into the parser. Test experiment demonstrates that our model significantly outperforms the previous Mongolian constituent parsers. We achieve 87.16% $F1$ on the development set and 86.23% $F1$ on the test.

The main contributions of the work can be summarized as follows:

- To the best of our knowledge, however, we are the first group to employ a deep neural network for the task of Mongolian constituent parsing.
- We propose morpheme representation and the last suffix tagging to improve performance.
- We compare the performance of three composition functions of morpheme representation and two schemes of POS tagging in Mongolian constituent parsing in details.

2   Mongolian Morphological Analysis

Due to lack of hand-annotated corpus and rich morphological varying, morphological knowledge parsing approaches were proposed to facilitate the Mongolian constituent parsing. Generally, morphological knowledge is summarized by hand, including syntactic template sets, rule base and dictionary base [2–6]. These methods given in [2–6] could give constituent parsing results automatically, but the problem also following. There are more than 2000 syntax rules in literature [5], and three dictionary bases and three rule bases in [2], however, only part of the linguistic phenomenon is covered. Another work [6] tries to deal Mongolian constituent parsing with open-source tools, Stanford Parser, which is a typical constituent parser for Chinese, English, German and other languages. However, the performance improvement is not significant because the constituent parsing is a language-related problem.

In the past, parsers optimize input by using a variety of pretrained morphological representations [10–15], such as suffixes, prefixes, special tokens and unsupervised morphemes to improve the performance. However, there is a very little similar study on Mongolian words representations [16], especially for Mongolian constituent parsing.

Mongolian is a morphologically-rich language, which is formed by attaching suffix to stem. The suffix falls into two groups: derivational suffix and inflection suffix. From example, Table 1 illustrates the grammatical and meaning functions of suffixes, where "ᠵᠢᠨ (jin)" and "ᠯᠠ (la)" are derivational suffixes, "ᠢ (-y′i)" and "ᠪᠠᠷ (-bar)" are inflection suffixes. Both of two groups indicate syntactic or semantic relations between words in a sentence. Therefore, we segmented the suffixes as a new token and extracted implicit knowledge to optimize our parser. After morphological segmentation, the sentence, in Fig. 1, will be turned into "arad-a′ ca erhile gsen svrgan homujil -u′n hogjilte -y′i jqrigji gvl vn jirvm ji gvl v n_a." Our key idea is to make the input embedding layer of Mongolian constituent parser more syntactic awareness. In order to realize this idea, we compare three different composition functions to compute the word representation at morpheme-level and find the best. We also replace POS with the last suffix tag, which makes the parser more efficient and easier to use.

Table 1. Examples of Mongolian suffix

Suffix	Stem	Meaning	New word	Meaning
ᠵᠢᠨ(jin)	ᠡᠪᠦᠯ (ebul)	winter	ᠡᠪᠦᠯᠵᠢᠨ (ebuljin)	in the whole winter
ᠯᠠ (la)	ᠤᠰᠤ (vsv)	water	ᠤᠰᠤᠯᠠ (vsvla)	watering
ᠢ (-y′i)	ᠰᠤᠷᠪᠠᠨ_᠎ᠠ (svrvn_a)	Surna	ᠰᠤᠷᠪᠠᠨ_᠎ᠠ ᠢ (svrvn_a-y′i)	Let Surna
ᠪᠠᠷ (-bar)	ᠰᠤᠷᠪᠠᠨ_᠎ᠠ (svrvn_a)	Surna	ᠰᠤᠷᠪᠠᠨ_᠎ᠠ ᠪᠠᠷ (svrvn_a-bar)	Through Surna

3   Method

Our method has three components: input embedding layer, encoder layer and decoder layer. It is shown in Fig. 2. Firstly, it learns the distributed representation of each input word by their morphemes. Secondly, the word representation, position and the last suffix tag of each word will be fed into the self-attention neural network. On the top of network, a chart decoder layer finds the optimal constituent parse tree. We will introduce our parser and its variants from bottom to top in following.

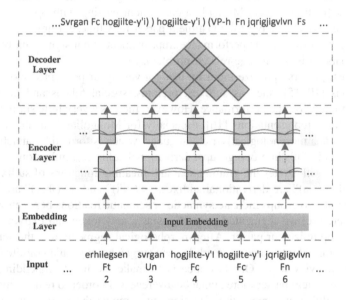

Fig. 2. The main architecture of our parser with layers

3.1   Input Embedding Layer

There are three kinds of embeddings will be fed into the encoder, word embeddings $[w_1, w_2, \cdots, w_L,]$, the last suffix tag embeddings $[s_1, s_2, \cdots, s_L,]$ and position embeddings $[p_1, p_2, \cdots, p_L,]$, all of which are generated from input embedding layer.

3.1.1   Word Representation Models

As outlined above, when parsing Mongolian, we characterized words with their morphemes to capture the syntactic information, thereby allowing better generalization between words with similar morphemes. In order to get better word representation for parsing, we compared three different composition functions that have commonly been used in recent works.

Suppose that a word w is made up of a sequence of morphemes where $m_i \in M$ is the embedding of morphemes and the $M \in \mathbb{R}^d$ is the vocabulary of morphemes, the d is the dimension of embeddings, and the $|w|$ stands for the number of constituent morphemes in the word. We use three composition functions to compute the word representations.

1. *Addition.* This composition function constructs the representation w of word w by simply adding together the embeddings of its morphemes. Formally, the equation is shown below:

$$w = \sum_{i=1}^{|w|} m_i \tag{1}$$

2. *Bidirectional LSTM Neural Network.* We adapt bidirectional long-short-term memory neural network (denoted Bi-LSTM) [17, 18] as our second composition function, which is widespread used for word representation in NLP tasks [19, 20]. Bi-LSTM use a pair of LSTMs to compute left-to-right $\overrightarrow{h_i} = LSTM\left(\overrightarrow{h_{i-1}}, m_i\right)$ and right-to-left $\overleftarrow{h_i} = LSTM\left(\overleftarrow{h_{i+1}}, m_i\right)$ for each morpheme, where $\overrightarrow{h_i}$ and $\overleftarrow{h_i}$ are the LSTM hidden states. Then, we fed them into multilayer perception with a single hidden layer and a tanh activation function to form the word representation:

$$w = MLP\left(\overrightarrow{h_{|w|}}, \overleftarrow{h_1}\right) \tag{2}$$

3. *Convolutional Neural Network.* Convolutional Neural Network. The Convolutional neural network (CNN) [14, 21] is the third strategy extensively employed as the composition function [22], which have achieved state-of-the-art results on various NLP task. The CNN composition function considers windows of l consecutive morphemes within the words, where a set of filters ($H_l \in \mathbb{R}^{d \times l}$) are applied to these morphemes windows to generate corresponding feature maps $f_w \in \mathbb{R}^{|w|-l+1}$, and the $i - th$ element of $f_w(i)$ is defined as:

$$f_w(i) = \left(<M_{|w|,i}, H_l> + b\right) \tag{3}$$

where $<A, B> = \sum_{i,j} A_{i,j} B_{i,j} = Tr(AB^T)$ denotes the Frobenius inner product, the $M_{|w|}$ is the morpheme embedding matrices, and the b is a bias. Then a max-pooling operation is used on the top of each feature map:

$$y_w = \max_i f_w(i) \tag{4}$$

To capture the interactions between the morpheme n-grams, which are picked up by the filters, we apply a highway network following. One layer of a highway network forms the word representation as following:

$$w = t \odot MLP(y_w) + (1 - t) \odot y_w \tag{5}$$

where $t = MLP_\sigma(y_w)$ is a sigmoid gating function, which is called the transform gate, and $(1 - t)$ is called the carry gate.

3.1.2 Last Suffix Embedding

POS tagging is a part of the input variable that has a great impact on the performance of the constituent parser. The POS of the central morpheme's (stem) was used in earlier Mongolian parsers. This approach ignores a lot of morpheme syntax information. To fully utilize morphological knowledge, we propose a suffix-based POS tagging approach to address this problem.

Suffix-based POS tagging approach is inspired by [10], who found it effective to use suffix information for Mongolian constituent parsing. The grammatical relationship, for instance, the grammatical subject or object of the sentence, is indicated in these languages by suffixes. Following [9], we replace the POS tag with the last suffix tag of each word and get the embedding s. There are 175 kinds of suffixes in our experiment, which is classified into 17 categories according to Mongolian Grammar Dictionary.

3.1.3 Position Embedding

There are various ways to encode positions. We adopt the signal timing approach from [13] for position embedding, which is formulated as follows:

$$
\begin{cases}
timing(p, 2i) = sin\left(\frac{p}{10000^{2i/d_m}}\right) \\
timing(p, 2i+1) = cos\left(\frac{p}{10000^{2i/d_m}}\right)
\end{cases}
\tag{6}
$$

where p represents the word position in a sentence.

3.2 Self-attention Encoder

Self-attention network (SAN), as its name suggests, is a special case of attention mechanism that only needs internal information of a sequence to compute its representation. Thus, it is more flexible at modeling both long-range and local dependencies comparing to RNN/CNN [23]. Following [9], we choose self-attention [23] as the key component in our architecture instead of LSTMs. The center of this SAN formulation is the multi-head attention sub-layer and the feed-forward sub-layer.

Multi-headed self-attention sublayer is a variant of dot-product (multiplicative) attention. Formally, for the $n - th$ head, given an input matrix X^n, $X^n = \mathrm{T} \times d_m$, where each row vector x_t^n corresponds to character t in the sentence and d_m is the model dimensionality. And the trainable parameter matrices C_Q, C_K, and C_V are used to map an input x_t^n to three vectors query $q_t^n = x_t C_Q^n$, key $k_t^n = x_t C_K^n$ and value $v_t^n = x_t C_V^n$, where $\left\{C_Q^n, C_K^n, C_V^n\right\} \in \mathbb{R}^d$, and the d is the number of hidden units of our network. We calculate the probability that character I attending to character j as $p^n(i \rightarrow j) \propto \exp\left(\frac{q_i^n \cdot k_j^n}{\sqrt{d}}\right)$, and the v_j for all characters that have been attended to are aggregated to form an average value $\overrightarrow{v}_i^n = \sum_j p^n(i \rightarrow j)v_j^n$. The scaled dot-product attention computes the attention scores based on the following mathematical formulation:

$$M^n = Attention\left(Q^n, K^n, V^n\right) = softmax\left(\frac{Q^n K^{n^T}}{\sqrt{d}}\right) V^n \tag{7}$$

where $Q^n = X^n C_Q^n$, $K^n = X^n C_K^n$, $V^n = X^n C_V^n$. Finally, all the vectors produced by parallel multi-heads are added together to form a single vector: $M = \sum_{n=1}^{N} M^n$. This allows a character to gather information from up to N remote locations in the sequence at each attentional layer.

Our feed-forward sub-layer is simple and following Vaswani et al. [23]. It consists of two linear layers with hidden ReLU (Rectified Linear Unit) nonlinearity in the middle. Formally, the equation is shown below:

$$FeedForward(X) = W_2 ReLU(W_1 X + c_1) + c_2 \tag{8}$$

where $W_1 \in \mathbb{R}^{d_m \times d}$ and $W_2 \in \mathbb{R}^{d \times d_m}$ are trainable matrices.

3.3 Chart Decoder

Given a Mongolian sentence $X = (x_1, x_2, \cdots, x_L)$ with L tokens, we aim to predict a constituent parse tree T. In this model, we apply the encoder-decoder architecture from [2], which the decoder assigns a real-valued score $s(T)$ to each T:

$$s(T) = \sum_{(i,j,l) \in T} s(i, j, l) \tag{9}$$

where $s(i, j, l)$ is a real-valued score for a constituent that is located between fencepost positions i and j in a sentence and has the label l. So, the objective function of our model is to find the optimal constituent parse tree $\widehat{T}$:

$$\widehat{T} = argmax_{T'} s(T') \tag{10}$$

The chart-based methods estimate the non-linear potential and perform precisely structured reasoning by dynamic programming [12, 24], which can incorporate structured loss functions during the training process. In the decoder, we use a chart-based approach to generate a parse tree to achieve the ultimate goal, as shown in formula (2) above. The chart decoder we used is proposed by [25] and additionally modified by [9, 10, 26], which contains two components, one is span representation and other is label scoring.

3.3.1 Span Representation

Stern et al. [25] define the $span(i, j)$ as r_{ij} which is concatenated by the corresponding forward and backward representations f_i and b_i for each fencepost i, where the f_i and b_i are the output of their encoder BiLSTM. In our parsing model, we follow [9] split the output of encoder SAN in half, the even coordinates contribute to f_i and the odd coordinates contribute to b_i. And then we can define span representation as [25]:

$$r_{ij} = [f_j - f_i, b_i - b_j] \tag{11}$$

3.3.2   Label Scoring

The label scoring function is a one-layer feed forward network whose input is feed with the span representation and output vector dimensionality equals the number of possible labels. The score of the label l is defined as:

$$s(i,j,l) = M_2 relu(LayerNorm(M_1 v + z_1) + z_2) \tag{12}$$

where *LayerNorm* denotes Layer Normalization, *relu* is the Rectified Linear Unit nonlinearity.

During the training, given the gold tree T^*, the model is trained to satisfy the constraints:

$$s(T^*) \geq s(T) + \Delta(T, T^*) \tag{13}$$

For each training sample, here Δ is the Hamming loss on labeled spans. The training objective is minimizing the hinge loss:

$$max(0, max_{T \neq T^*}[s(T) + \Delta(T, T^*)] - s(T^*)) \tag{14}$$

4   Experiments

4.1   Word Embedding Corpus

The word embedding training data were crawled from traditional Mongolian news web sites. After cleaning and Latin transliteration, we have got 50,000 sentences for training word embeddings and morpheme embeddings, which length are between 2 and 56. Morphemes are obtained from Mongolian Morphological Analyzer [27]. The token size and vocabulary of the corpus are shown in Table 2. The "morpheme-level" refers to take all of roots and suffixes as new tokens when segmenting the word, while "word-level" means without any segmentation. We use Gensim to obtain the pretrained word embedding and morpheme embedding with skip-gram method.

Table 2. The number of vocabulary and token

Level	Vocabulary	Tokens
Morpheme-level	19,672	1,508,007
Word-level	63,433	858,013

4.2   Constituent Parsing Corpus

Nowadays, there is no public annotated corpus about Mongolian Constituent Parsing. In this paper, we use the manually annotated corpus in [5, 6]. The corpus we used has been reviewed manually by a group of Mongolian native speakers and made minor modifications, which includes 5000 Mongolian sentences. We split it into training (4000 sentences, 80%), developing (500 sentences, 10%) and testing (500 sentences, 10%). This corpus was converted into phrase structure trees to training. In this paper, the tree label schema follows the works [5, 6], which is shown in Tables 3 and 4.

Table 3. Constituent tag set

Label	Description	Label	Description	Label	Description
NP	Noun Phrase	VP	Verb Phrase	OP	Orientation Phrase
AP	Adverb Phrase	QP	Quantifier Phrase	SP	Modal Particle
RP	Pronominal	MP	Numeric Phrase	DP	Adverb Phrase
TP	Temporal phrase	FP	Fixed Phrase	HP	Modal Phrase
S	Sentence	GP	Postpositional Phrase		

Table 4. Internal syntactic relation tag set

Label	Description	Label	Description
t	object-predicate	u	predicate-verb
b	adverb-predicate	s	auxiliary relationship
h	coordination relationship	d	attribute relationship
j	duplicate relationship	x	general relationship

4.3   Metrics and Baseline

We evaluated the results by the PASER-VAL metrics of *precision* (*P*), *recall* (*R*) and *F*1 [28], and we use CL to denote that the parser only marks the constituent tags in Table 3 and the CSL to denote that tags both in Tables 3 and 4 marked by the parser. We take two Mongolian constituent parsers as baseline systems which are described in the literature [5] (abbr. Wudan [5]) and literature [6] (abbr. Ning [6]).

4.4   Neural Network Training

All of our parsers use the same hyperparameters as standard SAN constituent parser [8]. Moreover, all LSTMs has 2 layers. We initialized all of the LSTM's parameters with the uniform distribution between −0.1 and 0.1. We used stochastic gradient descent without momentum, with a fixed learning rate of 0.8. After 50 epochs, we begin to half the learning rate every epoch.

5   Results and Discussion

5.1   The Effect of Different Composition Function

We compared our proposed Mongolian constituent parser, which is guided by morphological knowledge against baselines mentioned in Sect. 4.3. The input embedding layer of our parsers consists of morpheme representation, the last suffix tagging and position tagging. Our parsers are named after their composition function. Note that shown in Table 5 is the result of the development sets.

Table 5. Performance of our models and baseline systems (Dev)

Model	CL			CSL		
	P(%)	R(%)	F1(%)	P(%)	R(%)	F1(%)
Wudan [5]	77.01	77.07	77.04	–	–	–
Ning [6]	75.89	75.71	75.80	57.66	57.49	57.58
Addition model	83.75	83.81	83.78	79.19	80.55	79.86
Bi-LSTM model	87.10	87.22	**87.16**	85.49	85.14	**85.31**
CNN model	86.74	86.88	86.81	84.23	83.54	83.88

As shown in Table 5, all of our models perform better than the baseline models without any feature engineering or dictionary. Considering these evaluate metrics, the parser with Bi-LSTM composition function is the best of all. It establishes the performance of 87.16% (CL) and 85.31% (CSL) $F1$, outperforming the best of baseline 10.12% and 27.23% $F1$. The results indicated that our models can better extract the syntactic information from Mongolian morphemes, and the Bi-LSTM composition function is better than others.

5.2   The Effect of Word Representation

Table 6 shows the performance Mongolian constituent parsing with different level word representations. We observed that the performance of morpheme-level models is better than word-level models. Besides, about 97.25% morphemes can be found in the pretrained morpheme vocabulary, while about 82.4% words can be found in the pretrained embedding. This result shows that the parser benefits from additional word representations, which consistent with previous research.

5.3   The Effect of Different POS Tagging

To validate the effectiveness of the last suffix tagging, we evaluate their performance on the testing dataset and the scores are reported in Table 7. We also list the score of the different models with CHARLSTM POS tagging scheme [9]. According to the results, the following conclusions were obtained:

Table 6. Performance of word representation (Test)

	CL			CSL		
	P(%)	R(%)	F1(%)	P(%)	R(%)	F1(%)
Word-level	80.36	80.47	80.41	70.68	76.21	73.34
Morpheme-level	86.05	86.41	**86.23**	82.39	84.54	**83.45**

Table 7. Performance of different POS tagging (Test)

POS tagging	Model	CL			CSL		
		P(%)	R(%)	F1(%)	P(%)	R(%)	F1(%)
CHARLSTM	*Addition* model	81.33	82.49	81.91	77.72	79.23	78.47
	Bi-LSTM model	85.98	86.22	86.10	82.36	82.47	82.41
	CNN model	84.32	85.13	84.72	80.97	81.49	81.23
The last suffix	*Addition* model	82.24	82.61	82.42	79.17	79.53	79.35
	Bi-LSTM model	86.05	86.41	86.23	82.39	84.54	83.45
	CNN model	84.89	86.35	85.61	83.76	85.6	84.67

- Each parsing model with the last suffix tagging achieves a better result than that with CHARLSTM, because the last suffix tagging represents syntactic information.
- For all unsupervised POS Tagging schemes, the Bi-LSTM model performs better than other models, because it provides more temporal syntactic information than the Addition model and the CNN.

6 Conclusion

In this paper, we have proposed morphological knowledge guided approaches for Mongolian constituent parsing without resorting to dictionaries, rules, and large training corpus. Our key idea is to make the input embedding layer of Mongolian constituent parser have more syntactic awareness. We improved the word representations at morpheme-level and replaced POS with the last suffix tag to make them more syntactical and easier to use. Our experiments show that these models are able to obtain stranger competitive results compared to early methods. The BiLSTM model achieved state-of-the-art accuracy when BiLSTM composition function plus the last suffix embedding is used.

Acknowledgments. This work was funded by National Natural Science Foundation of China (Grant No. 61563040, 61773224, 61762069, 61866029), Natural Science Foundation of Inner Mongolia Autonomous Region (Grant No. 2017BS0601, 2016ZD06, 2018MS06025), and research program of science and technology at Universities of Inner Mongolia Autonomous Region (Grant No. NJZY18237).

References

1. Gómez-Rodríguez, C., Vilares, D.: Constituent parsing as sequence labeling (2018)
2. Wu, R., Mongh, J., Mo, R.: "From-bottom-to-top" to analyze sentence constituent of traditional Mongolian basing on the rule. In: IEEE International Conference on Information & Automation. IEEE (2017)
3. Arong, Xia, Y., Wang, S.: A research on constructing Mongolian Treebank based on phrase structure grammar. In: International Conference on Progress in Informatics & Computing. IEEE (2014)
4. Arong: The Research of Mongolian Statistical Parsing, Inner Mongolia Normal University, Hohhot (2014)
5. Wudanmuqier: A Study on Statistical and Rule-Based Combined Mongolian-Chinese Machine Translation. Inner Mongolia Normal University, Hohhot (2017)
6. Jing, N.: A Study on Tree to String Based Mongolian and Chinese Statistical Machine Translation. Inner Mongolia Normal University, Hohhot (2016)
7. Dyer, C., Kuncoro, A., Ballesteros, M., Smith, N.A.: Recurrent neural network grammars. In: Proceedings of the 2016 Conference of the North American Chapter of the Association for Computational Linguistics, pp. 199–209. Association for Computational Linguistics (2016)
8. Cross, J., Huang, L.: Span-based constituency parsing with a structure-label system and provably optimal dynamic oracles. In: Proceedings of the 2016 Conference on Empirical Methods in Natural Language Processing, pp. 1–11. Association for Computational Linguistics (2016)
9. Kitaev, N., Dan, K.: Constituency parsing with a self-attentive encoder (2018)
10. Gaddy, D., Stern, M., Klein, D.: What's going on in neural constituency parsers? An analysis (2018)
11. Hall, D., Durrett, G., Klein, D.: Less grammar, more features. In: Proceedings of the 52nd Annual Meeting of the Association for Computational Linguistics, vol. 1, pp. 228–237 (2014)
12. Finkel, J.R., Kleeman, A., Manning, C.D.: Efficient, feature-based, conditional random field parsing. In: Proceedings of ACL08: HLT, pp. 959–967. Association for Computational Linguistics, Columbus, Ohio (2008)
13. Kim, Y., Jernite, Y., Sontag, D., Rush, A.M.: Character-aware neural language models. In: Proceedings of the Thirtieth AAAI Conference on Artificial Intelligence, pp: 2741–2749. AAAI Press (2016)
14. Coavoux, M., Crabbé, B.: Multilingual lexicalized constituency parsing with wordlevel auxiliary tasks. In: Proceedings of the 15th Conference of the European Chapter of the Association for Computational Linguistics: Volume 2, Short Papers. Association for Computational Linguistics, pp. 331–336 (2017)
15. Liu, J., Zhang, Y.: Shift-reduce constituent parsing with neural lookahead features. Trans. Assoc. Comput. Linguist. 5, 45–58 (2017)
16. Wang, W., Bao, F., Gao, G.: Learning morpheme representation for Mongolian named entity recognition. Neural Process. Lett. 2019, 1–18 (2019)
17. Ling, W., Luís, T., Marujo, L., Astudillo, R.F., Amir, S.: Finding function in form: Compositional character models for open vocabulary word representation. arXiv preprint arXiv:1508.02096 (2015)
18. Ballesteros, M., Dyer, C., Smith, N.A.: Improved transition-based parsing by modeling characters instead of words with LSTMs. arXiv preprint arXiv:1508.00657 (2015)

19. Vylomova, E., Cohn, T., He, X., Haffari, G.: Word representation models for morphologically rich languages in neural machine translation (2016)
20. Vania, C., Lopez, A.: From characters to words to in between: do we capture morphology? (2017)
21. Shen, D., Wang, G., Wang, W., Min, M.R., Su, Q., Zhang, Y.: Baseline needs more love: on simple word-embedding-based models and associated pooling mechanisms (2018)
22. Kim, Y.: Convolutional neural networks for sentence classification. In: Proceedings of the 2014 Conference on Empirical Methods in Natural Language Processing (EMNLP), Doha, Qatar, pp. 1746–1751 (2014)
23. Vaswani, A., Shazeer, N., Parmar, N., Uszkoreit, J., et al.: Attention is all you need. In: Advances in Neural Information Processing Systems 30, NIPS 2017 (2017)
24. Durrett, G., Klein, D.: Neural CRF parsing. In: Proceedings of the 53rd Annual Meeting of the Association for Computational Linguistics and the 7th International Joint Conference on Natural Language Processing (Volume 1), pp. 302–312 (2015)
25. Stern, M., Andreas, J., Klein, D.: A minimal span-based neural constituency parser. In: Proceedings of the 55th Annual Meeting of the Association for Computational Linguistics (Volume 1), pp. 818–827 (2017)
26. Shen, Y., Lin, Z., Jacob, A.P., Sordoni, A., Courville, A., Bengio, Y.: Straight to the tree: constituency parsing with neural syntactic distance (2018)
27. Liu, N., Su, X., Gao, G., Bao, F.: Mongolian word segmentation based on three character level Seq2Seq models. In: Cheng, L., Leung, A.C.S., Ozawa, S. (eds.) ICONIP 2018. LNCS, vol. 11305, pp. 558–569. Springer, Cham (2018). https://doi.org/10.1007/978-3-030-04221-9_50
28. Grishman, R., Macleod, C., Sterling, J.: Evaluating parsing strategies using standardized parse files. In: Proceedings of Conference on Applied Natural Language Processing (1992)

BERT Based Hierarchical Sequence Classification for Context-Aware Microblog Sentiment Analysis

Jiahuan Lei[1], Qing Zhang[1(✉)], Jinshan Wang[2], and Hengliang Luo[1]

[1] Meituan-Dianping Group, Beijing, China
{leijiahuan,zhangqing31,luohengliang}@meituan.com
[2] Beijing University of Posts and Telecommunications, Beijing, China
wangjinshan@bupt.edu.cn

Abstract. In microblog sentiment analysis task, most of the existing algorithms treat each microblog isolatedly. However, in many cases, the sentiments of microblogs can be ambiguous and context-dependent, such as microblogs in an ironic tone or non-sentimental contents conveying certain emotional tendency. In this paper, we consider the context-aware sentiment analysis as a sequence classification task, and propose a Bidirectional Encoder Representation from Transformers (BERT) based hierarchical sequence classification model. Our proposed model extends BERT pre-trained model, which is powerful of dependency learning and semantic information extracting, with Bidirectional Long Short Term Memory (BiLSTM) and Conditional Random Field (CRF) layers. Fine-tuning such a model on the sequence classification task enables the model to jointly consider the representation with the contextual information and the transition between adjacent microblogs. Experimental evaluations on a public context-aware dataset show that the proposed model can outperform other reported methods by a large margin.

Keywords: Context-aware sentiment · Sentiment classification · BERT

1 Introduction

Since the inception of online microblog services such as Twitter and Weibo, increasing numbers of people are using such services to express their feelings and attitudes about different hot topics [2,12]. Identifying sentiments or opinions from microblogs can reveal if the online mood is positive, negative or even indifferent, and also facilitate many other disciplines, including social psychology, customer relationship management, and political science etc [19]. Therefore, how to provide an effective way to analyze users' sentiments has received significant attentions from both academic researchers and commercial companies.

J. Wang—This work was done while Jinshan Wang was an intern at Meituan-Dianping Group.

© Springer Nature Switzerland AG 2019
T. Gedeon et al. (Eds.): ICONIP 2019, LNCS 11955, pp. 376–386, 2019.
https://doi.org/10.1007/978-3-030-36718-3_32

There are three technical obstacles in determining the sentiment of microblogs effectively. First, users have very limited space to express their opinions in microblogs, thus the corresponding sentimental feature vectors generated from tweets are extremely sparse. Second, the sentiments embedded in microblog conversations are usually implicit and context-dependent, even a single nonsentimental word can express obvious sentiment in a given context. Third, long term memory is necessary to handle a microblog conversation. In a long conversation, all tweets usually share a common topic, namely background topic. If a target tweet of which polarity we want to determine, is at the tail of the conversation flow, the background topic can be distant from sentiment indicator since topic words are often omitted during the conversation [5].

Some deep learning models have been proposed to tackle above issues. Huang et al. [10] propose a hierarchical LSTM model to capture the long distance sentiment dependency in the microblog conversations. The performance of their proposed model is further improved by combining other social and text-based contextual features. Zhao et al. [20] use the following relationships in Twitter to build heterogeneous networks and incorporate random walks into the LSTM network for personalized sentiment classification. Ren et al. [16] extract the words in the training corpus as contextual features according to TF-IDF values and the Convolutional Neural Network (CNN) model is used to further process the text features for context-sensitive tweet sentiment classification. Feng et al. [5] introduce attention mechanism into hierarchical LSTM network models to classify context-aware sentiments in microblogs. The proposed Context Attention (CA)-LSTM model is capable of learning continuous representations and capturing context dependency by considering both the word order and tweet order in a conversation. However, none of these models can achieve very satisfying result for context-aware sentiment analysis task.

In this paper, we consider microblog conversation as a sequence ordered by time and utilize preceding and succeeding microblogs to enrich the representation of the target microblog. Besides, we use BERT [3] model to extract the contextual information at the char-level representation and it is pre-trained on a large scale of corpus with various topics. These can effectively alleviate sparsity problem and incorporate semantic contextual information. And we develop a hierarchical model with BERT and a BiLSTM layer, which can embed the contextual information at char level and incorporate the contextual information at tweet level. This can effectively model the long distance dependency for sentiment analysis. In addition, we adopt CRF layer in our model, which enables model to determine the sentiment not only considering the target microblog representation but also transitions between the neighboring sentiment. Experimental evaluations show that the proposed model can outperform other reported methods by a large margin.

The rest of the paper is organized as follows. Section 2 describes the details of the proposed BERT based sequence sentiment labeling model for context-aware microblog sentiment analysis. Experimental results are presented and analyzed in Sect. 3. Finally, Sect. 4 ends up with conclusions and discusses possible future work.

2   Methods

In this section, we will describe our proposed model for context-based microblog sentiment classification in detail. Firstly, we introduce the CA-LSTM model for sentiment classification, which is currently the stat-of-the-art model for COAE 2015 Context-Sensitive Microblog Sentiment Classification Task.[1] Then we will describe the improvement of our model compared with CA-LSTM model.

2.1   Overview of CA-LSTM Model for Baseline Comparison

To capture the hierarchical sequential structure for microblog sequence, the CA-LSTM model constructs a hierarchical architecture, as shown in Fig. 1 [5]. The input of the model is word embedding corresponding to each word. The first word-level LSTM layer generates representation of a single tweet using the last hidden state. And the second tweet-level LSTM layer is able to model the contextual information of the target tweet. Specifically, the inputs for the tweet-level LSTM are the representations of tweets in the conversation that is composed of the preceding tweets and the target tweet. The first tweet is root tweet, while the others are retweets or references of the root tweet ordered by time with the target tweet being the last one. It is worth noting that a contextual attention mechanism is adopted to improve the representation of those LSTM units. There are word-level and tweet-level context attention vectors in CA-LSTM model. Based on CA-LSTM model, the enhanced vector extracted from microblog sequences considers not only the features in target microblog, but also the contextual information from the preceding microblogs, which gives target microblog a better context-aware representation.

2.2   The Proposed BERT Based Sequence Sentiment Labeling Model

The overview of our proposed model architecture is shown in Fig. 2. We propose a BERT based hierarchical sequence sentiment classification model to build a context-aware sentiment classifier for microblogs. We firstly exploit BERT to incorporate contextual information implicitly and generate char-level representations of the target microblog. Then the representations are fed into an average pooling layer and BiLSTM layer to generate the tweet-level representation. Finally, representation is fed into CRF, which determines the sentiment not only considering the target microblog representation but also the neighboring sentiment transition.

Embedding Contextual Information Using BERT. The CA-LSTM model has achieved the state-of-the-art result for the context-aware sentiment classification task [5]. In CA-LSTM, LSTM units are used to learn long distance dependency and extract semantic information. In the first word-level LSTM layer, it

---

[1] http://www.ccir2015.com/.

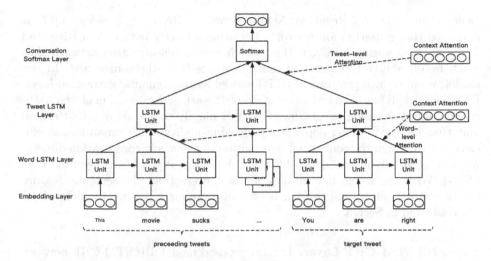

Fig. 1. The architecture of CA-LSTM network.

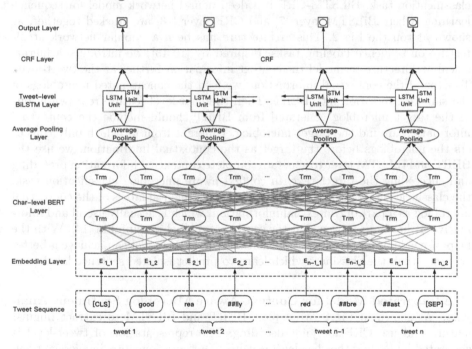

Fig. 2. The overall architecture of the proposed model.

can only generate the representation of a single tweet. Then the second tweet-level LSTM layer model the context information of the target tweet. However it has been proved theoretically and practically that self-attention unit achieves a better performance in terms of learning dependency and computational efficiency than traditional Recurrent Neural Networks (RNN) [9]. Besides, in [17], it is proved that self-attention networks perform distinctly better than RNN and CNN on word sense disambiguation, which means self-attention networks has much better ability to extract semantic features from the source text. In our model, we introduce pre-trained BERT model as the semantic extraction layer. BERT model [3] has achieved a new state-of-the-art performance in eleven natural language processing tasks. Since BERT is mainly composed of self-attention unit that has strong long dependency learning ability and computational efficiency, it can learn the contextual information of the whole conversation directly without separately modeling the different microblogs at word-level layer like CA-LSTM. With the whole information of the conversation, the semantic feature can be learned better, and this has been proven in our experiment which will be demonstrated in Sect. 3.4.

Extra BiLSTM-CRF Layer. In our proposed model, BiLSTM-CRF network architecture is utilized as an extension of BERT to finetune on the sequence classification task. BiLSTM-CRF is a deep neural network model for sequence learning, where BiLSTM layer [7] and CRF layer [13] are stacked together, as shown at top the Fig. 2. This architecture has been a popular network architecture on sequence labeling tasks. Inspired by [10,13], we introduce a hierarchical architecture to model the context information further at the tweet-level. To expand the contextual information, we feed the concatenated microblogs of the same conversation into BERT. Then the char-level feature representations of the target microblog generated from BERT should include the contextual information around the target microblog. Different from [5] which only considers the microblogs before the target as the contextual information, we use the BERT and BiLSTM layer to generate complete contextual information preceding and succeeding the target text. In context-aware microblog classification task, the classification models do not consider the sentimental labels of the contextual microblog as a part of contextual information, which is actually useful and informative. It has been proven that the sentimental label is helpful in [14]. With the help of neighboring sentiment information, the CRF model can achieve a better accuracy than the classifiers which learn to predict isolated sentence labels.

The Integrated Model for Context-Aware Microblog Sentiment Analysis. As shown in Fig. 2, we exploit BERT and BiLSTM to extract linguist feature and use CRF for joint decoding. The representation of tweet-level is generated by feeding the char-level feature representations into an average pooling layer separately. Then we feed the microblog conversation representation sequence into the BiLSTM layer. And we concatenate the representations from the forward and backward directional LSTM of each target microblog to generate the enhanced conversation representation sequence that composed of n tweets. Finally we feed them into the CRF model, which determines the sentiment not only considering the target microblog but also the sentimental dynamics of the conversation.

3 Experiment

In this section, the benchmark dataset for context-aware microblog sentiment classification task is introduced firstly. Then the experiment setup and baseline algorithms for comparison are described. Finally, the experimental results and the corresponding analysis are discussed.

Table 1. The statistics of the conversation length in the dataset.

	Length 2	Length 3	Length 3+
Percentage	57.8%	25.1%	17.1%

3.1 Dataset

The effectiveness of our proposed model is evaluated on COAE 2015 Context-Sensitive Microblog Sentiment Classification Task dataset.[2] In this dataset, the official training set were crawled from Weibo.com, the largest Chinese microblogging platform, and contains 2800 examples with *Positive, Neutral* and *Negative* as labels. Besides training set, the test set is also provided by the organization of COAE task, but the labels of this set are not disclosed. To evaluate models with the test set, two graduate students were asked to label the testing set [5], and only the examples with the consistent label are remained, which is about 65% of the whole testing set. Since Chinese context-sensitive microblog benchmark dataset is rare and to keep consistent with existing research, the dataset used in [5] is followed in our experiments.

Table 2. The sentiment drift information of the target and preceding adjacent microblog.

Target tweet	Preceding tweet		
	Positive	*Neutral*	*Negative*
Positive	764	286	120
Neutral	509	855	466
Negative	60	157	338

In the dataset, there are 4248 labeled Chinese microblogs, which form 555 threads by retweet and reference '@' relationships. From the point of labels, there are 1571 examples with *Positive* label, 1647 with *Neural* label and 1030 with *Negative* label. Among the threads, 57.8% threads have two microblog, 25.1%

---

[2] https://github.com/Jiahuan2019Sentiment-classification/coae2015/blob/master/data.

has three microblog and 17.1% has more than three microblogs as shown in Table 1. The statistics information of sentiment polarity drift between microblog and their preceding adjacent neighbor in the conversation chain are shown in Table 2. It can been seen that about 45% microblogs have changed polarities compared with their neighbors in the conversations. These polarity drifts are indicated by sentiment labels and features extracted from text, both of these two information can be captured by our model.

For each microblog thread, there are about 157 chars on average, and 35 chars on average for each microblog. In the dataset, 86.9% data are 'not-root' microblog. In our experiment, 4/5 of the whole dataset is selected as training set and the rest as testing set.

3.2   Baseline Methods for Comparison

We compare our proposed model with several baseline models including the state-of-art method for context based microblog sentiment classification. As deep learning models outperform existing traditional algorithms by a large margin, we focus on recent deep learning models, i.e. RNN models and its variants, such as RNN, Gated recurrent units (GRU), BiLSTM, Hierarchical LSTM (HLSTM), etc.

GRU. GRU is designed to have more persistent memory thus theoretically making it easier to capture long-term dependencies. The GRU model has two types of gates: the update gate and the reset gate. GRU model has fewer parameters to train and the training time can be less than the vanilla LSTM model [8].

BiLSTM. The basic idea of BiLSTM is to connect two LSTM hidden layers of opposite directions to the same output. Because the BiLSTM model looks at the sequence twice (from left to right and right to left), the output layer can get information from past and future states and the contextual information can be handled well [18].

HLSTM. Capturing this hierarchical sequential structure for text can potentially give the RNN models higher predictive accuracy [2], as seen in previous works [4,6,15,21]. The similar hierarchical LSTM network has been adopted by [10] for modeling the microblog conversations.

CA-LSTM. The CA-LSTM network has a hierarchical structure for modeling microblog sequence and allocates the words and tweets with different weights using attention mechanism [1,5]. With the help of the word-level and tweet-level attentions, CA-LSTM can capture the long distance dependency in microblog conversation and infer the sentiment polarities of context-sensitive words and tweets.

BERT. As aforementioned, BERT is pre-trained on a large scale of corpus, which can effectively alleviate the sparsity problem of feature space and give neural model a better training initialization [3]. In our experiments, we finetune BERT on the training set with a softmax output layer and without feeding the contextual text but only the target microblogs.

BERT with the Context. This model has a single different setting compared with BERT described in previous subsection, which is feeding the contextual information of the target microblogs to BERT directly. This is implemented by concatenating all the microblogs in the same conversation and feeding the whole string into BERT. By comparing the performance between BERT and BERT with contextual information, we can evaluate the improvement from the context.

BERT with the Context + CRF. This model is to finetune BERT pre-trained model with CRF layer on the training set, which converting the classification task of the target microblogs to a sequence labeling task. The CRF layer not only considers the input features extracted from source text, but also the sentiment from neighboring microblog in the same conversation. By comparing the performance of BERT with the context, we can evaluate the performance increment by the CRF layer.

3.3 Hyper-parameters

We use Chinese BERT-Base model[3] and it has 12 layers, 768 hidden states and 12 heads. For finetuning, all hyper-parameters are tuned on the training set. The maximum length is 400, the batch size is 16. Adam [11] is used for optimization with an initial learning rate of 2e-5. The dropout probability is 0.1. In BiLSTM and CRF layers, the hidden state size is 256. The maximum epoch number for training is 30.

3.4 Experimental Results

The hyper-parameters are tuned for all above mentioned models using training dataset to achieve the best performance [5]. The experimental results are shown in Table 3.

Table 3 shows that BERT-based models have better performance compared with the RNN networks by a large margin. Even without the contextual information, the performance of BERT exceeds CA-LSTM by a relative large margin. We think the reason is that the pre-trained BERT model can effectively alleviate the sparsity problem of feature space and give neural network model a good training initialization.

---

[3] https://github.com/google-research/bert.

Table 3. Experiment results of the DNN models.

Model	Context	Accuracy	Precision	Recall	MacroF1
GRU	No	0.5894	0.5959	0.5839	0.5794
	Yes	0.6188	0.6059	0.6012	0.6019
LSTM	No	0.6153	0.6100	0.5900	0.5815
	Yes	0.6205	0.6145	0.6058	0.6057
Bi-LSTM	No	0.6118	0.5921	0.5855	0.5802
	Yes	0.6268	0.6196	0.6189	0.6183
HLSTM	Yes	0.6401	0.6123	0.6320	0.6101
CA-LSTM	Yes	0.6518	0.6368	0.6369	0.6362
BERT	No	0.6745	0.6699	0.6755	0.6722
	Yes	0.8278	0.8168	0.8154	0.8147
BERT+CRF	Yes	0.8344	0.8254	0.8274	0.8256
BERT+Bi-LSTM+CRF	Yes	0.8461	0.8348	0.8381	0.8358

By comparing the performance between BERT and BERT with context, we can evaluate the gain brought by contextual information, which is 15.33% absolute increment on accuracy, while the performance increments by context in RNN networks are less than 3%. This demonstrates the effectiveness of learning contextual information by concatenating the sequential microblogs and feeding them directly into the BERT.

We can also see finetuning with the CRF layer also bring 0.66% absolute increment on accuracy compared with BERT+context, which indicates the effectiveness of considering the neighboring sentiment transitions.

We add the BiLSTM layer before feeding the tweet-level representation into the CRF layer. By comparing the performance between BERT+CRF with BiLSTM and without BiLSTM, we can see this BiLSTM layer can increase 1.17% absolute value on accuracy, this demonstrates that there is some scope at the tweet-level representation to improve.

According to the experimental results, the pre-trained BERT model is able to alleviate the sparsity problem of feature space and increase the sentiment classification performance by a large margin. Based on the Bert, adding the context and hierarchical architecture can effectively capture context-aware sentiments with long distance contextual dependency in microblog conversations. Besides, we adopt CRF layer to consider the sentimental dynamics and this results in further improvement.

4   Conclusion

In this work, we propose a BERT based sequence classification model which incorporates the contextual information with the target microblog for context-aware microblog sentiment classification task. By using the pre-trained BERT

with self-attention units and hierarchical architecture, our model can capture
the long distance dependency in microblog conversations. In addition, the CRF
layer determines the sentiment not only considering the target microblog representation but also the neighboring sentiment transitions. According to the
extensive experiments on a public Chinese context-aware microblog sentiment
classification dataset, it is demonstrated that our model outperforms the state-
of-the-art model by a large margin. The pre-trained BERT model adopted in this
work was trained using corpus of Chinese Wikipedia text, the expression style
in Wikipedia is much different from that of microblogs, thus post-training the
BERT-base model with microblog corpus will be further explored in our future
work.

References

1. Chen, H., Sun, M., Tu, C., Lin, Y., Liu, Z.: Neural sentiment classification with
   user and product attention. In: Proceedings of the 2016 Conference on Empirical
   Methods in Natural Language Processing, pp. 1650–1659 (2016)
2. Cheng, J., Zhang, X., Li, P., Zhang, S., Ding, Z., Wang, H.: Exploring sentiment
   parsing of microblogging texts for opinion polling on Chinese public figures. Appl.
   Intell. **45**(2), 429–442 (2016)
3. Devlin, J., Chang, M.W., Lee, K., Toutanova, K.: BERT: pre-training of
   deep bidirectional transformers for language understanding. arXiv preprint
   arXiv:1810.04805 (2018)
4. El Hihi, S., Bengio, Y.: Hierarchical recurrent neural networks for long-term dependencies. In: Advances in Neural Information Processing Systems, pp. 493–499
   (1996)
5. Feng, S., Wang, Y., Liu, L., Wang, D., Yu, G.: Attention based hierarchical LSTM
   network for context-aware microblog sentiment classification. World Wide Web
   22(1), 59–81 (2019)
6. Fernández, S., Graves, A., Schmidhuber, J.: Sequence labelling in structured
   domains with hierarchical recurrent neural networks. In: Proceedings of the 20th
   International Joint Conference on Artificial Intelligence, IJCAI 2007 (2007)
7. Graves, A., Mohamed, A., Hinton, G.: Speech recognition with deep recurrent
   neural networks. In: 2013 IEEE International Conference on Acoustics, Speech
   and Signal Processing, pp. 6645–6649. IEEE (2013)
8. Greff, K., Srivastava, R.K., Koutník, J., Steunebrink, B.R., Schmidhuber, J.:
   LSTM: a search space odyssey. IEEE Trans. Neural Netw. Learn. Syst. **28**(10),
   2222–2232 (2016)
9. Hochreiter, S., Bengio, Y., Frasconi, P., Schmidhuber, J., et al.: Gradient flow in
   recurrent nets: the difficulty of learning long-term dependencies (2001)
10. Huang, M., Cao, Y., Dong, C.: Modeling rich contexts for sentiment classification
    with LSTM. arXiv preprint arXiv:1605.01478 (2016)
11. Kingma, D.P., Ba, J.: Adam: a method for stochastic optimization. arXiv preprint
    arXiv:1412.6980 (2014)
12. Kwak, H., Lee, C., Park, H., Moon, S.: What is Twitter, a social network or a news
    media? In: Proceedings of the 19th International Conference on World Wide Web,
    pp. 591–600. ACM (2010)
13. Lafferty, J., McCallum, A., Pereira, F.C.: Conditional random fields: probabilistic
    models for segmenting and labeling sequence data (2001)

14. McDonald, R., Hannan, K., Neylon, T., Wells, M., Reynar, J.: Structured models for fine-to-coarse sentiment analysis. In: Proceedings of the 45th Annual Meeting of the Association of Computational Linguistics, pp. 432–439 (2007)
15. Mnih, A., Hinton, G.E.: A scalable hierarchical distributed language model. In: Advances in Neural Information Processing Systems, pp. 1081–1088 (2009)
16. Ren, Y., Zhang, Y., Zhang, M., Ji, D.: Context-sensitive twitter sentiment classification using neural network. In: Thirtieth AAAI Conference on Artificial Intelligence (2016)
17. Tang, G., Müller, M., Rios, A., Sennrich, R.: Why self-attention? A targeted evaluation of neural machine translation architectures. arXiv preprint arXiv:1808.08946 (2018)
18. Wang, Y., Feng, S., Wang, D., Zhang, Y., Yu, G.: Context-aware Chinese microblog sentiment classification with bidirectional LSTM. In: Li, F., Shim, K., Zheng, K., Liu, G. (eds.) APWeb 2016. LNCS, vol. 9931, pp. 594–606. Springer, Cham (2016). https://doi.org/10.1007/978-3-319-45814-4_48
19. Wu, F., Song, Y., Huang, Y.: Microblog sentiment classification with contextual knowledge regularization. In: Twenty-Ninth AAAI Conference on Artificial Intelligence (2015)
20. Zhao, Z., Lu, H., Cai, D., He, X., Zhuang, Y.: Microblog sentiment classification via recurrent random walk network learning. In: IJCAI, vol. 17, pp. 3532–3538 (2017)
21. Zhu, X., Sobihani, P., Guo, H.: Long short-term memory over recursive structures. In: International Conference on Machine Learning, pp. 1604–1612 (2015)

Topic Aware Context Modelling
for Dialogue Response Generation

Dali Chen, Wenge Rong$^{(\boxtimes)}$, Zhiyuan Ma, Yuanxin Ouyang, and Zhang Xiong

School of Computer Science and Engineering, Beihang University, Beijing, China
{dali_chen,w.rong,zhiyuan_ma,oyyx,xiongz}@buaa.edu.cn

Abstract. Response generation is an important direction in conversation systems. Currently a lot of approaches have been proposed and achieved significant improvement. However, an important limitation has been widely realized as most models tend to generate general answers. To cope with this limitation, besides the needs of more sophisticated generation models, how to use extra information is also an important direction. In this research, inspired by the importance of topics in conversation, we proposed a topic aware context modelling framework by utilizing similar question answer pairs in the repository. Furthermore, we use adversarial learning to improve the quality of generated response. The experimental study has shown the propose framework's potential.

Keywords: Dialogue response · Topic · Context · Adversarial

1 Introduction

Automatic chatbot has recently attracted much attention in the natural language processing area. It can be used in a lot of applications such as customer relationship management. In a chatbot system, how to generate proper response given a question is one of the most fundamental tasks. Earlier work focused on rule-based and instance-based methods. For example, Banchs et al. [2] introduced an instance-based dialog system based on a large conversational data set that uses a dual search strategy to complete the conversation. At the same time, Wang et al. [21] proposed a retrieval-based automatic question-and-answer model by constructing a short text dialogue data set of Sina Weibo, which is a popular social network service in China.

Recently, due to the development of deep learning, especially the emergence of end-to-end learning algorithms, a lot of advanced chatbot systems have been proposed. seq2seq is one of the most popular approaches and has been widely lauded as a promising solution for this task [7]. A typical seq2seq based model is an Encoder-Decoder model consisting of two recurrent neural networks to encode the source statement and map it to a fixed length. The vector space is decoded by another RNN to the vector space of the target statement [4].

Though seq2seq model has been widely employed and can generate smooth, grammatically compliant responses [8,10], it has a significant limitation, or called

© Springer Nature Switzerland AG 2019
T. Gedeon et al. (Eds.): ICONIP 2019, LNCS 11955, pp. 387–397, 2019.
https://doi.org/10.1007/978-3-030-36718-3_33

"safe response" problem [18], which means the model tends to generate some general responses, thereby making the chatbot far from practical use [14]. To overcome this challenge, some more sophisticated models are proposed, e.g, Hierarchical Recurrent Encoder-Decoder (HRED) [16], Conditional Variation Auto Encoder (CVAE) [5], Attention and so on. Such advanced methods have achieved significant improvement indeed.

Besides employing new models towards answer generation, another important thought is to add extra information to help generate more diverse responses. For example, Li et al. proposed to integrate user identity to help generate more personalized responses [9]. Asghar et al. discussed the importance and feasibility of employing emotion information to help generate diverse responses [1]. It has been justified that using extra knowledge is able to help generate more meaningful text [20].

In this research, we proposed a framework to help generate diverse response by utilizing the topics in improving meaningful response due to the importance of topic in conversation [20]. Furthermore, it is also expected that similar question answer pairs in related to the submitted question could probably help to generate diverse meaningful response since there are usually a lot of similar question answer pairs already existed in the repository. It is essential to utilize this kind of information to help find accurate topics. To further help improve the overall performance, in this research we employed the idea of adversarial learning [23] to further help the topic aware encoding and decoding during the response generation process. To verify the proposed framework, we generate a dataset from Tianya Wenda[1], one of the most popular social question answering platform in China and the experimental study on the dataset against popular benchmarks has shown the framework's potential.

The rest of the paper is organized as follows. Section 2 will briefly introduce the related work to the response generation and Sect. 3 will elaborate the proposed framework. The experimental study will be illustrated in Sect. 4 and Sect. 5 will conclude the paper.

2   Related Work

Response generation is a hot topic in recent years and has attracted much attention. Though most existed models have shown possible feasibility, there is a fundamental challenge in the community, normally referred as "safe response" problem [11]. To overcome this limitation, researchers put forward several different solutions and a lot of advanced response generation models have been proposed in the community.

Earlier approaches normally use rule-based and instance-based strategy to generate possible responses [2,21]. Though this kind of approaches is easy in implementation, the performance is not satisfied for open ended questions. Later on, seq2seq and its variant models have been widely lauded as promising solution for this task. For example, Shang et al. [17] proposed using a recurrent

---

[1] http://wenda.tianya.cn/.

neural network to generate responses to short text conversations. Based on the Encoder-Decoder framework, they proposed the Neural Responding Machine (NRM) and both encoding and decoding use recurrent neural networks. Similarly Shao et al. [18] proposed to add attention mechanism in the decoding stage. Li et al. [8] proposed an objective function based on mutual information based on the assumption that the original objective function tends to generate words with large marginal probability, which leads to a safe response by introducing source and target statements in the objective function. More recent advanced samples in this direction also include HRED and CVAE based approaches [16].

Besides proposing new models, some researchers have argued the importance of employing auxiliary information towards meaningful response [19]. For example, from the perspective of the speaker, Li et al. [9] proposed a speaker-based neural network dialogue model, which can capture the nature of dialogue between two speakers, including background information and style of speech. Their model has a large improvement in the perplexity and BLEU scores compared to the basic models, and the persistence of the dialogue. Similarly Xing et al. [22] proposed the introduction of topic information based on the sequence-to-sequence model. Its core idea is when constructing the dataset, a twitter-LDA [24] topic model is to used to infer the topic of the problem and selected the words with higher probability under the topic.

Another direction is to employ more sophisticated learning techniques to solve the problem. For example, Li et al. [10] used reinforcement learning directly on the generative question and answer. They proposed that the recent neural network model can be used to construct a dialogue system that automatically generates answers. Gasic et al. [6] proposed a dialogue management system based on POMDP (Partially Observable Markov Decision Process), which can quickly adapt to new fields by extending some core concepts and combining reinforcement learning. Yu et al. [23] applied the adversarial generation model to the generation of Chinese ancient poetry and achieved excellent results. The adversarial generation model can greatly alleviate the safe response problem, and it also has excellent performance when it is used as an evaluation standard by artificial scoring, which has great potential.

3   Methodology

In this framework, we will firstly try to find topics for the submitted question, and then also find similar question answer pairs in related to the submitted question to construct the context information for the submitted question. Afterwards we will utilize the context into the encode and decoder process to help generate diverse meaningful response.

3.1   Topic Aware Context Modeling

Considering there are normally a large number of question answering pairs in the repository, it is feasible to find similar question answer pairs as auxiliary background in relation to the given question. Based on this assumption, in this research, we employ classical BM25 [15] to find similar question answer pairs in related to the submitted question. The first step is to calculate the inverse document frequency (IDF) value of the word. The second step is to build an inverted index table and its purpose is to avoid redundant calculations and optimize the calculation speed. The third step is to calculate the most relevant question and answer pairs in the knowledge base for each submitted question. According to the above steps, the background information of the give question can be obtained.

After getting the background information of a question, the next step is to get the topics about the question and its related background information. In this research we utilize classical Latent Dirichlet Allocation (LDA) topic model [3] to infer the subject of the questions and take out the high probability words under the theme. By training the classical LDA theme model, we can calculate two probability distributions. One is the document-theme distribution and another is the topic-word distribution.

3.2 Topic Aware Context Based Encoder

The encoder proposed in this paper is as shown in Fig. 1, which consists of three parts. The first one is the recurrent neural network (RNN) based encoder for submitted question. The second one is also RNN based encoder for the relevant question and answer pairs. The third one is a multi-layer perception (MLP) responsible for the encoding topic words.

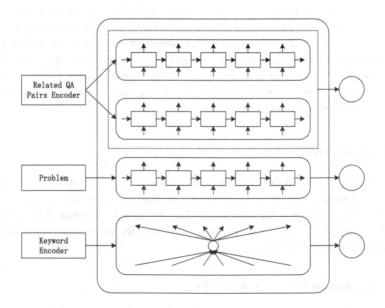

Fig. 1. Context aware encoder

The purpose of using this encoder structure is to explore the relevant questions and answers and the topic words that help generate high quality responses. The whole structure will generate four semantic vectors, among which the question answer pairs part will generate two independent vectors.

For submitted question and similar question answer pairs encoding, RNN is a typical model to generate semantic vectors, respectively. Assume the dimension of the word matrix E is $V \times emb_{size}$, V is the total number of words in the dictionary, and emb_{size} is the dimension of the word vector, we can define a mapping function named $look_{up}$, which is the output The word vector corresponding to the word number, such as the word numbered 0, outputs the first line vector of the word matrix E. The second step is to input w_1 to w_m into the RNN. As such the final output of $[h_1, h_2, h_3, ..., h_m]$ is a set of semantic vectors.

$$h_t = (1 - z_t)h_{t-1} + z_t^j \delta h_t \tag{1}$$

$$z_t^j = \sigma(W_z w_t + U_z h_{t-1}) \tag{2}$$

$$\delta h_t = tanh(W_\delta w_t + U_\delta(r_t \odot h_{t-1})) \tag{3}$$

$$r_t = \sigma(W_r w_t + U_r h_{t-1}) \tag{4}$$

For the multi-layer perception for encoding topics, assuming that the topic words vector is $x_i, i = 0, 1, ..., n, n$ refers to the index topics words, the topic words ca be encoded as follow:

$$v_i = tanh(M_T x_i + b) \tag{5}$$

where M_T is a matrix of Dimsize, Dim refers to the dimension of the word vector, and b is the bias term. The resulting $[v_0, v_1, ..., v_n]$ is the topic words vectors.

3.3 Topic Aware Context Based Decoder

The proposed decoder is shown in Fig. 2, where we need to consider the topics during the decode process. Assuming that the word probability vector output by the decoder is P_w, the word probability vector of the topic word is P_B by making the soft weight of the background word, and the weight of the i-th word in the vocabulary can de defined as w_i:

$$w_i = \begin{cases} 0, & i \notin B \\ \sum_i w_i^B, & i \in B \end{cases} \tag{6}$$

where the summation symbol in the formula refers to the sum of the weights of all the i-th words. w_i^B is the weight of the word in the background, and softmax can be obtained for w, i.e., $P_B = softmax(w)$. Therefore the final word probability generated is defined as::

$$P_{F_i} = \begin{cases} P_{W_{i'}}, & i \notin B \\ P_{W_i} + \alpha P_{B_{i'}}, & i \in B \end{cases} \tag{7}$$

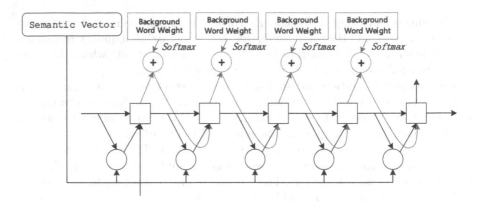

Fig. 2. Context aware decoder

where α is an enhancement factor, describing the size of the influence of background words on the generated response, and the larger the value, the greater the impact.

To further enhance the decode performance, we also use attention mechanism. Suppose that the hidden state in the i-th decode step is s_i, and the set of semantic vectors from the encoder is $[h_1, h_2, ...h_m]$, then the attention weight of each semantic vector is defined as:

$$a_{ij} = \frac{f(s_i, h_j)}{\sum_k f(s_i, h_k)} \tag{8}$$

$$f(s_i, h_j) = v_a^T tanh(W_1 s_i + W_2 h_j) \tag{9}$$

4   Experimental Study

4.1   Dataset and Configuration

The experimental data set contains 6 million question and answer pairs, crawled from Tianya Q&A. After segmentation using the word segmenter, the average length of the questions is 9.338 words, and the average length of the responses is 9.096 words. In order to satisfy the independence between the data set used to generate the model and the search model data set, we divided the 6 million questions and answers into two parts. The first part is called D1, which is the knowledge base as the retrieval model and used to train the LDA theme model. The second part is defined as D2, divided into training sets and test sets by 8:2, used to train the generated dialogue model.

In the experiment, we implemented BM25 algorithm on the data set D1. When the request is input, the program returns the k question and answer pairs most relevant to it. We also directly used the python gensim package to train the LDA theme model. Considering the total number of words and the size of the dictionary, the number of topics in the experiment is set to 50. Training the

LDA theme model will first save the strong 200 words under each theme. Due to computer performance limitations, only the top 50 words under the theme are involved in the training of the generated model.

Figure 3 shows the construction of a background-aware data set. First, use D1 to build the BM25 retrieval model, and train an LDA topic model, record the 50 most probable words under each topic to the file topic_words.txt; for each sample (q, a) in D2, use BM25 from Select the most relevant question and answer pair in D1, get the sample (q, a, c); use the LDA model to infer the subject t of (q, a), get the sample (q, a, t); merge (q, a, c) and (q, a, t), we can obtain samples (q, a, c, t).

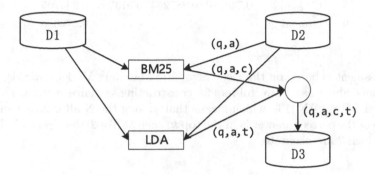

Fig. 3. Experimental data set construction

4.2   Results and Analysis

In order to better evaluate the performance of the model, we selected the evaluation metrics with Greedy Matching (GM), Embeding Average (EA) and Vector Extreme (VE) [12]. The baseline models are traditional Seq2Seq, RCNN, CA, Seq2seqBM, RCNNBM, CABM. In this section, we use CE to indicate the proposed model and two different α is also considered.

The overall performance of the proposed framework against all baselines are listed in Table 1. It is found from that table that the context aware encode decode framework can improve the diversity of the response, while the improvement in terms of similarity is not obvious. From the results of experiments of lines 7 and 8, it can be found that with the increase of the enhancement factor, the diversity is increased and the similarity slightly decreased. Considering the increase in the enhancement factor, the probability of background word generation increases, and the result is in line with our expectations. In addition, using the maximum likelihood estimation training model, considering the marginal probability of the security sample, it is difficult to improve the diversity of the model to a certain extent.

Table 2 shows the performance of the semantic evaluation, which is mainly used in the offline testing phase to select responses with higher semantic scores.

Table 1. Similarity assessment and diversity assessment

Seq	Model	GM	EA	VE	Distinct
1	Seq2seq	0.739995	0.891978	0.927852	0.162096
2	RCNN	0.738256	0.890657	0.926255	0.152166
3	CA	0.737784	0.889459	0.926193	0.154732
4	Seq2seqBM	0.745508	0.899429	0.930630	0.129898
5	RCNNBM	0.745356	0.899824	0.929974	0.128734
6	CABM	0.739452	0.891713	0.926812	0.157761
7	$CE_{a=1}$	0.741951	0.891856	0.921084	0.224890
8	$CE_{a=10}$	0.740210	0.887253	0.913598	0.244705
9	Ground	–	–	–	0.579080

The assessment is based on the Deep Semantic Matching Model (DSSM), which is mentioned above as a powerful tool for constructing sentence vectors. The indicator used is Topk@N [13], which means that among the N alternative answers, the score of the correct answer is in the top k, such as Top2@5 refers to 5 choices, among which 2 are accurate.

Table 2. Semantic evaluation model performance

Index	Accuracy
Top1@2	0.70944
Top1@5	0.40855
Top2@5	0.65421
Top1@10	0.26882
Top2@10	0.41702
Top5@10	0.77216

Table 3 shows the results of the semantic evaluation against other baselines. It can be seen from the table that the three models based on the greedy decoder (sequence 1, 2, 3) have similar scores, while the cluster based decoder scores are not satisfied.

Table 4 shows the results of the adversial assessment. The adversial assessment reflects the gap between the response and the real response. The higher the score, the better the performance of the model. From the results, it can be seen that the performance of the background enhancement decoder is significantly higher than other models. Combined with the results of diversity, we can infer that the diversity of responses is strongly correlated with the scores of adversial assessments, and increasing the diversity of models is conducive to generating closer to manual responses.

Table 3. Semantic evaluation result

Seq	Model	Score
1	Seq2seq	0.666681169
2	RCNN	0.656602106
3	CA	0.656193612
4	Seq2seqBM	0.636741288
5	RCNNBM	0.632538633
6	CABM	0.657613024
7	$CE_{\alpha=1}$	0.623462068
8	$CE_{\alpha=10}$	0.623878515

Table 4. Confrontation assessment results

Seq	Model	Score
1	Seq2seq	0.0185
2	RCNN	0.0150
3	CA	0.0185
4	Seq2seqBM	0.0175
5	RCNNBM	0.0190
6	CABM	0.0180
7	$CE_{\alpha=1}$	0.0440
8	$CE_{\alpha=10}$	0.0425

From the results of the whole experiment, the background perception generation model proposed by us has greatly improved the diversity, but the improvement in relevance and similarity is not obvious, and there is still room for improvement.

5   Conclusion

In this paper, we have conducted in-depth research on dialogue response generation model and tried to improve the problems of "safety response" challenge. The assumptions we put forward are that the information that the model can process is not rich enough. Based on this assumption, we proposed a topic aware context based encode/decode model for dialogue response generation. We firstly tried to get topic information for the submitted question by analyzing the similar question answer pairs. Afterwards an advanced encode decode framework is proposed. The experimental study has shown that this model can alleviate the problem of "safe reply".

Acknowledgement. This work was partially supported by the National Natural Science Foundation of China (No. 61977002).

References

1. Asghar, N., Poupart, P., Hoey, J., Jiang, X., Mou, L.: Affective neural response generation. In: Pasi, G., Piwowarski, B., Azzopardi, L., Hanbury, A. (eds.) ECIR 2018. LNCS, vol. 10772, pp. 154–166. Springer, Cham (2018). https://doi.org/10.1007/978-3-319-76941-7_12
2. Banchs, R.E., Li, H.: IRIS: a chat-oriented dialogue system based on the vector space model. In: Proceedings of the 50th Annual Meeting of the Association for Computational Linguistics: System Demonstrations, pp. 37–42 (2012)
3. Blei, D.M., Ng, A.Y., Jordan, M.I.: Latent dirichlet allocation. J. Mach. Learn. Res. **3**, 993–1022 (2003)
4. Cho, K., et al.: Learning phrase representations using RNN encoder-decoder for statistical machine translation. In: Proceedings of the 2014 Conference on Empirical Methods in Natural Language Processing, pp. 1724–1734 (2014)
5. Kingma, D.P., Welling, M.: Auto-encoding variational bayes. In: Proceedings of 2014 International Conference on Learning Representations (2014)
6. Gasic, M., et al.: Incremental on-line adaptation of POMDP-based dialogue managers to extended domains. In: Proceedings of 15th Annual Conference of the International Speech Communication Association, pp. 140–144 (2014)
7. Kalchbrenner, N., Blunsom, P.: Recurrent continuous translation models. In: Proceedings of the 2013 Conference on Empirical Methods in Natural Language Processing, pp. 1700–1709 (2013)
8. Li, J., Galley, M., Brockett, C., Gao, J., Dolan, B.: A diversity-promoting objective function for neural conversation models. In: Proceedings of the 2016 Conference of the North American Chapter of the Association for Computational Linguistics: Human Language Technologies, pp. 110–119 (2016)
9. Li, J., Galley, M., Brockett, C., Spithourakis, G.P., Gao, J., Dolan, W.B.: A persona-based neural conversation model. In: Proceedings of the 54th Annual Meeting of the Association for Computational Linguistics, pp. 994–1003 (2016)
10. Li, J., Monroe, W., Ritter, A., Jurafsky, D., Galley, M., Gao, J.: Deep reinforcement learning for dialogue generation. In: Proceedings of the 2016 Conference on Empirical Methods in Natural Language Processing, pp. 1192–1202 (2016)
11. Li, J., Monroe, W., Shi, T., Jean, S., Ritter, A., Jurafsky, D.: Adversarial learning for neural dialogue generation. In: Proceedings of the 2017 Conference on Empirical Methods in Natural Language Processing, pp. 2157–2169 (2017)
12. Liu, C., Lowe, R., Serban, I., Noseworthy, M., Charlin, L., Pineau, J.: How NOT to evaluate your dialogue system: an empirical study of unsupervised evaluation metrics for dialogue response generation, pp. 2122–2132 (2016)
13. Lowe, R., Pow, N., Serban, I., Pineau, J.: The ubuntu dialogue corpus: a large dataset for research in unstructured multi-turn dialogue systems. In: Proceedings of the 16th Annual Meeting of the Special Interest Group on Discourse and Dialogue, pp. 285–294 (2015)
14. Mou, L., Song, Y., Yan, R., Li, G., Zhang, L., Jin, Z.: Sequence to backward and forward sequences: a content-introducing approach to generative short-text conversation. In: Proceedings of the 26th International Conference on Computational Linguistics, pp. 3349–3358 (2016)
15. Robertson, S.E., Zaragoza, H., Taylor, M.J.: Simple BM25 extension to multiple weighted fields. In: Proceedings of the 2004 ACM CIKM International Conference on Information and Knowledge Management, pp. 42–49 (2004)

16. Serban, I.V., Sordoni, A., Bengio, Y., Courville, A.C., Pineau, J.: Building end-to-end dialogue systems using generative hierarchical neural network models. In: Proceedings of the 30th AAAI Conference on Artificial Intelligence, pp. 3776–3784 (2016)

17. Shang, L., Lu, Z., Li, H.: Neural responding machine for short-text conversation. In: Proceedings of the 53rd Annual Meeting of the Association for Computational Linguistics and the 7th International Joint Conference on Natural Language Processing of the Asian Federation of Natural Language Processing, pp. 1577–1586 (2015)

18. Shao, L., Gouws, S., Britz, D., Goldie, A., Strope, B., Kurzweil, R.: Generating long and diverse responses with neural conversation models. CoRR abs/1701.03185 (2017)

19. Song, Y., Yan, R., Li, X., Zhao, D., Zhang, M.: Two are better than one: an ensemble of retrieval- and generation-based dialog systems. CoRR abs/1610.07149 (2016)

20. Vougiouklis, P., Hare, J.S., Simperl, E.: A neural network approach for knowledge-driven response generation. In: Proceedings of 26th International Conference on Computational Linguistics, pp. 3370–3380 (2016)

21. Wang, H., Lu, Z., Li, H., Chen, E.: A dataset for research on short-text conversations. In: Proceedings of the 2013 Conference on Empirical Methods in Natural Language Processing, pp. 935–945 (2013)

22. Xing, C., et al.: Topic aware neural response generation. In: Proceedings of the 31st AAAI Conference on Artificial Intelligence, pp. 3351–3357 (2017)

23. Yu, L., Zhang, W., Wang, J., Yu, Y.: SeqGAN: sequence generative adversarial nets with policy gradient. In: Proceedings of the 31st AAAI Conference on Artificial Intelligence, pp. 2852–2858 (2017)

24. Zhao, W.X., et al.: Comparing Twitter and traditional media using topic models. In: Clough, P., et al. (eds.) ECIR 2011. LNCS, vol. 6611, pp. 338–349. Springer, Heidelberg (2011). https://doi.org/10.1007/978-3-642-20161-5_34

A Deep Neural Framework for Contextual Affect Detection

Kumar Shikhar Deep[(⊠)], Asif Ekbal, and Pushpak Bhattacharyya

Department of Computer Science and Engineering,
Indian Institute of Technology Patna, Patna, India
{shikhar.mtcs17,asif,pb}@iitp.ac.in

Abstract. A short and simple text carrying no emotion can represent some strong emotions when reading along with its context, i.e., the same sentence can express extreme anger as well as happiness depending on its context. In this paper, we propose a Contextual Affect Detection (CAD) framework which learns the inter-dependence of words in a sentence, and at the same time the inter-dependence of sentences in a dialogue. Our proposed CAD framework is based on a Gated Recurrent Unit (GRU), which is further assisted by contextual word embeddings and other diverse hand-crafted feature sets. Evaluation and analysis suggest that our model outperforms the state-of-the-art methods by 5.49% and 9.14% on Friends and EmotionPush dataset, respectively.

Keywords: Emotion classification · Emotion in dialogue · Contextual word embedding

1 Introduction

It becomes quite natural for us to gauge the emotion of a person if they explicitly mention that they are angry, sad or excited or even if they use the corresponding emojis at the end of the sentence, but what if there happens a drift in emotion while having a series of conversation between two people? And what if they stop using emotional emojis after a certain point of time even though they continue to be in the same state of emotion. Even human annotators may be confused if they do not consider context. Given that, even face-to-face conversation is confusing, sometimes, it should not be a matter of surprise if there could be a misinterpretation in textual conversations. The situation can get worse if there is a multi-party[1] conversation. In this scenario, emotion of one speaker can change due to the utterance of the second speaker, and can again be switched due to the intervening of the third speaker. We have to be attentive to every speaker in the conversation or else our context would be lost.

---

[1] Multi-Party conversation refers to the one having more than two speakers.

© Springer Nature Switzerland AG 2019
T. Gedeon et al. (Eds.): ICONIP 2019, LNCS 11955, pp. 398–409, 2019.
https://doi.org/10.1007/978-3-030-36718-3_34

Although a significant amount of research has been carried out for emotion analysis, only in the recent time there is a trend for performing emotion analysis of the dialogues in order to build an effective and human-like conversational agent.

Our current work focuses on detecting emotions in a textual dialogue system. We aim at labeling each utterance of a dialogue with one of the eight emotions, which comprises of Ekman's [4] six basic emotion tags, i.e., *anger, fear, sadness, happiness, disgust* and *surprise* plus *neutral* and *non-Neutral*[2] emotion. An example instance is depicted in Table 1. If we look at the last utterance in the table i.e., *There was no kangaroo!*, it can be considered as *neutral* but while we consider its previous context, it should be assigned with the *anger* class.

Table 1. Example utterances of a dialogue with their speaker and emotion label from EmotionLines [1] 2018 dataset

Speaker	Utterance	Emotion
Chandler	Good job Joe! Well done! Top notch!	Joy
Joey	You liked it? You really liked it?	Surprise
Chandler	Oh-ho-ho, yeah!	Joy
Joey	Which part exactly?	Neutral
Chandler	The whole thing! Can we go?	Neutral
Joey	Oh no-no-no, give me some specifics	Non-Neutral
Chandler	I love the specifics, the specifics were the best part!	Non-Neutral
Joey	Hey, what about the scene with the kangaroo? Did-did you like that part?	Neutral
Chandler	I was surprised to see a kangaroo in a World War I epic	Non-Neutral
Joey	You fell asleep!!	Anger
Joey	There was no kangaroo!	Anger

Our deep neural network framework follows a stacking structure which utilizes bidirectional gated recurrent unit (Bi-GRU) arranged in an hierarchical form. The lower Bi-GRU produces utterance level embeddings, and the upper-level Bi-GRU makes use of these embeddings to capture the contextual information in the dialogue. Some handcrafted features are incorporated at the different levels of the model to capture more linguistic evidences, which eventually found to be effective compared to the other models. We evaluate our proposed system on the benchmark dataset of EmotionLines 2018 [1]. We observe that our proposed framework attains better performance compared to the state-of-art model.

---

[2] Non-Neutral emotion refers to the one having no majority voting of any one emotion type.

2 Related Work

Emotion detection and Sentiment classification have always been a hot research topic in the area of Natural Language Processing (NLP). Existing research on emotion detection have mostly focused on textual contents. In recent times, deep neural nets are being used very extensively to perform emotion analysis in a variety of domains, mediums and languages. Some of the most widely used models for capturing emotions include Convolutional Neural Network (CNN) [11] and Recurrent Neural Networks (RNN) [14] like Long-Short Term Memory (LSTM) [12] and Gated Recurrent Unit (GRU) [2]. All these works focus on to classifying emotions at the sentence level or utterance level, and thus cannot capture the context and inter-dependence among the utterances in dialogue.

[17] proposed a network which made use of bidirectional long contextual short-term memory to detect the emotion of an utterance in dialogue and named it as bcLSTM. Later on, [6] improved bcLSTM by introducing a memory network which makes use of speaker information as well for context modeling. The authors in [13] used Bi-LSTM to capture word dependencies and to extract relevant features for detecting various emotions. On top of that, they applied self-attention [21] to capture the inter-dependencies between the utterances of a dialogue. The work reported in [18] uses hierarchical attention network model [22] to embed contextual information among the utterances in a dialogue. [8] used a bidirectional gated recurrent unit (Bi-GRU) [3] fused with self-attention [21] and its word embeddings to efficiently utilize word-level as well as utterance-level information.

Our proposed model differs from the existing models in the sense that we derive deep contextualized representation of each word in an utterance, and then incorporate it into the model as a feature along with the pre-trained Glove word embedding [15]. We acquire these word embedding from the pre-trained ELMo [16] model. These representations take the entire context into account. Being character based, they allow the network to use morphological cues to form robust representations for out-of-vocabulary words unseen in training. We use hierarchical Bi-GRU to learn the context in a dialogue fused with various handcrafted features obtained through transfer learning over similar tasks.

3 Proposed Methodology

In this section, we describe our proposed framework in details. Unlike the previous models, which performed exceptionally well in predicting some emotions follows complex architecture. Evaluation shows that a model which performs very well for a specific emotion class compensates with the lower performance in other emotion classes (i.e. performs at the cost of other classes). In contrast, our model is straightforward and efficient, and at the same time outperforms every different models with significant margins. It consists of two layers of hierarchy-the lower layer is for encoding the utterances (named as *utterance-encoder*), and the upper layer is for encoding the dialogues (named as *dialogue-encoder*).

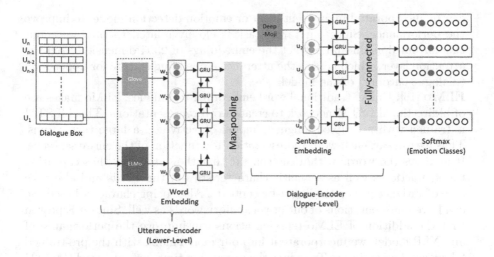

Fig. 1. Proposed architecture

Given a batch/dialogue[3], firstly the individual utterances are passed through utterance-encoder which comprises of a recurrent layer (biGRU) followed by a max-pooling layer. GRU learns the contextual representation of each word in an utterance, i.e., the representation of each word is learned based on the sequence of words in the utterance. Subsequently, we apply max-pooling over the hidden representation of each utterance to capture the most important features over time. The obtained utterance representations form the input to the dialogue-encoder, which again comprises of biGRU to capture the contextual information of each utterance in a dialogue. Since the task is to classify each utterance of a dialogue, the hidden representations of biGRU over the time are passed through fully connected layer followed by Softmax to obtain the corresponding emotion label. Further, the inputs to utterance encoder and dialogue encoder are assisted by a diverse set of hand-crafted features (c.f. Sect. 3.1) for the final prediction. Figure 1 depicts our proposed architecture.

3.1 Hand-Crafted Features

We make use of transfer learning to capture important evidences obtained from the various state-of-the-art pre-trained deep learning models. Following subsections explain these models in details:

- **DeepMoji** [5]: DeepMoji performs distant supervision on a very large dataset [20] (1.2 billion tweets) comprising of noisy labels (emojis). By incorporating transfer learning on various downstream tasks, they were able to outperform the state-of-the-art results on 8 benchmark datasets on 3 NLP tasks across the five domains. DeepMoji can give an excellent representation of text which

---

[3] We treat each dialogue as one batch.

can be incorporated in any sentiment or emotion detection model to improve the performance. Since our target task is closely related to this, we adopt this for our domain and extract the embeddings of 2304 dimension from the attention layer, which acts as the utterance embedding feature for upper-level (dialogue-encoder) of the model.

– **ELMo** [16]: Unlike traditional word embedding techniques, ELMo makes use of bidirectional LSTM network to create word representations. This biLSTM is trained with a coupled language model objective on a large text corpus. Thus we can say, each word representation is a function of the entire sentence. It analyses the words within the context that they are used, thus capturing the syntactic as well as semantic characteristics of the words and also take care of variance across the linguistic contexts. Also, being character based, we can have representations of out-of-vocabulary words as well. Since it is proven that the addition of ELMo representations can improve the performance of any NLP model, we incorporate it into our model along with the pre-trained Glove word embedding. To reduce the processing time, we extracted the 1024 dimensional ELMo word embeddings beforehand instead of creating it during the process.

3.2 Word Embedding

Embedding matrix is generated from the pre-processed text using a combination of pre-trained and deep contextualized word embedding:

1. **Pre-trained GloVe embeddings for tweets** [15]: We use 300-dimensional pre-trained GloVe word embeddings, trained on the Twitter corpus, for the experiments. The glove is a count-based model that captures the count of the word, i.e., how frequently it appears in a context.
2. **Deep contextualized ELMo embeddings** [16]: We extract 2304 dimensional word vectors from ELMo embedding model, which learns the embedding from an internal state of biLSTM and represents word-level contextual features of the input text.

We finally concatenate the word representation of both the embeddings, which act as input to the utterance-encoder (lower level).

4   Experiments and Results

4.1   Dataset Description

For experiments, we use the benchmark dataset of EmotionLines 2018 [1], which is an emotion annotated corpus of multi-party conversation. The dataset comprises of two individual corpus of dialogue set extracted from two different sources, one from the famous TV show scripts named Friends, and the other from human to human chat logs on Facebook messenger through an application called EmotionPush.

Table 2. Statistics of EmotionLines 2018 [1] dataset

Dataset	#Dialogues (#Utterances)			Emotion label distribution							
	Train	Validation	Test	Neu	Joy	Sad	Fea	Ang	Sur	Dis	Non
Friends	720 (10,561)	80 (1,178)	200 (2,764)	6530	1710	498	246	759	1657	331	2772
EmotionPush	720 (10,733)	80 (1,202)	200 (2,807)	9855	2100	514	42	140	567	106	1418

1. **Friends TV series data:** The Friends script was crawled, and each scene of an episode was treated as a dialogue. Thus each dialogue consists of multiple speakers. [1] separated the dialogues based on its window size[4] of [5, 9], [10, 14], [15, 19], and [20, 24]. Finally, they randomly collected 250 dialogues from each- thus creating a corpus of 1000 dialogues, which are further splitted up into 720, 80, and 200 dialogues for training, validation and testing, respectively.

2. **EmotionPush Chat log data:** This data was collected by crawling the private conversation among the friends on facebook messenger with the help of EmotionPush app. To protect the private information of the users like names, organizations, locations, email address, and phone numbers, they used a two-step masking procedure. They treated the conversations lasting not more than 30 min as a dialogue. Finally, they make use of the same procedure for sampling and categorizing as they used for Friends TV script and collected 1000 dialogues which were again divided in the same ratio for training, validation, and testing.

Table 2 shows the distribution of both Friends and EmotionPush datasets in terms of the number of dialogues, the number of utterances, and the number of emotion labels. To compare our model we follow the setup of [7] and evaluate its performance only on four emotions, i.e., anger, joy, sadness and neutral on both Friends and EmotoinPush datasets, and excluding all the other emotion classes during training of our model. We ignore other emotion classes by setting their corresponding loss weights to zero. Figure 2 depicts the distribution of emotion classes into train, validation, and test set for both Friends and EmotionPush datasets.

4.2 Pre-processing

Friends data consists of scene snippets containing multi-speaker conversation, while EmotionPush data includes Facebook messenger chats between two individuals. Both datasets contain some incomplete sentences and excessive use of punctuations. In addition to it, EmotionPush data also contains emoticons which are absent in the Friends data. We believe that the reason behind it is that Friends data is the script which is collected by converting audio to text. We perform the following pre-processing steps:

---

[4] Window size refers to number of utterances in a dialogue.

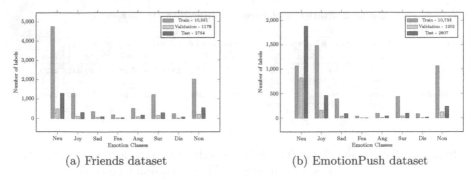

(a) Friends dataset   (b) EmotionPush dataset

Fig. 2. Emotion class distribution of Friends and EmotionPush dataset

(i) all the characters in text are converted to lower case; (ii) remove punctuation symbols except ! and ? because we believe '!' and '?' may contribute to a better understanding of intense emotions like surprise and anger; and (iii) remove extra space, emoticons and the newline character. Finally, we perform word tokenization to construct the vocabulary of words and symbols. The tokens, thus, collected are mapped to their corresponding 300-dimensional Glove vectors.

4.3   Experiments

We pad each utterance to a maximum length of 50 words. The GRU dimension is set to 300 for both lower and upper level. We employ 300 plus 1024 dimensional word embeddings and 300 plus 2304 dimensional sentence embeddings for the experiments. We use *Tanh* activation and set the *Dropout* [19] as 0.5 in order to prevent the model from overfitting. We optimize our model using *Adam* optimizer along with *weighted categorical cross-entropy* loss functions for emotion classification. From Table 2, it is clear that EmotionLines data suffers from class imbalance issue. We follow [9] to prevent our model from getting biased towards more frequently occurring emotion classes-thereby providing larger weights to the losses corresponding to less frequently occurring classes and vice-versa.

We conduct our experiments on the Pytorch framework[5]. We adopt the official evaluation metric of EmotionX 2018 [7] shared task, i.e. weighted accuracy (WA) (Eq. 1) and un-weighted accuracy (UWA) (Eq. 2), for measuring the performance of our model. We train our model for the maximum 50 epochs with early stopping criteria on validation accuracy, having the patience of 10. We initialize the learning rate by 0.00025 with the decaying factor of 0.5 on every 15 epochs.

$$WA = \sum_{c \epsilon C} p_c . a_c \qquad (1)$$

$$UWA = \frac{1}{|C|} \sum_{c \epsilon C} a_c \qquad (2)$$

---

[5] *Pytorch Home Page.* http://www.pytorch.org/.

where a_c refers to the accuracy of emotion class c and p_c refers to the percentage of emotion class c in the test set.

Table 3. Experimental results on Friends and EmotionPush datasets. F(E) denotes that the training is done on the corresponding dataset while F+E indicates that training is done on both Friends and EmotionPush dataset.

Framework used	Train data	Friends dataset		EmotionPush dataset	
		WA	*UWA*	*WA*	*UWA*
HiGRU [8]	F(E)	**74.4**	67.2	73.8	66.3
HiGRU-sf [8]	F(E)	74	**68.9**	73	68.1
HiGRU-sf	F+E	69	64.8	**77.1**	**70.2**
CAD	F(E)	*75.94*	*74.39*	*86.24*	*80.18*
Class accuracies		*Neu*: 75.14 *Joy*: 83.88		*Neu*: 87.62 *Joy*: 83.84	
		Sad: 65.88 *Ang*: 72.67		*Sad*: 73.56 *Ang*: 75.68	

Table 3 shows the evaluation results of the top-performing existing models so far compared with that of our proposed framework. In the table, HiGRU and HiGRU-sf are proposed by [8]. Results show that our model outperforms all the other models with a significant margin. Further, we observe the improvement to be statistically significant with 95% and 99% confidence on Friends and EmotionPush dataset, i.e., the p-value is less than 0.05 for paired T-test [10] of both the datasets. On Friends dataset, our model reports un-weighted and weighted accuracy of 74.39% and 75.94% as compared to that of 68.9% and 74.4% of the state-of-art models, thus improving them by 5.49% and 1.54%. On the other hand, our CAD framework performs better on EmotionPush dataset as well, reporting the unweighted and weighted accuracies of 80.18% and 86.24%, respectively, as compared to that of 70.2% and 77.1% in the state-of-art model, thus giving an increment of 9.14% and 9.98%. It is worth noticing that the accuracy of anger in EmotionPush dataset increases by 17.38 points without compensating with the other classes. This implies that for all the emotion classes our framework performs reasonably competent with the accuracies being balanced and not biased to any specific class.

To test the correctness of our prediction, we adopt some examples where the emotion drift occurs over an extended context. It can be seen from the Table 4 that rare emotions are predicted correctly. Thus we can say that our model captures the contextual information in the dialogue pretty well.

4.4 Error Analysis

In Fig. 3, we show the confusion matrices for both the datasets (i.e., Friends and EmotionPush) for quantitative analysis. We find that *joy* and *sad* emotions are mostly confused with *neutral*, possibly due to the absence of affective words and

Table 4. A set of two dialogues from Friends' test set showing the correct predictions of rare emotions

Speaker	Utterance	True emotion	Predicted emotion
Nurse	This room's available	Neutral	Neutral
Rachel	Okay!	Joy	Joy
	⋮		
	⋮		
Rachel	You listen to me!	Anger	Anger
Chandler	Hey!	Joy	Neutral
Monica	Hi!	Neutral	Neutral
	⋮		
	⋮		
Chandler	So, I guess this is over	Sadness	Sadness

large number of *neutral* class. Most of the *neutral* emotions get confused with *joy* due to the presence of some positive sentiment words. Majority of *anger* emotion in EmotionPush dataset are missclassified as *neutral* (mostly due to absence of any sentiment bearing words) while that of Friends dataset are misclassified as *joy* due to presence of exclaimation mark which shows strong emotion such as *joy* or *anger*. The presence of positive sentiment enforce it to predict *joy*.

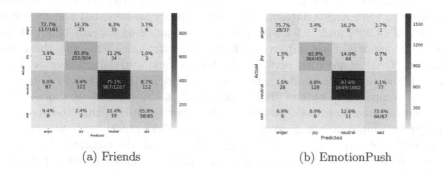

(a) Friends   (b) EmotionPush

Fig. 3. Confusion matrices for Emotion Classification.

We also perform a qualitative analysis to get better insights about the strength and weakness of the system. We found that, apart from dominating the effect of higher distribution class, few other error cases are present such as:

– **Loss of emotion drift:** When a strong emotion such as *anger* is encountered, it continues to be predicted. The reason behind it might be because we did not consider the speaker information while extracting contextual information from the utterances. An example is shown in the first part of Table 5.

– **Usage of expression like *lol, haha, etc.*:** Conversations involving such expressions have led to misclassifications of prediction by the model for some of the instances. An example is given in the second part of Table 5. The sentences are originally labeled *Sad*. However, due to the presence of a smiling expression-related term (*haha* and *lol*), the model has predicted it as *Joy*.

Table 5. Table showing loss of emotion drift in a dialogue of Friends dataset.

Utterances	True	Predicted
Don't ask me, I had it and I blew it!	Anger	Anger
Well, I want it!	Other	Anger
You can have it!	Other	Anger
I don't know, maybe I can't. I mean, maybe there's something wrong with me	Other	Anger
Oh, no! No!	Other	Anger
It's out there man! I've seen it! I got it!!	Joy	Anger
Then you hold on to it!!	Other	Anger
All right, man!!	Joy	Anger
All right, congratulations you lucky bastard!	Joy	Joy
I got it wrong lol	Sad	Joy
Gone but not forgotten haha	Sad	Joy

5 Conclusion

In this paper, we have presented a hybrid deep neural network framework (CAD) for detecting emotions in a dialogue. We propose a hierarchical BiGRU network which takes the assistance of various hand-crafted feature set on different levels of architecture to learn the contextual information of dialogue. The learned representation is fed to a fully connected layer over the time steps followed by softmax layer for the predictions. We have evaluated our model on the benchmark datasets of EmotionLines-2018, which consists of two corpora i.e., Friends and EmotionPush data. The evaluation suggests that our CAD framework obtains improved results against the state-of-art model so far. This model can be applied to various other similar datasets as well to improve their results.

Acknowledgement. Asif Ekbal acknowledges the Young Faculty Research Fellowship (YFRF), supported by Visvesvaraya Ph.D. scheme for Electronics and IT, Ministry of Electronics and Information Technology (MeitY), Government of India, being implemented by Digital India Corporation (formerly Media Lab Asia).

References

1. Chen, S.Y., Hsu, C.C., Kuo, C.C., Ku, L.W., et al.: EmotionLines: an emotion corpus of multi-party conversations. arXiv preprint arXiv:1802.08379 (2018)
2. Chung, J., Gulcehre, C., Cho, K., Bengio, Y.: Empirical evaluation of gated recurrent neural networks on sequence modeling. arXiv preprint arXiv:1412.3555 (2014)
3. Chung, J., Gulcehre, C., Cho, K., Bengio, Y.: Gated feedback recurrent neural networks. In: International Conference on Machine Learning, pp. 2067–2075 (2015)
4. Ekman, P.: Are there basic emotions? (1992)
5. Felbo, B., Mislove, A., Søgaard, A., Rahwan, I., Lehmann, S.: Using-millions of emoji occurrences to learn any-domain representations for detecting sentiment, emotion and sarcasm. In: Conference on Empirical Methods in Natural Language Processing (EMNLP) (2017)
6. Hazarika, D., Poria, S., Zadeh, A., Cambria, E., Morency, L.P., Zimmermann, R.: Conversational memory network for emotion recognition in dyadic dialogue videos. In: Proceedings of the 2018 Conference of the North American Chapter of the Association for Computational Linguistics: Human Language Technologies, Volume 1 (Long Papers), pp. 2122–2132 (2018)
7. Hsu, C.C., Ku, L.W.: SocialNLP 2018 emotionX challenge overview: recognizing emotions in dialogues. In: Proceedings of the Sixth International Workshop on Natural Language Processing for Social Media, pp. 27–31 (2018)
8. Jiao, W., Yang, H., King, I., Lyu, M.R.: HiGRU: hierarchical gated recurrent units for utterance-level emotion recognition. arXiv preprint arXiv:1904.04446 (2019)
9. Khosla, S.: EmotionX-AR: CNN-DCNN autoencoder based emotion classifier. In: Proceedings of the Sixth International Workshop on Natural Language Processing for Social Media, pp. 37–44 (2018)
10. Kim, T.K.: T test as a parametric statistic. Korean J. Anesthesiol. **68**(6), 540 (2015)
11. LeCun, Y., Bengio, Y., et al.: Convolutional networks for images, speech, and time series. Handbook Brain Theory Neural Netw. **3361**(10) (1995)
12. Liu, P., Qiu, X., Huang, X.: Recurrent neural network for text classification with multi-task learning. arXiv preprint arXiv:1605.05101 (2016)
13. Luo, L., Yang, H., Chin, F.Y.: EmotionX-DLC: self-attentive BiLSTM for detecting sequential emotions in dialogue. arXiv preprint arXiv:1806.07039 (2018)
14. Mikolov, T., Karafiát, M., Burget, L., Černocký, J., Khudanpur, S.: Recurrent neural network based language model. In: Eleventh Annual Conference of the International Speech Communication Association (2010)
15. Pennington, J., Socher, R., Manning, C.: GloVe: global vectors for word representation. In: Proceedings of the 2014 Conference on Empirical Methods in Natural Language Processing (EMNLP), pp. 1532–1543 (2014)
16. Peters, M.E., et al.: Deep contextualized word representations. In: Proceedings of NAACL (2018)
17. Poria, S., Cambria, E., Hazarika, D., Majumder, N., Zadeh, A., Morency, L.P.: Context-dependent sentiment analysis in user-generated videos. In: Proceedings of the 55th Annual Meeting of the Association for Computational Linguistics (Volume 1: Long Papers), pp. 873–883 (2017)
18. Saxena, R., Bhat, S., Pedanekar, N.: EmotionX-Area66: predicting emotions in dialogues using hierarchical attention network with sequence labeling. In: Proceedings of the Sixth International Workshop on Natural Language Processing for Social Media, pp. 50–55 (2018)

19. Srivastava, N., Hinton, G., Krizhevsky, A., Sutskever, I., Salakhutdinov, R.: Dropout: a simple way to prevent neural networks from overfitting. J. Mach. Learn. Res. **15**, 1929–1958 (2014)
20. Thelwall, M., Buckley, K., Paltoglou, G., Cai, D., Kappas, A.: Sentiment strength detection in short informal text. J. Am. Soc. Inform. Sci. Technol. **61**(12), 2544–2558 (2010)
21. Vaswani, A., et al.: Attention is all you need. In: Advances in Neural Information Processing Systems, pp. 5998–6008 (2017)
22. Yang, Z., Yang, D., Dyer, C., He, X., Smola, A., Hovy, E.: Hierarchical attention networks for document classification. In: Proceedings of the 2016 Conference of the North American Chapter of the Association for Computational Linguistics: Human Language Technologies, pp. 1480–1489 (2016)

Improving Student Forum Responsiveness: Detecting Duplicate Questions in Educational Forums

Manal Mohania[✉], Liyuan Zhou, and Tom Gedeon

College of Engineering and Computer Science, Australian National University,
Canberra, Australia
{manal.mohania,liyuan.zhou,tom.gedeon}@anu.edu.au

Abstract. Student forums are important for student engagement and learning in university courses but require high staff resources to moderate and answer questions. In introductory courses, the content can remain almost unchanged each year, so the questions asked in the course forums do not see a lot of variety over different iterations, which provides an opportunity for automation. This paper compiles a dataset of forum threads and meta-information of the participants from the Web Design and Development course at the Australian National University for the purposes of duplicate question detection in educational forums. A state of the art neural network model is trained on the dataset to measure its usefulness. An accuracy of 91.8% is achieved, which is on par with what is achieved on other datasets with similar features. A high performing neural network for this dataset could potentially be used to create a live system that detects and reuses answers for duplicate questions on course forums.

Keywords: Duplicate question detection · Neural networks · Duplicate question pair dataset

1 Introduction

The use of online forums as a medium for discussion and communication has become widespread in the field of education. One typical use case is for facilitating student discussions during an offering of a course. These forums are generally very rich in micro-collaborations [1] because all users have the ability to ask, answer and rate content. A study [2] reveals that discussions on these course forums promote collaborative learning by enhancing community building, developing self-identity, and improving relational dynamics, which in turn support learning at various knowledge levels and improve the cognitive process in learning.

However, while solving some problems, these discussion forums face problems of their own. While the forums are becoming more and more accessible by making the bar for participating on these forums quite low, it also inevitably leads to a

© Springer Nature Switzerland AG 2019
T. Gedeon et al. (Eds.): ICONIP 2019, LNCS 11955, pp. 410–421, 2019.
https://doi.org/10.1007/978-3-030-36718-3_35

lowering of the overall quality of the forum. In particular, while asking questions, it has been observed that a significant number of questions asked on a forum have previously been asked before. While no formal study that investigates this was found, this has been observed in some of the major web forums such as StackExchange, Quora and Yahoo! Answers.

With this paper, we release an anonymised dataset of questions and answers asked in a course forum for a Web Development and Design course at the Australian National University over the years 2015–2019. This course uses Piazza, a question and answer web service. We thus, henceforth, refer to this dataset as the "COMP1710 Piazza Dataset" (COMP1710 is the course code of the undergraduate version of the Web Design Development course at the Australian National University). This dataset will also feature metadata about the students in the course, such as their overall grade in the course, the mark they got for their participation on the course forum, their gender and ethnicity etc. Moreover, information about the questions that are duplicates of one another are also stored within the dataset.

After construction of the dataset, we perform some experiments by running a state-of-art-model built for natural language sentence matching on this dataset. We find that it achieves an impressive accuracy of 91.8% despite the average "sentence" length being much higher than what was previously used with that model. Upon experimenting with other duplicate question datasets where the average sentence is comparatively longer than the Quora Question Pairs Dataset (the original dataset on which it was tested), similar high accuracies were achieved. Surprisingly, this fact was not noted in the original paper.

2   Related Work

The task of detecting duplicate questions is a sub-task of the more general paraphrase detection task. However, the approaches used to solve the more general task are not always a step in the right direction towards detecting duplicate questions. In fact, it has been found that the performances achieved by different machine learning models on text paraphrase detection was significantly better than the ones achieved on detecting semantically equivalent questions [3].

2.1   Datasets

Numerous datasets related to the fields of question similarity have been published in recent years.

The Qatar Living Dataset. SemEval (Semantic Evaluation) is an ongoing series of evaluations of computational semantic analysis systems. In 2016, one of the tasks (Task 3) [4] in the SemEval workshops was related to answer selection in community question answering forums, which involves both detecting semantically equivalent questions and also selecting the best answer from a range of answers.

For evaluation of the models, they released the Qatar Living data corpus the source of which is the Qatar Living Forum[1]. This dataset contained 317 original questions, 3169 related questions and 31690 comments

The CQADupStack Dataset. CQADupStack is another benchmark dataset in the field of Community Question Answering. It contains threads from twelve StackExchange subforums, annotated with duplicate question information and comes with pre-defined training, development, and test splits, both for retrieval and classification experiments [5].

The dataset contains over 460,000 threads (an average of 38,362 threads per subforum). The percentage of duplicate questions has a high variation between subforums- ranging from 1.52% for the Wordpress[2] subforum to 9.31% for the English subforum[3]. The average number of duplicate questions per duplication, however, has a much smaller range (1.02 to 1.22).

The duplicate question annotations were manually performed by the users in these subforums. As a result, these labels are not guaranteed to be perfect. In fact, a study [6] concluded that the number of duplicates could be increased by around 45%, by annotating only 0.0003% of all the question pairs in the data set.

The Quora Question Pairs Datasets. In early 2017, Quora[4], a question and answer website, published a dataset of over 400,000 potential duplicate question pairs [7].

Questions on Quora differ from the questions on the Stackexchange and Yahoo! Forums in that they do not possess a separate question body. Questions on Quora are limited to a maximum length of 250 characters. This limitation compels the user to ask more general and less detailed questions. This is in contrast to most educational forums where the asker has the ability to explain their current understanding of the topic through the question bodies.

Despite the existence of a multitude of datasets relating to the field of community question answering, we construct another dataset due to the following reasons:

1. **Narrow Scope of Field:** Other datasets published so far are quite general in nature (with the exception of InsuranceQA). Quora Question Pairs for example, is not limited by scope in the types of questions contained. The Stackoverflow dataset, on the other hand, is somewhat more restricted in scope when compared to the Quora Question Pairs dataset. However, its scope (general programming) is still quite large to make it difficult to perform a detailed analysis. We create a dataset with a more restricted scope, one of questions asked during multiple offerings of a web design course at the

---

[1] www.qatarliving.com/forum.

[2] https://wordpress.stackexchange.com/.

[3] https://english.stackexchange.com/.

[4] www.quora.com.

Australian National University. The scope of this is small enough such that a significant fraction of duplicate question pairs are found, and large enough so that significantly many new questions can be added to it that are not duplicates of existing questions. This helps with the training of neural network models.

2. **Inclusion of Meta-data:** None of the datasets published so far include meta-data about the backgrounds of the users who participate in the forums. We include meta-data such as the ethnicity, gender, grade obtained in the course etc. This can potentially be used to deduce correlations between the quality of the posts made and the backgrounds of the users. A presence of a strong correlation would suggest that the background of the students could act as an effective heuristic measure when deciding the best answer to a given question.

3 The COMP1710 Piazza Dataset

Piazza is a question and answer platform that is used by many universities across the world. Piazza comes with a wide set of features which makes it an indispensable asset for many courses. For instance, the platform allows users to ask questions, post notes or hold a poll. These can be done anonymously, semi-anonymously or with the name visible to everyone. Piazza also provides a good rendering engine for code and LaTeX snippets.

The COMP1710 Piazza dataset is an anonymised dataset of questions and answers asked in the Piazza course forum for a Web Development and Design course at the Australian National University over the years 2015–2019. This dataset also features metadata about the students in the course, such as their overall grade in the course, the mark they got for their participation on the course forum, their gender and ethnicity etc. Moreover, information about the questions that are duplicates of one another are also provided within the dataset.

3.1 Dataset Format

The dataset is divided into three different files- one for the content of the threads, one for the metadata and one for information about duplicate questions.

One of the files (questions.json) is a JSON file that maps unique thread ids to information about them. The unique ids for the threads were created by hyphen separating the year of posting and the serial number of the thread in that year. For example, $2018 - 141$ refers to the 141st thread in the year 2018. These ids are mapped to information about the threads such as their title, body, answers, comments, votes, anonymous ids of the users that participated etc. Information on the history of the thread is also supplied along with the timestamps. The names used for their keys are self-explanatory. As mentioned previously, the choice of these keys was influenced by the visual structure of a Piazza thread page, and the information available to users.

The metadata is present in a separate JSON file (metadata.json). This file consists of a mapping from the anonymous students ids to their relevant meta information. References to the anonymised student mappings will also be present in the questions.json file.

Finally, the annotations for the duplicate questions are available in a CSV file of its own (duplicates.csv). Each row in the file contains the thread ids of questions that are duplicates of one another. Only the questions that have at least one duplicate have been mentioned in this file. Otherwise if a particular thread id is omitted from the file, it means that either the thread is not a question, or that it does not have any duplicates.

The dataset will be made available in December via www.hcc-workshop.anu. edu.au/comp1710-piazza-dataset.

3.2   Duplicate Question Definition

The definition for duplicate questions that was initially agreed upon by the dataset annotators was the same as the one that is used frequently in literature [8].

"Two questions are semantically equivalent if they can be adequately answered by the exact same answer."

However, this definition when used directly with the COMP1710 Piazza Dataset is not very useful. The primary reason for that is that the Piazza forums for the COMP1710 course are monitored for quality less rigorously than other real world forums such as StackExchange. In particular, asking multiple questions as part of the same thread is allowed in the former whereas, the latter follows the principle of "one question per thread"[5]. Keeping in mind that the eventual goal was to create a live question answering system, a few constraints were added to make it applicable to the majority of the questions in the dataset. The additional constraints added are listed below.

- If multiple questions are asked in two different threads, the threads would be considered duplicates if the majority of questions in one are duplicates of the majority of questions in another.
- In the case above, if there is no clear majority on the number of questions, the questions are then weighted by their word counts. As a consequence, if a particular thread consists of two questions where one uses a word count of 100 and the other uses 10 words only, the first question is assumed to be the "majority" of the given thread.
- Some questions when asked in different years get different responses. For example, "What is the location for the final exam?" is likely to receive different responses in each year. Such information retrieval questions where the answer may vary across years have still been annotated as duplicates.

---

[5] https://stackoverflow.com/help/how-to-ask.

Adding these additional constraints to the definition for duplicate questions made the annotation process more robust to human biases when performing annotations for questions that are in the inevitable grey areas due to ambiguities in the questions being considered.

3.3 Forum Statistics

The COMP1710 Piazza Dataset combines data from various different sources. Performing different statistical analyses may thus, reveal better insights about the dataset. Various statistical analyses are performed for the dataset, and the results obtained are then compared to existing datasets and discussed.

Number of Threads. The COMP1710 Piazza Dataset consists of 4,145 threads (inclusive of questions, notes and polls). When compared to other datasets from the domain, this is only larger than the Qatar Living Dataset. However, while the dataset size may seem orders of magnitude smaller relative to the larger ones, the smaller scope for the topic of discussion compensates for fewer threads, and is at the large end of what can plausibly collected from university course forums – the course has grown from 146 students in 2015 to 264 in 2019, and so has been on the medium to large size throughout.

Out of the 4,145 threads in the dataset, 3,262 of them are questions.

Average Length of Questions. On average, a question body contains 66.2 words (all HTML tags are stripped before this figure is calculated). This is on par with the average question length of the StackExchange datasets where the users have the ability to contextualise/describe their thoughts about the problem they are facing.

On the other hand, this statistic is much larger when compared to the Quora Question Pairs dataset, which has an average question length of under 10 words. The reduced length of questions on Quora allows the question to be more focused in scope. A longer question body, while allows the asker to explain the question with more rigour, also carries extra information that is often irrelevant to the question being asked.

3.4 Statistics for Duplicate Questions

The COMP1710 Piazza dataset has some interesting statistics for the duplicate questions present. We discuss these in this section and also compare the statistics with other datasets where possible. Due to the late arrival of the 2019 data, these statistics have been measured for the 2015–2018 subset.

Percentage of Duplicate Questions. There has been little change in the content and assignments of the COMP1710 course with each iteration. Unsurprisingly, a lot of the questions that are asked in a particular year are very similar to those that were asked in other years. In fact, around 42% of the questions that have been asked over the four years in the Piazza forums for this course have duplicates. When compared against question *pairs*, approximately 0.14% of the question pairs in this dataset are duplicates from all possible pairs of questions.

While the low percentage for the percentage of duplicate pairs is explicable, it does imply that there is a heavy imbalance in the labels of the classes of this dataset. This needs to be a consideration when trying to learn latent features from the dataset.

Number of Duplicate Questions per Duplicate Question. When a particular question has at least one duplicate, there are at least 4 of them on average in the COMP1710 Piazza Dataset. This number is significantly higher than the StackExchange datasets where this statistic has a value between 1 and 2 for all forums [6]. The higher number in this case is likely indicative of the fact that certain questions are very popular which push the average up. As an example, 20 various forms of the question "How do I submit my assignment?" were posted over the four years.

It should be noted that the feature of certain questions being very popular is not restricted to this dataset. In the StackExchange dataset, for example, on the webmasters subforum[6], a certain question appeared in 106 different forms. Due to the sheer size of the dataset, the value of the average number of duplicates is not heavily affected by such outliers.

4   Experiments and Results

4.1   The BiMPM Model

Wang et al. proposed the Bilateral Multi-Perspective Matching (Bi-MPM) model for the task of Natural Language Sentence Matching [9]. The model achieves state of the art performance for sentence paraphrase matching, when tested on the Quora Question Pairs Dataset. This model matches each time stamp of each of the two questions with every time stamp of the other question. A Bi-LSTM layer is then used to produce a fixed length matching vector, which is further as used as input for a fully connected layer that makes the final decision. We use this model to conduct our experiments.

4.2   Experiments Performed

Due to the late arrival of the 2019 data, we only utilised the 2015–2018 subset of the data for our experiments. That subset of the data contains 2,300 questions which corresponds to approximately 2.6 million question pairs (Fig. 1).

---

[6] https://webmasters.stackexchange.com.

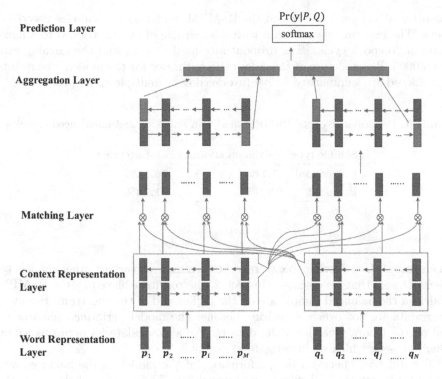

Fig. 1. The Bi-MPM model [9]

Preprocessing of the Data. The data was pre-processed in three stages- conversion to lowercase, removal of HTML tags (including images) and the removal of foreign characters. The final step was necessary because even though the course is taught in English, due to the significant number of international students, some question inadvertently contain non-English characters. We also used a list of stop words that contained standard greetings, as they add little value to the semantics of a question. However, it was also observed that removing this stop list did not affect results significantly.

4.3   Samples Generated

The first sample we generated consisted of 7,260 question pairs. This sample was created such that the number of question pairs labelled as duplicates was roughly equal to the number question pairs labelled non-duplicates. We created a 60%-20%-20% split for training, validation and testing respectively.

Another sample that we generated was one containing over 33,000 question pairs. This sample was purposefully created such that there is a heavy imbalance in the number of duplicate and non-duplicate questions. This sample contained around 2,200 duplicate question pairs. The validation and the test files used for this sample were the same as the ones used in the previous sample.

Results. We trained and tested the Bi-MPM model on the samples described above. The experiments were run with a batch size of 60 and trained to a maximum of 20 epoch cycles. The dropout rate used was 0.1 and the learning rate was 0.0005. We made use of the Adam [10] optimiser for the model. The results we achieved are summarised below (averaged over multiple runs) (Table 1).

Table 1. Performance of the Bi-MPM model on balanced and unbalanced samples

Sample type	Validation accuracy	Test accuracy
Unbalanced	77.14%	**76.11%**
Balanced	94.23%	**91.78%**

Discussion. Considering the average performance of various other models on other datasets that we discussed in Sect. 2, the results achieved by the Bi-MPM model on the balanced sample are on the higher end of the spectrum. However, the results are not overly surprising because the model performed remarkably well on the Quora Question Pairs dataset. We also validate its performance on other datasets, which we investigate in Sect. 4.3.

The difference between the performance of the model on the balanced and unbalanced samples is, however, not surprising. The heavy imbalance in the model causes the weights in the model to be trained such that the output is always biased towards marking question pairs as non-duplicates. However, since the test set itself is balanced, the overall accuracy is significantly lower on the test set.

Q1: the mark about assignment2: i have some questions about the mark and the feedback about it. 1. it is said that there is no forum posts nominated. however, apparently my questions are not anonymous. here is the photo about it. 2. it is said that there is no more than 3 links and no labels in the image map. however, there are 5 photos in the image map and each one has a label and a link. 3. it is said that there are no less than 10 photos in the photo gallery. however, i made two photo galleries and each one has five photos. in all, there are 10 photos here is the photo about the feedback. i strongly hope you can check my assignment again and give me a reasonable mark. thank you!

Q2: marking issues: i had included a portfolio page on my website showing some of my music, which was supposed to be my "something original", but received no marks for it. also, i accidentally added my new css file to every page rather than just 1, and received no marks. is there any chance of that being taken into consideration for my marks?

Model Output: Non-duplicates
Gold Standard: Duplicates

Fig. 2. Example of a question pair that was incorrectly classified as non-duplicates

A further analysis of questions that were incorrectly classified by the model trained on the balanced sample is performed below.

Figure 2 is an example of a question pair where the intent of both the questions is the same, in that they want to get their assignments remarked. The reasons, however, are very different which is evident from the context. This additional context is likely to be the reason why the model did not consider these two questions to be duplicates. The additional context, however, does not affect the true label of this question pair because all such questions in the dataset had the same answer along the lines of "It is best to bring this up with your tutor directly during your lab".

Q1: how do i make multiple page?
Q2: delete file in partch: hi all, i want to know how to delete files in partch with file name have symbol . or space in it? thanks so much for the answer.
Model Output: Duplicates
Gold Standard: Non-duplicates

Fig. 3. Example of a question pair that was incorrectly classified as duplicates

Finally, Fig. 3 is a question pair where one of the questions is quite short and harder to reason about. While there are not any common keywords between the two questions, they have been likely labelled as duplicates because the training set contained a few questions about "deleting multiple files on Partch" which may have ended up in the model parameters being updated such that the words "multiple", "delete" and "Partch" might be treated as near synonyms of one another resulting in the two questions being classified as duplicates.

With Other Datasets. To confirm that the results obtained by the Bi-MPM model on the COMP1710 Piazza dataset were not the result of an anomaly in the dataset, we ran the Bi-MPM model on a few other datasets, namely, AskUbuntu and Meta StackExchange. They were chosen primarily because the format of the questions in those are more similar to the ones in the COMP1710 Piazza dataset as compared to Quora Question Pairs.

The configuration of the model was the same as in the above experiment. The train, validation and test splits used for these datasets were the same ones used by Rodrigues et al. [11] to discredit the work of Bogdanova et al. [8]. These splits do not contain the clue in the question texts which had originally been left in by Bogdanova et al. The training, validation and testing sets in both the datasets have an almost equitable distribution for the two labels.

Running the Bi-MPM model for a maximum of 20 epochs on the respective datasets produced the results that are summarised in Table 2.

Discussion
The performance achieved by the Bi-MPM model on the other datasets is in a very similar range to what is achieved with the COMP1710 Piazza dataset.

Table 2. Performance of the Bi-MPM model on other duplicate question datasets

Dataset	Test set accuracy
Quora Question Pairs	88.17%[a]
Meta StackExchange	88.95%
AskUbunutu	92.34%
Comp1710 Piazza	91.78%

[a] As reported in the original paper

Surprisingly enough, not all of these results were reported in the original Bi-MPM paper [9]. There are two main points of discussion with these results.

Firstly, the average question length seems to have an inverse effect on the performance of the model. The model performs worst on the dataset with the smallest average question length. This is a bit surprising because a longer question often contains information that is not entirely relevant to the crux of the underlying question.

Secondly, despite major differences between the COMP1710 Piazza dataset and the AskUbuntu and Meta StackExchange datasets, the test accuracy achieved on the datasets is comparable. We believe that there are two conflicting factors at play here. Firstly, the narrow scope of field of the COMP1710 Piazza dataset makes it comparatively easier for the model to learn from the training set as it has a very limited vocabulary and can thus be better analysed. Secondly, the lack of incentive to maintain a high question quality results in the questions in the dataset having a high number of spelling errors and often, bad grammar. Considering these two points, it is not surprising that the accuracy achieved on the COMP1710 Piazza dataset is similar to the StackExchange datasets.

5   Conclusion and Future Work

In the previous section we saw that the Bi-MPM model performs very well on questions where the length is longer. This fact was surprisingly not noted in their original paper. In absolute terms, an accuracy of 91.8% is achieved on our test set. This is a lot higher than the test accuracies on other datasets by other models that we found during our research. However, this figure is on par with the accuracy achieved by the Bi-MPM model on other datasets, including those of StackExchange, where the questions are longer on average.

A substantial perceived benefit of the automated system is responsiveness, in being able to provide an answer essentially instantaneously to the large majority of questions. This work was used to create a pilot automated question answering system that automatically reuses answers from previous years if a new question that is semantically equivalent to a question from a previous year is asked. On limited testing by 11 students (9 males, 2 females with an average age of 22.18 and a standard deviation of 2.52) on a live version of the course, the average vote (on a scale from 1 to 5) on the ability of the bot to reuse answers from previous years was valued at 2.67. One of the reasons that the value was low was likely that the validity and the quality of the old answer was not taken into account when reusing it in another year, which should be possible given the 91.8% accuracy on duplicate question detection.

Finally, the inclusion of the metadata in the dataset makes it a useful dataset outside the fields of artificial intelligence and machine learning. As an example, one could use the metadata to study the correlation (and potential causation) between forum participation and the grade achieved in the course.

References

1. Shachaf, P.: Social reference: toward a unifying theory. Libr. Inform. Sci. Res. **32**(1), 66–76 (2010)
2. Blooma, M.J., Kurian, J.C., Chua, A.Y.K., Goh, D.H.L., Lien, N.H.: Social question answering: analyzing knowledge, cognitive processes and social dimensions of micro-collaborations. Comput. Educ. **69**, 109–120 (2013)
3. Rodrigues, J., Saedi, C., Branco, A., Silva, J.: Semantic equivalence detection: are interrogatives harder than declaratives? In: Proceedings of the 11th International Conference on Language Resources and Evaluation (2018)
4. AlessandroMoschitti, P.L., AbedAlhakimFreihat, W.H., Glass, J., Randeree, B.: Semeval-2016 task 3: community question answering. Proc. SemEval 525—545 (2016)
5. Hoogeveen, D., Verspoor K., Baldwin T.: CQADupStack: a benchmark data set for community question-answering research. In: Proceedings of the 20th Australasian Document Computing Symposium, p. 3. ACM (2015)
6. Hoogeveen, D., Verspoor F., Baldwin T.: CQADupStack: gold or silver. In: Proceedings of the SIGIR 2016 Workshop on Web Question Answering Beyond Factoids, vol. 16 (2016)
7. Quora dataset. https://data.quora.com/First-Quora-Dataset-Release-Question-Pairs. Accessed 7 Oct 2018
8. Bogdanova, D., dos Santos, C., Barbosa, L., Zadrozny, B.: Detecting semantically equivalent questions in online user forums. In: Proceedings of the 19th Conference on Computational Natural Language Learning, pp. 123–131 (2015)
9. Wang, Z., Hamza, W., Florian, R.: Bilateral multi-perspective matching for natural language sentences. In: Proceedings of the 26th International Joint Conference on Artificial Intelligence, pp. 4144–4150 (2017)
10. Kingma, D. P., Ba J.: Adam: a method for stochastic optimization. In: Proceedings of the 3rd International Conference for Learning Representations (2014)
11. Rodrigues, J.A., Saedi, C., Maraev, V., Silva, J., Branco, A.: Ways of asking and replying in duplicate question detection. In: Proceedings of the 6th Joint Conference on Lexical and Computational Semantics, pp. 262–270 (2017)

Time-Series and Related Models

On Probability Calibration of Recurrent Text Recognition Network

Xinghua Zhu, Jianzong Wang$^{(\boxtimes)}$, Zhenhou Hong, Junxiong Guo,
and Jing Xiao

Ping An Technology (Shenzhen) Co., Ltd., Shenzhen, China
{zhuxinghua889,wangjianzong347,hongzhenhou168,guojunxiong995,
jingxiao661}@pingan.com.cn, jzwang@188.com

Abstract. Optical text recognition has seen continual improvement in character accuracy over the past decade. However, as error persists, it is crucial to know when and where a recognition error occurs. Studies have shown that recent development of deep convolutional neural networks tends to increase calibration errors, compared to traditional classifiers such as SVM. Yet, the calibration error in deep neural networks for sequential text recognition has not been studied in the literature.

This paper addresses the probability misalignment problem in unsegmented text recognition models. We analyze the causes of probability misalignment in the popular recurrent text recognition model, the attention encoder-decoder model, and propose a novel probability calibration algorithm for individual character predictions. Experiments show that the proposed methods not only reduce expected calibration error, but also improve the character prediction accuracy. In our experiments, calibration error on authentic industrial datasets improved as much as 68% compared to original text recognizer outputs.

1 Introduction

In the past decade, deep neural networks (DNNs) have been successfully applied in many domains. The accuracy of DNN classifiers also grows rapidly with the development of deeper, and more sophisticated network structures and training techniques.

On the other hand, researches found that recent developments in convolutional neural networks (CNNs) lead to increased calibration error in the model [1]. In other words, the probability score given by the CNNs does not align with the true credibility of their predictions. In industrial applications, the misaligned probability score poses big challenges to subsequent decision making systems. For example, practitioners make treatment decisions based on probability of disease

---

J. Wang—This paper is supported by National Key Research and Development Program of China under grant No. 2018YFB1003500, No. 2018YFB0204400 and No. 2017YFB1401202.

T. Gedeon et al. (Eds.): ICONIP 2019, LNCS 11955, pp. 425–436, 2019.
https://doi.org/10.1007/978-3-030-36718-3_36

prediction [2]. Self-driving vehicles take correspondent actions based on probabilities of obstacle detection. In text recognition applications, the probability score is often used to filter false recognition results. Even though the text recognition model may have an overall character accuracy of 95% or above, it is not satisfactory in industrial applications. For instance, in an office document processing system, to alleviate human effort in logging identity information, names on the citizen identity card would be extracted by a text recognition model from scanned copies. An error in such text information is intolerable. Measures must be taken to filter out false predictions, which is usually done by thresholding the probability score from the predictions. If the model itself cannot discover an error from its output, human labour has to be allocated to double check the results from the text recognition model, increasing the total cost of the documenting system.

For general classification problems, model calibration methods have been proposed to reduce the error in probability scores. Guo et al experimented with series of contemporary CNNs and proposed that temperature scaling, a single-variant version of Platt scaling [3], is effective in reducing calibration error in all experiments [1]. Leethart et al. proposed a probability calibration tree to adapt calibration parameters according to original input data [4]. Pereyra et al. [5] and Kumar et al. [6] proposed an alternative option to enforce calibration during training. Yet, probability misalignment in recurrent neural networks and calibration methods on recurrent models have not been addressed in the literature.

In this paper, we analyze causes for probability misalignment in recurrent text recognition models. A novel calibration method, called *Calibration CNN*, is proposed for text recognition models. The performance of the proposed methods is demonstrated by experiments on authentic data in industry applications.

Contributions of this paper include:

1. Formulation of the probability misalignment problem in text recognition models.
2. Proposed a novel off-line probability calibration method for text recognizer.
3. Extensive comparison of the proposed model calibration method with existing methods on authentic industrial data.

2 Related Work

2.1 Text Recognition

Text recognition has always been an important branch of computer vision and scene understanding researches. Especially, for unsegmented character images, i.e., images containing a sequence of characters, recurrent neural networks (RNNs) are commonly adapted for text recognition models.

Connectionist temporal classification (CTC) [7] combines the probability maximization task with finding optimal sequence decoding for the output sequence from a recurrent network. Kim et al. improved the CTC network by incoporating attention mechanism [8] as well as a language model, which is also a recurrent network module itself [9].

Unlike CTC approaches, the encoder-decoder structure solves the feature-output vector alignment problem using the attention matrix. Its application in unsegmented character image labeling has proved very successful [10,11]. In [10], a fully convolutional network is used as the encoder. Given its uniformly shaped input images, a fully convolutional encoder has provided superior recognition accuracy compared to preceding methods. Whereas for input images with highly variable shapes, such as the equation images in [11], a recurrent encoder would be more robust in producing reliable features, as suggested in the original encoder-decoder proposition [12].

The contemporary text recognizers often achieve character accuracy above 95% given proper datasets. This paper bases on the encoder-decoder approach proposed in [11] for all experiments. Note that it is not our aim to discuss accuracy improvement for text recognizers, but rather the correctness of the confidence in the predicted individual characters.

2.2 Model Calibration

Classifiers are trained to minimize the overall error rate in given datasets. Yet, error rate is not the only criterion to measure the quality of a classifier. In many applications, it is also important to know the confidence of a prediction made by the classifier. The probability score that accompany the class prediction would be a convenient measurement of confidence. However, such probability scores are sometimes not available, or not reliable. The difference between a predicted confidence score and the actual extent of credibility is termed *probability misalignment*, and the process to correct such misalignment is termed *model calibration*.

Probability calibration can be incorporated with an existing classifier [6], or can be carried out off-line as post-processing steps with the classifier model untouched. Off-line calibration methods perform calibration on a hold-out validation dataset. Many classical calibration methods, such as histogram binning, isotonic regression, and Bayesian binning are designed for binary models. Extension for multinomial classification is often achieved by converting the problem into multiple one-versus-all problems. In contrast to the previous binning methods, Platt scaling [3] is a parametric approach to calibration. The non-probabilistic predictions of a classifier are used as input features for a logistic regression model. Guo et al. report that the *temperature scaling*, a single-parameter variant of Platt Scaling, is effective at calibrating predictions of various contemporary convolutional classification models [1].

Probability calibration trees [4] expands the Platt scaling method with a tree structure, where each leaf node is attached with a logistic regression model. The logistic model trees provides an adaptive calibration model, adjusting to the complexity in the input data distribution. Our proposed method is also an adaptive one. Instead of a decision tree, we train a convolutional neural network to extract features from character images. Logistic regression parameters are adaptively generated from the feature vectors.

3   Definitions

This paper addresses the per-character probability calibration problems in text recognition models. In this section, we lay out the formal definitions of related problems.

3.1   Text Recognition

The task of a text recognition model is to recognize unsegmented text strings from images. Given image input $\mathcal{I}$ of text string $\mathbf{y}$, a text recognition model T finds an estimate $\hat{\mathbf{y}} = T(\mathcal{I}; \theta)$, where θ is the collection of parameters of T.

In theory, the design of the recognition model $T(\cdot; \theta)$ should maximize the overall joint likelihood, i.e.,

$$\mathbb{P}\left(\hat{\mathbf{y}} = \mathbf{y} \mid \mathcal{I}; \theta\right) = \mathbb{P}\left(\hat{y}_0 = y_0, ..., \hat{y}_M = y_M \mid \mathcal{I}; \theta\right). \tag{1}$$

Yet, in practice, evaluating the joint probability in Eq. 1 is often infeasible. Therefore, most text prediction models assume Markov dependence [13] among characters in the text string, reducing the likelihood to

$$\mathbb{P}\left(\hat{\mathbf{y}} = \mathbf{y} \mid \mathcal{I}; \theta\right) = \prod_{t=1}^{T} \mathbb{P}\left(\hat{y}_t = y_t \mid \mathcal{I}; \hat{y}_{t-1}, \theta\right). \tag{2}$$

Given a set of training samples $\mathcal{X} = \{(\mathcal{I}^{(i)}, \mathbf{y}^{(i)}), i = 1, ..., N\}$, the negative log-likelihood loss is given by

$$\mathcal{L}_{\text{NLL}} = \sum_{i=1}^{N} \sum_{j=1}^{|\mathbf{y}^{(i)}|} -\log \mathbb{P}\left(\hat{y}_j^{(i)} = y_j^{(i)} \mid \mathcal{I}^{(i)}; \theta\right). \tag{3}$$

During training, the model parameters θ are optimized to minimize the total negative log-likelihood loss over the training dataset, i.e., $\theta^* = \arg\min_\theta \mathcal{L}_{\text{NLL}}$.

3.2   Model Calibration

A classification model is said to be *perfectly calibrated* if

$$\mathbb{P}\left(\hat{\mathbf{y}} = \mathbf{y} \mid \hat{p} = p\right) = p, \forall p \in [0, 1], \tag{4}$$

where $\hat{p}$ is the confidence of prediction $\hat{\mathbf{y}}$, given by the classification model. The left hand side of Eq. 4 is called the accuracy of the model. Therefore, in case of perfect calibration, the expected accuracy of the model is equal to its confidence.

In a finite sample validation set, the accuracy of the model is estimated by grouping predictions into segments with similar confidence $\hat{p}$. Specifically, predictions are grouped into M bins,

$$B_m = \left\{(\hat{\mathbf{y}}, \hat{p}) \mid \hat{p} \in \left(\frac{m-1}{M}, \frac{m}{M}\right]\right\}, m = 1, ..., M. \tag{5}$$

Then, the confidence and accuracy of B_m are estimated by taking the average values in the bin, respectively, i.e.,

$$\text{conf}(B_m) = \frac{1}{|B_m|} \sum_{i \in B_m} \hat{p}_i, \tag{6}$$

$$\text{acc}(B_m) = \frac{1}{|B_m|} \sum_{i \in B_m} \mathbf{1}(\hat{\mathbf{y}}_i = \mathbf{y}_i), \tag{7}$$

where $\mathbf{1}(\cdot)$ is the indicator function. The *reliability diagram* of a classification model is the plot of $\text{acc}(B_m)$ versus $\text{conf}(B_m)$ [14]. If the model is perfectly calibrated, the reliability diagram should be aligned with the identity line.

Note that the Eqs. 6 and 7 are unbiased estimates of the true confidence and accuracy of a model, only if the sample size $|B_m|$ is large enough. In modern classifiers, this assumption might not hold in most cases, because the predicted confidence $\hat{p}$ often clusters around 1.0. For such scenario, Leathart et al. proposed to divide the validation set into M equally populated bins for accuracy and confidence estimation [4].

Scalar statistic of the calibration, expected calibration error (ECE), is also defined based on the estimates of B_m's, i.e.,

$$\text{ECE} = \sum_{m=1}^{M} \frac{|B_m|}{n} |\text{acc}(B_m) - \text{conf}(B_m)|, \tag{8}$$

where n is the number of samples in the validation set.

In addition to the above calibration errors, other metrics of the classification model are also of interest to our applications.

4   Proposed Methods

4.1   Reasoning for the Cause of Miscalibration

As shown in Eq. 2, in recurrent text recognition models, the inference of character $\hat{\mathbf{y}}_t$ is conditioned on previous prediction $\hat{\mathbf{y}}_{t-1}$. The conditional probability increases overall prediction accuracy by exploiting prior distribution of character combinations in the training datasets. But it also causes bias towards frequent character combinations during inference. The conditional assumption might assert a prediction $\hat{\mathbf{y}}$ by looking at the previous prediction only, while rare combinations of characters are considered outliers. It further deepens the problem of class imbalance.

On the other hand, in [15], the authors found that a lot of the errors in text recognition originated from a shifted attention map. When the attended area shifts from the center of a character, the prediction of the character may be totally wrong, but has very high confidence score. By restraining the classifier to use features around the character centers only, these error can be alleviated in most cases [15].

We also investigated the connectionx between attention alignment and text recognition accuracy on our own datasets. The results are consistent with those in [15]. An example of misaligned attention is shown in Fig. 1.

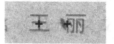   

Drifted attention centers, predicted by original SRN.   Correct attention centers, predicted by revised SRN with bounding box prediction.

Fig. 1. Example of attention center misalignment.

In Fig. 1, the depicted sample image contains Chinese characters " 王丽 ". Attention centers are marked with red "+" signs on the sample images. The results predicted by the original SRN (left) and the revised SRN (right) are " 王明 " (confidence 0.9999, 0.9936) and " 王丽 " (confidence 0.9987, 0.9999), respectively. In the results predicted by the original SRN, the attention center of the second character drifted only slightly to the left of the ground truth. Yet the predicted character is incorrect, while still holding extremely high confidence.

4.2   Calibration CNN

Based on the above reasoning, we propose the Calibration CNN to alleviate the probability misalignment in recurrent text recognition models.

Inspired by [4], the Calibration CNN is devised to perform adaptive calibration by referring to the original image data corresponding to a character prediction (see Fig. 2(a)).

Let $\hat{\mathbf{z}}$ denote the un-calibrated logits from the classification model. In [4], a decision tree is expanded on the original input data, where each leaf node n is attached to a logistic regression model $\{\mathbf{W}_n, \mathbf{b}_n\}$ for samples belonging to this leaf node. The calibrated probabilities in node n are given by vector scaling of $\hat{\mathbf{z}}$:

$$\tilde{\mathbf{z}} = \mathbf{W}_n \hat{\mathbf{z}} + \mathbf{b}_n, \tag{9}$$

$$\tilde{p} = softmax\left(\tilde{\mathbf{z}}\right). \tag{10}$$

Since the original input data in our problem are text images, we replace the decision tree with a CNN. On top of the CNN, parameters in the logistic regression model, $\mathbf{W}$ and $\mathbf{b}$, are inferred from the convoluted feature vector, i.e.,

$$\tilde{\mathbf{z}} = \mathbf{W}\left(\mathcal{I}_\mathbf{r}; \psi\right) \cdot \hat{\mathbf{z}} + \mathbf{b}\left(\mathcal{I}_\mathbf{r}; \psi\right), \tag{11}$$

$$\tilde{p} = softmax\left(\tilde{\mathbf{z}}\right), \tag{12}$$

where $\mathcal{I}_\mathbf{r}$ is the subimage corresponding to an individual character prediction in the original text image $\mathcal{I}$. ψ is the collection of parameters in the Calibration

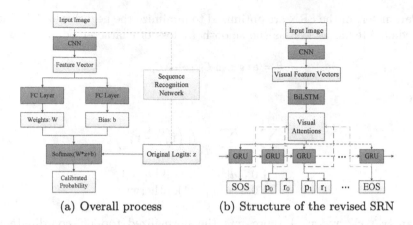

(a) Overall process   (b) Structure of the revised SRN

Fig. 2. Structure of the proposed neural networks.

CNN model. The original logits from the recognition model, and the logits from the character image CNN are combined in Eq. 11, to form the calibrated prediction of the individual character. The CNN learns how much to trust the original prediction through $\mathbf{W}$, and adjust the prediction by added bias $\mathbf{b}$ adaptively.

The proposed calibration CNN structure can also be interpreted as a residual structure, where the logits $\mathbf{z}_i$ from the SRN would be retained if it is coherent with ground truth labels. In other words, the accuracy of the calibration CNN predictions for individual characters could not be worse than the predictions from the SRN. It is also shown in experiments that the proposed calibration CNN improves character prediction accuracy even if the original accuracy of the SRN is extremely high.

Let $\mathcal{Y} = \left\{ \left(\mathcal{I}^{(i)}, \mathbf{r}^{(i)}, \hat{\mathbf{z}}^{(i)} \right) \mid i = 1, ..., N \right\}$ be the hold-out validation set. Parameters in the Calibration CNN are optimized to minimize the negative log-likelihood of individual character predictions, i.e.,

$$\psi = \underset{\psi^*}{\arg\min} \sum_{i=1}^{|\mathcal{Y}|} - \log \mathbb{P} \left(\tilde{\mathbf{y}}^{(i)} = \mathbf{y}^{(i)} \mid \mathcal{I}_{\mathbf{r}^{(i)}}^{(i)}; \psi^* \right) \tag{13}$$

To find out the image region $\mathbf{r}$ that corresponds to a character prediction of the recognizer, one might think of the using the attention map as an indirect reference. But the attention map is designed to gather contextual information for a single inference, it does not necessarily restrain in the character region itself. Therefore, instead of reusing the attention map, we add a branch to the decoder of our text recognition model, to obtain the correspondent image region with a character prediction.

The recurrent text recognition we used in our experiments is based on the sequential text recognition network (SRN) in [11]. The revised SRN is illustrated in Fig. 2(b).

Parameters in the SRN are optimized to minimize the negative log-likelihood of predicted texts, as well as the smooth L_1 loss of character bounding boxes, i.e.,

$$\theta = \arg\min_{\theta^*} \mathcal{L}_{\text{NLL}} + \lambda\mathcal{L}_{L_1}, \tag{14}$$

where

$$\mathcal{L}_{L_1} = \sum_{i=1}^{|\mathcal{Y}|} \sum_{j\in\{x,y,w,h\}} l_1\left(\hat{\mathbf{r}}_j^{(i)} - \mathbf{r}_j^{(i)}\right), \tag{15}$$

$$l_1(d) = \begin{cases} 0.5|d|^2, & \text{if } |d| \leq 1, \\ 0.5 + (|d| - 1), & \text{otherwise.} \end{cases} \tag{16}$$

$\mathbf{r}^{(i)} = \{\mathbf{r}_x^{(i)}, \mathbf{r}_y^{(i)}, \mathbf{r}_w^{(i)}, \mathbf{r}_h^{(i)}\}$ represents the normalized top-left coordinate and width/height of character bounding boxes.

Although we do not directly constrain the attention map to focus around character centers, the smooth L_1 loss on character bounding boxes imposes location sensitive constraints on the encoded features. In practice, adding the bounding box regression branch also helps to alleviate some of the errors caused by attention drift.

By singulating individual character input regions in the calibration, we turned the calibration problem into an image classification problem. Various techniques and structures developed for common image classification problems can be applied. In the experiments section, we compare performance of different CNN structures.

5   Experiments

5.1   Implementation Details

Models in our paper are implemented under the Tensorflow framework [16].

The input images are resized to have maximum heights of 32 pixels, and padded to size of 86 × 32 pixels. The encoder has 5 convolutional layers and 5 max pooling layers, reducing the input image to a 22 × 512 dimensional feature vector. A 2-layer bi-directional LSTM is applied on the top of the convolutional layers, each LSTM has 128 hidden units. For the decoder, GRU cells with 128 memory blocks are used. Character prediction logits $\mathbf{z}_i$ and bounding boxes are obtained by applying separate linear layers on shared GRU states.

The calibration CNN is also implemented on Tensorflow framework. Given an input text image $\mathcal{I}$ and a character prediction $(\hat{\mathbf{z}}, \mathbf{r})$ from the SRN, the image region $\mathcal{I}_\mathbf{r}$ is first pooled to fixed size 64 × 64. A CNN head is used to extract features from the character subimage. On top of the convolution layers of the backbone, we make two fully connected layers for the logistic regression parameters, $\mathbf{W}$ and $\mathbf{b}$, respectively.

All our experiments are carried out on a work station with a NVIDIA Tesla P100 GPU. The SRN is trained with an AdaDelta optimizer [17]. The batch size is set to 64. The initial learning rate is set to 1.0. The SRN model converges after about 100 epochs over the training dataset. The Calibration CNN is trained with an Adam optimizer [18] with initial learning rate 0.001. The batch size is set to 100. The Calibration CNN models typically converges after 20 epochs over the validation set.

5.2 Datasets

The proposed methods are experimented on two authentic industrial datasets, as well as an open dataset accessible to the public. Text images are cropped from optically scanned or photographed images of documents.

The composition of training/validation/testing sets are specified in Table 1. The samples in each dataset are divided into training/validation/testing sets by 6:3:1 ratio. In the licence plate number dataset, the lexicon is consisted of 25 upper-case letters (letter "I" is not allowed in license plate numbers), 10 digits, 34 Chinese characters representing provincial districts in China, and another 6 Chinese characters representing vehicles of police force or other specific uses. The ID name dataset contains 5,577 Chinese characters, with severe class imbalance in its lexicon. Last but not least, the SROIE dataset, published in the ICDAR2019 Robust Reading Challenge, has lexicon size 101, comprising of upper and lower case letters, numeric digits, punctuation signs, and 9 Chinese characters.

Table 1. Sample numbers and lexicon sizes for datasets in our experiments.

Dataset	Total sample size	Training	Validation	Testing	Lexicon size
License plate number	63,802	38,281	19,141	6,380	75
ID name	158,785	83,271	61,636	13,878	5,577
SROIE	30,158	18,094	9,049	3,015	101

5.3 Results Analysis

The proposed method is compared with existing parametric calibration methods, such as vector scaling [3] and temperature scaling [1]. We compared several popular CNN structures as the head feature extractor of Calibration CNN, namely VGGNet [19], ResNet50 [20], and DenseNet [21].

For computation of reliability diagram, we grouped test samples into 32 bins by their prediction confidence $\hat{p}$. Because the dominating majority of the samples are predicted with high confidence, many bins in the reliability diagrams do not contain enough examples for a meaningful statistical estimate of the accuracy and confidence. In the reliability diagrams included in this section, we have dropped bins that contain less than 10 samples.

Experiment results are summarized in Table 2 and Fig. 3.

On the license plate number dataset, all experimented methods perform reasonably well. The proposed calibration CNN with a DenseNet backbone has the

Table 2. Statistics comparison of original SRN predictions/calibrated predictions. Best calibrated score in each item is suffixed with • and the second best is suffixed with ○.

Dataset	Calibration method	ECE	ECE ratio
License plate number	Uncalibrated	0.003075	100.00%
	Vector Scaling	0.002913	65.46%
	Temperature Scaling	0.001513	49.20%
	VGGNet	0.001934	62.89%
	ResNet50	0.001433 ○	46.60%
	DenseNet	0.000983 •	31.97%
ID name	Uncalibrated	0.002572	100.00%
	Vector Scaling	0.003304	128.46%
	Temperature Scaling	0.003189	123.99%
	VGGNet	0.006116	237.79%
	ResNet50	0.002682 ○	104.28%
	DenseNet	0.002571 •	99.96%
SROIE	Uncalibrated	0.013817	100.00%
	Vector Scaling	0.003425 ○	24.79%
	Temperature Scaling	0.005481	39.67%
	DenseNet	0.003414 •	24.71%

lowest ECE. Compared to the uncalibrated predictions, the ECE is reduced by 68.03% by DenseNet calibrator.

For the ID name dataset, almost all calibration methods failed to reduce the ECE, except for the proposed DenseNet calibrator. Conventional methods, including vector scaling and temperature scaling, increased ECE by more than 20%. The proposed ResNet50 calibrator and DenseNet calibrator reported the lowest ECE, with only the DenseNet calibrator being able to reduce the ECE. ID name dataset is one with large corpus and severe class imbalance. This experiment also demonstrates that calibrating a text recognition model involving a comprehensive character corpus poses a different level of challenge on the cal-

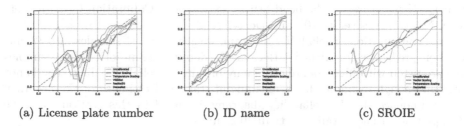

(a) License plate number   (b) ID name   (c) SROIE

Fig. 3. Reliability diagrams of the experimented datasets.

ibrators. The proposed CNN calibrator outperforms conventional methods in suppressing the ECE, but still has large room for improvement.

The performance of the proposed methods is also evaluated on the open dataset released by the SROIE Challenge. Due to time limit, we only compared the performance of the proposed DenseNet calibrator with vector scaling and temperature scaling algorithms. The performance of DenseNet calibrator is similar with that of vector scaling, both outperforming temperature scaling.

According to the above experiments, with a DenseNet or ResNet50 backbone, the proposed CNN calibrator outperforms the conventional scaling methods on both balanced and unbalanced datasets. With a VGGNet backbone, the proposed only works with a smaller-corpus, balanced dataset, such as the licence plate number dataset. Between datasets, the difficulty of calibration also varies by the corpus size and class balancedness.

6 Discussion

In this paper, we address the probability calibration problem for sequential text recognition systems. A novel calibration method is proposed for text recognition results calibration. The proposed calibration CNN takes the original image, as well as the output of the SRN as input, and performs adaptive calibration. Experiment results show that, with a DenseNet or ResNet50 backbone, the proposed CNN calibrator outperforms the conventional scaling methods on both balanced and unbalanced datasets. In future researches, more extensive experiments may be carried out to validate the performance of the proposed calibration method on more general text recognition frameworks.

Acknowledgement. This paper is supported by National Key Research and Development Program of China under grant No. 2018YFB1003500, No. 2018YFB0204400 and No. 2017YFB1401202.

References

1. Guo, C., Pleiss, G., Sun, Y., Weinberger, K.Q.: On calibration of modern neural networks. In: Proceedings of the 34th International Conference on Machine Learning, vol. 70, pp. 1321–1330. JMLR. org (2017)
2. Liao, Q., Ding, Y., Jiang, Z.L., Wang, X., Zhang, C., Zhang, Q.: Multi-taskdeep convolutional neural network for cancer diagnosis. Neurocomputing **348**, 66–73 (2018)
3. Platt, J., et al.: Probabilistic outputs for support vector machines and comparisons to regularized likelihood methods. In: Advances in Large Margin Classifiers, vol. 10, no. 3, pp. 61–74 (1999)
4. Leathart, T., Frank, E., Holmes, G., Pfahringer, B.: Probability calibration trees. In: Asian Conference on Machine Learning, pp. 145–160 (2017)
5. Pereyra, G., Tucker, G., Chorowski, J., Kaiser, Ł., Hinton, G.: Regularizing neural networks by penalizing confident output distributions. arXiv preprint arXiv:1701.06548 (2017)

6. Kumar, A., Sarawagi, S., Jain, U.: Trainable calibration measures for neural networks from kernel mean embeddings. In: International Conference on Machine Learning, pp. 2810–2819 (2018)
7. Graves, A., Fernández, S., Gomez, F., Schmidhuber, J.: Connectionist temporal classification: labelling unsegmented sequence data with recurrent neural networks. In: Proceedings of the 23rd International Conference on Machine Learning, pp. 369–376. ACM (2006)
8. Hori, T., Watanabe, S., Zhang, Y., Chan, W.: Advances in joint CTC-attention based end-to-end speech recognition with a deep CNN encoder and RNN-LM. arXiv preprint arXiv:1706.02737 (2017)
9. Kim, S., Hori, T., Watanabe, S.: Joint CTC-attention based end-to-end speech recognition using multi-task learning. In: 2017 IEEE International Conference on Acoustics, Speech and Signal Processing (ICASSP), pp. 4835–4839. IEEE (2017)
10. Wojna, Z., et al.: Attention-based extraction of structured information from street view imagery. In: 2017 14th IAPR International Conference on Document Analysis and Recognition (ICDAR), vol. 1, pp. 844–850. IEEE (2017)
11. Shi, B., Wang, X., Lyu, P., Yao, C., Bai, X.: Robust scene text recognition with automatic rectification. In: Proceedings of the IEEE Conference on Computer Vision and Pattern Recognition, pp. 4168–4176 (2016)
12. Vinyals, O., Kaiser, L., Koo, T., Petrov, S., Sutskever, I., Hinton, G.: Grammar as a foreign language. In: Advances in Neural Information Processing Systems, pp. 2773–2781 (2015)
13. Serfozo, R.: Basics of Applied Stochastic Processes. Springer, Heidelberg (2009)
14. DeGroot, M.H., Fienberg, S.E.: The comparison and evaluation of forecasters. J. Roy. Stat. Soc.: Ser. D (Stat.) 32(1–2), 12–22 (1983)
15. Cheng, Z., Bai, F., Xu, Y., Zheng, G., Pu, S., Zhou, S.: Focusing attention: towards accurate text recognition in natural images. In: Proceedings of the IEEE International Conference on Computer Vision, pp. 5076–5084 (2017)
16. Abadi, M., Agarwal, A., Barham, P., et al.: TensorFlow: large-scale machine learning on heterogeneous systems (2015). Software available from tensorflow.org. http://tensorflow.org/
17. Zeiler, M.D.: ADADELTA: an adaptive learning rate method. arXiv preprint arXiv:1212.5701 (2012)
18. Kingma, D.P., Ba, J.: Adam: a method for stochastic optimization. arXiv preprint arXiv:1412.6980 (2014)
19. Simonyan, K., Zisserman, A.: Very deep convolutional networks for large-scale image recognition. arXiv preprint arXiv:1409.1556 (2014)
20. He, K., Zhang, X., Ren, S., Sun, J.: Deep residual learning for image recognition. In: Proceedings of the IEEE Conference on Computer Vision and Pattern Recognition, pp. 770–778 (2016)
21. Iandola, F., Moskewicz, M., Karayev, S., Girshick, R., Darrell, T., Keutzer, K.: DenseNet: implementing efficient convnet descriptor pyramids. arXiv preprint arXiv:1404.1869 (2014)

On the Hermite Series-Based Generalized Regression Neural Networks for Stream Data Mining

Danuta Rutkowska[1] and Leszek Rutkowski[2]

[1] Information Technology Institute, University of Social Sciences, Lodz, Poland
drutkowska@san.edu.pl
[2] Institute of Computional Intelligence, Czestochowa University of Technology,
Czestochowa, Poland
leszek.rutkowski@iisi.pcz.pl

Abstract. In the paper, we develop the mathematically justified stream data mining algorithm for solving regression problems. The algorithm is based on the Hermite expansions of drifting regression functions. The global convergence, in the L_2 space, is proved both in probability and with probability one. The examples of several concept drifts to be handled by our algorithm, and the illustrative simulations are presented.

Keywords: Data streams · Regression function · Concept drift · Hermite series

1 Introduction

In the last decade, data stream mining has emerged as a very active and challenging area of research. For the excellent surveys and overviews of available techniques, the reader is referred to [2,4], and [18]. In many cases, data streams are characterized by the lack of stationarity and they require to develop new online algorithms working in a time-varying environment. Typical examples of changing environments include sensor networks, financial market or climate fluctuations. The environmental changes are known in the literature under the name concept drift and this phenomenon should be taken into account when designing stream data mining algorithms. In the excellent survey [4], the authors formalize the process of learning in non-stationary environments and describe the main strategies to cope with concept drift.

The vast majority of available algorithms are based on the classical methods developed for static data, often combined with windowing techniques to eliminate data elements coming from an old concept, see e.g. [2]. One of the first successful tools to stream data mining was the VFDT algorithm [5], based on the idea of the Hoeffding trees. This algorithm was later extended to the CVFDT algorithm [9] to work in a time-varying environment. The mathematical foundations of the VFDT and CVFDT were established in [16] and [17].

© Springer Nature Switzerland AG 2019
T. Gedeon et al. (Eds.): ICONIP 2019, LNCS 11955, pp. 437–448, 2019.
https://doi.org/10.1007/978-3-030-36718-3_37

From several dozen different well known other algorithms we mention here only a few, namely ensemble methods [10,14], nearest neighbor techniques [3, 15], Bayesian classifiers [21], spiking neural networks [11,12], and nonparametric density estimates [8].

The vast majority of available solutions in the world literature are devoted to classification problems in a time-varying environment, whereas regression problems are almost untouched. The VFDT and CVFDT methods, mentioned above, concern very fast decision trees, also used for classification.

In the recent papers [6] and [7], the authors studied the regression problems using the concept of the generalized regression neural networks, proposed by Specht [19]. They showed pointwise tracking properties of their algorithms.

Our goal is to extend those results to the L_2 (global) convergence. More precisely, in the paper, we assume that $\phi_n(\cdot)$, for $n = 1, 2, \ldots$, are the time-varying regression functions. Then, using the Hermite orthogonal expansions, we propose the online procedure $\hat{\phi}_n(\cdot)$, $n = 1, 2, \ldots$, and prove its ability to track regressions $\phi_n(\cdot)$, for $n = 1, 2, \ldots$, in the sense of the weak (in probability) and strong (with probability one) L_2 convergence. The convergence conditions, presented in Theorems 1 and 2, depend on the rate of changes of $\phi_n(\cdot)$, for $n = 1, 2, \ldots$, and their smoothness properties. We will show that the global convergence holds under weaker conditions and, consequently, the class of possible concept drifts can be wider than that presented in [6] and [7].

The rest of the paper is organized as follows. In Sect. 2, the basic properties of the Hermite series are introduced. In Sect. 3, the online algorithm is derived, whereas Sect. 4 presents its weak and strong convergence. The exemplary simulations are illustrated in Sect. 5. Finally, in Sect. 6, we draw conclusions and propose directions of future research.

2   Preliminaries

The online stream data mining algorithm, presented in this paper, is based on the Hermite orthonormal system, in the unidimensional case, defined by

$$g_j (x) = \left(2^j j! \, \pi^{\frac{1}{2}}\right)^{-\frac{1}{2}} e^{-\frac{x^2}{2}} H_j (x),\tag{1}$$

where

$$H_0 (x) = 1, \;\; H_j (x) = (-1)^j e^{x^2} \frac{d_j}{dx^j} e^{-x^2}, \;\; j = 1, 2, \ldots\tag{2}$$

are Hermite polynomials. Functions g_j of this system are bounded as follows [20]

$$\max_x |g_j (x)| \leq c_1 \, j^{-\frac{1}{12}}, \;\; j = 1, 2, \ldots\tag{3}$$

and can be generated in a recurrent way

$$g_0 (x) = \pi^{-\frac{1}{4}} e^{\frac{-x^2}{2}}, \qquad g_1 (x) = 2^{\frac{1}{2}} \pi \, x \, e^{-\frac{x^2}{2}} = 2^{\frac{1}{2}} x \, g_0 (x),$$

$$g_{j+1}(x) = -\left(2/(j+1)\right)^{\frac{1}{2}} x \, g_j(x) - \left(j/(j+1)\right)^{\frac{1}{2}} g_{j-1}(x) \tag{4}$$

for $j = 1, 2, \ldots$.

Since $g_j(.)$ is a complete orthonormal system in $L_2(R)$, for $j = 1, 2, \ldots$ then, the system composed of all possible products

$$\Psi_{j_1, \ldots, j_p}\left(x^{(1)}, \ldots, x^{(p)}\right) = g_{j_1}\left(x^{(1)}\right) \cdots g_{j_p}\left(x^{(p)}\right) \tag{5}$$

for $j_k = 0, 1, 2, \ldots$, and $k = 1, \ldots, p$, is a complete orthonormal system in $L_2(R^p)$, where $p > 1$, see [13].

In the paper, for any square integrable function $h(x)$, we use the following notation:

$$\|h(x)\|_{L_2} = \left(\int h^2(x) dx\right)^{\frac{1}{2}}. \tag{6}$$

The most important property of the Hermite orthonormal system is the ability to approximate any function defined in $\mathbb{R}^p$. Therefore, it is suitable for the situation when drifting regression functions, defined in this space, are considered.

3 The Stream Data Mining Algorithm

In the paper, we study a time-varying data stream model of the form:

$$Y_n = \phi_n(X_n) + Z_n, \qquad n = 1, 2, \ldots, \tag{7}$$

where $\phi_n(\cdot)$ is a sequence of unknown functions, X_n is a sequence of independent and identically distributed random variables in $\mathbb{R}^p$ with the same density function $f(x)$; and Z_n is a sequence of independent random variables such that:

$$\mathbb{E}Z_n = 0, \qquad Var[Z_n] = \sigma_z^2, \qquad n = 1, 2, \ldots. \tag{8}$$

Based on the learning sequence $(X_1, Y_1), (X_2, Y_2), \ldots$, we will design a nonparametric procedure tracking changes of $\phi_n(\cdot)$, for $n = 1, 2, \ldots$. Let us represent functions $\phi_n(\cdot)$ in model (7) in the form:

$$\phi_n(x) = \frac{\phi_n(x) f(x)}{f(x)} = \frac{R_n(x)}{f(x)} \tag{9}$$

at each point x at which $f(x) \neq 0$, $n = 1, 2, \ldots$. Without loss of generality, we assume that the density function, $f(x)$, is known. If it is unknown, it can be estimated by a number of various sequential procedures, including the orthogonal series [6] and the Parzen kernel-based methods [7]. Under that assumption, the estimate of $\phi_n(\cdot)$ is given by

$$\hat{\phi}_n(x) = \frac{\hat{R}_n(x)}{f(x)}. \tag{10}$$

Now, the challenge is to design a procedure $\hat{R}_n(\cdot)$ tracking for changes of functions $R_n(\cdot)$ in formula (9). Assuming that

$$\|R_n(x)\|_{L_2} <= \infty, \qquad n = 1, 2, \ldots, \tag{11}$$

using (1) and (5), we expand functions $R_n(\cdot)$ in the Hermite orthogonal series as follows:

$$R_n(x) \sim \sum_{j_1=0}^{\infty} \cdots \sum_{j_p=0}^{\infty} a_{j_1,\ldots,j_p,n} \, \Psi_{j_1},\ldots,_{j_p}(x), \tag{12}$$

for $n = 1, 2, \ldots$, with

$$a_{j_1,\ldots,j_p,n} = \int R_n(x) \, \Psi_{j_1},\ldots,_{j_p}(x) \, dx, \tag{13}$$

where $x \in \mathbb{R}^p$.

Let us denote the partial expansion of (12) by

$$S_n(x) = \sum_{j_1=0}^{q(n)} \cdots \sum_{j_p=0}^{q(n)} a_{j_1,\ldots,j_p,n} \, \Psi_{j_1},\ldots,_{j_p}(x) \tag{14}$$

where $q(n) \longrightarrow \infty$ as $n \longrightarrow \infty$.

In the next section, we require, in Theorems 1 and 2, that partial expansions $S_n(x)$ approach unknown functions $R_n(x)$ as $n \longrightarrow \infty$.

Replacing coefficients $a_{j_1,\ldots,j_p,n}$ in (14) by their estimates would give a natural estimate of functions $R_n(x)$, for $n = 1, 2, \ldots$. However, the tracking procedure would not work in the online mode. Therefore, here for tracking $R_n(x)$, $n = 1, 2, \ldots$, we propose the procedure:

$$\hat{R}_{n+1}(x) = \hat{R}_n(x)+$$

$$\gamma_{n+1} \left(Y_{n+1} \sum_{j_1=0}^{q(n)} \cdots \sum_{j_p=0}^{q(n)} g_{j_1}(x^{(1)})g_{j_1}(X_{n+1}^{(1)}) \cdots g_{j_p}(x^{(p)})g_{j_p}(X_{n+1}^{(p)}) - \hat{R}_n(x) \right), \tag{15}$$

where $\hat{R}_0(x) = 0$ and γ_n is a sequence of numbers such that

$$\sum_{n=1}^{\infty} \gamma_n = \infty, \qquad \gamma_n \xrightarrow{n} 0, \qquad \gamma_n > 0. \tag{16}$$

Equation (15) can be considered as a counterpart of the online Parzen kernel-based procedure:

$$\hat{R}_{n+1}(x) = \hat{R}_n(x) + \gamma_{n+1} \left(Y_{n+1} \, h_{n+1}^{-p} \, K\left(\frac{x - X_{n+1}}{h_{n+1}}\right) - \hat{R}_n(x) \right) \tag{17}$$

where $K(\cdot)$ is the Parzen kernel, and h_n is a sequence of numbers such that $h_n \longrightarrow 0$ as $n \longrightarrow \infty$, see [7]. On the other hand, procedure (17) is the online version of the generalized regression neural networks introduced by Specht in [19].

4   Convergence Theorems

In this section, we investigate the tracking properties of algorithm (10) where $\hat{R}_n(x)$ is given by (15). Let us denote:

$$d_n = \int_{\mathbb{R}^p} \phi_n^2(x) f(x) dx + \sigma_z^2, \tag{18}$$

for $n = 1, 2, \ldots$.

Theorem 1. *Assume that condition (18) holds and sequence γ_n satisfies conditions (16). Suppose that the unknown functions, $\phi_n(x)$ in model (7), vary in such a way that*

$$\gamma_n^{-1} \|\phi_{n+1}(x) - \phi_n(x)\|_{L_2} \xrightarrow{n} 0, \tag{19}$$

sequence $q(n)$ satisfies

$$\gamma_n^{-1} (q(n))^{\frac{11p}{6}} d_n \xrightarrow{n} 0, \qquad q(n) \xrightarrow{n} \infty, \tag{20}$$

and

$$\gamma_n^{-1} \|S_n(x) - R_n(x)\|_{L_2} \xrightarrow{n} 0, \tag{21}$$

then

$$\mathbb{E}\|(\hat{\phi}_n(x) - \phi_n(x)) f(x)\|_{L_2}^2 \xrightarrow{n} 0, \tag{22}$$

and

$$\|(\hat{\phi}_n(x) - \phi_n(x)) f(x)\|_{L_2} \xrightarrow{n} 0 \quad \text{in probability.} \tag{23}$$

Proof. See Appendix.

Remark 1. Let us assume that $t_n^l(x; R_n) \in L_2(\mathbb{R}^p)$ where

$$t_n^l(x; R_n) = \prod_{k=1}^{p} \left(x^{(k)} - \partial/\partial x^{(k)} \right)^l R_n \left(x^{(1)}, \ldots, x^{(p)} \right). \tag{24}$$

Then, it can be shown (see [18], p. 259) that

$$\|S_n(x) - R_n(x)\|_{L_2} \leq \|t_n^l(x; R_n)\|_{L_2} \left(q(n)^{\frac{-pl}{2}} \right). \tag{25}$$

The bound given by (25) will be useful to find sequences γ_n and $q(n)$ satisfying condition (21).

Example 1. (incremental concept drift)
We consider the incremental concept drift in the regression model:

$$\phi_n(x) = n^\alpha \phi(x) \tag{26}$$

where $\alpha > 0$ and $\phi(x) \in L_2$. It is easily seen that, using (25), conditions (19), (20), and (21) take the form:

$$\gamma_n^{-1} n^{\alpha-1} \xrightarrow{n} 0, \qquad \gamma_n (q(n))^{\frac{11p}{6}} n^{2\alpha} \xrightarrow{n} 0, \qquad \gamma_n^{-1} (q(n))^{\frac{-pl}{2}} n^\alpha \xrightarrow{n} 0. \tag{27}$$

Let us choose

$$\gamma_n = c_1 n^{-\gamma}, \quad q(n) = [c_2 n^q] \tag{28}$$

for $c_1, c_2, \gamma, q > 0$, where $[a]$ means the integer part of a.

Then, conditions (27) are satisfied if

$$\gamma + \alpha < 1, \qquad \frac{11qp}{6} + 2\alpha - \gamma < 0, \qquad \gamma + \alpha - \frac{qpl}{2} < 0. \tag{29}$$

It is easily seen that, for a given α, parameters γ and q shoud satisfy:

$$\gamma < 1 - \alpha, \qquad \frac{2(\gamma + \alpha)}{pl} < q < \frac{6(\gamma - 2\alpha)}{11p}. \tag{30}$$

If $0 < \alpha < 0.5$, one can choose sequences γ_n and $q(n)$ in procedure (15), assuring convergence (22) and (23). Comparing with the recent pointwise convergence [7], which holds for $0 < \alpha < 1/3$, the L_2 convergence allows a bigger incremental concept drift.

Example 2. (reoccurring and mixed concept drifts)
The algorithm presented in the previous section is also applicable to tracking reoccurring concept drift, e.g. in the model:

$$Y_n = \phi(X_n)\,(C_1 \sin A_n + C_2 \cos B_n) + Z_n \tag{31}$$

or it also can handle the mixed concept drift of the form:

$$Y_n = \phi(X_n)\,(C_1 n^t + C_2 \sin A_n + C_3 \cos B_n) + Z_n \tag{32}$$

where $A_n = k_1 n^{\alpha_1}$, $B_n = k_2 n^{\alpha_2}$, and C_1, C_2, C_3, k_1, k_2 are real numbers, $\alpha_1, \alpha_2, t > 0$.

For models (31) and (32), we can determine sequences γ_n and $q(n)$ guaranteeing convergence (22) and (23) if $t < 0.5$ and $\alpha_1, \alpha_2 < 1$.

Theorem 2. *Assume that condition* (11) *holds and sequence* γ_n *satisfies conditions* (16). *Suppose that the unknown functions,* $\phi_n(x)$ *in model* (7), *vary in such a way that*

$$\sum_{n=1}^{\infty} \gamma_n^{-1} \|(\hat{\phi}_n(x) - \phi_n(x))f(x)\|_{L_2}^2 < \infty, \tag{33}$$

sequence $q(n)$ *satisfies functions,* $\phi(x)$ *in model* (7) *vary in such a way that*

$$\sum_{n=1}^{\infty} \gamma_n^2 (q(n))^{\frac{11p}{6}} d_n < \infty \tag{34}$$

and

$$\sum_{n=1}^{\infty} \gamma_n^{-1} \|S_n(x) - R_n(x)\|_{L_2}^2 < \infty, \tag{35}$$

then

$$\|(\hat{\phi}_n(x) - \phi_n(x))f(x)\|_{L_2} \xrightarrow{n} 0 \quad \text{with probability one.} \tag{36}$$

Proof. See Appendix.

Example 3. Assuming the incremental concept drift, as in model (26), conditions (33), (34), and (35) take the form:

$$\sum_{n=1}^{\infty} \gamma_n^{-1} n^{2(\alpha-1)} < \infty, \tag{37}$$

$$\sum_{n=1}^{\infty} \gamma_n^2 (q(n))^{\frac{11p}{6}} n^{2\alpha} < \infty, \tag{38}$$

$$\sum_{n=1}^{\infty} \gamma_n^{-1} (q(n))^{-pl} n^{2\alpha} < \infty. \tag{39}$$

For sequences γ_n and $q(n)$, given by (28), the above conditions are satisfied if

$$\gamma < 1 - 2\alpha, \qquad \frac{\gamma + 2\alpha + 1}{pl} < q < \frac{6(2\gamma - 2\alpha - 1)}{11p}. \tag{40}$$

It is easly seen that we can find parameters γ and q if $0 < \alpha < 0.5$, and again this interval is wider than interval $0 < \alpha < 1/6$ determined in [7] for the pointwise convergence.

5   Simulation Results

In this section, we show the performance of algorithm (10) with recursion (15), assuming that input data $X_1, X_2, \ldots,$ are coming from the following mixture of three normal distributions: $0.4N(0, 0.2) + 0.3N(-1.2, 0.5) + 0.3N(0.8, 0.5)$, and the time-varying data stream model is given by (7) and (26) with

$$\phi(x) = \sin(2x + 3)(x + 8)(x - 8)(x + 1)/10 \tag{41}$$

whereas Z_n are from the normal distribution, $N(0, 1)$, moreover γ_n, and $q(n)$ are given by (28) with $q = 0.19$ and $\gamma = 0.75$, for $c_1 = 1$ and $c_2 = 20$, chosen in the experiment.

Plots of the *MSE* are shown in Fig. 1, for $\alpha = 0.1; 0.2; 0.25$. The conditions of the convergence theorem are satisfied for $\alpha = 0.1$ and $\alpha = 0.2$, but violated for $\alpha = 0.25$.

In Fig. 2, we depict the fit of the tracking algorithm to the data points, for $\alpha = 0.2$, whereas Fig. 3 shows its perfect performance after processing 100000 data items. Figures 3 and 4 portray plots of estimator $\hat{\phi}_n(x)$ and estimated function $\phi_n(x)$. In Fig. 4, the tracking properties are demonstrated for $x = 1$.

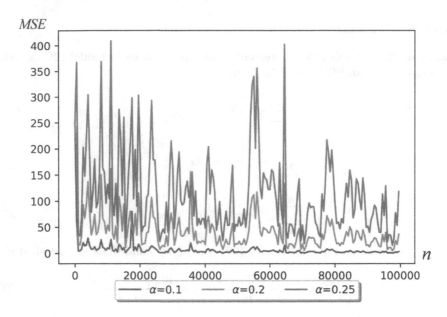

Fig. 1. Plots of the *MSE* for $\alpha = 0.1; 0.2; 0.25$.

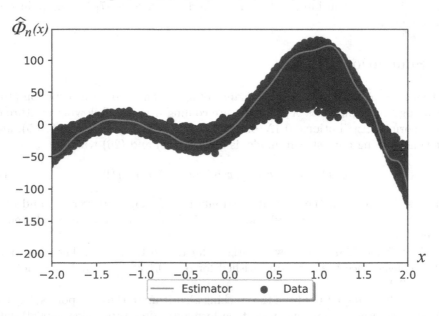

Fig. 2. The fit of the tracking algorithm to the data points.

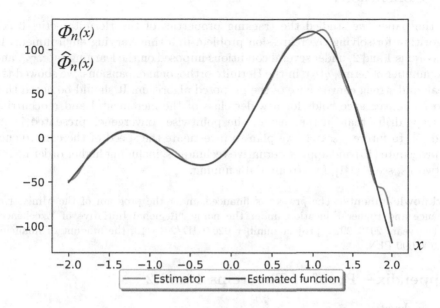

Fig. 3. Comparison of the estimator and estimated function after 100000 iterations

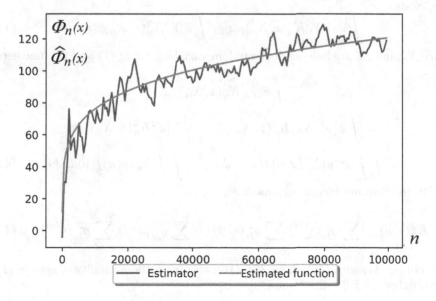

Fig. 4. Tracking of the estimated function by its estimator at point $x = 1$

6   Conclusions

In the paper, we studied the tracking properties of the Hermite series-based algorithm for solving the regression problem in a time-varying environment. In Theorems 1 and 2, under several conditions imposed on the learning rate, γ_n, and the number of terms, $q(n)$, in the Hermite orthogonal expansions, we showed the weak and strong convergence of the proposed algorithm. It should be noted that the L_2 convergence holds for a wider class of the incremental and reoccurring concept drifts than in the case of the pointwise convergence presented in [6] and [7]. In future research, we plan to investigate the speed of the convergence of procedure (15) and apply alternative techniques, including higher order neural networks, see e.g. [1], for stream data mining.

Acknowledgments. The project is financed under the program of the Minister of Science and Higher Education under the name "Regional Initiative of Excellence" in the years 2019–2022, project number 020/RID/2018/19, the amount of financing 12,000,000 PLN.

Appendix – Proof of Theorems 1 and 2

Let us denote:

$$K_n(x, u) = \sum_{j_1=0}^{q(n)} \cdots \sum_{j_p=0}^{q(n)} g_{j_1}(x^{(1)}) g_{j_1}(u^{(1)}) \cdots g_{j_p}(x^{(p)}) g_{j_p}(u^{(p)}). \qquad (42)$$

Obviously,

$$\int Var[Y_n K_n(x, X_n)] dx \leq \int \mathbb{E}[Y_n^2 K_n^2(x, X_n)] dx. \qquad (43)$$

Since X_n and Z_n are independent random variables, using (7) and (8), one gets:

$$\int \mathbb{E}[Y_n^2 K_n^2(x, X_n)] dx$$

$$= \int \mathbb{E}[\phi_n^2(X_n) K_n^2(x, X_n)] dx + \int \mathbb{E}[Z_n^2 K_n^2(x, X_n)] dx$$

$$= \int \int \phi_n^2(u) K_n^2(x, u) f(u) dx du + \sigma_z^2 \int \int K_n^2(x, u) f(u) dx du. \qquad (44)$$

By the Schwarz inequality, one has:

$$K_n^2(x, u) \leq \sum_{j_1=0}^{q(n)} g_{j_1}^2(x^{(1)}) \sum_{j_1=0}^{q(n)} g_{j_1}^2(u^{(1)}) \cdots \sum_{j_p=0}^{q(n)} g_{j_p}^2(x^{(p)}) \sum_{j_p=0}^{q(n)} g_{j_p}^2(u^{(p)}) \qquad (45)$$

Combining (44) with (45), using (3), (18), and the orthonormality of system (1), one obtains the following bound:

$$\int Var[Y_n K_n(x, X_n)] dx \leq q^p(n) \left(\sum_{j=0}^{q(n)} G_j^2 \right)^p d_n. \qquad (46)$$

In view of (25) and (46), a proper application of Theorems 9.3 and 9.4 in [18] concludes the proof of Theorems 1 and 2.

References

1. Akdeniz, E., Egrioglu, E., Bas, E., Yolcu, U.: An ARMA type Pi-sigma artificial neural network for nonlinear time series forecasting. J. Artif. Intell. Soft Comput. Res. **8**(2), 1–21 (2018)
2. Bifet, A., Gavalda, R., Holmes, G., Pfahringer, B.: Machine Learning for Data Streams with Practical Examples in MOA. MIT Press, Cambridge (2018)
3. Devi, V.S., Meena, L.: Parallel MCNN (PMCNN) with application to prototype selection on large and streaming data. J. Artif. Intell. Soft Comput. Res. **7**(3), 155–169 (2017)
4. Ditzler, G., Roveri, V., Alippi, C., Polikar, V.: Learning in nonstationary environments: a survey. IEEE Comput. Intell. Mag. **10**(4), 12–25 (2015)
5. Domingos, P., Hulten, G.: Mining high-speed data streams. In: Proceedings of 6th ACM SIGKDD International Conference on Knowledge Discovery and Data Mining, pp. 71–80 (2000)
6. Duda, P., Jaworski, M., Rutkowski, L.: Knowledge discovery in data streams with the orthogonal series-based generalized regression neural networks. Inf. Sci. **460**, 497–518 (2018)
7. Duda, P., Jaworski, M., Rutkowski, L.: Convergent time-varying regression models for data streams: tracking concept drift by the recursive Parzen-based generalized regression neural networks. Int. J. Neural Syst. **28**, 1–23 (2018)
8. Duda, P., Rutkowski, L., Jaworski, M., Rutkowska, D.: On the Parzen kernel-based probability density function learning procedures over time-varying streaming data with applications to pattern classification. IEEE Tran. Cybern. 1–14 (2018)
9. Hulten, G., Spencer, L., Domingos, P.: Mining time-changing data streams. In: Proceedings of the 7th ACM SIGKDD International Conference on Knowledge Discovery and Data Mining, pp. 97–106 (2001)
10. Krawczyk, B., Minku, L.L., Gama, J., Stefanowski, J., Wozniak, M.: Ensemble learning for data stream analysis: a survey. Inf. Fusion **37**, 132–156 (2017)
11. Lobo, J.L., Lana, I., Ser, J.D., Bilbao, M.N., Kasabov, N.: Evolving spiking neural networks for online learning over drifting data streams. Neural Netw. **108**, 1–19 (2018)
12. Nobukawa, S., Nishimura, H., Yamanishi, T.: Pattern classification by spiking neural networks combining self-organized and reward-related spike-timing-dependent plasticity. J. Artif. Intell. Soft Comput. Res. **9**(4), 283–291 (2019)
13. Nikolsky, S.: A Course of Mathematical Analysis. Mir Publishers, Moscow (1977)
14. Pietruczuk, L., Rutkowski, L., Jaworski, M., Duda, P.: How to adjust an ensemble size in stream data mining? Inf. Sci. **381**, 46–54 (2017)
15. Ramirez-Gallego, S., Krawczyk, B., Garcia, S., Wozniak, M., Benitez, J.M., Herrera, F.: Nearest neighbor classification for high-speed big data streams using spark. IEEE Trans. Syst. Man Cybern. Syst. **47**, 2727–2739 (2017)
16. Rutkowski, L., Pietruczuk, L., Duda, P., Jaworski, M.: Decision trees for mining data streams based on the McDiarmid's bound. IEEE Trans. Knowl. Data Eng. **25**, 1272–1279 (2013)
17. Rutkowski, L., Jaworski, M., Pietruczuk, L., Duda, P.: A new method for data stream mining based on the misclassification error. IEEE Trans. Neural Netw. Learn. Syst. **26**, 1048–1059 (2015)

18. Rutkowski, L., Jaworski, M., Duda, P.: Stream Data Mining: Algorithms and Their Probabilistic Properties. Springer, Heidelberg (2019)
19. Specht, D.F.: A general regression neural network. IEEE Trans. Neural Netw. **2**(6), 568–576 (1991)
20. Szego, G.: Orthogonal Polynomials, vol. 23. American Mathematical Society Coll. Publ. (1959)
21. Yuan, J., Wang, Z., Sun, Y., Zhang, W., Jiang, J.: An effective pattern-based Bayesian classifier for evolving data stream. Neurocomputing **295**, 17–28 (2018)

Deep Hybrid Spatiotemporal Networks for Continuous Pain Intensity Estimation

Selvarajah Thuseethan[(⊠)], Sutharshan Rajasegarar, and John Yearwood

Deakin University, Geelong, VIC 3220, Australia
{tselvarajah,srajas,john.yearwood}@deakin.edu.au

Abstract. Humans use rich facial expressions to indicate unpleasant emotions, such as pain. Automatic pain intensity estimation is useful in a variety of applications in social and medical domains. However, the existing pain intensity estimation approaches are limited to either classifying the discrete intensity levels in pain or estimating the continuous pain intensities without considering the key-frame. The first approach suffers from abnormal fluctuations while estimating the pain intensity levels. Further, continuous pain estimation approaches suffer from low prediction capabilities. Hence, in this paper, we propose a deep hybrid network based approach to automatically estimate the continuous pain intensities by incorporating spatiotemporal information. Our approach consists of two key components, namely *key-frame analyser* and *temporal analyser*. We use one conventional and two recurrent convolutional neural networks to design key-frame and temporal analysers, respectively. Further, the evaluation on a benchmark dataset shows that our model can estimate the continuous emotions better than existing state-of-the-art methods.

Keywords: Pain intensity estimation · Hybrid deep network · Convolutional neural network · Recurrent convolutional neural network

1 Introduction

Highly social species such as human use face as the primary medium to express emotional states, such as pain during everyday interactions [5]. Due to the fact that the pain assessment is inevitable in applications related to medical, sports and social environments, it is essential to devise efficient mechanisms to estimate the pain in-the-wild automatically. For, instance, accurate pain evaluation during a medical intervention can help the practitioner to provide appropriate treatment at the right time. Meanwhile, the fine-grained analysis of many basic and non-basic emotions has become an emerging topic in the past [25]. For example, in [21], we have recognised different intensity levels of micro-expressions from images. Further, in [22], a metric-based intensity estimation mechanism for primary emotions is proposed. However, in general, estimating the level of pain is subjective, and hence complicated. In the past, researchers have used

© Springer Nature Switzerland AG 2019
T. Gedeon et al. (Eds.): ICONIP 2019, LNCS 11955, pp. 449–461, 2019.
https://doi.org/10.1007/978-3-030-36718-3_38

various techniques to define the pain intensities, manually and automatically, from acute facial expressions. So far, two widely known manual pain intensity estimation methods, namely, self and observer reports, have been used by medical practitioners. Moreover, the computer-aided pain intensity estimation from facial expressions has always been in the centre of attraction for computer vision researchers.

In practice, the lack of labelled data and standard rules cause the automatic pain intensity estimation challenging. The action units (AUs) of the facial action coding system (FACS) [3] provide a universal standard to define the pain intensity levels. In [17], authors proposed *Prkachin and Solomon Pain Intensity (PSPI) metric* to estimate the pain intensities in sixteen-scale ordinal scale from a combination of six AUs. Following the work [17], in the recent past, plenty of research have utilized the PSPI metric to classify the pain intensity levels into a various number of classes. For instance, Rudovic et al. [20] have adopted the original PSPI metric to classify the pain intensities into six classes, namely, none, mild, discomforting, distressing, intense and excruciating. A few emotional states, such as distress, discomfort and excruciating, can be extracted from the pain levels defined in the PSPI metric. More importantly, the pain intensity levels can become a critical ingredient of other non-basic emotions, such as non-confidence or distress. Hence, it is important to accurately classify these pain intensity levels in order to explore new non-basic emotions.

This paper proposes a hybrid deep neural network framework that utilizes the features extracted from both target and adjacent frames, to estimate the frame-level pain intensity continuously from facial expressions. We carefully construct the conventional and recurrent versions of the convolutional neural networks (CNNs) together to achieve accurate intensity estimation in our framework. According to the best of our knowledge, the proposed framework is the first one to use the features obtained from both *target* and *adjoint* frames to estimate the frame-level emotion intensity levels. In addition, to obtain the final pain estimation, we present a comprehensive neural network based feature fusion mechanism that combines the features extracted from different CNNs. Below we list the key contributions of this paper.

- We present an efficient hybrid pain intensity estimation framework, comprised of one conventional and two recurrent CNNs (RCNNs), to extract features from the target and adjoint frames, respectively. We use a selected number of frames before and after the target frame (i.e., key-frame) as adjoint frames in our frame-by-frame regression model to encode the additional temporal changes.
- We evaluate the method on UNBC-McMaster Shoulder Pain Expression Archive Database [11], and show that our approach outperforms the state-of-the-art pain intensity estimation methods in terms of stability, accuracy and efficiency. Further, we perform an ablation study to show that our final model yields significant performance improvement compared to using only the intermediate components, such as considering only the past frames.

The remaining sections of this paper are structured as follows. In Sect. 2, the preliminaries are defined. Section 3 describes our proposed pain intensity estimation method. The experimental results and a summary of the discussion are presented in Sect. 4. The conclusion and remarks to future works are presented in the final section of the paper.

2 Preliminaries

In this section, we outline the background of PSPI metric and briefly discuss the existing state-of-the-art pain intensity estimation approaches.

2.1 PSPI Metric

Empirical studies in pain intensity estimation from facial expressions suggest that four facial action units (AUs); brow lowering ($AU4$), orbital tightening ($AU6$ and $AU7$), levator contraction ($AU9$ and $AU10$) and eye closure ($AU43$) reveal majority of the information about pain. As mentioned previously, Prkachin proposed a pain metric, namely PSPI in [16], and as a follow-up work, Prkachin and Solomon recently confirmed the metric in [17]. Authors defined the pain intensity metric as the summation of the AU intensities mentioned above, as shown in Eq. (1).

$$PSPI = AU4 + (AU6|AU7) + (AU9|AU10) + AU43 \qquad (1)$$

As illustrated in Eq. (1), in PSPI metric, the pain intensity values are calculated by adding the intensity values of $AU4$, maximum of $AU6$ or $AU7$, maximum of $AU9$ or $AU10$ and $AU43$. For example, if the intensity values of $AU4$, $AU6$, $AU7$, $AU9$, $AU10$ and $AU43$ are 4, 5, 3, 1, 2 and 1 respectively, then the pain intensity value is calculated as $PSPI = 4 + max(5,3) + max(1,2) + 1$, which is 12. PSPI metric generates a 16-point pain intensity scale based on the intensity scales of the corresponding AUs. The intensity scale of each AU spans from absent (0) to maximum (5), while $AU43$ takes only the binary values; 1 when the eye is closed and 0 otherwise. Hence, the pain intensity score ranges from a minimum of 0 to a maximum of 16.

Using the PSPI metric as the standard pain intensity definition, many researchers in the recent past have proposed different approaches to estimate the emotion intensities. Next, we survey a few noteworthy works in this area.

2.2 Related Work

Early research works in pain intensity estimation had a tendency of classifying the pain into a binary class; pain and non-pain. However, in recent years, a vast number of studies have started focusing on a fine-grained pain intensity level estimation rather than a simple twofold classification. Typical handcrafted feature based techniques, such as [6,9,11,14,18–20,25], were started a decade ago. Yet, handcrafted feature extraction methods are effective due to the fact that they require less computational power. Although the handcrafted feature extraction techniques are straightforward in general, they are not effective. On the other hand, due to the recent advances in computational power (i.e., the invention of powerful GPU based chips), researchers have started working on automatic feature extractive deep learning techniques [12,23,26]. A simple deep architecture has outperformed handcrafted feature extraction based pain intensity estimation techniques comprehensively [23].

Binary classification of pain, commonly known as detection, is less complicated than estimating multiple intensity levels of pain. Kalkhoran and Fatemizadeh [9] eliminated a few intensity levels, and proposed a slightly different regression-based approach to detect the pain. Unlike other existing pain detection approaches, this method considered observer-rated pain intensity (OPI) value. In [14], Neshov and Manolova proposed a similar binary classification method of pain based on PSPI value. Although the authors stated that the proposed method clearly outperforms all the existing regression-based methods after a careful comparison, binary classification is not capable to cater the needs of present day applications. However, estimation of pain intensity at fine-grained levels, such as using PSPI value from 0 to 16, is challenging due to the limited deviations available in painful facial expressions between subsequent PSPI scales. Hence, researchers in the past tend to curtail the number of pain intensity classes. Hammal and Cohn [6] proposed one such approach to define the pain intensity in four levels, namely $PSPI = 0$ as none, $PSPI = 1$ as trace, $PSPI = 2$ as weak and $PSPI \geq 3$ as strong. Roy et al. [19] proposed another novel framework to estimate the pain intensity levels, in the medical domain using four class definition of [6] and achieved an improved performance. Rudovic et al. [20] presented another novel pain estimation approach that does not use any previously proposed standard classification of pain intensity levels. The authors categorized the pain intensity levels into six meaningful emotions, namely, none, mild, discomforting, distressing, intense and excruciating. Further, Zhao et al. [25] extended the [20] in their approach and showed better classification accuracies under a fully supervised setting.

In order to initiate the fine-grained pain level estimation, Lucey et al. [11] investigated the automatic pain estimation problem through the 16-level PSPI scale. In a follow-up work, Rathee and Ganotra [18] demonstrated a slightly higher accuracy of 96% for the 16-level pain intensity estimation with their model. More recently, in [12], authors designed a recurrent neural network based feature extractor for 16-level pain intensity estimation. However, all these approaches used single frame static features to estimate the frame-wise pain intensity levels, which gives abnormal fluctuations when estimating the continuous pain from a sequence of images. In order to overcome this drawback, [7,8,23,26] and [4] considered the pain intensity estimation using regression-based approaches, and shown substantial performance enhancement. In particular, [23] and [26] examined a set of prior frames to estimate the pain intensity of the target frame. Evaluations demonstrated that the use of historical informa-

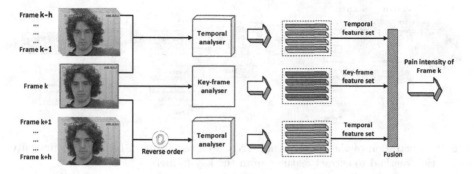

Fig. 1. The overall architecture of our proposed deep pain intensity estimation framework.

tion improves the pain assessment in a sequence of images with continuous pain annotations (i.e., a video). Lastly, considering [23] and [26], the key observations is that less attention is paid for the pain related features that can be extracted from the key-frame. More importantly, the frames located after the key-frame were not considered. In this work, we incorporate both the past and subsequent frames in addition to the key-frame when estimating the pain intensity. Next, we present our proposed model.

3   Proposed Model

Our proposed method consists of two main components and a fusion unit, namely *key-frame analyser* and *temporal analyser*. The key-frame analyser is a conventional deep CNN model used to extract features from a target frame in each step of a sliding window. The second component, namely temporal analyser, estimates the pain related features from the adjacent frames of a target frame. We use two identical RCNNs to extract features from h number of frames located prior and posterior to the key-frame. Lastly, to construct the pain intensity level estimator, we use a fusion mechanism to combine the features extracted by the deep networks. The overall architecture of our proposed pain intensity estimation framework is illustrated in Fig. 1. In this figure, note that we have described one of multiple feature extraction and fusion steps available in a sliding window process. This step will be repeated multiple times for a long sequence of pain frames.

3.1   Key-Frame Analyser

In this sub-section, we describe the architecture of the proposed key-frame analyser in detail. Motivated by the recent successes of deep CNNs in computer vision, the proposed frame-wise feature extractor is constructed to utilize the spatial features extracted from a key-frame during pain intensity estimation

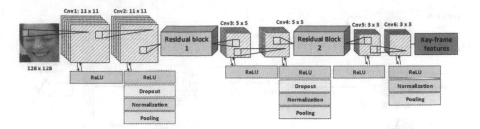

Fig. 2. Illustration of the conventional CNN architecture used in our pain intensity estimation method to extract features from the key-frame.

task. Figure 2 illustrates the deep CNN architecture used in the frame-wise feature extractor. As shown in the figure, our CNN network consists of six convolutional networks and two deep residual blocks. In addition, rectifier linear unit (ReLU), dropout, normalization and pooling layers are appropriately staked in our architecture. The first layer accepts the input frames in sizes of 128 × 128.

As can be seen, we use multiple ReLU regularly after each convolution layer. In a deep neural network, sparse representations can be obtained effortlessly through a ReLU activation function. Additionally, ReLU allows a deep neural network to achieve a better gradient propagation. We have added a dropout layer after the convolution layers 2 and 4 to prevent over-fitting. As indicated in [13], the max pooling layer drastically cut down the computational complexity by progressively reducing the parameters and spatial feature size. The training time can further be reduced by placing cross-channel normalization layers appropriately. Hence, after the convolution layers 2, 4 and 6, we have stacked in a normalization and pooling layers in our architecture. In deep networks, accuracy starts to degrade after a saturation point when we increase the number of convolutional layers; this situation is commonly known as a degradation issue. The degradation problem can be avoided using properly designed residual networks with short connections. Thus, in our architecture, two deep residual blocks are placed after convolution layers 2 and 4. Both residual blocks have six convolution layers with appropriately linked short and long skip connections.

3.2   Temporal Analyser

As described in the previous sub-section, the proposed keyframe analyser considers only the spatial features of the keyframe in each step. However, from the previous studies related to emotion estimation, it has been observed that the adjacent frames have an impact on a keyframe's pain intensity level. Hence, in addition to the extracted spatial features of a keyframe, we also incorporate the temporal features extracted from a few frames located before and after each corresponding keyframe.

Recently, the RCNN has shown a rapid success in various sequential image classification tasks, such as continuous emotion estimation [2] and tracking [15]. In order to improve the performance of RCNN, researchers have proposed diverse

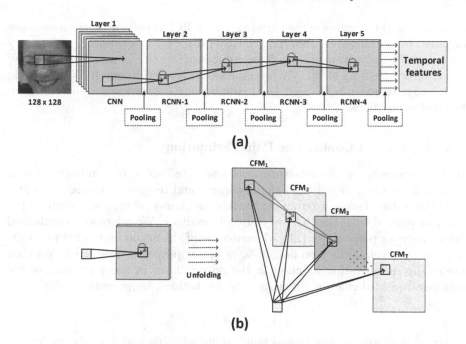

Fig. 3. (a) The overall RCNN architecture used as the temporal analyser in our approach (b) The unfolded illustration of an RCNN layer for T time steps. In both (a) and (b), the black and red arrows indicate feedforward and recurrent connections respectively (Colour figure online).

architectures and experimented on different sequential computer vision tasks. The hidden layers of several adjacent frames in a sequence, including the current layer, are connected in RCNN. Commonly, in sequential tasks, an RCNN demonstrates better performance due to the fact that the temporal information of a sequential input is preserved. In particular, an appropriately designed RCNN can effortlessly outperform existing state-of-the-art pain estimation methods that use only the spatial features. Inspired by [10], in our approach, we use two similar RCNNs to extract temporal features from the adjacent frames. The overall architecture of the RCNN used in the temporal analyser unit is presented in Fig. 3(a). We designed our proposed RCNN architecture using five layers (i.e., layers 1–5) with four RCNN layers after a conventional CNN layer placed upfront. The input size of the first layer is same as the keyframe analyser, which is 128×128. Apart from convolution and recurrent layers, after each layer in our architecture, we place a max pooling layer. We get the temporal features map for a sequence of frames after the last convolutional layer as the output, which will be combined with features extracted by the keyframe analyser.

Figure 3(b) provides an illustration of an unfolded RCNN layer with multiple conventional CNN layers. In each RCNN layer, the hidden layer weights obtained in $t + 1$ steps are shared. Unlike a conventional CNN network with $(t + 1)$ layers that takes only the values of the current step, an RCNN network keeps a sequence of values from 0 to current step (i.e., t). Generally, the model appears to be a very deep feed-forward network with a fixed number of ($4(t+1)+1$ in our architecture) layers after unfolding all RCNN layers. As can be seen, in our RCNN network, there exist shared weights and local connections between recurrent and feed-forward connections.

3.3   Fusion and Continuous Pain Estimation

In our approach, we use a feature level fusion technique to combine the pain related features extracted from the key-frame and temporal analysers. To perform the feature fusion, we combine the intermediate-level representations of the features derived from the last layer of each analyser. We adopted a regularised fusion network proposed in [24]. The outcome of the fusion unit is fed to a softmax layer, which is the final output layer of our proposed framework. We then used a linear activation function in the output layer in order to activate the continuous-valued emotion intensity level predictions, as presented in Eq. 2.

$$\hat{y} = w^T(x + y) \tag{2}$$

where, $\hat{y}$ indicates the continuous pain predicted value and $x + y$ is the feature vector after the fusion. We have modified the loss function to regression-based mean squared error and minimized it during the training process using back-propagation through time (BPTT) technique [1].

4   Results and Experiments

4.1   Settings

We evaluated our proposed spatiotemporal based continuous pain intensity estimation framework on a benchmark dataset, namely, UNBC-McMaster Shoulder Pain Expression Archive (UNBC) [11]. In the past, UNBC dataset has been used widely in most pain intensity estimation studies since it provides a well-annotated facial expression based pain intensity labels. The videos in this dataset were recorded under the clinical and controlled environment, and the subjects experienced a variety of chronic shoulder pain. The original UNBC benchmark dataset contains spontaneous videos of 129 human subjects distributed evenly for each gender, with 63 males and 66 females. However, the database portion available for distribution consists of 200 sequences of 25 subjects with 48,398 FACS [3] coded frames. Along with 16-level PSPI values, annotations for self-rated Sensory Scale (SEN), Affective Motivational Scale (AFF) and Visual Analog Scales (VAS) are also provided. In this paper, to perform our proposed continuous pain intensity estimation experiments, we use the images of publicly released dataset with the corresponding 16-level PSPI ground-truth values.

We also performed a series of preprocessing steps to improve the performance of our proposed framework. We use a preprocessing pipeline, which is similar

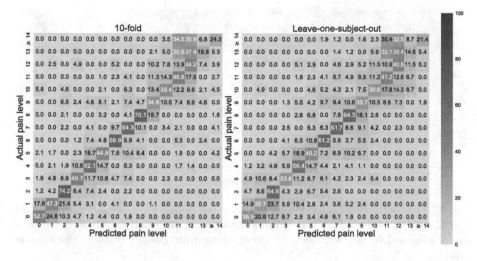

Fig. 4. Illustration of the pain intensity classification results using key-frame analyser proposed as a component in our approach. Results are presented based on 10-fold and leave-one-subject-out cross-validations.

to the one proposed in [21]. It mainly consists of two primary phases: data augmentation and normalisation. The preprocessed images are then used in the training and testing phases. We use both leave-one-subject-out and 10-fold cross-validation during the training and testing phase of the experiment. In leave-one-subject-our cross-validation, we use 1 subject to test on a model which is trained on the other subjects. On the contrary, we split the dataset into 10 partitions, to train the model on 9 and test on last. In both cross-validations, we repeated the same step multiple times to obtain the average performance metric values. The stochastic gradient descent (SGD) has been used as the optimization objective function for the deep learning components, with the learning parameters set to $learning rate = 0.001$, $momentum = 0.9$ and $weight decay = 0.00005$.

4.2 Ablation Study

In this sub-section, we perform a component-wise evaluation to demonstrate the importance of the complete framework in estimating the continuous pain intensity levels. As mentioned previously, our proposed framework has two major components. The first component, key-frame analyser, is to extract the spatial features from the key-frame. We use key-frame analyser alone to estimate the pain intensity values from a sequence of images. Note that the results obtained are the discrete pain intensity levels (i.e., pain levels $0, 1, 2, ..., 16$) since the key-frame analyser is a traditional feed-forward deep CNN network. Therefore, we have not compared the results achieved in this step against other steps which are described later in the ablation study. However, the classification accuracies for the pain intensity levels are reported in Fig. 4. Due to the lack of annotated samples for the higher pain intensity levels, such as 14, 15 and 16, we have grouped

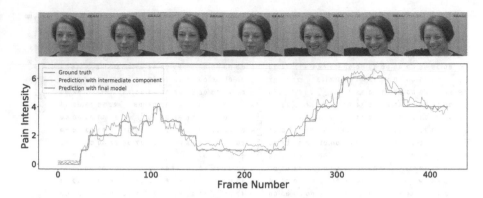

Fig. 5. The continuous prediction of the pain intensities for a sequence taken from UNBC dataset is presented. The results obtained by an intermediate and the final model proposed in our approach is shown along with ground truth (Colour figure online).

them to a single intensity class in our experiment and denoted as ≥ 14. As can be seen, the key-frame analyser achieved the highest classification accuracies for the pain intensity level prediction in 10-fold cross-validation. For example, the pain intensity prediction accuracies are 52.7% and 38.5% for 10-fold and leave-one-subject-out cross-validations, respectively. Next, we will demonstrate how we have improved this detection accuracy by incorporating our temporal features.

In order to extract the temporal features from the frames located before and after the key-frame, we use the second component. In order to demonstrate the significance of the frames located before and after the key-frame, we have structured this experiment as follows. We design an intermediate component with key-frame extractor and one RCNN network to extract only the features from frames located before the key-frame. Next, we combine the next RCNN network that extracts the features from frames located after the key-frame to obtain our final model.

Figure 5 illustrates the predicted continuous pain intensities for a sequence from UNBC dataset using the aforementioned variations of our proposed framework. The ground truth frame-level pain intensity annotations are indicated using blue line in the figure. The results demonstrate that our final model achieved better results (indicated in green colour) in terms of estimating continuous pain intensities compared to the intermediate component (indicated in orange colour).

4.3 Comparison with the State-of-the-art

Additionally, we compare our model with other noteworthy techniques proposed for continuous pain intensity estimation on UNBC dataset. The comparison results are illustrated in Table 1. After exploiting the features extracted from both key-frame and temporal analyser, our approach shows promising results and outperforms all the state-of-the-art methods proposed in the literature. Our final framework achieved an average mean squared error (MSE) and Pearson's inner-product correlation coefficient (PCC) of 1.29 and 0.73 for the fused features key-frame and temporal analysers, which shows that our framework is effective.

Table 1. Comparison of the pain intensity estimation results of the proposed hybrid approach with other state-of-the-art methods in the literature.

Methods	Variations	MSE	PCC
Kaltwang et al. [8]	PTS	2.59	0.36
	DC	1.71	0.55
	LBP	1.81	0.48
	(DCT+LBP)/RVR	1.39	0.59
Florea et al. [4]	Hessian Histograms	3.76	0.25
	Gradient Histograms	4.76	0.34
Hong et al. [7]	2Standmap	1.42	0.55
Zhou et al. [26]	RCNN regression	1.54	0.65
Our method	Before	1.51	0.62
	Before+After	1.37	0.69
	Before+After+key-frame	**1.29**	**0.73**

5 Conclusion

This paper introduces a deep hybrid network based continuous pain intensity estimation framework. The combination of key-frame and temporal analysers allowed us to devise a sophisticated mechanism that works effectively on a continuous pain sequence. The robustness of our approach was further enhanced by including a feature set extracted from a few prior and posterior frames by the temporal analyser. Experiments on the benchmark UNBC-McMaster Shoulder Pain Expression Archive dataset demonstrated that our approach is capable of estimating continuous pain intensities effectively. Further, the comparison with other existing state-of-the-art methods proved that our approach outperformed the state-of-the-art continuous pain intensity estimation methods. As a future direction, we aim to expand this continuous pain intensity estimation framework to estimate other complex emotions, such as confidence, depression and distress.

References

1. De Jeses, O., Hagan, M.T.: Backpropagation through time for a general class of recurrent network. In: Proceedings of the International Joint Conference on Neural Networks, IJCNN 2001, (Cat. No. 01CH37222), vol. 4, pp. 2638–2643. IEEE (2001)
2. Ebrahimi Kahou, S., Michalski, V., Konda, K., Memisevic, R., Pal, C.: Recurrent neural networks for emotion recognition in video. In: Proceedings of the 2015 ACM on International Conference on Multimodal Interaction, pp. 467–474. ACM (2015)
3. Ekman, R.: What the Face Reveals: Basic and Applied Studies of Spontaneous Expression Using the Facial Action Coding System (FACS). Oxford University Press, Cary (1997)
4. Florea, C., Florea, L., Vertan, C.: Learning pain from emotion: transferred hot data representation for pain intensity estimation. In: Agapito, L., Bronstein, M.M., Rother, C. (eds.) ECCV 2014. LNCS, vol. 8927, pp. 778–790. Springer, Cham (2015). https://doi.org/10.1007/978-3-319-16199-0_54
5. Frank, M.G., Ekman, P., Friesen, W.V.: Behavioral markers and recognizability of the smile of enjoyment. J. Pers. Soc. Psychol. **64**(1), 83 (1993)
6. Hammal, Z., Cohn, J.F.: Automatic detection of pain intensity. In: Proceedings of the 14th ACM International Conference on Multimodal Interaction, pp. 47–52. ACM (2012)
7. Hong, X., Zhao, G., Zafeiriou, S., Pantic, M., Pietikäinen, M.: Capturing correlations of local features for image representation. Neurocomputing **184**, 99–106 (2016)
8. Kaltwang, S., Rudovic, O., Pantic, M.: Continuous pain intensity estimation from facial expressions. In: Bebis, G., et al. (eds.) ISVC 2012. LNCS, vol. 7432, pp. 368–377. Springer, Heidelberg (2012). https://doi.org/10.1007/978-3-642-33191-6_36
9. Kalkhoran, H.M., Fatemizadeh, E.: Pain level estimation in video sequences of face using incorporation of statistical features of frames. In: 2015 9th Iranian Conference on Machine Vision and Image Processing (MVIP), pp. 172–175. IEEE (2015)
10. Liang, M., Hu, X.: Recurrent convolutional neural network for object recognition. In: Proceedings of the IEEE Conference on Computer Vision and Pattern Recognition, pp. 3367–3375 (2015)
11. Lucey, P., Cohn, J.F., Prkachin, K.M., Solomon, P.E., Matthews, I.: Painful data: the UNBC-McMaster shoulder pain expression archive database. In: Face and Gesture 2011, pp. 57–64. IEEE (2011)
12. Martinez, L., Rosalind Picard, D.: Personalized automatic estimation of self-reported pain intensity from facial expressions. In: Proceedings of the IEEE Conference on Computer Vision and Pattern Recognition Workshops, pp. 70–79 (2017)
13. Mendes, C.C.T., Frémont, V., Wolf, D.F.: Exploiting fully convolutional neural networks for fast road detection. In: 2016 IEEE International Conference on Robotics and Automation (ICRA), pp. 3174–3179. IEEE (2016)
14. Neshov, N., Manolova, A.: Pain detection from facial characteristics using supervised descent method. In: 2015 IEEE 8th International Conference on Intelligent Data Acquisition and Advanced Computing Systems: Technology and Applications (IDAACS), vol. 1, pp. 251–256. IEEE (2015)
15. Ondruska, P., Posner, I.: Deep tracking: seeing beyond seeing using recurrent neural networks. In: Thirtieth AAAI Conference on Artificial Intelligence, March 2016
16. Prkachin, K.M.: The consistency of facial expressions of pain: a comparison across modalities. Pain **51**(3), 297–306 (1992)

17. Prkachin, K.M., Solomon, P.E.: The structure, reliability and validity of pain expression: evidence from patients with shoulder pain. Pain **139**(2), 267–274 (2008)
18. Rathee, N., Ganotra, D.: A novel approach for pain intensity detection based on facial feature deformations. J. Vis. Commun. Image Represent. **33**, 247–254 (2015)
19. Roy, S.D., Bhowmik, M.K., Saha, P., Ghosh, A.K.: An approach for automatic pain detection through facial expression. Procedia Comput. Sci. **84**, 99–106 (2016)
20. Rudovic, O., Pavlovic, V., Pantic, M.: Automatic pain intensity estimation with heteroscedastic conditional ordinal random fields. In: Bebis, G., et al. (eds.) ISVC 2013. LNCS, vol. 8034, pp. 234–243. Springer, Heidelberg (2013). https://doi.org/10.1007/978-3-642-41939-3_23
21. Thuseethan, S., Rajasegarar, S., Yearwood, J.: Detecting micro-expression intensity changes from videos based on hybrid deep CNN. In: Yang, Q., Zhou, Z.-H., Gong, Z., Zhang, M.-L., Huang, S.-J. (eds.) PAKDD 2019. LNCS (LNAI), vol. 11441, pp. 387–399. Springer, Cham (2019). https://doi.org/10.1007/978-3-030-16142-2_30
22. Thuseethan, S., Rajasegarar, S., Yearwood, J.: Emotion intensity estimation from video frames using deep hybrid convolutional neural networks. In: 2019 International Joint Conference on Neural Networks (IJCNN). IEEE (2019)
23. Wang, F., et al.: Regularizing face verification nets for pain intensity regression. In: 2017 IEEE International Conference on Image Processing (ICIP), pp. 1087–1091. IEEE (2017)
24. Wu, Z., Wang, X., Jiang, Y.G., Ye, H., Xue, X.: Modeling spatial-temporal clues in a hybrid deep learning framework for video classification. In: Proceedings of the 23rd ACM International Conference on Multimedia, pp. 461–470. ACM (2015)
25. Zhao, R., Gan, Q., Wang, S., Ji, Q.: Facial expression intensity estimation using ordinal information. In: Proceedings of the IEEE Conference on Computer Vision and Pattern Recognition, pp. 3466–3474 (2016)
26. Zhou, J., Hong, X., Su, F., Zhao, G.: Recurrent convolutional neural network regression for continuous pain intensity estimation in video. In: Proceedings of the IEEE Conference on Computer Vision and Pattern Recognition Workshops, pp. 84–92 (2016)

Sales Demand Forecast in E-commerce Using a Long Short-Term Memory Neural Network Methodology

Kasun Bandara[1]([✉]), Peibei Shi[2], Christoph Bergmeir[1], Hansika Hewamalage[1], Quoc Tran[2], and Brian Seaman[2]

[1] Faculty of Information Technology, Monash University, Melbourne, Australia
{herath.bandara,christoph.bergmeir,hansika.hewamalage}@monash.edu
[2] @Walmart Labs, San Bruno, USA
{pshi,qtran,brian}@walmartlabs.com

Abstract. Generating accurate and reliable sales forecasts is crucial in the E-commerce business. The current state-of-the-art techniques are typically univariate methods, which produce forecasts considering only the historical sales data of a single product. However, in a situation where large quantities of related time series are available, conditioning the forecast of an individual time series on past behaviour of similar, related time series can be beneficial. Since the product assortment hierarchy in an E-commerce platform contains large numbers of related products, in which the sales demand patterns can be correlated, our attempt is to incorporate this cross-series information in a unified model. We achieve this by globally training a Long Short-Term Memory network (LSTM) that exploits the non-linear demand relationships available in an E-commerce product assortment hierarchy. Aside from the forecasting framework, we also propose a systematic pre-processing framework to overcome the challenges in the E-commerce business. We also introduce several product grouping strategies to supplement the LSTM learning schemes, in situations where sales patterns in a product portfolio are disparate. We empirically evaluate the proposed forecasting framework on a real-world online marketplace dataset from Walmart.com. Our method achieves competitive results on category level and super-departmental level datasets, outperforming state-of-the-art techniques.

Keywords: E-commerce · Time series · Demand forecasting · LSTM

1 Introduction

Generating product-level demand forecasts is a crucial factor in E-commerce platforms. Accurate and reliable demand forecasts enable better inventory planning, competitive pricing, timely promotion planning, etc. While accurate forecasts can lead to huge savings and cost reductions, poor demand estimations are proven to be costly in this domain.

© Springer Nature Switzerland AG 2019
T. Gedeon et al. (Eds.): ICONIP 2019, LNCS 11955, pp. 462–474, 2019.
https://doi.org/10.1007/978-3-030-36718-3_39

The business environment in E-commerce is highly dynamic and often volatile, which is largely caused by holiday effects, low product-sales conversion rate, competitor behaviour, etc. As a result, demand data in this domain carry various challenges, such as highly non-stationary historical data, irregular sales patterns, sparse sales data, highly intermittent sales, etc. Furthermore, product assortments in these platforms follow a hierarchical structure, where certain products within a subgroup of the hierarchy can be similar or related to each other. In essence, this hierarchical structure provides a natural grouping of the product portfolio, where items that fall in the same subcategory/category/department/su per-department are considered as a single group, in which the sales patterns can be correlated. The time series of such related products are correlated and may share key properties of demand. For example, increasing demand of an item may potentially cause to decrease/increase sales demand of another item, i.e., substituting/complimentary products. Therefore, accounting for the notion of similarity between these products becomes necessary to produce accurate and meaningful forecasts in the E-commerce domain.

The existing demand forecasting methods in the E-commerce domain are largely influenced by state-of-the-art forecasting techniques from the exponential smoothing [1] and the ARIMA [2] families. However, these forecasting methods are univariate, thus treat each time series separately, and forecast them in isolation. As a result, though many related products are available, in which the sales demand patterns can be similar, these univariate models ignore such potential cross-series information available within related products. Consequently, efforts to exploit the enormous potentials of such multiple related time series is becoming increasingly popular [3–8]. More recently, Recurrent Neural Networks (RNN) and Long Short-Term Memory Networks (LSTM), a special group of neural networks (NN) that are naturally suited for time series forecasting, have achieved promising results by globally training the network across all related time series that enables the network to exploit any cross-series information available [5,6,8].

Therefore, with the primary objective of leveraging demand forecasts in the E-commerce domain, we identify the main research contributions of this study as follows:

- We exploit sales correlations and relationships available in an E-commerce product hierarchy, while introducing a systematic preprocessing framework to overcome the data challenges in the E-commerce domain.
- We analyse and compare two different LSTM learning schemes with different back-propagation error terms, and include a mix of static and dynamic features to incorporate potential external driving factors of sales demand.
- We empirically evaluate our framework using real-world retail sales data from the internal database of Walmart.com, in which we use state-of-the-art forecasting techniques to compare against our proposed framework.

The rest of the paper is organized as follows. We describe the proposed preprocessing scheme in Sect. 2. Next, in Sect. 3, we outline the key learning properties included in our LSTM network architecture. We summarise the overall architecture of our forecasting engine in Sect. 4. Our experimental setup is presented in Sect. 5, where we demonstrate the results obtained by applying our framework to a large dataset from Walmart.com. Finally, Sect. 6 concludes the paper.

2   Data Preprocessing

Sales datasets in the E-commerce domain experience various issues that we aim to address with the following preprocessing mechanisms in our framework.

2.1   Handling Data Quality Issues

Nowadays, data extract, transform, load (ETL) [24] is the main data integration process in data warehousing pipelines. However, the ETL process is often unstable in real-time processing, and may cause false "zero" sales in the dataset. Therefore, we propose a method to distinguish the actual zero sales from the false zero sales ("fake zeros") and treat the latter as missing observations.

Our approach is mostly heuristic, where we initially compute the minimum non-zero sales of each item in the past 6 months. Then, we treat the zero sales as "fake" zero sales if the minimum non-zero sales of a certain item are higher than a threshold $\gamma = 10$. We treat these zero sales as missing observations. It is also noteworthy to mention that the ground truth of zero sales is not available, thus potential false positives can appear in the dataset.

2.2   Handling Missing Values and Sales Normalization

We use a forward-filling strategy to impute missing sales observations in the dataset. This approach uses the most recent valid observation available to replace the missing values. We performed preliminary experiments that showed that this approach outperforms more sophisticated imputation techniques such as linear regression and Classification And Regression Trees (CART).

Also, the product assortment hierarchy is composed of numerous commodities that follow various sales volume ranges, thus performing a data normalisation strategy becomes necessary before building a global model like ours. We use the *mean-scale* transformation proposed by [5], where the mean sales of a product is considered as the scaling factor. This transformation can be formally defined as follows:

$$X_{i,new} = \frac{X_i}{1 + \frac{1}{k} \sum_{t=1}^{k} X_{i,t}} \tag{1}$$

Here, $X_{i,new}$ represents the normalised sales vector, and k denotes the number of sales observations of product i.

2.3 Product Grouping

According to [8], employing a time series grouping strategy can improve the LSTM performance in situations where time series are disparate. Therefore, we introduce two product grouping mechanisms in our preprocessing scheme.

In the first approach, the target products are grouped based on available domain knowledge. Here, we use the sales ranking and the percentage of zero sales as primary business metrics to form groups of products. The first group (G1) represents the product group with a high sales ranking and a low zero sales density. Whereas, group 2 (G2) represents the product group with a low sales ranking and a high zero sales density. Group 3 (G3) represents the rest of the products. From an E-commerce perspective, products in G1 are the "head items" that bring the highest contribution to the business, thus improving the sales forecast accuracy in G1 is most important. Details of the above groupings are summarized in Table 2.

The second approach is based on time series clustering, where we perform K-means clustering on a set of time series features to identify the product grouping. Table 1 provides an overview of these features, where the first two features are business specific features, and the rest are time series specific features. The time series features are extracted using the *tsfeatures* package developed by [23]. Finally, we use a *silhouette analysis* to determine the optimal number of clusters in the K-means clustering algorithm.

Table 1. Time series and sales-related features used for product clustering

Feature	Description
Sales.quantile	Sales quantile over total sales
Zero.sales.percentage	Sales sparsity/percentage of zero sales
Trend	Strength of trend
Spikiness	Strength of spikiness
Linearity	Strength of linearity
Curvature	Strength of curvature
ACF1-e	Autocorrelation coefficient at lag 1 of the residuals
ACF1-x	Autocorrelation coefficient at lag 1
Entropy	Spectral entropy

Table 2. Sales sparsity thresholds used for domain-based product grouping

Group-ID	Sales ranking	Sales sparsity
1	Sales.quantile ≤ 0.33	Zero.sales.percentage.quantile ≥ 0.67
2	Sales.quantile ≥ 0.67	Zero.sales.percentage.quantile ≤ 0.33
3	Other	Other

3   LSTM Network Architecture

LSTMs are an extension of RNNs that have the ability to learn long-term dependencies in a sequence, overcoming the limitations of vanilla RNNs [9,11,12]. The cohesive gating mechanism, i.e., input, output, and forget gates, together with the self-contained memory cell, i.e., "Constant Error Carousel" (CEC) allow the LSTM to regulate the information flow across the network. This enables the LSTM to propagate the network error for much longer sequences, while capturing their long-term temporal dependencies.

In this study, we use a special variant of LSTMs, known as "LSTM with peephole connections" that requires the LSTM input and forget gates to incorporate the previous state of the LSTM memory cell. For further discussions of RNN and LSTM architectures, we refer to [8]. In the following, we describe how exactly the LSTM architecture is used in our work.

3.1   Learning Schemes

We use the input and output data frames generated from the Moving Window (MW) strategy procedure as the primary training source of LSTM. Here, MW strategy transforms a time series (X_i) into pairs of $<input, output>$ patches, which are used as the training data of the LSTM. As recommended by Bandara et al. [8], in the MW generation process, we follow the Multi-Input Multi-Output (MIMO) strategy [14] and employ a local normalization process to avoid possible network saturation effects, which are caused by the bounds of the network activation functions [15]. In particular, the mean value for each input window $(\bar{X}_i)$ is calculated and subtracted from each data point of the corresponding input and output window. This also enables the network to generate conservative forecasts, which is particularly beneficial in the E-commerce domain, as this reduces the risk of generating large demand forecasting errors.

Figure 1 summarizes the LSTM learning schemes used in our study, LSTM-LS1 and LSTM-LS2. Here, $W_t \in \mathbb{R}^n$ represents the input window at time step t, $h_t \in \mathbb{R}^p$ represents the hidden state at time step t, and the cell state at time step t is represented by $C_{t-1} \in \mathbb{R}^p$. Note that p denotes the dimension of the memory cell of the LSTM. Additionally, we introduce $\hat{Y}_t \in \mathbb{R}^m$ to represent the projected output of the LSTM at time step t. Here, m denotes our output window size, which is equivalent to the forecasting horizon M. Here, each LSTM layer is followed by a fully connected neural layer (excluding the bias component) to project each LSTM cell output h_t to the dimension of the output window m.

The proposed learning schemes can be distinguished by the overall error term E_t used in the network back-propagation, which is back-propagation through time (BPTT; [10,13]). Given $Y_t \in \mathbb{R}^m$ are the actual observations of values in the output window at time step t, which are used as the teacher inputs for the predictions $\hat{Y}_t$, the LSTM-LS1 scheme accumulates the error e_t of each LSTM cell instance to compute the error E_t of the network. Here, e_t refers to the prediction error at time step t, where $e_t = Y_t - \hat{Y}_t$. Whereas in LSTM-LS2, only the error term of the final LSTM cell instance e_{t+1} is used as the error E_t for the network training. For example, in Fig. 1, the E_t of LSTM-LS1 scheme is equivalent to $\sum_{j=t-2}^{t+1} e_j$, while the error term in the final LSTM cell state e_{t+1} gives the error E_t of LSTM-LS2. These error terms are eventually used to update the network parameters, i.e., the LSTM weight matrices. In this study, we use TensorFlow, an open-source deep-learning toolkit [16] to implement the above LSTM learning schemes.

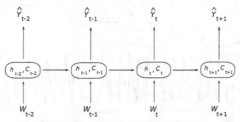

(a) An unrolled representation of learning scheme LSTM-LS1

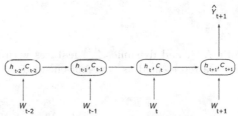

(b) An unrolled representation of learning scheme LSTM-LS2

Fig. 1. The architectures of LSTM learning schemes, LSTM-LS1 and LSTM-LS2. Each squared unit represents a peephole connected LSTM cell, where h_t provides short-term memory and C_t retains the long-term dependencies of LSTM.

3.2   Exogenous Variables

We use a combination of static and dynamic features to model external factors that affect the sales demand. In general, static features include time invariant information, such as product type, product category, etc. Dynamic features include calendar features (e.g., holidays, season, weekday/weekend). These features can be useful to capture sales demand behaviours of products in a certain period of time.

Figure 2 demonstrates an example of applying the MW approach to include static and dynamic features in an input window. Now, the input window W_t is a unified vector of past sales observations X_t, static features $Z_t^{(s)}$, and dynamic features $Z_t^{(d)}$. As a result, in addition to historical sales observations $\{x_1, x_2, ..., x_n\}$, we also include the input windows of the holidays $\{h_1, h_2, ..., h_n\}$, seasons $\{s_1, s_2, ..., s_n\}$, day of the week $\{d_1, d_2, ..., d_n\}$, and the sub category

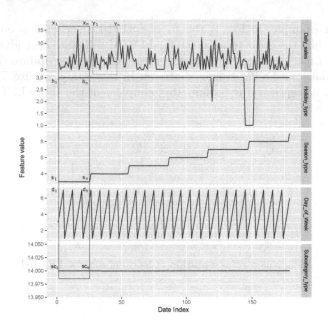

Fig. 2. Using both static $Z_t^{(s)}$, and dynamic $Z_t^{(d)}$ features with the MW approach. All categorical variables are represented as "one-hot-encoded" vectors in the LSTM training data.

types $\{sc_1, sc_2, ..., sc_n\}$. Later, LSTM uses a concatenation of these input windows to learn the actual observation of the output window $\{y_1, y_2, ..., y_m\}$.

4   Overall Procedure

The proposed forecasting framework is composed of three components, namely (1) pre-processing layer, (2) LSTM training layer, and (3) post-processing layer. Figure 3 gives a schematic overview of our proposed forecasting framework.

As described in Sect. 2, we initially perform several preprocessing techniques to arrange the raw data for the LSTM training procedure. Afterwards, the LSTM models are trained according to the LSTM-LS1 and LSTM-LS2 learning schemes. Then, in order to obtain the final forecasts, we rescale and denormalize the predictions generated by the LSTM. Here, the rescaling process back-transforms the generated forecasts to their original scale of sales, whereas the denormalization process (see Sect. 3) adds back the mean sales of the last input window to the forecasts.

5   Experiments

In this section, we describe the experimental setup used to empirically evaluate our proposed forecasting framework. This includes the datasets, error metrics,

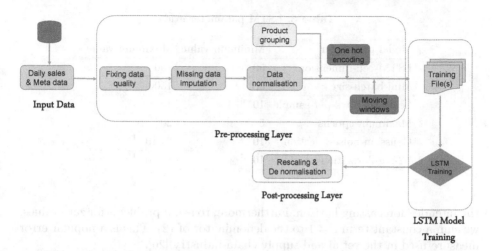

Fig. 3. The overall summary of the proposed sales demand forecasting framework, which consists of a pre-processing, an LSTM training, and a post-processing part.

hyper-parameter selection method, benchmark methods and LSTM variants used to perform the experiments, and the results obtained.

5.1   Datasets

We evaluate our forecasting framework on two datasets collected from the internal database of Walmart.com. We first evaluate our framework on a subset of 1724 items that belong to the product *household* category, which consists of 15 different sub-categories. Next, we scale up the number of products to 18254 by extracting a collection from a single super-department, which consists of 16 different categories.

We use 190 consecutive days of daily sales data in 2018. The last 10 days of data are reserved for model testing. We define our forecasting horizon M as 10, i.e., training output window size n is equivalent to 10. Following the heuristic proposed by Bandara et al. [8], we choose the size of the training input window n as 13 (10 * 1.25).

5.2   Error Measure

We use a modified version of the mean absolute percentage error (mMAPE) as our forecasting error metric. We define the mMAPE for each item as:

$$\text{mMAPE} = \frac{1}{m} \sum_{t=1}^{m} \left(\frac{|F_t - A_t|}{1 + |A_t|} \right). \tag{2}$$

Here, A_t represents the actual sales at time t, and F_t is the respective sales forecast generated by a prediction model. The number m denotes the length of

Table 3. LSTM parameter grid

Model parameter	Minimum value	Maximum value
LSTM-cell-dimension	50	100
Mini-batch-size	60	1500
Learning-rates-per-sample	10^{-6}	10^{-3}
Maximum-epochs	5	20
Gaussian-noise-injection	10^{-4}	$8 \cdot 10^{-4}$
L2-regularization-weight	10^{-4}	$8 \cdot 10^{-4}$

the intended forecasting horizon. Furthermore, to avoid problems for zero values, we sum a constant term $\epsilon = 1$ to the denominator of (2). This is a popular error measure used in the retail and supply chain industry [26].

To report the overall mMAPE for a set of items, we use both mean of the mMAPEs (Mean mMAPE) and the median of the mMAPEs (Median mMAPE). Here, median mMAPE is suitable to summarise the error distribution in situations where the majority of the observations are zero sales, i.e., long tailed sales demand items.

5.3   Hyperparameter Selection and Optimization

Our LSTM based learning framework contains various hyper-parameters, including LSTM cell dimension, model learning rate, number of epochs, mini-batch-size, and model regularization terms, i.e., Gaussian-noise and L2-regularization weights. We use two implementations of a Bayesian global optimization methodology, *bayesian-optimization* and *SMAC* [17,19] to autonomously determine the optimal set of hyper-parameters in our model [18]. Table 3 summarises the bounds of the hyper-parameter values used throughout the LSTM learning process, represented by the respective minimum and maximum columns.

Moreover, we use the gradient-based *Adam* [20] and *COntinuous COin Betting (COCOB)* [21] algorithms as our primary learning optimization algorithms to train the network. Unlike in other gradient-based optimization algorithms, *COCOB* does not require tuning of the learning rate.

5.4   Benchmarks and LSTM Variants

We use a host of different univariate forecasting techniques to benchmark against our proposed forecasting framework. This includes forecasting methods from the exponential smoothing family, i.e., *exponentially weighted moving average (EWMA), exponential smoothing (ETS)* [22,23], and a model from the moving average family, i.e., *autoregressive moving-average model (ARIMA)* [22,23]. Though some of these benchmarks have been proposed in the literature decades ago, they are used in many businesses as the forecasting work-horses on a daily basis, and recent forecasting competitions have shown that even today these methods are able to obtain very competitive accuracies [25]. We also use *Prophet*, a forecasting technique recently introduced by Facebook Research [27], as a benchmark. In addition to the well-established benchmarks in this domain, we include standard benchmarks such as Naïve, and Naïve Seasonal. Some of these benchmarks are also currently used in the forecasting framework at Walmart.com. Furthermore, in our experiments, we add the following variants of our baseline LSTM model.

- *LSTM.ALL*: The baseline LSTM model, where one model is globally trained across all the available time series.
- *LSTM.GROUP*: A separate LSTM model is built on each subgroup of time series, which are identified by the domain knowledge available.
- *LSTM.FEATURE*: The subgroup labels identified in the *LSTM.GROUP* approach is used as an external feature (one-hot encoded vector) of LSTM.
- *LSTM.CLUSTER*: The time series sub-grouping is performed using a time series feature based clustering approach (refer Sect. 2). Similar to *LSTM.GROUP*, a separate LSTM model is trained on each cluster.

5.5   Results and Discussion

Tables 4 and 5 show the results for the category level and super-department level datasets. Here, k corresponds to the number of items in each group, and $G1/G2/G3$ represent the product sub-groups introduced in Sect. 2.3. We use a weekly seasonality in the seasonal benchmarks, i.e., ETS (seasonal), Naïve Seasonal. It is also worth to mention that for the super-department dataset, we only employ one grouping strategy, namely LSTM.GROUP, and include only the best-performing learning scheme in the category level dataset, which is LSTM-LS1, to examine the robustness of our forecasting framework.

In the tables, under each LSTM variant, we present the results of the different learning schemes, i.e., LSTM-LS1 and LSTM-LS2, hyper-parameter selection methods, i.e., Bayesian and SMAC, and optimization learning algorithms, i.e., Adam and COCOB, and achieve comparable results. According to Table 4, considering all the items in the category, the proposed LSTM.Cluster variant obtains the best Mean mMAPE, while the Naïve forecast gives the best Median mMAPE. Meanwhile, regarding G1, which are the items with most business impact, the LSTM.Cluster and LSTM.Group variants outperform the rest of the benchmarks, in terms of the Mean mMAPE and Median mMAPE respectively. We also observe in G1 that the results of the LSTM.ALL variant are improved after applying our grouping strategies. Furthermore, on average, the LSTM variants together with the Naïve forecast achieve the best-performing results within G2 and G3, where the product sales are relatively sparse compared to G1.

We observe a similar pattern of results in Table 5, where in general, the LSTM.GROUP variant gives the best Mean mMAPE, while the Naïve forecast ranks as the first in Median mMAPE. Likewise in G1, the LSTM.GROUP variant performs superior amongst other benchmarks, and in particular outperforms the LSTM.ALL variant, while upholding the benefits of item grouping strategies

Table 4. Results for category level dataset

Model	Configuration	mMAPE (All) k=1724		mMAPE (G1) k=549		mMAPE (G2) k=544		mMAPE (G3) k=631	
		Mean	Median	Mean	Median	Mean	Median	Mean	Median
LSTM.ALL	LSTM-LS1/Bayesian/Adam	0.888	0.328	1.872	0.692	0.110	0.073	0.640	0.283
LSTM.ALL	LSTM-LS1/Bayesian/COCOB	0.803	0.267	1.762	0.791	0.070	0.002	0.537	0.259
LSTM.ALL	LSTM-LS2/Bayesian/Adam	0.847	0.327	1.819	0.738	0.103	0.047	0.582	0.326
LSTM.GROUP	LSTM-LS1/Bayesian/Adam	0.873	0.302	1.882	**0.667**	0.093	0.016	0.604	0.283
LSTM.GROUP	LSTM-LS1/Bayesian/COCOB	1.039	0.272	2.455	0.818	0.074	**0.000**	0.549	**0.250**
LSTM.GROUP	LSTM-LS2/Bayesian/Adam	0.812	0.317	1.818	0.738	0.091	0.022	0.587	0.314
LSTM.FEATURE	LSTM-LS1/Bayesian/Adam	1.065	0.372	2.274	0.889	0.135	0.100	0.738	0.388
LSTM.FEATURE	LSTM-LS1/Bayesian/COCOB	0.800	0.267	1.758	0.772	**0.069**	**0.000**	0.533	0.255
LSTM.FEATURE	LSTM-LS2/Bayesian/Adam	0.879	0.324	1.886	0.750	0.091	0.022	0.611	0.324
LSTM.CLUSTER	LSTM-LS1/Bayesian/Adam	0.954	0.313	2.109	0.869	0.135	0.110	0.625	0.322
LSTM.CLUSTER	LSTM-LS1/Bayesian/COCOB	**0.793**	0.308	**1.695**	0.748	0.077	0.005	0.562	0.302
LSTM.CLUSTER	LSTM-LS2/Bayesian/Adam	1.001	0.336	2.202	0.863	0.084	0.017	0.664	0.347
EWMA	-	0.968	0.342	1.983	1.026	0.107	0.021	0.762	0.412
ARIMA	-	1.153	0.677	2.322	0.898	0.103	0.056	0.730	0.496
ETS (non-seasonal)	-	0.965	0.362	2.020	0.803	0.113	0.060	0.713	0.444
ETS (seasonal)	-	0.983	0.363	2.070	0.804	0.116	0.059	0.713	0.445
Naïve	-	0.867	**0.250**	1.803	0.795	0.124	**0.000**	0.632	**0.250**
Naïve Seasonal	-	0.811	0.347	1.789	0.679	0.086	**0.000**	**0.523**	0.320
Prophet-Facebook	-	0.892	0.342	1.923	0.842	0.103	0.042	0.609	0.325

Table 5. Results for super-department level dataset

Model	Configuration	mMAPE (All items) k=18254		mMAPE (G1) k=5682		mMAPE (G2) k=5737		mMAPE (G3) k=6835	
		Mean	Median	Mean	Median	Mean	Median	Mean	Median
LSTM.ALL	LSTM-LS1/Bayesian/Adam	1.006	0.483	2.146	1.285	0.191	0.079	0.668	0.434
LSTM.ALL	LSTM-LS1/Bayesian/COCOB	0.944	0.442	2.041	1.203	0.163	0.053	0.614	0.394
LSTM.GROUP	LSTM-LS1/Bayesian/Adam	**0.871**	0.445	**1.818**	**1.009**	0.189	0.067	**0.603**	0.377
LSTM.GROUP	LSTM-LS1/Bayesian/COCOB	0.921	0.455	1.960	1.199	0.173	0.053	0.618	0.394
LSTM.FEATURE	LSTM-LS1/Bayesian/Adam	0.979	0.424	2.117	1.279	**0.151**	0.050	0.653	0.377
LSTM.FEATURE	LSTM-LS1/Bayesian/COCOB	1.000	0.443	2.143	1.282	0.215	0.092	0.676	0.398
EWMA	-	1.146	0.579	2.492	1.650	0.229	0.091	0.805	0.562
ARIMA	-	1.084	0.536	2.305	1.497	0.198	0.094	0.734	0.510
ETS (non-seasonal)	-	1.097	0.527	2.314	1.494	0.204	0.092	0.755	0.509
ETS (seasonal)	-	1.089	0.528	2.290	1.483	0.204	0.092	0.756	0.510
Naïve	-	0.981	**0.363**	2.008	1.122	0.204	**0.000**	0.713	**0.286**
Naïve Seasonal	-	1.122	0.522	2.323	1.513	0.219	0.050	0.803	0.475
Prophet-Facebook		1.087	0.554	2.266	1.400	0.210	0.113	0.765	0.534

under these circumstances. Similarly, on average, the LSTM variants and Naïve forecast obtain the best results in G2 and G3. In both tables, we observe several methods producing zero Median mMAPE in the G2 subgroup. This is due to the high volume of zero sales present among the items in G2. In E-commerce business, items in the G2 are called "tail items", which are usually seasonal products. These items follow low sales during most time of a year and high sales during certain period of time. Therefore, generating demand forecast for these items is still essential, although their sales are sparse.

Overall, the majority of the LSTM variants show competitive results under both evaluation settings, showing the robustness of our forecasting framework with large amounts of items. More importantly, these results reflect the contribution made by the time series grouping strategies to uplift the baseline LSTM performance.

6   Conclusions

There exists great potential to improve sales forecasting accuracy in the E-commerce domain. One good opportunity is to utilize the correlated and similar sales patterns available in a product portfolio. In this paper, we have introduced a novel demand forecasting framework based on LSTMs that exploits non-linear relationships that exist in the E-commerce business.

We have used the proposed approach to forecast the sales demand by training a global model across the items available in a product assortment hierarchy. Our developments also present several systematic grouping strategies to our base model, which are in particular useful in situations where product sales are sparse.

Our methodology has been evaluated on a real-world E-commerce database from Walmart.com. To demonstrate the robustness of our framework, we have evaluated our methods on both category level and super-department level datasets. The results have shown that our methods have outperformed the state-of-the-art univariate forecasting techniques.

Furthermore, the results indicate that E-commerce product hierarchies contain various cross-product demand patterns and correlations are available, and approaches to exploit this information are necessary to improve the sales forecasting accuracy in this domain.

References

1. Hyndman, R., et al.: Forecasting with Exponential Smoothing: The State Space Approach. Springer, Heidelberg (2008). doi: 10.1007/978-3-540-71918-2
2. Box, G.E.P., et al.: Time Series Analysis: Forecasting and Control. Wiley, Hoboken (2015)
3. Trapero, J.R., Kourentzes, N., Fildes, R.: On the identification of sales forecasting models in the presence of promotions. J. ORS **66**, 299–307 (2015)
4. Borovykh, A., Bohte, S., Oosterlee, C.W.: Conditional time series forecasting with convolutional neural networks. arXiv [cs.AI] (2017)
5. Flunkert, V., Salinas, D., Gasthaus, J.: DeepAR: probabilistic forecasting with autoregressive recurrent networks. arXiv [cs.AI] (2017)
6. Wen, R. et al.: A multi-horizon quantile recurrent forecaster. arXiv [stat.ML] (2017)
7. Chapados, N.: Effective Bayesian modeling of groups of related count time series. In: Proceedings of the 31st ICML (2014)

8. Bandara, K., Bergmeir, C., Smyl, S.: Forecasting across time series databases using RNNs on groups of similar series: a clustering approach. arXiv [cs.LG] (2017)
9. Elman, J.L.: Finding structure in time. Cogn. Sci. **14**(2), 179–211 (1990)
10. Williams, R.J., Zipser, D.: Gradient-based learning algorithms for RNNs and their computational complexity (1995)
11. Bengio, Y., Simard, P., Frasconi, P.: Learning long-term dependencies with gradient descent is difficult. IEEE Trans. Neural Netw. **2**, 157–166 (1994)
12. Hochreiter, S., Schmidhuber, J.: Long short-term memory. Neural Comput. **9**(8), 1735–1780 (1997)
13. Sutskever, I., Vinyals, O., Le, Q.V.: Sequence to sequence learning with neural networks. In: Ghahramani, Z., et al. (eds.) Proceedings of the 27th NIPS (2014)
14. Ben Taieb, S., et al.: A review and comparison of strategies for multi-step ahead time series forecasting based on the NN5 forecasting competition. Expert Syst. Appl. **39**(8), 7067–7083 (2012)
15. Ord, K., Fildes, R.A., Kourentzes, N.: Principles of Business Forecasting, 2nd edn. Wessex Press Publishing Co., New York (2017)
16. Abadi, M., et al.: TensorFlow: Large-scale machine learning on heterogeneous distributed systems. arXiv [cs.DC] (2016)
17. Hutter, F., Hoos, H.H., Leyton-Brown, K.: Sequential model-based optimization for general algorithm configuration. In: Proceedings of the 5th International Conference on Learning and Intelligent Optimization, Italy, Rome, pp. 507–523 (2011)
18. Fernando, Bayesian-optimization: Bayesian Optimization of Hyper-parameters. Github (2017). https://bit.ly/2EssG1r
19. Snoek, J., Larochelle, H., Adams, R.P.: Practical Bayesian optimization of machine learning algorithms. In: Proceedings of the 25th NIPS (2012)
20. Kingma, D.P., Ba, J.: Adam: a method for stochastic optimization. arXiv [cs.LG] (2014)
21. Orabona, F., Tommasi, T.: Training deep networks without learning rates through coin betting. arXiv [cs.LG] (2017)
22. Hyndman, R.J., Khandakar, Y.: Automatic time series forecasting: the forecast package for R. J. Stat. Softw. **26**(3), 1–22 (2008)
23. Hyndman, R.J., et al.: Time series features R package (2018). https://bit.ly/2GekHql
24. Kornelson, K.P., Vajjiravel, M., Prasad, R., Clark, P.D., Najm, T.: Method and system for developing extract transform load systems for data warehouses (2006)
25. Makridakis, S., Spiliotis, E., Assimakopoulos, V.: The M4 competition: results, findings, conclusion and way forward. Int. J. Forecast. **34**, 802–808 (2018)
26. Weller, M., Crone, S.: Supply chain forecasting: best practices & benchmarking study. Technical report, Lancaster Centre for Forecasting (2012)
27. Taylor, S.J., Letham, B.: Forecasting at scale. Am. Stat. **72**(1), 37–45 (2018)

Deep Point-Wise Prediction for Action Temporal Proposal

Luxuan Li[1], Tao Kong[2(✉)], Fuchun Sun[1(✉)], and Huaping Liu[1]

[1] Department of Computer Science and Technology,
Beijing National Research Center for Information Science and Technology (BNRist),
Tsinghua University, Beijing, China
llx17@mails.tsinghua.edu.cn, {fcsun,hpliu}@tsinghua.edu.cn
[2] ByteDance AI Lab, Beijing, China
taokongcn@gmail.com

Abstract. Detecting actions in videos is an important yet challenging task. Previous works usually utilize (a) sliding window paradigms, or (b) per-frame action scoring and grouping to enumerate the possible temporal locations. Their performances are also limited to the designs of sliding windows or grouping strategies. In this paper, we present a simple and effective method for temporal action proposal generation, named Deep Point-wise Prediction (DPP). DPP simultaneously predicts the action existing possibility and the corresponding temporal locations, without the utilization of any handcrafted sliding window or grouping. The whole system is end-to-end trained with joint loss of temporal action proposal classification and location prediction.

We conduct extensive experiments to verify its effectiveness, generality and robustness on standard THUMOS14 dataset. DPP runs more than 1000 frames per second, which largely satisfies the real-time requirement. The code is available at https://github.com/liluxuan1997/DPP.

Keywords: Temporal action proposal · Deep point-wise prediction · Untrimmed videos

1 Introduction

Despite huge success in understanding a single image, understanding videos still needs further more exploration. Temporal action proposal generation, which aims to extract temporal intervals that may contain an action, has drawn lots of attention recently. It is a challenging task since high quality proposals not only require accurate classification of an action, but also require precise starting time and ending time.

Previous temporal action proposal generation methods can be generally classified into two main types. The first type is to generate proposals by sliding windows. These methods first predefine a series of temporal windows with fixed

---

L. Li and T. Kong—The first two authors contribute equally to the paper.

© Springer Nature Switzerland AG 2019
T. Gedeon et al. (Eds.): ICONIP 2019, LNCS 11955, pp. 475–487, 2019.
https://doi.org/10.1007/978-3-030-36718-3_40

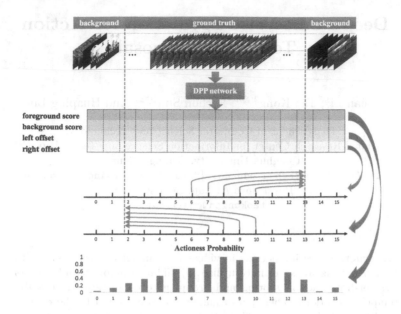

Fig. 1. Overview of DPP. For time points in the sequence of an untrimmed video, DPP directly predicts the probability of action existence and the corresponding starting and ending offsets.

lengths as proposal candidates. Then those proposal candidates are scored to indicate the probability of action existence. Finally ranking is applied to get top proposals. Early works like SST [1] and SCNN-prop [19] try to get high recall by generating dense proposal candidates. SST generates k proposals at each time step by utilizing RNN. TURN [6] and S3D [23] add boundary regression network to get more precise starting and ending time. However, the disadvantages of the sliding window methods are obvious: (1) High-density sliding windows cause great cost of time; (2) Without boundary regression network, the temporal boundaries are not so precise; (3) Sliding windows require multiple predefined lengths and strides, thus introducing additional hyper-parameters of design choices (Fig. 1).

The second type is to generate proposals by actioness grouping. These methods evaluate the probability of action existence for each temporal point and group points with high actioness scores to form final proposals. For example, TAG [24] first uses an actioness classifier to evaluate the actioness probabilities of individual snippets and generates proposals by classic watershed algorithm. BSN [13] adopts three binary classifiers to evaluate starting, ending and actioness probabilities of each snippet separately. Then it combines all candidate starting and ending locations as proposals when the gaps between them are not too far. Methods based on actioness score tend to generate more precise boundaries. However, quality of proposals generated by this type of methods highly depends on the grouping strategy. Besides, evaluating actioness probabilities for all points and grouping them limit the processing efficiency.

How we humankind recognize and localize a video action? Do we need predefined windows and scanning the whole video sequence? The answer is obviously no. For any single frame in a video, human can directly distinguish if an action happens. And sometimes, human even do not need to see the very start or end of the action but can predict the location.

Inspired by this, we present a simple yet effective system named Deep Point-wise Prediction Network (DPP) to generate temporal action proposals. Our method can be divided into two sibling streams: (1) predicting action existing probability for each temporal point in feature maps; (2) predicting starting time and ending time respectively for each position that potentially contains an action. The whole architecture consists of three parts. The first part is backbone network to extract high level spatio-temporal features. The second part is Temporal Feature Pyramid Network (TFPN), which is inspired by Feature Pyramid Network (FPN) [14] for object detection task. The third part includes a binary classifier for actioness score and a predictor for starting and ending time. The whole system is end-to-end trained with joint loss of classification and localization.

In summary, the main contributions of our work are three-fold:

- We propose a novel method named Deep Point-wise Prediction for temporal action proposal generation, which can generate high quality temporal action proposals with precise boundaries in real time.
- Our proposed DPP breaks through the performance limitation of sliding window based methods. It needs no extra design for predefined sliding windows or anchors. Also, with different backbone networks, DPP gets promising results.
- We evaluate DPP on standard THUMOS 2014 dataset, and achieve state-of-the-art performance.

2   Related Work

Action Recognition. Action Recognition is an important task of video understanding. Architectures of this task always consist of two part: spatio-temporal feature extraction network and category classifier. Since action recognition and temporal action proposal generation both need spatio-temporal features for the following steps, this task is worthy of investigation. Earlier works like improved Dense Trajectory (iDT) [21] use traditional feature extraction method consists of HOF, HOG, and MBH. With the development of convolutional neural network, many researchers adopt two-stream network [5] for this task. It combines 2D convolutional neural network and optical flow to capture appearance and motion features respectively. Recently, as kinds of 3D convolutional neural networks such as C3D [20], P3D [17], I3D [2] and 3D-ResNet [8] appear, adopting 3D convolutional neural network to extract spatio-temporal feature is getting more and more popular [1–3,23].

Temporal Action Proposals and Detection. Since natural videos are always long and untrimmed, temporal action proposals and detection have aroused intensive interest from researchers [1,3,6,8,23,24]. DAP [4] leverages LSTM to encode the video sequence for temporal features. SST [1] presents a method combined C3D and GRU to generate temporal action proposals, trying to capture long-time dependency. SCNN-prop [19] adopts multi-scale sliding windows to generate segment proposals. Then it uses 3D convolution neural network and fully-connected layers to extract features and classify proposals separately. Recent studies focus more on how to get proposals with precise boundaries. TURN [6] applies a coordinate regression network to adjust proposal boundaries. CBR [7] proposes cascaded boundary regression for further boundary refinement. Other methods like TAL-net [3] modifies Faster-RCNN to fit temporal action proposal generation task.

For temporal action detection, methods can be divided into two main types: one-stage [7,12,19,23,24] and two-stage [1,6,13]. One-stage methods like S3D [23] generate temporal action proposals and make classification simultaneously. While two-stage methods such as TURN [6] and BSN [13] generate proposals first and re-extract features to classify those proposals.

3   Approach

In this section, we introduce the proposed Deep Point-wise Prediction Network and how it works in details.

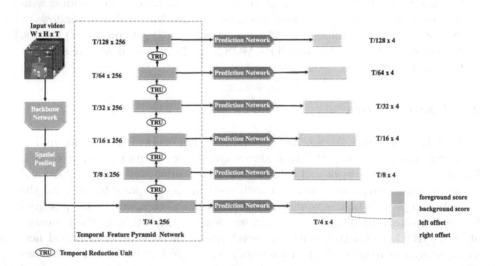

Fig. 2. The architecture of our Deep Point-wise Prediction Network.

3.1 Deep Point-Wise Prediction Network

As shown in Fig. 2, Deep Point-wise Prediction Network consists of three sub-networks, which are backbone network, Temporal Feature Pyramid Network, and prediction network.

Backbone Network. We use backbone network and spatial pooling to generate the first-level feature map from a video sequence[1]. More specifically, given a video sequence with shape of $T \times H \times W \times 3$, through backbone network, we get a feature map with shape of $\frac{T}{8} \times \frac{H}{16} \times \frac{W}{16} \times C$, where T is the frame number, H and W are height and width respectively, C is output channel varying with backbone networks. Then we adopt a transpose 3D convolutional layer to upsample the feature map in T dimension and a 2D average pooling layer to pool the spatial features. Finally, we get our first-level temporal feature map with the shape of $\frac{T}{4} \times 256$.

Temporal Feature Pyramid Network. The core unit of Temporal Feature Pyramid Network is the Temporal Reduction Unit. It receives current feature map as input and outputs next feature map with larger receptive field in each point. And it consists of four 1D temporal convolutional layers with the first three layers of stride 1 and last layer of stride 2. As a result, every feature map is half size of last feature map in temporal dimension. TRU between different levels share the same weights.

Prediction Network. Prediction Network is applied on different feature maps and generates predictions for every point. The first part is a binary classifier to generate foreground and background score. The second part is a predictor to generate left offset and right offset of proposals. Both parts are achieved by 1D convolutional operation.

3.2 Label Assignment

During training, we need to assign actioness label to every output point according to the ground truth. We design a simple but effective label assignment strategy here. First, points in feature maps are mapped into time points in the original video. For example, for a point in l_{th}-level feature map with position $t = \{0, 1, \cdots, T_l\}$, its corresponding position in the original video is $2^{l+1}(t+0.5)$. If the corresponding position of a point is inside any ground truth, we define it as a positive point. Further restriction for positive labels is introduced in Sect. 3.3. Since there is no overlap in adjacent ground truths, a point can only be inside one ground truth. While previous methods whether sliding window based or actioness grouping based adopt a temporal Intersection over Union (tIOU) threshold strategy to define positive proposals and assign corresponding ground truth proposals [1,4,6,7,23,24]. Their predefined segments may have overlap with more than one ground truths simultaneously. Compared with the tIoU based matching strategy, our label assignment process is more simple and straightforward.

---

[1] We contrast different backbones in our experiments.

3.3   Scale Assignment

To predict the proposal location for every point, we try to learn transformation of left offset and right offset between ground truths and current point. Specifically, for points in l_{th}-level feature map with position $t = \{0, 1, \cdots, T_l\}$ and corresponding ground truth proposal with boundary (t_{start}, t_{end}), our localization target is:

$$s_1 = \lambda \log \frac{2^{l+1}(t + 0.5) - t_{start}}{2^{l+1}}, s_2 = \lambda \log \frac{t_{end} - 2^{l+1}(t + 0.5)}{2^{l+1}} \qquad (1)$$

where l indicates that the point is from l_{th} feature map, T_l is the length of this feature map, $2^{l+1}(t + 0.5)$ projects the point in feature map into the original input video sequence. λ is a coefficient which is set as 3.0 in our training to control the importance of localization part in final loss.

As we can learn from label assignment strategy in Sect. 3.2, a ground truth may be assigned to different points in different level feature maps. And if we keep all these positive points for training, it can be difficult with large scale variations in boundary offsets. Also, as a result of fixed sizes of convolutional kernels, receptive fields of points in the same level feature map are same and points in higher level feature map tend to have bigger receptive fields. And it is hard for a point to predict proposal boundaries far from its receptive field. In l_{th} feature map, the stride of adjacent points is 2^{l+1}. And its receptive field size is several times as the stride. Here, we want to restrict target left offset and right offset around receptive field of current point. So we divide the original localization targets by default stride of corresponding feature maps to regularize them. For target offsets close to default stride of corresponding feature maps, this operation centers them around 1. And the log function further centers them around 0. We add additional restrictions for positive points as below:

$$s_1, s_2 \in [-\eta, \eta] \qquad (2)$$

where η is a parameter to control the localization range. Note that points regarded as positive in Sect. 3.2 but do not satisfy condition in this Eq. 2 will be ignored during training. As η increases, a ground truth is likely to be optimized by more feature maps.

In conclusion, Eq. (1) computes the regularized left offset and right offset between each time point in feature maps and corresponding ground truth proposals. With predictions from our regressor, we can easily get the final boundaries by inverse transformation of Eq. (1). Equation (2) selects valuable boundary prediction targets for training.

3.4   Loss Function

Our loss consists of two parts which are action loss and localization loss respectively. The overall loss is combination of above two loss defined as:

$$L = L_{act} + L_{loc}. \qquad (3)$$

For action loss, we use cross entropy loss, which is effective for classification task

$$L_{act} = -\frac{1}{N}\Sigma_i^N \left(a_i \log q_i^1 + (1 - a_i)q_i^0\right),$$ (4)

where a_i is the actioness label for i_{th} sample, q_i is a vector contains two elements which are predicted foreground and background score with Softmax activation. For localization loss, we adopt the widely used Smooth L_1 loss [18].

$$L_{loc} = \frac{1}{N_{pos}}\Sigma_i^{N_{pos}}\Sigma_{j=1}^2 smooth_{L1}(r_i^j - s_i^j)$$ (5)

where N_{pos} is the number of points we define as positive samples, r_i is boundary prediction of i_{th} point and s_i is the target defined in Sect. 3.3.

4   Experiments

4.1   Dataset and Setup

THUMOS 2014. We evaluate the proposed method on THUMOS 2014 dataset [10], which is a standard and widely used dataset for temporal action proposal generation task. It contains 200 validation and 213 test untrimmed videos whose action instances are annotated temporally. Following the conventions [1, 6, 13, 16, 23, 24], We train our models on validation set and evaluate them on testing set.

Evaluation Metrics. For temporal action proposal generation, we adopt the conventional evaluation metric. We calculate Average Recall (AR) which is mean value of recall over different tIOU thresholds under various Average Number of proposals, denoted as AR@AN. Specifically, tIOU set of [0.5 : 0.05 : 1.0] is used in our experiments.

Experiments Setup. During training, we used the stochastic gradient descent (SGD) as our optimizer. Momentum factor is set as 0.9 and weight decay factor is set as 0.0001 to regularize weights. We apply a multi-step learning scheduler to adjust learning rate. For all models, the training process lasts for 10 epochs. The initial learning rate is set as 0.0001. It is divided by 10 at epoch 7 and divided by 10 again at epoch 10. Training for one epoch means iterating over the dataset once. To form a batch while training, we clip videos as segments with equivalent length, which is 256 frames in our experiments specifically. The overlap of adjacent clips is 128 frames. We adopt sampling frequency of 8 fps in our experiments. According to our network architecture introduced in Sect. 3.1, we finally get 126 samples for one clip regardless of assignment strategy. To reduce overfitting, we adopt a multi-scale crop strategy [22] for per frame in addition to random horizontal flip transformation. Like most foreground/background tasks, huge imbalance of positive and negative samples exists in our experiments. Thus, we randomly sample negative samples in each batch to keep the ratio of positive and negative samples about 1:1. This strategy is proved to be efficient and results in more stable training.

During inference, We predict actioness score and boundary offset for each point in all feature maps. Final boundary can be computed by inverse transformation of Eq. (1). Then proposals of different clips in the same video are gathered. Finally, all proposals of a video are sorted according to the actioness score and filterd by Non-Maximum Suppression (NMS) with threshold value of 0.7.

4.2   Ablation Study

Comparison with Pre-defined Sliding Windows. For sliding window based methods, the density of sliding windows at each timestamp is an important factor that influences the performance. Most of them adopt a multi-scale anchor strategy to cover more ground truth proposals [12,23]. It may come to an assumption that more dense pre-defined sliding windows will lead to a better result. To explore the influence of sliding window density, we setup a fair contrast experiment and results are shown in Table 1. For better comparison with our methods, we use the same architecture in Fig. 2 and assign a base sliding window for each point in feature maps. The ratios in Table 1 means the number of sliding windows in each point. For example, in second row, there are two pre-defined sliding windows for each position in feature maps. One is the base sliding window, the other is a sliding window with same center but half length as base sliding window. Thus, the amount of output proposals is twice as our method. During training for sliding window based methods, we assign positive labels for pre-defined sliding windows when their tIOU with any ground truth exceeds 0.5 [7,12,23].

Table 1. Contrast of sliding windows with various ratios and DPP

Method	Ratios	AR@50	AR@100	AR@200
Sliding window	1	24.2	32.05	39.63
Sliding window	2	24.25	32.3	40.76
Sliding window	3	24.42	32.79	41.09
Sliding window	5	23.07	31.08	39.78
DPP	n/a	**25.88**	**34.79**	**43.37**

With a certain limit, more sliding windows do result in a higher average recall. However, over-density sliding windows do not help. While our method is superior to the best performance of sliding window based methods. This may be caused by many reasons. One possible reason is that multi-ratio sliding windows cause the ambiguous problem. Sliding windows at the same position with different ratios share the same input features, but expected to have different predictions. And our scale assignment strategy restricts target predictions of each point inside its receptive field, likely to result in better performance. Meanwhile, more sliding windows mean more outputs both in training and inference, undoubtedly leading to decrease in speed. In conclusion, compared with sliding window based methods, DPP has the following advantages: (1) no ambiguous problem thus making optimization much easier; (2) fewer hyper-parameters which needs to be manually designed; (3) fewer proposal candidates resulting in faster processing.

Analysis of Scale Assignment. We design a novel scale assignment strategy in Sect. 3.3. And according to Eq. (1), η decides the localization target range of each pyramid. As η increases, the localization target range will be larger. Thus a ground truth is more likely to match different pyramids, resulting in more positive proposal candidates.

Table 2. Influence of η for DPP

η	Backbone	AR@50	AR@100	AR@200
2	ResNet-50	25.58	33.29	41.52
2.5	ResNet-50	25.79	33.54	42.24
3	ResNet-50	**25.88**	**34.79**	**43.37**
4	ResNet-50	25.47	33.74	42.26

Table 2 shows the influence of η on the performance of DPP. And $\eta = 3$ gets the best performance, which is used in all the following experiments. We can compute by the inverse transformation of Eq. (1) that, when $\eta = 3$, the lower bound and upper bound of localization target are about $\frac{1}{3}$ and three times of default size for each pyramid.

Exploration of Backbone Network. For the test of different backbones, we fix the pyramid amount as 6. As Table 3 shows, 3D ResNet-50, 3D ResNet-101 [8] and C3D [20] are compared in our experiments. Backbone network with heavier weights tends to get better performances. We also test the performance of different backbone networks in speed. C3D outperforms other backbones in average recall but loses in speed competition. With almost the same average recall, 3D ResNet-101 attains about the twice speed of C3D. Note that all fps data is evaluated on a single GeForce GTX 1080 Ti. And for each experiment, fps is computed as mean fps of three epochs.

Table 3. Performance of different backbones

Backbone network	AR@50	AR@100	AR@200	fps
ResNet-50	25.88	34.79	43.37	1804
ResNet-101	28.01	36.27	44.36	1294
C3D	**28.57**	**36.65**	**44.55**	676

Varying Pyramids for DPP. DPP adopts a pyramid structure to generate feature maps with different scales. We make a contrast experiment here to explore how pyramid amounts affect the performance of DPP.

Table 4. Varying pyramids for DPP

Pyramids	npc	AR@50	AR@100	AR@200
6	126	28.57	**36.65**	**44.55**
5	124	27.14	35.61	43.51
4	120	27.28	35.69	42.89
3	112	**28.75**	36.22	43.05

Table 4 shows results of different pyramid amounts varying from 3 to 6, where npc means number of proposals in one clip. Here, all experiments in Table 4 use C3D as backbone network. It is found that under metrics of AR@100 and AR@200, 6 pyramids performs best. And under metirc of AR@50, 3 pyramids performs best. Since the difference among results of all these experiments is slight, we can infer that our proposed DPP is robust for pyramids variation.

4.3   Comparison with State-of-the-art Methods

We compare the proposed DPP with other state-of-the-art methods on action temporal proposal generation in Table 5. To illustrate effectiveness of DPP, all methods adopt C3D [20] to extract spatio-temporal features and our method outperforms other methods. All methods in the top part of the table adopt pre-defined sliding windows to generate proposal candidates, which is similar to anchor-based methods in object detection such as SSD [15]. As we can see, DPP surpasses all sliding-window based method by a large margin. Specifically, DPP outperforms TURN, which performs best in sliding-window based methods, by improvement of 16.2% in AR@200.

Actioness-grouping methods like BSN group temporal points with high actioness scores to form temporal action proposals. Compared to BSN, DPP increases AR@200 with 2%. MGG ensembles actioness-grouping based method which is proposed in [24] and sliding-window based method to get higher results. Such methods cost much time when predicting, while our method generates high quality proposals with a high speed. Fps for the four methods in the top part of Table 5 are evaluated on a Geforce Titan X GPU and our method is evaluated on a Geforce GTX 1080 Ti GPU. Though BSN and MGG do not report their fps, according to the difference in principles, sliding-window based methods are expected to run faster than actioness-grouping based methods. Thus, compared to ensemble methods, DPP achieves comparative even better results with a much faster speed.

Table 5. Comparison with other temporal action proposal generation methods

	Features	AR@50	AR@100	AR@200	fps
Sliding-window methods					
DAPs [4]	C3D	13.56	23.83	33.96	134.1
SCNN-prop [19]	C3D	17.22	26.17	37.01	60
SST [1]	C3D	19.90	28.36	37.90	308
TURN [6]	C3D	19.63	27.96	38.34	880
Actioness-grouping methods					
BSN [13]	C3D	27.19	35.38	43.61	–
Ensemble methods					
MGG [16]	C3D	29.11	36.31	44.32	–
Our method					
DPP	C3D	28.57	36.65	44.55	676
DPP	ResNet-101	28.01	36.27	44.36	1294

5   Conclusion

In this paper, We present a simple yet efficient method named Deep Point-wise Prediction to generate high quality temporal action proposals. Unlike previous work, we do not use any pre-defined sliding windows to generate proposal candidates, but predict left and right offsets for each point in different feature maps directly. We also note that there are also previous works in 2D object detection sharing similar ideas [9,11]. Without ambiguity of using same feature to regress different proposal candidates, our method gets better performance on localization and generates higher quality proposals. In experiments, we explore different settings of our methods and prove its robustness. DPP is evaluated on standard THUMOS 2014 dataset to demonstrate its effectiveness.

Acknowledgement. This work was jointly supported by National Natural Science Foundation of China under Grant No. 61621136008 and 91848206.

References

1. Buch, S., Escorcia, V., Shen, C., Ghanem, B., Carlos Niebles, J.: SST: single-stream temporal action proposals. In: Proceedings of the IEEE Conference on Computer Vision and Pattern Recognition, pp. 2911–2920 (2017)
2. Carreira, J., Zisserman, A.: Quo vadis, action recognition? A new model and the kinetics dataset. In: proceedings of the IEEE Conference on Computer Vision and Pattern Recognition, pp. 6299–6308 (2017)
3. Chao, Y.W., Vijayanarasimhan, S., Seybold, B., Ross, D.A., Deng, J., Sukthankar, R.: Rethinking the faster R-CNN architecture for temporal action localization. In: Proceedings of the IEEE Conference on Computer Vision and Pattern Recognition, pp. 1130–1139 (2018)

4. Escorcia, V., Caba Heilbron, F., Niebles, J.C., Ghanem, B.: DAPs: deep action proposals for action understanding. In: Leibe, B., Matas, J., Sebe, N., Welling, M. (eds.) ECCV 2016. LNCS, vol. 9907, pp. 768–784. Springer, Cham (2016). https://doi.org/10.1007/978-3-319-46487-9_47

5. Feichtenhofer, C., Pinz, A., Zisserman, A.: Convolutional two-stream network fusion for video action recognition. In: Proceedings of the IEEE Conference on Computer Vision and Pattern Recognition, pp. 1933–1941 (2016)

6. Gao, J., Yang, Z., Chen, K., Sun, C., Nevatia, R.: Turn tap: temporal unit regression network for temporal action proposals. In: Proceedings of the IEEE International Conference on Computer Vision, pp. 3628–3636 (2017)

7. Gao, J., Yang, Z., Nevatia, R.: Cascaded boundary regression for temporal action detection. arXiv preprint arXiv:1705.01180 (2017)

8. Hara, K., Kataoka, H., Satoh, Y.: Learning spatio-temporal features with 3D residual networks for action recognition. In: Proceedings of the IEEE International Conference on Computer Vision, pp. 3154–3160 (2017)

9. Huang, L., Yang, Y., Deng, Y., Yu, Y.: DenseBox: unifying landmark localization with end to end object detection. arXiv preprint arXiv:1509.04874 (2015)

10. Idrees, H., et al.: The thumos challenge on action recognition for videos "in the wild". Comput. Vis. Image Underst. 155, 1–23 (2017)

11. Kong, T., Sun, F., Liu, H., Jiang, Y., Shi, J.: FoveaBox: beyond anchor-based object detector. arXiv preprint arXiv:1904.03797 (2019)

12. Lin, T., Zhao, X., Shou, Z.: Single shot temporal action detection. In: Proceedings of the 25th ACM International Conference on Multimedia, pp. 988–996. ACM (2017)

13. Lin, T., Zhao, X., Su, H., Wang, C., Yang, M.: BSN: boundary sensitive network for temporal action proposal generation. In: Proceedings of the European Conference on Computer Vision (ECCV), pp. 3–19 (2018)

14. Lin, T.Y., Dollár, P., Girshick, R., He, K., Hariharan, B., Belongie, S.: Feature pyramid networks for object detection. In: Proceedings of the IEEE Conference on Computer Vision and Pattern Recognition, pp. 2117–2125 (2017)

15. Liu, W., et al.: SSD: single shot multibox detector. In: Leibe, B., Matas, J., Sebe, N., Welling, M. (eds.) ECCV 2016. LNCS, vol. 9905, pp. 21–37. Springer, Cham (2016). https://doi.org/10.1007/978-3-319-46448-0_2

16. Liu, Y., Ma, L., Zhang, Y., Liu, W., Chang, S.F.: Multi-granularity generator for temporal action proposal. arXiv preprint arXiv:1811.11524 (2018)

17. Qiu, Z., Yao, T., Mei, T.: Learning spatio-temporal representation with pseudo-3D residual networks. In: proceedings of the IEEE International Conference on Computer Vision, pp. 5533–5541 (2017)

18. Ren, S., He, K., Girshick, R., Sun, J.: Faster R-CNN: towards real-time object detection with region proposal networks. In: Advances in Neural Information Processing Systems, pp. 91–99 (2015)

19. Shou, Z., Wang, D., Chang, S.F.: Temporal action localization in untrimmed videos via multi-stage CNNs. In: Proceedings of the IEEE Conference on Computer Vision and Pattern Recognition, pp. 1049–1058 (2016)

20. Tran, D., Bourdev, L., Fergus, R., Torresani, L., Paluri, M.: Learning spatiotemporal features with 3D convolutional networks. In: Proceedings of the IEEE International Conference on Computer Vision, pp. 4489–4497 (2015)

21. Wang, H., Schmid, C.: Action recognition with improved trajectories. In: Proceedings of the IEEE International Conference on Computer Vision, pp. 3551–3558 (2013)

22. Wang, L., Xiong, Y., Wang, Z., Qiao, Y.: Towards good practices for very deep two-stream convnets. arXiv preprint arXiv:1507.02159 (2015)
23. Zhang, D., Dai, X., Wang, X., Wang, Y.F.: S3D: single shot multi-span detector via fully 3D convolutional networks. arXiv preprint arXiv:1807.08069 (2018)
24. Zhao, Y., Xiong, Y., Wang, L., Wu, Z., Tang, X., Lin, D.: Temporal action detection with structured segment networks. In: Proceedings of the IEEE International Conference on Computer Vision, pp. 2914–2923 (2017)

Real-Time Financial Data Prediction Using Meta-cognitive Recurrent Kernel Online Sequential Extreme Learning Machine

Zongying Liu[1], Chu Kiong Loo[1], and Kitsuchart Pasupa[2(✉)]

[1] Faculty of Computer Science and Information Technology, University of Malaya,
50603 Kuala Lumpur, Malaysia
liuzongying@siswa.um.edu.my, ckloo.um@um.edu.my
[2] Faculty of Information Technology,
King Mongkut's Institute of Technology Ladkrabang, Bangkok 10520, Thailand
kitsuchart@it.kmitl.ac.th

Abstract. This paper proposes a novel algorithm called Meta-cognitive Recurrent Kernel Online Sequential Extreme Learning Machine with a kernel filter and a modified Drift Detector Mechanism (Meta-RKOS-ELM$_{ALD}$-DDM). The algorithm aims to tackle a well-known concept drift problem in time series prediction by utilising the modified concept drift detector mechanism. Moreover, the new meta-cognitive learning strategy is employed to solve parameter dependency and reduce learning time. The experimental results show that the proposed method can achieve better performance than the conventional algorithm in a set of financial datasets.

Keywords: Financial data · Real-time prediction · Kernel filter · Concept drift · Meta-cognitive learning

1 Introduction

Many researchers and professional workers have been paid attention to real-time financial prediction [1–4]. In the real world, forecasting the movement is a practical issue that affects the decision of traders in the trading process. Real-time time series prediction for financial data is in demand because the investors want to make trading decisions based on the most recent data and how it fits into historical context. Therefore, this paper focuses on real-time financial prediction problem.

It is required to select an appropriate technique which can handle the problem. The selection depends on data type, quality of models, and pre-defined assumption [5]. Considering an example, Autoregressive Moving-Average model, it requires data that are a normal distribution. However, the majority of real-world data distribution is not a normal distribution. Moreover, removing outlier

© Springer Nature Switzerland AG 2019
T. Gedeon et al. (Eds.): ICONIP 2019, LNCS 11955, pp. 488–498, 2019.
https://doi.org/10.1007/978-3-030-36718-3_41

values from the data prior to utilising most of the statistical models is essential because these models cannot handle non-stationary data. In real-world applications, time-series data is almost non-stationary—which causes some limited conditions for the statistical models.

Nowadays, machine learning algorithms have been widely applied in the stock market analysis and prediction due to its capability of handling non-linearity in financial market data and extracting useful features from a vast amount of data without relying on prior knowledge of predictors [6,7]. One of the well-known and effective algorithms is the Extreme Learning Machine (ELM) that has been proved to have good generalisation performance and fast learning speed [8]. However, ELM is unable to update its model when new data is entering. Therefore, Online Sequential ELM (OS-ELM) was proposed [9]. Although its performance is satisfying, it is still not stable due to the characteristic of random input weights. Hence, the kernel method is employed to replace the random part of OS-ELM to stabilise the model [10]. However, when introducing the kernel method to the algorithm, the complexity is scaled by the number of training sample. Therefore, kernel filter is considered to save computational complexity [10].

Financial data are non-stationary. It also generally appears concept drift problem, in which the statistical properties of the target variable changes over time. This problem can reduce the accuracy of the model because the data may become obsolete quickly over time. There are three types of method that have been successfully applied to solve the concept drift problem as follows: (i) Using a unified framework to detect the drift–an ensemble algorithm to detect using incremental learning manner [11]; (ii) Feature extraction for explicit concept drift detection [12]–using time series features to monitor how concepts evolve over time; and (iii) monitoring the change of error distribution in the learning part [13]. According to [13], detecting the change of error distribution by Drift Detection Method (DDM) is the most efficient way for concept drift detection, but it is only applicable for a classification task. In this work, we employ DDM to detect concept drift in the learning part for regression task.

Moreover, our regression prediction model utilises a new meta-cognitive learning strategy that can decide to retrain the model, adding or discarding the neuron in the learning part when there is a new incoming sample. At the same time, it also can automatically define the threshold of kernel filter, that can directly reduce the training time.

2   Methodology

This section first describes the data processing method. Then Recurrent Kernel OS-ELM is explained and followed by a kernel filter method–is employed to select useful training samples. Next, DDM that is employed to detect the concept drift problem and a new meta-cognitive learning strategy that can automatically define the threshold of kernel filter are explained in the following subsections.

2.1 Data Transformation and Processing

Time series data is defined as a series of data points listed in time order. Assuming that the data is given as $\boldsymbol{x} = [x_1, x_2, \ldots, x_N]$, where N is the data size. The time series data x is transformed to be a matrix X with a dimension of $[(N - W - P + 1) \times (W + P)]$ as shown in (1).

$$
X = \begin{bmatrix}
X_{1,1} & \cdots & X_{1,W} & X_{1,W+1} & \cdots & X_{1,W+P} \\
\vdots & \ddots & \vdots & \vdots & \ddots & \vdots \\
X_{L,1} & \cdots & X_{L,W} & X_{L,W+1} & \cdots & X_{L,W+P} \\
\vdots & \ddots & \vdots & \vdots & \ddots & \vdots \\
X_{N-W-P+1,1} & \cdots & X_{N-W-P+1,W} & X_{N-W-P+1,W+1} & \cdots & X_{N-W-P+1,W+P}
\end{bmatrix},
\tag{1}
$$

where W is the time window size, P is the number of prediction horizon, and L is the training size. More details can be found in [7]. Then, the data is normalised and separated into the training input data (X_{Tr}), its corresponding target data in the p-th step ($\boldsymbol{y}_p$), testing input data (X_{Te}), and its corresponding target data in the p-th step ($\hat{\boldsymbol{ty}}_p$), which are shown as follows:

$$
X_{Tr} = \begin{bmatrix} X_{1,1} & \cdots & X_{1,W} \\ \vdots & \ddots & \vdots \\ X_{L,1} & \cdots & X_{L,W} \end{bmatrix} ; \boldsymbol{y}_p = \begin{bmatrix} X_{1,W+p} \\ \vdots \\ X_{L,W+p} \end{bmatrix},
\tag{2}
$$

$$
X_{Te} = \begin{bmatrix} X_{L+1,1} & \cdots & X_{L+1,W} \\ \vdots & \ddots & \vdots \\ X_{N-W-P+1,1} & \cdots & X_{N-W-P+1,W} \end{bmatrix} ; \hat{\boldsymbol{ty}}_p = \begin{bmatrix} X_{L+1,W+p} \\ \vdots \\ X_{N-W-P+1,W+p} \end{bmatrix}.
\tag{3}
$$

2.2 Recurrent Kernel OS-ELM

Scardapane et al. proposed an algorithm for online learning with Kernel ELM [10] that is called Online Sequential Extreme Learning Machine with Kernel (KOS-ELM). It overcomes the drawbacks of OS-ELM that is unstable prediction results due to random input weights. Liu and his colleagues proposed a recurrent algorithm with KOS-ELM (RKOS-ELM) that handle the multi-step time series prediction [14,15]. The size of the output weight will increase when the new training samples are received. In the update phase, $l \in \{2, \ldots, L\}$, the output weights ($\boldsymbol{\beta}_l$) with interval coefficient matrix Q_l can be calculated by the following equations:

$$
Q_l = \begin{bmatrix} Q_{l-1} r_l + z_l z_l^T & -z_l \\ -z_l^T & 1 \end{bmatrix},
\tag{4}
$$

$$
\boldsymbol{\beta}_l = \begin{bmatrix} \boldsymbol{\beta}_{l-1} - z_l r_l^{-1} e_l \\ r_l^{-1} e_l \end{bmatrix},
\tag{5}
$$

where $\boldsymbol{g}_l = [k(\boldsymbol{X}_{Tr_l}, \boldsymbol{X}_{Tr_1}), \ldots, k(\boldsymbol{X}_{Tr_l}, \boldsymbol{X}_{Tr_{l-1}})]^T$, $z_l = Q_{l-1} \boldsymbol{g}_l$, $r_l = C^{-1} + k(\boldsymbol{X}_{Tr_1}, \boldsymbol{X}_{Tr_1}) - z_l^T \boldsymbol{g}_l$, and $e_l = y_l - \boldsymbol{g}_l^T \boldsymbol{\beta}_{l-1}$. k is a kernel function, C is a regularisation parameter that generally is set to 1, and e stands for prediction error.

According to the theory of recurrent multi-step-ahead prediction algorithm, the training data in the p-th step can be defined as

$$
X_{Tr,p} = \begin{bmatrix} X_{1,p} & \cdots & X_{1,W} & \hat{y}_{1,1} & \cdots & \hat{y}_{1,p-1} \\ \vdots & \ddots & \vdots & \vdots & \ddots & \vdots \\ X_{L,p} & \cdots & X_{L,W} & \hat{y}_{L,1} & \cdots & \hat{y}_{L,p-1} \end{bmatrix},
\tag{6}
$$

where $\hat{y}_{p-1}$ represents the predicted values of training data in the $(p-1)$-th step and $(W+1) \geq P$.

2.3   Kernel Filters in RKOS-ELM

Although the kernel method plays a vital role in the aspect of improving forecasting performance in RKOS-ELM, it takes time in the learning process of RKOS-ELM. A kernel filter, Approximate Linear Dependency (ALD), achieved superior performance in filtering incoming samples for classification [10]. Therefore, RKOS-ELM employs ALD to filtering samples in the process of time series prediction in this work, that is referred as RKOS-ELM$_{\text{ALD}}$.

In RKOS-ELM$_{\text{ALD}}$, the initialisation phase is similar to KOS-ELM. In the updating phase, RKOS-ELM$_{\text{ALD}}$ employs ALD criteria that bases on the distance (Δ) between a sample and the linear span of the current dictionary (D) in the feature space. Δ can be calculated by

$$
\Delta_l = ktt_l - \mathbf{kt}_l^T Q_l \mathbf{kt}_l,
\tag{7}
$$

where Q_l is an interval coefficient matrix with information of the previous input data in RKOS-ELM, $ktt_l = k(\mathbf{X}_{Tr,l}, \mathbf{X}_{Tr,l})$ that is a kernel of $\mathbf{X}_{Tr,l}$, and $\mathbf{kt}_l = [k(\mathbf{D}(1), \mathbf{X}_{Tr,1}), \dots, k(\mathbf{D}(l), \mathbf{X}_{Tr,l})]$ that is the kernels of dictionary (D) and the input data $(\mathbf{X}_{Tr,l})$. If Δ is more than or equal to a constant φ, the corresponding input sample will update the output weights that leads to an increasing of hidden neuron. Then, the sample will be added into D. If Δ is less than or equal to φ the output weights will be updated without adding any neurons. It is noted that the kernel filter aims to reduce the training cost.

2.4   Modified DDM in RKOS-ELM$_{\text{ALD}}$

Perceptron, neural network, and decision tree employed DDM and were found to be affective to learn a new concept in classification task [16]. Therefore, DDM is modified to use in time series prediction.

The binomial distribution is closely approximated by a normal distribution with the same mean and variance when there is a sufficiently large number of sample [16]. Therefore, this study focuses on a probability distribution that is a key flag that represents changes in context. In the learning phase of RKOS-ELM$_{ALD}$, the l-th error rate $ER_{l,p}$ in the p-step can be defined as

$$ER_{l,p} = \frac{|y_{l,p} - \hat{y}_{l,p}|}{y_{l,p}}, \tag{8}$$

where y and $\hat{y}$ is a target and a predicted target, respectively. The standard deviation ($SD_{l,p}$) can be calculated as

$$SD_{l,p} = \sqrt{\frac{ER_{l,p} \times (1 - ER_{l,p})}{l}}, \tag{9}$$

Hence, the error rate, $ER_{l,p}$, in the $1 - \alpha/2$ confidence interval is approximately $ER_{l,p} \pm \alpha \cdot SD_{l,p}$ when there are a large number ($L \geq 30$), where α depends on the confidence level. When the first data point is fed into the model, the initial minimum value of error rate ER_{min} and standard deviation SD_{min} are defined as $ER_{1,p}$ and $SD_{1,p}$, respectively. Then, the new data of the p-th step coming in the learning part is processed and updates ER_{min} and SD_{min}. In this work, the warning confidence level has been set to 95%. This means that the warning level is reached if $ER_i + SD_i \geq ER_{min} + 2 \cdot SD_{min}$. The confidence level for the concept drift is set to 99%. Therefore the concept drift problem appears if $ER_i + SD_i \geq ER_{min} + 3 \cdot SD_{min}$. Otherwise, there is no concept drift, ($ER_i + SD_i \leq ER_{min} + SD_{min}$). At the same time, the minimum of error rate and standard deviation will be updated. Therefore, DDM is used in the learning of RKOS-ELM$_{ALD}$ in order to decide that the incoming data should be added into the output weight or update the output weight. The output weights can be updated by the following equation:

$$\beta_l = \beta_{l-1} + U_l v_l (y_l - kt\beta_{l-1}), \tag{10}$$

where U and V are the interval matrices for output weights that can be calculated as (11) and (12), respectively.

$$U_l = \frac{1}{\Delta_l} \begin{bmatrix} \Delta_l U_{l-1} + op_{l-1} op_{l-1}^T & -op_{l-1} \\ -op_{l-1}^T & 1 \end{bmatrix}, \tag{11}$$

$$v_l = v_{l-1} - \frac{v_{l-1}}{1 + op_l v_{l-1} op_l} (op_l v_{l-1}), \tag{12}$$

where $op_l = U_l kt$. It is noted that the initialised interval matrices can be defined as $U_1 = \frac{1}{k(X_{Tr,1}, X_{Tr,1})}$ and $op_1 = U_1 k(X_{Tr,1}, X_{Tr,1})$. The pseudocode of RKOS-ELM$_{ALD}$ with DDM is shown in Algorithm 1.

2.5 New Meta-cognitive Learning Strategy

Searching for the optimal ALD threshold directly leads to the growth of learning time. To solve this problem, meta-cognitive learning strategy is considered in the model. When there is a new incoming data, the strategy not only decides to add,

---

Algorithm 1. Learning of $RKOS - ELM_{ALD}$ with DDM

Require: Prediction horizon size P; Time window size W; Number of training data
  L; Training data X_{Tr} and y by (2); Kernel parameter δ; Output weight
  of RKELM in the p-th step β_p; Prediction value in the p-th step $\hat{y}_p$; ALD
  threshold φ;
Ensure: Output weight β_p; Prediction value $\hat{y}_p$.
 1: **for** $p \in \{1, \ldots, P\}$ **do**
 2:     Initialise $Q_{1,p}$ and $\beta_{1,p}$ based on data $([X_{Tr_{1,p}}, y_{1,p}])$;
 3:     $D_p = X_{Tr_{1,p}}$;
 4:     $v_{1,p} = 1$;
 5:     Calculate $ER_{1,p}$, $SD_{1,p}$, $ER_{\min}$ and $SD_{\min}$;
 6:     **for** $l \in \{2, \ldots, L\}$ **do**
 7:         Calculate $\Delta_{l,p}$ by (7);
 8:         Compute $ER_{l,p}$, $SD_{l,p}$ by (8) and (9), respectively;
 9:         **if** an incoming sample has concept drift problem and $\Delta_{l,p} \geq \varphi_l$ **then**
10:             Update $Q_{l,p}$ by (4);
11:             Update $\beta_{l,p}$ by (5);
12:             Add the current sample into D_p;
13:         **else**
14:             Update V_p by (12);
15:             Update β_p by (10);
16:             $ER_{\min} = ER_{l,p}$;
17:             $SD_{\min} = SD_{l,p}$;
18:         **end if**
19:     **end for**
20:     Add the predicted value into training data as a new training sample for the
      next step by (6);
21: **end for**

---

retrain or discard neuron but also automatically defines ALD threshold. It contains four parts, including under-sampling, neuron addition, updating sample, and discarding samples.

Under-sampling is the first phase–initialisation for the model–which requires the minimum number of hidden neurons. In the online learning models, the minimum number of hidden neurons is defined as one. At the same time, the initial threshold of ALD (φ) is equal to the current prediction error (e_1). The second phase is neuron addition, which contains φ and DDM criteria for incoming data. The hidden neuron will be increased, and input data is added into the dictionary memory when the incoming data fulfills the requirement of ALD and DDM. Then the current φ for the l-th input sample can be defined by the following equation:

$$\varphi_l = \lambda(\varphi_{l-1}) + (1 - \lambda)e_l, \tag{13}$$

where λ is the slope that controls the rate of self-adaptation and set close to 1. If the incoming sample does not have concept drift problem or is close to the samples in dictionary memory, it will go to the updating phase. The output weight will be updated by (10). The last phase is discarding phase. If the number

---

Algorithm 2. The new strategy of meta-cognitive learning.

1: Initialise the output weight of model β_1;   ▷ Undersampling:
2: Calculate the prediction error e_1;
3: Initialise the threshold of ALD ($\varphi_1 = e_1$);
4: **for** $p \in \{2, \ldots, P\}$ **do**
5:     **if** There is a concept drift **then**
6:         $CD = 1$;
7:     **else**
8:         $CD = 0$;
9:     **end if**
10:    Calculate Δ by (7);
11:    **if** $CD = 1$ *and* $\Delta \geq \varphi_{p-1}$ **then**   ▷ Neuron Addition:
12:        Increase a hidden neuron;
13:        Adding the incoming sample into D;
14:    **end if**
15:    Update the threshold of ALD by (13);
16:    **if** $CD = 0$ *and* $\Delta \leq \varphi_{p-1}$ **then**   ▷ Updating Phase
17:        Update the output weights by (10);
18:        Update the threshold of ALD by (13);
19:    **end if**
20:    **if** $HiddenNode \geq \#HiddenNode_{\max}$ **then**   ▷ Discarding Phase
21:        Employ FB algorithm to discard the row with minimum error pattern of
    the kernel matrix;
22:        Update the output weights by updated kernel matrix and memory;
23:        Update the threshold of ALD by (13);
24:    **end if**
25: **end for**

---

of hidden neurons is more than the maximum number of hidden nodes (1000 in this work), the corresponding sample with the minimum error pattern that is determined by Fixed Budget (FB) will be discarded from dictionary memory. The detail of FB algorithm can be found in [17]. The pseudocode of new strategy of meta-cognitive learning is shown in Algorithm 2.

3   Experimental Results and Discussion

In this section, we evaluate the proposed model–RKOS-ELM$_{ALD}$-DDM and Meta-RKOS-ELM$_{ALD}$-DDM–with the state-of-the-art–Recurrent OS-ELM–in a set of financial data. This work aims to predict the daily closing value for each stock. We use eighteen historical data to predict the next eighteen steps in the future, similar to [7]. All data sets are collected from Yahoo! Finance as follows: Nikkei 225 (Nikkei) is retrieved from January 5, 1965 to January 5, 2000; Hang Seng Index (HSI) is collected from January 1, 1990 to December 31, 2010; Shanghai Stock Exchange Composite Index (SSE) is collected from January 1, 1991 to January 6, 2017; Standard & Poor's 500 Index (S&P500) is from December 1, 2006 to December 1, 2016. After data transformation process, Nikkei, HSI, SSE, and S&P500 has the dimension of (12796×36), (8205×36), (6558×36), and (1270×36), respectively.

The experiments were conducted on a computer with Window 10 OS, 8th Gen Intel Core i7 Processor with 16 GB of memory. Each model was selected based on their minimum Symmetric Mean Absolute Percentage Error on each dataset. The optimal number of hidden neurons (σ) of ROS-ELM was searched in the range of $\{5, 10, 15, 20, \ldots, 1000\}$. A threshold φ of RKOS-ELM$_{ALD}$ was search in range of $\{0.00010, 0.00011, \ldots, 0.00100\}$. In RKOS-ELM$_{ALD}$-DDM, we simply set the threshold as the same value as of RKOS-ELM$_{ALD}$ for each dataset. This can show how DDM play a role in the model.

Table 1 compares the Mean Square Error (MSE) of ROS-ELM, RKOS-ELM$_{ALD}$, and RKOS-ELM$_{ALD}$-DDM in the average values of four periods of prediction horizons. RKOS-ELM$_{ALD}$-DDM can perform best in all periods in Nikkei and SSE, except for 13–18 period in Nikkei. In other datasets, RKOS-ELM$_{ALD}$-DDM yields the best performance only in 13–18 period while ROS-ELM achieves the best accuracy in 1–7 and 8–12 periods. However, considering at long period prediction (1–18), it is clearly seen that RKOS-ELM$_{ALD}$-DDM is the best contender in all four datasets.

Table 1. Comparison of Mean Square Error of multi-step-ahead prediction for the ROS-ELM, RKOS-ELM$_{ALD}$, and RKOS-ELM$_{ALD}$-DDM. The best performance is in boldface.

Dataset	Model	Average period			
		1–7	8–12	13–18	1–18
Nikkei	ROS-ELM	3.46E-04	1.70E-03	9.95E-04	9.39E-04
	RKOS-ELM$_{ALD}$	7.73E-05	2.09E-04	**3.29E-04**	1.98E-04
	RKOS-ELM$_{ALD}$-DDM	**7.71E-05**	**2.09E-04**	3.30E-04	**1.98E-04**
HSI	ROS-ELM	**7.76E-04**	**1.32E-03**	1.65E-02	6.16E-03
	RKOS-ELM$_{ALD}$	9.55E-04	1.94E-03	4.15E-03	2.29E-03
	RKOS-ELM$_{ALD}$-DDM	1.03E-03	2.02E-03	**3.54E-03**	**2.14E-03**
SSE	ROS-ELM	8.00E-04	1.37E-03	1.73E-03	1.27E-03
	RKOS-ELM$_{ALD}$	3.46E-04	1.13E-03	5.01E-03	2.12E-03
	RKOS-ELM$_{ALD}$-DDM	**2.81E-04**	**8.89E-04**	**1.69E-03**	**9.20E-04**
S&P500	ROS-ELM	**2.35E-05**	**8.30E-05**	4.23E-04	1.73E-04
	RKOS-ELM$_{ALD}$	5.07E-05	9.58E-05	1.53E-04	9.78E-05
	RKOS-ELM$_{ALD}$-DDM	4.90E-05	1.13E-04	**1.42E-04**	**9.77E-05**

We further compare RKOS-ELM$_{ALD}$-DDM and Meta-RKOS-ELM$_{ALD}$-DDM in order to show the ability of meta-cognitive learning strategy in the learning process as shown in Table 2. Employing meta-cognitive learning strategy in RKOS-ELM$_{ALD}$-DDM can only improve the prediction performance in 8–12, 13–18, 1–18 periods for Nikkei, and in 1–7 for HSI only. Although the meta-cognitive learning strategy degrades the performances in other datasets, the difference of MSE between employing and not employing the meta-learning strategy are very small. However, the benefit of employing meta-learning strategy is a huge reduction of computational times compared to without the strategy, RKOS-ELM$_{ALD}$-DDM. The learning time in RKOS-ELM$_{ALD}$-DDM is much more approximately a hundred of times than that of Meta-RKOS-ELM$_{ALD}$-DDM. Therefore, meta-cognitive learning strategy plays a significant role in the learning part of RKOS-ELM$_{ALD}$-DDM. It helps RKOS-ELM$_{ALD}$-DDM to reduce the learning time and solve the parameter dependency.

Table 2. Comparison of Mean Square Error of multi-step-ahead prediction and learning time for the RKOS-ELM$_{ALD}$-DDM and Meta RKOS-ELM$_{ALD}$-DDM. The best performance is in boldface.

Dataset	Model	Average period				Learning time
		1–7	8–12	13–18	1–18	Time
Nikkei	RKOS-ELM$_{ALD}$-DDM	**7.71E-05**	2.09E-04	3.30E-04	1.98E-04	4139.26
	Meta-RKOS-ELM$_{ALD}$-DDM	7.76E-05	**2.08E-04**	**3.28E-04**	**1.97E-04**	**40.58**
	Difference	5.86E-07	−8.81E-07	−1.88E-06	−6.43E-07	−4098.68
HSI	RKOS-ELM$_{ALD}$-DDM	1.03E-03	**2.02E-03**	**3.54E-03**	2.24E-03	18265.56
	Meta-RKOS-ELM$_{ALD}$-DDM	**9.47E-04**	2.35E-03	3.58E-03	**2.21E-03**	171.42
	Difference	−7.88E-05	3.28E-04	−3.85E-05	3.01E-05	−18094.14
SSE	RKOS-ELM$_{ALD}$-DDM	**2.81E-04**	**8.89E-04**	**1.69E-03**	**9.20E-04**	1417.05
	Meta-RKOS-ELM$_{ALD}$-DDM	2.85E-04	9.91E-04	1.76E-03	9.72E-04	12.70
	Difference	4.00E-06	1.02E-04	7.00E-05	5.20E-05	−1404.35
S&P500	RKOS-ELM$_{ALD}$-DDM	**4.90E-05**	**1.13E-04**	**1.42E-04**	**9.77E-05**	1935.98
	Meta-RKOS-ELM$_{ALD}$-DDM	7.67E-05	1.44E-04	1.74E-04	1.28E-04	21.73
	Difference	2.77E-05	3.10E-05	3.20E-05	3.03E-05	−1914.25

4 Statistical Analysis

We employ the Mann-Whitney U Test to compare Meta-RKOS-ELM$_{ALD}$-DDM with RKOS-ELM$_{ALD}$-DDM in multi-step-ahead time series prediction. The null hypothesis is that there is no difference between the ranks of each method. Firstly, all samples of the two models are ranked based on their MSE as shown in Table 3. Then we can calculate the sum of ranks in each model that corresponds to $U_1 = 121$ and $U_2 = 135$. According to the table of critical values of the Mann-Whitney U, the critical value of U is 75 at $\alpha = 0.05$ for $n_1 = 16$ and $n_2 = 16$. The $\min(U_1, U_2)$ is greater than the critical value U. This means that we cannot reject the null hypothesis, hence the performance of Meta-RKOS-ELM$_{ALD}$-DDM is competitive to RKOS-ELM$_{ALD}$-DDM. However, our proposed model is approximately thousands time faster than RKOS-ELM$_{ALD}$-DDM. This shows that meta-cognitive learning strategy plays a significant role in saving training time.

Table 3. The comparison of RKOS-ELM$_{ALD}$-DDM (Model 1) and Meta-RKOS-ELM$_{ALD}$-DDM (Model 2).

#	Model 1	Model 2	Rank 1	Rank 2
1	7.71E-05	7.76E-05	3	4
2	1.03E-03	9.47E-04	24	21
3	2.81E-04	2.85E-04	15	16
4	4.90E-05	7.67E-05	1	2
5	2.09E-04	2.08E-04	14	13
6	2.02E-03	2.35E-03	27	30
7	8.89E-04	9.91E-04	19	23
8	1.13E-04	1.44E-04	6	9
9	3.30E-04	3.28E-04	18	17
10	3.54E-03	3.58E-03	31	32
11	1.69E-03	1.76E-03	25	26
12	1.42E-04	1.74E-04	8	10
13	1.98E-04	1.97E-04	12	11
14	2.24E-03	2.21E-03	29	28
15	9.20E-04	9.72E-04	20	22
16	9.77E-05	1.28E-04	5	7
Sum of ranks			257	271

5 Conclusion

We propose an approach called Meta-RKOS-ELM$_{ALD}$-DDM. The experimental results show that the proposed algorithm can improve the forecasting performance to some extent in different prediction periods in financial datasets. ALD and DDM enable RKOS-ELM$_{ALD}$-DDM to yield the best performance in the long term prediction (1–18) for all datasets. Moreover, meta-cognitive learning strategy can deal with the incoming samples in the learning process–when to add neuron, to discard sample, or to retrain the output weight. In each step, it also can automatically define the ALD threshold. The major benefits of Meta-RKOS-ELM$_{ALD}$-DDM are as follows: a good generalisation model for financial datasets; a new modified DDM which is a method of dealing with concept drift in time series prediction; meta-cognitive learning strategy that does not only reduce the learning time but also solves the parameter dependency problem.

Acknowledgement. This research was supported by the Frontier Research Grant from the University of Malaya (Project No. FG003-17AFR), the International Collaboration Fund from MESTECC (Project No. CF001-2019), ONRG NICOP grant (Project No: IF017-2018) from Office of Naval Research Global, UK, and the Faculty of Information Technology, King Mongkut's Institute of Technology Ladkrabang.

References

1. Altman, E.I., Iwanicz-Drozdowska, M., Laitinen, E.K., Suvas, A.: Financial distress prediction in an international context: a review and empirical analysis of Altman's z-score model. J. Int. Financ. Manage. Acc. **28**(2), 131–171 (2017)
2. Dixon, M., Klabjan, D., Bang, J.H.: Classification-based financial markets prediction using deep neural networks. Algorithmic Financ. **6**(3–4), 67–77 (2017)
3. Das, S., Behera, R.K., Kumar, M., Rath, S.K.: Real-time sentiment analysis of twitter streaming data for stock prediction. Proc. Comput. Sci. **132**, 956–964 (2018)
4. Liu, C., Arunkumar, N.: Risk prediction and evaluation of transnational transmission of financial crisis based on complex network. Clust. Comput. **22**(Suppl. 2), 4307–4313 (2019). https://doi.org/10.1007/s10586-018-1870-3
5. Haykin, S.: Neural Networks and Learning Machines, 3rd edn. Pearson Education, London (2009)
6. Fischer, T., Krauss, C.: Deep learning with long short-term memory networks for financial market predictions. Eur. J. Oper. Res. **270**(2), 654–669 (2018)
7. Liu, Z., Loo, C.K., Masuyama, N., Pasupa, K.: Recurrent kernel extreme reservoir machine for time series prediction. IEEE Access **6**, 19583–19596 (2018). https://doi.org/10.1109/ACCESS.2018.2823336
8. Huang, G.B., Zhu, Q.Y., Siew, C.K.: Extreme learning machine: a new learning scheme of feedforward neural networks. Neural Netw. **2**, 985–990 (2004)
9. Huang, G.B., Liang, N.Y., Rong, H.J., Saratchandran, P., Sundararajan, N.: Online sequential extreme learning machine. In: Proceedings of the IASTED International Conference on Computational Intelligence (CI 2005), Calgary, Canada, 4–6 July 2005, pp. 232–237 (2005)
10. Scardapane, S., Comminiello, D., Scarpiniti, M., Uncini, A.: Online sequential extreme learning machine with kernels. IEEE Trans. Neural Netw. Learn. Syst. **26**(9), 2214–2220 (2015)
11. Elwell, R., Polikar, R.: Incremental learning of concept drift in nonstationary environments. IEEE Trans. Neural Netw. **22**(10), 1517–1531 (2011)
12. Cavalcante, R.C., Minku, L.L., Oliveira, A.L.: FEDD: feature extraction for explicit concept drift detection in time series. In: Proceedings of the International Joint Conference on Neural Networks (IJCNN 2016), pp. 740–747 (2016)
13. Mittal, V., Kashyap, I.: Online methods of learning in occurrence of concept drift. Int. J. Comput. Appl. **117**(13), 18–22 (2015). https://doi.org/10.5120/20614-3280
14. Liu, Z., Loo, C.K., Pasupa, K.: Handling concept drift in time-series data: meta-cognitive recurrent recursive-kernel OS-ELM. In: Cheng, L., Leung, A.C.S., Ozawa, S. (eds.) ICONIP 2018. LNCS, vol. 11306, pp. 3–13. Springer, Cham (2018). https://doi.org/10.1007/978-3-030-04224-0_1
15. Liu, Z., Loo, C.K., Seera, M.: Meta-cognitive recurrent recursive kernel OS-ELM for concept drift handling. Appl. Soft Comput. **75**, 494–507 (2019)
16. Gama, J., Medas, P., Castillo, G., Rodrigues, P.: Learning with drift detection. In: Bazzan, A.L.C., Labidi, S. (eds.) SBIA 2004. LNCS (LNAI), vol. 3171, pp. 286–295. Springer, Heidelberg (2004). https://doi.org/10.1007/978-3-540-28645-5_29
17. Chen, B., Liang, J., Zheng, N., Príncipe, J.C.: Kernel least mean square with adaptive kernel size. Neurocomputing **191**, 95–106 (2016)

Deep Spatial-Temporal Field for Human Head Orientation Estimation

Zhansheng Xiong[1], Zhenhua Wang[1(✉)], Zheng Wang[2], and Jianhua Zhang[1]

[1] Zhejiang University of Technology,
288 Liuhe Rd., Hangzhou 310023, People's Republic of China
zhhwang@zjut.edu.cn
[2] Fudan University, 220 Handan Rd.,
Shanghai 200433, People's Republic of China

Abstract. We present a human-head-orientation estimation approach which enables effective estimation of head orientations of multiple individuals appeared within the same scene. Our approach bases deep representation in order to obtain adequate visual features of head orientations. To boost the estimation performance, we propose a conditional random field which fuses shallow feature, deep feature and spatial-temporal contextual cues, where the fusing parameters are learned from data via structured support vector machine. We demonstrate that the three components of fusion are complementary to each other in terms of head orientation estimation. Meanwhile, the proposed spatial-temporal field outperforms the state-of-the-art significantly on public dataset.

Keywords: Head orientation estimation · Spatial-temporal representation · Fusion

1 Introduction

Head pose estimation is essential to many applications such as human computer interaction, human activity recognition, pedestrian tracking [17–19] and scene understanding. For instance, in scene understanding, head pose information helps to determine the interaction between people [1]. Head orientation can also represent the visual focus of attention. In particular, if a person oriented his head towards some direction, probably something interesting happens in that direction.

Most existing approaches estimate 3D head orientations including yaw, pitch and roll. These approaches can be classified into two categories: appearance based methods and model based methods. The first category learns discriminative models from visual features of head images, which are robust against large head pose variation [2, 4, 5, 10, 11, 13]. Model based approaches rely on geometric cues and non-rigid 3D facial models which are able to estimate precise continuous values of yaw, pitch and roll [3, 6–8]. However, they are typically sensitive to

© Springer Nature Switzerland AG 2019
T. Gedeon et al. (Eds.): ICONIP 2019, LNCS 11955, pp. 499–509, 2019.
https://doi.org/10.1007/978-3-030-36718-3_42

large variation of head poses as they rely on the localization of local features and estimated 3D information.

In this paper, we consider the problem of estimating discrete head orientations for multiple persons appeared within the same scene. To our knowledge, most existing approaches for such a problem treat different individuals independently [4,10,13]. However, relations among objects can provide significant contextual cues which fix incorrect recognition when objects lack discriminative cues caused by factors like low image resolution, motion blur, poor lighting. We address the problem by exploiting the complementary characteristic of various discriminative cues including deep CNN representation, hand-engineered features and spatial-temporal context. To this end, we build a conditional random field for fusing such representations and learn the model parameters via structured support vector machine. Experimental results show our approach outperforms the state-of-the-art on public dataset.

2   Related Work

With respect to appearance based methods, Tran *et al.* [2] matched local HoG feature with a pre-trained codebook to get the closest extended templates which provide the corresponding rotation angles. Foytik *et al.* [3] presented a two layer framework, which dissected global nonlinear manifold into local linear neighborhood. Lee et al. [4] designed a filter bank to generate sparse responses, which were compressed via random projections and utilized for pose estimation with a random forest. Lu et al. [5] proposed an ordinary preserving manifold analysis approach to seek a low-dimensional subspace for head pose and age estimation. Patron-Perez et al. learned a simple set of one-vs-all linear support vector machine (SVM) classifiers using HoG features [11], and the scores of SVM classifiers are temporally smoothed by applying a quadratic smoothing.

With respect to model based approaches, Breitenstein et al. [6] aligned a range image with pre-computed pose images of an average face model. Li et al. [8] reconstructed a face template by fitting a 3D morphable face model, and the head pose is then determined by registering this user-specific face template to the input depth video. These methods rely on the accurate localization of facial features, which are typically sensitive to large variation of head poses and facial expression, as well as low resolution of input image.

Our approach is novel compared with existing methods. First, this work considers a much more challenging task, which is estimating head orientations of multiple persons simultaneously, whereas the aforementioned approaches deal with single person only. Second, we combine deep features, shallow features and contextual information for the recognition of head orientations, which has yet been exploited for this task. Finally, in terms of accuracy, the proposed approach is competitive compared against both baselines and the state-of-the-art.

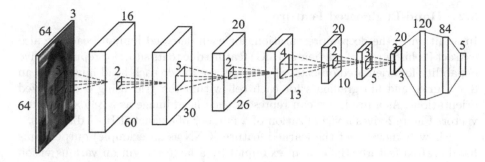

Fig. 1. Convolutional neural network for head orientation classification. The input is 64×64 pixels RGB image. The network outputs five classification scores, one for each orientation class.

3 Methodology

We now present our approach for the classification of head poses of multiple individuals. We assume that the human heads have been detected beforehand using detectors like [14]. Here we consider a standard way of discretizing head orientations proposed in [10]. This discretization includes five classes of head orientations, *i.e.* profile-left (right), frontal-left (right) and backwards.

3.1 Deep CNN Feature

Our deep representation of head orientations is illustrated by Fig. 1 (layer-wise parameters are provided in Table 1). It uses 64×64 pixels RGB scale image as input. We normalize the intensity values of head images such that the mean and variance are 0 and 1 respectively. Max-pooling follows each of the first four convolutional layers. The first, the second and the third fully connected (FC) layers contain 120, 84 and 5 neurons respectively. We use ReLU as the activation function for all layers except for the last FC layer, where Tanh function is employed. We train the parameters of the network using stochastic gradient descent with momentum.

Table 1. Summary of the CNN structure for head-orientation classification. $I(s, s, c)$ means a square c-channel input image of s pixels. $C(k, n)$ denotes convolutional layer with square filters of k pixels., where n is the number of filters. Pooling Layer is denoted by $P(p)$, where p is the size of the square pooling regions. $F(e)$ indicates fully connected layer of e neurons.

L0	L1	L2	L3	L4	L5	L6	L7	L8	L9	L10
I(64,64,3)	C(5,16)	P(2)	C(5,20)	P(2)	C(4,20)	P(2)	C(3,20)	C(3,120)	F(84)	F(5)

3.2   Hand-Engineered Feature

In addition to the deep representation, for each detected human head, we also extract its histogram of gradients (HoG) feature due to its superior representative capability for orientated objects. Specifically, we divide each head image into an 8×8 grid, and bin gradients for each cell within the grid using 6 discretized orientations. As a result, we can represent each head image as a 386×1 feature vector. Figure 2 gives a visualization of a number of extracted HoG diagrams.

It is well-known that the learned feature (CNN as an example) outperforms hand-crafted feature (HoG as an example) by a large margin on various vision tasks. We can draw the same conclusion from our experimental results in Sect. 4. However, it is interesting to find that the combination of deep and hand-crafted feature representations delivers much better estimation of head orientations compared with using each individual representation only, see Sect. 4 for details.

3.3   Spatial Temporal Model

Our goal is to estimate the orientation of M_t persons within frame t. We cast the estimation problem as finding a discriminative function $F(\mathbf{x}, \mathbf{y}, \mathbf{w})$ such that for an image $\mathbf{x}$, the assignment of head orientations $\mathbf{y}$ exhibits the best score calculated by F, which is given by:

$$\mathbf{y}^* = \arg\max_{\mathbf{y} \in \mathcal{Y}} F(\mathbf{x}, \mathbf{y}, \mathbf{w}). \tag{1}$$

As in many learning framework, we consider functions linear in some feature representation Φ,

$$F(\mathbf{x}, \mathbf{y}, \mathbf{w}) = \mathbf{w}^\top \Phi(\mathbf{x}, \mathbf{y}). \tag{2}$$

Let $(\mathbf{x}, \mathbf{y})$ denote a training instance, where $\mathbf{x} = (\mathbf{x}_1, \ldots, \mathbf{x}_T)$ is the video sequence including T frames, $\mathbf{y} = (\mathbf{y}_1, \ldots, \mathbf{y}_T)$ is the pose labelling of all frames in the sequence. Here $\mathbf{y}_t = (y_t^1, \ldots, y_t^{M_t})$ is the labelling of a number of M_t persons within frame t. For each time-stamp t, we consider the dependency among the head orientations of different people, which can be modelled by a graphical representation $G_t = (V_t, E_t)$. Here V_t is the node set of the graph with each node representing the head orientation of the associated person. $E_t = V_t \times V_t$ is the edge set of the graph G_t. Hence G_t is fully-connected. For an arbitrary $(\mathbf{x}, \mathbf{y})$, the discriminative function F is formulated as:

$$F(\mathbf{x}, \mathbf{y}, \mathbf{w}) =$$
$$\sum_{t \in \{1 \ldots T\}} \left\{ \mathbf{w}_1^\top \sum_{i \in V_t} \Phi_1(\mathbf{x}_t, y_t^i) + \mathbf{w}_2^\top \sum_{(i,j) \in E_t} \Phi_2(y_t^i, y_t^j) + \mathbf{w}_3^\top \sum_{s \in V_t} \Phi_3(y_t^s, y_{t-1}^s) \right\}, \tag{3}$$

where $\mathbf{w} = [\mathbf{w}_1, \mathbf{w}_2, \mathbf{w}_3]$ are the model parameters to be learned during training. The local feature $\Phi_1(\mathbf{x}_t, y_t^i)$ is defined as:

$$\Phi_1(\mathbf{x}_t, y_t^i) = \mathbf{e}_1(y_t^i) S(\mathbf{x}_t, y_t^i), \tag{4}$$

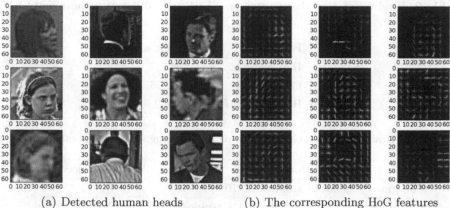

(a) Detected human heads   (b) The corresponding HoG features

Fig. 2. An illustration of hand-engineered feature. The left represents detected human heads. The right depicts the extracted HoG features.

where $S(\mathbf{x}_t, y_t^i)$ denotes the belief of assigning an orientation label y_t^i to person i in the t-th frame $\mathbf{x}_t$, which is the discriminant score of SVM classification using a concatenation of CNN and HoG features. $\mathbf{e}_1(y_t^i) \in \{0,1\}^{|\mathcal{Y}|}$ denotes a vector takes 1 at its y_t^i-th position, and takes 0 elsewhere.

The spatial feature $\Phi_2(y_t^i, y_t^j)$ is defined as:

$$\Phi_2(y_t^i, y_t^j) = \left(\mathbf{e}_2(y_t^i - 1) \times |\mathcal{Y}| + y_t^j \right), \tag{5}$$

where $\mathbf{e}_2 \in \{0,1\}^{|\mathcal{Y}|^2}$ denotes a vector takes 1 at its $(y_t^i - 1) \times |\mathcal{Y}| + y_t^j$-th position, and takes 0 elsewhere. This joint feature enables us to learn the compatibility between the labelling of head orientations appeared within the identical frame.

The temporal feature $\Phi_3(y_t^s, y_{t-1}^s)$ is defined as:

$$\Phi_3(y_t^s, y_{t-1}^s) = \mathbf{e}_2 \left((y_{t-1}^s - 1) \times |\mathcal{Y}| + y_t^s \right), \tag{6}$$

which enables the learning of transitions of head orientations of the same person across time. To train $\mathbf{w}$, we use the structured SVM package [15], with the inference problem (that is, finding the most violated constraints) solved via loopy belief propagation.

4 Experiment

Here we provide experimental results to show (1) combining CNN feature and HoG feature improves head orientation estimation significantly. (2) the classification results can be further improved by considering the spatio-temporal relations among heads of different individuals. For CNN training, we use TensorFlow library.

Table 2. Head orientation classification on TVHI using different features and SVM classifiers.

	Features	Test accuracy
F1	HoG features	67.1%
F2	CNN features	71.9%
F3 (ours)	HoG + CNN features	**76.1%**

Table 3. Head orientation classification on TVHI using spatio-temporal context.

	Model terms	Test accuracy
The state-of-the-art	Patron *et al.* [10]	72.0%
M1 (ours)	Concatenated + temporal	76.2%
M2 (ours)	Concatenated + spatial	77.0%
M3 (ours)	Concatenated + temporal + spatial	**77.5%**

4.1 Result on TV Human Interaction Dataset (TVHI)

TV Human Interaction dataset [9] is composed of 300 videos clips cut from 23 different TV shows. Each clip contains one to six people (mostly two or three people). The dataset contains 55,678 upper body bounding boxes, and five discrete head orientation categories including frontal-left (fl), frontal-right (fr), profile-left (pl), profile-right (pr) and backwards (bw). As prefect frontal orientations are rare, they are moved to either of the two frontal categories. We split the dataset as is suggested in [9], which generates two mutually exclusive groups: one subset contains 30,148 bounding boxes while the other contains 25,530 bounding boxes. For each group, we train a model on it and test the model on the other such that we can evaluate the performance of our approach on the entire dataset. Results are reported by summarizing the results on both subsets.

To obtain the bounding boxes of human heads, we empirically estimate the location and size of human head for each human upper body. We collect such estimations for both training and testing, and take the annotations of upper body orientations as the groundtruth of head orientations.

Data augmentation is a common way to create additional samples to train the deep model sufficiently. To this end, we apply transformations, flipping and RGB jittering to the extracted head patches. In terms of transformation, we first apply a random rotating within ten degrees to the head patches. Then the resulting images are randomly shifted within five pixels. Next random noise is added to one channel of the head image picked by random. At last all patches are resized to 64 × 64 pixels.

We now compare three types of feature representations for head orientation estimation: (1) HoG feature, (2) CNN feature, (3) the concatenation of both features. For each cell of an 8 × 8 grid overlay onto a head image, we extract 6

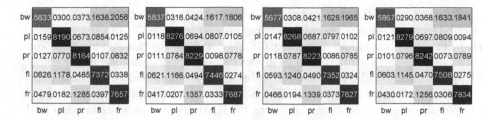

Fig. 3. Confusion matrices for head orientation classification on TVHI. From left to right, it shows results of *concatenated features, concatenated + temporal, concatenated + spatial* and *concatenated + temporal + spatial* respectively. Note our full model (that is, *concatenated + temporal + spatial*) obtains best results on all classes.

Table 4. Head orientation classification on HH dataset using different features with SVM classifiers and spatial context.

	Features	Test accuracy
F3 (without data augmentation)	CNN features	45.4%
F4 (without data augmentation)	HoG features	68.3%
F5 (with data augmentation)	CNN features	53.6%
F6 (with data augmentation)	HoG features	68.9%
F7 (ours)	HoG + CNN features	**75.9%**
M4 (ours)	Concatenated + spatial	**77.4%**

oriented gradients as its local features. As result, each head image can be represented by a 384 dimensions HOG feature vectors. In Fig. 2 we visualize the hog features extracted from a few head images. We extract CNN features from convolutional layers. Specifically, we evaluate the effectiveness of CNN features from different convolutional layers and found that the second to last convolutional layer performs best. We normalize the CNN feature (180 dimensions) and the HoG feature (384 dimensions) separately, which are then concatenated to obtain a 564 dimensional feature vector. For each representation, we use the LIBLIN-EAR toolbox [16] to train a discriminative model to predict head orientations. Table 2 demonstrates classification results using different features. Clearly CNN performs much better than the HoG representation. Evidently, the concatenated representation outperforms each component significantly, which is interesting given the fact that the first component, that is, the HoG representation performs much worse than the CNN feature. This suggests that these features are complementary to each other in terms of representing head orientations.

Next we compare our spatio-temporal model against (1) the concatenated feature, (2) the spatio-temporal model without using spatial term, (3) the spatio-temporal model without using temporal term. Results are provided in Table 3. Two conclusions can be drawn here. First, the spatio-temporal model outperforms the concatenated feature representation by 1.4%, mainly due to the modeling of contextual relations among head orientations of people within our spatio-temporal model. Second, modeling spatial context (77.0%) is more effective than modeling temporal context (76.2%), at least for this experiment. Note that our full spatio-temporal model gives the best classification accuracy among all approaches. We also compare the state-of-the-art proposed by [10], where the overall classification accuracy (72.0%) is 3.5% worse than ours.

We also plot the confusion matrices for head orientation classification with different approaches. Results are shown in Fig. 3. One can see that when the contextual information is used, the classification performance is significantly improved. Note our full model (that is, *concatenated + temporal + spatial*) obtains best results on all classes of head orientations.

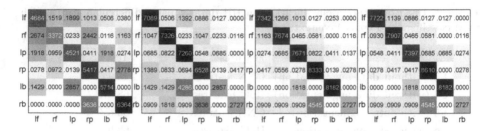

Fig. 4. Confusion matrices for head orientation classification on HH dataset. From left to right, it shows results of *CNN Features without data augmentation, HoG Features without data augmentation, HoG + CNN Features* and *concatenated + spatial*, respectively (temporal information is not available for this dataset). Note that our approach (that is, *concatenated + spatial*) obtains best results on most classes.

4.2   Result on Hollywood Heads Dataset (HH)

This dataset contains a set of images extracted from Hollywood movies where people have been annotated at both head and upperbody-level. It includes six head orientations: left-profile (lp), right-profile (pr), left-frontal (fl), right-frontal (fr), left-back (lb) and right-back (rb). Here we also compare three types of feature representation for head orientation estimation: (1) HoG feature, (2) CNN feature, (3) the concatenation of both features. For each cell of an 8×8 grid overlay onto a head image, we extract 6 oriented gradients as its local representation. As result, each head image can be represented by a 384 dimensions HOG feature vectors. We extract deep representation from each head region using CNN. Afterwards we normalize the extracted CNN feature (180 dimensions) and HoG feature (384 dimensions) separately, and the resulting normalized features are concatenated to obtain a 564 dimensional feature vector. For each representation, we use the LIBLINEAR toolbox [16] to train a discriminative model to classify head orientations. Table 4 demonstrates the classification results using (1) HoG and CNN features without data augmentation, (2) HoG and CNN features with data augmentation, (3) the spatial context model (excluding the temporal context term in Eq. (3) as spatial information is not available for this dataset). Interestingly, HoG performs significantly better than the deep representation. The reason might be that the number of training examples is extremely small for HH, which is insufficient to train an effective deep model. SVM is well known for its generalization ability against small dataset, and the SVM model trained on HoG feature is more accurate on this dataset. Remarkably, when concatenating the deep and hand-engineered features, again the classification result is improved significantly, which indicates that HoG and CNN features are complementary to each other with respect to the head orientation prediction task. We also compare the results of models trained with and without data augmentation. Clearly results using data augmentation are much better (especially when using HoG feature) than the results without using augmentation. Finally, our spatial model (M4) gives the best result (outperforms HoG + CNN features by 1.5%), which suggests that modeling the relations among people is important to the head orientation classification task. We also plot the confusion matrices for head orientation classification with different approaches in Fig. 4. Some visualization results are provided in Fig. 5.

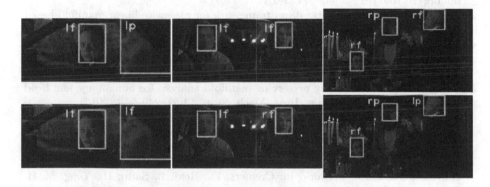

Fig. 5. Visualization of head orientation classification results using three examples. The top row shows the result of *HoG + CNN features*, and the bottom row lists the result of *concatenated + spatial*, which is able to correct misclassified results by local representation (*i.e. HoG + CNN features*).

5   Conclusion

In this paper, we have presented a spatial temporal field for the learning discrete head orientations from video clips, with each video contains possibly an arbitrary number of persons. Our spatial temporal model combined the learned feature, the handcrafted feature and the contextual information to represent the relations of head orientations of different individuals, which admitted superior performance on benchmark dataset. We found that the deep feature, the hand-engineered feature and the contextual feature are complementary to each other in terms of head orientation recognition, and fusing these features with our spatial temporal model boosted recognition accuracy. In addition, data augmentation is important to learn effective local features of head orientations, especially when the training set is small. In future, a sufficiently large dataset is essential to further improve the recognition performance of discrete head orientations.

Acknowledgement. This work is partially supported by National Natural Science Foundation of China (61802348, 61876167) and National Key R&D Program of China (2018YFB1305200).

References

1. Wang, Z., Shi, Q., Shen, C., Hengel, A.: Bilinear programming for human activity recognition with unknown MRF graphs. In: Computer Vision and Pattern Recognition (2013)
2. Tran, D.T., Lee, J.-H.: A robust method for head orientation estimation using histogram of oriented gradients. In: Kim, T., Adeli, H., Ramos, C., Kang, B.-H. (eds.) SIP 2011. CCIS, vol. 260, pp. 391–400. Springer, Heidelberg (2011). https://doi.org/10.1007/978-3-642-27183-0_41
3. Foytik, J., Asari, V.K.: A two-layer framework for piecewise linear manifold-based head pose estimation. Int. J. Comput. Vis. **101**(2), 270–287 (2013)
4. Lee, D., Yang, M.H., Oh, S.: Fast and accurate head pose estimation via random projection forests. In: Proceedings of the IEEE International Conference on Computer Vision, pp. 1958–1966 (2015)
5. Lu, J., Tan, Y.P.: Ordinary preserving manifold analysis for human age and head pose estimation. IEEE Trans. Hum.-Mach. Syst. **43**(2), 249–258 (2013)
6. Breitenstein, M.D., Kuettel, D., Weise, T., Van Gool, L., Pfister, H.: Real-time face pose estimation from single range images. In: Computer Vision and Pattern Recognition, pp. 1–8 (2008)
7. Li, S., Chan, A.B.: 3D human pose estimation from monocular images with deep convolutional neural network. In: Cremers, D., Reid, I., Saito, H., Yang, M.-H. (eds.) ACCV 2014. LNCS, vol. 9004, pp. 332–347. Springer, Cham (2015). https://doi.org/10.1007/978-3-319-16808-1_23
8. Li, S., Ngan, K.N., Paramesran, R., Sheng, L.: Real-time head pose tracking with online face template reconstruction. IEEE Trans. Pattern Anal. Mach. Intell. **38**(9), 1922–1928 (2016)
9. Patron-Perez, A., Marszalek, M., Reid, I., Zisserman, A.: TV Human Interaction Dataset. http://www.robots.ox.ac.uk/~alonso/tv_human_interactions.html
10. Patron-Perez, A., Marszalek, M., Reid, I., Zisserman, A.: Structured learning of human interactions in TV shows. IEEE Trans. Pattern Anal. Mach. Intell. **34**(12), 2441–2453 (2012)
11. Ahn, B., Park, J., Kweon, I.S.: Real-time head orientation from a monocular camera using deep neural network. In: Cremers, D., Reid, I., Saito, H., Yang, M.-H. (eds.) ACCV 2014. LNCS, vol. 9005, pp. 82–96. Springer, Cham (2015). https://doi.org/10.1007/978-3-319-16811-1_6
12. Fan, R.E., Chang, K.W., Hsieh, C.J., Wang, X.R., Lin, C.J.: LIBLINEAR: a library for large linear classification. J. Mach. Learn. Res. **9**, 1871–1874 (2008)

13. Kang, M.J., Lee, J.K., Kang, J.W.: Combining random forest with multi-block local binary pattern feature selection for multiclass head pose estimation. Plos One **12**(7), e0180792 (2017)
14. Joseph, R., Santosh, D., Ross, G., Ali, F.: You only look once: unified, real-time object detection. In: Computer Vision & Pattern Recognition (2016)
15. Ioannis, T., Thorsten, J., Thomas, H., Yasemin, A.: Large margin methods for structured and interdependent output variables. J. Mach. Learn. Res. **6**(2), 1453–1484 (2006)
16. Fan, R.E., Chang, K.W., Hsieh, C.J., Wang, X.R., Lin, C.J.: LIBLINEAR: a library for large linear classification. J. Mach. Learn. Res. **9**(9), 1871–1874 (2008)
17. Yao, R., Xia, S., Zhang, Z., Zhang, Y.: Real-time correlation filter tracking by efficient dense belief propagation with structure preserving. IEEE Trans. Multimedia **19**(4), 772–784 (2017)
18. Yao, R., Lin, G., Shen, C., Zhang, Y., Shi, Q.: Semantics-aware visual object tracking. IEEE Trans. Circ. Syst. Video Technol. **29**, 1687–1700 (2018)
19. Yao, R., Xia, S., Shen, F., Zhou, Y., Niu, Q.: Exploiting spatial structure from parts for adaptive kernelized correlation filter tracker. IEEE Sig. Process. Lett. **23**(5), 658–662 (2016)

Prediction-Coherent LSTM-Based Recurrent Neural Network for Safer Glucose Predictions in Diabetic People

Maxime De Bois[1]([✉])(iD), Mounîm A. El Yacoubi[2](iD), and Mehdi Ammi[3](iD)

[1] CNRS-LIMSI and Université Paris Saclay, Orsay, France
maxime.debois@limsi.fr
[2] Samovar, CNRS, Télécom SudParis, Institut Polytechnique de Paris, Évry, France
mounim.el_yacoubi@telecom-sudparis.eu
[3] Université Paris 8, Saint-Denis, France
ammi@ai.univ-paris8.fr

Abstract. In the context of time-series forecasting, we propose a LSTM-based recurrent neural network architecture and loss function that enhance the stability of the predictions. In particular, the loss function penalizes the model, not only on the prediction error (mean-squared error), but also on the predicted variation error.

We apply this idea to the prediction of future glucose values in diabetes, which is a delicate task as unstable predictions can leave the patient in doubt and make him/her take the wrong action, threatening his/her life. The study is conducted on type 1 and type 2 diabetic people, with a focus on predictions made 30-min ahead of time.

First, we confirm the superiority, in the context of glucose prediction, of the LSTM model by comparing it to other state-of-the-art models (Extreme Learning Machine, Gaussian Process regressor, Support Vector Regressor).

Then, we show the importance of making stable predictions by smoothing the predictions made by the models, resulting in an overall improvement of the clinical acceptability of the models at the cost in a slight loss in prediction accuracy.

Finally, we show that the proposed approach, outperforms all baseline results. More precisely, it trades a loss of 4.3% in the prediction accuracy for an improvement of the clinical acceptability of 27.1%. When compared to the moving average post-processing method, we show that the trade-off is more efficient with our approach.

Keywords: Glucose prediction · Recurrent neural network · Loss function · Stability · Clinical acceptability

1 Introduction

With 1.5 milion inputed deaths in 2012, diabetes is one of the leading diseases in the modern world [26]. Diabetic people, due to the non-production of insulin

© Springer Nature Switzerland AG 2019
T. Gedeon et al. (Eds.): ICONIP 2019, LNCS 11955, pp. 510–521, 2019.
https://doi.org/10.1007/978-3-030-36718-3_43

(type 1) or an increased resistance to its action (type 2), have a lot of trouble managing their blood glucose. In one hand, when their glycemia falls too low (state of hypoglycemia), they are at risk of short-term complications (e.g., coma, death). In the other hand, if their glycemia is too high (hyperglycemia), the complications are long-term (e.g., cardiovascular diseases, blindness).

A lot of efforts are focused towards helping diabetic people in their daily life, with, for instance, continuous glucose monitoring (CGM) devices (e.g., FreeStyle Libre [18]), artificial pancreas (e.g., MiniMed 670G [16]), or coaching smartphone applications for diabetes (e.g., mySugr [20]). Thanks to the advances in the field of machine learning and the increased availability of data, a lot of researchers are following the lead of the prediction of future glucose values. The goal is to build data-driven models that, using the patient's past information (e.g., glucose values, carbohydrate intakes, insulin boluses), predict glucose values multiple minutes ahead of time (we call those models multi-step predictive models).

While a lot of the early work in the glucose prediction field were focused on the use of autoregressive (AR) models [22], the models that are used nowadays are more complex. Georga et al. explored the use of Support Vector Regression (SVR) in predicting glucose up to 120 min ahead of time in type 1 diabetes [9]. Valletta et al. proposed the use of Gaussian Process regressor (GP) to include a measure of the physical activity of type 1 diabetic patients into the predictive models [25]. In their work, Daskalaki et al. demonstrated the superiority of feed-forward neural networks compared to AR models [2]. As for them, Georga et al. studied the use of Extreme Learning Machine models (ELM) in short-term (PH of 30 min) type 1 diabetes glucose prediction [10]. Finally, recurrent neural networks (RNN) have shown a lot of interest in the field [27], and in particular those with long short-term memory (LSTM) units [5,15,17,24].

However, neural-network-based models, while exhibiting very promising results, often show instability in the predictions. This comes from the training of the models that, most of the time, aims at minimizing the mean-squared error (MSE) loss function. It makes the model focus on getting a good point-accuracy, without questioning the coherence of consecutive predictions.

The stability of the predictions is very important in predicting future glucose values. Predicting towards the wrong direction or with consecutive inconsistent directions can make the diabetic patient take the wrong action, potentially threatening his/her life. This is why the accuracy of the predicted glucose variations is taken into account when assessing the clinical acceptability of glucose predictive models, with, for instance, the widely-used Continuous Glucose-Error Grid Analysis (CG-EGA) [19]. We identified that this issue is not specific to the field of glucose prediction and can be extended to other multi-step forecasting applications, such as stock market prediction [6] or flood levels forecasting [1].

In this paper, to enhance the stability of the predictions, we propose a new LSTM-based RNN architecture and loss function. We demonstrate the usefulness of the idea by applying it to the challenging task of predicting future glucose values of diabetic patients which directly benefits from an increased stability.

We can summarize our contributions as follows:

1. We propose a new loss function that penalizes the model simultaneously during its training, not only on the classical MSE, but also on the predicted variation error. To be able to compute the penalty, we propose to use the loss function in a two-output LSTM-based RNN architecture. We validate the proposed approach by comparing it to four other state-of-the-art models.
2. We demonstrate the importance of making stable predictions in the context of glucose predictions as accurate but unstable predictions lead the models to have a bad clinical acceptability.
3. We confirm the overall usefullness of using LSTM-based RNN in predicting future glucose values by comparing it to other state-of-the-art models. In particular, the LSTM model shows more clinical acceptable results.
4. We have conducted the study on two different datasets, one with type 1 and one with type 2 diabetic patients. This is worth mentioning as glucose prediction studies are very rarely done on type 2 diabetes (although it represents around 90% of the whole diabetic population).
5. Finally, we have made all the source code and a standalone implementation of the CG-EGA available in Github.

The rest of the paper is organized as follows. First, we introduce the proposed architecture and loss function. Then, we present its application to the prediction of future glucose values. Finally, we provide the reader with the results and takeaways from the experiments.

2   Prediction-Coherent LSTM-Based Recurrent Neural Network

2.1   Presentation of the Model

In multi-step time-series forecasting, at time t, the model takes a set of features X to predict the future value of the time-series y at a prediction horizon PH: $\hat{y}_{t+PH}$. Most of the time, the input features X comprises the past H known values of the time-series y as well as other time-related features.

RNN, and in particular those based on LSTM cells, are neural networks that are particularly suited for time-series forecasting as they include the temporal component of the features and the predictions into their architecture [13]. Such models are usually trained with the MSE loss function (see Eq. 1) which estimates the mean accuracy of the predictions.

$$MSE(\boldsymbol{y}, \hat{\boldsymbol{y}}) = \frac{1}{n} \sum_{i=1}^{n} (y_i - \hat{y}_i)^2 \qquad (1)$$

However, using the MSE does not incentivize the model to make successive predictions that are coherent with their respective true values. More formally, we can call two consecutive predictions, $\hat{y}_{t+PH-1}$ and $\hat{y}_{t+PH}$, coherent with the true values when the predicted variation from one to the other, $\Delta\hat{y}_{t+PH}$, reflect the true variation of the time-series Δy_{t+PH}.

To enhance to coherence of consecutive predictions, we propose the idea of using a two-output LSTM that takes advantage of its architecture to penalize incoherent successive predictions during its training. We call this neural network a Prediction-Coherent LSTM-based recurrent neural network (pcLSTM).

Two-Output LSTM. The two-output LSTM is a standard LSTM unrolled H times and that outputs the predictions of the last two steps (see Fig. 1).

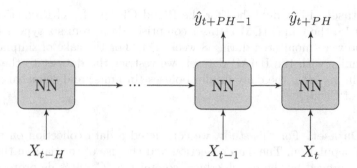

Fig. 1. Two-output LSTM which has been unrolled H times. X_t are the input features at time t and $\hat{y}_{t+PH}$ is the forecast of the time-series y at a time $t + PH$.

Variations Penalized Loss Function. To enhance the coherence between two consecutive predictions, we propose to penalize the network on the error of the predicted variation. We define the cMSE (see Eq. 2), which is the weighted sum of the MSE of the predictions and the MSE of the predicted variations. We call the parameter c the *coherence factor*. It represents the relative importance of the variation-based penalty compared to the accuracy of the predictions.

$$cMSE(\boldsymbol{y}, \hat{\boldsymbol{y}}) = MSE(\boldsymbol{y}, \hat{\boldsymbol{y}}) + c \cdot MSE(\boldsymbol{\Delta y}, \boldsymbol{\Delta \hat{y}})$$
$$= \frac{1}{n} \sum_{i=1}^{n} (y_i - \hat{y}_i)^2 + c \cdot (\Delta y_i - \Delta \hat{y}_i)^2 \qquad (2)$$

The coherence factor c is a problem-dependent parameter that has to be optimized depending on the relative importance of having coherent or stable predictions versus having accurate predictions.

We note that, if the coherence factor, c, is set to 0, the $cMSE$ becomes the MSE and the model then behaves like a standard one-output LSTM model.

3 Methods

In this section, we go through the experimental details of the study, and, in particular, the data we used, the preprocessing steps we followed, the models we implemented, and the evaluation metrics we used.

We made the source code used in this study available in the pcLSTM Github repository [4].

3.1 Experimental Data

Our data come from two distinct datasets: the Ohio T1DM dataset and the IDIAB dataset accounting for 6 type 1 and 5 type 2 diabetic patients respectively.

Ohio Dataset. First published for the Blood Glucose Level Prediction Challenge in 2018, the OhioT1DM Dataset comprises data from six type 1 diabetic people who were monitored during 8 weeks [14]. For the sake of simplicity and the uniformity with the IDIAB dataset, we restrict the dataset to the glucose readings (in mg/dL), the daily insulin boluses (in units) and the meal information (in g of CHO).

IDIAB Dataset. For this study, we conducted a data collection on the type 2 diabetic population. The data collection and the use of the data in this study has been approved by the french ethical committee "Comités de protection des personnes" (ID RCB 2018-A00312-53).

Five people with type 2 diabetes (4F/1M, age 58.8 ± 8.28 years old, BMI 30.76 ± 5.14 kg/m^2, HbA1c 6.8 ± 0.71 %), have been monitored for 31.8 ± 1.17 days in free-living conditions. The patients were equipped with FreeStyle Libre (FSL) CGM devices (Abbott Diabetes Care) [18], which were recording their glucose levels (in mg/dL), and with the mySugr (mySugr GmbH) coaching app for diabetes [20], in which the patient logged his/her food intakes (in g of CHO) and insulin boluses (in units).

3.2 Preprocessing

The goal of the preprocessing part is to uniformize the two datasets and prepare them for the training and testing of the models.

Data Cleaning. To balance the training and the testing sets regarding the distribution of the samples on the daily timeline, we have chosen to remove incomplete days from the datasets. As a result, for every patient, we ended up with an average of 38.5 (±4.82) and 29.4 (±1.62) days worth of data for the Ohio and IDIAB datasets respectively.

We noticed that several glucose readings in the IDIAB dataset were erroneous (characterized by high amplitude spikes). As this is not particularly surprising (a study by Fokkert *et al.* reported that only 85.5% of the FSL readings were within ±20% of the reference sensor values [7]), we removed them to prevent them from disturbing the training of the model.

Resampling and Interpolation. To synchronize the data between them, we have resampled both datasets to get a sample every 5 min. During the resampling process, glucose values have been averaged, insulin boluses and CHO intakes have been summed up.

To make up for the introduced missing glucose values in the IDIAB dataset (which has one reading every 15 min, instead of 5), we interpolated the glucose signals as it has already been done in the context of glucose prediction [23]. In particular, we used a piecewise cubic hermite interpolating polynomial (PCHIP) [8] to avoid oscillations in the interpolated signal (which occurred with a single polynomial interpolation) and to preserve the monotonicity of the fitted signal (which was an issue with a spline interpolation) [12].

Datasets Splitting. To ready up the datasets for the training and testing of the models, we have to create the training, validation and testing sets. The splitting of the data has been done on full days of data to ensure an uniform distribution of the daily sequences across the datasets. We split the data into training, validation and testing sets following a 50%/25%/25% distribution.

Input Scaling. Lastly, the training sets data have been standardized (zero-mean and unit-variance). The same transformation has then been applied to the validation and testing sets.

3.3 Models

In this study, we compare the proposed approach (pcLSTM) to four other state-of-the-art models, namely an Extreme Learning Machine neural network (ELM), a Gaussian Process regressor (GP), a LSTM recurrent neural network (LSTM), and a Support Vector Regression model (SVR).

Every model is personalized to the patient. To be able to model long-term dependencies, every model takes the past 3 h of glucose, insulin, and CHO values as input. The hyperparameters of every model have been tuned on the validation sets by grid search.

ELM. The ELM architecture has 10^5 neurons in its single hidden layer. To reduce the impact of overfitting, we applied a L2 penalty (500) to the weights.

GP. The GP model has been implemented with a dot-product kernel. The dot-product has been chosen instead of a traditional radial basis function kernel as it has been shown to perform better in the context of glucose prediction [5]. The inhomogeneity parameter of the kernel has been set to 10^{-8}. To ease the fitting of the model, white noise (value of 10^{-2}) has been added to the observations.

LSTM. The LSTM model is made of a single hidden layer of 128 LSTM units. It has been trained to minimize the MSE loss function using the Adam optimizer with batches of 10 samples and a learning rate of 5×10^{-3}. To prevent the overfitting of the network to the training data, we added a L2 penalty (10^{-4}) and used the early stopping methodology.

pcLSTM. The pcLSTM recurrent neural network shares the same characteristics with the LSTM model. The only difference is its two-output architecture and its associated cMSE loss function (see Sect. 2). In particular, the coherence factor has been optimized through grid search to ensure a good trade-off between the accuracy of the predictions and the accuracy of the predicted variations. We settled down with a coherence factor of 2.

SVR. The SVR model has been implemented with a radial basis function (RBF) kernel. The coefficient of the kernel has been set to 5×10^{-4}. The wideness of the no-penalty tube has been set to 0.1 and the penalty itself has been set to 50.

3.4   Post-processing

By using the cMSE loss function, we incentivize the model to make consecutive predictions reflecting the actual glucose rate of change. In a way, it can be viewed as a smoothing effect integrated to the training of the model.

Some post-processing time-series smoothing techniques exist, such as the exponential smoothing or the moving average smoothing [21]. The latter, yielding a better trade-off between the accuracy of the predictions and the accuracy of the predicted variations, has been used with a window of the last 3 predictions.

3.5   Evaluation Metrics

In this study, three evaluation metrics have been used: the Root-Mean-Squared prediction Error (RMSE), the Root-Mean-Squared predicted variation Error (dRMSE), and the Continuous Glucose-Error Grid Analysis (CG-EGA) measuring the clinical acceptability of the predictions.

RMSE. The RMSE is the most used metric in the world of glucose prediction as it measures the overall accuracy of the predictions [19].

dRMSE. We call the dRMSE the RMSE applied to the difference between two consecutive predictions. Therefore, it measures the accuracy of the predicted variations and can be used to estimate the impact of the variation-based penalty in the cMSE loss function.

CG-EGA. The CG-EGA provides a measure of the clinical acceptability of the predictions [19]. Indeed, predictions, depending on the current state of the patient's glycemia (hypoglycemia, euglycemia[1], or hyperglycemia), can be more or less dangerous, which is not taken into account in metrics such as the RMSE.

Technically, the CG-EGA is made of two grids: the Point-Error Grid Analysis (P-EGA) and the Rate-Error Grid Analysis (R-EGA). Whereas the P-EGA provides an acceptability score (from A to E) to the glucose predictions, the R-EGA gives each prediction a score (also from A to E) based on the variation from the previous prediction to the current one [11]. The CG-EGA combines both grids and gives, for every prediction, in its simplified representation, a clinical acceptability category: accurate prediction (AP), benign error (BE), or erroneous prediction (EP). For a prediction to be categorized as an AP, it needs to have a score of A or B in both the P-EGA and the R-EGA.

We published the source code of the CG-EGA implementation in Github [3].

4   Results and Discussion

The results of the models, presented with and without the moving average smoothing technique discussed in Sect. 3.4, are reported in Table 1. Figure 2 gives a graphical representation of the effect of the proposed approach on the predictions. A detailed graphical clinical acceptability classification of the predictions is given by Fig. 3.

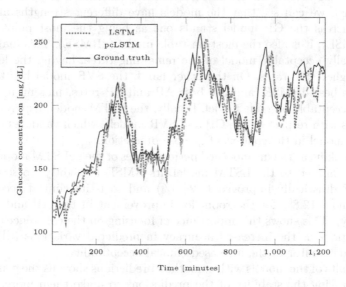

Fig. 2. Glucose predictions of the unsmoothed LSTM and pcLSTM against the ground truth, for a given day of one of the patients.

---

[1] The euglycemia region is the region between hypoglycemia and hyperglycemia.

Table 1. Performances of the ELM, GP, LSTM, pcLSTM, and SVR models, evaluated at a prediction horizon of 30 min with and without the smoothing of the predictions (mean ± standard deviation, averaged on the subjects from both datasets).

Model	RMSE	dRMSE	CG-EGA		
			AP	BE	EP
Without smoothing					
ELM	25.54 ± 5.02	1.90 ± 0.45	79.34 ± 7.53	14.92 ± 5.50	5.74 ± 2.33
GP	**18.92 ± 4.56**	2.21 ± 0.44	81.70 ± 6.21	13.88 ± 4.09	4.41 ± 2.28
LSTM	19.48 ± 4.42	1.95 ± 0.40	82.98 ± 5.65	12.42 ± 3.73	4.60 ± 2.06
pcLSTM	20.32 ± 4.56	**1.47 ± 0.31**	**87.60 ± 4.74**	**8.76 ± 3.23**	**4.01 ± 1.84**
SVR	20.08 ± 4.24	1.74 ± 0.44	83.92 ± 6.10	11.75 ± 4.24	4.32 ± 2.01
With smoothing					
ELM	26.64 ± 5.17	1.42 ± 0.31	86.13 ± 5.26	9.31 ± 3.89	4.57 ± 1.79
GP	**20.42 ± 4.70**	1.48 ± 0.31	87.17 ± 4.38	9.08 ± 3.03	**3.74 ± 1.65**
LSTM	21.21 ± 4.63	1.41 ± 0.30	87.51 ± 4.45	8.60 ± 3.15	3.89 ± 1.60
pcLSTM	22.42 ± 4.85	**1.29 ± 0.28**	**88.82 ± 4.43**	**7.36 ± 3.18**	3.81 ± 1.68
SVR	21.81 ± 4.43	1.42 ± 0.32	87.38 ± 4.78	8.79 ± 3.37	3.83 ± 1.63

First, when looking at the unsmoothed baseline results, apart from the ELM model that has overall the worse performances (excluding it from the following analysis), we can see that the models have different strengths and weaknesses. Whereas the GP model stands out as being the most point-accurate model (RMSE), it is also the most unstable model (dRMSE). This makes it the least clinically acceptable model of the remaining three, having the lowest AP and the highest EP rates. On the other hand, the SVR model has the worse RMSE, the best dRMSE, and the best AP and EP rates, making it the most clinically acceptable baseline model. Finally, the LSTM model displays competitive results with respect to the GP and SVR models, which validates the use of the LSTM model in the context of glucose prediction.

When looking at the unsmoothed performances of the pcLSTM model, we can see that, compared to the LSTM model, its RMSE is slightly worse (+4.3%), its dRMSE drastically improved (−24.6%) and so is its clinical acceptability (+27.1% and −12.8% for the room for improvement in the AP and EP rates respectively). This shows the importance of focusing on the coherence of successive predictions as the increased accuracy in predicted variations (dRMSE) is the main contributor to the increased clinical acceptability.

The results of the models with smoothed predictions show us the general benefit of improving the stability of the predictions to make them more clinically acceptable. Even though all the models see their clinical acceptability improved, the improvement varies from model to model: the models with the highest instability benefit from the smoothing the most. In average, the improvement due to the smoothing applied on the baseline models (still excluding the ELM model) is

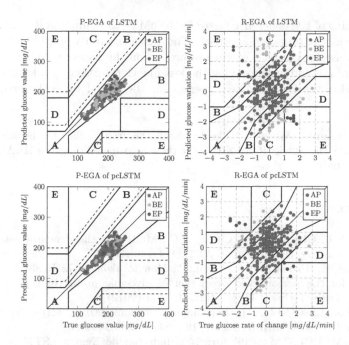

Fig. 3. P-EGA (left) and R-EGA (right) for LSTM (top) and pcLSTM (bottom) models for a patient during a given day. The CG-EGA classification (AP, BE, or EP) is computed by combining both P and R-EGA ranks.

of $+8.5\%$, -24.3%, $+26.0\%$, and -14.14% in RMSE, dRMSE, AP and EP rates respectively. Those results show us that the trade-off made by the pcLSTM is much more efficient ($+8.5\%$ against $+4.3\%$ in RMSE for overall the same improvement in the other metrics).

5 Conclusion

In this paper, we have presented a new loss function for recurrent neural networks which, by penalizing the model on the predicted variation errors in addition to the prediction errors, helps the network making more stable predictions.

We apply the proposed model to the prediction of future glucose values in diabetes. First, we validate the use of recurrent neural networks (in particular with LSTM units) by showing that our baseline LSTM model is competitive when compared to other state-of-the-art models. Then, we demonstrate the importance of the proposed approach as it greatly improves the clinical acceptability of the predictions. Lastly, we compare the proposed approach to another smoothing technique. While the effect on the clinical acceptability is the same, the loss in the accuracy of the prediction is higher, making our proposed approach more efficient.

The tuning of the coherence factor in the cMSE loss function is of paramount importance for the proposed approach. The desired stability is application dependant and must, in the case of glucose prediction, be assessed by practitioners. In the future we plan on improving the loss function further by adding penalties directly tied to the CG-EGA (e.g., penalizing the model when the prediction is an EP).

Acknowledgments. We would like to thank the french diabetes health network Revesdiab and Dr. Sylvie JOANNIDIS for their help in building the IDIAB dataset used in this study.

References

1. Chang, F.J., Chiang, Y.M., Chang, L.C.: Multi-step-ahead neural networks for flood forecasting. Hydrol. Sci. J. **52**(1), 114–130 (2007)
2. Daskalaki, E., Prountzou, A., Diem, P., Mougiakakou, S.G.: Real-time adaptive models for the personalized prediction of glycemic profile in type 1 diabetes patients. Diab. Technol. Ther. **14**(2), 168–174 (2012)
3. De Bois, M.: CG-EGA python implementation (2019). https://github.com/dotXem/CG-EGA, https://doi.org/10.5281/zenodo.3459590
4. De Bois, M.: PCLSTM (2019). https://github.com/dotXem/pcLSTM, https://doi.org/10.5281/zenodo.3459566
5. De Bois, M., El Yacoubi, M., Ammi, M.: Study of short-term personalized glucose predictive models on type-1 diabetic children. In: IJCNN (2019, accepted)
6. Dong, G., Fataliyev, K., Wang, L.: One-step and multi-step ahead stock prediction using backpropagation neural networks. In: 2013 9th International Conference on Information, Communications & Signal Processing, pp. 1–5. IEEE (2013)
7. Fokkert, M., et al.: Performance of the freestyle libre flash glucose monitoring system in patients with type 1 and 2 diabetes mellitus. BMJ Open Diabetes Res. Care **5**(1), e000320 (2017)
8. Fritsch, F.N., Carlson, R.E.: Monotone piecewise cubic interpolation. SIAM J. Numer. Anal. **17**(2), 238–246 (1980)
9. Georga, E.I., et al.: Multivariate prediction of subcutaneous glucose concentration in type 1 diabetes patients based on support vector regression. IEEE J. Biomed. Health Inf. **17**(1), 71–81 (2013)
10. Georga, E.I., Protopappas, V.C., Polyzos, D., Fotiadis, D.I.: Online prediction of glucose concentration in type 1 diabetes using extreme learning machines. In: Engineering in Medicine and Biology Society (EMBC), 2015 37th Annual International Conference of the IEEE, pp. 3262–3265. IEEE (2015)
11. Kovatchev, B.P., Gonder-Frederick, L.A., Cox, D.J., Clarke, W.L.: Evaluating the accuracy of continuous glucose-monitoring sensors: continuous glucose-error grid analysis illustrated by therasense freestyle navigator data. Diabetes Care **27**(8), 1922–1928 (2004)
12. Li, C.S.R., Yan, P., Bergquist, K.L., Sinha, R.: Greater activation of the "default" brain regions predicts stop signal errors. Neuroimage **38**(3), 640–648 (2007)
13. Mandic, D.P., Chambers, J.: Recurrent Neural Networks for Prediction: Learning Algorithms, Architectures and Stability. John Wiley & Sons, Inc. (2001)

14. Marling, C., Bunescu, R.: The ohiot1dm dataset for blood glucose level prediction. In: The 3rd International Workshop on Knowledge Discovery in Healthcare Data, Stockholm, Sweden (2018)
15. Martinsson, J., Schliep, A., Eliasson, B., Meijner, C., Persson, S., Mogren, O.: Automatic blood glucose prediction with confidence using recurrent neural networks. In: 3rd International Workshop on Knowledge Discovery in Healthcare Data, KDH@ IJCAI-ECAI 2018, 13 July 2018, pp. 64–68 (2018)
16. Messer, L.H., et al.: Optimizing hybrid closed-loop therapy in adolescents and emerging adults using the minimed 670g system. Diabetes Care **41**(4), 789–796 (2018)
17. Mirshekarian, S., Bunescu, R., Marling, C., Schwartz, F.: Using LSTMS to learn physiological models of blood glucose behavior. In: Engineering in Medicine and Biology Society (EMBC), 2017 39th Annual International Conference of the IEEE, pp. 2887–2891. IEEE (2017)
18. Ólafsdóttir, A.F., et al.: A clinical trial of the accuracy and treatment experience of the flash glucose monitor freestyle libre in adults with type 1 diabetes. Diabetes Technol. Ther. **19**(3), 164–172 (2017)
19. Oviedo, S., Vehí, J., Calm, R., Armengol, J.: A review of personalized blood glucose prediction strategies for t1dm patients. Int. J. Num. Methods Biomed. Eng. **33**(6), e2833 (2017)
20. Rose, K., Koenig, M., Wiesbauer, F.: Evaluating success for behavioral changein diabetes via mhealth and gamification: mysugr's keys to retention andpatient engagement. Diabetes Technol. Ther. **15**, A114 (2013)
21. Shumway, R.H., Stoffer, D.S.: An approach to time series smoothing and forecasting using the em algorithm. J. Time Ser. Anal. **3**(4), 253–264 (1982)
22. Sparacino, G., Zanderigo, F., Corazza, S., Maran, A., Facchinetti, A., Cobelli, C.: Glucose concentration can be predicted ahead in time from continuous glucose monitoring sensor time-series. IEEE Trans. Biomed. Eng. **54**(5), 931–937 (2007)
23. Stahl, F., Johansson, R.: Short-term diabetes blood glucose prediction based on blood glucose measurements. In: 2008 30th Annual International Conference of the IEEE Engineering in Medicine and Biology Society, pp. 291–294. IEEE (2008)
24. Sun, Q., Jankovic, M.V., Bally, L., Mougiakakou, S.G.: Predicting blood glucose with an LSTM and Bi-LSTM based deep neural network. In: 2018 14th Symposium on Neural Networks and Applications (NEUREL), pp. 1–5, November 2018. https://doi.org/10.1109/NEUREL.2018.8586990
25. Valletta, J.J., Chipperfield, A.J., Byrne, C.D.: Gaussian process modelling of blood glucose response to free-living physical activity data in people with type 1 diabetes. In: 2009 Annual International Conference of the IEEE Engineering in Medicine and Biology Society, pp. 4913–4916. IEEE (2009)
26. World Health Organization, et al.: Global Report on Diabetes. World Health Organization (2016)
27. Zarkogianni, K., Vazeou, A., Mougiakakou, S.G., Prountzou, A., Nikita, K.S.: An insulin infusion advisory system based on autotuning nonlinear model-predictive control. IEEE Trans. Biomed. Eng. **58**(9), 2467–2477 (2011)

Teacher-Student Learning and Post-processing for Robust BiLSTM Mask-Based Acoustic Beamforming

Zhaoyi Liu[1(✉)], Qiuyuan Chen[2], Han Hu[3], Haoyu Tang[4], and Y. X. Zou[1]

[1] School of Shenzhen Graduate, Peking University, Shenzhen 518055, China
1701213615@sz.pku.edu.cn
[2] College of Computer Science and Technology, Zhejiang University,
Hangzhou, China
chenqiuyuan@zju.edu.cn
[3] School of Software, Tsinghua University, Beijing, China
hh17@mails.tsinghua.edu.cn
[4] Department of Electronic Systems,
Norwegian University of Science and Technology, 7050 Trondheim, Norway
haoyut@stud.ntnu.no

Abstract. In real-world environments, automatic speech recognition (ASR) is highly affected by reverberation and background noise. A well-known strategy to reduce such adverse interferences in multi-microphone scenarios is microphone array acoustic beamforming. Recently, time-frequency (T-F) mask-based acoustic beamforming receives tremendous interest and has shown great benefits as a front-end for noise-robust ASR. However, the conventional neural network (NN) based T-F mask estimation approaches are only trained in parallel simulated speech corpus, which results in poor performance in the real data testing, where a data mismatch problem occurs. To make the NN-based mask estimation, termed as NN-mask, more robust against data mismatch problem, this paper proposes a bi-directional long short-term memory (BiLSTM) based teacher-student (T-S) learning scheme, termed as BiLSTM-TS, which can utilize the real data during student network training stage. Moreover, in order to further suppress the noise in the beamformed signal, we explore three different mask-based post-processing methods to find a better way to utilize the estimated masks from NN. The proposed approach is evaluated as a front-end for ASR on the CHiME-3 dataset. Experimental results show that the data mismatch problem can be reduced significantly by the proposed strategies, leading to relative 4% Word Error Rates (WER) reduction compared to conventional BiLSTM mask-based beamforming, in the real data test set.

Keywords: Teacher-student learning · Mask estimation · Robust acoustic beamforming · Post-processing · Speech recognition

---

Z. Liu, Q. Chen, H. Hu and H. Tang—Equal contribution.

T. Gedeon et al. (Eds.): ICONIP 2019, LNCS 11955, pp. 522–533, 2019.
https://doi.org/10.1007/978-3-030-36718-3_44

1   Introduction

Automatic speech recognition (ASR) has attracted amounts of attention in recent years with the growing demands for many applications [9,17], such as mobile devices with speech-enabled personal assistants and interaction among smart home devices and people by speech [17]. However, for such real-world far-field practical application scenarios, background noise and reverberation degrades speech quality as well as the performance of the ASR system, especially under low signal-to-noise ratio (SNR) conditions.

Multi-channel speech enhancement [4,8], especially NN-mask for acoustic beamforming [2,7,11], significantly improves the performance of ASR under these circumstances. For example, CHiME-3 and CHiME-4 challenges [1], the NN-mask has been developed for beamforming [2,15], which achieves the state-of-art. In [2], a BiLSTM mask network has been designed and trained. In this study, researchers treat the multi-channel signals separately where one speech mask and one noise mask are learned for one channel signal. Finally, the masks are combined to generate the final mask by median pooling. The beamforming weights are computed as the principal generalized eigenvector of the speech and noise covariance matrices.

In principle, the key idea of those mask-based acoustic beamforming is to estimate a monaural time-frequency (T-F) mask with a well-trained NN in advance, so that the spatial covariance matrices of speech and noise can be derived for beamforming. Therefore, accurately estimating the T-F mask is essential to perform beamforming efficiently. Note that there are two types of NN training T-F mask targets [16]: one is hard mask target, which is a binary mask constructed from premixed speech and noise signals, such as ideal binary mask (IBM); while the second is soft mask target, which contains the probabilistic information among noise signal class and speech signal class, such as ideal ratio mask (IRM). However, the conventional NN-mask only using parallel simulated speech corpus to train shows the poor performance when it predicts masks in the real data testing, where a data mismatch problem occurs [18].

In this paper, in order to reduce the impact of the data mismatch problem of NN-mask, our proposed approach uses bi-directional long short-term memory based teacher-student (BiLSTM-TS) learning [3,10,14] architecture to utilize the real data information in training phase. Specifically, two BiLSTM mask estimation networks, are designed as a teacher network and a student network, respectively. The teacher network is trained with simulated data, and it is then employed to generate the soft labels for both simulated and real data separately. Then, the student network can be trained by the simulated data and real data with generated soft labels from the well-trained teacher network. In addition, in order to further suppress the noise in the beamformed signal, we explore three different mask-based post-processing methods to find a better way to utilize the estimated masks. The proposed approach and mask-based post-processing methods are evaluated on CHiME-3 dataset [1]. Our proposed approach leads to relative 4% average Word Error Rates (WER) reduction compared to conventional BiLSTM mask-based beamforming, in the real data test set.

In summary, our contributions are as follows:

- We propose a BiLSTM-based teacher-student learning scheme for mask estimation (BiLSTM-TS), which enable the NN-based mask estimator to utilize the real training data in the training stage, in order to reduce the impact of the data mismatch problem.
- We explore various mask-based post-processing ways to utilize the estimated masks to further suppress the noise in the beamformed signal.

The remainder of this work is organized as follows: Sect. 2 shows the related work of mask-based acoustic beamforming. Our approach is presented in Sect. 3 in detail. Detailed experimental corpus, metric, setups, and results are discussed in Sect. 4. Finally, Sect. 5 summarizes the conclusions.

2 Background

In the short-time Fourier transform (STFT) domain, the received noisy signal from multiple microphones can be expressed as:

$$\mathbf{Y}_{\tau,\omega} = \mathbf{X}_{\tau,\omega} + \mathbf{N}_{\tau,\omega} \tag{1}$$

where $\mathbf{Y}_{\tau,\omega}$, $X_{\tau,\omega}$ and $\mathbf{N}_{\tau,\omega}$ represent STFT vectors of the noisy signal, clean speech and noise respectively. τ and ω denote time index and frequency channel, respectively. The beamformer applies a linear filter $\mathbf{w}_\omega^{\mathbf{H}}$ to observed noisy signal $\mathbf{Y}_{\tau,\omega}$ to produce an beamformed speech signal, $\tilde{s}_{\tau,\omega}$, as follow:

$$\tilde{s}_{\tau,\omega} = \mathbf{w}_\omega^{\mathbf{H}} \mathbf{Y}_{\tau,\omega} \tag{2}$$

where superscript H denotes conjugate transpose.

Figure 1 shows the diagram of the recently proposed mask-based acoustic beamforming. In the stage of time-frequency mask estimation, multiple microphones receive a set of noisy speech signals, generate a speech mask and a noise mask for each microphone by treating the microphone array as several independent microphones. Then the estimated masks are condensed to a single speech mask and a single noise mask by using a median filter.

With the estimated clean speech mask $M_X(\tau, \omega)$ and noise mask $M_N(\tau, \omega)$ by BiLSTM network, spatial covariance matrices of speech $\Phi_X(\omega)$ and noise $\Phi_N(\omega)$ are computed as:

$$\Phi_v(\omega) = \sum_{\tau=1}^{T} M_v(\tau, \omega) \mathbf{Y}_{\tau,\omega} \mathbf{Y}_{\tau,\omega}^{\mathbf{H}} \qquad \mathbf{v} \in \{\mathbf{X}, \mathbf{N}\} \tag{3}$$

Then these spatial covariance matrices compute beamformer coefficients $\mathbf{w}_\omega$. In this study, we propose to maximize the SNR of the beamformer output in each frequency bin separately leading to the Generalized Eigenvalue (GEV) beamformer [2] with coefficients:

$$\mathbf{w_{GEV}}(\omega) = \underset{\mathbf{w}}{\operatorname{argmax}} \frac{\mathbf{w}^{\mathbf{H}} \Phi_{\mathbf{X}}(\omega) \mathbf{w}}{\mathbf{w}^{\mathbf{H}} \Phi_{\mathbf{N}}(\omega) \mathbf{w}} \tag{4}$$

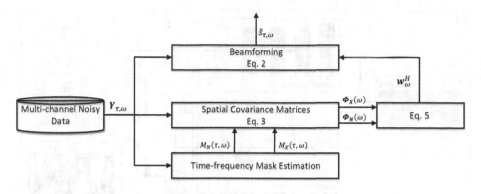

Fig. 1. Processing flow of mask-based beamforming.

This optimization problem is equivalent to solving the following eigenvalue problem:

$$\left\{\Phi_N^{-1}\Phi_X\right\} \mathbf{w_{GEV}}(\omega) = \lambda \mathbf{w_{GEV}}(\omega) \tag{5}$$

where $\mathbf{w_{GEV}}(\omega)$ is the eigenvector of $\left\{\Phi_N^{-1}\Phi_X\right\}$ and λ is the corresponding eigenvalue. Finally, the blind analysis normalization (BAN) [2] is used as a post-filter of beamformer to reduce arbitrary distortion of the GEV beamformer.

3   Approach

3.1   BiLSTM Teacher-Student Learning for Mask Estimation

This work focuses on the data mismatch problem in NN-mask. Considering that the NN-mask is a supervised training which requires target labels in training stage. Hence, parallel speech corpus, such as original clean speech and simulated noisy speech, is required to prepare the corresponding labels. This means the conventional NN-mask can only be trained with simulated data, which may lead to a poor performance of the mask estimation network under the real data conditions where a data mismatch problem occurs. In order to reduce the impact of the data mismatch problem, our idea is quite intuitive that the real data can be pooled with the simulated data in the NN-mask training stage to train a better mask estimation network. In this work, we introduce teacher-student (T-S) scheme to reduce data mismatch problem. The training strategy is that the well-trained teacher network is used as the label generator which processes the original simulated and real data in order to predict soft labels. Then the student network can utilize real-data information and simulated data information to train a mask estimator. Figure 2 illustrates the framework of proposed BiLSTM teacher-student learning (BiLSTM-TS).

Teacher Network. For teacher network, in the training stage, the magnitude spectrum of noisy signal in STFT-domain is given as the input of the teacher network. Note that the teacher network is only trained by using simulated training

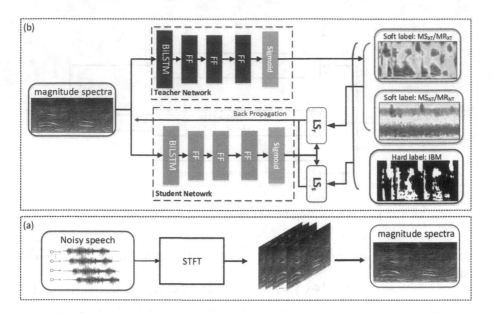

Fig. 2. The framework of our proposed BiLSTM teacher-student learning mask estimation (BiLSTM-TS). (a) **Feature extraction**. Obtain the short-time Fourier transforms (STFT) of the noisy signals and calculate their magnitude spectra $|\mathbf{Y}|_{\tau,\omega}$. (b) **Proposed BiLSTM-TS model**. Use magnitude spectrum of ith channel $Y_i^m(\tau,\omega)$ as the input of NN. The well-trained BiLSTM teacher network generates the estimated clean speech soft labels MS_{XT} and MR_{XT} as well as noise soft label MS_{NT} and MR_{NT} as additional labels to student network.

data. We employ the ideal binary mask (IBM) as the training target. There are two types of IBM are estimated: one is the clean speech mask $IBM_X(\tau,\omega) \in 0,1$, the other is the noise mask $IBM_N(\tau,\omega) \in 0,1$, which are defined as:

$$\mathbf{IBM_N} = \begin{cases} 1, & \frac{\|X(\tau,\omega)\|}{\|N(\tau,\omega)\|} < 10^{th_N}, \\ 0, & else. \end{cases} \tag{6}$$

$$\mathbf{IBM_X} = \begin{cases} 1, & \frac{\|X(\tau,\omega)\|}{\|N(\tau,\omega)\|} > 10^{th_X}, \\ 0, & else. \end{cases} \tag{7}$$

where $\|X(\tau,\omega)\| \in \mathbb{R}_{\geqslant 0}$ and $\|N(\tau,\omega)\| \in \mathbb{R}_{\geqslant 0}$ are power spectra of the clean speech signal and the noise signal at each T-F unit (τ,ω), respectively. To obtain the better results, the two thresholds th_X and th_N are manually selected to be different from each other.

The teacher network is trained to predict the clean speech mask $MS_{XT}(\tau,\omega) \in [0,1]$ and $MR_{XT}(\tau,\omega) \in [0,1]$ as well as the noise mask $MS_{NT}(\tau,\omega) \in [0,1]$ and $MR_{NT}(\tau,\omega) \in [0,1]$ at each T-F bin (τ,ω). We use the NN proposed in [2] as the architecture of our teacher network, including a

BiLSTM layer followed with three-feed forward layers. Table 1 shows the configurations of teacher network.

Table 1. Configurations of BiLSTM teacher mask network.

Layer	Units	Type	Activation	Dropout
L1	256	BiLSTM	Tanh	0.5
L2	513	Feedforward 1	ReLU	0.5
L3	513	Feedforward 2	ReLU	0.5
L4	1026	Feedforward 3	Sigmoid	0.0

We use the binary cross-entropy (BCE) as the loss function of teacher network which is defined as:

$$Loss = BCE(IBM_v, M_{vT})$$

$$\overset{def}{=} \frac{1}{T}\frac{1}{W} \sum_{v \in \{X,N\}} \sum_{\tau=1}^{T} \sum_{\omega=1}^{W} IBM_v(\tau,\omega) log(M_{vT}(\tau,\omega)) \qquad (8)$$

$$+ (1 - IBM_v(\tau,\omega))log(1 - M_{vT}(\tau,\omega))$$

As shown in Fig. 2, in our design, the well-trained teacher network is used as the soft label generator for the real data and the simulated data. Then the student network can utilize the generated masks of clean speech $M_{XT}(\tau,\omega)$ and noise $M_{NT}(\tau,\omega)$ as the soft labels.

Student Network. The structure of the student network is the same as the teacher network described in Sect. 3.1. In the training stage of student network, we use different loss functions to train our SMM with the simulated data and the real-recording data, respectively. For simulated data, we consider the following lost functions for speech LS_{sX} and noise LS_{sN}, as follow:

$$LS_{sX} = (1 - \pi)BCE(IBM_X(\tau,\omega), MS_{XS}(\tau,\omega))$$
$$+ \pi BCE(MS_{XT}(\tau,\omega), MS_{XS}(\tau,\omega)) \qquad (9)$$

$$LS_{sN} = (1 - \pi)BCE(IBM_N(\tau,\omega), MS_{NS}(\tau,\omega))$$
$$+ \pi BCE(MX_{NT}(\tau,\omega), MS_{NS}(\tau,\omega)) \qquad (10)$$

where $MS_{XS}(\tau,\omega)$ and $MS_{NS}(\tau,\omega)$ denotes the estimated clean speech mask and noise mask by student network, respectively. The hyper-parameter π is the imitation parameter adjusting the relative attention of two type of targets. The $IBM_X(\tau,\omega)$ and $IBM_N(\tau,\omega)$ are the hard mask labels of speech and noise, respectively. The final cost function of SMM for simulated data, termed as L_{Ss} is expressed as:

$$LS_s = (LS_{sX} + LS_{sN})/2 \qquad (11)$$

For real data, the conventional NN-mask can only utilize parallel data combined by the clean speech and noise, which are not usually obtained in the practical application. However, the student network is able to obtain the soft labels of the real data generated by teacher network. Therefore, the loss function for the student network for real data, termed as LS_r, is defined as:

$$LS_r = [BCE(MR_{XT}(\tau, \omega), MR_{XS}(\tau, \omega)) \\ + BCE(MR_{NT}(\tau, \omega), MR_{NS}(\tau, \omega))]/2 \tag{12}$$

where $MR_{XS}(\tau, \omega)$ and $MR_{NS}(\tau, \omega)$ represent the estimated noise mask and clean speech mask by student network, respectively.

With this setup, the student network has been trained on the simulated data and real-recording data with loss LS_s and loss LS_r, respectively. When the student predicts the clean speech mask and noise mask for each microphone channel, we calculate the beamforming coefficients using the method shown in Sect. 2.

3.2   Mask-Based Post-processing

For the beamformer, the aim of the method is to improve the signal-to-noise ratio (SNR) without distorted the clean speech, but it is hard to completely eliminate the noise. There are many post-processing approaches can be utilized to eliminate the noise in the beamformed speech, and obtain the extra enhanced signals. However, the enhanced speech need to avoid being distorted to further improve the ASR performance. We explore three different mask-based post-processing for the beamformed speech:

1. Apply the estimated clean speech mask $M_X(\tau, \omega)$ directly (**direct-mask**), after beamforming as post-processing. After this post-processing, we can obtain enhanced speech $\tilde{x}_{\tau, \omega}$ as follow:

$$\tilde{x}_{\tau, \omega} = \tilde{s}_{\tau, \omega} \odot M_X(\tau, \omega) \tag{13}$$

where $\odot$ presents dot multiplication. And the M_X is estimated by the mask estimation network.

2. In order to simultaneously control the noise reduction level and speech distortion, the beamformed speech $\tilde{s}_{\tau, \omega}$ can be conditionally used $M_X(\tau, \omega)$ by piecewise function (**condition-mask**) as follows:

$$\tilde{x}_{\tau, \omega} = \begin{cases} \tilde{s}_{\tau, \omega} & M_X(\tau, \omega) \geqslant 0.8 \\ \tilde{s}_{\tau, \omega} \odot M_X(\tau, \omega) & 0.2 \leqslant M_X(\tau, \omega) < 0.8 \\ \tilde{s}_{\tau, \omega} \odot 0.2 & otherwise \end{cases} \tag{14}$$

Note that the value of $M_X(\tau, \omega)$ are real numbers within the range [0,1]. If the value of estimated $M_X(\tau, \omega)$ is very large indicating that it has very high SNR at certain T-F unit, it is not necessary to perform noise reduction which can potentially result in the speech distortion.

3. Apply the **threshold-mask** post-processing method. Firstly, we compute the global SNR for each frequency ω, termed as $gSNR(\omega)$, as follow:

$$gSNR(\omega) = 10log_{10}\frac{\sum_{\tau=1}^{T} M_X(\tau,\omega)\tilde{s}_{\tau,\omega}^2}{\sum_{\tau=1}^{T} M_N(\tau,\omega)\tilde{s}_{\tau,\omega}^2} \qquad (15)$$

Secondly, we use $gSNR(\omega)$ to calculate a threshold, $th(\omega)$, as:

$$th(\omega) = \frac{1}{1 + e^{(\alpha gSNR - \beta)/\gamma}} \qquad (16)$$

The Eq. (16) is a sigmoidal function, hence the threshold is ranged $[0,1]$. We use parameters α, β and γ to adjust the shape of the sigmoidal function. Through cross-validation, their values are set to 1.5, -5 and 2, respectively. Then, the threshold-mask can be obtained, termed as $M_{th}(\tau,\omega)$, as:

$$M_{th}(\tau,\omega) = M_X(\tau,\omega)^{th(\omega)} \qquad (17)$$

From Eqs. (16) and (17), we can find that when $gSNR(\omega)$ is high the value of $th(\omega)$ will be close 0. This makes the threshold-mask $M_{th}(\tau,\omega)$ be close to 1, which is independent of the value of clean speech mask $M_X(\tau,\omega)$. If not, $M_{th}(\tau,\omega)$ is close to $M_X(\tau,\omega)$ when $gSNR(\omega)$ is low. Finally, we can obtain the enhanced speech $\tilde{x}_{\tau,\omega}$ by:

$$\tilde{x}_{\tau,\omega} = \tilde{s}_{\tau,\omega} \odot M_{th}(\tau,\omega) \qquad (18)$$

4   Experiments

In this work, we evaluate the proposed acoustic beamforming approach on ASR tasks using the CHiME-3 corpus [1]. The proposed algorithm is used as a frontend for ASR systems.

4.1   Corpus

CHiME-3. The CHiME-3 corpus includes real and simulated data generated by artificially mixing the incorporations of Wall Street Journal (WSJ) corpus [5] sentences spoken with 4 different noisy environments which selected: cafe (CAFE), street junction (STR), public transport (BUS) and pedestrian area (PED). This corpus is recorded by using a 6-channel microphone array attached to a tablet device. The corpus is divided into 3 respective subset:

- Training set: composing 8738 (1600 real + 7138 simulated) noisy utterances.
- Development set (dt_05): containing 3280 (1640 real + 1640 simulated) noisy utterances.
- Evaluation set (et_05): including 2640 (1320 real + 1320 simulated) noisy utterances.

4.2 Metric

Word Error Rate (WER). WER is a common metric to evaluate the performance of ASR system [6]. The WER compares a reference to an hypothesis and is defined as:

$$WER = \frac{S + D + I}{N} \tag{19}$$

where S is the number of substitutions, D is the number of deletions, I is the number of insertions and N is the number of total words in the reference. The lower the value of WER, the better the ASR performance.

4.3 Experimental Setups

To compare the performance of different masking models, the standard back-end ASR provided by the CHiME-3 challenge is directly used, which contains based on a relatively simple Gaussian Mixture Model (GMM) acoustic model [12] trained using Kaldi speech recognition toolkit [13]. For language model, A standard the Wall Street Journal (WSJ) speaker-independent medium-vocabulary (5K) word tri-gram language model is used for decoding in this work. We use a common metric word error rate (WER) to denote the performance of ASR.

4.4 Evaluation on BiLSTM-TS

As frontend processing, the mask-based beamforming approach proposed by Heymann *et al.* [2] which is described in Sect. 2 as well as set as our teacher network, is used for comparison with our proposed student models with different values of hyper-parameter π.

Table 2. Comparison of the performance (%WER) of different mask estimation networks for ASR systems on CHiME-3.

Parameters	BiLSTM mask	DEV		EVAL	
		simu	*real*	*simu*	*real*
−	Baseline/Teacher	10.8	11.97	11.59	17.97
$\pi = 0.0$	Student	10.87	11.84	11.62	17.34
$\pi = 0.2$	Student	10.61	11.67	11.84	16.89
$\pi = 0.5$	Student	10.2	11.26	11.79	15.53
$\pi = 0.8$	Student	10.4	10.78	9.96	14.75
$\pi = 1.0$	Student	**8.4**	**9.37**	**8.89**	**13.79**

The results of these experiments are shown in Table 2. From the results, we can see that the performance of most student models with different configurations are better than that of the teacher network as expected, although the teacher model has already been robust. The results also reveal that except for the student model with hyper-parameter $\pi = 0.0$, the improvements are largely achieved not only on the real test condition but also on the simulated test condition. This is an interesting finding, since the data mismatch problem between the original simulation training and the test conditions is small, only adding the real data in the training actually increases the mismatch for the simulated test conditions. Specifically, adding the teacher-student (T-S) learning scheme results in a relative improvement rate of up to 4.1% and 2.7% for the real and simulated evaluation data, respectively. In contrast, utilizing T-S learning scheme can reduce the impact of the data mismatch problem of mask estimation for acoustic beamforming by pooling real data with simulated data in the training stage with soft labels from teacher model, thus contributes to better performance for real applications.

4.5   Evaluation on Different Post-processing Methods

We also compared the three different mask-based post-processing methods described in Sect. 4 on two BiLSTM mask estimation networks for beamforming by using same ASR back-end. In detail, the two BiLSTM mask models are the teacher model and the student model with hyper-parameter $\pi = 0.0$. And we use the BiLSTM teacher model and student model without the post-processing as the baselines.

Table 3 lists the ASR performance of direct-mask, condition mask and threshold-mask approaches. First, for the direct-mask method, we can find that since directly applying the mask to the beamformed signal is very sensitive to the mask estimation error. And the performance of direct-mask method underperforms that of the baselines. Second, for the condition-mask method, the results of this method show the improvements on the real data, while the performances

Table 3. Comparison of the performance (%WER) of the BiLSTM teacher and student mask estimation network with direct-mask, condition mask, and threshold-mask methods as well as without post-processing for ASR systems on CHiME3.

BiLSTM MASK	Post-processing	DEV		EVAL	
		simu	*real*	*simu*	*real*
Baseline	None	10.8	11.97	11.59	17.97
Student	None	**8.4**	9.37	**8.89**	13.79
Baseline	Direct-mask	12.37	13.12	13.01	19.85
Student	Direct-mask	11.81	12.58	10.36	16.27
Baseline	Condition-mask	10.27	11.43	11.63	17.86
Student	Condition-mask	8.22	9.35	9.09	13.52
Baseline	Threshold-mask	10.97	12.08	11.27	17.42
Student	Threshold-mask	8.42	**8.96**	9.1	**13.46**

of condition-mask post-processing on the simulated data are slightly decreased. From the results of the threshold-mask method, we can find that threshold-mask post-processing for beamformed speech can suppress the noise, which can further improve the ASR performance for both real-recording data and simulated data.

5 Conclusion

In this work, motivated by the data mismatch problem for NN-based mask estimation acoustic beamforming results from training simulated data and testing real data, we propose BiLSTM teacher-student learning (BiLSTM-TS) approach. With the aim of utilizing the real record data in mask estimation training, the T-S is applied on the real record data to produce the soft labels, hence the real data can be combined with the simulated data for mask estimation. Experimental results show that, as a frontend, the student model of BiLSTM-TS improves ASR performance. Furthermore, through exploring the different mask-based post-processing methods, we find that the threshold-mask can further suppress the noise in the beamformed signal. For the future work, by using strong ASR back-end, we believe that the ASR performance can be further improved.

References

1. Barker, J., Marxer, R., Vincent, E., Watanabe, S.: The third 'CHiME' speech separation and recognition challenge: analysis and outcomes. Comput. Speech Lang. **46**, 605–626 (2017)
2. Heymann, J., Drude, L., Haebumbach, R.: Neural network based spectral mask estimation for acoustic beamforming. In: IEEE International Conference on Acoustics, Speech and Signal Processing (ICASSP), pp. 196–200 (2016)
3. Hinton, G.E., Vinyals, O., Dean, J.: Distilling the knowledge in a neural network. arXiv Machine Learning (2015)
4. Hoshen, Y., Weiss, R.J., Wilson, K.W.: Speech acoustic modeling from raw multichannel waveforms. In: IEEE International Conference on Acoustics, Speech and Signal Processing (ICASSP) (2015)
5. Garofalo, J., Graff, D., Paul, D., Pallett, D.: CSR-I (WSJ0) complete. Linguistic Data Consortium, Philadelphia (2007)
6. Klakow, D., Peters, J.: Testing the correlation of word error rate and perplexity. Speech Commun. **38**(1), 19–28 (2002)
7. Kubo, Y., Nakatani, T., Delcroix, M., Kinoshita, K., Araki, S.: Mask-based MVDR beamformer for noisy multisource environments: introduction of time-varying spatial covariance model. In: IEEE International Conference on Acoustics, Speech and Signal Processing (ICASSP) (2019)
8. Kumatani, K., Mcdonough, J.W., Raj, B.: Microphone array processing for distant speech recognition: from close-talking microphones to far-field sensors. IEEE Signal Process. Mag. **29**(6), 127–140 (2012)
9. Mofrad, M.H., Mosse, D.: Speech recognition and voice separation for the Internet of Things. In: Proceedings of the 8th International Conference on the Internet of Things, p. 8 (2018)

10. Mosner, L., et al.: Improving noise robustness of automatic speech recognition via parallel data and teacher-student learning. In: IEEE International Conference on Acoustics, Speech and Signal Processing (ICASSP) (2019)
11. Pfeifenberger, L., Zohrer, M., Pernkopf, F.: DNN-based speech mask estimation for eigenvector beamforming. In: IEEE International Conference on Acoustics, Speech and Signal Processing (ICASSP) (2017)
12. Povey, D., et al.: The subspace Gaussian mixture model-a structured model for speech recognition. Comput. Speech Lang. **25**(2), 404–439 (2011)
13. Povey, D., et al.: The Kaldi speech recognition toolkit. In: IEEE Workshop on Automatic Speech Recognition and Understanding (ASRU) (2011)
14. Subramanian, A.S., Chen, S.J., Watanabe, S.: Student-teacher learning for BLSTM mask-based speech enhancement. In: Interspeech, pp. 3249–3253 (2018)
15. Tu, Y., Du, J., Sun, L., Ma, F., Lee, C.: On design of robust deep models for CHiME-4 multi-channel speech recognition with multiple configurations of array microphones. In: INTERSPEECH, pp. 394–398 (2017)
16. Wang, D., Chen, J.: Supervised speech separation based on deep learning: an overview. IEEE Trans. Audio Speech Lang. Process. **26**(10), 1702–1726 (2018)
17. Yu, D., Li, J.: Recent progresses in deep learning based acoustic models. IEEE/CAA J. Autom. Sin. **4**(3), 396–409 (2017)
18. Zhou, Y., Qian, Y.: Robust mask estimation by integrating neural network-based and clustering-based approaches for adaptive acoustic beamforming. In: IEEE International Conference on Acoustics, Speech and Signal Processing (ICASSP), pp. 536–540 (2018)

Maxout into MDLSTM for Offline Arabic Handwriting Recognition

Rania Maalej[1](✉) 🆔 and Monji Kherallah[2]

[1] National School of Engineers of Sfax, University of Sfax, Sfax, Tunisia
rania.mlj@gmail.com
[2] Faculty of Sciences, Sfax University, Sfax, Tunisia

Abstract. Research on Arabic handwriting recognition has been seriously challenged due to its cursive appearance, the variety of writers and the diversity of styles. In fact, motivated by a series of success cases in computer vision, we try to explore the Maxout units in Multidirectional neural networks for the offline task. Therefore, in this work, we model an Arabic handwritten word with a deep MDLSTM-based system. This architecture can directly work on raw input images since it enables us to model the script variations on both axes of the image due to recurrence over them. However, several problems, such as the vanishing gradient, can affect the training of this recognition system. To overcome this problem, we should integrate Maxout units into MDLSTM system in order to enhance it and improve its performance. In this context, different integration modes are carried out to draw out the best topology. Proposed systems are evaluated on a large database IFN/ENIT. According to the experimental results and compared to the baseline system, the best tested architecture reduced the label error rate by 6.86%.

Keywords: LSTM · MDLSTM · Maxout · Offline Arabic handwriting recognition

1 Introduction

Recurrent Neural Network (RNN) is a powerful learning model that achieves state-of-the-art results in a wide range of computer vision and deep neural network-based solution. In particular, the Long Short-Term Memory (LSTM) [1] has been a very successful recurrent neural network architecture in various recognition systems. The LSTM units enable the network to store information for longer amounts of time. Besides, an LSTM unit is integrated into the Multi-Dimensional Recurrent Neural Network (MDRNN), which generalize the standard RNN by providing recurrent connections along all spatio-temporal dimensions present in the input data. The MDRNN's connections enable the network to create a flexible representation of the context. Then, the combination of the MDRNN and LSTM, which has been used to achieve state of the art results in offline handwriting recognition systems [2], is called the Multi-Dimensional Long Short-Term Memory MDLSTM [3]. However, the deep MDLSTM architecture can suffer from the vanishing gradient problem which can be solved by integrating Maxout units with different locations and group size in order to

© Springer Nature Switzerland AG 2019
T. Gedeon et al. (Eds.): ICONIP 2019, LNCS 11955, pp. 534–545, 2019.
https://doi.org/10.1007/978-3-030-36718-3_45

draw out the best topology that improves the accuracy of the baseline system, based on MDLSTM, for offline Arabic handwriting recognition. The obtained recognition systems have been tested and compared on the IFN/ENIT corpus [4].

The remainder of the paper is organized as follows. Section 2 introduces the MDLSTM network and explains how it outperforms for Arabic offline handwriting recognition. Section 3 describes the Maxout units and their different integration modes into the baseline system. The experiments and results are presented in Sect. 4. Finally, the conclusion is drawn and some future perspectives are suggested in Sect. 5.

2 MDLSTM Baseline System Overview

Recently, MDLSTM networks, which can deal with higher-dimensional data, were won handwriting recognition competitions [5, 6]. In fact, recognition systems based on MDLSTM have been shown to yield promising results due to recurrence used over both axes of an input image which allows to model the writing variations on both axes and to directly work on raw input images. Several works were done to improve the MDLSTM performance, for a better offline Arabic handwriting recognition system, such as applying dropout technique during training [7] to prevent network from overfitting. Indeed, dropout improves the network performance and significantly reduces the error rate when it is applied before, after or between LSTM layers [8] (Table 1).

Table 1. MDLSTM-based recognition systems comparison with IFN/ENIT database

Approach	Label Error Rate (LER)
Baseline system: MDLSTM w/CTC	16.97%
MDLSTM w/CTC w/dropout 1 [7]	12.09%
MDLSTM w/CTC w/dropout 2 [8]	11.62%

MDLSTM layers are composed by several LSTM nodes. Each one consists of multiple recurrent connections, called memory blocks (see Fig. 1). Each block contains a set of internal cells, whose activation is controlled by three multiplicative 'gate' units. those gates allow the cells to store and to access information over long periods of time.

Network computes the input gate i, the forget gate f, the cell activation vectors c, the output gate o and the hidden vector sequence h. where W denotes weight matrices, the b terms denotes bias vectors, τ and ϕ are *Tanh* functions and σ is the logistic sigmoid function.

$$i_t = \sigma(W_{xi}x_t + W_{hi}h_{t-1} + W_{ci}c_{t-1} + b_i) \tag{1}$$

$$f_t = \sigma(W_{xf}x_t + W_{hf}h_{t-1} + W_{cf}c_{t-1} + b_f) \tag{2}$$

$$a_t = \tau(W_{xc}x_t + W_{hc}h_{t-1} + b_c) \tag{3}$$

$$c_t = f_t c_{t-1} + i_t tanh(W_{xc}x_t + W_{hc}h_{t-1} + b_c) \tag{4}$$

$$o_t = \sigma(W_{xo}x_t + W_{ho}h_{t-1} + W_{co}c_t + b_o) \tag{5}$$

$$h_t = o_t \phi(c_t) \tag{6}$$

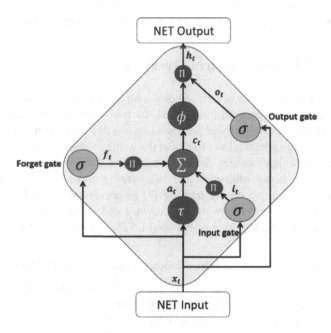

Fig. 1. LSTM memory cell

To recognize offline handwriting script, and when we need to use images as input data for neural networks, we need to put the images on a vertical line at a time so that input images can be converted into a 1D series. It would therefore be unlikely for the recognition system to manage deformations along the vertical axis. In fact, a simple one-pixel transformation of an image makes it regarded as a new image by the process.

In this context, the proposed MDRNN [3] is an easier solution that consists in presenting a special case of a directed acyclic graph network, which is a stronger generalization of a standard RNN by offering recurrent connections across all the spatio-temporal dimensions found in the data. (Figure 2 shows the case of two dimensional MDRNN). Such links enable the network to build an internal dynamic internal representation, which makes the system strong to handle distortions such as image rotations and shears. The MDRNN allows to model multidimensional context in a flexible way. In fact, there are four parallel MDRNN layers that process each input in one of the four possible directions (Fig. 2). Then, the four directions will be brought together to get the full context from all directions at every spatial position.

The hidden state $h(i, j)$ for position (i, j) of an MDRNN layer is computed based on the previous hidden states $h(i - 1, j)$ and $h(i, j - 1)$ of both axes and the current input x (i, j) by

$$h(i, j) = \sigma(W \, x(i, j) + I \, h(i - 1, j) + J \, h(i, j - 1) + b) \tag{7}$$

where W, I and J are weight matrices, b a bias vector and σ a nonlinear activation function.

To make network able to access long-range context, a Multidimensional LSTM is proposed, this neural network is the combination of two networks: LSTM and MDRNN.

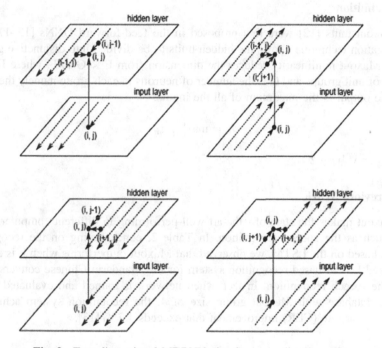

Fig. 2. Two dimensional MDRNN give four scan directions [3].

The challenge with MDLSTM network is to transform two-dimensional images into one-dimensional label sequences. This problem can be solved by the use of a hierarchy structure of MDLSTM layers. In fact, the data is transmitted through recurrent layers with blocks of activations gathered together after each level. The heights of the blocks are fixed to incrementally collapse the 2D images into 1D sequences able to be labelled by the output layer. The output layer based on CTC [9] is added to the MDLSTM network to label non-segmented sequence data. In fact, the CTC layer allows the network to directly map input sequences to the conditional probabilities of possible labelling. Their activations are interpreted as the probabilities of observing the corresponding characters at specific timesteps. The CTC-based output layer has 121 units, 120 of which are required to present our 120 labels. The last one's activation is the chance of no observation or 'blank' observation. By adding all the possible probabilities, this output layer can easily interpret all possible ways of aligning each label sequence.

The MDLSTM is a deep feedforward neural network, however, despite the use of powerful LSTM units, MDLSTM network can suffer from the vanishing gradient problem [10, 11], which can be solved by adding Maxout units in different locations in this network in order to draw out the best one that improves the baseline system.

3   Maxout

3.1   Definition

The Maxout units [12] were first proposed in the feed-forward DNNs [13–17] This regularization technique allows the hidden units to be divided into disjunctive groups. So, the Maxout nonlinearity reduces the dimension from F × G to F, where F is the number of unit groups and G is the number of neurons in each group namely the group size. The output is the maximum of all the inputs:

$$h_i = \max_{i=1}^{G} z_{ij} \tag{8}$$

where $z_{ij} = x^T W_{ij} + b_{ij}$

3.2   Previous Work

The Maxout makes the state-of - the-art well-performing in different computer vision tasks, such as the speech recognition. In Table 2, concentrating on the recognition systems based on the LSTM, we observed that Maxout outperforms when it is applied on stacked LSTM-based recognition system for the Mandarin Chinese conversational telephone speech recognition. In fact, when network is trained and evaluated on the HKUST database with Maxout group size of 4, the recognition system achieves a character error rate (CER) improvement that exceeds 1.75%[13].

Table 2. Error recognition rate reduced with Maxout.

Authors	Network	Error rate	Dataset	Reduction
Li and Wu [13]	Stacked LSTM	CER	HKUST	1.75%
Cai and Liu [18]	LSTM	CER	Cantonais	1.7%
Cai and Liu [18]	LSTM	SER	Vietnamiens	1.8%
Cai and Liu [18]	LSTM	WER	Pashto	2.4%
Cai and Liu [18]	LSTM	WER	Turque	2.5%
Cai and Liu [18]	LSTM	WER	Tagalog	2.2%
Cai and Liu [18]	LSTM	WER	Tamil	1.6%
Maalej and kherallah [19]	BLSTM (1)	LER	ADAB	10.62%
Maalej and kherallah [19]	BLSTM (2)	LER	ADAB	10.99%

Similarly, according to [18], the Maxout operates well on the IARPA Babel datasets in recognition of six different languages. In fact, this function reduces the Cantonese Character Error Rate (CER) by 1.7% and the Vietnamese Syllable Error Rate (SER) by 1.8%. On the other hand, the Maxout function decreases the Pashto Word Error Rate (WER) by 2.4%, the Turkish one by 2.5%, the Tagalog by 2.2% and the Tamil by 1.6%. Such recurrent Maxout neural networks are trained with a dropout rate of 0.2 added only on the fully-connected layers.

Moreover, for an online Arabic handwriting recognition system based on BLSTM [19], two modes of Maxout integration are proposed. First, Maxout function is used inside the LSTM nodes, with the Maxout group size of 3, the Label Error Rate (LER) of 23.78% are founded, hence the error rate reduction reaches 10.62%; in a second step Maxout layers are stacked after the BLSTM layers and this last architecture was the most powerful and the reduction in the label error rate reached 10.99%.

According to these previous works, we can conclude that the Maxout is an elegant activation function that significantly enhance LSTM-based systems. In next section, we presented the two different ways of the Maxout integration into baseline system based on the MDLSTM of the offline Arabic handwriting recognition.

3.3   Architecture of Maxout on MDLSTM

Two approaches have been suggested to connect the Maxout to our MDLSTM network-based recognition system. The first is to add the Maxout function within the LSTM unit, whereas the second consists in adding a Maxout layer in feedforwards layers, after each MDLSTM layers.

3.3.1   Maxout Inside LSTM Units

Certainly, the Maxout enhances the performance of several LSTM-based recognition systems. Indeed, this technique was found to be well suited inside the LSTM unit and we attempted to use it to improve the accuracy of the offline Arabic handwriting recognition system based on the MDLSTM.

In order to avoid the explosion of the hidden state activation over time and calculate the hidden state at each step, the recurrent neural network uses mostly saturating nonlinear activation functions, such as the *Tanh*, which results in a more stable dynamic learning system. Hence, at the first thought, this does not enable us to create an LSTM network with a non-saturating activation function, such as the Maxout.

Nonetheless, when we investigated the structure of the LSTM (see Fig. 1), we discovered that this RNN uses self-connected unbounded internal memory cells that are kept by multiplicative non-linear gates. In fact, apart from the activation of these three gates, two non-linear functions τ and ϕ in our system are a saturating non-linearity *Tanh*. On the other hand, since the output is the multiplication of the ϕ output vector and the o_t output gate, in this ϕ non-linear function there will no longer a dimension reduction. As a consequence, we can add a Maxout unit rather than the τ function (see Fig. 3).

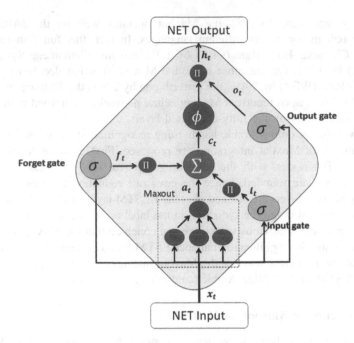

Fig. 3. LSTM with Maxout group Size of 3.

Moreover, Maxout improves the efficiency of different recognition systems based on LSTM. In fact, since this technique is found to be well adapted to the LSTM networks, we are trying to use it to improve the accuracy of the MDLSTM-based offline Arabic handwriting recognition system.

The output activation ϕ in Eq. (6) is keeping the same saturating nonlinearity function *tanh*, in this proposed network. Therefore, the hidden states h_t are kept bounded for the memory blocks. Consequently, we can allocate any non-saturating nonlinear function for τ, such as the Maxout non-linearity. For Eq. (3), the formula for cell output activation will be:

$$a_t = \max_{i=1}^{G}(W_{xci}x_t + W_{hci}h_{t-1} + b_{ci}) \tag{9}$$

Where G is the group size.

3.3.2   Maxout in Feedforward Layers on MDLSTM

The second way to integrate Maxout into MDLSTM network is to add Maxout units in feedforward layers as illustrated in Fig. 4. We get a hybrid model that can be called a recurrent Maxout network, it combines MDLSTM and Maxout layers. The MDLSTM network is used in the lower layers of this recognition system, to model the long-term dependencies of the data at the input. Fully connected layers with Maxout neurons are used after LSTM recurrent layers and finally, the CTC layer is used as an output layer. This architecture has already proven its success in the field of voice recognition [18].

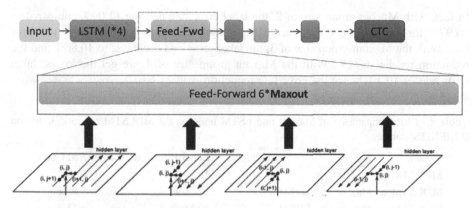

Fig. 4. MDLSTM with Maxout in feedforward layers.

4   Experimental Results

4.1   IFN/ENIT Database

The IFN/ENIT Database [4] contains 32492 images of Arabic words written by more than 1000 writers, which are used to validate and compare different proposed architectures. Those words are the names of 937 Tunisian towns and villages. The IFN/ENIT database is divided in 5 sets (see Table 3). To compare our architectures with those of other systems we chose the same circumstances. In fact, *set a, b* and *c* are used for training while *set d* and *e* are used for testing. The IFN/ENIT database was triumphantly exploited by several research groups as it was used for offline Arabic handwriting recognition competition in ICDAR 2009 [6].

Table 3. The IFN/ENIT dataset.

Sets	Words	Characters
a	6537	51984
b	6710	53862
c	6477	52155
d	6735	54166
e	6033	45169

In order to integrate Maxout into the baseline recognition system based on MDLSTM, two methods are detailed in Sect. 3. The first is to add the Maxout function inside LSTM nodes and the second method is to switch from *tanh* to Maxout at the activation function in the feed-forward layers.

4.2   Maxout Inside LSTM Units

As illustrated in Table 4, Maxout decreases the label error rate of the offline handwriting recognition system based on MDLSTM when it is added inside LSTM nodes.

In fact, with Maxout group size of 2, the label error rate became 11.09% compared to 16.97% for the baseline system, achieving a significant 5.88% reduction in the error rate. With the Maxout group size of 3, the label error rate decreases to 10.86% and the reduction reaches 6.11%. With the Maxout group size of 4, we get the lowest label error rate of 10.3% hence the error rate reduction reaches 6.67%.

Table 4. LER comparaison of Maxout into LSTM node on the MDLSTM network, tested on IFN/ENIT database.

System	Group size	Label Error Rate (LER)	Reduction
MDLSTM baseline system	–	16.97%	–
MDLSTM w\ Maxout into LSTM	2	11.09%	5.88%
MDLSTM w\ Maxout into LSTM	3	10.86%	6.11%
MDLSTM w\ Maxout into LSTM	4	**10.30%**	**6.67%**

Table 4 shows that Maxout significantly improves the performance of our offline Arabic handwriting recognition system based on MDLSTM for all three examinated group sizes. It is worth noting that the lowest error rate was reached with the group size of 4.

4.3 Maxout Nodes in Feedforward Layers

Regarding the second MDLSTM extension manner with Maxout, it is worth noting that when added, the Maxout layer reduces the label error rate of the offline handwriting recognition system, firstly with group size of 2 to achieve a substantial reduction of the error rate by 6.37%, the formed label error rate is 10.60% when it was equivalent to 16.97% for the baseline system. Secondly, the group size of 3 to achieve a better reduction of the error rate of 6.44%, given that the new founded label error rate is 10.53%. Thirdly, with group size of 4, to achieve the best reduction, which this architecture that reaches 6.86%, given the 10.11% new label error rate.

Table 5. LER comparaison of Maxout layers with MDLSTM network tested on IFN/ENIT database.

System	Group size	Label Error Rate	Reduction
MDLSTM baseline system	0	16.97%	–
Maxout layers with MDLSTM	2	10.60%	6.37%
Maxout layers with MDLSTM	3	10.53%	6.44%
Maxout layers with MDLSTM	4	**10.11%**	**6.86%**

As illustrated in Table 5, we can therefore conclude that adding of the Maxout layers in the MDLSTM network significantly reduces the label error rate. In fact, the lowest error rate was achieved with a size of group equal to 4.

Finally, we found that our solution for offline Arabic handwriting recognition, which is based on a deep learning architecture combining MDLSTM and Maxout units, gives a competitive result against the other systems, as illustrated in Table 6. In fact, the label error rate of a recognition system based on the Dynamic Bayesian Network reached 18% [20], while the one based on MDLSTM with CTC and on which dropout is applied was 11.62%. However, for a hybrid recognition system with CNN and HMM, the label error rate was 10.77%. In fact, all cited research studies gave worse results than the present work in which the recognition system is based on Maxout and MDLSTM as the LER reached 10.11%. On the other hand, a hybrid system based on CNN-BLSTM and trained with an extended IFN/ENIT database, created by some augmentation data techniques, has the best label error rate estimated at 7.79%.

Table 6. Comparison of offline Arabic handwriting recognition systems trained and tested with IFN/ENIT database.

Authors	Networks	Label Error Rate
Jayech et al. [20]	Dynamic Bayesian network	18.00%
Maalej et al. [8]	MDLSTM w/CTC w/dropout	11.62%
Amrouch et al. [21]	CNN-HMM	10.77%
Maalej et al. [22]	CNN-BLSTM	07.79%
Present work	MDLSTM-Maxout	**10.11%**

5 Conclusions

In this paper, we have proposed on offline Arabic handwriting recognition system based on the architecture of MDLSTM. We have integrated Maxout units in the MDLSTM to counter against vanishing gradients problem common to deep neural networks. Two methods of Maxout incorporation are tested and compared with different Maxout group sizes. First, we added a Maxout unit inside the LSTM units instead of τ the tanh function. The best result was recorded with group size of 4. The second way to combine Maxout with MDLSTM is to add Maxout units in the feedforward layers instead of the sigmoid functions. The performance of the new system outdoes the MDLSTM baseline system and the reduction of the error label rate, which reached 6.86%. As a future perspective, we propose to evaluate the effect of other regularization methods such as DropConnect, ReLU and leaky ReLU on the MDLSTM network.

References

1. Hochreiter, S., Schmidhuber, J.: Long short-term memory. Neural Comput. **9**, 1735–1780 (1997)
2. Bluche, T., Louradour, J.J., Messina, R.: Scan, attend and read: end-to-end handwritten paragraph recognition with mdlstm attention. In: 14th IAPR International Conference on Document Analysis and Recognition (ICDAR), pp. 1050–1055. IEEE (2017)

3. Graves, A., Schmidhuber, J.A.: Offline handwriting recognition with multidimensional recurrent neural networks. In: Advances in Neural Information Processing Systems, pp. 545–552 (2009)
4. Pechwitz, M., Maddouri, S.S., Märgner, V., et al.: IFN/ENIT-database of handwritten Arabic words. In: Proceedings of CIFED. Citeseer, pp. 127–136 (2002)
5. Strauß, T., Grüning, T., Leifert, G., Labahn, R.: Citlab ARGUS for historical handwritten documents (2014). arXiv Prepr arXiv:14123949
6. El, H., Volker Märgner, A.: ICDAR 2009-Arabic handwriting recognition competition, pp. 14:3–13 (2011)
7. Maalej, R., Tagougui, N., Kherallah, M.: Recognition of handwritten Arabic words with dropout applied in MDLSTM. In: Campilho, A., Karray, F. (eds.) ICIAR 2016. LNCS, vol. 9730, pp. 746–752. Springer, Cham (2016). https://doi.org/10.1007/978-3-319-41501-7_83
8. Maalej, R., Kherallah, M.: Improving MDLSTM for offline Arabic handwriting recognition using dropout at different positions. In: Villa, A., Masulli, P., Pons Rivero, A. (eds.) ICANN 2016. LNCS, vol. 9887, pp. 431–438. Springer, Cham (2016). https://doi.org/10.1007/978-3-319-44781-0_51
9. Graves, A., Fernández, S., Gomez, F., et al.: Connectionist temporal classification: labelling unsegmented sequence data with recurrent neural networks. In: Proceedings of the 23rd International Conference on Machine Learning, pp 369–376. ACM (2006)
10. Pascanu, R., Mikolov, T., Bengio, Y.: On the difficulty of training recurrent neural networks. In: International Conference on Machine Learning, pp 1310–1318 (2013)
11. Bengio, Y., Simard, P., Frasconi, P.: Learning long-term dependencies with gradient descent is difficult. IEEE Trans. Neural Netw. 5, 157–166 (1994)
12. Goodfellow, I.J., Warde-Farley, D., Mirza, M., et al.: Maxout Networks, arXiv preprint arXiv:1302.4389 (2013)
13. Li, X., Wu, X.: Improving long short-term memory networks using maxout units for large vocabulary speech recognition. In: ICASSP 2015, pp. 4600–4604 (2015)
14. Swietojanski, P., Li, J., Huang, J.-T.: Investigation of maxout networks for speech recognition. In: IEEE International Conference on Acoustics, Speech and Signal Processing (ICASSP), pp. 7649–7653 (2014)
15. Miao, Y., Metze, F., Rawat, S., et al.: Deep maxout networks for low-resource speech recognition. In: IEEE Workshop on Automatic Speech Recognition and Understanding (ASRU), pp. 398–403 (2013)
16. Zhang, X., Trmal, J., Povey, D., et al.: Improving deep neural network acoustic models using generalized maxout networks. In: IEEE International Conference on Acoustics, Speech and Signal Processing (ICASSP), pp. 215–219 (2014)
17. Glorot, X., Bordes, A., Bengio, Y.: Deep sparse rectifier neural networks. In: Proceedings of the Fourteenth International Conference on Artificial Intelligence and Statistics, pp 315–323 (2011)
18. Cai, M., Liu, J.: Maxout neurons for deep convolutional and LSTM neural networks in speech recognition. Speech Commun. 77, 53–64 (2016)
19. Maalej, R., Kherallah, M.: Improving the DBLSTM for on-line Arabic handwriting recognition. Multimed. Tools Appl. (in press)
20. Jayech, K., Mahjoub, M., Amara, N.B.: Arabic handwritten word recognition based on dynamic Bayesian network. Int. Arab J. Inf. Technol. 13(6B), 1024–1031 (2016)

21. Amrouch, M., Rabi, M., Es-Saady, Y.: Convolutional feature learning and CNN based HMM for Arabic handwriting recognition. In: Mansouri, A., El Moataz, A., Nouboud, F., Mammass, D. (eds.) ICISP 2018. LNCS, vol. 10884, pp. 265–274. Springer, Cham (2018). https://doi.org/10.1007/978-3-319-94211-7_29
22. Maalej, R., Kherallah, M.: Convolutional neural network and BLSTM for offline Arabic handwriting recognition. In: IEEE International Arab Conference on Information Technology (ACIT), pp. 1–6 (2018)

Unsupervised Neural Models

Unsupervised Feature Selection Based on Matrix Factorization with Redundancy Minimization

Yang Fan[1], Jianhua Dai[2(✉)], and Siqi Xu[1]

[1] College of Intelligence and Computing, Tianjin University, Tianjin, China
{fany,siqixu}@tju.edu.cn
[2] Hunan Provincial Key Laboratory of Intelligent Computing and Language
Information Processing, College of Information Science and Engineering,
Hunan Normal University, Changsha, Hunan, China
jhdai@hunnu.edu.cn

Abstract. Unsupervised feature selection (UFS) based on matrix factorization (MF) is an efficient technique for dimensionality reduction in image processing task. Most MF based methods learn cluster indicator matrix and bases matrix, and exploit the bases matrix for feature selection via ranking weights. Since correlated features tend to have similar rankings and these methods select the top ranked features with large correlations, the selected features might contain redundant information. Toward this end, we propose a novel matrix factorization with redundancy minimization method, in which performing MF and removing redundant features are incorporated into a coherent model. To reduce the redundancy, we define a regularization to penalize the high-correlated features. The effective $\ell_{2,p}$-norm ($0 < p \leq 1$) imposed on bases matrix is suitable for feature selection. Experimental results on image datasets validate the effectiveness of the proposed approach.

Keywords: Image processing · Unsupervised feature selection · Matrix factorization · Redundancy minimization

1 Introduction

Many image processing tasks have witnessed images represented by high dimensional features, such as local features (SIFT) [5]. In most cases, not all features of visual contents of real-life images are significant for pattern recognition, computer vision and multimedia applications and most of them are even noisy and redundant, which would demand more on computational time and storage requirements and weaken the performance of model [2,8]. Feature selection which can keep data properties and select the most representative features is a main technique to overcome the over-fitting, low efficiency of model and poor performance of the learning tasks.

© Springer Nature Switzerland AG 2019
T. Gedeon et al. (Eds.): ICONIP 2019, LNCS 11955, pp. 549–560, 2019.
https://doi.org/10.1007/978-3-030-36718-3_46

From the perspective of availability of labels, feature selection can be grouped into three categories: supervised [11], semi-supervised [10,15] and unsupervised cases [14,16]. Supervised and semi-supervised methods can select discriminative features according to the power of distinguishing instances from different classes, which can achieve higher performance. Since images often have incomplete labels and assigning labels to images is an expensive and time consuming task, UFS is more challenging and promising [13].

In recent years, UFS has drawn increasingly attention, and a number of alternative criteria have been proposed. One type of UFS algorithms adopts MF technique to learn the cluster indicator matrix and bases matrix, and perform feature selection by using the bases matrix with sparse learning, which has been extensive studied by researchers. RUFS [9] performs robust clustering by local learning regularized nonnegative MF and robust feature selection via joint $\ell_{2,1}$-norms minimization. EUFS [12] directly embeds feature selection into a clustering algorithm by MF without transforming UFS into supervised case. However, the aforementioned methods do not explicitly consider the redundancy among features, which may result in the redundancy existing in the results. More specifically, since correlated features have similar ranking and be considered to be equally significant for UFS, these methods select the top ranked features which might be highly correlated to each other and contain redundant information.

To address the above issue, we propose a novel UFS algorithm, namely Matrix Factorization with Redundancy Minimization (MFRM). Different from existing MF based UFS methods, a main advantage of our approach is that it take the redundancy among features into consideration. Besides, the joint learning of MF and spectral analysis enables to learn more accurate cluster labels of input images. The main contributions of this work are summarized as:

(1) A novel UFS method based on matrix factorization with redundancy minimization is proposed. We formulate the proposed model as an optimization problem and design an efficient alternating minimization algorithm for it.
(2) We define a redundancy minimization regularization to penalize the high-correlated features.
(3) We conduct extensive experiments on image datasets to demonstrate the superiority of the proposed model.

2   Matrix Factorization

For an arbitrary matrix A, we denote its i-th row, its j-th column and (i, j)-th entry as a_i, a^j and A_{ij}, and its Frobenius norm is denoted as $||A||_F = \sqrt{\sum_i \sum_j A_{ij}^2}$, and $\mathrm{Tr}(A)$ is the trace of A if A is square. I_c is an $c \times c$ identity matrix.

Let $X \in \mathbb{R}^{n \times d}$ be the data matrix, where each row $x_i \in \mathbb{R}^{1 \times d}$ denotes an instance. The feature matrix is denoted as $X = \{f^1, f^2, \ldots, f^d\}$, where f^j is the j-th feature vector. Suppose these n samples are clustered into c clusters $(U^1, U^2, \ldots, U^c)$ by the matrix factorization as:

$$\min_{U^T U=I, U\geq 0, W} \|X - UW^T\|_F^2 \tag{1}$$

where $U \in \mathbb{R}^{n \times c}$ is the cluster indicator matrix and $W \in \mathbb{R}^{d \times c}$ is the bases matrix. According to the following theorem [12], we perform feature selection via the bases matrix.

Theorem 1. *Given* $X = \{f^1, f^2, \ldots, f^d\}$ *and* $\|f^i\|_1 = 1, \forall i$, *we use* UW^T *to reconstruct* X, *i.e,* $\hat{X} = UW^T$, *and perform feature selection via* W *with the orthogonal on* U.

Proof. Since $\hat{X} = UW^T$, we get $f^i = Uw_i^T$.

$$\|\hat{f}^i\|_2^2 = \|Uw_i^T\|_2^2 = w_i U^T U w_i^T = \|w_i^T\|_2^2 \tag{2}$$

3   Methodology

To select the most representative features and reduce the redundancy among features for UFS, we propose to adopt the matrix factorization and redundancy minimization, simultaneously. Our main task of this work is to obtain the cluster labels of input images and remove the redundancy among the selected features of visual contents of images. Matrix factorization technique is used to learn cluster labels U and bases matrix W (which can be regarded as the weights of features). Redundancy minimization is designed to be imposed on W to remove the redundant features which are highly correlated to each other and have similar rankings. Therefore, the framework of MFRM is formulated as:

$$\min_{U^T U=I, U\geq 0, W} \|X - UW^T\|_F^2 + \mathcal{G}(W) + \mathcal{R}(W) \tag{3}$$

where $\mathcal{G}(W)$ is a regularization function which is usually imposed on feature selection matrix to make model more robust and suitable for feature selection, and $\mathcal{R}(W)$ is a redundancy minimization regularization to penalize the high-correlated features and make the difference of similar features larger.

Most existing UFS methods adopt multiple criteria to compute feature scores, use different strategies to rank features and select the top ranked features. Consequently, the selected features may contain much redundancy due to the fact that correlated features have similar ranking and be considered to be equally significant for UFS. To penalize the framework (3) for redundant features, the first thing we need to do is to calculate the correlation between features. There are many correlation strategies, such as Pearson correlation coefficient and mutual information. Here, we adopt the Pearson correlation coefficient $C \in \mathbb{R}^{d \times d}$ which between the i-th feature f^i and the j-th feature f^j is defined as:

$$C_{ij} = \frac{1}{n-1} \sum_{m=1}^{n} \left(\frac{f_m^i - \overline{f^i}}{\sigma_{f^i}}\right)\left(\frac{f_m^j - \overline{f^j}}{\sigma_{f^j}}\right) \tag{4}$$

where $\frac{f_m^i - \overline{f^i}}{\sigma_{f^i}}$, $\overline{f^i}$ and σ_{f^i} are the standard score, mean and standard deviation of i-th feature.

To make high-correlated features with similar rankings far away from each other, we define a redundancy minimization regularization imposed on W as:

$$\mathcal{R}(W) = \min_W \quad -\sum_{l=1}^{c} \sum_{i,j=1}^{d} (W_{il} - W_{jl})^2 C_{ij}$$

$$\Rightarrow \quad \min_W \quad -Tr(W^T L_C W) \tag{5}$$

where $L_C = D_C - C$ is a Laplacian matrix and the (i,i)-th element of diagonal matrix D_C equals $\sum_{j=1}^{d} C_{ij}$. By minimizing the above defined term $\mathcal{R}(W)$, the framework (3) can reduce the redundancy during feature selection.

For the regularization function $\mathcal{G}(W)$, we impose effective $\ell_{2,p}$-norm ($0 < p \leq 1$) on bases matrix W, which can perform sparse feature selection and get a better sparsity solution than $\ell_{2,1}$-norm. The formulation of the group sparsity regularization $\ell_{2,p}$-norm added on W is:

$$\mathcal{G}(W) = ||W||_{2,p}^p = \sum_{i=1}^{d} (\sum_{j=1}^{c} W_{ij}^2)^{p/2} = \sum_{i=1}^{d} ||w_i||^p \tag{6}$$

where w_i is i-th row of W, d is the number of features and c is the number of cluster labels. The weight of i-th feature is calculated by $||w_i||_2$. The sparsity of W is affected by the value of p. When $p = 1$, the above formulation is $\ell_{2,1}$-norm. Obviously, the sparsity of W increases as p decreases.

By incorporating the redundancy minimization regularization (5) and the group sparsity regularization $\ell_{2,p}$-norm into the proposed framework (3), we have:

$$\min_{U,W} \quad ||X - UW^T||_F^2 + ||W||_{2,p}^p - Tr(W^T L_C W)$$

$$s.t. \quad U^T U = I, U \geq 0 \tag{7}$$

Although we use MF to learn the cluster labels of input images, we fail to capture the local data structure. Inspired by that similar images should have similar cluster labels, we apply spectral analysis to detect the manifold structure and force similar images with similar cluster labels:

$$\min Tr(U^T L_S U) \tag{8}$$

where $L_S = D_S - S$ is a Laplacian matrix and D_S is a diagonal matrix with its elements defined as $D_{S_{ii}} = \sum_{j=1}^{n} S_{ij}$. $S \in \mathbb{R}^{n \times n}$ is the sample similarity matrix which is obtained by RBF kernel in this work. By considering manifold information of input images, the problem (7) can be rewritten as:

$$\min_{U,W} \quad ||X - UW^T||_F^2 + \alpha Tr(U^T L_S U)$$

$$+ \quad \beta||W||_{2,p}^p - Tr(W^T L_C W)$$

$$s.t. \quad U^T U = I, U \geq 0 \tag{9}$$

where α and β are nonnegative trade-off parameters. The first two terms are joint learning of MF and spectral analysis which learn more accurate cluster labels and bases matrix while the last two terms are to make the bases matrix be sparse and select non-redundant representative features correspondingly.

4   Optimization

In this section, an alternating minimization strategy is derived to effectively solve the optimization problem of MFRM. We iteratively update W and F by the alternating minimization method which decomposes the problem into two subproblems where only one variable is involved.

First, when the cluster label U is fixed, the optimization problem in (9) is rewritten as:

$$\min_{W} \quad ||X - UW^T||_F^2 + \beta||W||_{2,p}^p - Tr(W^T L_C W) \tag{10}$$

When $p = 1$, the problem (10) is convex but non-smooth. However, in our model, the range of values of p is $(0, 1]$ and the problem is non-convex when $0 < p < 1$. To this end, we use Iterative Reweighted Least Square (IRLS) algorithm to solve the subproblem of W with the $\ell_{2,p}$-norm.

We define the diagonal weighting matrice $G^t \in \mathbb{R}^{d \times d}$ by the given current W^t:

$$g_j^t = \frac{p}{2}||w_j^t||_2^{p-2} \tag{11}$$

where w_j^t is j-th row of W^t and g_j^t is the j-th diagonal element of G^t. The solution of IRLS algorithm at the $t+1$ step involves the following weighted least squares problem:

$$
\begin{aligned}
W^{t+1} &= \arg\min_{W} Q(W|W^t) \\
&= \arg\min_{W} Tr((X - UW^T)^T (X - UW^T)) \\
&+ \beta Tr(W^T G^t W) - Tr(W^T L_C W)
\end{aligned}
\tag{12}
$$

By setting the derivative of (12) w.r.t W to zero, we can get the closed-form solution of W^{t+1} as:

$$W^{t+1} = (I + \beta G^t - L_C)^{-1} X^T U \tag{13}$$

After getting the W^{t+1}, we can update G^{t+1} by the definition (11). According to [17], the problem (10) monotonically decreases and is guaranteed to converge to a stationary point by iteratively updating W^t and G^t. We also introduce a sufficiently small value ϵ to redefine g_j^t to get a stable solution:

$$g_j^t = \frac{p}{2\max(||w_j^t||_2^{2-p}, \epsilon)} \tag{14}$$

Algorithm 1. Algorithm for the proposed MFRM.

Input: Data matrix $X \in \mathbb{R}^{n \times d}$; Parameters α, β and θ; cluster number c; Number of
   selected features t;
 1: Construct sample similarity matrix S and calculate L_S;
 2: Construct correlation coefficient C and calculate L_C;
 3: Initialize $\theta = 10^6$, U and W;
 4: **repeat**
 5:    Update W by solving (10) via IRLS;
 6:    Update U by (17);
 7: **until** Convergence criterion satisfied
Output: Sort all d features according to $\|w_i\|_2$ in descending order and select the
   top-t ranked features.

Next, when the bases matrix W is fixed, we rewrite the objective function
(9) with relaxing the orthogonal constraint:

$$\min_U \quad \|X - UW^T\|_F^2 + \alpha Tr(U^T L_S U) + \frac{\theta}{2}\|U^T U - I_c\|_F^2$$
$$s.t. \quad U \geq 0 \tag{15}$$

where $\frac{\theta}{2}\|U^T U - I_c\|_F^2$ is a penalty term and θ is a parameter which should be
large enough to ensure the orthogonality satisfied. Since the problem (15) is a
convex optimization with nonnegative constraint, we introduce the Lagrangian
multiplier Δ_{ij} for constraint $U_{ij} \geq 0$ and get the Lagrangian function:

$$\mathcal{L}(U, \Delta) = \quad \|X - UW^T\|_F^2 + \alpha Tr(U^T L_S U)$$
$$+ \quad \frac{\theta}{2}\|U^T U - I_c\|_F^2 - Tr(\Delta^T U) \tag{16}$$

By setting the derivative of (16) w.r.t U to zero and applying the Karush-
Kuhn-Tuckre (KKT) condition $\Delta_{ij} U_{ij} = 0$, we can get the following updating
method:

$$U_{ij} \leftarrow U_{ij} \frac{(XW + \theta U)_{ij}}{(UW^T W + \alpha L_S U + \theta UU^T U)_{ij}} \tag{17}$$

Then we normalize U with $(U^T U)_{ii} = 1, i = 1, \ldots, c$. The algorithm for solving
MFRM is summarized in Algorithm 1. The loop will stop if the loss variation
ratio is less than 10^{-6} or the number of iterations reach the maximum iteration.

Complexity and Convergence. There are two subproblems in the proposed
algorithm: subproblem W and subproblem U. In each iteration, the time com-
plexities of W and U are $O(T(d^3 + d^2 n + dnc))$ and $O(cn^2)$, respectively, where
d is the number of features, n is number of samples, c is the number of pseudo
classes and T is the iteration number of the IRLS algorithm. The convergence of
subproblem W depends on the IRLS algorithm whose convergence has been well

Table 1. Detailed information of the datasets.

Dataset	Instances	Features	Classes	Domain
ORL	400	1024	40	Image, Face
AR	130	2400	10	Image, Face
PIE	210	2420	10	Image, Face
Yale	165	1024	15	Image, Face
pixraw10P	100	10000	10	Image, Face
COIL20	1440	1024	20	Image, Object

studied and proved [17]. The optimization problem for U is a convex function. Hence, the objective function value is guaranteed to decrease in each iteration and our algorithm will eventually converge due to the lower bound 0.

5   Experiments

In this section, we conduct extensive experiments to evaluate the performance of the proposed method on six image datasets. We compare MFRM with comparison methods in terms of clustering performance. We also give the performance of selected features with the proposed method on face images.

5.1   Datasets

In our experiments, six diverse image datasets are collected to evaluate the performance of the proposed method and comparison methods, including five face image datasets (ORL, AR, PIE, Yale and pixraw10P) and one object image dataset (COIL20). The detail information of chosen datasets is shown is Table 1.

5.2   Experimental Settings

To validate the effectiveness of the proposed MFRM, we compare it with the following UFS methods:

- LapScore [4]: LapScore is a filter method that evaluates features by the power of preserving the local manifold structure.
- MCFS [1]: MCFS adopts spectral clustering with ℓ_1-norm regularization to maintain data distribution.
- NDFS [7]: NDFS uses the nonnegative spectral analysis to select the most discriminative features.
- RUFS [9]: RUFS combines robust nonnegative matrix factorization and local learning to perform robust feature learning.

– EUFS [12]: EUFS is an embedded method that applies orthogonal matrix factorization to select features without transforming unsupervised feature selection into supervised learning.

For all methods, we specify the size of neighborhoods k as 5. In our model
MFRM, we set the value of p for $\ell_{2,p}$-norm as 0.8 and denote $\theta = 10^6$ to guarantee the orthogonality satisfied. For fair comparison, we adopt grid-search strategy to traverse the parameters from $\{10^{-6}, 10^{-4}, \ldots, 10^6\}$ and record the best
results. We set the number of selected features as $\{50, 100, \ldots, 300\}$ and report
the average results due to the fact that it is still an open problem to determine
the optimal number of selected features in unsupervised feature selection [3,6].
We evaluate the performance of k-means clustering on selected features via two
widely used metrics, i.e., Normalized Mutual Information (NMI) and Clustering
Accuracy (ACC) [6]. The lager NMI and ACC are, the better the performance
is. Since k-means algorithm is sensitive to the initialization, we repeat k-means
clustering 20 times with random initialization and record the mean and standard
deviation of results for all methods.

5.3 Results and Analysis

The clustering performance in terms of NMI and ACC on six image datasets for
the compared methods are reported in Tables 2 and 3, respectively. The results
are given in the format of "average ± standard deviation". The best results are
highlighted in bold.

Table 2. Clustering results (NMI% ± std) of the compared methods.

	ORL	AR	PIE	Yale	pixraw10P	COIL20
Baseline	72.01 ± 2.97	13.88 ± 3.57	22.36 ± 4.66	44.55 ± 2.51	80.61 ± 3.33	70.47 ± 3.92
LapScore	66.38 ± 2.58	22.00 ± 3.09	22.27 ± 2.23	43.10 ± 3.95	79.75 ± 6.12	65.64 ± 3.81
MCFS	72.49 ± 2.63	17.26 ± 2.96	50.38 ± 2.80	44.74 ± 2.88	82.57 ± 3.98	70.95 ± 1.60
NDFS	71.29 ± 2.98	35.74 ± 2.74	48.02 ± 4.00	40.65 ± 2.71	**88.42 ± 2.92**	72.20 ± 3.00
RUFS	73.48 ± 3.88	40.17 ± 5.23	43.93 ± 5.11	45.34 ± 2.08	84.18 ± 3.76	72.56 ± 2.70
EUFS	70.46 ± 3.09	53.59 ± 3.52	63.39 ± 3.30	47.82 ± 2.72	81.29 ± 5.19	66.19 ± 7.35
MFRM	**75.67 ± 2.47**	**55.95 ± 2.86**	**65.01 ± 2.94**	**49.70 ± 3.02**	86.69 ± 2.99	**73.89 ± 2.10**

Table 3. Clustering results (ACC% ± std) of the compared methods.

	ORL	AR	PIE	Yale	pixraw10P	COIL20
Baseline	47.75 ± 2.83	19.23 ± 3.61	24.74 ± 2.54	35.76 ± 2.74	74.88 ± 3.45	58.65 ± 4.82
LapScore	42.78 ± 3.35	21.60 ± 3.45	21.65 ± 2.77	37.44 ± 2.88	66.47 ± 7.99	52.37 ± 4.71
MCFS	51.40 ± 2.95	21.40 ± 2.93	38.29 ± 3.74	37.93 ± 2.54	76.33 ± 4.71	58.07 ± 2.31
NDFS	50.12 ± 2.31	33.10 ± 2.68	39.56 ± 2.93	33.13 ± 3.05	**79.95 ± 2.89**	59.57 ± 3.63
RUFS	52.11 ± 3.78	37.77 ± 4.88	33.71 ± 4.97	38.01 ± 3.44	77.36 ± 4.52	61.61 ± 3.68
EUFS	48.18 ± 2.81	48.97 ± 3.71	53.01 ± 4.11	39.96 ± 3.95	76.18 ± 5.34	53.59 ± 5.75
MFRM	**56.76 ± 2.69**	**49.83 ± 2.70**	**55.22 ± 2.85**	**41.51 ± 3.08**	78.77 ± 3.21	**63.05 ± 2.81**

From these two tables, it is noticed that feature selection can not only select the most representative features, but also improve the performance by comparing with baseline which adopts all features. We can see that simultaneous clustering and feature selection can outperform the strategies that select features one by one. NDFS, RUFS, EUFS and MFRM all outperform MCFS by using the orthogonal nonnegative constraint. RUFS performs robust clustering by local learning regularized nonnegative MF and robust feature selection, which resulting in relatively good results. EUFS yields larger values of NMI and ACC, which demonstrates that it is significant to directly embed feature selection into a clustering algorithm by MF for unsupervised feature selection. Our method MFRM achieves the best performance on five datasets and the second best result on pixraw10P dataset by explicitly taking the redundancy among high-correlated features in account.

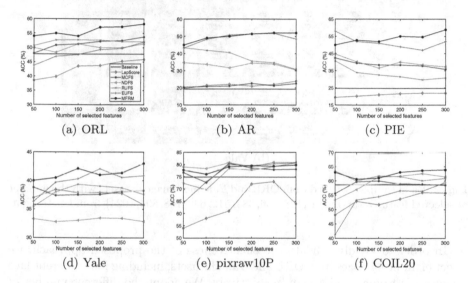

Fig. 1. Clustering results (ACC) of all methods with different features on six image datasets.

Additionally, we also conduct experiments to evaluate the performance of all methods with increasing number of features. The experimental results in terms of ACC of all methods are shown in Fig. 1. It is observed that as the number of features increases, the ACC of the competing methods usually begins to decrease after reaching the maximum, which denotes that the selected features by these methods may contain redundant features that degrade the performance. Our method can handle this case and has better results of ACC regarding most feature numbers, which demonstrates that it is necessary to consider the redundancy among features. However, these unsupervised feature selection methods are all sensitive to the number of selected features.

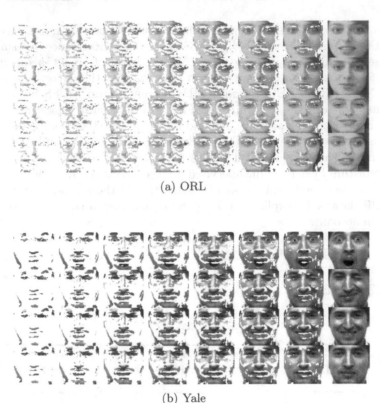

(a) ORL

(b) Yale

Fig. 2. Eight samples selected from ORL and Yale face image datasets with the number of selected features varying in $\{128, 256, 384, 512, 640, 768, 896, 1024\}$ from left to right.

In order to vividly validate the effectiveness of the proposed approach, we select eight face images from ORL and Yale datasets, including four different face images of a woman and a man, respectively. We adopt the different number of features of every face image for reconstruction. As shown in Fig. 2, the proposed MFRM can reconstruct the outline of the facial features with a small number of features which are useful to distinguish a people. Obviously, the proposed method can select the valuable and discriminative features (e.g., eyes, nose, mouth, etc) primarily and remove the redundant features (cheek and background).

6   Conclusion

In this paper, we propose a novel unsupervised feature selection method which could jointly learn cluster labels of images and select the non-redundant representative features. A redundancy minimization regularization has been defined to penalize high-correlated features to minimize the redundancy among features. The effective $\ell_{2,p}$-norm is introduced to perform sparse feature selection.

Experimental results on different image datasets demonstrate the proposed method MFRM outperforms the state-of-the-art methods.

Acknowledgment. This work was partially supported by the National Natural Science Foundation of China (Nos. 61976089, 61473259, 61070074, 60703038) and the Hunan Provincial Science & Technology Program Project (Nos. 2018RS3065, 2018TP1018).

References

1. Cai, D., Zhang, C., He, X.: Unsupervised feature selection for multi-cluster data. In: Proceedings of the 16th ACM SIGKDD International Conference on Knowledge Discovery and Data Mining, pp. 333–342 (2010)
2. Cheng, K., Li, J., Liu, H.: Unsupervised feature selection in signed social networks. In: Proceedings of the 23rd ACM SIGKDD International Conference on Knowledge Discovery and Data Mining, pp. 777–786 (2017)
3. Du, L., Shen, Y.: Unsupervised feature selection with adaptive structure learning. In: Proceedings of the 21th ACM SIGKDD International Conference on Knowledge Discovery and Data Mining, pp. 209–218 (2015)
4. He, X., Cai, D., Niyogi, P.: Laplacian score for feature selection. Adv. Neural Inf. Process. Syst. **18**, 507–514 (2005)
5. Kaya, G.T., Kaya, H., Bruzzone, L.: Feature selection based on high dimensional model representation for hyperspectral images. IEEE Trans. Image Process. **26**(6), 2918–2928 (2017)
6. Li, J., Wu, L., Dani, H., Liu, H.: Unsupervised personalized feature selection. In: Proceedings of the Thirty-Second AAAI Conference on Artificial Intelligence (2018)
7. Li, Z., Yang, Y., Liu, J., Zhou, X., Lu, H.: Unsupervised feature selection using nonnegative spectral analysis. In: Proceedings of the Twenty-Sixth AAAI Conference on Artificial Intelligence (2012)
8. Qi, M., Wang, T., Liu, F., Zhang, B., Wang, J., Yi, Y.: Unsupervised feature selection by regularized matrix factorization. Neurocomputing **273**, 593–610 (2018)
9. Qian, M., Zhai, C.: Robust unsupervised feature selection. In: Proceedings of the 23rd International Joint Conference on Artificial Intelligence, IJCAI 2013, pp. 1621–1627 (2013)
10. Sheikhpour, R., Sarram, M.A., Gharaghani, S., Chahooki, M.A.Z.: A survey on semi-supervised feature selection methods. Pattern Recogn. **64**, 141–158 (2017)
11. Tang, J., Alelyani, S., Liu, H.: Feature selection for classification: a review. In: Data Classification: Algorithms and Applications, pp. 37–64 (2014)
12. Wang, S., Tang, J., Liu, H.: Embedded unsupervised feature selection. In: Proceedings of the Twenty-Ninth AAAI Conference on Artificial Intelligence, pp. 470–476 (2015)
13. Yang, S., Nie, F., Li, X.: Unsupervised feature selection with local structure learning. In: 2018 IEEE International Conference on Image Processing, ICIP 2018. pp. 3398–3402 (2018)
14. Yang, Y., Shen, H.T., Ma, Z., Huang, Z., Zhou, X.: $l_{2,1}$-norm regularized discriminative feature selection for unsupervised learning. In: IJCAI, pp. 1589–1594 (2011)
15. Yuan, G., Chen, X., Wang, C., Nie, F., Jing, L.: Discriminative semi-supervised feature selection via rescaled least squares regression-supplement. In: Proceedings of the Thirty-Second AAAI Conference on Artificial Intelligence, pp. 8177–8178 (2018)

16. Zhao, Z., Liu, H.: Spectral feature selection for supervised and unsupervised learning. In: Proceedings of the Twenty-Fourth International Conference on Machine Learning, pp. 1151–1157 (2007)
17. Zhu, P., Hu, Q., Zhang, C., Zuo, W.: Coupled dictionary learning for unsupervised feature selection. In: Proceedings of the Thirtieth AAAI Conference on Artificial Intelligence, pp. 2422–2428 (2016)

Distance Estimation for Quantum Prototypes Based Clustering

Kaoutar Benlamine[1](✉), Younès Bennani[1](✉), Ahmed Zaiou[1](✉),
Mohamed Hibti[2], Basarab Matei[1](✉), and Nistor Grozavu[1](✉)

[1] LIPN UMR 7030 CNRS, Université Paris 13 - Sorbonne Paris Cité,
Villetaneuse, France
{kaoutar.benlamine,younes.bennani,ahmed.zaiou,basarab.matei,
nistor.grozavu}@lipn.univ-paris13.fr
[2] EDF Lab Saclay, PERICLES, Gaspard Monge Street, Palaiseau, France
mohamed.hibti@edf.fr

Abstract. Quantum machine learning is a new area of research with the recent work on quantum versions of supervised and unsupervised algorithms. In recent years, many quantum machine learning algorithms have been proposed providing a speed-up over the classical algorithms. In this paper, we propose an analysis and a comparison of three quantum distances for protoptypes-based clustering techniques. As an application of this work, we present a quantum K-means version which gives a good classification just like its classical version, the difference resides in the complexity: while the classical version of K-means takes polynomial time, the quantum version takes only logarithmic time especially in large datasets. Finally, we validate the benefits of the proposed approach by performing a series of empirical evaluations regarding the quantum distance estimation and its behavior versus the stability of finding the nearest centers in the right order.

Keywords: Quantum machine learning · K-means · Unsupervised learning · Prototypes based clustering

1 Introduction

Machine learning techniques are applied for solving a large variety of problems such as sorting, regression and classifying information. In supervised machine learning, the learner is provided a set of training examples with features presented in the form of high-dimensional vectors and with corresponding labels to mark its category. The aim is to classify new examples based on these training sets. In unsupervised learning, the machine tries to find a hidden structure in unlabeled data.

As the amount of data generated in our society is drastically increasing, it is necessary to have more powerful ways of handling information. That's why recent

A. Zaiou—Partially supported by and co-financed through the European Erasmus+ Programme.

studies and applications are focusing on the problem of large-scale machine learning. A lot of works have been devoted to quantum machine learning. For example, the development of quantum procedures for linear algebra as: matrix multiplication, eigenvectors and eigenvalues of matrices and estimating distances between quantum states. Efforts have also been made to solve the problem of pattern recognition [9] and to develop the quantum version of artificial neural networks [6] widely used in machine learning.

In this paper, we are interested in the estimation of the distance for quantum prototypes based clustering as the main task of machine learning algorithm is analyzing the similarity between the vectors that is done through the evaluation of the distance and the inner products between the large vectors. The notion of distance in quantum clustering algorithms differs from the conventional one, in the sense that it may vary depending on the probabilistic effects due to the quantum nature of the states.

The rest of paper is organized as follows. Section 2 presents the distance estimation. Section 3 describes grover's algorithm. Section 4 would be the description of the proposed quantum K-means. Section 5 is devoted to experimental results. Finally, the conclusion summarizes our work and its advantages.

2   How to Estimate the Distances Between a Given Data and Centroids?

Distance measurements to the different centroids are necessary for a clustering algorithm. To do this, how can we translate the idea of measuring distances into something that can be easily and efficiently done on a quantum computer? For a conventional computer, calculating Euclidean distances is easy, but doing it in the same way on a quantum computer would be much more complicated and would require more qubits than we can afford. On the other hand, the probabilistic nature of qubits makes it easier to measure phase differences and probability amplitudes.

For clustering algorithms, distances are necessary just to assign data points to different clusters. The objective is then to know which cluster is closest to a data point. This measure does not need to be proportional to the real distance, but only in positive correlation with it. Indeed, we only need the nearest centroid, not the exact values of the real distances.

In quantum computing, many distance-type measurements are available when we process qubits [2,7,10], such as the inner product between two (normalized) vectors and the probabilities of measuring a qubit in the states $|0\rangle$ or $|1\rangle$.

2.1   Fidelity as a Similarity Measure

Fidelity is a measure of similarity between two quantum states, which is defined in the case of two pure states $|\psi\rangle$ and $|\phi\rangle$ by $Fid(|\psi\rangle, |\phi\rangle) = |\langle\psi|\phi\rangle|^2$. The fidelity varies between 0 if the states are orthogonal (that's to say, perfectly distinguishable) to 1 if the states are identical.

Fidelity is similar to a measure commonly used in classical information, called cosine similarity. The properties of fidelity include symmetry: $Fid(|\psi\rangle, |\phi\rangle) = Fid(|\phi\rangle, |\psi\rangle)$, as well as invariance under unitary transformation, which means that if we apply the same unitary transformation U to two quantum states this does not change their fidelity: $Fid(|U\psi\rangle, |U\phi\rangle) = Fid(|\phi\rangle, |\psi\rangle)$.

The fidelity $|\langle\psi|\phi\rangle|$ [1] of two quantum states $|\psi\rangle$ and $|\phi\rangle$ can be obtained through the quantum circuit Swap test presented in Fig. 1.

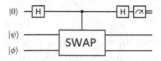

Fig. 1. Swap test circuit

The circuit of swap test allows to compare two quantum states. It is composed of two Hadamard gates and a Control-Swap gate.

The control qubit is on the state: $|+\rangle = \frac{|0\rangle+|1\rangle}{\sqrt{2}}$

After applying the Controlled Swap test, we get:

$$CSWAP|+\rangle\,|\psi\rangle\,|\phi\rangle \rightarrow \frac{|0\rangle\,|\psi\rangle\,|\phi\rangle + |1\rangle\,|\phi\rangle\,|\psi\rangle}{\sqrt{2}}$$

By applying the second Hadamard gate, we obtain:

$$CSWAP|+\rangle\,|\psi\rangle\,|\phi\rangle \rightarrow \frac{|0\rangle\,(|\psi\rangle\,|\phi\rangle + |\phi\rangle\,|\psi\rangle) + |1\rangle\,(|\psi\rangle\,|\phi\rangle - |\phi\rangle\,|\psi\rangle)}{2}$$

While measuring the ancillary qubit, we get:

$$P(|0_A\rangle) = \left|\frac{1}{2}\langle0|0\rangle\,|\psi\rangle\,|\phi\rangle + |\phi\rangle\,|\psi\rangle\right|^2$$

$$= \frac{1}{4}\Big|\,|\psi\rangle\,|\phi\rangle + |\phi\rangle\,|\psi\rangle\,\Big|^2$$

$$= \frac{1}{2} + \frac{1}{2}\,|\langle\psi|\phi\rangle|^2$$

After measurement, we have $P(|0_A\rangle) = \frac{1}{2} + \frac{1}{2}|\langle\psi|\phi\rangle|^2$. A probability of $1/2$ consequently shows that the two quantum states $|\psi\rangle$ and $|\phi\rangle$ do not overlap at all (they are orthogonal), while a probability of 1 indicates that they have maximum overlap.

2.2 States Construction to Estimate the Distance-Type Measurements

Several works have been made to compute the fidelity between two quantum states, all these works use the swap test circuit to obtain the similarity measure but they use different data preparation and construction of the states. In this section, we present the preparation and the construction of the states $|\psi\rangle$ and $|\phi\rangle$ of each method. Let's consider that we want to compute the distance between the two quantum states $|x\rangle$ and $|w\rangle$.

Wiebe et al. Approach

1. *Data preparation*

Given $N = 2^n$ dimensional complex vectors $\boldsymbol{x}$ and $\boldsymbol{w}$ with components $x_j = |x_j|e^{-i\alpha_j}$ and $w_j = |w_j|e^{-i\beta_j}$ respectively. Assume that $\{|x_j|, \alpha_j\}$ and $\{|w_j|, \beta_j\}$ are stored as floating point numbers in quantum random access memory.

2. *Construction of the states*

Wiebe, Kapoor and Svore [10] suggested a representation of the states that aims to write the parameters into amplitudes of the quantum states.

$$|\psi\rangle = \frac{1}{\sqrt{d}} \sum_j |j\rangle \left(\sqrt{1 - \frac{|x_j|^2}{r_{max}^2}} e^{-i\alpha_j} |0\rangle + \frac{x_j}{r_{max}} |1\rangle \right) |1\rangle$$

$$|\phi\rangle = \frac{1}{\sqrt{d}} \sum_j |j\rangle |1\rangle \left(\sqrt{1 - \frac{|w_j|^2}{r_{max}^2}} e^{-i\beta_j} |0\rangle + \frac{w_j}{r_{max}} |1\rangle \right)$$

Where $j = \{1, ..., n\}$, and r_{max} is an upper bound on the maximum value of any feature in the dataset. The input vectors are d-sparse, i.e., contain no more than d non-zero entries.

Using the swap test, the inner product is evaluated by:

$$d_{q_1}(|x\rangle, |w\rangle) = d^2 r_{max}^4 (2P(|0\rangle) - 1) \tag{1}$$

Lloyd et al. Approach

1. *Data preparation*

To use the forces of quantum mechanics without being limited to the classical ideas of data encoding; Lloyd, Mohseni and Rebentrost [7] proposed a way to encode the classical vectors into a quantum state.
Consider $N = 2^n$ dimensional complex vectors $\boldsymbol{x}$ and $\boldsymbol{w}$, we have:

$$|x\rangle = \frac{\boldsymbol{x}}{|\boldsymbol{x}|}, |w\rangle = \frac{\boldsymbol{w}}{|\boldsymbol{w}|}$$

2. *Construction of the states*

Seth Lloyd and his co-workers proposed a way to construct the state $|\psi\rangle$ and $|\phi\rangle$. The idea is to adjoin an ancillary qubit to states creating an entangled state $|\psi\rangle$. The greater the difference between the states $|x\rangle$ and $|w\rangle$, the more the resulting state is entangled [3].

$$|\psi\rangle = \frac{1}{\sqrt{2}} (|0\rangle |x\rangle + |1\rangle |w\rangle)$$

$$|\phi\rangle = \frac{1}{\sqrt{Z}}(|\boldsymbol{x}|\,|0\rangle - |\boldsymbol{w}|\,|1\rangle)$$

Where $Z = |\boldsymbol{x}|^2 + |\boldsymbol{w}|^2$

After applying the swap test circuit, the distance is evaluated by:

$$d_{q2}(|x\rangle, |w\rangle) = 2Z(2P(|0\rangle) - 1) \tag{2}$$

Anagolum Approach

1. *Data preparation*

   For simplification, we assume that we are in 2-dimensional space. Let's consider that we have two vectors $\boldsymbol{x}(x_0, x_1)$ and $\boldsymbol{w}(w_0, w_1)$.

   We can map data values to θ and α values using these equations.

   For x we get:

   $$\alpha_0 = (x_0 + 1)\frac{\pi}{2}, \quad \theta_0 = (x_1 + 1)\frac{\pi}{2} \tag{3}$$

   Similarly for w we get:

   $$\alpha_1 = (w_0 + 1)\frac{\pi}{2}, \quad \theta_1 = (w_1 + 1)\frac{\pi}{2} \tag{4}$$

2. *Construction of the states*

   To construct the two states $|\psi\rangle$ and $|\phi\rangle$ Anagolum [2] proposed to use U gate as follows:

   $$|\psi\rangle = U(\theta_0, \alpha_0, 0)|0\rangle \tag{5}$$

   $$|\phi\rangle = U(\theta_1, \alpha_1, 0)|0\rangle \tag{6}$$

Indeed, U gate implement the rotations we need to perform to encode our data points.

$$U(\theta, \alpha, \lambda) = \begin{pmatrix} \cos\frac{\theta}{2} & -e^{i\lambda}\sin\frac{\theta}{2} \\ e^{i\alpha}\sin\frac{\theta}{2} & e^{i\lambda+i\alpha}\cos\frac{\theta}{2} \end{pmatrix}$$

This instruction would cause the qubit to move θ radians away from the positive z-axis, and α radians away from the positive x-axis.

Using the swap test, the distance is evaluated by:

$$d_{q3}(|x\rangle, |w\rangle) = P(|1\rangle) \tag{7}$$

3 How to Search for the Nearest Centroid to a Given Data?

In quantum computing, Grover's algorithm allows to search for one or more element in an unsorted database with N entries in $O(\sqrt{N})$ time. Grover's algorithm begins with a quantum register of n qubit initialized to $|0\rangle$, when n is the number necessary to represent the search space, we have $2^n = N$ which means $|0\rangle^{\otimes n} = |0\rangle$.

Equal Superposition: The first step is to apply the Hadamard transform $H^{\otimes n}$ to put the system into an equal superposition of states:

$$|\psi\rangle = H^{\otimes n}|0\rangle^{\otimes n} = \frac{1}{\sqrt{2^n}} \sum_{x=0}^{2^n-1} |x\rangle$$

Quantum Oracle O: An oracle is a black-box function and a quantum oracle is a quantum black-box, which means that it can observe and modify the system without collapsing it to a classical state. It will recognize if the system is in the correct state: if the system is in the correct state, then the oracle will rotate the phase by π radians, otherwise it will do nothing. To create the circuit that represents this oracle it is necessary to implement this transformation of $|x\rangle$:

$$O|x\rangle \rightarrow (-1)^{y(x)}|x\rangle, \text{where } y(x) = \begin{cases} 1 \text{ if } x \text{ is the correct state} \\ \\ 0 \text{ else} \end{cases}$$

Diffusion Transform: It performs inversion about the average. This part consists of another application of the Hadamard transform $H^{\otimes n}$, followed by a conditional phase shift that shifts every state except $|0\rangle$ by -1, followed by another Hadamard transform. The diffusion transform can be represented by this equation, using the notation $|\psi\rangle$:

$$H^{\otimes n}[2|0\rangle\langle 0| - I]H^{\otimes n} = 2H^{\otimes n}|0\rangle\langle 0|H^{\otimes n} - I = 2|\psi\rangle\langle\psi| - I$$

The entire Grover iteration is given by: $[2|\psi\rangle\langle\psi| - I]O$.

The runtime of Grover's entire algorithm is $O(2^{\frac{n}{2}})$, as it performs $O(\sqrt{N}) = O(2^{\frac{n}{2}})$ iterations each with a runtime of $O(n)$.

4   Proposed Quantum Clustering Approach

4.1   General Concept

K-means clustering [8] is a type of unsupervised machine learning that aims to find groups in the data by dividing the dataset into K clusters. In this section, we give the algorithm of quantum K-means, this algorithm is adaptable for the three approaches explained above.

Assume that we have a set of quantum states $|X\rangle = \{|x_n\rangle \in \mathbb{C}^M, n = 1, ..., N\}$, and a set of K clusters C_k, $|C_k|$ is the number of vectors within the cluster k. K-means clustering aims to partition the N observations into K clusters C_k with $|W\rangle = |w_1\rangle, |w_2\rangle, ..., |w_K\rangle$ centroids, so as to minimize the within-cluster variance. Formally, the objective is to find:

$$\operatorname*{argmin}_{W} D(|x\rangle, |w\rangle)) = \operatorname*{argmin}_{C} \sum_{k=1}^{K} \sum_{|x_n\rangle \in C_k} d_{q_i}^2(|x_n\rangle, |w_k\rangle) \qquad (8)$$

We compute the distance between each training state and each cluster centroid using the swap test circuit Fig. 1. Then, we assign each state to the closest centroid using Grover's algorithm as explained in Sect. 3.

The second step of QK-means is updating the centroid of each cluster. To do so, the update centroid of each cluster is given by:

$$|w_k^{(t+1)}\rangle = |(Y_k^{(t)})^T X\rangle$$

where

$$|Y_k^{(t)}\rangle = \frac{1}{\sqrt{|C_k|}} \sum_{n=1}^{N} y_{nk} |n\rangle \quad \text{and} \quad y_{nk} = \begin{cases} 1 \text{ if } x_n \in C_k \\ 0 \text{ else} \end{cases}$$

4.2   Quantum Learning Algorithm

We give the main steps of the proposed algorithm in the following. The distance $d_{q_i}(|x_n\rangle, |w_k\rangle)$ is at the user's choice, in our case we opt for the distance d_{q_1} as it gives the best result. For the stopping criterion, we use the relative distortion between two iterations with respect to a threshold ϵ.

Algorithm 1: Quantum K-means algorithm

Input: $|X\rangle = \{|x_n\rangle \in \mathbb{C}^M, n = 1, ..., N\}$, K number of clusters C_k, initial centroids of the clusters at $t = 0$: $|w_1^{(0)}\rangle, |w_2^{(0)}\rangle, ..., |w_K^{(0)}\rangle$.

Output: K clusters C_k.

  repeat

  Assignment step (clustering): Each data is assigned to the cluster with the nearest center using Grover's search:

$$C_k^{(t)} \longleftarrow \{|x_n\rangle : d_{q_i}^2(|x_n\rangle, |w_k^{(t)}\rangle) \le d_{q_i}^2(|x_n\rangle, |w_j^{(t)}\rangle)), \forall j, 1 \le j \le K\}$$

  where each $|x_n\rangle \in |X\rangle$ is assigned to exactly one $C_k^{(t)}$, even if it could be assigned to more of them.

  Update step: The center of each cluster C_k is recalculated as being the average of all data belonging to this cluster (following the previous assignment step):

$$|w_k^{(t+1)}\rangle \longleftarrow |(Y_k^{(t)})^T X\rangle$$

  until Convergence is reached

Convergence can be considered as achieved if the relative value of the distortion level $D(|x\rangle, |w^{(t)}\rangle)$ falls below a small prefixed threshold ϵ:

$$\frac{D(|x\rangle, |w^{(t-1)}\rangle) - D(|x\rangle, |w^{(t)}\rangle)}{D(|x\rangle, |w^{(t)}\rangle)} < \epsilon$$

4.3   Validation Criteria

As a validation criteria, we use the Davies-Bouldin (DB) index and quantum Davies-Bouldin (QDB) index. As the estimation of the distance in the classical version it's not the same as the quantum version.

The Davies Bouldin index [4] can be calculated with the following formula:

$$DB = \frac{1}{K} \sum_{k=1}^{K} \max_{k \neq k'} \frac{d_n(w_k) + d_n(w_{k'})}{d(w_k, w_{k'})} \tag{9}$$

where K is the number of clusters, d_n is the average distance of all elements from the cluster C_k to their cluster center w_k, $d(w_k, w_{k'})$ is the distance between clusters centers w_k and $w_{k'}$. This index well evaluates the quality of unsupervised clustering because it's based on the ratio of the sum of within-clusters scatter to between-clusters separation. More the value of DB is lower, more the clustering is better. The main objective is to evaluate how well the clustering has been done.

As we have already mentioned before, the notion of distance in quantum approaches is different from the classical case. Quantum distance does not need to be proportional to the real distance, but only have a positive correlation with it. We need only the nearest centroid, not the exact value of the real distance. To evaluate the quality of quantum clustering with a Davies-Bouldin index-type based on intra- and inter-cluster distances, we propose to adapt it to the quantum case. To do this, we will define the Quantum Davies-Bouldin (QDB) quality index as follows:

$$QDB = \frac{1}{K} \sum_{k=1}^{K} \max_{k \neq k'} \frac{\delta_n(w_k) + \delta_n(w_{k'})}{\delta(w_k, w_{k'})} \tag{10}$$

where

$$\delta_n(w_k) = \frac{1}{|C_k|} \sum_{i=1}^{|C_k|} d_{q_1}(|x_i\rangle_{x_i \in C_k}, |w_k\rangle) \text{ and } \delta(w_k, w_{k'}) = d_{q_1}(|w_k\rangle, |w_{k'}\rangle)$$

5   Empirical Evaluations

5.1   Datasets

The classical and quantum version of K-means was tested on three real world datasets available for public use in the UCI Machine learning repository [5]. Iris data set contains 3 classes of 50 instances each, where each class refers to a type of iris plant. Wine is a dataset that is related to a chemical analysis of wines grown in the same region in Italy but derived from different cultivars. The data Breast Cancer has 569 instances with 32 variables (ID, diagnosis, 30 real-valued input variables). Each data observation is labeled as benign (357) or malignant (212).

5.2   Comparison of Different Quantum Distances

Which Quantum Distance Has a High Probability of Finding the Right Nearest Center? Because of the probabilistic nature of the qubits, the distance between two states is hard to compute as we will get a probabilistic result; the distance is unstable. However, it's easier to assign data points to different groups because we don't need the exact distances to each one but only the closest centroid. Thus, we can just put the new data point in the cluster associated with the smallest value that our parameter takes. To illustrate more our idea, we gave an example of two distributions. Figures 2 and 3 represent two distributions where the black dot X is the test data and the three crosses are the centers ($C1$, $C2$, $C3$).

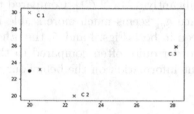
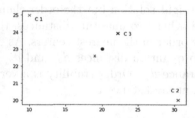

Fig. 2. Distribution 1   **Fig. 3.** Distribution 2

From Table 1, we can notice that the distance changes from an iteration to another but the assignment to the closest centroid is correct. Wiebe et al. approach gives a higher confidence interval in a time lower than other approaches.

Table 1. Distance-types comparison

Distance	Distribution	Green	Blue	Black	Probability of success
Wiebe et al. approach	1	665 times	9322 times	13 times	[92.71%, 93.70%]
(d_{q_1})	2	0 times	0 times	10000 times	[99.96%, 100%]
Lloyd et al. approach	1	2190 times	7620 times	190 times	[75.35%, 77.02%]
(d_{q_2})	2	0 times	515 times	9485 times	[94.40%, 95.26%]
Anagolum approach	1	2722 times	6530 times	748 times	[64.36%, 66.22%]
(d_{q_3})	2	2486 times	2175 times	5339 times	[52.41%, 54.36%]

Which Quantum Distance Has a High Probability of Finding the Nearest Centers in the Right Order with a Good Stability? After analyzing the performance of the different quantum distances in terms of the stability of the values allowing the choice of the right center, we will study the behaviour of these quantum distances, but this time in terms of the stability of the order of the nearest centers. In other words, how far away is it possible to find the nearest centers in the right order whatever the iteration? To do this, we carried out 10,000 searches for the nearest centers for the two studied distributions. We analyzed the stability of the order of the nearest centers found by each quantum distance. The results show that the distance d_{q_1} is the best one which offers a very good stability in the order of the nearest centers in the case of the two studied distributions. As shown in Table 1, the distance d_{q_1} exhibits a very good stability in the order of the nearest centers compared to the other two quantum distances. For distribution 1, the correct order of the nearest centers is $[C2\ C1\ C3]$. The distance d_{q_1} finds this order with a probability of 85.32% (8532 times out of 10,000 searches), while the distance d_{q_2} and d_{q_3} find the order with a probability of 53.26% (5326/10,000) and 26.10% (261/10,000) respectively. In the case of distribution 2, the situation is more complicated because the test point is almost halfway between two centers. This situation is confirmed by the results obtained in Fig. 5. Indeed, the distance d_{q_1} always finds the right order of the nearest centers $[C3\ C1\ C2]$. Nevertheless, this distance continues to provide the right solution but the order changes significantly $[C3\ C2\ C1]$. Compared to the other two quantum distances, the distance d_{q_1} seems much more stable in the order of the nearest centers. As can be seen in both Figs. 4 and 5, the other two quantum distances d_{q_2} and d_{q_3} change order quite often compared to the distance d_{q_1}. Order stability is a very relevant information on the behaviour of quantum distances.

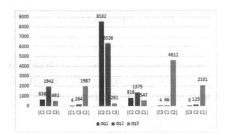

Fig. 4. Stability in distribution 1   **Fig. 5.** Stability in distribution 2

5.3   Clustering Through Quantum K-means

We used three different datasets to show the experimental results of QK-means. Figures 6, 7 and 8 represent the projection of the datasets iris, wine and breast cancer respectively using the principal component analysis. We can notice that the algorithm of QK-means has identified the different clusters (groups) which are significantly different (distant) from each other. Therefore, the quantum K-means gives a good classification just like it's classical version, but the advantage of the quantum version is that it can deal with high dimensional spaces in a time much more quicker than the classical version, which is crucial in nowadays.

For each data set we compare the Davies-Bouldin (DB) index for both the classical and the quantum version of K-means. These results are represented in Table 2. DB and QDB index are not calculated with the same distances. Direct comparison is therefore difficult, but we can see that QDB shows a decreasing

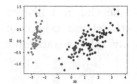

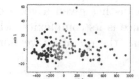

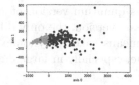

Fig. 6. QK-means clustering on Iris data

Fig. 7. QK-means clustering on Wine data

Fig. 8. QK-means clustering on Breast Cancer data

behaviour during different iterations of learning process, indicating an improvement in the quality of quantum clustering. We can therefore consider that QDB is a good quality indicator for quantum clustering (Figs. 9 and 10).

Table 2. K-means & QK-means using DB index

Dataset	K-means (DB)	QK-means (QDB)
Iris	0.66	$[0.37, 0.56]$
wine	0.53	$[0.40, 0.59]$
Breast Cancer	0.50	$[0.38, 0.57]$

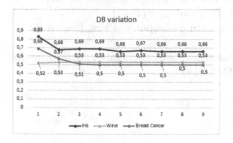

Fig. 9. Davies-Bouldin variation

Fig. 10. QDavies-Bouldin variation

6 Conclusion

In this paper, we implemented a new logarithmic time complexity quantum algorithm for K-means clustering. We analyzed three different methods to estimate the distance for quantum prototypes based clustering algorithms. Through this analysis, we noticed that the notion of distance in quantum computing is different from the classical one. Because what counts in the quantum computation is the correlation not the real values of the distance. This analysis is so crucial as it can solve any prototype based clustering algorithm. To measure the quality of clustering, we have adapted a classical criterion to the quantum case.

This quantum version of K-means has given a good classification just like its classic version, the only difference is its complexity; while the classic version of K-means takes polynomial time, the quantum version only takes logarithmic time, especially in large data sets.

References

1. Aïmeur, E., Brassard, G., Gambs, S.: Machine learning in a quantum world. In: Lamontagne, L., Marchand, M. (eds.) AI 2006. LNCS (LNAI), vol. 4013, pp. 431–442. Springer, Heidelberg (2006). https://doi.org/10.1007/11766247_37
2. Anagolum, S.: Quantum machine learning: distance estimation for k-means clustering (2019). https://towardsdatascience.com/quantum-machine-learning-distance-estimation-for-k-means-clustering-26bccfbfcc76
3. Cai, X.D., et al.: Entanglement-based machine learning on a quantum computer. Phys. Rev. Lett. **114**(11), 110504 (2015)
4. Davies, D.L., Bouldin, D.W.: A cluster separation measure. IEEE Trans. Pattern Anal. Mach. Intell. **2**, 224–227 (1979)
5. Dua, D., Graff, C.: UCI machine learning repository (2017). http://archive.ics.uci.edu/ml
6. Gupta, S., Zia, R.: Quantum neural networks. J. Comput. Syst. Sci. **63**(3), 355–383 (2001)
7. Lloyd, S., Mohseni, M., Rebentrost, P.: Quantum algorithms for supervised and unsupervised machine learning (2013). arXiv preprint arXiv:1307.0411
8. MacQueen, J., et al.: Some methods for classification and analysis of multivariate observations. In: Proceedings of the Fifth Berkeley Symposium on Mathematical Statistics and Probability, vol. 1, pp. 281–297, Oakland (1967)
9. Schützhold, R.: Pattern recognition on a quantum computer. Phys. Rev. A **67**(6), 062311 (2003)
10. Wiebe, N., Kapoor, A., Svore, K.M.: Quantum nearest-neighbor algorithms for machine learning. Quant. Inf. Comput. **15** (2018)

Accelerating Bag-of-Words with SOM

Jian-Hui Chen[1,2,3,4], Zuo-Ren Wang[1,3,4], and Cheng-Lin Liu[2,3,4(✉)]

[1] State Key Laboratory of Neuroscience, Institute of Neuroscience,
Chinese Academy of Sciences, Shanghai, People's Republic of China
{jhchen,zuorenwang}@ion.ac.cn
[2] NLPR, Institute of Automation, Chinese Academy of Sciences,
Beijing, People's Republic of China
liucl@nlpr.ia.ac.cn
[3] University of Chinese Academy of Sciences, Beijing, People's Republic of China
[4] CAS Center for Excellence of Brain Science and Intelligence Technology,
Chinese Academy of Sciences, Beijing, People's Republic of China

Abstract. We propose a fast Bag-of-Words (BoW) method for image classification, inspired by the mechanism that arrangement of neurons in visual cortex can preserve the topology of mapping from inputs, and the fact that human brain can retrieve information almost instantly. We propose algorithms for accelerating both Self-Organizing Map (SOM) training and BoW coding. First, we modify the traditional SOM based on the matrix factorization form of K-means. Utilizing the topology-preserving property of dictionary learned by SOM, the coding process of BoW can be accelerated by fast search of k-nearest neighbor codewords in the grid of SOM dictionary. We evaluate the proposed method in different coding scenarios for image classification task on MNIST and CIFAR-10 datasets. The results show that the proposed method accelerates BoW classification greatly with little loss of classification accuracy.

Keywords: Bag-of-Words · Self-Organizing Map · Fast coding · Image classification

1 Introduction

Bag-of-Words (BoW) is a classical framework used for pattern representation and classification. It has been widely used in various recognition tasks, such as face recognition, image classification, and natural language processing.

The process of BoW-based image classification consists of five basic steps: patch extraction, patch feature extraction, dictionary learning, feature coding and pooling [8]. The coding and pooling steps enable representing the image of various size as a global vector of fixed dimensionality. In recent years, deep neural networks (DNNs) have achieved higher classification performance than BoW in image classification, but there are close links between DNN and BoW, making space for combining DNN with BoW. The deep convolutional neural network can be considered as an end-to-end BoW model, it behaves like BoW on ImageNet

© Springer Nature Switzerland AG 2019
T. Gedeon et al. (Eds.): ICONIP 2019, LNCS 11955, pp. 573–584, 2019.
https://doi.org/10.1007/978-3-030-36718-3_48

[2]. In the BoW framework, using DNN to extract patch features is effective to improve the classification performance. It has been demonstrated that BoW can also realize deep models [3] and achieve comparable performance with deep models [2]. Bag-of-Words has its own advantages of shift invariance and stable performance [22]. As hybrids of BoW and DNN, spatial pyramid pooling can handle arbitrary size/scale inputs [7], neural BoW models can outperform RNN on text classification [9] and scale coding bag of deep features can improve the performance of action recognition [12]. Nowadays, BoW model still has its own advantages in the era of deep learning.

Feature coding is an important step in BoW model, and there are a variety of coding methods which use k nearest neighbors to code local descriptors. The computation of coding can be large in each training or testing step because each patch descriptor is compared with all the codewords in the dictionary. On the other hand, the accuracy of BoW models on test set can be improved by increasing the size of dictionary, which further makes computation larger [4].

This paper proposes a method using Self-Organizing Map (SOM) instead of K-means clustering to generate dictionary to accelerate the coding process for BoW. The dictionary generated by SOM is featured by the topology of code-words that neurons (corresponding to codewords) neighboring in a grid are also close in the data space. With this feature, the search of k nearest neighbors in the dictionary will be simplified by searching for the nearest neighbor only. This will significantly accelerate the coding step during training and testing. By taking advantage of these features, we develop algorithms for both fast SOM training and fast coding in BoW classification. The main contributions of this paper are as follows. (1) we propose to use topologically ordered prototypes generated by SOM to accelerate the feature coding step of BoW framework; (2) we modify classical Self-Organizing Map algorithm to make it converge faster; (3) we analyze the effects of acceleration and performance under different coding methods.

The rest of this paper is organized as follows. Section 2 reviews the background methods of BoW and SOM; Sect. 3 describes the proposed acceleration methods; Sect. 4 presents experimental results, and Sect. 5 draws concluding remarks.

2   Background

Before describing our proposed methods, we briefly review the Bag-of-Words framework [8] in Sect. 2.1 and the Self-Organizing Map (SOM) model [21] in Sect. 2.2.

2.1   Bag-of-Words

The BoW framework has been widely used for text categorization and image classification by representing the text/image as a vector of weights of code-words. Typically, the coding process for image classification consists of five steps:

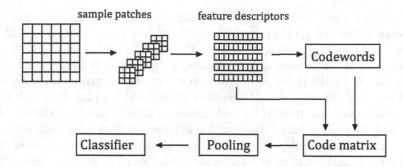

Fig. 1. The Bag-of-Words framework.

patches extraction, feature extraction, dictionary learning, feature coding, and feature pooling [8], see Fig. 1. Assume input images have $w \times w$ pixels, the steps are illustrated as follows.

Patches Extraction. Each image is divided into small blocks and sampled. Grid sampling [17] is the most common method. Each block is represented as a vector. Assume patch size of $p \times p$, then for step size s, $((w - p)/s + 1)^2$ patches are obtained per image.

Patch Feature Extraction. Each block (patch) is described as a vector by extracting local features. Common descriptors include the histogram of oriented gradients (HOG) [6] and scale-invariant feature transform (SIFT) [16] descriptor, both of which use local gradient information. Other types of features can be extracted from a block by using, e.g., deep neural network.

Dictionary Learning. For representing the whole image, a dictionary of codewords is learned for weighting patch features. The codewords are usually generated by unsupervised or supervised methods [10]. Each codeword is a vector of the same dimensionality as patch descriptor, and all codewords together compose a dictionary which is a matrix.

Feature Coding. This is to assign weights for codewords to each patch. Each patch descriptor is compared with codewords and assigned a weight to each codeword according to the similarity between descriptor and codewords. The weights form a vector with dimensionality equal to the number of codewords.

Feature Pooling. This step is to summarize the weights of all the patches of an image to obtain the global representation of the image. Classical pooling methods include max-pooling [20] and average-pooling [5]. Pooling makes the final code invariant to small perturbation, such as translation, rotation or scaling.

2.2   Self-Organizing Map

Self-Organizing Map [13] is a topology-preserving vector quantization algorithm. It not only learns codewords (cluster centers), but also organizes the centers into an ordered map in which similar centers will be gathered as close as possible.

In SOM, neurons representing codewords are often arranged in a 2-D rectangular or hexagonal grid. From the input data $\mathbf{X} = (x_1, \cdots, x_N), x_i \in \mathbb{R}^D$, a dictionary of codewords (weight vectors) $\mathbf{W} = (w_1, \cdots, w_M), w_j \in \mathbb{R}^D$ will be generated. M is the number of neurons, and w_i corresponds to the weights of a neuron. Let Ω be the index of neurons on a rectangular grid. Now for neuron k and neuron v, where $k, v \in \Omega$, the distance on grid is $\eta(k, v, t)$, which is the neighborhood function defined on grid. If two neurons locate near to each other in the grid, then the value of this function is large, otherwise is small. There are many ways to define neighborhood function. "Mexican-hat" function resulted by lateral inhibition is found to be biologically plausible [11]. Step function outputs 1 for neighbors and 0 otherwise. The Gaussian-like function is more practical and frequently-used [21]. Gaussian-like function is defined as

$$\eta(k, v, t) = \exp(-\frac{\|k - v\|^2}{2\sigma(t)^2}), \tag{1}$$

where σ represents the effective range of the neighborhood and often decreases with time t.

Algorithm 1. SOM Algorithm

---

1 Initialize the SOM grid map and Neuron weights $(w_1, \cdots, w_M)$;
2 **repeat**
3 | At each time t, sample an input $x(t)$ from dataset $\mathbf{X}$;
4 | Match the input to all Neurons and select the winner:
   | $\nu(t) = \arg\max_{j \in \Omega}[w_j^T x(t)]$;
5 | Update the weights of winner and its neighbors:
   | $w_j(t+1) = \begin{cases} \frac{w_j + \alpha(t)x(t)}{\|w_j + \alpha(t)x(t)\|} & j \in \eta_{v(t)} \\ w_j & j \notin \eta_{v(t)} \end{cases}$
6 **until** *the map converges*;
7 **return** *The SOM model*;

The learning process of SOM is shown in Algorithm 1. Here because normalized weight vectors (unit norm) are used, the inner product is used as similarity measure, and the neighborhood function uses step function for simplicity. The learning rate $\{a(t), t > 0\}$ decreases monotonically. Finally on termination, this algorithm returns the weights of the neurons, each neuron corresponding to a prototype of vector quantization in the data space.

3   Accelerated Bag-of-Words

The motivation of our work is to make feature coding faster using SOM dictionary to accelerate the BoW framework. For fast training of SOM, we also propose a modified SOM algorithm.

3.1 Modified Self-Organizing Map

Classical SOM is an online learning algorithm [21]. It takes a long time to converge [13]. K-means is a kind of matrix factorization and can be accelerated [1]. Since SOM can be considered as a kind of extension to K-means algorithm, it is reasonable to predict that SOM can also be accelerated. What we base here is spherical K-means [3] defined as follows:

$$\min_{D,c} \sum_i \|c_i D - x_i\|^2 + \|D - D_{old}\|^2, \tag{2}$$

subject to

$$\|c_i\|_0 \leq 1, \|D_j\|_2 = 1, \; i \in 1, 2, \cdots, N; \; j \in 1, 2, \cdots, M, \tag{3}$$

where c_i is the code vector of x_i, and $c_i \in \mathbb{R}^M$. Let $C = (c_1, c_2, \cdots, c_N), C \in \mathbb{R}^{N \times M}$. D_j is the jth row of dictionary, which is a single prototype. The goal is to find a dictionary that can minimize the error of x_i and its reconstruction $c_i D$. Each input x_i only belong to one cluster in spherical K-means, so the code vectors c_i have at most one non-zero entry. D_j has a unit length so that c_i and D cannot scale along with each other. Unit length dictionary will not learn different magnitude of the same pattern. This makes quantization more efficient.

However, SOM would prefer $\|c_i\|_0$ to be larger than 1 to update similar centers simultaneously. Thus, the SOM loss can be defined as:

$$\min_{D,c} \sum_i \|(c_i \odot \eta_i)D - x_i\|^2 + \|D - D_{old}\|^2, \tag{4}$$

$$\eta_{i,j} = \eta(v_i, j, t) \; with \; v_i = \arg\max_{j \in \Omega}[D_j x_i], \; i \in 1, 2, \cdots, N, \tag{5}$$

subject to

$$\|D_j\|_2 = 1, \; j \in 1, 2, \cdots, M, \tag{6}$$

where η will decay respect to time t. From Spherical K-means update rules [3], we can infer the same conclusion:

$$D_{new} \propto ((C \odot \eta)^T X + D_{old}), \tag{7}$$

here $\odot$ denotes the element-wise multiplication, and the regulation term $\|D - D_{old}\|^2$ can prevent small clusters from being pulled too far in a single iteration. The total SOM process becomes a matrix multiplication that can be parallelized. According to the results of the original paper [3], the objective function converges extremely fast using this method.

The learning process of fast SOM is shown in Algorithm 2. Calculating distance matrix in advance can further accelerate the process. We use a one-hot vector to index the distance matrix and output the corresponding distance with all other neurons on the grid for each input. Altogether, we generate a neighbor matrix for the whole dataset, and each row represents the neighbor coefficient of neurons over the dictionary for a single input.

Algorithm 2. Fast SOM Algorithm

---

1 Initialize the SOM grid map and Neuron weights $(w_1, \cdots, w_M)$;
2 **for** $(k, v) \in \Omega^2$ **do**
3 $\quad\mid\quad H_{k,v} = \|k - v\|^2$
4 **end**
5 **repeat**
6 $\quad\mid\quad$ At each time t, decay effective range of the neighborhood:
7 $\quad\mid\quad \sigma(t) = M * \exp(-\frac{t}{decay\ step})$
8 $\quad\mid\quad$ Select the winner and calculate the coefficient η:
9 $\quad\mid\quad$ **for** $i \in 1, 2, \cdots, N$ **do**
10 $\quad\mid\quad\mid\quad v_i = \arg\max_{j \in \Omega} |D_j x_i|$;
11 $\quad\mid\quad\mid\quad \zeta_i = \text{Onehot}(v_i) \in \mathbb{R}^M$
12 $\quad\mid\quad$ **end**
13 $\quad\mid\quad \eta = \exp^{\frac{\zeta H}{2\sigma(t)^2}}, \eta \in \mathbb{R}^{N \times M}$
14 $\quad\mid\quad C = X D^T$
15 $\quad\mid\quad D = D + \alpha(t)(C \odot \eta)^T X$
16 $\quad\mid\quad D_j = \frac{D_j}{\|D_j\|^2}, j \in 1, 2, \cdots, M$
17 **until** *the map converges;*
18 **return** *The SOM model;*

3.2   Feature Coding by Fast K-Nearest Neighbor Search

Assume each image has already been sampled into L patches, and SOM has learned M prototypes for the patches throughout the dataset. Now coding step would be mainly applied on similarity matrix for the given dictionary. For an image that has L patches, each patch would be compared to M prototypes, thus similarity matrix $S \in \mathbb{R}^{N \times L \times M}$. There are many ways to evaluate similarity between patches and codewords in dictionary, here we choose the inner product which shows advantages in parallelization.

Feature coding includes global coding and local coding [8]. Local coding uses a combination of the nearest codewords for approximating the manifold of inputs, and is more effective than global coding that uses all codewords which is excess.

Assume results of comparison between patches and codewords are stored in similarity matrix S. A transform function is applied on the top k similarity vectors to fit certain constraints, unitization for example. Because SOM organizes similar codewords together on grid and the neighborhood relationship on grid is fixed, so we can retrieve approximate k nearest neighbor with two steps: find the top nearest neighbor and then retrieve its k − 1 neighbors on grid by indexing, shown in Algorithm 3. Thus, a neighboring mask can be prepared in advance and then we can identify the top k nearest neighbors in similarity matrix S by element-wise multiply. These are all operations on matrixes, they can be parallelized on GPU. Furthermore, there are fewer operations in fast encoding than traditional k nearest neighbor search, thus it is much faster than the traditional one.

Algorithm 3. Fast Encoding

---

1 Calculating distances of clustering centers on grid:
2 **for** $(k, v) \in \Omega^2$ **do**
3 $\quad \big|\quad H_{k,v} = \|k - v\|^2$
4 **end**
5 Defined neighboring mask on grid organizing centers:
6 $Mask_{k,v} = \begin{cases} 1 \; if \; H_{k,v} \in topk(H_k) \\ 0 \qquad otherwise \end{cases}$
7 Calculate similarity matrix between patches $P \in \mathbb{R}^{N \times L \times (p \times p)}$ and dictionary D:
8 $S = PD^T$
9 **for** $i \in 1, 2, \cdots, N$ **do**
10 $\quad \big|\quad v = \arg\max_{j \in \Omega} |S_i|;$
11 $\quad \big|\quad S_i = S_i \odot Mask_v$
12 $\quad \big|\quad$ Encode with a non-linear function f:
13 $\quad \big|\quad code = f(S_i)$
14 **end**
15 **return** *code*;

The difference in function f results in distinct coding results. We use four local coding methods in this paper: hard coding, soft coding, threshold coding, and salient coding [8]. Hard coding usually uses one-hot vector, we use k-hot vector here instead for k nearest neighbors and then normalize it. Soft coding utilizes k-nearest neighbor in the form of $\frac{\exp^{S_{i,j}}}{\sum_j \exp^{S_{i,j}}}$, increasing the signal to noise ratio. Threshold coding outputs the signal when it surpasses the threshold. Salient coding [8] uses the ratio between outputs from the nearest neighbor and k-1 next nearest neighbors:

$$\Psi_{i,j} = \Phi(\frac{S_{i,j}}{\frac{1}{K-1}\sum_{j \neq i}^K S_{i,j}}), \tag{8}$$

here use $\Phi(z) = 1 - z$ for convenience. After coding the descriptors of all patches, the codes of patched are pooled to obtain the global representation of image.

4 Experiments

In this section, we validate our proposal on the classic MNIST and CIFAR-10 datasets. MNIST is a widely-used handwritten digits dataset, which contains 10 classes of 60,000 training samples and 10,000 testing samples, where each image has 28×28 pixels [15]. CIFAR-10 dataset consists of 60000 color images, which are sized 32×32 from 10 classes, including 50000 training images and 10000 test images [14]. First, we generate codewords for patches using the proposed fast SOM method. Then, we test the dictionary on different coding methods. Finally, we use fast encoding to accelerate the whole BoW framework. The classifier used here is a multiple layer perceptron (MLP) with 512 hidden units and 10 outputs.

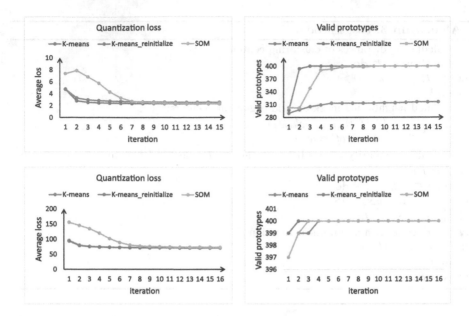

Fig. 2. Average loss and number of non-empty prototypes for K-means and fast SOM model. Top: MNIST, bottom: CIFAR-10. The K-means_reinitialize will re-initialize empty prototypes after each iteration, K-means that doesn't re-initialize will get stuck in local optimum for MNIST.

4.1   Dictionary Generation

We adapt fast SOM algorithm inspired by Spherical K-means [3]. The latter also serves as a baseline to compare against. For MNIST, we use patch size of 5×5 as feature descriptor directly, and there should be 23×23 descriptors for each image. For CIFAR-10, we trained a VGG-19 [19] with 92.75% test accuracy and feed the images directly to the model, then use output of the second block, with 256 8×8 filters, as feature descriptors. The dictionary size that we use is 400. From Fig. 2, we can see that for both datasets, fast SOM converges in 7 iterations, and each iteration only costs 2.7 s. This is remarkably faster than popular SOM package pyclustering [18] that use classical online training, which takes 427 s for one iteration in the python version. The resulted prototypes for MNIST are shown in Fig. 3, we can see that the similar prototypes locate more closely than dissimilar pairs.

4.2   Bag-of-Words Classification

Each descriptor is compared to the dictionary, and there should be k non-zero elements in each code of descriptor, which is selected by k nearest mask $Mask_v$ in Algorithm 3. Then we use a max-pooling of stride 2 upon coding results and feed them into the MLP. The final output of MLP indicates the probability for each

Fig. 3. The codewords for MNIST generated by fast Self-Organizing Map arranged on a rectangular grid. We can see that similar orientation codewords are located near to each other.

Table 1. Run time for coding methods on MNIST (M) and CIFAR-10 (C), $k = 50$. Suffixes -400 and -1600 show the size of dictionary.

Run time (s) M/C	Threshold	Soft	Hard	Salient
K-means-400	36.5/20.3	37.5/20.4	36.6/19.6	45.5/21.9
SOM-400	37.2/20.7	38.8/20.6	41.3/19.5	43.5/22.1
SOM_ANN-400	12.6/9.4	13.0/9.9	10.9/8.5	15.2/10.34
K-means-1600	199.6/102.8	201.0/109.6	193.1/104.9	222.6/112.6
SOM-1600	219.8/101.2	224.9/107.8	212.6/101.5	242.3/111.2
SOM_ANN-1600	60.7/35.9	62.8/38.5	52.2/32.8	67.7/39.5

class. Using 400 codewords generated by K-means and fast SOM, we compared the performance of four coding methods and varies k from 10 up to 400, where there are 10 repetitions under each setting of k. The results on MNIST are shown in Fig. 4 and CIFAR-10 in Fig. 5. We did not see an obvious difference in test accuracy between the results using SOM dictionary and K-means dictionary.

To accelerate BoW, we approximate the nearest neighbor coding method by Algorithm 3. The index of the maximal similarity between patch and codewords in dictionary are used to retrieve k-nearest neighbors that are organized together (neighborhood) in the pre-defined grid. This method saves a lot of time when compared to the conventional k nearest search over the dictionary. The performance of approximate k nearest neighbors for SOM (SOM_ANN) is shown in Figs. 4 and 5, it is similar to the conventional k-nearest neighbor coding on SOM dictionary. The running time when $k = 50$ is shown in Table 1, and we can see that SOM_ANN spends much shorter time than K-means and SOM that use conventional k-nearest neighbors search: one third for 23×23 feature map in MNIST and half for 8×8 feature map in CIFAR-10 for small dictionary. The

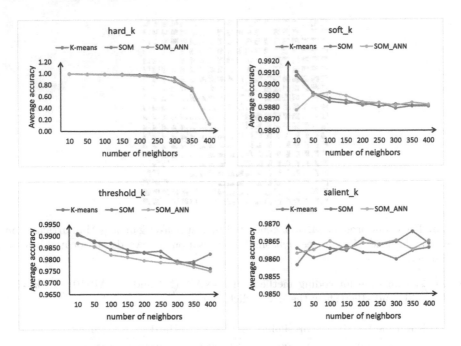

Fig. 4. For MNIST dataset, SOM_ANN behaves similar to K-means and SOM that uses true k nearest neighbor for coding (dictionary size 400).

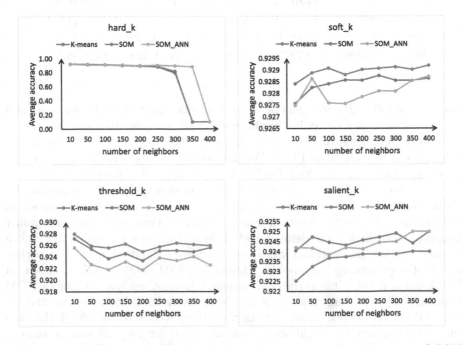

Fig. 5. For CIFAR-10 dataset, SOM_ANN behaves similarly to K-means and SOM that use true k nearest neighbor for coding (dictionary size 400).

degree of acceleration become one forth in MNIST and one third in CIFAR-10 for bigger dictionary.

A higher degree of acceleration can be achieved by using larger feature map and bigger dictionary which cost of more running time. Thus, our method is especially suitable for those tasks in which big dictionary and high-resolution images are used.

5 Conclusion

In this paper, we introduce a method for accelerating Bag-of-Words (BoW) framework in image classification. The code dictionary is learned using SOM, which arranges the codewords (cluster centers) on a grid with topology preserved (neurons neighboring on the grid have similar codewords). The topology-preserving properties can be utilized to accelerate the search of k-nearest neighbors in feature coding in BoW-based classification. We also modify the original SOM for faster convergence in training than popular packages at the present time, this will make big dictionary learning more easily. Our experimental results on the MNIST and CIFAR-10 datasets show that using SOM learned dictionary, the coding can be largely accelerated while the classification accuracy is comparable to that of coding without utilizing the grid topology.

In future work, we plan to improve the image classification performance using better feature extraction using deep neural networks.

Acknowledgements. Supported by the Major Project for New Generation of AI Grant No. 2018AAA0100400, the National Natural Science Foundation of China (NSFC) Grant No. 61721004, the Strategic Priority Research Program of Chinese Academy of Science, Grant No. XDB32010300, Shanghai Municipal Science and Technology Major Project (Grant No. 2018SHZDZX05).

References

1. Bauckhage, C.: K-means clustering is matrix factorization. arXiv preprint arXiv:1512.07548 (2015)
2. Brendel, W., Bethge, M.: Approximating CNNs with bag-of-local-features models works surprisingly well on imagenet. arXiv preprint arXiv:1904.00760 (2019)
3. Coates, A., Ng, A.Y.: Learning feature representations with k-means. In: Montavon, G., Orr, G.B., Müller, K.-R. (eds.) Neural Networks: Tricks of the Trade. LNCS, vol. 7700, pp. 561–580. Springer, Heidelberg (2012). https://doi.org/10.1007/978-3-642-35289-8_30
4. Coates, A., Ng, A.Y., Lee, H.: An analysis of single-layer networks in unsupervised feature learning. In: Proceedings of the Fourteenth International Conference on Artificial Intelligence and Statistics, AISTATS 2011, Fort Lauderdale, USA, 11–13 April 2011, pp. 215–223 (2011)
5. Csurka, G., Dance, C., Fan, L., Willamowski, J., Bray, C.: Visual categorization with bags of keypoints. In: Workshop on Statistical Learning in Computer Vision, ECCV, Prague, vol. 1, pp. 1–2 (2004)

6. Dalal, N., Triggs, B.: Histograms of oriented gradients for human detection. In: 2005 IEEE Conference on Computer Vision and Pattern Recognition (CVPR 2005), pp. 886–893 (2005)

7. He, K., Zhang, X., Ren, S., Sun, J.: Spatial pyramid pooling in deep convolutional networks for visual recognition. IEEE Trans. Pattern Anal. Mach. Intell. **37**(9), 1904–1916 (2015)

8. Huang, Y., Wu, Z., Wang, L., Tan, T.: Feature coding in image classification: a comprehensive study. IEEE Trans. Pattern Anal. Mach. Intell. **36**(3), 493–506 (2014)

9. Iyyer, M., Manjunatha, V., Boyd-Graber, J., Daumé III, H.: Deep unordered composition rivals syntactic methods for text classification. In: Proceedings of the 53rd Annual Meeting of the Association for Computational Linguistics and the 7th International Joint Conference on Natural Language Processing, Long Papers, vol. 1, pp. 1681–1691 (2015)

10. Jiang, Z., Zhang, G., Davis, L.S.: Submodular dictionary learning for sparse coding. In: 2012 IEEE Conference on Computer Vision and Pattern Recognition (CVPR 2012), pp. 3418–3425 (2012)

11. Kandel, E.R., et al.: Principles of Neural Science, vol. 4. McGraw-Hill, New York (2000)

12. Khan, F.S., Van De Weijer, J., Anwer, R.M., Bagdanov, A.D., Felsberg, M., Laaksonen, J.: Scale coding bag of deep features for human attribute and action recognition. Mach. Vis. Appl. **29**(1), 55–71 (2018)

13. Kohonen, T.: Self-organized formation of topologically correct feature maps. Biol. Cybern. **43**(1), 59–69 (1982)

14. Krizhevsky, A., Hinton, G.: Learning multiple layers of features from tiny images. Technical report, Citeseer (2009)

15. LeCun, Y., Bottou, L., Bengio, Y., Haffner, P., et al.: Gradient-based learning applied to document recognition. Proc. IEEE **86**(11), 2278–2324 (1998)

16. Lowe, D.G.: Distinctive image features from scale-invariant keypoints. Int. J. Comput. Vis. **60**(2), 91–110 (2004)

17. Marszalek, M., Schmid, C., Harzallah, H., van de Weijer, J.: Learning representations for visual object class recognition. In: Proceedings of the PASCAL Visual Object Classes Challenge 2007 (2007)

18. Novikov, A.: PyClustering: data mining library. J. Open Source Softw. **4**(36), 1230 (2019)

19. Simonyan, K., Zisserman, A.: Very deep convolutional networks for large-scale image recognition. arXiv preprint arXiv:1409.1556 (2014)

20. Yang, J., Yu, K., Gong, Y., Huang, T.S.: Linear spatial pyramid matching using sparse coding for image classification. In: 2009 IEEE Conference on Computer Vision and Pattern Recognition (CVPR 2009), pp. 1794–1801 (2009)

21. Yin, H.: The self-organizing maps: background, theories, extensions and applications. In: Fulcher, J., Jain, L.C. (eds.) Computational Intelligence: A Compendium. SCI, vol. 115, pp. 715–762. Springer, Heidelberg (2008). https://doi.org/10.1007/978-3-540-78293-3_17

22. Zhou, H., Wei, L., Lim, C.P., Creighton, D., Nahavandi, S.: Robust vehicle detection in aerial images using bag-of-words and orientation aware scanning. IEEE Trans. Geosci. Remote Sens. **99**, 1–12 (2018)

A Deep Clustering-Guide Learning
for Unsupervised Person Re-identification

Guo Chen, Song Wu, and Guoqiang Xiao[✉]

College of Computer and Information Science,
National and Local Joint Engineering Laboratory of Intelligent Transmission
and Control Technology, Southwest University, Chongqing, China
lawrencefyi@163.com, {songwu,gqxiao}@swu.edu.cn

Abstract. Unsupervised person re-identification (RE-ID) has attracted
increasing attentions due to its ability to overcome the scalability problem of supervised RE-ID methods. However, it is hard to learn discriminative features without pairwise labels and identity information
in unlabeled target domains. To address this problem, we propose a
deep clustering-guided model for unsupervised RE-ID that focuses on
full mining of supervisions and a complete usage of the mined information. Specifically, we cluster person images from unlabeled target and
labeled auxiliary datasets together. On the one hand, although the clustering IDs of unlabeled person images could be directly used as pseudo-
labels to supervise the whole model, we further develop a non-parametric
softmax variant for cluster-level supervision. On the other hand, since
clustering badly suffers from intra-person appearance variation and inter-
person appearance similarity in the unlabeled domain, we propose a reliable and hard mining in both intra-cluster and inter-cluster. Concretely,
labeled persons (auxiliary domain) in each cluster are used as *comparators* to learn comparing vectors for each unlabeled persons. Following
the consistency of the visual feature similarity and the corresponding
comparing vector similarity, we mine reliable positive and hard negative
pairs in the intra-cluster, and reliable negative and hard positive pairs
in the inter-cluster for unlabeled persons. Moreover, a weighted point-
to-set triplet loss is employed to adaptively assign higher (lower) weights
to reliable (hard) pairs, which is more robust and effective compared
with the conventional triplet loss in unsupervised RE-ID. We train our
model with these two losses jointly to learn discriminative features for
unlabeled persons. Extensive experiments validate the superiority of the
proposed method for unsupervised RE-ID.

Keywords: Unsupervised person re-identification · Clustering ·
Supervision

1 Introduction

Person re-identification (RE-ID), a task that consists of matching pairs of person images across non-overlapping camera views, has attracted significant attention in the computer vision community [1]. In recent years, RE-ID has achieved

T. Gedeon et al. (Eds.): ICONIP 2019, LNCS 11955, pp. 585–596, 2019.
https://doi.org/10.1007/978-3-030-36718-3_49

impressive progress due to the significant development of deep learning [2,3]. However, most existing RE-ID methods require tremendous labeled data, which incurs unaffordable manual efforts, limiting the scalability for large-scale real-world application scenarios. To address this, some studies have focused on unsupervised learning by improving hand-crafted feature representation [4,5], clustering [6–8] and resorting to the auxiliary labeled dataset [9–11]. However, these methods do not achieve satisfying performance against supervised RE-ID methods; hence, they are far from practical application to large-scale real-world data. Obviously, great intra-person appearance variation is the major challenging for supervised RE-ID. Even worse, lacking the pairwise labeling and identity information in unsupervised RE-ID, it is more difficult to identify the discriminative information. Therefore, mining the potential supervision information as learning guidance is reasonable and necessary for unsupervised RE-ID.

Recent works focus on mining such desired supervision. The most common techniques are based on clustering. Fan *et al.* [6] propose the progressive unsupervised learning framework, which integrates clustering and self-paced learning. Lin *et al.* [7] develop the bottom-up clustering framework with diversity regularization. Yu *et al.* [8] propose to learn the cross-view asymmetric distance metric based on clustering labels. However, these clustering-based methods are unable to learn discriminative enough feature embeddings, since clustering badly suffers from intra-person appearance variation and inter-person appearance similarity. Meanwhile, Yu *et al.* [10] propose to learn a soft multilabel vector for each unlabeled image based on an auxiliary dataset, which can be used to mine positive and hard negative samples. The main difference in [10] is that such soft multilabel could leverage the auxiliary reference information other than only visual feature similarity, while clustering-based methods only use pseudo-labels to encode the visual feature similarity of a pair of unlabeled images. Nevertheless, the latter method fails to make full mining of supervisions and take full advantage of the mined label information.

To address the shortcomings of existing methods, this study proposes a novel deep clustering-guided method (i.e., CEG) to achieve full mining of supervisions and a full usage of the mined information. The key strategy is to cluster the unlabeled target and labeled auxiliary datasets, which can mine two types of supervision signals. On the one hand, the cluster IDs of unlabeled person images could be used as pseudo-labels to train the whole model, which can achieve cluster-level discrimination. Nevertheless, it is error-prone and unable to learn discriminative enough feature embeddings, as clustering results badly suffer from intra-person appearance variation and inter-person appearance similarity in the unlabeled dataset. Therefore, on the other hand, in each cluster we further propose to use labeled persons as *comparators* and learn a comparing vector for each unlabeled image, which could be used to mine the latent discriminative pairwise label information. Essentially, such comparing vector encodes the indirect comparative characteristic of the unlabeled person, and images of the same person should have similar comparing vectors. Integrating the clustering results and comparing vectors, we propose a reliable and hard mining in intra- and inter-clustering. When a pair of person images are in the same cluster (intra-cluster) and *sufficiently* visual similar, with similar comparing vectors, they are considered as a reliable positive pair; otherwise, they are regarded as a hard negative pair. A pair of person images in different clusters (inter-cluster) and *sufficiently* visual dissimilar, with dissimilar comparing vectors, are considered as a reliable negative pair; otherwise, they are regarded as a hard positive pair. In our hands, merely mining reliable pairs is unable to learn discriminative enough feature embeddings, and only mining hard pairs and selecting the hardest pair is error-prone. Therefore, we propose a weighted point-to-set (P2S) triplet loss to consider both reliable and hard pairs. The weight of a sample against the anchor lies in its visual feature and comparing vector; the reliable (hard) samples are assigned higher (lower) weights to maintain stability and effectiveness. Historically, multi-loss joint training has shown superiority in supervised RE-ID [1]. In unsupervised RE-ID, without pedestrian annotations existing unsupervised RE-ID methods fail to make full usage of the mined label information (i.e., only single loss could be used.). Fortunately, we mine two kinds of supervision signals used as two types of losses to jointly supervise the CNN model, which achieves full mining of supervisions and a full usage of the mined information.

2   Related Works

2.1   Unsupervised RE-ID

According to whether the auxiliary dataset is used, unsupervised RE-ID can be categorized into two types: (1) *Fully unsupervised RE-ID without the auxiliary dataset.* This includes designing hand-craft features [4,5], exploiting localized salience statistics [12,13], and clustering-based methods [6–8]. The most related works are clustering-based methods. For example, Yu et al. [8,14] proposed to learn the cross-view asymmetric distance metric based on clustering labels. Meanwhile, Fan *et al.* [6] proposed the progressive unsupervised learning framework, which integrates clustering and self-paced learning, and Lin *et al.* [7] developed the bottom-up clustering framework with diversity regularization. However, due to the lack of pairwise labels, these methods are unable to learn discriminative enough features, and fail to achieve a satisfying performance. (2) *Unsupervised RE-ID with the auxiliary dataset.* Lv et al. [9] proposed the transfer learning of the pedestrians' spatio-temporal patterns from labeled source dataset to the unlabeled target domain. Peng *et al.* [11] developed a cross-dataset transfer method based on dictionary learning. Furthermore, Yu *et al.* [10] proposed to learn a soft multilabel vector for each unlabeled person based on labeled persons from an auxiliary dataset. Different from these methods, our model combines clustering and guidance of the auxiliary dataset, mining not only cluster-level supervision but also potential pairwise label information.

2.2   Unsupervised Domain Adaptation

Our work is also related to unsupervised domain adaptation (UDA), where the target dataset is unlabeled during training. Most UDA approaches learn a mapping between source and target distributions. Yang *et al.* [15] proposed to learn a domain-shared group-sparse dictionary to align condition and distributions. Cao *et al.* [16] propose to learn a transfer support vector machine. Tsai *et al.* [17] proposed to learn a common feature space for joint adaptation and classification. Shekhar *et al.* [18] proposed to learn a latent dictionary which can represent both domains. Different from the UDA setting which assumes that both source and target domains have the same class, distinct RE-ID datasets contain entirely varying person identities (classes). Hence, UDA methods cannot be directly utilized for unsupervised RE-ID.

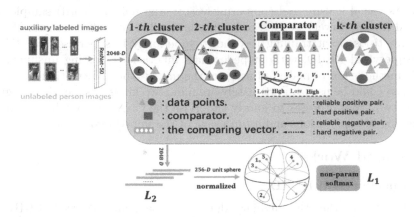

Fig. 1. Illustration of the proposed model. We cluster unlabeled (yellow dots) and labeled person images (red dots). With the clustering IDs of unlabeled person images, we propose a non-parametric softmax variant L_1 to achieve basic cluster-level discrimination. Moreover, in each cluster, labeled persons are used as *comparators* $\mathbf{r}$ (red squares), which are compared with each unlabeled person images to obtain their comparing vectors $\mathbf{v}$ (green rectangles with hollow circles). In intra-clustering, two unlabeled images are considered as a reliable positive pair (green solid arrows) with similar visual features and comparing vectors; otherwise, they are regarded as a hard negative pair (black dotted arrows). Accordingly, in inter-clustering, two unlabeled images are viewed as a reliable negative pair (black solid arrows) with dissimilar visual features and comparing vectors; otherwise, they are regarded as a hard positive pair (green dotted arrows). With this mining scheme, we further propose a weighted point-to-set loss L_2 to adaptively assign higher (lower) weights to reliable (hard) pairs. We train our model with the above joint losses to learn discriminative feature embeddings of unlabeled images. Best viewed in color. (Color figure online)

3   Deep Clustering-Guided Learning

3.1   Preliminary

Given the unlabeled target dataset $\mathcal{X} = \{x_i\}_{i=1}^{N_u}$ with N_u person images and a labeled auxiliary dataset $\mathcal{S} = \{s_i, y_i\}_{i=1}^{N_a}$ with N_a labeled person images where

y_i denotes the label for the i-th image s_i. The total number of person images is $N = N_u + N_a$. Note that identities in the target dataset are non-overlapping with those in the source dataset. Our goal is to learn a discriminative feature embedding function $f(\cdot)$ from the unlabeled dataset $\mathcal{X}$ with the guidance of the labeled dataset $\mathcal{S}$. Specifically, our framework mainly contains two iterative procedures as follows: (1) The feature embeddings of unlabeled target and labeled auxiliary datasets $\mathcal{X}$ and $\mathcal{S}$ are clustered to mine two types of supervision signals. (2) The network is retrained with two joint losses to learn discriminative feature embeddings for unlabeled person images. The overall illustration of this model is shown in Fig. 1. Note that we enforce a unit norm constraint in feature embedding ($\| f(\cdot) \|_2 = 1, \| \mathbf{r} \|_2 = 1$).

3.2   Cluster-Level Supervision

We follow a standard clustering algorithm (e.g. k-means) to group the feature embeddings of both unlabeled dataset $\mathcal{X}$ and labeled dataset $\mathcal{S}$ into predefined K distinct clusters. Thus, we can obtain the cluster assignments $\mathbf{c} = [c_i]_{N \times 1}$ with $c_i = 1, \cdots, K$ and a centroid matrix $\mathbf{C} \in \mathbf{R}^{d \times K}$, where d is the feature dimension. Obviously, the cluster assignments of unlabeled person images could be viewed as their pseudo-labels to train the whole model (the classifier parameter $\mathbf{W}$ and the embedding parameter θ) using the softmax criterion [19]:

$$P(k|x) = \frac{exp(\mathbf{W}^\top f(\theta; x))}{\sum_{j=1}^K exp(\mathbf{W}^\top f(\theta; x))}. \tag{1}$$

However, this conventional parametric softmax formulation with the weight parameter $\mathbf{W}$ in fully connected layer may not be suitable for our model, since we mainly focus on the feature embedding function $f(\theta; \cdot)$. Therefore, according to [20], we propose its non-parametric variant by defining the probability that an unlabeled image x belongs to the k-th cluster:

$$P(k|x, \hat{\mathbf{C}}) = \frac{exp(\hat{\mathbf{C}}_k^\top f(\theta; x)/\tau)}{\sum_{j=1}^K exp(\hat{\mathbf{C}}_j^\top f(\theta; x)/\tau)}, \tag{2}$$

where τ is a temperature parameter and $\hat{\mathbf{C}}_k$ denotes the k-th cluster center of only unlabeled person images. We do not adopt the original centroid matrix $\mathbf{C}$, encoded by both the unlabeled domain $\mathcal{X}$ and the labeled auxiliary domain $\mathcal{S}$, due to domain shift [21]. Against the parametric softmax classifier, the above Eq. (2) entirely focuses on the feature embedding function. The final objective is to minimize the negative log-likelihood over the unlabeled dataset $\mathcal{X}$:

$$L_1 = -\sum_{i=1}^{N_u} \frac{1}{N_{c_i}} log P(c_i|x_i, \hat{\mathbf{C}}), \tag{3}$$

where c_i is the cluster ID of the unlabeled image x_i, and N_{c_i} is the size of the c_i-th cluster, which addresses the trivial parametrization problem by weighting the contribution of each cluster to the loss function [19]. However, since there are intra-person appearance variation and inter-person appearance similarity in the unlabeled dataset $\mathcal{X}$, visually similar person images of different identities may be assigned to the same cluster ID and visually dissimilar person images of same identities may be in different clusters. Therefore, it could not learn discriminative enough feature embeddings only based on cluster-level supervision. To address this problem, we next mine another type of supervision to jointly learn the discriminative feature embeddings of unlabeled person images.

3.3   Reliable and Hard Mining

Generally, each cluster is composed of both unlabeled and labeled person images. In each cluster, such labeled person images could serve as *comparators*, which are compared with each unlabeled person image to encode its indirect comparative characteristics defined as comparing vector. We use a simple way to establish these *comparators* by averaging feature embeddings of images of each labeled person. Formally, the i-th *comparator* in the k-th cluster is denoted by $\mathbf{r}_i^k = \sum_{j=1}^{N_i^k} f(s_j)/N_i^k$, where N_i^k is the number of person images of the i-th labeled person in the k-th cluster. Based on the inner product of the feature embeddings of unlabeled person images and corresponding *comparators*, the comparing vector $\mathbf{v}$ for the unlabeled person image x in the k-th cluster is as follows:

$$v^i = \frac{exp(\mathbf{r}_i^{k\top} f(\theta; x))}{\sum_{j=1}^{N^k} exp(\mathbf{r}_j^{k\top} f(\theta; x))}, \tag{4}$$

where v^i is the i-th element of vector $\mathbf{v}$, and N^k is the number of *comparators* in the k-th cluster. Each unlabeled person image is only compared with *comparators* in the same cluster. Generally, different clusters have different numbers of *comparators*, thus the dimension of comparing vector is expanded to the total number of *comparators* for easily comparing them among different clusters.

In supervised RE-ID, hard sample mining has the outstanding performance in learning discriminative feature embeddings [1,22]. However, it is very challenging to perform such mining in the absence of pairwise labels, as it is error-prone to determine whether visually dissimilar (similar) images have the same identity or not. Obviously, a pair of images in the same cluster cannot be directly identified as a positive pair (same identity), and a pair of images in different clusters cannot also be directly identified as a negative pair (different identities). Based on the visual feature and the comparing vector, we propose to mine reliable positive pairs and hard negative pairs in the intra-cluster, and reliable negative pairs and hard positive pairs in the inter-cluster. Specifically, we make the following assumptions:

Assumption 1. *When a pair of unlabeled person images x_i, x_j are in the same cluster, i.e., $c_i = c_j$, if they are sufficiently visually similar and have highly similar comparing vectors, they are considered as a reliable positive pair, otherwise, they are defined as a hard negative pair.*

Assumption 2. *When a pair of unlabeled person images x_i, x_j are in different clusters, i.e., $c_i \neq c_j$, if they are highly visually dissimilar and have dissimilar comparing vectors, they are defined as a reliable negative pair, otherwise, they are considered as a hard positive pair.*

The feature similarity measure of unlabeled person images adopts the cosine similarity, which is simplified as the inner product of their feature embeddings. For the similarity measure of comparing vectors of two unlabeled person images x_i and x_j, we apply the agreement function [10], i.e., $z(\mathbf{v}_i, \mathbf{v}_j) = 1- \parallel \mathbf{v}_i - \mathbf{v}_j \parallel_1 / 2$, where $\parallel \cdot \parallel_1$ is the well-defined L_1 distance. We define two threshold values σ_1 and η_1 for the visual feature and comparing vector similarity in the intra-cluster, and two threshold values σ_2 and η_2 in the inter-cluster (specific threshold scheme is based on a mining ratio and shows in Sect. 4.2). Based on Assumptions 1 and 2, for an unlabeled person image pair (x_i, x_j), we formally propose:

Intra-cluster:

$$relia\_P = \{(i,j)|c_i = c_j; f(x_i)^\top f(x_j) \geq \sigma_1; z(\mathbf{v}_i, \mathbf{v}_j) \geq \eta_1\}$$
$$hard\_N = \{(i,j)|c_i = c_j; f(x_i)^\top f(x_j) \leq \sigma_1; z(\mathbf{v}_i, \mathbf{v}_j) \leq \eta_1\}, \quad (5)$$

Inter-cluster:

$$hard\_P = \{(i,j)|c_i \neq c_j; f(x_i)^\top f(x_j) \geq \sigma_2; z(\mathbf{v}_i, \mathbf{v}_j) \geq \eta_2\}$$
$$relia\_N = \{(i,j)|c_i \neq c_j; f(x_i)^\top f(x_j) \leq \sigma_2; z(\mathbf{v}_i, \mathbf{v}_j) \leq \eta_2\}. \quad (6)$$

In unsupervised RE-ID, merely mining reliable pairs cannot learn discriminative enough feature embeddings, and only mining hard pairs and selecting the hardest pair is error-prone. Hence, we propose a reliable and hard mining strategy, which considers both reliable and hard samples with adaptive weights. Intuitively, reliable samples should be assigned higher weights to maintain stability, and the hard samples should be assigned lower weights to reduce the impact of identity error. Therefore, we adopt the weighted point-to-set (P2S) triplet loss [22] to consider all reliable and hard samples, which is robust and effective. Given an anchor x_a without its label, let $P_a^+ = relia\_P_a \cup hard\_P_a$ denote the whole positive set which contains the reliable and hard positive samples, and $N_a^- = relia\_N_a \cup hard\_N_a$ denote the whole negative set. The P2S triplet loss is defined as:

$$L_2 = \frac{1}{N_{batch}} \sum_{a=1}^{N_{batch}} \{D(f(x_a), P_a^+) - D(f(x_a), N_a^-) + m\}_+, \quad (7)$$

where $\{\cdot\}_+ = max(\cdot, 0)$, margin m is a constant, and D denotes the P2S distance which assigns larger (lower) weights to reliable (hard) samples in both positive and negative sets as

$$
\begin{cases}
D(f(x_a), P_a^+) = \dfrac{\sum_{x_i} d(f(x_a), f(x_i)) w_i^+}{\sum_{x_i} w_i^+} \\[4mm]
D(f(x_a), N_a^-) = \dfrac{\sum_{x_j} d(f(x_a), f(x_i)) w_j^-}{\sum_{x_j} w_j^-} ,
\end{cases}
\tag{8}
$$

where w_i^+ and w_j^- denote the weights of $f(x_i)$ and $f(x_j)$ in the positive and negative sets respectively, and d is a predefined distance metric. The weight of a sample against the anchor is considered to lies in its visual feature and comparing vector. Accordingly, we propose the following exponential weighting schemes:

$$
\begin{cases}
w_i^+ = exp(\dfrac{z(\mathbf{v}_a, \mathbf{v}_i)}{d(f(x_a), f(x_i))\delta}), & if \quad x_i \in P_a^+ \\[4mm]
w_j^- = exp(\dfrac{d(f(x_a), f(x_j))}{z(\mathbf{v}_a, \mathbf{v}_j)\delta}), & if \quad x_j \in N_a^- ,
\end{cases}
\tag{9}
$$

where $\delta > 0$ is a coefficient. In the positive set, reliable samples with small distances against the anchor and high contrast values of comparing vectors are assigned higher weights than hard ones. On the contrary, in the negative set, hard samples with small distances against the anchor and low contrast values of comparing vectors are assigned lower weights than reliable ones.

To summarize, the loss objective of the proposed model is formulated by:

$$
L_{CEG} = L_1 + \lambda L_2,
\tag{10}
$$

where λ is the hyperparameter. We train our model end to end by the Stochastic Gradient Descent (SGD) method. For testing, we compute the cosine feature similarity of each probe(query)-gallery pair, and obtain the ranking list of probe images against the gallery images.

4 Experiments

4.1 Datasets

Evaluation Benchmarks. We apply our model to two benchmark datasets, including Market-1501 [23] and DukeMTMC-reID [24]. For simplicity, they will be referred as Market and Duke respectively. **Market** contains 32,668 images of 1,501 identities from six cameras, while **Duke** has 36,411 images of 1,404 identities from 8 cameras. Following the standard protocol [23], we utilize half of identities for training and the other half for testing. Target image labels are not utilized during training. We evaluate the accuracy of Rank-1/Rank-5/Rank-10 and the mean average precision (MAP) [23].

Auxiliary Dataset. We select MSMT17 [25] as the auxiliary dataset. It contains 126,441 images of 4,101 identities from 15 cameras, which is beneficial for the diversity of *comparators*.

4.2 Implementation Details

We choose the ResNet-50 [26] as the CNN backbone and initialize it with pre-trained parameters on ImageNet [27]. Additionally, the last fully-connected layer is removed and the stride of the last residual block is set to 1. The batch size is set to 128, randomly sampling unlabeled images. We use the SGD [28] as the optimization algorithm, and the learning rate is set to 0.0001 initially and decay by 0.1 every 40 epochs. Totally there are 120 training epochs. For threshold values, we define the mining ratio $\rho = 0.05$ for indirect assignment [10]. We set λ to 0.001 which balances the two losses. The number of clusters K is set to 700 for Duke and 750 for Market.

Table 1. Comparison with state-of-the-art methods in the Market and Duke datasets.

Methods	Venue	Market-1501				DukeMTMC-reID			
		Rank-1	Rank-5	Rank-10	MAP	Rank-1	Rank-5	Rank-10	MAP
LOMO	CVPR15	27.2	41.6	49.1	8.0	12.3	21.3	26.6	4.8
BoW	ICCV15	35.8	52.4	60.3	14.8	17.1	28.8	34.9	8.3
UDML	CVPR16	34.5	52.6	59.6	12.4	18.5	31.4	37.6	7.3
TJ-AIDL	CVPR18	58.2	74.8	81.1	26.5	44.3	59.6	65.0	23.0
PTGAN	CVPR18	38.6	57.3	66.1	15.7	27.4	43.6	50.7	13.5
SPGAN	CVPR18	51.5	70.1	82.7	27.1	41.1	56.6	68.0	22.3
PUL	ToMM18	45.5	60.7	66.7	20.5	30.0	43.4	48.5	16.4
CAMEL	ICCV17	54.5	73.1	–	26.3	40.3	57.6	–	19.8
DECAMEL	TPAMI2019	60.2	76.0	81.1	32.4	–	–	–	–
CEG w/o L1	Ours	61.4	78.2	82.5	33.8	47.5	73.4	70.4	30.1
CEG w/o L2	Ours	59.8	77.4	80.6	31.2	45.1	73,4	68.5	28.6
CEG	Ours	**64.5**	**80.5**	**83.8**	**38.5**	**54.5**	**73.4**	**79.5**	**35.6**

4.3 Comparison to the State of the Art

Hand-crafted feature representation based methods [11,23,29] are comparatively assessed, and the proposed method significantly outperforms them by a large margin. This is because the previous methods are mostly based on heuristic design and cannot learn discriminative features.

Compared with unsupervised domain adaptation based methods [25,30,31], the proposed method achieves superior performance. The reason is that the previous methods focus on adapting the knowledge from the source domain to the target one, while the proposed method directly mines the discriminative supervision in the unlabeled dataset, which is more effective for unsupervised RE-ID.

Compared with clustering-based methods [6,8,14], the proposed method also achieves superior performance. The key reason is that the previous methods assign pseudo-labels only based on visual feature similarity, which may assign the same pseudo-label to similar images of different identities, and cannot mine discriminative supervision.

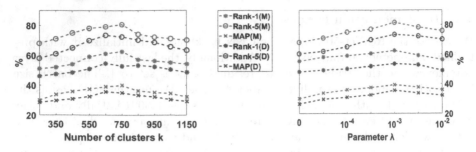

Fig. 2. Evaluation of the important hyperparameters K and λ on Market (red curves) and Duke (blue curves). (M/D), Market/Duke. (Color figure online)

4.4 Ablation Study

We perform an ablation study to demonstrate the effectiveness of both L_1 and L_2. As shown in Table 1, "CEG w/o L_1" ("CEG w/o L_2") indicates that our model is trained without L_1 (L_2). Specifically, on Market/Duke, CEG outperforms "CEG w/o L_1" by 3.1%/7.0% on Rank-1 accuracy, and CEG outperforms "CEG w/o L_2" by 4.7%/9.4% on Rank-1 accuracy. This is because either methods makes full usage of the mined label information. Only with L_1 (w/o L_2) the basic cluster-level discrimination of feature embeddings is merely guaranteed; only with L_2 (w/o L_1), the method fails to take advantage of the identity label information; With two losses L_1 and L_2, the method achieves the best performance. Thus, the effectiveness of CEG (with both L_1 and L_2) is demonstrated.

4.5 Further Analysis

Various Numbers of Clusters K. We evaluate how the number of clusters affects model learning (λ is fixed to 0.001). K is sampled from $\{300, 350, 500, 550 \cdots 1100, 1150\}$. As shown in Fig. 2 (left panel), the best performance occurs with $K = 750/700$ on Matket/Duke.

Parameter λ. We evaluate the impact of λ (K is set to 750/700). As shown in Fig. 2 (right panel), it is significant to balance the two losses.

5   Conclusion

In this paper, we propose a clustering-guide approach (CEG) to address the unsupervised RE-ID task. Specifically, we cluster unlabeled and auxiliary datasets, aiming to achieve full mining of supervisions and a complete usage of the mined information. On the one hand, we develop a non-parametric softmax variant for cluster-level supervision. On the other hand, using labeled persons in each cluster as *comparators*, each unlabeled person image maintains a comparing vector, which is utilized to mine reliable and hard pairs in intra- and inter-clusters. We further propose a weighted point-to-set loss, which is robust and effective. We train our model with these two losses jointly to learn discriminative features for unlabeled person images. Extensive experiments validate the superiority of the proposed method for unsupervised RE-ID.

Acknowledgement. This work was supported by the National Natural Science Foundation of China (NO. 61806168), Fundamental Research Funds for the Central Universities (NO. SWU117059), and Venture & Innovation Support Program for Chongqing Overseas Returnees (NO. CX2018075).

References

1. Zheng, L., Yang, Y., Hauptmann, A.G.: Person re-identification: past, present and future. CoRR, abs/1610.02984 (2016)
2. Sarfraz, M.S., Schumann, A., Eberle, A., Stiefelhagen, R.: A pose-sensitive embedding for person re-identification with expanded cross neighborhood re-ranking. In: CVPR, pp. 420–429 (2018)
3. Xu, J., Zhao, R., Zhu, F., Wang, H., Ouyang, W.: Attention-aware compositional network for person re-identification. In: CVPR, pp. 2119–2128 (2018)
4. Farenzena, M., Bazzani, L., Perina, A., Murino, V., Cristani, M.: Person re-identification by symmetry-driven accumulation of local features. In: CVPR, pp. 2360–2367 (2010)
5. Kodirov, E., Xiang, T., Fu, Z., Gong, S.: Person re-identification by unsupervised ℓ_1 graph learning. In: Leibe, B., Matas, J., Sebe, N., Welling, M. (eds.) ECCV 2016. LNCS, vol. 9905, pp. 178–195. Springer, Cham (2016). https://doi.org/10.1007/978-3-319-46448-0_11
6. Fan, H., Zheng, L., Yan, C.C., Yang, Y.: Unsupervised person re-identification: clustering and fine-tuning. ToMM **14**, 83:1–83:18 (2018)
7. Lin, Y., Dong, X., Zheng, L., Yan, Y., Yang, Y.: A bottom-up clustering approach to unsupervised person re-identification. In: AAAI (2019)
8. Yu, H.-X., Wu, A., Zheng, W.-S.: Unsupervised person re-identification by deep asymmetric metric embedding. TPAMI, 1 (2018)
9. Lv, J., Chen, W., Li, Q., Yang, C.: Unsupervised cross-dataset person re-identification by transfer learning of spatial-temporal patterns. In: CVPR, pp. 7948–7956 (2018)
10. Yu, H.-X., Zheng, W.-S., Wu, A., Guo, X., Gong, S., Lai, J.-H.: Unsupervised person re-identification by soft multilabel learning. In: CVPR (2019)
11. Peng, P., et al.: Unsupervised cross-dataset transfer learning for person re-identification. In: CVPR, pp. 1306–1315 (2016)
12. Wang, H., Gong, S., Xiang, T.: Unsupervised learning of generative topic saliency for person re-identification (2014)
13. Rui, Z., Ouyang, W., Wang, X.: Unsupervised salience learning for person re-identification. In: CVPR (2013)
14. Yu, H.-X., Wu, A., Zheng, W.-S.: Cross-view asymmetric metric learning for unsupervised person re-identification. In: ICCV, pp. 994–1002 (2017)
15. Yang, B., Ma, A.J., Yuen, P.C.: Domain-shared group-sparse dictionary learning for unsupervised domain adaptation. In AAAI (2018)
16. Cao, Y., Long, M., Wang, J.: Unsupervised domain adaptation with distribution matching machines. In: AAAI (2018)

17. Tsai, Y.-H.H., Hou, C.-A., Chen, W.-Y., Yeh, Y.-R., Wang, Y.-C.F.: Domain-constraint transfer coding for imbalanced unsupervised domain adaptation. In: AAAI (2016)
18. Shekhar, S., Patel, V.M., Nguyen, H.V., Chellappa, R.: Generalized domain-adaptive dictionaries. In: CVPR, pp. 361–368 (2013)
19. Caron, M., Bojanowski, P., Joulin, A., Douze, M.: Deep clustering for unsupervised learning of visual features. In: Ferrari, V., Hebert, M., Sminchisescu, C., Weiss, Y. (eds.) Computer Vision – ECCV 2018. LNCS, vol. 11218, pp. 139–156. Springer, Cham (2018). https://doi.org/10.1007/978-3-030-01264-9_9
20. Wu, Z., Xiong, Y., Yu, S.X., Lin, D.: Unsupervised feature learning via non-parametric instance discrimination. In: CVPR, pp. 3733–3742 (2018)
21. Pan, S.J., Yang, Q.: A survey on transfer learning. TKDE **22**, 1345–1359 (2010)
22. Yu, R., Dou, Z., Bai, S., Zhang, Z., Xu, Y., Bai, X.: Hard-aware point-to-set deep metric for person re-identification. In: Ferrari, V., Hebert, M., Sminchisescu, C., Weiss, Y. (eds.) ECCV 2018. LNCS, vol. 11220, pp. 196–212. Springer, Cham (2018). https://doi.org/10.1007/978-3-030-01270-0_12
23. Zheng, L., Shen, L., Tian, L., Wang, S., Wang, J., Tian, Q.: Scalable person re-identification: a benchmark. In: ICCV, pp. 1116–1124 (2015)
24. Ristani, E., Solera, F., Zou, R., Cucchiara, R., Tomasi, C.: Performance measures and a data set for multi-target, multi-camera tracking. In: Hua, G., Jégou, H. (eds.) ECCV 2016. LNCS, vol. 9914, pp. 17–35. Springer, Cham (2016). https://doi.org/10.1007/978-3-319-48881-3_2
25. Wei, L., Zhang, S., Gao, W., Tian, Q.: Person transfer GAN to bridge domain gap for person re-identification. In: CVPR, pp. 79–88 (2018)
26. He, K., Zhang, X., Ren, S., Sun, J.: Deep residual learning for image recognition. In: CVPR, pp. 770–778 (2016)
27. Krizhevsky, A., Sutskever, I., Hinton, G.E.: Imagenet classification with deep convolutional neural networks. Commun. ACM **60**, 84–90 (2012)
28. Bottou, L.: Stochastic gradient descent tricks. In: Montavon, G., Orr, G.B., Müller, K.-R. (eds.) Neural Networks: Tricks of the Trade. LNCS, vol. 7700, pp. 421–436. Springer, Heidelberg (2012). https://doi.org/10.1007/978-3-642-35289-8_25
29. Liao, S., Hu, Y., Zhu, X., Li, S.Z.: Person re-identification by local maximal occurrence representation and metric learning. In: CVPR, pp. 2197–2206 (2015)
30. Wang, J., Zhu, X., Gong, S., Li, W.: Transferable joint attribute-identity deep learning for unsupervised person re-identification. In: CVPR, pp. 2275–2284 (2018)
31. Deng, W., Zheng, L., Kang, G., Yang, Y., Ye, Q., Jiao, J.: Image-image domain adaptation with preserved self-similarity and domain-dissimilarity for person re-identification. In: CVPR, pp. 994–1003 (2018)

Semi-supervised Deep Learning Using Improved Unsupervised Discriminant Projection

Xiao Han, Zihao Wang, Enmei Tu$^{(\boxtimes)}$, Gunnam Suryanarayana, and Jie Yang

School of Electronics, Information and Electrical Engineering,
Shanghai Jiao Tong University, Shanghai, China
{hanxiao2015,wangzihao33}@sjtu.edu.cn, hellotem@hotmail.com

Abstract. Deep learning demands a huge amount of well-labeled data to train the network parameters. How to use the least amount of labeled data to obtain the desired classification accuracy is of great practical significance, because for many real-world applications (such as medical diagnosis), it is difficult to obtain so many labeled samples. In this paper, modify the unsupervised discriminant projection algorithm from dimension reduction and apply it as a regularization term to propose a new semi-supervised deep learning algorithm, which is able to utilize both the local and nonlocal distribution of abundant unlabeled samples to improve classification performance. Experiments show that given dozens of labeled samples, the proposed algorithm can train a deep network to attain satisfactory classification results.

Keywords: Manifold regularization · Semi-supervised learning · Deep learning

1 Introduction

In reality, one of the main difficulties faced by many machine learning tasks is manually tagging large amounts of data. This is especially prominent for deep learning, which usually demands a huge number of well-labeled samples. Therefore, how to use the least amount of labeled data to train a deep network has become an important topic in the area. To overcome this problem, researchers proposed that the use of a large number of unlabeled data can extract the topology of the overall data's distribution. Combined with a small amount of labeled data, the generalization ability of the model can be significantly improved, which is the so-called semi-supervised learning [5,18,21].

This work is supported by NSFC China (61806125, 61802247, 61876107) and Startup Fund for Youngman Research at SJTU (SFYR at SJTU).
X. Han and Z. Wang—Make equal contributions.

Recently, semi-supervised deep learning has made some progress. The main ideas of existing works broadly fall into two categories. One is generative model based algorithms, for which unlabeled samples help the generative model to learn the underly sample distribution for sample generation. Examples of this type algorithms include CatGAN [15], BadGAN [7], variational Bayesian [10], etc. The other is discriminant model based algorithms, for which the role of the unlabeled data may provide sample distribution information to prevent model overfitting, or to make the model more resistant to disturbances. Typical algorithms of this type include unsupervised loss regularization [1,16], latent feature embedding [8,14,18,20], pseudo label [11,19]. Our method belongs to the second category, in which an unsupervised regularization term, which captures the local and global sample distribution characteristics, is added to the loss function for semi-supervised deep learning.

The proposed algorithm is based on the theory of manifold regularization, which is developed by Belkin et al. [3,4] and then introduced into deep learning by Weston et al. [18]. Given L labeled samples $x_1, x_2, ... x_L$ and their corresponding labels $y_1, y_2, ..., y_L$, recall that manifold regularization combines the idea of manifold learning with the idea of semi-supervised learning, and learns the manifold structure of data with a large amount of unlabeled data, which gets the model better generalization. Compared to the loss function in tradition supervised learning framework, the manifold regularization based semi-supervised learning algorithm adds a new regularization term to penalize the complexity of the discriminant function f over the sample distribution manifold, as shown in the Eq. (1):

$$\frac{1}{L} \sum_{i=1}^{L} V(x_i, y_i, f) + \gamma_A \|f\|_K^2 + \gamma_I \|f\|_I^2 \tag{1}$$

where $V(\cdot)$ is an arbitrary supervised loss term, and $\|\cdot\|_K$ is a kernel norm, such as a Gaussian kernel function, that penalizes the model complexity in the ambient (data) space. $\|\cdot\|_I$ is the introduced manifold regularization term, which penalizes model complexity along the data distribution manifold to make sure that the prediction output have the same distribution as the input data. γ_A and γ_I are used as weights. As shown in Fig. 1, after the manifold regularization term is introduced, the decision boundary tries not to destroy the manifold structure of the data distribution and meanwhile, keeps itself as simple as possible, so that the boundary finally passes through where the data is sparsely distributed.

However, the research on the application of manifold regularization in the field of semi-supervised deep learning has not been fully explored. The construction of manifold regularization only considers the local structural relationship of samples. For classification problems, we should not only preserve the positional relationship of neighbor data to ensure clustering, but also consider distinguishing data from different manifolds and separating them in the embedded space. Therefore, in this paper, we propose a novel manifold loss term based on the improved Unsupervised Discriminant Projection (UDP) [9], which incorporates both local and nonlocal distribution information, and we conduct experiments

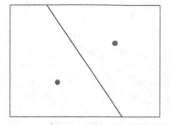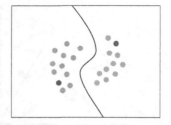

Fig. 1. Manifold regularization makes the decision boundary where the data distribution is sparse. Left: traditional supervised learning results; right: manifold regularized semi-supervised learning.

on real-world datasets to demonstrate that it can produce better classification accuracy for semi-supervised deep learning than its counterparts.

The following contents are organized as follows: The theory and the proposed algorithm are presented in Sect. 2; then the experimental results are given in Sect. 3, followed by conclusions and discussions in Sect. 4.

2 Improved UDP Regularization Term

In this section, we first review the UDP algorithm and then introduce an improved UDP algorithm. Then we propose a semi-supervised deep learning algorithm which is based on the improved UDP algorithm.

2.1 Basic Idea of UDP

The UDP method is proposed by Yang et al. originally for dimensionality reduction of small-scale high-dimensional data [9]. As a method for multi-manifold learning, UDP considers both local and non-local quantities of the data distribution. The basic idea of UDP is shown in Fig. 2. Suppose that the data is distributed on two elliptical manifolds denoted by c_1 and c_2, respectively. If we only require that the distances of neighboring data are still close after being projected along a certain direction, then the projection along $\mathbf{w}_1$ will be the optimal direction, but at this time the two data clusters will be mixed with each other and difficult to separate after projection. Therefore, while requiring neighbor data to be sufficiently close after projection, we should also optimize the direction of the projection so that the distance between different clusters is as far as possible. Such projected data are more conducive to clustering after dimensionality reduction.

For this reason, UDP uses the ratio of local scatter to non-local scatter, to find a projection which will draw the close data closer, while simultaneously making the distant data even more distant from each other. The local scatter can be characterized by the mean square of the Euclidean distance between any pair of the projected sample points that are neighbors. The criteria for judging

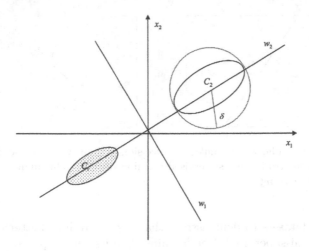

Fig. 2. Illustration of clusters of two-dimensional data and optimal projection directions [9].

neighbors can be K-nearest neighbors or ϵ neighbors. Since the value of ϵ is difficult to determine and it may generate an unconnected graph, the K-nearest neighbor criterion is used here to define the weighted adjacency matrix **H** with kernel weighting:

$$
H_{ij} = \begin{cases} exp(-\||x_i - x_j\||^2/t) & \text{if } x_j \text{ is among } K \text{ nearest neighbors of } x_i, \\ & \text{or } x_i \text{ is among } K \text{ nearest neighbors of } x_j \quad (2) \\ 0 & \text{otherwise} \end{cases}
$$

Then given a training set containing M samples $x_1, x_2, ..., x_M$, denote the local set $U^K = \{(i,j)|x_j \text{ is the neighbor of } x_i\}$. After projecting x_i and x_j onto a direction **w**, we get their images y_i and y_j. The local scatter is defined as

$$
J_L(\mathbf{w}) = \frac{1}{MM} \sum_{i=1}^{M} \sum_{j=1}^{M} K_{ij}(y_i - y_j)^2 \tag{3}
$$

Similarly, the nonlocal scatter can be defined by the mean square of the Euclidean distance between any pair of the projected sample points that are not in any set of neighborhoods. It is defined as

$$
J_N(\mathbf{w}) = \frac{1}{MM} \sum_{i=1}^{M} \sum_{j=1}^{M} (K_{ij} - H_{ij})(y_i - y_j)^2 \tag{4}
$$

The optimal projection vector $\mathbf{w}^*$ minimizes the following final objective function

$$
\mathbf{w}^* = \arg\min J(\mathbf{w}) = \frac{J_L}{J_N} \tag{5}
$$

2.2   An Improved UDP for Large Scale Dimension Reduction

Since the original UDP method is developed for dimensionality reduction of small-scale data sets, the data outside the K-nearest neighbors of a sample are regarded as nonlocal data and participate in the calculation of a nonlocal scatter. However, when the scale of training data is large, this way of calculating the nonlocal scatter will bring a prohibitive computational burden, because each sample has $M - K$ nonlocal data. To overcome this problem, we propose an improved UDP for large scale dimension reduction.

Suppose there are training data $x_1, x_2, ..., x_M$, and the desired output of x_i after dimension reduction is y_i. Using the Euclidean distance as a measure, similar to the definition of the K-nearest neighbor set, we define a set of N-distant data set $D^N = \{(i,j)|x_j$ is one of the N farthest data from $x_i\}$. Similarly, we define a non-adjacency matrix $\mathbf{W}$:

$$W_{ij} = \begin{cases} exp(-|||x_i - x_j|||^2/t) & \text{if } x_j \text{ is among } N \text{ farthest samples away from } x_i, \\ & \text{or } x_i \text{ is among } N \text{ farthest samples away from } x_j \\ 0 & \text{otherwise.} \end{cases}$$

(6)

Then we define the distant scatter as

$$J_D = \frac{1}{m} \sum_{i=1,j \in D^N}^{M} W_{ij} \|y_i - y_j\|_2^2$$

(7)

for the local scatter J_L, we use the same one as the original UDP. So the objective function of the improved UDP is

$$J_R(\mathbf{w}) = \frac{J_L}{J_D}$$

(8)

$$= \sum_{i=1}^{M} \frac{\sum_{j \in U^K} H_{ij} \|y_i - y_j\|_2^2}{\sum_{b \in D^N} W_{ib} \|y_i - y_b\|_2^2}$$

(9)

The improved UDP also requires that after the mapping of the deep network, the outputs of similar data is as close as possible, while simultaneously "pushing away" the output of dissimilar data. Although only the data with extreme distance is used, in the process of making the dissimilar data far away from each other, the data similar to them will gather around them respectively, thus widening the distance between the classes and making the sparse area of data distribution more sparse, densely areas denser.

2.3   The Improved UDP Based Semi-supervised Deep Learning

Suppose we have a dataset $\{x_1, ..., x_L, x_{L+1}, ...x_M\}$, in which the first L data points are labeled samples with labels $\{y_1, y_2, ..., y_L\}$, and the rest data points are unlabeled samples. Let $\{g_1, g_2, ..., g_M\}$ be the embeddings of the samples through a deep network. Our aim is to train a deep network $f(x)$ using both labeled and unlabeled samples, such that different classes are well separated and meanwhile, cluster structures are well preserved. Putting all together, we have the following objective function

$$J = \sum_{i=1}^{L} l(f_i, y_i) + \lambda \sum_{i=1, j \in U^K, k \in D^N}^{L+U} J_R(g_i, g_j, g_k, H_{ij}, W_{ik}) \tag{10}$$

where L is the number of labeled data and U is the number of unlabeled data. $l(\cdot)$ is the supervised loss function and $J_R(\cdot)$ is the UDP regularization term. λ is the hyperparameter, which is used to balance the supervisory loss and unsupervised loss. We use the softmax function as our supervised loss, but other type of loss function (e.g. mean square error) are also applicable.

We use error backpropagation (BP) to train the network. The details of the training process are given in the following algorithm.

Algorithm 1. Semi-supervised deep learning based on improved UDP

Require: labeled data x_i and corresponding label $y_i, i = 1, 2, ..., L$, unlabeled data $x_j, j = 1, 2, ..., U$, output of neural network $f(\cdot)$, output of the embedded UDP regularization item $g(\cdot)$
1: Find K-nearest neighbors and N-distant samples of each sample
2: Calculated the kernel weights H_{ij} for neighbors and W_{ij} for distant samples
3: **repeat**
4:     Randomly select a group of labeled data and their labels (x_i, y_i)
5:     Gradient descend $l(f(x_i), y_i)$
6:     Select x_i and its K-nearest data x_j and N-distant data x_k
7:     Gradient descend $J_R(g(x_i), g(x_j), g(x_k), H_{ij}, W_{ik})$
8: **until**
9: Meet accuracy requirements or complete all iterations

---

3   Experimental Results

3.1   Results of Dimensionality Reduction

Firstly, we test the dimensionality reduction performance of the improved UDP method in two different image datasets, MNIST and ETH-80[1]. Then we compare the improved UDP with original UDP, as well as several popular dimension reduction algorithms (Isomap [2], Multidimensional scaling (MDS) [6], t-SNE [13] and spectral embedding [12]), to show its performance improvement.

MNIST is a dataset consisting of 28×28 grayscale images of handwritten digits. We randomly selected 5000 samples from the dataset to perform our

---

[1] ETH-80: https://github.com/Kai-Xuan/ETH-80.

experiments because the original UDP usually applies to small-scale datasets. ETH-80 is a small-scale but more challenging dataset which consists of 256×256 RGB images from 8 categories. We use all the 820 samples from "apples" and "pears" categories and convert the images from RGB into grayscale for manipulation convenience. The parameters of the baseline algorithms are set to their suggested default values and the parameters (kernel width t, number of nearest neighbors K and number of farthest points N) of the improved UDP are set empirically. The experimental results on the two datasets are shown in Figs. 3 and 4, respectively.

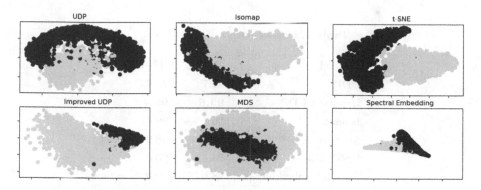

Fig. 3. Dimension reduction of digits 1 and 2 in MNIST ($t = 4, K = 10$ and $N = 300$).

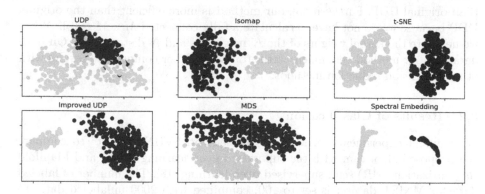

Fig. 4. Dimension reduction of 'apples' and 'pears' categories in ETH-80 ($t = 12.0, K = 10$ and $N = 50$).

From these results we can see that after dimension reduction, the improved UDP maps different classes more separately than the original UDP on both datasets. This is important because while adopting the new UDP into semi-supervised learning in Eq. (10), better separation means more accurate classification. It is also worth mentioning that although on the ETH-80 dataset, the improved UDP achieves comparable results as the rest baseline algorithms, its results on MNIST is much better (especially than MDS, Isomap) in terms of classes separation.

To quantitatively measure the classes separation, Table 1 shows the cluster purity given by k-means clustering algorithm on these two datasets after dimensionality reduction. The purity is calculated based maximum matching degree [17] after clustering.

Table 1. Cluster purity of 6 methods.

Method	MNIST	ETH-80
UDP	81.7	77.7
Improved UDP	**93.8**	**99.4**
Isomap [2]	86.1	99.9
MDS [6]	53.7	98.9
t-SNE [13]	93.1	100.0
Spectral embedding [12]	98.6	100.0

Table 1 demonstrates that our improved UDP method improves the cluster purity by a large margin compared to the original UDP. It can also be seen from Figs. 3 and 4 that our improved UDP method is more appropriate for clustering than original UDP. Furthermore, our method is more efficient than the original UDP because we do not have to calculate a fully connected $M \times M$ graph. What we need are the kernel weights of the K neighbors and N distant data. On both datasets, our method gets much better (on MNIST) or competitive results with other dimension reduction methods.

3.2 Results of Classification

We conduct experiments on MNIST dataset and SVHN dataset[2] to compare the proposed algorithm with the supervised deep learning (SDL) and Manifold Regularization (MR) semi-supervised deep learning [18]. The number of labeled data for MNIST dataset is set to 100, combined with 2000 unlabeled data, to train a deep network. For SVHN, from the training set we randomly selected 1000 samples as labeled data and 20000 samples as unlabeled data to train a network. For both experiments, we test the trained network on the testing set

---

[2] SVHN the Street View House Numbers (SVHN) Dataset (http://ufldl.stanford.edu/housenumbers/), which consists of color images for real-world house number digits with various appearance and is a highly challenging classification problem.

(of size 10000 in MNIST and 26032 in SVHN) to obtain testing accuracy. The optimizer we choose Adam. The parameters are manually tuned using a simple grid search rule. K and N take 10 and 50 and kernel width is within $[3.5, 4.0]$.

We adopt the three embedding network structures described in [18] and the results of MNIST and SVHN are shown in Table 2. For supervised deep learning, we apply entropy loss at the network output layer only, since middle layer embedding and auxiliary network do not make any sense. From the table we can see, MR is better for middle layer embedding. Our method is better for output embedding and auxiliary network embedding and achieves better classification results for most network structures. The results also suggest that it may be helpful to combine MR with UDP together, using MR for hidden layer and UDP for output layer[3].

Table 2. Classification correct rate.

Number of labled data	MNIST			SVHN		
	SDL	MR	Improved UDP	SDL	MR	Improved UDP
Output layer embedding	74.31	82.95	**83.19**	55.21	64.70	**72.66**
Middle layer embedding	–	**83.52**	83.07	–	**72.10**	69.35
Auxiliary neural network	–	87.55	**87.79**	–	62.61	**71.32**

4 Conclusions and Future Work

Training a deep network using a small number of labeled samples is of great practical significance, since many real-world applications have big difficulties to collect enough labeled samples. In this paper, we modify the unsupervised discriminant projection (UDP) algorithm to make it suitable for large data dimension reduction and semi-supervised learning. The new algorithm simultaneously takes both local and nonlocal manifold information into account and meanwhile, could reduce the computational cost. Based on this, we proposed a new semi-supervised deep learning algorithm to train a deep network with a very small amount of labeled samples and many unlabeled samples. The experimental results on different real-world datasets demonstrate its validity and effectiveness.

The construction of the neighbor graph is based on Euclidean distance in data space, which may not be a proper distance measure on data manifold. In the future, other neighbor graph construction methods, such as the measure on the Riemannian manifold, will be tried. The limitation of the current method is that

---

[3] We leave this to our future work. We should also point out that although the classification accuracies are somehow lower than the state-of-the-art results, the network we employed is a traditional multilayer feedforward network and we do not utilize any advanced training techniques such as batch-normalization, random data augmentation. In the future, we will try to train a more complex network with advanced training techniques to make thorough comparisons.

it can attain good results for tasks that are not too complex, such as MNIST, but for more challenging classification datasets, such as CIFAR10, which the direct K nearest neighbors may not reflect the actual similarity, the method may not perform very well. Our future work will try to use some pre-learning techniques, such as auto-encoder or kernel method, to map origin data to a much concise representation.

References

1. Bachman, P., Alsharif, O., Precup, D.: Learning with pseudo-ensembles. In: Advances in Neural Information Processing Systems, vol. 4, pp. 3365–3373 (2014)
2. Balasubramanian, M., Schwartz, E.L.: The isomap algorithm and topological stability. Science **295**(5552), 7 (2002)
3. Belkin, M., Niyogi, P., Sindhwani, V., Bartlett, P.: Manifold regularization: a geometric framework for learning from examples. J. Mach. Learn. Res. **7**(1), 2399–2434 (2006)
4. Belkin, M., Niyogi, P., Sindhwani, V.: On manifold regularization. In: AISTATS, p. 1 (2005)
5. Chapelle, O., Scholkopf, B., Zien, A. (eds.): Semi-supervised learning (2006). IEEE Trans. Neural Netw. **20**(3), 542 (2009)
6. Cox, T.F., Cox, M.A.: Multidimensional Scaling. Chapman and Hall/CRC, New York (2000)
7. Dai, Z., Yang, Z., Yang, F., Cohen, W.W., Salakhutdinov, R.R.: Good semi-supervised learning that requires a bad GAN. In: Advances in Neural Information Processing Systems, pp. 6510–6520 (2017)
8. Hoffer, E., Ailon, N.: Semi-supervised deep learning by metric embedding. arXiv preprint arXiv:1611.01449 (2016)
9. Jian, Y., David, Z., Jing-Yu, Y., Ben, N.: Globally maximizing, locally minimizing: unsupervised discriminant projection with applications to face and palm biometrics. IEEE Trans. Pattern Anal. Mach. Intell. **29**(4), 650–664 (2007)
10. Kingma, D.P., Mohamed, S., Rezende, D.J., Welling, M.: Semi-supervised learning with deep generative models. In: Advances in Neural Information Processing Systems, pp. 3581–3589 (2014)
11. Lee, D.H.: Pseudo-label: the simple and efficient semi-supervised learning method for deep neural networks. In: Workshop on Challenges in Representation Learning, ICML, vol. 3, p. 2 (2013)
12. Luo, B., Wilson, R.C., Hancock, E.R.: Spectral embedding of graphs. Pattern Recogn. **36**(10), 2213–2230 (2003)
13. Van der Maaten, L., Hinton, G.: Visualizing data using t-SNE. J. Mach. Learn. Res. **9**(Nov), 2579–2605 (2008)
14. Rasmus, A., Valpola, H., Honkala, M., Berglund, M., Raiko, T.: Semi-supervised learning with ladder networks, pp. 3546–3554 (2015)
15. Springenberg, J.T.: Unsupervised and semi-supervised learning with categorical generative adversarial networks. arXiv preprint arXiv:1511.06390 (2015)
16. Thulasidasan, S., Bilmes, J.: Semi-supervised phone classification using deep neural networks and stochastic graph-based entropic regularization. arXiv preprint arXiv:1612.04899 (2016)
17. Tu, E., Cao, L., Yang, J., Kasabov, N.: A novel graph-based k-means for nonlinear manifold clustering and representative selection. Neurocomputing **143**, 109–122 (2014)

18. Weston, J., Ratle, F., Mobahi, H., Collobert, R.: Deep learning via semi-supervised embedding. In: Montavon, G., Orr, G.B., Müller, K.-R. (eds.) Neural Networks: Tricks of the Trade. LNCS, vol. 7700, pp. 639–655. Springer, Heidelberg (2012). https://doi.org/10.1007/978-3-642-35289-8_34
19. Wu, H., Prasad, S.: Semi-supervised deep learning using pseudo labels for hyperspectral image classification. IEEE Trans. Image Process. **27**(3), 1259–1270 (2018)
20. Yang, Z., Cohen, W.W., Salakhutdinov, R.: Revisiting semi-supervised learning with graph embeddings. arXiv preprint arXiv:1603.08861 (2016)
21. Zhu, X., Goldberg, A.B.: Introduction to semi-supervised learning. In: Synthesis Lectures on Artificial Intelligence and Machine Learning, vol. 3, no. 1, pp. 1–130 (2009)

Unsupervised Pre-training of the Brain Connectivity Dynamic Using Residual D-Net

Youngjoo Seo[1(✉)], Manuel Morante[2(✉)], Yannis Kopsinis[3(✉)],
and Sergios Theodoridis[2(✉)]

[1] Signal Processing Laboratory 2, EPFL, Lausanne, Switzerland
youngjoo.seo@epfl.ch
[2] Department of Informatics and Telecommunications,
University of Athens (Greece), Athens, Greece
morante@cti.gr, stheodor@di.uoa.gr
[3] Computer Technology Institute and Press "Diophantus" (CTI) Patras (Greece),
Patras, Greece
kopsinis@ieee.org

Abstract. In this paper, we propose a novel unsupervised pre-training method to learn the brain dynamics using a deep learning architecture named residual D-net. As it is often the case in medical research, in contrast to typical deep learning tasks, the size of the resting-state functional Magnetic Resonance Image (rs-fMRI) datasets for training is limited. Thus, the available data should be very efficiently used to learn the complex patterns underneath the brain connectivity dynamics. To address this issue, we use residual connections to alleviate the training complexity through recurrent multi-scale representation and pre-training the architecture unsupervised way. We conduct two classification tasks to differentiate early and late stage Mild Cognitive Impairment (MCI) from Normal healthy Control (NC) subjects. The experiments verify that our proposed residual D-net indeed learns the brain connectivity dynamics, leading to significantly higher classification accuracy compared to previously published techniques.

1 Introduction

Alzheimer's Disease (AD) is the most common degenerative brain disease associated with dementia in elder people [5], and it is characterized by a progressive decline of memory, language and cognitive skills. The transition from cognitive health to dementia flows throw different stages, and it may require decades until the damage is noticeable [25]. Unfortunately, the precise biological mechanisms behind the AD remain unknown, to a large extent, and this makes the development of an effective treatment difficult. Moreover, the costs of Alzheimer's care constitutes a substantial burden on families, which exacerbates through the evolution of the disease [4]. For these reasons, early detection is crucial to prevent, slow down and, hopefully, stop the development of the AD.

© Springer Nature Switzerland AG 2019
T. Gedeon et al. (Eds.): ICONIP 2019, LNCS 11955, pp. 608–620, 2019.
https://doi.org/10.1007/978-3-030-36718-3_51

Towards this goal, several studies point out that an intermediate stage of cognitive brain dysfunction, referred as Mild Cognitive Impairment (MCI), is a potential precursor of AD [4] (especially with respect to memory problems, referred as amnesic MCI). Although the final transition from MCI to AD varies per individual, a recent systematic review of 32 available studies reported that at least 3 out 10 patients with MCI developed the AD over the period of five or more years [23]. During the early stages of the AD and MCI, the brain operates so that to allow the individuals to function normally by inducing abnormal neuronal activity, that compensates for the progressive loss of neurons. These fluctuations can be measured using rs-fMRI, which is a powerful non-invasive technique to examine the brain behavior. Therefore, the rs-fMRI provides valuable information to study the brain connectivity dynamics and, potentially, to detect individuals with AD or MCI from healthy subjects.

Nowadays, several methods have been proposed to classify subjects with MCI from healthy subjects using fMRI data [6]. The most basic approach consists of a direct study of the mean Functional Connectivity (FC). For example, features from the FC matrix [27] or graph theoretical approach [12] are proposed to perform the classification task. However, two practical limitations restrict these approaches: first, the manual feature designing requires an extensive domain knowledge of the brain connectivity dynamics and, second, the limited number of the available data samples makes it difficult to find a proper model that will generalize in different datasets.

On the other hand, a more sophisticated approach is proposed in [21] to address these two problems: this method automatically learns the features from the data using a Deep Auto-Encoder (DAE) by avoiding potential human biases. Nevertheless, the DAE does not consider any information regarding the brain connectivity dynamics, which is crucial to understand the AD. Accordingly, any alternative deep learning method must simultaneously consider the structure and the dynamics of the brain functional connectivity, for automatically extracting significant features from the data. However, since complex deep learning architectures usually require a large number of training samples, the lack of sufficient data constitutes the major practical limitation of such methods.

For all these reasons, in this paper, we introduce a recurrent multi-scale deep neuronal network, named residual D-net, to analyze the brain behavior. The main novelty of the presented architecture is that it allows us to unravel the brain connectivity dynamics, but, efficiently learning with a limited number of samples, which constitutes the most common scenario in practice. Therefore, we applied our proposed residual D-net to learn the brain connectivity dynamics of our subjects. Then, we feed the learned brain dynamic features into a classifier to distinguish subjects with MCI from healthy individuals.

2 Materials and Preprocessing

In this study, we use a public rs-fMRI cohort from the Clinical Core of Alzheimer's Disease Neuroimaging Initiative (ADNI)[1], which has established a competitive collaboration among academia and industry investigation focused on the early identification and intervention of AD [1].

Among the different datasets of ADNI (including the latest studies *ADNI go* and *ADNI 2*), there are data sets referring to patient with early stage of Mild Cognitive Impairment (eMCI), and patients with an advanced stage of the condition referred as Late stage Mild Cognitive Impairment (LMCI). In this paper, we report studies for both datasets separately.

Table 1. Demographics of the healthy control subjects (NC), patients with eMCI and patients with LMCI

	NC	eMCI	LMCI
Number of subjects	36	31	26
Male/Female	14/22	15/16	15/11
Number of scans	100	100	77
Male/Female	37/63	58/42	41/36
Age (mean $\pm$ SD)	72.7 $\pm$ 4.5	72.4 $\pm$ 3.8	74.3 $\pm$ 3.4

2.1 ADNI Cohorts

The final used cohort comprises 277 scans from 36 Normal healthy Control (NC) subjects, 31 patients with eMCI and 26 patients with LMCI (see Table (1)). With respect to the data acquisition, all the rs-fMRI scans were collected at different medical centers using a 3 Tesla Philips scanners following the same acquisition protocol [11]: Repetition Time (TR) = 3000 ms, Echo Time (TE) = 30 ms, flip angle = 80°, matrix size 64 × 64, number of slices = 48 and voxel thickness = 3.313 mm. Each scan was performed during 7 min producing a total number of 140 brain volumes.

2.2 Preprocessing

The functional images were preprocessed using the Data Processing Assistant for Resting-State fMRI (DPARSF) toolbox[2] and the SPM 12 package[3] following standard preprocessing steps:

---

[1] Availiable at http://adni.loni.usc.edu/.

[2] DPARSF: Available at http://rfmri.org/DPARSF.

[3] SPM 12: Available at http://www.fil.ion.ucl.ac.uk/spm.

- First, we discarded the first 10 volumes of each scan to avoid T1 equilibrium effects and we applied a slice-timing correction to the slice collected at TR/2 to minimize T1 equilibrium errors across each TR.
- After correcting the acquisition time, we realigned each time-series using a six-parameter rigid-body spatial transformation to compensate for head movements [9]. During this step, we excluded any scanner that exhibited a movement or rotation in any direction bigger than 3 mm or 3° respectively.
- Then, we normalized the corrected images over the Montreal Neurological Institute (MNI) space and resampled to 3 mm isotropic voxels. The resulted images were detrended in time through a linear approximation and spatially smoothed using a Gaussian filtering with FWHM = 4 mm.
- Finally, we removed the nuisance covariates of the white matter and the cerebrospinal fluid to avoid further effects and focused on the signal of the grey matter, and we band-pass filtered (0.01–0.08 Hz) the remaining signals to reduce the effects of motion and non-neuronal activity fluctuations.

2.3   Brain Network Analysis

In order to investigate the behavior of the brain functional connectivity, we labeled each brain volume into 116 Regions of Interest (ROIs), using the Automated Anatomical Labeling (AAL) atlas[4]. This atlas divides the brain into macroscopic brain structures: 45 ROIs for each hemisphere and 26 cerebellar ROIs. In this study, we excluded the 26 cerebellar ROIs, because theses areas are mainly related to motor and cognitive functional networks [16]. Then, we estimated a representative time course by averaging the intensity of all the voxel within each ROI, and we normalized the values in the range −1 to 1. Finally, we folded all the time courses into a matrix $\mathbf{R} \in \mathbb{R}^{90 \times 130}$, where each row contains the time evolution of one specific ROI.

3   Proposed Methods

In this paper, we propose a novel residual D-net framework to model the brain connectivity dynamics. First, the selective brain functional connectivity dynamics, used as input for the residual D-net is presented. Then, the details of residual D-net will be described.

3.1   Selective Brain Functional Connectivity Dynamics

In order to capture the brain connective dynamics in the rs-fMRI, we examine the time-varying functional connectivity (FC) variability via windowing correlation matrices [2], which provides a fair estimate of the natural dynamics of the functional brain connectivity. However, our goal is to identify individuals that will potentially develop AD. Consequently, we restricted our study of the

---

[4] AAL documentation available at http://www.gin.cnrs.fr/en/tools/aal-aal2/.

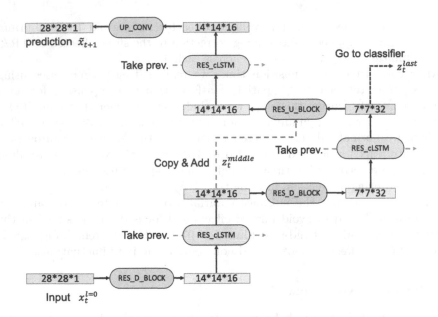

Fig. 1. Residual D-net architecture

whole-brain dynamics to just a few areas that may suffer damage due to the AD, which, also, reduces the pattern complexity of the brain functional connectivity. In this way, severals studies have pointed that certain brain areas are more likely to be affected by the AD. These areas are localized in the Frontal Lobe [7], the Hypocampus [19] and the Temporal Lobe [18,19]. Therefore, we limited our study of the brain connectivity dynamics to 28 ROIs that are vulnerable to AD.

Thus, using this specific set of ROIs and following the method described in [2], for each scan $(\mathbf{R}_i)$, with $i = 1, 2, \ldots, N$, where N is the total number of analyzed scans, we estimated the dynamic FC through a sliding window approach, and we computed each covariance matrix from a windowed segment of $\mathbf{R}_i$. We applied a tapered window created by convolving a rectangle (with $= 10$ TRs $= 30$) with a Gaussian ($\sigma = 4$TRs) and a sliding window in steps of 2 TRs, resulting in a total number of 56 windows. Accordingly, the result of each scan contains a sequence of 56 covariance matrices that encode the connectivity dynamics of the studied ROIs. These sequential matrices comprise the FC dynamics of the 28 ROIs, and we will use them as an input to the proposed method. Figure (4.a) shows examples of input sequences of these covariance matrices.

3.2   Residual D-Net

The proposed model needs to understand the dynamics of brain FC; that is, how the pattern within the covariance matrix changes along time. Furthermore, the model should be very efficient to learn the dynamics given a limited number of training data.

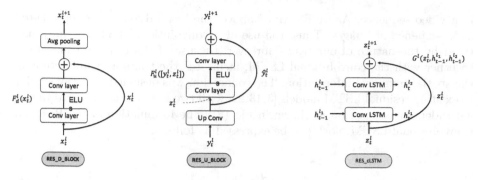

Fig. 2. Major component of the residual D-net: Donw/up Residual Block and Residual convLSTM Block

To address these issues, the proposed residual D-net has three major properties that allow the model to learn with relatively few training samples, while retaining its capacity to learn complex dynamics. Figure (1) shows the main architecture of the proposed residual D-net, which is formed by three main components: up residual block, down residual block (RES_U/D_Block) and a residual convolutional long short-term memory block (RES_cLSTM).

RES_U/D_Block: The residual network (resNet) [10] is a competitive deep architecture capable to produce a detailed decomposition of the input data. The residual connection in the resNet constrains the network to learn a residual representation, so that to facilitate the training. We exploit this property to learn complex patterns in the input, while keeping the training to be simple. In addition, we add an "average pooling" layer and "up convolution" layer, to express the multi-scale representation. The formulations of each down/up residual block can be expressed as follows:

$$x_t^{l+1} = \text{avgpool}(F_d^l(x_t^l) + x_t^l), \tag{1}$$

$$y_t^{l+1} = F_u^l([\hat{y}_t^l, z_t^l]) + y_t^l, \tag{2}$$

where x_t^l and y_t^l are the inputs of the l_{th} RES_D/U_Block, respectively. Each block has a bypass identity connection to fit the residual mapping from the input. We denote each convolutional layer in the block as $F_d^l(x_t^l)$ and $F_u^l(y_t^l)$ in Fig. (2), which are composed of two 3×3 convolutional layers and we employ the exponential linear units (ELUs) [8] as the nonlinear activation function. The major difference lies in their "up/down sampling" layer. In the RES_D_BLOCK, a average pooling layer is attached to down sample the input. In the RES_U_BLOCK, we use a up-conv layer for up-sampling $(\hat{y}_t^l)$ the input and it is concatenated with z_t^l, which comes from the high resolution feature map in the upper RES_cLSTM Block.

RES_cLSTM Block: The convolutional LSTM [26] is a well-known Recurrent Neural Network (RNN) model, capable of capturing spatial-temporal features in a video sequence. As we described above, the brain dynamics is represented as a sequence of images. Thus, the use of a convolutional LSTM is fully justified by the nature of our task. Moreover, the use of the residual connection, together with the convolutional LSTM, facilitates the training, while retaining the spatial-temporal information. The connection was designed in a way similar to existing residual LSTM models [3,13,22] with two concatenated LSTM blocks with identity connection as shown in Fig. (2). The formulation of the Residual Convolutional LSTM block can be expressed as follows:

$$z_t^{l+1} = h_t^{l_2} + z_t^l, \tag{3}$$

$$h_t^{l_2} = G^l(z_t^l, h_{t-1}^{l_1}, h_{t-1}^{l_2}). \tag{4}$$

Here, z_t^l is the input of the l_{th} RES_cLSTM Block and $h_{t-1}^{l_1}$, $h_{t-1}^{l_2}$ represents hidden states of the convolutional LSTM layer from previous $t-1$ time step. The function $G^l(z_t^l, h_{t-1}^{l_1}, h_{t-1}^{l_2})$ represents the l_{th} two-layered convolutional LSTM that maps dynamics of the input pattern into the current hidden states(H_t^l : $[h_t^{l_1}, h_t^{l_2}]$). Similarly to the residual block, all convolutional layer uses 3×3 size filter.

Structure of Residual D-net: Using the residual blocks as components, we build a 2-depth U-net architecture for multi-scale representation. The U-net framework [17] was developed for dealing with deep representative learning tasks with few training samples. We adopt the same framework to take advantage of the rich feature representation and the efficient learning scheme. In addition, we add a recurrent flow to capture the dynamic behavior, so that the architecture forms **D-shape**. As shown in Fig. (1), The input $x_t^{l=0}$ comprises 28×28 images of the correlation map at t time step. RES_D_Block decreases the input size by half and increases the feature map by two starting from the initial 16-feature map size. The feature maps are contracting until they reach the last RES_cLSTM block. These abstract embeddings (z_t^{last}) are finally used later on for the classification. During the expansion path, the feature map from the middle-depth layer, z_t^{middle}, is concatenated via a skip-connection. This multi-scale way of training allows to learn the complex patterns of the input sequences and to capture the dynamic changes in the hidden state of the convolutional LSTM.

3.3   Unsupervised Pre-training and Fine-Tuning

First, we train our residual D-net with sequences of correlation maps by predicting a few steps ahead of the sequences. Given T-time step input sequences, residual D-net predicts the output until next $2T$ time points $(\tilde{x}_{T+1,...,2T})$. By predicting the future steps, model can be trained unsupervised way [20], see Fig. (3). We use mean square error (MSE) of prediction as the loss, and the adam [14] optimizer for updating the parameter with learning rate 0.0005. In Fig. (4.b), we can see an example of the predicted sequences, and it shows that unsupervised pre-training of the residual D-net learns the dynamic behavior of the human brain. After unsupervised training, we take all the output of the

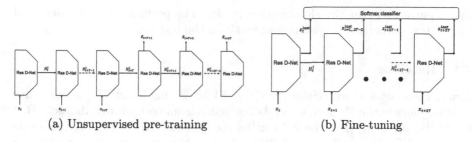

(a) Unsupervised pre-training   (b) Fine-tuning

Fig. 3. Training scheme of the (a) unsupervised pre-training and (b) supervised fine-tuning using the residual D-net.

(b) Target sequences

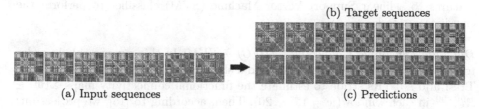

(a) Input sequences   (c) Predictions

Fig. 4. (a) shows the sequences of the dynamic functional connectivity that used for input, and (b) shows the target sequences to be predicted and (c) represents the sequences of the predictions from residual D-net.

last layer of RES_cLSTM block (z_t^{last}) for classification task. During the classification learning, the parameters in the contracting path($2 \times$(RES_D_BLOCK + RES_cLSTM)) can be fine-tuned with concatenated softmax-classifier such as Fig. (3.b). And the final decision will be made by averaging the result from classifier as follows:

$$logit = \frac{1}{T} \sum_{t=1}^{N} \text{softmax}(w_{cl} \times z_t^{last} + b_{cl}). \qquad (5)$$

Here, w_{cl} and b_{cl} are the softmax-classifier projection weights and bias, respectively. We use the binary cross-entropy as a loss function to fine-tune the architecture with a learning rate 0.00001. We found that involving unsupervised pre-training is crucial, in order to avoid over-fitting during the training of the networks, see Fig. (5). After the fine-tuning, the classifier learns the differences between the two dynamic pattern in each class.

4   Performance Evaluation

We conducted two classification experiments (NC vs. eMCI and NC vs. LMCI) to evaluate the proposed residual D-net and compare it with three baselines techniques. For this, we performed a five-fold subject-wise cross-validation to avoid using the same subject. Each validation set was used for selecting the optimal hyper-parameters for the classification model. The performance was measured by the total accuracy, precision, and recall on the test set.

4.1 Baselines

Static Functional Connectivity (SFC) + SVM: Zhang *et al.* [27] suggest five specific pairs of the Pearson's correlation coefficients on each raw dataset ($\mathbf{R} \in \mathbb{R}^{90 \times 130}$), assuming that the FC can be used to distinguish the MCI subjects from the NC. The authors explicitly selected these features after applying a two-sample T-test on 40 subjects. In this paper, we further investigated twenty alternative coefficients using Fisher feature selection [24], and we fed the selected features to a linear Support Vector Machine (SVM) classifier to perform the classification task.

Dynamic Functional Connectivity (DFC) + SVM: In this experiment, in order to consider the brain dynamics, we used a sliding rectangular window (width: 30 TRs) and a 5 TRs stride to estimate the functional connectivity maps $\Sigma(w) \in \mathbb{R}^{90 \times 90}$ in each window($w = 1, \ldots, 20$). Then, according to [15], we project our data into a $K \times 20$-dimensional feature map and then, we selected the best 100 features using Fisher feature selection, and we measured the performance with a linear SVM classifier.

Deep Auto-Encoder (DAE) + HMM: Suk *et al.* [21] propose an unsupervised feature learning using a DAE. First, they trained a four-layer DAE (hidden layers: 200-100-50-2) using as an input all the ROIs directly. Afterward, for each specific time instance, they converted the information of all the ROIs (a 116 real vector) into a 2-dimensional feature map. Then, they fit these 2-dimensional feature maps into two Hidden Markov Models (HMM) to model the NC and the MCI classes. Similarly, we implemented this method but using 6 hidden states with 2-mixtures of Gaussian HMM via the Baum-Welch algorithm.

Table 2. Values of the Accuracy (Acc), Precision (Pre) and Recall (Rec) for each five-fold subject-wise cross-validation for the eMCI dataset.

CV	SFC + SVM			DFC + SVM			DAE + HMM			Res. D-net		
	Acc	Pre	Rec	Acc	Pre	Rec	Acc	Pre	Rec	Acc	Pre	Rec
1	57.1	52.0	68.4	50.0	46.2	63.2	59.5	54.5	63.2	**71.4**	62.1	94.7
2	52.5	61.1	47.8	42.5	50.0	30.4	45.0	53.8	30.4	**70.0**	66.7	95.7
3	27.8	36.8	33.3	63.9	78.6	52.4	63.9	65.4	81.0	**72.2**	72.0	85.7
4	50.0	48.0	57.1	43.2	40.0	38.1	43.2	41.7	47.6	**72.7**	66.7	85.7
5	36.8	33.3	50.0	42.1	38.5	62.5	52.6	45.5	62.5	**65.8**	56.0	87.5
Total	45.5	45.9	51.0	48.0	48.0	48.0	52.5	52.3	56.0	**70.5**	64.7	90.0

Table 3. Values of the Accuracy (Acc), Precision (Pre) and Recall (Rec) for each five-fold subject-wise cross-validation for the LMCI dataset.

CV	SFC + SVM			DFC + SVM			DAE + HMM			Res. D-net		
	Acc	Pre	Rec	Acc	Pre	Rec	Acc	Pre	Rec	Acc	Pre	Rec
1	50.0	44.4	42.1	50.0	41.7	26.3	38.1	37.9	57.9	**73.8**	68.2	78.9
2	48.5	44.4	25.0	54.5	55.6	31.3	60.6	80.0	25.0	**75.8**	75.0	75.0
3	**74.1**	85.7	50.0	33.3	25.0	25.0	51.9	46.7	58.3	66.7	60.0	75.0
4	61.1	47.1	61.5	50.0	27.3	23.1	61.1	46.7	53.8	**72.2**	61.5	61.5
5	48.7	40.0	35.3	61.5	57.1	47.1	56.4	50.0	52.9	**64.1**	55.6	88.2
Total	55.4	48.5	41.6	50.8	41.4	31.2	53.1	46.3	49.4	**70.6**	63.4	76.6

4.2 Discussion and Results

As we discussed during the description of the experiment, we adopted a five-fold subject-wise cross-validation, in order to ensure the reliability of the different methods.[5] Tables (2) and (3) show the results associated with the accuracy, precision and recall obtained for the different methods, for the eMCI and LMCI dataset respectively.

The main conclusion is that all the baseline techniques turned out significantly inferior results. First, the inferior performance of SFC + SVM is expected because it does not consider any brain dynamics. Moreover, a further analysis turned out that this method performed well on the training set, in contrast to the test set. This observation evidences that the method fails to generalize among different datasets. On the other hand, although the DFC + SVM takes into account the time evolution of the FC, the method does not learn the relationships within the brain dynamics and, consequently, fails to perform the classification task.

Regarding to the DAE + HMM, the major limitation of this approach is that is not an end-to-end learning method. That is, although it incorporates an HMM that tries to model the dynamics, the DAE does not capture any information from the brain connectivity dynamics. Leading to a inferior performance. In contrast, further analysis during the training and the pre-training have shown that our proposed method effectively learns the brain dynamics. Thus, Fig. (4) shows the original and the predicted covariance matrices, which assembles the FC brain dynamics. Observe that our proposed approach captures and reproduces the true dynamics of the brain behavior. This explains why the proposed method exhibits the best performance and it properly generalizes among the different cross-validation sets.

Pre-training vs. Overfitting
Considering the limited number of samples of the studied datasets, the primary risk of our proposed method is that of overfitting. However, we faced this

---

[5] The code and pre-processed data is available at https://github.com/youngjoo-epfl/residualDnet.

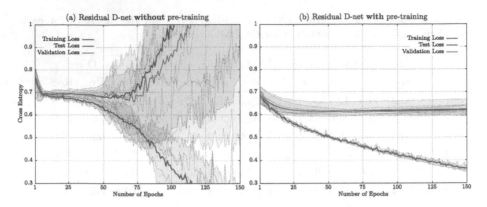

Fig. 5. Cross-entropy errors on the LMCI dataset obtained by the proposed method without pre-training (a) and with pre-training (b).

challenge by introducing the residual D-net architecture, and also by pre-training the model prior to the classification task.

Although we have already discussed the advantages the residual D-net architecture, we illustrate the benefits of the pre-training in Fig. (5), where we plotted the loss errors for the LMCI dataset with and without pre-training. Observe that the model overfits without pre-training (see Fig. (5.a)); that is, we can not guarantee that the method had generalized correctly, making it impossible to establish any proper stopping criterion. However, the behavior of the loss curves radically changes after pre-training the model (see Fig. (5.b)). Now, the method has converged and we can define a proper stopping criterion.

5   Conclusions

In this paper, we presented a new method named residual D-net to identify MCI from NC subjects. In contrast to the previous methods, proposed residual D-net can be efficiently trained with few number of training samples, while unravels the brain connectivity dynamics in unsupervised learning. Furthermore, the proposed pre-training approach enforces the generalization performance of the proposed method and offers an adequate selection of a stopping criterion.

Acknowledgment. This research was supported in part by the European Union's H2020 Framework Programme (H2020-MSCA-ITN-2014) under grant No. 642685 MacSeNet.

References

1. Aisen, P.S., et al.: Clinical core of the Alzheimer's disease neuroimaging initiative: progress and plans. Alzheimer's Dement. J. Alzheimer's Assoc. **6**(3), 239–246 (2010)
2. Allen, E.A., Damaraju, E., Plis, S.M., Erhardt, E.B., Eichele, T., Calhoun, V.D.: Tracking whole-brain connectivity dynamics in the resting state. Cereb. Cortex **24**(3), 663–676 (2014)
3. Alom, M.Z., Hasan, M., Yakopcic, C., Taha, T.M., Asari, V.K.: Recurrent residual convolutional neural network based on u-net (R2U-Net) for medical image segmentation. arXiv preprint. arXiv:1802.06955 (2018)
4. Alzheimer's Association: 2016 Alzheimer's disease facts and figures. Alzheimer's Dement. **12**(4), 459–509 (2016)
5. Barker, W.W., et al.: Relative frequencies of Alzheimer disease, lewy body, vascular and frontotemporal dementia, and hippocampal sclerosis in the state of Florida brain bank. Alzheimer Dis. Assoc. Disord. **16**(4), 203–212 (2002)
6. Brown, C.J., Hamarneh, G.: Machine learning on human connectome data from MRI. arXiv preprint. arXiv:1611.08699 (2016)
7. Buckner, R.L., Kelley, W.M., Petersen, S.E.: Frontal cortex contributes to human memory formation. Nat. Neurosci. **2**(4), 311–314 (1999)
8. Clevert, D.A., Unterthiner, T., Hochreiter, S.: Fast and accurate deep network learning by exponential linear units (ELUs). arXiv preprint. arXiv:1511.07289 (2015)
9. Friston, K.J., Frith, C.D., Frackowiak, R.S., Turner, R.: Characterizing dynamic brain responses with fMRI: a multivariate approach. NeuroImage **2**(2, Part A), 166–172 (1995)
10. He, K., Zhang, X., Ren, S., Sun, J.: Deep residual learning for image recognition. In: Proceedings of the IEEE Conference on Computer Vision and Pattern Recognition, pp. 770–778 (2016)
11. Jack, C.R., et al.: The Alzheimer's disease neuroimaging initiative (ADNI): MRI methods. J. Magn. Reson. Imaging **27**(4), 685–691 (2008)
12. Khazaee, A., Ebrahimzadeh, A., Babajani-Feremi, A.: Application of advanced machine learning methods on resting-state fMRI network for identification of mild cognitive impairment and Alzheimer's disease. Brain Imaging Behav. **10**(3), 799–817 (2016)
13. Kim, J., El-Khamy, M., Lee, J.: Residual LSTM: design of a deep recurrent architecture for distant speech recognition. arXiv preprint. arXiv:1701.03360 (2017)
14. Kingma, D.P., Ba, J.: Adam: a method for stochastic optimization. arXiv preprint. arXiv:1412.6980 (2014)
15. Leonardi, N., et al.: Principal components of functional connectivity: a new approach to study dynamic brain connectivity during rest. NeuroImage **83**, 937–950 (2013)
16. Middleton, F.A., Strick, P.L.: Basal ganglia and cerebellar loops: motor and cognitive circuits. Brain Res. Rev. **31**(2–3), 236–250 (2000)
17. Ronneberger, O., Fischer, P., Brox, T.: U-Net: convolutional networks for biomedical image segmentation. In: Navab, N., Hornegger, J., Wells, W.M., Frangi, A.F. (eds.) MICCAI 2015. LNCS, vol. 9351, pp. 234–241. Springer, Cham (2015). https://doi.org/10.1007/978-3-319-24574-4_28
18. Squire, L.R.: Memory and the hippocampus: a synthesis from findings with rats, monkeys, and humans. Psychol. Rev. **99**(2), 195 (1992)

19. Squire, L.R., Stark, C.E.L., Clark, R.E.: The medial temporal lobe. Ann. Rev. Neurosci. **27**(1), 279–306 (2004)
20. Srivastava, N., Mansimov, E., Salakhudinov, R.: Unsupervised learning of video representations using LSTMs. In: International Conference on Machine Learning, pp. 843–852 (2015)
21. Suk, H.I., Wee, C.Y., Lee, S.W., Shen, D.: State-space model with deep learning for functional dynamics estimation in resting-state fMRI. NeuroImage **129**, 292–307 (2016)
22. Wang, Y., Tian, F.: Recurrent residual learning for sequence classification. In: Proceedings of the 2016 Conference on Empirical Methods in Natural Language Processing, pp. 938–943 (2016)
23. Ward, A., Tardiff, S., Dye, C., Arrighi, H.M.: Rate of conversion from prodromal alzheimer's disease to alzheimer's dementia: a systematic review of the literature. Dement. Geriatr. Cogn. Disord. Extra **3**(1), 320–332 (2013)
24. Weston, J., Mukherjee, S., Chapelle, O., Pontil, M., Poggio, T., Vapnik, V.: Feature selection for SVMs. In: Advances in Neural Information Processing Systems, pp. 668–674 (2001)
25. Wilson, R.S., Segawa, E., Boyle, P.A., Anagnos, S.E., Hizel, L.P., Bennett, D.A.: The natural history of cognitive decline in Alzheimer's disease. Psychol. Aging **27**(4), 1008–1017 (2012)
26. Xingjian, S., Chen, Z., Wang, H., Yeung, D.Y., Wong, W.K., Woo, W.C.: Convolutional LSTM network: a machine learning approach for precipitation nowcasting. In: Advances in Neural Information Processing Systems, pp. 802–810 (2015)
27. Zhang, X., Hu, B., Ma, X., Xu, L.: Resting-state whole-brain functional connectivity networks for MCI classification using L2-regularized logistic regression. IEEE Trans. NanoBiosci. **14**(2), 237–247 (2015)

Clustering Ensemble Selection
with Determinantal Point Processes

Wei Liu[1], Xiaodong Yue[1,2(✉)], Caiming Zhong[3], and Jie Zhou[4]

[1] School of Computer Engineering and Science,
Shanghai University, Shanghai 200444, China
`ldachuan@outlook.com, yswantfly@shu.edu.cn`
[2] Shanghai Institute for Advanced Communication and Data Science,
Shanghai University, Shanghai, China
[3] College of Science and Technology, Ningbo University, Ningbo 315211, China
`zhongcaiming@nbu.edu.cn`
[4] College of Computer Science and Software Engineering, Shenzhen University,
Guangdong 518060, China
`jie_jpu@163.com`

Abstract. Clustering ensemble selection methods choose qualified and diverse base clusterings for ensemble. Existing methods rank base clusterings according to validity indices as quality measures and select diverse clusterings in top qualified ones. However, the ranking-based selection is hard to filter out base clusterings and may miss important diverse clusterings of moderate quality for ensemble. Aiming at the problem, we revisit the base clustering selection from the view of stochastic sampling and propose a Clustering Ensemble Selection method with Determinantal Point Processes (DPPCES). DPP sampling of base clusterings adds the randomness to the clustering selection while guaranteeing quality and diversity. The randomness is helpful to avoid the local optimal solution and provide a flexible way to select qualified and diverse base clusterings for ensemble. Experimental results verify the effectiveness of the proposed DPP-based clustering ensemble selection method.

Keywords: Clustering ensemble selection · Determinantal Point
Process

1 Introduction

Clustering Ensemble methods utilize consensus functions to integrate a group of base clusterings to obtain the final clustering results [20]. Not all the base clusterings play a positive role in ensemble process and therefore Clustering Ensemble Selection methods have been proposed to select significant base clusterings from candidate ones [6]. Clustering quality and diversity are two critical factors to evaluate the significance of base clusterings for ensemble [6]. Clustering ensemble selection methods aim to find qualified and diverse base clusterings to generate final clustering results.

© Springer Nature Switzerland AG 2019
T. Gedeon et al. (Eds.): ICONIP 2019, LNCS 11955, pp. 621–633, 2019.
https://doi.org/10.1007/978-3-030-36718-3_52

Existing clustering ensemble selection methods adopt both external validity indices [6] and internal validity indices [3] to evaluate the quality of base clusterings. Based on the quality evaluations, base clusterings are ranked and the top ones are chosen for ensemble. Among the qualified base clusterings, considering the clustering diversity, the distance measures between data distributions, such as normalized mutual information are used to further select diverse base clusterings to generate final ensemble results [6]. However, the ranking-based selection methods are hard to filter out base clusterings according to their quality and may miss important diverse clusterings of moderate quality for ensemble [10]. Moreover, the quality and diversity measures can be linearly combined to obtain the overall evaluation of base clusterings [19]. But it is difficult to define a general combination function for diverse data distributions.

To tackle the problems above, we model the base clustering selection problem as a stochastic sampling process and propose a clustering ensemble selection method with Determinantal Point Processes (DPPs) in this paper. DPPs provide a class of precise probabilistic models for subset selection problems where diversity is preferred [15]. In DPPs, diverse items are selected according to the probabilities which are computed from the determinants of item-correlation matrices. The correlation matrices can be constructed based on the measures of item quality and diversity [15]. As to the attractive properties of selecting important and diverse items, DPPs have gained substantial research interests and been extended to k-DPPs [14], structured DPPs, sequential DPPs and low-rank DPPs. DPP sampling adds the randomness to the selection process on the premise of guaranteeing quality and diversity. The randomness is helpful to avoid the local optimal solution and thereby provides a flexible way to select qualified and diverse base clusterings for ensemble. The contributions of this paper are summarized as follows.

- *Formulate base clustering selection with DPP sampling.* We revisit the selective clustering ensemble from the view of stochastic sampling and construct k-DPPs for sampling subsets of significant base clusterings. The probability in DPP clustering sampling is computed based on the determinants of correlation matrix L of base clusterings, and each element of the matrix consists of the quality and diversity evaluations of base clusterings.
- *Implement a clustering ensemble selection algorithm with DPP sampling (DPPCES).* The algorithm of sampling base clusterings from DPPs consists of two stage. In the first stage, a subset of eigenvectors of correlation matrix L is selected to form an elementary DPP. In the second stage, a subset of k base clusterings is sampled in probability from the elementary DPP.

The rest of this paper is organized as follows. Section 2 overall introduces the clustering ensemble selection method based on DPPs sampling, which includes the sampling model of base clustering selection, probability computation and algorithm implementation. In Sect. 3, experiment results validate the effectiveness of the DPP-based selective clustering ensemble. The work conclusion is given in Sect. 4.

2   Clustering Ensemble Selection with DPPs

The key problem of clustering ensemble selection is how to choose a subset of significant base clusterings. Traditional methods rank the base clusterings according to their quality and diversity and thereby select the top ones for ensemble. Different from the ranking-based selection strategies, we revisit the selection of base clusterings as a stochastic sampling process. Given a set of M base clusterings $C = \{c_1, c_2, \cdots, c_M\}$, we randomly select a subset of k base clusterings from C in probability, $C^S \subseteq C$ and $|C^S| = k$. The probability of subset selection $P(C^S)$ depends on the quality and diversity of the base clusterings contained in C^S.

$$P(C^S) \sim P\left(quality\left(C^S\right), diversity\left(C^S\right)\right) \qquad (1)$$

The base clusterings of both high quality and diversity will be considered significant and have high probabilities being selected. As to the characteristics of DPPs for sampling qualitative and diverse items [15], we formulate the selection of base clusterings with k-DPP sampling. The k-DPP sampling model of base clusterings and the corresponding probability computation will be further introduced in next subsections.

2.1   Modeling Base Clustering Selection with DPP Sampling

Revisiting the clustering ensemble selection from the view of DPP sampling, we can define a determinantal point process for sampling base clusterings with the item-correlation matrix in the form of marginal kernel [14].

Definition 1. *DPP of base clustering sampling.* *Given a set of M base clusterings $C=\{c_1, c_2, \cdots, c_M\}$, a point process $\mathcal{P}$ defines a probability measure on all the clustering subsets of C. $\mathcal{P}$ is a determinantal point process if drawing a random set C^S from C according to $\mathcal{P}$, the probability of C^S being selected is*

$$P\left(C^S\right) = det\left(K_{C^S}\right) \qquad (2)$$

where K is a $M \times M$ symmetric matrix indexed by the elements of C, which presents the correlation between M base clusterings. It is required that K is positive semidefinite and all the eigenvalues of K should be less than or equal to one. The matrix K is referred as the marginal kernel to compute the probability of any subset C^S being selected. $K_{C^S} = [K_{ij}]_{c_i, c_j \in C^S}$ denotes the sub-matrix indexed by the base clusterings in C^S and $det(K_{C^S})$ is the determinant of the sub-matrix. For the empty set, $det(K_{C^S}) = 1$. If $C^S = \{c_i\}$ is a singleton, $P(c_i) = K_{ii}$, which means the diagonal of the marginal kernel K gives the probabilities of selecting individual base clusterings.

In general, it is difficult to construct the marginal kernel K. Therefore, we utilize L-ensemble to construct DPPs for sampling base clusterings referring to [15]. Comparing with the marginal kernel, L-ensemble defines a DPP via a positive semidefinite correlation matrix L but without the constraints of eigenvalues.

Definition 2. *DPP of base clustering sampling with L-ensemble.* A *point process $\mathcal{P}$ on the clustering subsets of C is a determinantal point process if drawing a random set C^S from C according to $\mathcal{P}$, the probability of C^S being selected is*

$$P\left(C^S\right) = \frac{\det\left(L_{C^S}\right)}{\det\left(L + I\right)} \tag{3}$$

where L is a $M \times M$ positive semidefinite matrix indexed by elements of C, I is the $M \times M$ identity matrix and $\det\left(L + I\right) = \sum_{C' \subseteq C} \det\left(L_{C'}\right)$ is used to normalize the matrix determinants to probabilities.

Based on the DPPs of clustering sampling with L-ensemble, we can further define the probability of selecting a subset of k base clusterings for ensemble referring to k-DPP models which are used to sample fixed-size subsets from DPPs [14].

Definition 3. *k-DPP of base clustering sampling with L-ensemble.* Sup*pose any sampled subset C^S consists of k base clusterings, the k-DPP of clustering sampling is defined by the following probability measure of subset selection with L-ensemble,*

$$P^k(C^S) = \frac{\det\left(L_{C^S}\right)}{\sum\limits_{C' \subseteq C \wedge |C'| = k} \det\left(L_{C'}\right)} \tag{4}$$

where $\left|C^S\right| = k$ and L_{C^S} is the $k \times k$ submatrix of L indexed by C^S.

Based on the definition above, we can compute the probabilities of selecting subsets of k base clusterings with the eigenvalues of matrix L. Suppose $L = \sum_{i=1}^{M} \lambda_i v_i v_i^T$, λ_i refers to the eigenvalue corresponding to the eigenvector v_i, the probability of selecting a k-size subset C^S is

$$
\begin{aligned}
P^k(C^S) &= \frac{\det\left(L_{C^S}\right)}{\sum\limits_{C' \subseteq C \wedge |C'| = k} \det\left(L_{C'}\right)} \\
&= \frac{\prod_{c_i \in C^S} \lambda_i}{\sum\limits_{C' \subseteq C \wedge |C'| = k} \left\{ \prod_{c_j \in C'} \lambda_j \right\}},
\end{aligned} \tag{5}
$$

The probability calculations of DPP samplings of base clusterings need to construct the correlation matrix L. Decomposing the matrix L as a Gram matrix $L = B^T B$, we can reformulate the probability measure of DPP sampling with the diversity and quality of elements [15]. Suppose each vector B_i in B has the form of $B_i = q_i \cdot \phi_i$, in which q_i is a positive real number to measure the element quality and the normalized feature vector ϕ_i, $\|\phi_i\|_2 = 1$ denotes the direction of the ith element. We rewrite the matrix L as

$$L = [L_{ij}]_{1 \le i,j \le M}, \quad L_{ij} = q_i \phi_i^T \cdot \phi_j q_j \tag{6}$$

We can see that the inner product $\phi_i^T \cdot \phi_j \in [-1, +1]$ indicates the similarity between the elements i and j. L_{ij} consists of the quality and diversity of the pair of elements. Denoting the similarity $\phi_i^T \cdot \phi_j = s_{ij}$, we rewrite

$$L = \{L_{ij} = q_i \cdot s_{ij} \cdot q_j \,|\, 1 \leq i \leq M, 1 \leq j \leq M\} \tag{7}$$

Next we adopt multiple diversity and quality measures of clusterings to construct the L matrix of base clusterings.

Quality Measure of Base Clusterings. Without loss of generality, we adopt internal validity indices which measure the data partitions by clusterings without external class labels to evaluate the quality of base clusterings. Specifically, we adopt four popular internal indices which include Compactness Index (CPI), Davies-Bouldin Index (DBI) [5], Calinski Harabasz Index (CHI) [3] and $\mathcal{I}$ Index [16]. CHI and $\mathcal{I}$ Index have positive correlations with clustering quality, high index values indicate the high quality of clustering results. For consistency, we also transform DBI and CPI to make the indexes have a positive correlation with clustering quality, $DBI = \exp(-DBI)$ and $CPI = \exp(-CPI)$. Moreover, we map the values of all the internal indexes to [0,1] with min-max normalization. Based on the consistent and normalized internal validity indices, we can directly obtain the quality evaluation q_i of a base clustering c_i through averaging the values of four internal validity indexes.

$$q_i = q(c_i) = \frac{CPI(c_i) + DBI(c_i) + \mathcal{I}(c_i) + CHI(c_i)}{4} \tag{8}$$

Diversity Measure of Base Clusterings. As to the characteristic of Normalized Mutual Information (NMI) to measure nonlinear correlations between distributions [17], we adopt NMI to measure the similarity between two base clusterings c_i and c_j.

$$s_{i,j} = s(c_i, c_j) = NMI(c_i, c_j) \tag{9}$$

Based on the quality and diversity measures of base clusterings, we can construct L matrix to compute the probability of DPP clustering sampling. In the algorithm implementation, we further set factors to balance the clustering quality and diversity in the elements of L matrix to select significant base clusterings for ensemble.

2.2   Algorithm Implementation

The probability of k-DPP clustering sampling in Definition 3 requires computing the determinants of all the $k \times k$ submatrices of L, which is an exponential task and difficult to apply. To tackle this problem, Kulesza and Taskar proposed an efficient two-stage DPP sampling method [14]. To implement the two-stage k-DPP sampling, a k-DPP is decomposed into a mixture of elementary DPPs as

$$P^k \left(C^S \right) = \frac{1}{e_k^M} \sum_{J \subseteq \{1,\ldots,M\} \wedge |J|=k} P^{V_J} \left(C^S \right) \prod_{t \in J} \lambda_t \tag{10}$$

in which P^{V_J} is an elementary DPP which is defined by a subset of k eigenvectors $V_J = \{v_t \,|\, t \in J\}$ of matrix L and the marginal kernel of the elementary DPP P^{V_J} is given by $\sum_{t \in J} v_t v_t^T$, the mixture weight of P^{V_J} is $\prod_{t \in J} \lambda_t \big/ e_k^M$ which is determined by the eigenvalues of k eigenvectors in V_J, $e_k^M = \sum_{|J|=k} \prod_{t \in J} \lambda_t$ is a shorthand for the kth elementary symmetric polynomial for normalization.

Based on the formula (10), we can further define the marginal probability for selecting a single clustering as

$$P^k \left(c_i \in C^S \right) = \frac{1}{e_k^M} \sum_{|J|=k} P^{V_J} \left(c_i \in C^S \right) \prod_{t' \in J} \lambda_{t'} \tag{11}$$

Because the diagonal of the marginal kernel gives the probabilities of individual items being included in the selected subset. We can infer that

$$
\begin{aligned}
P^k \left(c_i \in C^S \right) &= \frac{1}{e_k^M} \sum_{|J|=k} P^{V_J} \left(c_i \in C^S \right) \prod_{t' \in J} \lambda_{t'} \\
&= \frac{1}{e_k^M} \sum_{|J|=k} \left(\sum_{t \in J} \left(v_t^T \rho_i \right)^2 \right) \prod_{t' \in J} \lambda_{t'} \\
&= \frac{1}{e_k^M} \sum_{t=1}^M \left(v_t^T \rho_i \right)^2 \sum_{J \supseteq \{t\}, |J|=k} \prod_{t' \in J} \lambda_{t'} \\
&= \sum_{t=1}^M \left(v_t^T \rho_i \right)^2 \lambda_t \frac{e_{k-1}^{-t}}{e_k^M}
\end{aligned}
\tag{12}
$$

where e_{k-1}^{-t} denotes the $(k-1)$-order elementary symmetric polynomial for all the eigenvalues of L except λ_t, ρ_i is the ith standard basis M-vector, which is all zeros except for a one in the ith position.

Referring to formula (12), the marginal probability of selecting the ith item is the sum of the contributions $\left(v_t^T \rho_i \right)^2$ made by each eigenvector scaled by the respective probabilities that the eigenvectors are selected. The probability for selecting an eigenvector v_t is computed as $\lambda_t \left(e_{k-1}^{-t} \big/ e_k^M \right)$. Based on this, we can implement a two-stage k-DPP sampling to select k base clusterings from M candidates for clustering ensemble. In the first stage, a subset of $k \leq M$ eigenvectors is selected from M eigenvectors of the matrix L to form a subspace, where the probability of selecting each eigenvector depends on its associated eigenvalue. In the second stage, a subset of k base clusterings is sampled based on the selected eigenvectors. The details are shown in Algorithm 1.

Algorithm 1. Clustering Ensemble Selection with k-DPP Sampling (DPPCES)

Input: Set of M base clusterings, $C = \{c_1, c_2, \cdots, c_M\}$,
               Number of selected base clusterings, k;

Output: Set of selected k base clusterings, C^S.

1: Initialize $C^S = \emptyset$;

2: Compute the quality of base clusterings in C according to formula (8), $Q(C) = 0.7 * \{q_1, q_2, \cdots, q_M\}$;

3: Construct the similarity matrix of M base clusterings according to formula (9), $S(C) = 0.3 * \{s_{ij} \,|\, 1 \le i \le M, 1 \le j \le M\}$;

4: Construct L matrix, $L = \mathrm{Diag}(Q(C)) \cdot S(C) \cdot \mathrm{Diag}(Q(C))$;

5: Decompose L matrix into eigenvalues and eigenvectors, $(\lambda_i, v_i), 1 \le i \le M$;

6: Set $t = M, l = k$;

7: //First stage: select k eigenvectors to form an elementary DPP;

8: **while** $l > 0$ **do**

9:    **if** $rand \sim U[0,1] < \lambda_t \frac{e_{l-1}^{t-1}}{e_l^t}$ **then**

10:      $V = V \cup \{v_t\}$;

11:      $l = l - 1$;

12:    **end if**

13:    $t = t - 1$

14: **end while**

15: //Second stage: sample k base clusterings from the elementary DPP;

16: **while** $|V| > 0$ **do**

17:    Select one clustering c_i from C with probability $P(c_i) = \frac{1}{|V|} \sum_{v \in V} \left(v^T \rho_i\right)^2$;

18:    Add c_i into C^S, $C^S = C^S \cup \{c_i\}$;

19:    Compute $V_\perp$, which is the orthonormal basis of the subspace of V orthogonal to e_j;

20:    Update the subspace $V \leftarrow V_\perp$;

21: **end while**

---

3   Experimental Results

We implement two experiments to verify the proposed clustering ensemble selection method based on DPP sampling (DPPCES). In the first experiment, we validate the superiority of DPP sampling for base clustering selection. The second experiment overall evaluates the performance of DPPCES through comparing with other elegant clustering ensemble selection methods. The descriptions of test data sets are shown in Table 1.

In the experiments, we adopt three external criteria and two internal criteria to evaluate the performances of clustering ensemble selection methods. The external criteria include Clustering Accuracy (CA), Adjusted Rand Index (ARI) and Normalized Mutual Information (NMI), and the internal criteria include Silhouette Coefficient (SC) and Calinski Harabasz Index (CHI) [3]. The high values of criteria indicate the clustering ensemble selection methods produce good results. The other experiment settings are listed below.

- K-means algorithm is adopted to generate candidate base clusterings and the cluster centers are randomly initialized.

Table 1. Description of data sets

Data sets	Feature	Instance	Class	Sources
DS1 (S1)	2	5000	15	[7]
DS2 (Jain)	2	373	2	[12]
DS3 (Flame)	2	240	2	[8]
DS4 (Pathbased)	2	300	3	[4]
DS5 (Aggregation)	2	788	7	[9]
DS6 (D31)	2	3100	31	[18]
DS7 (Iris)	4	150	3	[1]
DS8 (Heart)	13	270	2	UCI [1]
DS9 (Wine)	13	178	3	UCI [1]
DS10 (Protein localization sites)	7	336	8	UCI [1]
DS11 (Australian credit approval)	14	690	2	UCI [1]
DS12 (Waveform)	21	5000	3	UCI [1]

- The number of candidate base clusterings is set 30 and the selection ratio ranges from 20% to 60%.
- The number of clusters in each base clustering is set $\sqrt{N}$ as default, N denotes the number of items in the data set. Specially, for Two-level-refined Co-association Matrix Ensemble (TOME) method, the cluster numbers of base clusterings are randomly initialized in the range of $[2, \sqrt{N}]$.
- LinkCluE [11] is utilized as a consensus function to ensemble the selected base clusterings to generate the final clustering results.
- We perform the clustering ensemble selection methods 10 times on each data set and present the average evaluation of the clustering results.

3.1   Test of Base Clustering Selection Strategy

In this experiment, we utilize DPPCES and other four clustering selection strategies to select base clusterings and compare the ensemble results. The comparative base clustering selection strategies include Full Clustering Ensemble (FCE), Top-k Quality Clustering Ensemble Selection (TQCES), Random Clustering Ensemble Selection (RCES) and Top-k of Diversity Clustering Ensemble Selection (TDCES). FCE strategy ensembles all the base clusterings to obtain the final results and thus can be considered as the baseline for comparison.

Because of the limitation of paper length, we just present the average evaluations of the selective clustering ensemble results generated by different selection strategies on all the data sets as shown in Fig. 1. The selection ratio of base clusterings ranges from 20% to 60%. We can find that, under all the evaluation criteria, the selection strategy based on DPP sampling achieves the best clustering ensemble results. Synthesizing both the clustering quality and diversity measures in the selection probability computation, DPP clustering sampling is effective to capture significant base clusterings and thus produce more precise clustering ensemble results than the other selection strategies which rank and filter out base clusterings according to only quality or diversity measure.

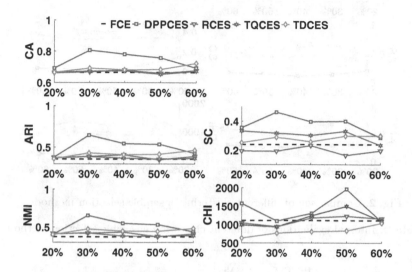

Fig. 1. Comparison of different base clustering selection strategies.

3.2 Comparison with Other Clustering Ensemble Selection Methods

Besides the validation of base clustering selection, in the second experiment, we overall evaluate the proposed DPPCES method through comparing with three elegant clustering ensemble selection methods, which include Cluster and Selection algorithm (CAS) [6], Adaptive Cluster Ensemble Selection algorithm (ACES) [2] and Selective Spectral Clustering Ensemble algorithm (SELSCE) [13].

Figure 2 illustrates the average evaluations of the selective clustering ensemble results produced by different methods on all the test data sets. It is obvious that DPPCES outperforms the other clustering ensemble selection methods under both internal and external evaluation criteria. Based on the superiority of DPP sampling to select important and diverse items, DPPCES can select a limited number of significant base clusterings to achieve precise ensemble results.

Tables 3 and 2 show the external and internal evaluations of the best results generated by different clustering ensemble selection methods against the selection ratio on each data set. We can see that on most data sets, DPPCES produces more precise ensemble results than the other methods. Abundant experiments indicate that the clustering ensemble selection method based on DPP sampling is effective to select qualified and diverse base clusterings and thereby produce precise clustering ensemble results.

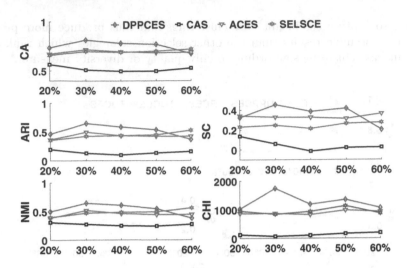

Fig. 2. Comparison of different clustering ensemble selection methods.

Table 2. Internal evaluations of different clustering ensemble selection methods.

Data sets	SC			
	DPPCES	CAS	ACES	SELSCE
DS1	**0.82 (30%)**	−0.23 (40%)	0.60 (20%)	0.75 (50%)
DS2	**0.61 (30%)**	0.36 (40%)	0.39 (20%)	0.61 (40%)
DS3	0.44 (50%)	0.32 (30%)	0.44 (40%)	**0.44 (30%)**
DS4	0.42 (20%)	0.19 (20%)	0.60 (60%)	**0.70 (30%)**
DS5	**0.62 (20%)**	−0.10 (20%)	0.62 (20%)	0.62 (40%)
DS6	**0.61 (60%)**	0.54 (50%)	0.50 (50%)	0.22 (20%)
DS7	0.69 (20%)	**0.70 (20%)**	0.60 (30%)	0.60 (20%)
DS8	**0.32 (30%)**	0.20 (60%)	0.32 (20%)	0.32 (20%)
DS9	**0.46 (50%)**	0.31 (30%)	0.40 (30%)	0.42 (20%)
DS10	**0.57 (30%)**	0.10 (20%)	0.52 (40%)	0.41 (60%)
DS11	0.41 (50%)	0.20 (20%)	**0.41 (20%)**	0.38 (20%)
DS12	0.23 (40%)	0.01 (60%)	**0.30 (30%)**	0.15 (20%)
Data sets	CHI			
DS1	**13607 (30%)**	255 (40%)	6385 (50%)	10061 (50%)
DS2	**371 (30%)**	157 (40%)	82 (20%)	371 (40%)
DS3	118 (50%)	86 (20%)	116 (40%)	**118 (30%)**
DS4	125 (20%)	31 (20%)	244 (60%)	**330 (30%)**
DS5	**1156 (20%)**	45(60%)	1155 (20%)	1156 (40%)
DS6	**5072 (50%)**	1327 (60%)	4136 (50%)	1881 (20%)
DS7	349 (20%)	**358 (20%)**	249 (30%)	249 (20%)
DS8	**62 (30%)**	44 (30%)	60(20%)	60 (20%)
DS9	**81 (50%)**	47 (30%)	40 (30%)	55 (30%)
DS10	**106 (30%)**	47 (20%)	51 (30%)	64 (60%)
DS11	**228 (30%)**	102 (20%)	2 (20%)	222 (20%)
DS12	1220 (40%)	398 (50%)	**1481 (30%)**	1059 (20%)

Table 3. External evaluations of different clustering ensemble selection methods.

Data sets	CA			
	DPPCES	CAS	ACES	SELSCE
DS1	**0.91 (30%)**	0.35 (40%)	0.80 (50%)	0.85 (50%)
DS2	**1.00 (30%)**	0.82 (50%)	0.81 (20%)	1.00 (40%)
DS3	**0.98 (20%)**	0.63 (20%)	0.97 (30%)	0.96 (30%)
DS4	**0.97 (40%)**	0.41 (40%)	0.88 (40%)	0.77 (50%)
DS5	1.00 (50%)	0.40 (50%)	1.00 (20%)	**1.00 (20%)**
DS6	**0.85 (60%)**	0.65 (20%)	0.79 (50%)	0.61 (60%)
DS7	**0.96 (40%)**	0.89 (20%)	0.75 (30%)	0.75 (20%)
DS8	**0.74 (30%)**	0.70 (60%)	0.73 (20%)	0.73 (20%)
DS9	**0.97 (50%)**	0.60 (20%)	0.65 (30%)	0.73 (60%)
DS19	**0.82 (30%)**	0.50 (20%)	0.65 (20%)	0.70 (60%)
DS11	**0.86 (30%)**	0.63 (20%)	0.56 (20%)	0.83 (20%)
DS12	**0.77 (40%)**	0.61 (40%)	0.58 (20%)	0.59 (20%)
Data sets	ARI			
DS1	**0.91 (30%)**	0.13 (40%)	0.81 (50%)	0.86 (50%)
DS2	**1.00 (30%)**	0.31 (50%)	0.26 (20%)	1.00 (40%)
DS3	**0.92 (20%)**	0.05 (20%)	0.90 (30%)	0.84 (30%)
DS4	**0.91 (40%)**	0.01 (40%)	0.69 (40%)	0.51 (60%)
DS5	1.00 (50%)	0.10 (50%)	**1.00 (20%)**	1.00 (40%)
DS6	**0.82 (60%)**	0.45 (20%)	0.78 (50%)	0.57 (60%)
DS7	**0.89 (40%)**	0.72 (20%)	0.57 (30%)	0.57 (20%)
DS8	**0.23 (30%)**	0.16 (60%)	0.20 (20%)	0.20 (20%)
DS9	**0.90 (50%)**	0.48 (30%)	0.47 (30%)	0.56 (60%)
DS10	**0.77 (30%)**	0.24 (40%)	0.47 (20%)	0.57 (60%)
DS11	**0.50 (30%)**	0.07 (20%)	0.01 (20%)	0.44 (20%)
DS12	**0.43 (40%)**	0.14 (40%)	0.34 (30%)	0.18 (20%)
Data sets	NMI			
DS1	**0.96 (30%)**	0.46 (40%)	0.90 (50%)	0.92 (50%)
DS2	**1.00 (30%)**	0.24 (40%)	0.18 (20%)	1.00 (40%)
DS3	**0.86 (20%)**	0.16 (20%)	0.84 (30%)	0.77 (30%)
DS4	**0.88 (40%)**	0.08 (20%)	0.73 (40%)	0.60 (50%)
DS5	1.00 (50%)	0.31 (30%)	**1.00 (20%)**	0.99 (40%)
DS6	**0.92 (60%)**	0.80 (20%)	0.90 (50%)	0.80 (60%)
DS7	**0.86 (40%)**	0.74 (20%)	0.63 (30%)	0.63 (20%)
DS8	**0.18 (30%)**	0.14 (60%)	0.17 (20%)	0.17 (20%)
DS9	**0.88 (50%)**	0.56 (30%)	0.50 (30%)	0.57 (30%)
DS10	**0.69 (30%)**	0.46 (40%)	0.46 (20%)	0.56 (60%)
DS11	**0.43 (30%)**	0.13 (20%)	0.01 (20%)	0.38 (20%)
DS12	**0.44 (40%)**	0.29 (40%)	0.38 (30%)	0.22 (20%)

4 Conclusion

The ranking-based clustering ensemble selection methods are hard to filter out base clusterings and may miss important diverse clusterings for ensemble. In this paper, we revisit the base clustering selection from the view of stochastic sampling and propose a clustering ensemble selection method with Determinantal Point Processes. DPP sampling of base clusterings provide a flexible way to select qualified and diverse base clusterings in probability. Experimental results verify the effectiveness of the proposed DPP-based clustering ensemble selection method. The efficiency of DPP clustering sampling will be further improved in our future works.

Acknowledgment. This work was supported by National Natural Science Foundation of China (Nos. 61573235, 61976134), and Open Project Foundation of Intelligent Information Processing Key Laboratory of Shanxi Province (No. CICIP2018001).

References

1. Asuncion, A., Newman, D.: UCI machine learning repository (2007)
2. Azimi, J., Fern, X.: Adaptive cluster ensemble selection. In: Twenty-First International Joint Conference on Artificial Intelligence (2009)
3. Caliński, T., Harabasz, J.: A dendrite method for cluster analysis. Commun. Stat.-theory Methods **3**(1), 1–27 (1974)
4. Chang, H., Yeung, D.Y.: Robust path-based spectral clustering. Pattern Recogn. **41**(1), 191–203 (2008)
5. Davies, D.L., Bouldin, D.W.: A cluster separation measure. IEEE Trans. Pattern Anal. Mach. Intell. **2**, 224–227 (1979)
6. Fern, X.Z., Lin, W.: Cluster ensemble selection. Stat. Anal. Data Min.: ASA Data Sci. J. **1**(3), 128–141 (2008)
7. Fränti, P., Virmajoki, O.: Iterative shrinking method for clustering problems. Pattern Recogn. **39**(5), 761–775 (2006)
8. Fu, L., Medico, E.: Flame, a novel fuzzy clustering method for the analysis of dna microarray data. BMC Bioinf. **8**(1), 3 (2007)
9. Gionis, A., Mannila, H., Tsaparas, P.: Clustering aggregation. ACM Trans. Knowl. Disc. Data (TKDD) **1**(1), 4 (2007)
10. Hadjitodorov, S.T., Kuncheva, L.I., Todorova, L.P.: Moderate diversity for better cluster ensembles. Inf. Fusion **7**(3), 264–275 (2006)
11. Iam-on, N., Garrett, S., et al.: LinkCluE: a MATLAB package for link-based cluster ensembles. J. Stat. Softw. **36**(9), 1–36 (2010)
12. Jain, A.K., Law, M.H.C.: Data clustering: a user's dilemma. In: Pal, S.K., Bandyopadhyay, S., Biswas, S. (eds.) PReMI 2005. LNCS, vol. 3776, pp. 1–10. Springer, Heidelberg (2005). https://doi.org/10.1007/11590316_1
13. Jia, J., Xiao, X., Liu, B., Jiao, L.: Bagging-based spectral clustering ensemble selection. Pattern Recogn. Lett. **32**(10), 1456–1467 (2011)
14. Kulesza, A., Taskar, B.: k-DPPs: Fixed-size determinantal point processes. In: Proceedings of the 28th International Conference on Machine Learning (ICML 2011), pp. 1193–1200 (2011)
15. Kulesza, A., Taskar, B.: Learning determinantal point processes (2011)

16. Maulik, U., Bandyopadhyay, S.: Performance evaluation of some clustering algorithms and validity indices. IEEE Trans. Pattern Anal. Mach. Intell. **24**(12), 1650–1654 (2002)
17. Strehl, A., Ghosh, J.: Cluster ensembles-a knowledge reuse framework for combining multiple partitions. J. Mach. Learn. Res. **3**(Dec), 583–617 (2002)
18. Veenman, C.J., Reinders, M.J.T., Backer, E.: A maximum variance cluster algorithm. IEEE Trans. Pattern Anal. Mach. Intell. **24**(9), 1273–1280 (2002)
19. Zhao, X., Liang, J., Dang, C.: Clustering ensemble selection for categorical data based on internal validity indices. Pattern Recogn. **69**, 150–168 (2017)
20. Zhong, C., Hu, L., Yue, X., Luo, T., Fu, Q., Xu, H.: Ensemble clustering based on evidence extracted from the co-association matrix. Pattern Recogn. **92**, 93–106 (2019)

Generative Histogram-Based Model Using Unsupervised Learning

Parisa Rastin[1(✉)], Guénaël Cabanes[2], Rosanna Verde[3], Younès Bennani[2], and Thierry Couronne[1,2,3]

[1] LORIA, UMR-CNRS 7503, University of Lorraine, Nancy, France
`parisa.rastin@loria.fr`
[2] LIPN, UMR-CNRS 7030, UP13, Sorbonne Paris Cité, Villetaneuse, France
[3] Dipartimento Matematica e Fisica, Università della Campania Luigi Vanvitelli, Naples, Italy

Abstract. This paper presents a new generative unsupervised learning algorithm based on a representation of the clusters distribution by histograms. The main idea is to reduce the model complexity through cluster-defined projections of the data on independent axes. The results show that the proposed approach performs efficiently compared with other algorithms. In addition, it is more efficient to generate new instances with the same distribution than the training data.

Keywords: Unsupervised learning · Clustering · Generative model · Histogram distribution

1 Introduction

Unsupervised learning is a branch of machine learning able to compute a model of the data distribution without any external information. Unsupervised learning is a very important tool for data analysis and popular application have been proposed in various field such as marketing [13], bioinformatic [1] or fraud detection [4]. One of the most common family of unsupervised learning approaches are clustering algorithms. Their task is to detect groups (clusters) of objects (instances) having similar features, compared to objects belonging to different groups. Some clustering algorithms compute a model representing the distribution of each cluster. The simplest models compute only the mean vector of each cluster: the most cited being the K-means family [9]. Others propose a more complex model, for example the Gaussian Mixture Model (GMM) [12] which assumes a mixture of Gaussian functions, usually one for each cluster, as model of the data distribution. Other clustering algorithms do not propose an explicit model of the data distribution: they perform the clustering of the training data, but in order to classify new objects, they require a comparison with all the objects of the training data-set. These algorithms are, for example, density-based algorithms such as BDSCAN [7], or hierarchical clustering approaches such as the Hierarchical Agglomerative Clustering [11].

© Springer Nature Switzerland AG 2019
T. Gedeon et al. (Eds.): ICONIP 2019, LNCS 11955, pp. 634–646, 2019.
https://doi.org/10.1007/978-3-030-36718-3_53

Among the wide panel of family of clustering algorithms, we are interested in probabilistic approaches. The main idea is to be able to predict, given a set of observations, a probability distribution over a set of classes, instead of only delivering the most similar class that the observation should belong to. Probabilistic approaches can be divided into two families. Generative approaches compute, given the data X and the clusters labels C, a statistical model of the joint probability distribution on $X \times C$, $P(X, C)$, the probabilities to observe an object x in a cluster c [10]. These models are called generative because the join probability distribution can be used to generate new samples following the same distribution as the training data. On the contrary, discriminative models compute the conditional probability of the cluster label C, given an object x: $P(C|X = x)$ [10]. Such approaches can compute membership probabilities, but are not suited to estimate the generative functions. Most of the time, the Expectation - Maximization (EM) algorithm [5] is used to estimate the parameter of the models.

A popular algorithm for discriminative clustering is Fuzzy C-Mean (FCM) [3]. FCM is similar to K-Means algorithm [9], except for the assignment of the objects to the clusters according to a membership value. First, the number of clusters must be chosen by the user and the membership values are initialized randomly, then the centroid of each cluster is computed based on the memberships' values (maximization step) and new memberships are computed based on the centroids (expectation step). These two steps are repeated until convergence. In Fuzzy C-Mean, the centroid of a cluster is the mean of all data points, weighted by their degree of membership to the cluster. When a generative approach is preferable, one of the most used algorithm is the above mentioned Gaussian Mixture Model (GMM) [12]. Again, the number of clusters is given as input and the model's parameters (the weight, the center and the covariance matrix of each Gaussian) are computed by alternating expectation and maximization steps.

GMM can produce very good results when the clusters' distributions are not too different from Gaussian distributions. When it is not the case, however, the data distribution cannot be modelled with a small number of Gaussian. Few approaches have been proposed to try to compute more general models. The algorithm presented in [2] is based on a (usually Gaussian) kernel density estimation made under a couple of constraints. In [16], the authors propose approaches based on different family of distributions (e.g. mixed logit model). As far as we are aware, there is no work using histograms as a true non-parametric representation of the data distribution. Histograms are a simple way of describing the empirical distribution as observed from the data. We propose here a non-parametric generative approach based on the EM algorithm, able to compute a histogram mixture model, allowing to deal with a much wider range of distributions than in previous algorithms.

The remainder of this paper is organized as follows. Section 2 describes the proposed approach and a complexity analysis is given in Sect. 3. The experimental protocol and the obtained results are detailed in Sect. 4. Finally, Section 5 concludes the paper and introduces future works.

2   General Framework

In this section, we introduce a new histogram-based clustering algorithm. The principle is to represent each cluster k with a set H_k of d histograms where d is the number of dimensions of the data-set X. H_k is a distribution represented with d histograms: $H_k = (h_{k,1}, \ldots, h_{k,d})$. Each $h_{k,l}$ is an empirical distribution and it is represented by a sequence of B continuous and no-overlapped intervals (or bins) $I_{k,l}^j$ with an associated weight (or relative frequency) $\pi_{k,l}^j$, for $j = 1, \ldots, B$, such that $\sum_{j=1}^{B} \pi_{k,l}^j = 1$:

$$h_{k,l} = [(I_{k,l}^1, \pi_{k,l}^1), \ldots, (I_{k,l}^B, \pi_{k,l}^B)]. \tag{1}$$

Let $X = (x_1, x_2, \ldots, x_n)$ be a data-set of N independent observations from a mixture of K distributions of dimension d, each represented by a set H_k of d histograms, and let $Z = (z_1, z_2, \ldots, z_n)$ be the latent variables that determine the component (i.e. the cluster) from which the observation originates.

The aim is to estimate the unknown parameters of the histograms:

$$\theta = (\theta_1, \ldots, \theta_K) \tag{2}$$

with

$$\theta_k = (\tau_k, h_{k,1}, \ldots, h_{k,B}). \tag{3}$$

The expected values of θ minimize the following likelihood function :

$$L(\theta; X, Z) = p(X, Z \mid \theta). \tag{4}$$

This minimization can be done via an Expectation - Maximization (EM) algorithm.

2.1   Maximization Step

In the Maximization step of the algorithm, the parameters of the histogram distribution are updated in order to maximize the expected value of the likelihood function of the model based on the current membership matrix of the data X, as computed is the Expectation step. To compute the membership matrix, however, we expect the histograms $(h_{k,1}, \ldots, h_{k,d})$ in H_k, for each cluster (component) k, to be independents from each other.

As each histogram $h_{k,l}$ represents a distribution along one dimension, we compute a set of d new independent axes and project the data belonging in cluster k in this new space. The projection is performed via Weighted Principal Component Analysis (WPCA [19]) to compute the eigenvectors of the covariance matrix of the data, weighed by their membership values for cluster k. We obtain d new independent axes representing the principal components of the data in cluster k, according to their membership values.

The data are then projected on each of the d new axes and d histogram are computed. To compute the parameters of an histogram $h_{k,l}$, the range between the minimal and the maximal value of the data projected on axis l is divided into B equal intervals (bins) $I_{k,l}^j, j \in (1, \ldots, B)$. For each of these interval, the relative frequency $\pi_{k,l}^j$ is computed as the normalized sum of the membership for cluster k of the objects projected in this interval:

$$\pi_{k,l}^j = \frac{\sum_{i/x_i^l \in I_{k,l}^j} T_{k,i}}{\sum_{j=1}^B \sum_{i/x_i^l \in I_{k,l}^j} T_{k,i}} \tag{5}$$

with x_i^l the value on the i^{st} data point projected on axis l and $T_{k,i} := P(Z_i = k \mid X_i = x_i; \theta)$ is the membership for cluster k of an observation x_i, according the current parameters θ, as computed in the Expectation step.

The mixing parameters τ_k for each cluster k are simply computed as the sum of the membership values for this cluster:

$$\tau_k = \sum_{i=1}^N T_{k,i}. \tag{6}$$

This process is repeated for each cluster k, in order to obtain the values of all the parameters in θ.

2.2 Expectation Step

The expectation step computes the $K \times N$ membership matrix $T = [T_{k,i}]$, such as $T_{k,i} := P(Z_i = k \mid X_i = x_i; \theta)$, with K the number of clusters (components) and N the number of observations in the training data-set.

The probability $P_k(x_i^l) := P(X_i^l = x_i^l \mid Z_i = k; \theta)$ of an unique value x_i^l for a distribution represented by a histogram $h_{k,l}$ is simply the weight $\pi_{k,l}^j$ (we recall that $\sum_{j=1}^B \pi_{k,l}^j = 1$ and $\pi_{k,l}^j \in [0,1]$) so that x_i^l is in the corresponding interval $I_{k,l}^j$:

$$P_k(x_i^l) = \pi_{k,l}^j \text{ with } j \mid x_i^l \in I_{k,l}^j \tag{7}$$

As the representation space of each cluster have been redefined such as the new axes are independents, the multivariate probability of an observation x_i for the full distribution H_k associated to cluster k is proportional to the product of the individual probabilities and can be computed with the Bayesian formalism:

$$T_{k,i} = \frac{\tau_k \prod_{l=1}^d P_k(x_i^l)}{\sum_{k=1}^K \tau_k \prod_{l=1}^d P_k(x_i^l)} \tag{8}$$

Note that this equation is only valid because of the WPCA projections computed for each cluster in the Maximization step. Without this trick, we would have needed to compute the full multivariate histogram, with a weight π associated to each combination of intervals in all dimensions. The number of parameters to learn would have been in $\mathcal{O}(B^d)$, instead of $\mathcal{O}(B.d)$ in the proposed approach.

2.3 Proposed Algorithm

The approach is described in Algorithm 1. It takes as input the data X, the expected number of components (clusters) K and the number of intervals (bins) B for the histograms.

Algorithm 1. Histogram-based generative clustering

     Input: X, K and B.
     Output: Adapted parameters θ.
1: Initialize $T = [T_{k,i}]$ and τ_k for each component k.
2: **repeat**
       MAXIMIZATION STEP
3:    **for each** component k **do**
4:       Compute a WPCA projection of X weighted by $T_{k,\cdot}$.
5:       Compute the histogram distributions on each WPCA axes l:

$$\pi_{k,l}^j = \frac{\sum_{i/x_i^l \in I_{k,l}^j} T_{k,i}}{\sum_{j=1}^B \sum_{i/x_i^l \in I_{k,l}^j} T_{k,i}}.$$

6:       Compute the mixing parameter τ_k:

$$\tau_k = \sum_{i=1}^N T_{k,i}$$

      EXPECTATION STEP
7:    **for each** component k and instance $x_i \in X$ **do**
8:       Compute the membership $T_{k,i}$:

$$T_{k,i} = \frac{\tau_k \prod_{l=1}^d P_k(x_i^l)}{\sum_{k=1}^K \tau_k \prod_{l=1}^d P_k(x_i^l)}$$

      with $P_k(x_i^l) = \pi_{k,l}^j$ for $j \mid x_i^j \in I_{k,l}^j$.

9: **until** convergence.

The mixing parameters are initialized such that $\tau_k = N/K$ for $k = 1, \ldots, K$, with N the number of instances in the training data-set. The membership matrix $T = [T_{k,i}]$ can be initialized randomly, but we choose to optimize the initialization using a Fuzzy C-means algorithm [3] trained on the data with a number of cluster equal to K. Fuzzy C-means computes a membership matrix T_{init} based on the distances between data points and clusters' centers. After normalization, it is a good starting point for the proposed model.

3 Complexity

In this section we analyze the complexity of the proposed approach in comparison to a classical Gaussian Mixture Model (GMM).

In term of time complexity, the maximization step of the proposed algorithm requires, for each cluster, the computation of the covariance matrix ($\mathcal{O}(K.N.d^2)$, with K the number of clusters, N the data size and d the number of dimensions) and the computation of the eigenvectors of the covariance matrix, usually around $\mathcal{O}(d^3)$, though some decomposition approaches are known to have a lower complexity. The projection is in $\mathcal{O}(N.d)$, and the histograms computation have a complexity of $\mathcal{O}(B.N.d)$, with B the number of chosen bins. The expectation step requires the computation of a probability for each histogram in each cluster, for each data point, leading to a complexity of $\mathcal{O}(K.B.N.d)$. The number of bins B being a constant user-chosen parameter, the overall complexity is $\mathcal{O}(K.N.d^3)$. It is the same complexity as the classical EM algorithm used to compute a full GMM [5]. Non-generative approaches, such as K-means, have a lower complexity regarding the number of dimension ($\mathcal{O}(K.N.d)$), because of the simplicity of the produced model.

In term of model complexity, the proposed approach is actually at least as parsimonious as a full GMM. Indeed, thanks to the projections, for each cluster only d histograms (size B) are computed, leading to global model size in $\mathcal{O}(B.K.d)$. A full GMM is composed of K mean vectors (size d) and K covariance matrices (size d^2), for a model complexity of $\mathcal{O}(K.d^2)$. If we chose a number of bins $B < d$, the histograms model is at the same time smaller than the GMM and not limited to a family of distributions. In addition, in most cases, B does not need to be large, values between 5 to 20 have shown very good results in our preliminaries experiments. Note that a GMM computing only the diagonal covariance (i.e. the variance in each dimension) results in a more compact model ($\mathcal{O}(K.d)$), at the expense of ignoring all possible correlations between features.

The proposed approach is therefore no more complex than a GMM, both in term of computation and model complexity. However, the histograms model should be a better representation of the data distribution than a GMM, because it can model a much larger range of distributions.

4 Experimental Validation

In this section, we compare experimentally the proposed approach with several classical algorithms. We compared it with two well-known "discriminative" approaches, K-means [9] and Fuzzy C-means (FCM) [3]. As the proposed approach initializes its membership matrix using FCM, it is important to check that the obtained clustering improves from the initial partition. We also compared with two generative approaches, a Gaussian Mixture Model learning only the diagonal covariance (GMM diag) and Gaussian Mixture Model learning the full covariance matrix (GMM full). In order to validate the proposed algorithm, we tested two criteria in particular: the quality of the algorithm for the clustering task and its ability to generate new samples with the same distribution as the training data.

In order to evaluate these criteria, the algorithms are applied on sixteen data-sets. Eight of them are artificial data-set generated from various distributions (Sect. 4.1). Knowing the distributions allows an easier interpretation of the experimental results. In real data-sets, however, the range of possible distributions are usually more diverse, thus we also tested the algorithms on eight real data-sets with various sizes, dimensions and expected number of clusters.

To test the clustering quality of the proposed algorithm in comparison to its competitors, we chose two external quality indexes (see Sect. 4.2) able to compare the obtained clustering to an expected partition of the data. Internal quality indexes, which estimate the compactness and the separability of the clusters, are usually biased toward hyper-spherical distributions and are, therefore, not well adapted to the type of approaches proposed in this paper.

To test the quality of the generated samples, we compare the dissimilarity between the distribution of the original training data and the distribution of the generated data (Sect. 4.3). The computation of the dissimilarity measures between each pair of empirical distributions is based on the Wasserstein metric [14], seen as a solution of an optimal transport problem.

In all experiments, we chose a value of K matching the expected number of clusters and we fixed the number of bins to $B = 20$. All experiments have been done using Python 3.7, with the *scikit-learn* package for the classical algorithms and the quality indexes and the *Python Optimal Transport* package for the computation of the Wasserstein distance.

4.1 Data-Sets

Sixteen data-sets have been used for the experiments. They were chosen to propose a high diversity of challenges in order to validate the proposed approach in comparison to classical algorithms. Table 1 summarizes the data-sets characteristics.

Eight of them are artificial data. "Gauss 1" and "Gauss 2" data-sets are structured with several Gaussian clusters, in respectively 3 and 50 dimensions. "Rect 1" and "Rect 2" have rectangular clusters in two dimensions, with some overlap between clusters. Clusters in "Comets" and "Gradients" are drawn from gamma distributions, resulting in non-symmetrical shapes. Finally, two data-sets with non-linearly separable clusters in three dimensions, "Atom" and "Chainlink" were chosen from the Fundamental Clustering Problems Suite (FCPS) [17].

The eight real data-sets come from the Open Machine Learning (OpenML) data base [18]. The data-sets were chosen for their variety of shapes, size, dimensions and number of expected clusters. We selected four data-sets with a small number of objects, under 500, as it is usually more difficult to compute the empirical distribution in such case. We also tested the approaches on bigger data-sets, from 5000 to 20000 objects, with a number of dimensions going up to 40 and a number of expected clusters ranging from 5 to 26.

4.2 Quality

Evaluating the performance of a clustering algorithm is not as trivial as counting the number of errors or the precision and recall of a supervised classification

Table 1. Data-sets description

Name	Size	Dimension	#Clusters	Type
Gauss 1	10000	3	3	Artificial
Gauss 2	10000	50	10	Artificial
Rect 1	3000	2	3	Artificial
Rect 2	3000	2	3	Artificial
Comets	3000	2	3	Artificial
Gradients	3000	2	3	Artificial
Atom	800	3	2	Artificial
Chainlink	1000	3	2	Artificial
Ecoli	336	7	2	Real
Letter	20000	16	26	Real
Page-blocks	5473	10	5	Real
Satimage	6430	36	6	Real
Seeds	210	7	3	Real
Texture	5500	40	11	Real
Transplant	131	3	2	Real
Galaxy	323	4	2	Real

algorithm. A popular strategy is to evaluate if the obtained clustering defines separations of the data similar to some ground truth set of classes [6].

In this paper, we used two external quality indexes which provide a measure of similarity between the cluster assignment proposed by the algorithms and the "true" labels, when they are known. Here we evaluate the clustering results using the Adjusted Rand Index (ARI) [8] and the Normalized Mutual Information score (NMI) [15]. These two indexes were computed for each data-set and each algorithm. We also computed a global measurement score following [20]:

$$Score(A_i) = \frac{1}{N_d} \sum_j \frac{Ind(A_i, X_j)}{\max_i Ind(A_i, X_j)} \tag{9}$$

where $Ind(A_i, X_j)$ indicates the quality index value of algorithm A_i for data-set X_j and N_d the number of tested data-sets. This score gives an overall evaluation of the performance of each approach relatively to the others. A value of 1 means that the approach is always the more efficient regarding the quality index. The lower the values in $[0, 1]$, the less efficient is the algorithm in comparison to its competitors. The results are very similar between the two indexes and we chose to show here only the results obtained for the ARI index (Table 2).

The quality of the proposed approach is either comparable to the classical approaches, especially when the clusters' distributions follow a Gaussian law ("Gauss 1" and "Gauss 2"), or better than the other algorithms. In average, generative models perform better than K-means or Fuzzy C-means (FMC).

Table 2. Adjusted Rand Index (ARI) for each data-set and each algorithm.

Data-set	K-means	FCM	GMM diag	GMM full	Proposed
Gauss 1	0.97	0.97	0.97	0.97	0.97
Gauss 2	1.00	1.00	1.00	1.00	0.98
Rect 1	0.77	0.72	0.99	0.98	1.00
Rect 2	0.68	0.68	0.49	0.68	0.80
Comets	0.65	0.67	0.65	0.94	0.92
Gradients	0.81	0.78	0.94	0.85	0.96
Atom	0.18	0.22	0.02	0.03	0.72
Chainlink	0.09	0.09	0.91	0.91	0.99
Ecoli	0.23	0.53	0.00	0.37	0.72
Letter	0.15	0.00	0.11	0.18	0.19
Page-blocks	0.10	0.01	0.06	0.19	0.22
Satimage	0.53	0.53	0.50	0.47	0.51
Seeds	0.77	0.77	0.68	0.72	0.78
Texture	0.51	0.47	0.44	0.69	0.75
Transplant	0.61	0.77	0.74	0.59	0.85
Galaxy	0.27	0.27	0.27	0.22	0.33
Score	**0.70**	**0.66**	**0.70**	**0.82**	**0.99**

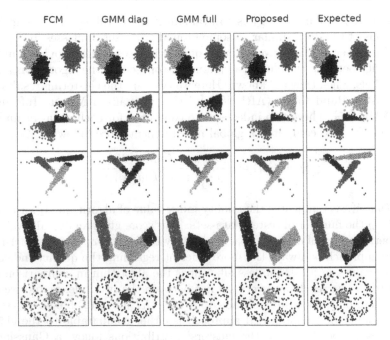

Fig. 1. Visual examples of clustering results obtain by various algorithms. Top to bottom: "Gauss 1", "Gradients", "Comets", "Rect 1" and "Atom".

We also see a clear increase of quality with the increase of generality of the model, a full Gaussian Mixture Model (GMM) being better than the diagonal GMM and the proposed approach being in average better than the GMM.

It is interesting to note that the proposed algorithm, despite using a FMC to initialize its membership matrix, shows much better clustering results than FMC. The GMM approaches are very good for many of the tested data-sets, but sometime fail to produce the desired clustering (remarkable examples are data-sets "Atom" and "Ecoli"). In this experiment, there is no clear impact of the number of observations, dimensions or clusters on the quality of the obtain clustering. We suppose that the complexity of the data structure, in term of clusters' distributions and overlapping, plays a much more important role.

Figure 1 illustrates the observed differences in quality among the algorithms. In these examples, some of the algorithms' limitations are clearly visible. In particular, FCM is suited for hyper-spherical clusters such as in "Gauss 1", but lack the flexibility to detect correctly clusters from other type of distributions. Diagonal GMM is slightly better, but is unable to model correlations between features ("Comets", "Rect 1"). Finally, the full GMM is more efficient, but have difficulties with far-from-Gaussian distributions (e.g. "Rect 1" or "Atom").

4.3   Generation of New Samples

Generative models are powerful tools to model the data distribution and can be used to generate new samples following the same distribution. As the proposed approach compute an estimation of the empirical distribution instead of a mixture of Gaussian, we expect that its ability to generate new data is better than the GMM. To test this assumption, we generated samples following the distributions learn from the sixteen training data-sets, and we compared the distribution of the generated data to the distribution of the original data. The similarity between the two distribution, based on the data, were computed with a Earth mover's distance (EMD) also known as the Wasserstein metrics. The EMD between two distributions is proportional to the minimum amount of work required to convert one distribution into the other [14]. The Wasserstein distance between two distributions u and v is:

$$l_1(u, v) = \inf_{\pi \in \Gamma(u,v)} \int_{\mathbb{R} \times \mathbb{R}} |x - y| \mathrm{d}\pi(x, y) \tag{10}$$

where $\Gamma(u, v)$ is the set of (probability) distributions on $\mathbb{R} \times \mathbb{R}$ whose marginals are u and v on the first and second factors respectively. Note that the input distributions can be empirical, i.e. described from data samples.

All distances for each algorithm and each data-sets are presented in Fig. 2. Note that the values can vary a lot from a data-set to another, based on their size and dimension. In order to increase the readability of the results, the distances have been normalized such that the less efficient approach for each data-set have a score of 1. A score of 0 would indicate a perfect match between the two distributions. The results show that, as expected, the proposed approach is usually much better than the GMM to generate new data matching the distribution of a training data-set. For some data-set, a full GMM is as efficient as the histogram-based model (see data-sets "Satimage" or "Texture"), but in other cases the proposed algorithm is much better (for example "Rect 1", "Gradients", "Ecoli" or "Letter").

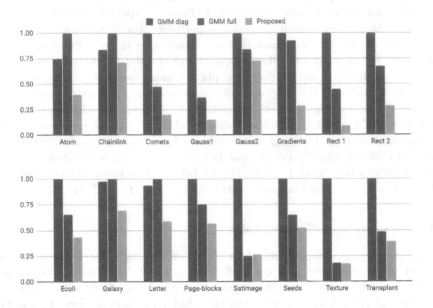

Fig. 2. For each generative algorithm, Normalized Wasserstein distance between each training data-set and the generated data. Smaller values indicate a better fit.

5   Conclusion

In this paper, we introduced a new generative unsupervised learning algorithm based on the computation of histograms to representation the data distributions. The main idea is to reduce the model complexity for each class via different projections on independent axes and to compute a one-dimensional histogram for each of these axes. Axes being independent, the computation of the join probability distribution is greatly simplified.

The proposed algorithm has a complexity comparable to the complexity of a Gaussian Mixture Model (GMM), while being able to model a wider variety of distributions. To validate its quality experimentally, we compared the proposed approach to several classical algorithms. The results show that the obtained model is in average better than models obtained with other algorithms. In addition, the proposed approach is more efficient than a GMM to generate new instances with the same distribution as the training data.

To pursue this study, we plan to test the use of non-linear projections instead of the current linear projections. We expect that this will improve the performances of the model when the data distribution have non-convex components. We also plan to reduce the complexity of the algorithm by limiting the number of principal components in the projections.

Acknowledgements. This work was supported in part by the Pro-TEXT project (No ANR-18-CE23-0024) financed by the ANR (Agence Nationale de la Recherche).

References

1. Baldi, P., Brunak, S., Bach, F.: Bioinformatics: The Machine Learning Approach. MIT press, Cambridge (2001)
2. Benaglia, T., Chauveau, D., Hunter, D.R.: An EM-like algorithm for semi- and nonparametric estimation in multivariate mixtures. J. Comput. Graph. Stat. **18**(2), 505–526 (2009)
3. Bezdek, J.C., Ehrlich, R., Full, W.: FCM: the fuzzy c-means clustering algorithm. Comput. Geosci. **10**(2–3), 191–203 (1984)
4. Cabanes, G., Bennani, Y., Grozavu, N.: Unsupervised learning for analyzing the dynamic behavior of online banking fraud. In: IEEE 13th International Conference on Data Mining, pp. 513–520 (2013)
5. Dempster, A.P., Laird, N.M., Rubin, D.B.: Maximum likelihood from incomplete data via the EM algorithm. J. Roy. Stat. Soc. B **39**(1), 1–38 (1977)
6. Dudoit, S., Fridlyand, J.: A prediction-based resampling method for estimating the number of clusters in a dataset. Genome Biol. **3**(7), 1–21 (2002)
7. Ester, M., Kriegel, H.P., Sander, J., Xu, X.: A density-based algorithm for discovering clusters in large spatial databases with noise. In: International Conference on Knowledge Discovery and Data Mining, pp. 226–231 (1996)
8. Hubert, L., Arabie, P.: Comparing partitions. J. Classif. **2**(1), 193–218 (1985)
9. Jain, A.K.: Data clustering: 50 years beyond k-means. Pattern Recogn. Lett. **31**(8), 651–666 (2010)
10. Jebara, T.: Machine Learning: Discriminative and Generative, vol. 755. Springer, Heidelberg (2012)
11. Maimon, O., Rokach, L.: Data Mining and Knowledge Discovery Handbook. Springer, New York (2005). https://doi.org/10.1007/b107408
12. McLachlan, G.J., Basford, K.E.: Mixture models: inference and applications to clustering, vol. 84. M. Dekker, New York (1988)
13. Rastin, P., Cabanes, G., Matei, B., Bennani, Y., Marty, J.M.: A new sparse representation learning of complex data: application to dynamic clustering of web navigation. Pattern Recogn. **91**, 291–307 (2019)
14. Ruschendorf, L.: Wasserstein metric. In: Hazewinkel, H. (ed.) Encyclopedia of Mathematics. Springer, Berlin (2001). https://doi.org/10.1007/978-94-009-5991-0
15. Strehl, A., Ghosh, J.: Cluster ensembles – a knowledge reuse framework for combining multiple partitions. J. Mach. Learn. Res. **3**, 583–617 (2003)
16. Train, K.E.: Mixed Logit, p. 138–154. Cambridge University Press (2003)
17. Ultsch, A.: Fundamental Clustering Problems Suite (FCPS) (2005)
18. Vanschoren, J., van Rijn, J.N., Bischl, B., Torgo, L.: OpenML: networked science in machine learning. SIGKDD Explorations **15**(2), 49–60 (2013)

19. Yue, H.H., Tomoyasu, M.: Weighted principal component analysis and its applications to improve FDC performance. In: IEEE Conference on Decision and Control (CDC), vol. 4, pp. 4262–4267 (2004)
20. Zhao, H., Fu, Y.: Dual-regularized multi-view outlier detection. In: International Conference on Artificial Intelligence, pp. 4077–4083. AAAI Press (2015)

Author Index

Printed in the United States
By Bookmasters